ACCOUNTING
DESK BOOK

ACCOUNTING DESK BOOK

The Accountant's Everyday Instant Answer Book

ELEVENTH EDITION

TOM M. PLANK
LOIS R. PLANK

PRENTICE HALL

Library of Congress Cataloging-in-Publication Data

Plank, Tom M.
    Accounting desk book: the accountant's everday instant answer
book / Tom M. Plank—11ed.
      p. cm
    Includes index.
    ISBN 0-13-084471-3
    1. Accounting. II. Title.
HF5635.B668 1995
657′.02′02—dc19   88-39352
                                                  CIP

© 2000 *by Prentice Hall*

Printed in the United States of America

10 9 8 7 6 5 4 3 2

This publication is designed to provide accurate and authoritative information in regard to the subject matter covered. It is sold with the understanding that the publisher is not engaged in rendering legal, accounting, or other professional service. If legal advice or other expert assistance is required, the services of a competent professional person should be sought.

—*From a Declaration of Principles jointly adopted by a Committee of the American Bar Association and a Committee of Publishers and Associations.*

ISBN 0-13-084471-3

90000

ATTENTION: CORPORATIONS AND SCHOOLS

Prentice Hall books are available at quantity discounts with bulk purchase for educational, business, or sales promotional use. For information, please write to: Prentice Hall Special Sales, 240 Frisch Court, Paramus, NJ 07652. Please supply: title of book, ISBN number, quantity, how the book will be used, date needed.

 Prentice Hall Press Paramus, NJ 07652

http://www.phdirect.com

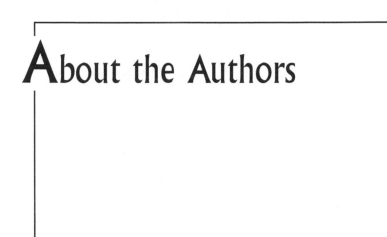

About the Authors

Tom M. Plank is a specialist in SEC Accounting Rules and Regulations, new security issues registrations, and annual reports and filings required by the SEC. He holds his degrees from the Graduate School of Management, University of California at Los Angeles.

Mr. Plank has served on the accounting, finance and economics faculties of various major universities in Chicago and Los Angeles. His business experience includes that of an officer and economist for a large commercial bank, a securities analyst for an investment banking firm, an account executive for a large securities firm, and a consultant for various corporations for Securities and Exchange Commission filings.

Mr. Plank has published many articles in various journals and is the author of several business books: *SEC Accounting Rules and Regulations, The Age of Automation, The Science of Leadership*, and several editions and supplements to the *Accounting Desk Book*. He is also the co-editor of the *Encyclopedia of Accounting Systems*.

Lois R. Plank received her B.A. degree in Public Administration and International Relations from Miami University in Oxford, Ohio, with additional work in investments at the University of California at Los Angeles and at the University of Illinois.

Mrs. Plank is the co-editor of the *Encyclopedia of Accounting Systems* and co-author of several of the supplements to the *Accounting Desk Book*. She has been involved in budgeting and financial management with a government agency in Washington, D.C., and instituted a public relations and marketing program for a suburban Chicago school district.

v

She is an editor of professional publications and books, and is a public relations consultant. Additional experience includes chief copy consultant for a national magazine, and newspaper reporting.

Introduction

This eleventh edition of the *Desk Book* was created for several reasons. First, the passage of time required the updating and substantial revision of the material from prior editions. There has been a continuing inundation of new accounting rules Generally Accepted Accounting Principles (GAAP). Changes in accounting treatment have resulted from extensive Security and Exchange Rule adoptions, the "new" Internal Revenue Service's Regulations, increased emphasis on and consideration of Financial Accounting Standards Board decisions and a revolutionary shift in direction of the Government Accounting Standards Board.

The importance of current information to keep pace with the fast movement of the state-of-the-art cannot be overemphasized. Coverage of topics, application, examples, and definitions of terms where necessary to be consistent with contemporary literature in accounting, finance and taxation. Care has been taken to avoid abstract theory, technical jargon, complex "legalese" or textbook type prose which can needlessly complicate the understanding of rules and procedures. All topics are covered in a straightforward, plain English style.

In addition, the years since the publication of the tenth edition, have seen far-reaching developments in global business and commerce requiring the attention of accountants. Evidence of this is reflected in the three chapters dealing specifically with international accounting considerations: "The International Federation of Accountants," "The International Accounting Standards Committee," and "The G+4: Representation of National Accounting Standard-Setting Bodies." Another aspect of the changing business world is considered in the chapter, "E-Communication and E-Commerce."

The discussions throughout the *Desk Book* are self contained. A review of the topics does not require references to other sources. The Contents clearly sets forth the subject matter discussed. Users will also find the Index helpful in locating needed information rapidly.

It should be emphasized that the *Desk Book* is not a textbook. It is essentially a reference manual to provide the user with immediate answers to a large number of practical accounting, finance, tax, and general business management questions.

ACKNOWLEDGMENTS

We would like to acknowledge the invaluable editorial assistance of Christie Ciraulo and Bryan R. Plank.

Contents

CHAPTER 5   90
BUSINESS COMBINATIONS

CHAPTER 6   116
INTERNATIONAL FEDERATION OF ACCOUNTANTS

CHAPTER 9   182
INSURANCE ACCOUNTING

CHAPTER 10   196
DERIVATIVES

CHAPTER 11   211
FOREIGN CURRENCY TRANSLATIONS
AND DERIVATIVE DISCLOSURE

CHAPTER 12   229
GOVERNMENTAL FUND ACCOUNTING

CHAPTER 13   246
"NEW" GOVERNMENTAL ACCOUNTING

CHAPTER 14   262
NOT-FOR-PROFIT OR EXEMPT ORGANIZATIONS

CHAPTER 15   277

BUDGETING FOR PROFIT PLANNING
AND BUDGETARY CONTROL

CHAPTER 16   302

CHANGE IN ACCOUNTING METHODS
AND CONSIDERATION OF ACCOUNTING PERIODS

CHAPTER 17   326
THE SECURITIES AND EXCHANGE COMMISSION —
ORGANIZATION AND THE ACTS

Chapter 1

Principles of Financial Statements, Disclosure, Analysis, and Interpretation

The general objective is to provide reliable information on resources, obligations and progress. The information should be useful for comparability, completeness and understandability. The basic features involved in financial accounting are: the individual accounting entity, the use of approximation and the preparation of fundamentally related financial statements.

The financial statements—balance sheet, income statement, change in stockholders' equity and statement of cash flows, as well as segment reports and interim reports—will summarize a firm's operations and ending financial position. Analysts, investors, creditors and potential investors and creditors will analyze these documents in their decision-making processes.

FAIR PRESENTATION IN CONFORMITY WITH GAAP

1. GAAP applicable in the circumstances have been applied in accumulating and processing the accounting information; and
2. Changes from period to period in GAAP have been properly disclosed; and
3. The information in the *underlying* records is properly *reflected* and *described* in the financial statements in conformity with GAAP; and
4. A proper balance has been achieved between:
    a. The conflicting needs to disclose the important aspects of financial position and results of operation in conformity with conventional concepts, and to

1

b. Summarize the voluminous underlying data with a limited number of financial statement captions and supporting notes.

12 PRINCIPLES OF FINANCIAL STATEMENT PRESENTATION

1. Basic Financial Statements—minimum requirements:
   a. Balance Sheet
   b. Statement of Income
   c. Statement of Changes in Stockholders' Equity
   d. Statement of Cash Flows
   e. Disclosure of Accounting Policies
   f. Disclosure of Related Notes

   Usually presented for two or more periods.

   Other information may be presented, and in some cases required, as supplemental information: price-level statements; information about operations in different industries; foreign operations and export sales; major customers (segment reporting).
2. A Complete Balance Sheet
   a. All Assets
   b. All Liabilities
   c. All classes of Stockholders' Equity.
3. A Complete Income Statement
   a. All Revenues
   b. All Expenses
4. A Complete Statement of Cash Flow

   Includes and describes all important aspects of the company's financing and investing activities.
5. Accounting Period

   Basic time period is one year

   An interim statement is for less than one year.
6. Consolidated Financial Statements

   They are presumed to be more meaningful than separate statements of the component legal entities

   They are *usually* necessary when one of the group owns (directly or indirectly) *over 50 percent* of the outstanding voting stock

   The information is presented as if it were a *single enterprise*.
7. The Equity Basis

For unconsolidated subsidiaries (where over 50 percent is owned) *and for investments in 50 percent or less* of the voting stock of companies in which the investor has significant influence over investees, 20 percent or more ownership presumes this influence, unless proved otherwise. The investor's share of the net income reported by the investee is picked up and shown as income and an adjustment of the investment account—for all earnings subsequent to the acquisition. Dividends are treated as an adjustment of the investment account.

8. Translation of Foreign Branches

   Translated into U.S. Dollars by conventional translation procedures involving foreign exchange rates.

9. Classification and Segregation:

   (Must separately disclose these important components)

   a. *Income Statement*—Sale (or other source of revenue); Cost of Sales; Depreciation; Selling Administration Expenses; Interest Expense; Income Taxes.

   b. *Balance Sheet*—Cash; Receivables; Inventories; Plant and Equipment; Payables; and Categories of Stockholder's Equity:
      - Par or stated amount of capital stock; Additional paid-in capital
      - Retained earnings: (affected by—
        1. Net income or loss,
        2. Prior period adjustments,
        3. Dividends, or
        4. Transfers to other categories of equity).
      - Working Capital—current assets and current liabilities should be classified as such to be able to determine working capital—useful for enterprises in: manufacturing, trading, some service enterprises.
      - Current assets—include cash and other items that can reasonably be expected to be realized in cash in one year or a shorter business cycle.
      - Current liabilities—include those that are expected to be satisfied by the use of those assets shown as current; or the creation of other current liabilities; or expected to be satisfied in one year.
      - Assets and liabilities should *not* be offset against each other unless a legal right to do so exists, which is a rare exception.
      - Gains and Losses—arise from other than products or services, may becombined and shown as one item. Examples: write-downs of inventories, receivables, capitalized research and development costs, *all sizable*. Also, gains and losses on: temporary investments,

non-monetary transactions, currency devaluations are a few typical items.

- Extraordinary items or gain or loss—should be shown separately under its own title, distinguished by unusual nature and infrequent occurrence should be shown net of taxes.
- Net Income—should be separately disclosed and clearly identified on the income statement.

10. Other disclosures: (Accounting policies and notes)

a. Customary or routine disclosures:

- Measurement bases of important assets
- Restrictions on assets
- Restriction on owners' equity
- Contingent liabilities
- Contingent assets
- Important long-term commitments not in the body of the statements
- Information on terms of equity of owners
- Information on terms of long-term debt
- Other disclosures required by AICPA

b. Disclosure of changes in accounting policies.

c. Disclosure of important subsequent events—between balance sheet date and date of the opinion.

d. Disclosure of accounting policies ("Summary of Significant Accounting Policies").

11. Form of Financial Statement Presentation:

No particular form is presumed better than all others for all purposes. Several are used.

12. Earnings Per Share:

Must be disclosed on *the face of the Income Statement.*

Should be disclosed for:

a. Income before extraordinary items

b. Net Income.

Should consider:

a. Changes in number of shares outstanding

b. Contingent changes

c. Possible dilution from potential conversion of:

- Preferred stock
- Options
- Warrants

MATERIALITY

There have been attempts by authoritative rule-making bodies, scholars of accounting, users of fnanicial statements, and others to develop quantitative criteria for determining the materiality of items in the financial statements. They postulate that if Item A is X percent of a total, Item A is material. If Item B is Y percent of a total, then Item B is material, but . . . .. All efforts have proved fruitless, and there are no accepted quantitative standards that can be wholly relied upon for an unquestioned determination of whether an item is material or immaterial (and can be omitted from the financial statements or notes thereto).

The courts to some extent have helped. However, it should be cautioned that different jurisdictions in different geographic areas of the country have established many different opinions and definitions of materiality. For example, the Tenth Circuit Court of Appeals ruled that information is material if ". . . the trading judgment of reasonable investors would not have been left untouched upon receipt of such information." (*Mitchell v. Texas Gulf Sulphur Co.*) In the "landmark" *Bar Chris* case the judge said that a material fact is one ". . . which if it had been correctly stated or disclosed would have deterred or tended to deter the average prudent investor from purchasing the securities in question" (*Escott et al. v. Bar Chris Construction Corporation et al.*).

Principally because the U.S. Supreme Court defined materiality in the *TSC Industries Inc. v. Northway Inc.* case, the following statement of the Court is considered to be an authoritative basis upon which to render a judgment of materiality:

"An omitted fact is material if there is a substantial likelihood that a reasonable shareholder would consider it important in deciding how to vote. This standard is fully consistent with the general description of materiality as a requirement that the defect have a significant *propensity* to affect the voting process."

(Note: This decision dealt with omissions of material information.)

"The Securities and Exchange Commission defines *material information:* '*The term* material *when used to qualify a requirement for the furnishing of information as to any subject, limits the information required to those matters as to which an average prudent investor ought reasonably to be informed.*'"

What's Material?   The accountant must decide precisely what information requires disclosure. The accountant must exercise judgment according to the circumstances and facts concerning material matters and their conformity with Generally Accepted Accounting Principles. A few examples of material matters are:

1. The form and content of financial statements.
2. Notes to the statements.
3. The terminology used in the statements.
4. The classification of items in the statements.
5. Amount of detail furnished.
6. The bases of the amounts presented, i.e., for inventories, plants, liabilities, etc.
7. The existence of affiliated or controlling interests.

A clear distinction between materiality and disclosure should be noted. Material information involves both quantitative (data) and qualitative information. Additionally, the information must be disclosed in a manner that enables a person of "average" comprehension and experience to understand and apply it to an investment decision. Contra speaking, information disclosed in a manner that only an "expert" can evaluate is not considered within the meaning and intent of disclosure requirements.

Materiality should be thought of as an abstract concept. Many efforts to define the term can be found in the literature, e.g., accounting and auditing books, law books, and Regulation S-X. Nevertheless, in the final analysis, judgments with respect to what is material resulting from court decisions, SEC actions, accountants' interpretations, and corporate and financial officers' judgments have ultimately evolved into the subjective judgment of individuals (accountants and management) responsible for deciding what is and is not material.

DISCLOSURES REQUIRED IN FINANCIAL STATEMENTS

Below is an outline of the most important disclosures required in financial statements with a brief comment on the substance of each requirement.

Accounting Policies. APB Opinion 22 *Disclosure of Accounting Policies* is the applicable GAAP. (See the discussion at the end of this chapter.) The disclosure should set forth the accounting principles underlying the statements that materially affect the determination of financial position, changes in financial position, and results of operations. Also included are the accounting principles relating to recognition of revenue, allocation of asset costs to current and future periods, the selection from existing acceptable alternatives, such as the inventory method chosen, and any accounting principles and methods unique to the industry of the reporting entity.

As a general rule, the preferred position of the review of accounting policies is footnote No. 1, but a section summarizing the policies preceding the footnotes is acceptable.

Who decides what information is material? This decision is the responsibility of management working with the company's accountant. Listed below are a few items considered material that *must* be recognized. As a generalization, the *causes* for material changes in financial statement items must be noted to the extent necessary for users to understand the business as a whole. This requirement applies to all financial statements, not just to the income statement.

1. Sales and revenues. Increases or decreases in sales and revenues that are temporary or nonrecurring and their causes.
2. Unusually increased costs.
3. Informative generalizations with respect to each important expense category.
4. Financial expenses. Changes in interest expenses (and interest income); changes in the company's cost of borrowing; changes in the borrowing mix, e.g., long-term vs. short-term.
5. Other income and expense items. These may include dividend income from investees; the equity in the income or losses of investees or of unconsolidated subsidiaries.
6. Income taxes. The effective tax rate paid by corporations should be reconciled to the statutory rates. The reconciliation provides the basis for a description of the reasons for year-to-year variations in the effective tax rate to which a business is subject. Changes caused by the adoption of new or altered policies of tax-deferred accounting are considered material.
7. Material changes in the relative profitability of lines of business.
8. Material changes in advertising, research and development, new services, or other discretionary costs.
9. The acquisition or disposition of a material asset.
10. Material and unusual charges or gains, including credits or charges associated with discontinuance of operations.
11. Material changes in assumptions underlying deferred costs and the plan for the amortization of such costs.
12. The cost of goods sold, where applicable. The gross margin of an enterprise can be affected by important changes in sales volume, price, unit costs, mix of products or services sold, and inventory profits and losses. The composition of cost among fixed, semi-variable and variable elements influences profitability. Changes in gross margins by an analysis of the interplay between selling prices, costs, and volume should be explained.

13. Cash flow information.
14. Dilution of earnings per share.
15. Segmental reporting.
16. Rental expense under leases.
17. Receivables from officers and stockholders.

FULL DISCLOSURE

Full Disclosure is an attempt to present all essential information about a company in the following reports:

1. Balance Sheet
2. Income Statement
3. Statement of Changes in Stockholders' Equity
4. Statement of Cash Flows
5. Accompanying Footnotes

The objectives of financial reporting are set forth in *FASB Concepts Statement No. 1*. The financial statements, notes to the financial statements, and necessary supplementary information are governed by FASB standards. Financial reporting includes other types of information, such as *Management's Discussion and Analysis*, letters to stockholders, order backlogs, statistical data, and the like, commonly included in reports to shareholders.

The Full Disclosure Principle

Financial facts significant enough to influence the judgment of an informed person should be disclosed. The financial statements, notes to the financial statements, summary of accounting policies, should disclose the information necessary to prevent the statements from being misleading. The information in the statements should be disclosed in a manner that the intended meaning of the information is apparent to a reasonably informed user of the statements.

DISCLOSURE IN FINANCIAL REPORTING

Disclosure.   The heart of the compilation and disclosure of financial information is *accounting*. Yet, the idea of "adequate disclosure" stands alone as the one concept in accounting that involves all of the good things and all of the dangers inherent in the professional practice of accounting and auditing. Probably the use of the colloquialism "disclosure" best describes the all-embracing nature of the concept. That is to say, *disclosure is the name of the financial reporting game.*

For decades the profession has been inundated with disclosure literature, rules, regulations, statements, government agencies' accounting regulations, court decisions, tax decisions, intellectualizing by academics, books and seminars, all concerning what disclosure is all about.

Yet nobody has answered precisely what continues to remain the essential question: Disclosure of *what*, by *whom*, for *whom?*

The lack of definitive qualitative and quantitative criteria for what information must or need not be disclosed forces upon the independent accountant the responsibility to decide what constitutes a matter requiring disclosure, requiring an exercise of judgment in light of the circumstances and facts available at the time. The *accountant's* responsibility is confined to the expression of an opinion based upon an examination. The representations made through the statements are *management's* responsibility.

What is a material fact, and for whom does a disclosed fact have material significance? What substantive standards of disclosure must the accountant maintain? Who is to promulgate these standards? The profession? One or all of the governmental regulatory agencies? A federal board of accounting? The courts? The Congress?

One conclusion is clear, however. There is an unmistakable trend toward increasing demands upon the accounting profession for more financial information. What better evidence can be cited than the conclusion of the AICPA Study Group on the Objectives of Financial Statements? The group's report said that" . . . financial statements should meet the needs of those with *LEAST* ability to obtain information."

The confusion between what is and is not *material* is caused by a widely held concept—different facts have different meanings for the individual user of financial information. Information that is important to one user may be insignificant to another.

> "All information must adapt *itself* to the perception of those towards whom the information is intended."
>
> -Anonymous

It is neither possible nor economically feasible, however, for an accountant to cover in the statements every single small detail concerning a client's business. Where should the accountant draw the line? (Not many years ago, a large accounting firm had to defend a lawsuit up to the U.S. Supreme Court at a cost of several million dollars because the accountant did not question the company's chief executive officer's policy that he, alone, open the company's mail.)

Recent trends in financial reporting reflect an increase in the amount of disclosure found in financial statements. The information is communicated in the footnotes, which are an integral part of the financial statements. Although the footnotes are usually drafted in somewhat technical language, they are the accountant's means of amplifying or explaining the items present in the main body of the statements. Footnote information can generally be classified as follows:

1. *Disclosure of Accounting Policies Applied* . This information is required in order to inform the user of the statements of the accounting methods used in preparing the information that appears in statements.
2. *Disclosure of Gain or Loss Contingencies.* Because many contingent gains or losses are not properly included in the accounts, their disclosure in the footnotes provides relevant information to financial statement users.
3. *Examination of Credit Claims.* A liability, such as a bank loan, may have numerous covenants that are not conveniently disclosed in the liability section of the balance sheet.
4. *Claims of Equity Holders.* The rights of various equity security issues along with certain unique features that may apply to certain issues are commonly disclosed in footnotes to the statements.
5. *Executory Commitments.* These refer to contract obligations undertaken by the company that have not been performed, or have been only partially performed at the statement date.

In some cases a company is faced with a sensitive issue that requires disclosure in a footnote. Some examples are:

1. related party transactions
2. errors
3. irregularities
4. illegal acts

DISCLOSURES ITEMIZED

Following is an alphabetical listing of items requiring disclosure including short comments if applicable.

> Accelerated Depreciation Methods—when methods are adopted.
> Accounting Policies—(see the discussion of APB 22 at the end of this chapter.)

Allowances (depreciation, depletion, bad debts)—deduct from asset with disclosure .

Amortization of Intangibles—disclose method and period.

Amounts Available for Distribution—note the needs for any holdback retention of earnings.

Arrangements with Reorganized Debtor—disclose if a subsequent event.

Arrears on Cumulative Preferred Stock—the rights of senior securities must be disclosed on the face of balance sheet or in the notes.

Assets (interim changes in)—only significant changes required for interims.

Business Segments.

Cash-Basis Statements—fact must be disclosed in the opinion with delineation of what would have been had accrual basis been used, its significant variance.

'Change in Stockholders' Equity Accounts—in a separate schedule. This does not include the changes in retained earnings statement, which is also a basic requirement.

Change to Declining Balance Method—disclose change in method and effect of it.

Changes, Accounting—see Chapter 16.

Commitments, Long-Term—disclose unused letters of credit, assets pledged as security for loans, pension plans, plant expansion or acquisition; obligations to reduce debt, maintain working capital or restrict dividend.

Commitments to Complete Contracts—only the extraordinary ones.

Consolidation Policy—method used.

Construction Type Contracts—method used.

Contingencies—disclose when reasonable possibility of a loss, the nature of, and estimated loss. Threats of expropriation, debtor bankruptcy if actual. Those contingencies which might result in gains, but not misleading as to realization. Disclosure of uninsured risks is advised, but not required. Gain contingencies should be disclosed, but not reflected in the accounts.

Contingencies in Business Combinations—disclose escrow items for contingencies in the notes.

Control of Board of Directors—disclose any stock options existing.

Corporate Officer Importance—disclose if a major sales or income factor to the company.

Current Liabilities—disclose why, if any, omitted (in notes).

Dating (Readjusted) Earned Surplus—no more than 10 years is the term now required.

Deferred Taxes—disclose and also see Timing Differences in this text.

Depreciation and Depreciable Assets—disclose the following:

1. Depreciation expense for the period.
2. Balances of major classes of depreciable assets by nature or function.
3. Accumulated depreciation by classes, or in total.
4. A general description of the methods used in computing depreciation.

Development Stage Enterprises—are required to use the same basic financial statements as other enterprises, with certain additional disclosures required. Special type statements are not permissible.

Discontinued Operations—disclose separately below continuing-operating income, net of tax, but before extraordinary items. Show separate EPS.

Diversified Company's Foreign Operations.

Earnings per share—see discussion in this text, but the following is also required in addition to the data stated there (does not apply to nonpublic enterprises):

1. Restatement for a prior period adjustment
2. Dividend preference
3. Liquidation preference
4. Participation rights
5. Call prices and dates
6. Conversion rates and dates
7. Exercise prices and dates
8. Sinking fund requirements
9. Unusual voting rights
10. Bases upon which primary and fully diluted earnings per share were calculated
11. Issues which are common stock equivalents
12. Issues which are potentially dilutive securities
13. Assumptions and adjustments made for earnings per share data
14. Shares issued upon conversion, exercise, and conditions met for contingent issuances
15. Recapitalization occurring during the period or before the statements are issued

16. Stock dividends, stock splits or reverse splits occurring after the close of the period before the statements are issued
17. Claims of senior securities entering earnings per share computations
18. Dividends declared by the constituents in a pooling
19. Basis of presentation of dividends in a pooling on other than a historical basis
20. Per share and aggregate amount of cumulative preferred dividends in arrears.

Equity Method—as follows:

1. Financial statements of the investor should disclose in the notes, separate statements or schedules, or parenthetically:
    a. The name of each investee and percent of ownership,
    b. The accounting policies of the investor, disclosing if, and why, any over 20 percent holdings are not under the equity method,
    c. Any difference between the carrying value and the underlying equity of the investment, and the accounting treatment thereof.
2. Disclose any investments which have quoted market prices (common stocks) showing same—do not write down.
3. Present summary balance sheet and operating information when equity investments are material.
4. Same as above for any unconsolidated subsidiaries where ownership is majority.
5. Disclose material effects of contingent issuances.

Extinguishment (Early) of Debt—gains or losses should be described, telling source of funds for payoff, income tax effect, per share amount.

Extraordinary Items—describe on face of income statement (or in notes), show effect net of tax after income from continuing operations, also after business disposals if any, show EPS separately for extraordinary item. May aggregate immaterial items.

Fiscal Period Differences (in Consolidating)—disclose intervening material.

Fiscal Year Change—disclose effect only.

Foreign Items—Assets, must disclose any significant ones included in U.S. statements; gains or losses shown in body of U.S. statement; disclose significant "subsequent event" rate changes; operations, adequate disclosure to be made of all pertinent dollar information, regardless of whether consolidating or not (for foreign subsidiaries).

Headings and Captions—may be necessary to explain.

Income Taxes (and Deferred Taxes)—(see Timing Differences in this text.)

Income Taxes of Sole Proprietor or Partnership—may be necessary to disclose personal taxes to be paid if the money will come from and put a drain on the firm's cash position.

Infrequent Events—show as separate component of income and disclose nature of them.

Interim Statements—(see discussion in Appendix E.)

Inventories—disclose pricing policies and flow of cost assumption in "Summary of Significant Accounting Policies"; disclose changes in method and effect on income. Dollar effect based upon a change should be shown separately from ordinary cost of sales items.

Investment Tax Credits—disclose method used, with amounts if material. Also, disclose substantial carryback or carryforward credits.

Leases.

Legal Restrictions on Dividend Payments—put in notes.

Liability for Tax Penalties—if significant, disclose in notes. May have to take exception in opinion.

Market Value of Investments in Marketable Securities—should be written down to market value and up again, but not to exceed cost for entire portfolio per classification.

Noncumulative Preferred Stock—should disclose that no provision has been made because it is noncumulative.

Obligations (Short-Term)—disclose in notes the reason any short-term obligations are not displayed as current liabilities.

Partnerships, Limited—disclose fact that it's a limited partnership.

Patent Income—disclose if income is ending.

Pension Plans—must disclose the following:

1. Describe and identify employee groups covered by plan.
2. The accounting and funding policy.
3. The provision for pension cost for the period.
4. Excess, if any, of vested benefits over fund total; any balance sheet deferrals, accruals, prepays.
5. Any significant matters affecting comparability of periods presented.

Political Contributions—must disclose if material or not deductible for taxes, or if they are beneficial to an officer.

Pooling of Interests.

Price-Level Restatements.

Prior Period Adjustments—must disclose with tax effects. Must disclose in interim reports.

Purchase Commitment Losses—should be separately disclosed in dollars in income statement.

Purchase Method. (See Business Combinations.)

Purchase Option Cancellation Costs—yes, disclose.

Real and Personal Property Taxes—disclose if using estimates, and if substantial. All adjustments for prior year estimates should be made through the current income statement.

Real Estate Appraisal Value—for development companies, footnote disclosure might be useful.

Receivables, Affiliated Companies, Officers and Employees—should be segregated and shown separately from trade receivables.

Redemption Call of Preferred Stock—disclose in the equity section.

Renegotiation Possibilities—use dollars if estimable or disclose inability to estimate.

Research and Development Costs—disclosure must be made in the financial statements of the total research and development costs charged to expenses in each period for which an income statement is presented. Government-regulated enterprises should disclose the accounting policy for amortization and the totals expensed and deferred, but not the confidential details of specific projects, patents, new products, processes or company research philosophy. Apply the above provision for disclosure to business combinations.

Restricted Stock Issued to Employee—disclose circumstance and the restrictions.

Retained Earnings Transferred to Capital Stock—arises usually with "splitups effected as dividends" and with stock dividends; must disclose and include schedule showing transfers from retained earnings to capital stock. Also, must disclose number of shares for EPS; must show subsequent event effects.

Sale and Leaseback.

Seasonal Business (Interim Statements)—must disclose, and advisable to include 12-month period, present and past.

Stock Dividends, Split-up—must disclose even if a subsequent event and use as if made for and during all periods presented.

Stock Options—disclose status. Has effect on EPS.

Stockholders Buy/Sell Stock Agreements—disclose.

Subleases.

Termination Claims (War and Defense Contracts)—shown as current receivable, unless extended delay indicated; usually shown separately and disclosed if material, in income statement.

Treasury Stock—Shown in body of balance sheet (equity section ordinarily); should, in notes, indicate any legal restrictions.

Unconsolidated Subsidiaries—if using cost method, should also give independent summary information about position and operations.

Undistributed Earnings of Subsidiaries.

Unearned Compensation.

Unremitted Taxes—disclose only if going concern concept is no longer valid.

RESTATEMENTS

The following alphabetical listing indicates those areas that *require* a restatement (with disclosure) for all prior periods presented in the comparative financial statements:

Appropriations of Retained Earnings—any change made for the reporting of contingencies requires retroactive adjustment.

Changes in Accounting Principle Requiring Restatement:

1. Change from LIFO to another method.
2. Change in long-term construction method.
3. Change to or from "full cost" method in the extractive industries.
4. Must show effect on both net income and EPS for all periods presented.

Change in Reporting Entity—must restate.

Contingencies—restate for the cumulative effect applying the rules for contingencies.

Earnings Per Share—the effect of all restatements must be shown on EPS, separating as to EPS from continuing operations, EPS from disposals, EPS from extraordinary items and EPS from net income.

Equity Method—restatement required when first applying the method, even though it was not required before.

Extraordinary Items—if a similar one in prior period was not classified as extraordinary, but is now, reclassify now for comparison.

Foreign Currency Translations—restate to conform with adoption of standards; if indeterminable, use the cumulative method. Disclose nature of restatement and effect (or cumulative effect) on income before extraordinary items, on net income, and on related per share amounts.

Income Taxes (Equity Method)—restate to comply.

Interim Financial Statements—restate for changes in accounting principle and for prior period adjustments. If it's a cumulative type change, the first interim period should show the entire effect; if in later period, full effect should be applied to the first period and restated for other periods.

Leases.

Oil and Gas Producing Companies—in conforming with standards, restatement is not required, but it is permissible.

Pooling of Interests

1. A change in accounting method for pooled unit should be applied retroactively.
2. In initial pooling, combine year-to-date, restate prior periods presented, show separate information for independent operations and positions. Purchase method shows pro forma combine.
3. Until pooling is consummated, include the proportion of earnings in ordinary financials; but also present statements (retroactively applied) as if pooling had occurred.

Prior Period Adjustments—must restate the details affected for all periods presented, disclose and adjust opening retained earnings. Must also do it for interim reports.

Refinancing Short-Term Obligations—restatement is permitted, but not required.

Research and Development Costs—In conforming with standards, apply retroactively as a prior period adjustment.

(*No* retroactive recapitalization of costs is permissible. Applies to *purchase* combinations also. Basic rule: expense as incurred.)

Statistical Summaries (5 years, 10 years, etc.)—restate all prior years involved in prior period adjustments.

Stock Dividends and Splits—must restate earnings per share figures and number of shares to give effect to stock dividends and splits *including* those occurring after close of period being reported on (for all periods presented).

Revision based on FASB Opinions—retroactive restatement is not required *unless* the new standard *specifically* states that it is required.

(Note that restatements are *not* required for a change from FIFO to LIFO, nor for a change in the method of handling investment tax credits.)

Timing and Permanent Differences—Income Taxes

Those which will not reverse or "turn around" in other periods:

1. Specific *revenues exempt* from taxability (examples):
   Dividend exclusions interest on tax-exempt securities
   Life insurance proceeds
   Negative goodwill amortization
   Unrealized gains on marketable securities
   Unrealized gains on foreign currency translations
   Tax benefits arising from stock-option compensatory plans (when booked as income)
2. Expenses which are *not* tax deductible:
   Depreciation taken on appraisal increases or donated property
   Goodwill amortization
   Premiums on officer life insurance
   Tax penalties and fines
   Unrealized losses on securities or currency translations
3. Those expenses which are predicated upon different bases for financial and tax purposes:
   Depreciation on trade-ins
   Statutory depletion vs cost depletion
   Business combinations which treat purchase as "pooling for tax return or pooling as purchase."

Timing Differences

Those which *will* turn around or reverse in one or more subsequent periods. Four broad categories:

1. Income—for Accounting NOW—for Taxes LATER
2. Expenses—for Accounting NOW—for Taxes LATER
3. Income—for Accounting LATER—for Taxes NOW
4. Expenses—for Accounting LATER—for Taxes NOW

Below is an explanation of these four categories

1. Items of *income* included for accounting financial statement purposes NOW not taken on the tax return until a LATER time (examples):
   a. Gross profit on installment method date of sale/when collected on tax return.
   b. Percentage of completion method on books/completed contract method for tax return.
   c. Leasing rentals on books under financing method/actual rent less depreciation for tax return.
   d. Subsidiary earnings reported now/as received for tax return.
2. Items of *expense* taken on financial statements NOW, not taken on tax returns until LATER (examples):
   a. Accelerated depreciation used for financials/not for tax return.
   b. Contributions on financials over 5% limit/carried over for taxes.
   c. Deferred compensation accruals/taken when paid on tax return.
   d. Estimated costs of various kinds/taken when cost or loss becomes actual and known, such as: guarantees, product warranties, inventory losses, legal settlements, segment disposals, major repairs.
   e. Depreciation based on shorter life for books than for tax return.
   f. Organization costs taken now/amortized for tax return.
3. Items of *income* taken into financial books LATER, but reported as income NOW on tax returns:
   a. Rents and royalties deferred until earned/reported when collected for tax return.
   b. Deferred fees, dues, services contracts/reported when collected for tax returns.
   c. Intercompany consolidation gains and losses/taxed now if filing separate return.
   d. Leaseback gains, amortized gains over lease-term/date of sale for tax return.
4. Items of *expense* taken into financial books LATER, but taken NOW on tax returns:
   a. Depreciation; shorter lives used for tax purposes accelerated rates on tax return/straight-line on books;certain emergency facility amortization taken on tax returns/later on books.
   b. Bond discount, premium costs taken on return/amortized on books.
   c. Certain costs which are taken for tax purposes/but deferred for financial purposes, as:
   d. Incidental costs of property acquisitions

e. Preoperating costs

f. Certain research and development costs (deferred for financial purposes).

Other Considerations Regarding Income Taxes

Interperiod tax allocation should be followed under the deferred method. Timing differences may be considered individually or grouped by similarity. Tax carryback losses (including investment tax credit carrybacks) should be recognized in the loss period in which the carryback originated. Carryforwards should not be recognized until realized (then show as *extraordinary* item) unless there is no doubt of realization (then show as part of operating profit or loss).

Balance Sheet Presentation of Income Taxes

Tax accounts on the balance sheet should be classified separately as to:

1. Taxes estimated to be paid currently.
2. *Net* amount of current deferred charges and deferred credits related to timing differences.
3. *Net* amount of noncurrent deferred taxes related to timing differences.
4. Receivables for carryback losses.
5. When realization is beyond doubt, show an asset for the benefit to be derived from a carryforward of losses.
6. Deferred investment credits, when this method is employed.

Income Statement Presentation of Income Taxes

All taxes based on income, including foreign, federal, state and local, should be reflected in income tax expense in the income statement.

The following components should be disclosed separately and put on the income statement before extraordinary items and prior period adjustments:

1. Taxes estimated to be payable.
2. Tax effects of timing differences.
3. Tax effects of operating losses.

In addition, the following general disclosures are required:

1. Amounts of any operating loss carryforwards not recognized in the loss period, with expiration dates and effect on deferred tax accounts.

2. Significant amounts of any other unused tax deductions or credits, with expiration dates.

3. Any reasons for significant differences between taxable income and pre-tax accounting income.

4. Deferred income taxes related to an asset or liability are classified the same as the related asset or liability. A deferred tax charge or credit is related to an asset or liability if reduction of the asset or liability would cause the underlying timing difference to reverse. Deferred income taxes that are not related to an asset or liability are classified according to the expected reversal date of the timing difference.

FINANCIAL STATEMENT ANALYSIS AND INTERPRETATION

Analysis techniques applied to financial statements are of interest to the corporate financial officer of any entity for a number of reasons. For one thing, that particular company's financial statements will be subject to analysis by creditors, credit grantors, and investors. Furthermore, the financial officer will want to analyze the company's statements for internal management use as well as analyze other companies' financial statements for credit purposes and perhaps for investment purposes (where an acquisition is being considered).

The financial statements are a systematic and convenient presentation of the financial position and operating performance of a business entity. The question is: What can be learned by analyzing and interpreting the information available in the statements?

There is much valuable information to be learned, as ratio analysis answers questions concerning the financial facts of a business:

1. GAAP permits a variety of accounting procedures and practices that significantly affect the results of operation reported in the statements. Statement analysis helps to evaluate the choices of alternative accounting decisions.

2. The statements for a number of successive years can be compared by the use of ratios and unusual trends and changes can be noted.

3. A company's statements can be compared with those of other similar companies in the same industry.

4. Statement analysis is the basis for estimating, or projecting, potential operating results by the development of pro forma statements.

5. The effects of external economic developments on a company's business can be applied to results as shown in the statements.

6. The balance sheet valuations can be related to the operating results disclosed in the income statement, since the balance sheet is the link between successive income statements.

7. Since ratios are index numbers obtained by relating data to each other, they make comparisons more meaningful than using the raw numbers without relating an absolute dollar figure to another statement item.

FOUR GROUPS OF RATIOS

Ratios are usually classified into four groups:

1. *Liquidity Ratios:* Measures of the ability of the enterprise to pay its short-term obligations.
2. *Profitability Ratios:* Measures of the profits (losses) over a specified period of time.
3. *Coverage Ratios:* Measures of the protection for the interest and principal payments to long-term creditors and investors.
4. *Activity Ratios:* Measures of how efficiently the company is employing its assets.

The ratios in the following discussion are those most commonly applied to measure the operating efficiency and profitability of a company. (There are hundreds of possible relationships that can be computed and trends identified.) The discussion includes an explanation of the answers that each ratio provides; each ratio's application to a specific area of a business will be noted.

THE ACCOUNTANT'S RESPONSIBILITY

In evaluating the ratios, the accountant must be mindful that the ratios are simply a measuring tool, not the final answers nor the end in themselves. They are one of the tools for evaluating the *past* performance and providing an indication of the future performance of the company. Ratios are a *control* technique and should be thought of as furnishing management with a "red flag" when a ratio has deviated from an established norm, or average, or predetermined standard.

Accordingly, ratio analysis is meaningless without an *adequate feedback* system by which management is promptly informed of a problem demanding immediate attention and correction.

While accountants are concerned primarily with the *construction* of the financial statements, particularly their technical accuracy and validity, the accountant is also relied upon by the many different users of the statements for assistance in the interpretation of the financial information. The accountant must use experience and technical skill to evaluate information and to contribute to management decisions that will maximize the optimum allocation of an organization's economic resources.

Basic Analysis Techniques

Much of the analytical data obtained from the statements is expressed in terms of ratios and percentages. (Carrying calculations to one decimal place is sufficient for most analysis purposes.) The basic analysis technique is to use these ratios and percentages in either a *horizontal* or *vertical* analysis, or both.

Horizontal analysis.   Here, similar figures from several years' financial statements are compared. For example, it may be useful to run down two years' balance sheets and compare the current assets, plant assets, current liabilities, long-term liabilities, etc., on one balance sheet with the similar items on the other and note the amount and percentage increases or decreases for each item. Of course, the comparison can be for more than two years. A number of years may be used, each year being compared with the base year or the immediate preceding year.

Vertical analysis.   Here, component parts are compared to the totals in a single statement. For example, it can be determined what percentage each item of expense on the income statement is of the total net sales, or, what percentage of the total assets the current assets comprise.

Ratios.   Customarily, the *numerator* of the equation is expressed first, then the denominator. For example, fixed assets to equity means fixed assets *divided by* equity. Also, whenever the numerator is the larger figure, there is a tendency to use the word "turnover" for the result.

As indicated above, these techniques are widely used, generally in the course of one analysis.

BALANCE SHEET ANALYSIS

The significance of the balance sheet is that it shows relationships between classes of assets and liabilities. From long experience, businessmen have learned that certain relationships indicate the company is in actual or potential trouble or is in good financial shape. For example, these relationships may indicate that the business is short of working capital, is undercapitalized generally, or has a bad balance between short- and long-term debt.

It must be emphasized that there are no fixed rules concerning the relationships. There are wide variations between industries and even within a single industry. It is often more valuable to measure these relationships against the past history of the same company than to use them in comparison with other businesses. If sharp disparities do show, however, it is usually wise not to ignore them. Many of the so-called "excesses" that in the past have led to recessions often show up in the balance sheets of individual companies. The most important balance sheet ratios and their implications for the business are discussed below.

Ratio of Current Assets to Current Liabilities

The *current ratio* is probably the most widely-used measure of liquidity, i.e., a company's ability to pay its bills. It measures the ability of the business to meet its current liabilities. The current ratio indicates the extent to which the current liabilities are covered. For example, if current assets total $400,000 and current liabilities are $100,000, the current ratio is 4 to 1.

Good current ratios will range from about 2 to almost 4 to 1. However, the ratio will vary widely in different industries. For example, companies which collect quickly on their accounts and do not have to carry very large inventories can usually operate with a lower current ratio than those companies whose collections are slower and inventories larger.

If current liabilities are subtracted from current assets, the resulting figure is the *working capital* of the company; in other words, the amount of free capital which is immediately available for use in the business. One of the most significant reasons for the failure of small businesses is the lack of working capital, which makes it difficult or impossible for the business to cope with sudden changes in worsening economic conditions. Conversely, lack of a comfortable amount of working capital may prevent a small business from taking advantage of opportunities to expand in a growing economy.

The details of working capital flow are presented in the two-year comparative Statement of Cash Flows, a mandatory part of the financial statements.

An important feature of the ratios to remember is that when both factors are decreased by the same amount, the ratio is increased:

	Old	Change	New
Current Assets	$100,000	$(25,000)	75,000
Current Liabilities	50,000	(25,000)	25,000
Working Capital	50,000	—0—	50,000
Ratio	2 to 1		3 to 1

By paying off $25,000 worth of liabilities (depleting Cash), you have increased the ratio from 2 to 1 to 3 to1. Note that the *dollar* amount of *working capital* remains the same $50,000.

Conversely, should you borrow $50,000 on short-terms (increasing Cash and Current Liabilities), you would *reduce* the ratio to *11/2 to 1* ($150,000/ 100,000), again with the dollar amount of working capital remaining at $50,000.

A variation of the current ratio is the *acid test*. This is the ratio of *quick assets* (cash, marketable securities, and accounts receivable) to *current liabilities*. This ratio eliminates the inventory from the calculation, since inventory may not be readily convertible to cash.

Acid-Test Ratio

The current ratio does not disclose the fact that a portion of the current assets may be tied up in slow-moving inventories, which leaves the question of how long it will take to transform the inventories into finished product and how much will be realized on the sale of the merchandise. Elimination of inventories and prepaid expenses from the current assets will give better information for short-term creditors. A *quick* or *acid-test ratio* relates total current liabilities to cash, marketable securities, and receivables. If this total is $150 divided by current liabilities of $100, the acid-test ratio is 11/2 to 1 which is low compared to an industry average of 3 to 1. This means a company would have difficulty meeting its short-term obligations and would have to obtain additional current assets from other sources.

Defensive-Interval Ratio

The defensive-interval ratio is computed by dividing defensive assets— cash, marketable securities, and receivables—by projected daily expenditures from operations. This ratio measures the time span a firm can operate with present liquid assets without resorting to revenues from next year's sources. Projected daily expenditures are computed by dividing cost of goods sold plus selling and administrative expenses and other ordinary expenses by 365 days. Assuming a company has a defensive-interval measure of 150 days and an industry average of 75 days, the 150 days provides a company with a high degree of protection, and can offset the weakness indicated by low current and acid-test ratios that a company might have.

Ratio of Current Liabilities to Stockholders' Equity

This ratio measures the relationship between the short-term creditors of the business and the owners. Excessive short-term debt is frequently a danger sign, since it means that the short-term creditors are providing much or all of the company's working capital. If anything happens to concern the short-term creditors, they will demand immediate repayment and create the risk of insolvency. Short-term creditors are most often suppliers of the business, and the company's obligation to them is listed under accounts payable. However, short-term creditors may also include short-term lenders.

A general rule occasionally cited for this ratio is that for a business with a tangible capital and earnings (net worth) of less than $250,000, current liabilities should not exceed two-thirds of this tangible net worth. For companies having a tangible net worth over $250,000, current liabilities should not exceed three-fourths of tangible net worth.

Tangible net worth is used instead of total net worth because intangible assets (such as patents and copyrights) may have no actual market value if the company is forced to offer them in distress selling.

Ratio of Total Liabilities to Stockholders' Equity

The ratio differs from the preceding one in that it includes only long-term liabilities. Since the long-term creditors of a company are normally not in a position to demand immediate payment, as are short-term creditors, this ratio may be moderately greater than the preceding one without creating any danger for the company. However, the ratio should never exceed 100 percent in an industrial company. If it did, this would mean that the company's creditors have a larger stake in the enterprise than the owners themselves. Under such circumstances, it is very likely that credit would not be renewed when the existing debts matured. Utilities and financial companies can operate safely with much higher ratios because more of their liabilities are long-term.

Ratio of Fixed Assets to Stockholders' Equity

The purpose of this ratio is to measure the relationship between fixed and current assets. The ratio is obtained by dividing the book value of the fixed assets by the tangible value of stockholders' equity. A rule sometimes used is that if tangible net worth is under $250,000, fixed assets should not exceed two-thirds of tangible net worth. If tangible net worth is over $250,000, fixed assets should not exceed three-fourths of tangible net worth.

Ratio of Fixed Assets to Long-Term Liabilities

Since long-term notes and bonds are often secured by mortgages on fixed assets, a comparison of the fixed assets with the long-term liabilities reveals what "coverage" the note or bondholders have—i.e., how much protection they have for their loans by way of security. Furthermore, where the fixed assets exceed the long-term liabilities by a substantial margin, there is room for borrowing additional long-term funds on the strength of the fixed asset position.

Ratio of Cost of Goods Sold to Inventory —Inventory Turnover

One of the most frequent causes of business failure is lack of inventory control. A firm that is optimistic about future business may build up its inventory to greater than usual amounts Then, if the expected business does not materialize, the company will be forced to stop further buying and may also have difficulty paying its creditors. In addition, if a company is not selling off its inventory regularly, that item, or part of it, is not really a *current* asset. Additionally, there may be a considerable amount of unsalable inventory included in the total. For all these reasons, a business is interested in knowing how often the inventory "turns over" during the year. In other words, how long will the current inventory be on the shelves, and how soon will it be turned into money?

To find out how often inventory turns over, the average inventory is compared to the cost of goods sold shown on the income statement. (Typically, average is computed by adding opening and closing inventories and dividing the total by two.) For example, if average inventory is $2 million and cost of goods sold adds up to $6 million, during the course of the year, the company has paid for three times the average inventory. Therefore, it can be said that the inventory turned over three times, and at year-end there remained about a four months' supply of inventory on hand.

Because information about cost of goods sold and average inventory may not be readily available in published reports, another way to measure the same results is by using the ratio of net sales to inventory. In this ratio, net sales is substituted for cost of goods sold. Since net sales will always be a larger figure (because it includes the business's profit margin), the resulting inventory turnover will be a higher figure.

How large an inventory should a company carry? That depends upon many factors within a particular business or industry. What may be large or small may vary with the type of business or the time of year. An automobile dealer with a large inventory at the beginning or middle of a model year will be in a strong position. A large inventory at the end of the season places him in a weak financial position.

Ratio of Inventory to Working Capital

This is another ratio to measure over- or under-inventory. Working capital is current assets minus current liabilities. If inventory is too high a proportion of working capital, the business is short on quick assets—cash and accounts receivable. A general rule for this ratio is that businesses of tangible net worth of less than $250,000 should not have an inventory which is more than three-fourths of net working capital. For a business with tangible net worth in excess of $250,000, inventory should not exceed net working capital. The larger-size business can tolerate a condition where there are no quick assets because its larger inventory can be borrowed against; in addition, it presumably has fixed assets which can be mortgaged if necessary.

Inventory as a percentage of current assets may indicate a significant relationship when comparison is made between companies in the same industry, but not between different types of companies because of other variables.

Receivables Turnover

An important consideration for any business is the length of time it takes to collect its accounts receivable. The longer accounts receivable are outstanding, the greater the need for the business to raise working capital from other sources. In addition, a longer collection period increases the risk of bad debts. A general rule for measuring the collection period is that it should not be more than one-third greater than the net selling terms offered by the company. For example, if goods are sold on terms of 30 days net, the average collection period should be about 40 days, though this varies from industry to industry. Special rules apply in the case of installment selling.

Another way of measuring the collection rate of accounts receivable is to divide the net sales from the income statement by the average accounts receivable. This gives the accounts receivable turnover; i.e., how many times during the year the average accounts receivable were collected. A comparison with prior years reveals whether the company's collection experience is getting better or worse. The faster the turnover, the more reliable the current and acid-test ratios are for financial analytical purposes.

Asset Turnover

This ratio indicates how efficiently a company utilizes its assets. If the turnover rate is high, the indication is that a company is using its assets efficiently to generate sales. If the turnover ratio is low, a company either has to use its assets more efficiently or dispose of them. The asset turnover ratio is affected by the depreciation method used. If an accelerated method of depreciation is used, the results would be a higher turnover rate than if the straight-line method is used, all other factors being equal.

Book Value of the Securities

This figure represents the value of the outstanding securities according to the values shown on the company's books. This may have little relationship to market value—especially in the case of common stock. Profitable companies often show a low net book value, but report very substantial earnings.

Railroads, on the other hand, may show a high book value for their common stock, but have such low or irregular earnings that the stock's market price is much less than the book value. Insurance companies, banks and investment companies are exceptions. Since most of their assets are liquid—cash, accounts receivable, marketable securities—the book value of their common stock may well present a fair approximation of the market value.

Nevertheless, book value is an important test of financial strength. It is computed by simply subtracting all liabilities from total assets. The remaining sum represents the book value of the equity interest in the business. In computing this figure, it is a good idea to include only tangible assets—land, machinery, inventory, etc. A patent right or other intangible may be given a large dollar value on the balance sheet, but in the event of liquidation may not be salable at all. The theory underlying the measurement of book value is that it is a good measure of how much cash and credit the company may be able to raise if it comes upon bad times. Book value is usually expressed per share outstanding.

Book value is also an important measure for the bondholders of the company. For them, the value has the significance of telling them how many dollars per bond outstanding the company has in available assets. Since they have a call on the company's assets before either the preferred stockholders or the common stockholders, a substantial book value per bond in excess of the face amount of the bond offers relative assurance of the safety of the bond—assurance that funds will be available to pay off the bonds when they become due. To find the book value of the bonds, add together the total stockholders' equity and the amount of the bonds outstanding.

For example, stockholders' equity totals $5 million. Bonded indebtedness is $2 million. From this $7 million total we subtract $1 million of intangibles. That leaves $6 million of net tangible assets. This represents a coverage of three times the total bond indebtedness, usually a fairly substantial coverage.

INCOME STATEMENT ANALYSIS

Just as with the balance sheet, most of the figures obtained from the income statement acquire real meaning only by comparison with other figures, either with similar figures of previous years of the same company or with the corresponding figures of other companies in the same or similar business.

For example, comparisons can be made between each significant item of expense and cost and net sales to get a percentage of net sales (vertical analysis) which can then be compared with other companies. Percentages are more meaningful to compare than absolute dollar amounts, since the volume of business done by one company in the same industry may vary substantially from the volume of another company.

Comparison can also be made of each of the significant figures on the income statement with the same figures for prior years (horizontal analysis). Here, too, comparisons of percentages rather than absolute dollar amounts might be more meaningful if the volume of sales has varied substantially from year to year.

Other significant comparisons are covered in the following paragraphs.

Ratio of Long-Term Debt to Equity

This ratio measures the leverage potential of the business; that is, the varying effects which changes in operating profits will have on net profits. The rule is that the higher the debt ratio, the greater will be the effect on the common stock of changes in earnings because of increased interest expenses.

Many security analysts feel that in an industrial company equity should equal at least half the total of all equity and debt outstanding. Railroads and utilities, however, are likely to have more debt (and preferred stock) than common stock because of the heavy investments in fixed assets, much of which is financed by the use of debt and preferred stock.

A stock is considered to have high leverage if the issuing company has a high percentage of bonds and preferred stock outstanding in relation to the amount of common stock. In good years, this will mean that after bond interest and preferred stock dividends are paid, there will be an impressive earnings per share figure because of the small amount of common stock outstanding.

On the other hand, that same high leverage situation could cause real difficulty with even a moderate decline in earnings. Not only would the decline eliminate any dividends for the common stock, but also could even necessitate drawing from accumulated earnings to cover the full interest on its bonds.

Earnings Per Share (EPS)

Probably, the most important ratio used today is the earnings per share (EPS) figure. It is a *mandatory* disclosure on all annual financial (income) statements (for public companies) and mandatory for all interim statements (though unaudited) for public companies. Moreover, the EPS must be broken out separately for extraordinary items. The standards of calculation are quite complex where preferred stock, options and convertibility are involved.

FASB 128, *Earnings per Share*

FASB 128 established new standards for computing and presenting earning per share (EPS) and applies to entities with publicly held common stock or potential common stock.

It simplifies the admittedly complicated methods used for computing earnings per share previously found in APB 15, *Earnings Per Share,* and makes the requirements comparable to new international EPS standards adopted recently. In doing this, FASB 128 replaces the presentation of primary EPS with a presentation of basic EPS. It also requires dual presentation of basic and diluted EPS on the face of the income statement for all entities with complex capital structures and requires a reconciliation of the numerator and denominator of the basic EPS computation to the numerator and denominator of the diluted EPS computation.

The oft interpreted, reinterpreted, and much maligned APB 15 had required that entities with simple capital structures present a single "earnings per common share" on the face of the income statement, whereas those with complex capital structures had to present both "primary" and "fully diluted" EPS. Primary EPS showed the amount of income attributed to each share of common stock if every common stock equivalent were converted into common stock. Fully diluted EPS considers common stock equivalents and all other securities that could be converted into common stock. The two EPS figures required under FASB 128 follow:

1. Basic Earnings Per Share is computed by dividing income available to stockholders by the weighted average number of common shares outstanding during the period. Shares issued during the period and shares reacquired during the period should be weighted for the portion of the period they were outstanding. The formula would be: (Net income minus preferred dividends) divided by common stock.

   Under the old rules, U.S. companies with complex capital structures could not present a basic earnings per share figure. (A company has a complex capital structure when it has issued securities convertible into common stock or has agreements to issue common stock at some future date.) The principal difference between basic and primary earnings per share is that the latter takes into account so-called common share equivalents. In nearly every country outside of the U.S. that requires an earnings per share disclosure, the requirement calls for a basic earnings per share presentation rather than a primary EPS figure. An entity's basic earnings per share will show higher earnings per share than primary earnings per share did, but this will mean no change as far as a company's actual equity valuation is concerned.

2. Diluted EPS reflects the potential dilution that could occur if securities or other contracts to issue common stock were exercised or converted into common stock or resulted in the issuance of common stock that would then share in the earnings of the entity. It is figured in a similar manner to basic EPS after adjusting the numerator and denominator for the possible dilution. Since it is, therefore, computed in a similar man-

ner to fully diluted EPS under APB 15, it will produce a similar earnings per share figure.

Equity Valuation Unchanged. The new standard did not change U.S. equity valuations because:

1. Even though basic earnings per share show a higher figure than primary earnings per share, informed investors do not use basic earnings per share anyway for companies with complex capital structures because it does not take into account the potential dilutive effect of convertibles, options, warrants, and the like.
2. Most entities' dilutive earnings per share are substantially the same as their fully diluted earnings per share had been.

Resulting Changes. Of course, the most important change introduced by the FASB 128 is the elimination of the complicated calculations necessary to arrive at primary earnings per share and replace them with the simpler calculations necessary to obtain basic earnings per share for disclosure.

In addition, diluted EPS is somewhat different from "fully diluted earnings per share." Not only is "fully" dropped, but the calculation of the figure is changed in several ways:

1. Elimination of the provision that the diluted earnings per share need not be given if the potential dilution is less than three percent.
2. Elimination of the use of the end of period stock price in the treasury stock method calculation to determine maximum dilution.
3. Elimination of the modified treasury stock method that was used to calculate potential dilution in cases when an unusually large number of options or warrants were outstanding.
4. Use of the earnings from continuing operations as the "control figure" to determine if a security or contingent issuance is antidilutive in certain situations.

The new statement not only supersedes APB 15 and AICPA Accounting Interpretation 1–102 of APB 15, but it also supersedes or amends other accounting pronouncements scattered throughout accounting literature. The provisions in this Statement are substantially the same as those in International Accounting Standard 33, *Earnings per Share,* issued by the International Accounting Standards Committee at the same time.

Sales Growth

The raw element of profit growth is an increase in sales (or revenues when the company's business is services). While merely increasing sales is no guarantee that higher profits will follow, it is usually the first vital step; therefore, in analyzing a company, the sales figures for the past four or five years are important. If they have been rising and there is no reason to believe the company's markets are near the saturation point, it is reasonable to assume that the rise will continue.

When a company's sales have jumped by the acquisition of another firm, it is important to find out if the acquisition was accomplished by the issuance of additional common stock, by the assumption of additional debt, or for cash. If the company was paid for by common stock and if the acquired firm's earnings are the same on a per-share basis as those of the acquiring firm, the profit picture remains exactly as it was before. The additional sales growth is balanced by the *dilution of the equity*—that is, the larger number of shares now sharing in the earnings.

The situation is quite different if the purchase was for cash or in exchange of bonds or preferred stock. Here, no dilution of the common stock has occurred. The entire profits of the new firm (minus the interest which must be paid on the new debt or the interest formerly earned on the cash) benefit the existing shareholders.

In any event, acquisitions of new companies often require a period of consolidation and adjustment, frequently followed by a decreased rate of sales growth.

Consideration should be given to the effect of inflation on sales. A situation can exist where the increase in sales may be caused by the increase in prices. The result may be that unit sales have dropped in relation to the previous year's, but the dollar sales have increased. Comparing unit sales may be a better method of ascertaining the sales increase under certain circumstances.

Computing Operating Profit

A company's costs of operations fall into two groups: *cost of goods sold* and *cost of operations*. The first relates to all the costs of producing the goods or services matched to the revenues produced by those costs. The second includes all other costs not directly associated with the production costs, such as selling and administrative costs (usually called period expenses).

Subtracting both of these groups of costs from sales leaves *operating profit*. Various special costs and special forms of income are then added or subtracted from operating income to get *net income before taxes* After deducting state and federal income taxes, the final figure (which is commonly used for computing the profit per share) is *net income*. When analyzing a company, however, you will often be most interested in the operating profit figure, since this reflects the real earning capacity of the company.

The best way to look at cost figures is as a percentage of sales. Thus, a company may spend 90 cents out of every dollar in operating costs. We say its cost percentage is 90 percent or, more commonly, its *operating profit margin* is 10 percent. Profit margins vary a great deal among industries, running anywhere from 1 percent to 20 percent of sales; thus comparisons should not be made between companies in different industries. The trend of the operating profit margin for a particular company, however, will give an excellent picture of how well management is able to control costs. If sales increases are obtained only by cutting prices, this will immediately show as a decrease in the margin of profit. In introducing a new product it is sometimes necessary to incur special costs to make initial market penetration, but this should be only temporary.

The most used, examined and discussed ratio within a company is the *gross profit ratio*. More significance is probably attached to this ratio than to any other because increases usually indicate improved performance (more sales, more efficient production) and decreases indicate weaknesses (poor selling effort, waste in production, weak inventory controls).

When comparing a company with others in the same field, if the company's profit margin is low by comparison, it signals troubles ahead; if it is high, the company appears to be a worthy competitor.

The terminology in the gross profit percentages is sometimes confusing and misinterpreted, especially when the word "markup" is used. As an example:

	$	%
Sales	$ 100	100%
Cost of Sales	80	80%
Gross Profit	$ 20	20%

In conventional usage, there is a 20 percent gross profit or margin on the sale (20/100). However, to determine the *markup*, the cost of sales is the denominator and the gross profit is the numerator (20/80 equals a 25 percent markup).

Starting with gross profit *percentage desired*, to gross 20 percent, what should the selling price be? (The only known factor is cost.)

	%	Known	As calculated
Selling price	100%	?	$ 150
Cost	80%	$ 120	120
Gross Profit	20%	?	$ 30

Selling price is always 100 percent. If cost is $120 and is equal to 80 percent of the selling price (it must be 80 percent because a gross of 20 percent was set), divide $120 by 80 percent to get the 100 percent selling price of $150.

Ratio of Net Sales to Stockholders' Equity

A company acquires assets in order to produce sales which yield a profit. If tangible assets yield too few sales, the company is suffering from underselling: i.e., the underutilization of its assets. On the other hand, the company may suffer from overtrading; i.e., too many sales in proportion to its tangible net worth. In other words, there is too heavy a reliance on borrowed funds to generate sales.

Another way of measuring the effective utilization of assets is to determine the ratio of net sales to total assets (excluding long-term investments).

In either case, comparisons of these ratios with similar ratios of other companies in the same industry can indicate the relative efficiency in utilization of assets of the company being analyzed.

Ratio of Net Sales to Working Capital

This is similar to the preceding ratio, since it measures the relationship between sales and assets. In this case, however, the ratio measures whether the company has sufficient net current assets to support the volume of its sales or, on the other hand, if the capital invested in working capital is working hard enough to produce sales.

Profit Margin on Sales

The profit margin on sales is obtained by dividing net income by net sales for the period. A ratio of 7.5 percent compared to an industry average of 4.6 percent indicates a company is achieving an above-average rate of profits on each sales dollar received.

The profit margin on sales does not indicate how profitable a company is for a given period of time. Only by determining how many times the total assets turned over during a period of time is it possible to ascertain the amount of net income earned on total assets. The rate of return on assets is computed by using net income as the numerator and average total assets as a denominator. An average of 6.2 percent compared to an industry average of 4.9 percent is above the average of an industry and results from a high profit margin on sales.

Rate of Return on Common Stock Equity

This ratio is defined as net income after interest, taxes, and preferred stock dividends (if any) divided by average common stockholders' equity. When the rate of return on common stock equity is higher than the rate of return on total assets, the company is considered to be trading on the equity. Trading on the equity increases a company's financial risk, but it increases a company's earnings.

Dividend Yield

The dividend yield is the cash dividend per share divided by the market price of the stock at the time the yield is determined. This ratio gives the rate of return that an investor will receive at the time on an investment in a stock or bond.

Times Interest Earned

This ratio is computed by dividing income before interest charges and taxes by the interest charge. The ratio indicates the safety of a bondholder's investment. A company that has an interest earned ratio of 5 to 1 shows a significantly safer position for meeting its bond interest obligations than a company with a lower ratio.

STATEMENT OF CHANGES IN STOCKHOLDERS' EQUITY

This statement presents an equity analysis of changes from year to year in each shareholder's account, records any additional shares issued, foreign currency translation gains/losses, dividends per share (if paid), retained earnings. This last figure indicates how well the company itself is doing by revealing how much of the profits it can retain to finance further growth opportunities. In an era of corporate raiding and takeovers, management may be wise to be sure that retained earnings are not too high, but are put to good use in increasing total earnings per share for the benefit of current stockholders.

Return on Equity

This ratio is another method of determining earning power. Here, the opening equity (capital stock plus retained earnings, plus or minus any other equity section items) is divided into the net income for the year to give the percentage earned on that year's investment.

Return to Investors

This is a relatively new ratio used mostly by financial publications, primarily for comparison of many companies in similar industries. The opening equity is divided into the sum of the dividends paid plus the market price appreciation of the period. In addition, the ratio is sometimes extended to cover five years, ten years or more.

Dividend Payout Ratio

The *dividend* per common share is divided by the *earnings* per common share to get the *percentage* of dividend payout.

The dividends on common stock will vary with the profitability of the company but other considerations also affect the percent of payout:

1. the relative stability of the earnings
2. the need for new capital
3. the directors' judgment concerning the outlook for earnings
4. the general views of management relating to the advisability of
   a. plowing back a large part of earnings into the business, or
   b. raising additional funds from outside sources

Dividends on the preferred stock are not subject to a year-to-year fluctuation. If the fixed dividend on *cumulative* preferred stock for any year cannot be met, the payments would accumulate and be paid before any dividends could be declared on the common stock.

FASB 130, *REPORTING COMPREHENSIVE INCOME*

FASB 130 began in conjunction with the Exposure Draft (ED) on derivatives and hedging. However, since there is much less in it to cause prolonged controversy, this Standard was issued requiring reporting and display of comprehensive income effective in 1998, while the new derivatives standard became effective on June 15, 2000. Financial statements from previous periods used for comparison must be reclassified in line with the provisions of Statement 130.

At the time the EDs were issued, U.S. GAAP did not use a comprehensive income concept. The idea was to issue the two EDs simultaneously in anticipation of employing the concept in connection with the derivative and other future standards.

All of the items that are required to be recognized under accounting standards as components of comprehensive income must now be reported in a financial statement that is displayed with the same degree of prominence as other financial statements.

Comprehensive Income Defined

Comprehensive income is defined in FASB Concepts Statement 6, *Elements of Financial Statements* as, ". . . the change in equity (net assets) of a business enterprise during a period from transactions and other events and circumstances from non-owner sources. It includes all changes in equity during a period except those resulting from investments by owners and distributions to owners."

FASB 130 considers that comprehensive income consists of two major components—net income and "other comprehensive income." The latter refers to revenues, expenses, gains and losses, that according to GAAP are included in comprehensive income, but excluded from net income. They are direct debits or credits to owners' equity that do not involve transactions with owners, such as foreign currency translation gains and losses, unrealized gains or losses on marketable securities classified as available-for-sale, and minimum pension liability adjustments. Thus, comprehensive income is the total of net income plus the revenue, expense, gain and loss changes in equity during a period which now is not included in net income.

Equity Valuation Not Affected

This new display and related disclosures will not influence equity valuations, nor is any new or additional information disclosed. It merely repackages existing disclosed data in a new format. FASB 130 may not be of particular interest to sophisticated investors, creditors, and securities firms, but it should be of interest to accountants who have the task of implementing the new format. However, this should not be a particularly onerous job since it is largely a matter of displaying known financial data rather than calculating additional figures that would change recognition of income.

On the other hand, the FASB does appear to believe that, used in conjunction with related disclosures and other information in the financial statements, the comprehensive income information could help the knowledgeable user in assessing an entity's activities, and the timing and extent of future cash flows. Further, the Board emphasizes that while a total comprehensive income figure is useful, information about its components may give more insight into an enterprise's activities.

Format for Presentation of Comprehensive Income

One aspect for the accountant to consider is the best way to use this new display to inform, but not confuse, the less sophisticated user of financial statements. Since the Statement does not require a specific financial statement format for the display of comprehensive income and its components, the accountant may be expected to make some choices.

1. The requirement to report a new "income" figure for the quarter may be displayed as *either* a performance measurement or a change in equity. Which to choose?

2. Companies are permitted to display total comprehensive income and its components in either an income statement type format or in a statement of changes in equity format. Would it be better to preserve the current income statement as a separate display and show a company's net income figure as the bottom line? Or not? (With the equity format, a statement of changes in equity must be displayed as a primary financial statement.)

3. The Standard permits companies to report only a total for comprehensive income in condensed interim financial statements issued to shareholders. Would it be less confusing to show total comprehensive income as a part of a complete display of the calculations every time rather than as a single figure?

Application of Requirements

FASB 130 applies to all companies that present a full set of general-purpose financial statements. Investment companies, defined benefit pension plans, and other employee benefit plans that are exempt from the requirement to provide a statement of cash flows by FASB 102, *Statement of Cash Flows—Exemption of Certain Enterprises and Certification of Cash Flows from Certain Securities Acquired for Resale,* are not exempt from requirements of FASB 130 if it applies in all other respects. However, it does not apply to organizations that have no items of comprehensive income in any period presented, or to not-for-profit organizations that are covered by FASB 117, *Financial Statements of Not-for-Profit Organizations.*

As mentioned above, the Statement suggests how to report and display comprehensive income and its components, but does not provide guidance on items that are to be included. For this guidance, the existing and future accounting standards mentioned earlier will need to be consulted.

Components of Comprehensive Income

At this time, eight items qualify, according to GAAP, as components of other comprehensive income that, under prior standards, bypassed the income statement and had to be reported as a balance within a separate component of equity in a statement of financial position.

1. Foreign currency translation adjustments.
2. Gains and losses on foreign currency transactions that are designated as, and are effective as, economic hedges of a net investment in a foreign entity, commencing as of the designation date.
3. Gains and losses on intercompany foreign currency transactions that are of a long-term-investment nature (i.e., settlement is not planned or anticipated in the foreseeable future), when the entities to the transaction are consolidated, combined, or accounted for by the equity method in the reporting enterprise's financial statements.
4. A change in the market value of a futures contract that qualifies as a hedge of an asset reported at fair value according to FASB 115, *Accounting for Certain Investments in Debt and Equity Securities.*
5. A net loss recognized under FASB 87, *Employers' Accounting for Pensions,* as an additional pension liability not yet recognized as net periodic pension cost.
6. Unrealized holding gains and losses on available-for-sale securities.
7. Unrealized holding gains and losses that result from a debt security being transferred into the available-for-sale category from the held-to-maturity category.
8. Subsequent decreases (if not an other-than-temporary impairment) or increases in the fair value of available for-sale securities previously written down as impaired.

(This list will be expanded now that the derivatives and hedging standard is promulgated. Some gains and/or losses from those transactions will be included as part of other comprehensive income.)

Terminology

The Statement does not require that the descriptive terms "comprehensive income," "total comprehensive income," or "other comprehensive income" be used in financial statements. It permits companies to use equivalent terms, such as "total non-owner changes in equity," "comprehensive loss" or other appropriate descriptive labels. It may be that most entities will choose to use alternative terms since "comprehensive income" still has a rather hollow ring to it.

Cash Flow and Equity Valuation Not Affected

Inasmuch as all of the items included in other comprehensive income are noncash items, the FASB decided that indirect-method cash flow statement presentation would continue to begin with net income as required by FASB 95, *Statement of Cash Flows.*

FASB 130 should clarify the extent to which revenue, expense, gain and loss items are being taken directly to owners' equity, but, as mentioned above, the display of comprehensive income and its components will not affect equity valuation. Unlike the requirements in FASB 131, *Disclosures About Segments of an Enterprise and Related Information,* which calls for greatly expanded reporting on segments, the requirements of FASB 130 call for no new data. Since informed investors have always examined owners' equity to evaluate the material now collected under the other comprehensive income items, the new display should have little impact on the public's conception of a company's financial condition.

APB Opinion 22, *Disclosure of Accounting Policies*

APB 22 covers *Disclosure of Accounting Policies.* A description of all significant accounting policies of the reporting entity should be included as an integral part of all financial statements. Whether these statements are issued in presenting the entity's financial position, changes in the financial position, or in showing results of operations in accordance with GAAP, a description of all significant accounting policies, methods and practices of the reporting entity should be included as an integral part of all financial statements. When it is appropriate to issue one or more basic financial statements without the others, these statements should also comprise the pertinent accounting policies. Not-for-profit entities should also present details of their accounting policies as an integral part of their financial statements.

Content and Format of Disclosures

1. Disclosure of accounting policies should identify and describe the accounting principles employed by the reporting business and the methods of applying those principles which are important in the determination of financial position, changes in financial position, or results of operations. The disclosure should include decisions concerning applica-

bility of principles relating to recognition of revenue and allocation of asset costs to current and future periods. The disclosure statement should comprise all the reasoning behind the choice of, or an explanation of, the accounting principles and methods employed that involve any of the following:

a. Selection of one practice over another from existing acceptable alternatives.

b. Principles and methods peculiar to the industry of the reporting firm, even when such principles and methods are characteristically followed in that industry

c. Unusual or innovative applications of generally accepted accounting principles or of practices and methods peculiar to that industry.

2. Examples of disclosures commonly required in regard to accounting policies include those relating to basis of consolidation, depreciation methods, amortization of intangibles, inventory pricing, accounting for research and development costs and the basis for amortization thereof, translation of foreign currencies, recognition of profit on long-term construction-type contracts, recognition of revenue from franchising and leasing operations, and any other items deemed pertinent to give a complete picture of a firm's financial status.

3. The format follows a plan of having a separate *Summary of Significant Accounting Policies* preceding the notes to the financial statements or, in some cases, as the initial note of the statement.

Chapter 2
Revenue and Expenses

REVENUE (INCOME)

The principles upon which net income is determined derive from the pervasive measurement principles, such as realization, and the modifying conventions, such as conservatism.

The entire process of income determination ("matching") consists of identifying, measuring and relating revenue and expenses for an accounting period. Revenue is usually determined by applying the realization principle, with the changes in net asset value interrelated with the recognition of revenue. Revenue arises from three general activities:

1. Selling products;
2. Rendering services or letting others use owned resources, resulting in interest, rent, etc;
3. Disposing of other resources (not products), such as equipment or investments.

Revenue does not include proceeds from stockholders, lenders, asset purchases or prior period adjustments.

Revenue, in the balance sheet sense, is a gross increase in assets or a gross decrease in liabilities recognized and measured in conformity with GAAP, which results from those profit-directed activities that can change owners' equity.

Revenue is considered *realized* when:

1. The earning process is complete or virtually complete, and
2. An exchange has taken place.

The objectives of accounting determination of income are not always the same as the objectives used for tax purposes.

There are various acceptable ways of determining income:

Revenue (see three general activities above):

1. Accrual method—this is financial accounting and GAAP.
2. Cash method—this is *not* considered financial accounting, and not GAAP, since one of the characteristics of GAAP is the *accrual* of appropriate items.
3. Installment sales method—generally for retail stores.
4. Completion of production method—used for precious metals.
5. For long-term construction contracts:
   a. Completed contract method.
   b. Percentage-of-completion method.
6. For leasing activities:
   a. The direct financing method.
   b. The operating method.
   c. The sales method.
7. The cost recovery method (used for installment sales).
8. Consolidation method—for majority-owned subsidiaries (over 50%).
9. Equity method—for non-consolidated subsidiaries and for controlled non-subsidiaries.

Other types of income requiring special determination:

1. Extraordinary items of income.
2. Unrealized income arising from:
   a. Foreign currency holdings or transactions.
   b. Ownership of marketable securities shown as current assets.

A *shareholder* in a corporation does *not* have income when that corporation earns income (except for a Sub-S corporation). The shareholder has, and reports for tax purposes, income only upon *distribution* of that income in the form of dividends. Generally, distributions of stock—stock dividends and stock splits—are *not* income to the shareholder, but merely an adjustment of the number of shares he holds (for the same original cost plus token costs, if any). However, there are some situations which call for the stockholder to report stock dividends as income.

If a buyer has a right of return to the seller, revenue is recognized if *all* of the following criteria are met:

1. Buyer is obligated to pay (and not contingent upon resale of the product) or has paid the seller.
2. Buyer's obligation would not be changed by theft, damage, or destruction of the product.
3. Seller does not have any significant obligation to buyer related to resale of the product by the buyer.
4. Buyer's business must have economic substance separate from the seller's business.

If these criteria are met, sales revenue and cost of sales reported in the income statement are reduced to reflect estimated returns; expected losses are accrued.

EXPENSES

Expenses are one of the six basic elements of financial accounting, along with assets, liabilities, owners' equity, revenue and net income.

> Expenses are determined by applying the expense recognition principles on the basis of relationships, between acquisition costs [the term "cost" is commonly used to refer to the amount at which assets are initially recorded, regardless of how determined], and either the independently determined revenue or accounting periods. Since the point in time at which revenue and expenses are recognized is also the time at which changes in amounts of net assets are recorded, income determination is interrelated with asset valuation.

All costs are not expenses. Some costs are related to later periods, will provide benefits for later periods, and are carried forward as assets on the balance sheet. Other costs are incurred and provide no future benefit, having expired in terms of usefulness or applicability—these expired costs are called "expenses." All expenses, therefore, are part of the broader term "cost." These expired costs are not assets and are shown as deductions from revenue to determine net income.

> Expenses are gross decreases in assets or gross increases in liabilities recognized and measured in conformity with GAAP that result from those types of profit-directed activities that can change an owner's equity.

Recognizing Expenses

Three pervasive principles form the basis for recognizing expenses to be deducted from revenue to arrive at net income or loss:

1. Associating cause and effect ("matching"):

For example, manufacturing cost of goods sold is measured and matched to the *sale* of the product. Assumptions must be made as to how these costs attach to the product—whether on machine hours, space used, labor expended, etc. Assumptions must also be made as to how the costs flow out (LIFO, FIFO, average costs).

2. Systematic and rational allocation:

When there is no direct way to associate cause and effect and certain costs are known (or presumed) to have provided benefits during the accounting period, these costs are allocated to that period in a systematic and rational manner and to appear so to an unbiased observer. The methods of allocation should be consistent and systematic, though methods may vary for different types of costs. Examples are: Depreciation of fixed assets, amortization of intangibles, interperiod allocation of rent or interest. The allocation referred to here is not the allocation of expired manufacturing costs with the "cost" area to determine unit or job costs; it is rather the broader area of allocation to the manufacturing area from the unexpired asset account: Depreciation on factory building, rather than overhead-depreciation on Product A, B, or C.

3. Immediate recognition (period expenses):

Those costs which are expensed during an accounting period because:

a. They cannot be associated on a cause-and-effect basis with revenue, yet no useful purpose would be achieved by delaying recognition to a future period, or
b. They provide no discernible future benefits, or
c. They were recorded as assets in a prior period and now no longer provide discernible future benefits.

Examples are: Officer salaries, most selling expenses, legal fees, most general and administrative expenses.

OTHER EXPENSES (AND REVENUE)

Gains and losses.   Expenses and revenue from *other* than sales of products, merchandise or services may be separated from (operating) revenue and disclosed net separately.

Unusual items.   Unusual items of expense or income not meeting the criteria of "extraordinary" should be shown as a separate component of income from continuing operations.

Extraordinary items.   Extraordinary items are discussed elsewhere in this book. They should be shown separately—net of applicable taxes—*after* net income from continuing operations. If there are any disposals of business segments, they should be shown immediately prior to extraordinary items—also with tax effect.

IMPUTED INTEREST ON NOTES RECEIVABLE OR PAYABLE

Accounting Considerations

The AICPA sets forth the appropriate accounting when the face amount of certain receivables or payables ("notes") does not reasonably represent the present value of the consideration given or received in certain exchanges. The objective of these rules is to prevent the form of the transaction from prevailing over its economic substance.

(*Present value* is the sum of future payments, discounted to the present date at an appropriate rate of interest.)

APB Opinion 21 states that:

1. When a note is received or issued solely for cash, the note is presumed to have a present value equal to the cash received. If it is issued for cash equal to its face amount, it is presumed to earn the stated rate of interest.

2. When a note is received for cash and some other rights or privileges, the value of the rights or privileges should be given accounting recognition by establishing a note discount or premium account, with the offsetting amount treated as appropriate. An example is a five-year noninterest-bearing loan made to a supplier in partial consideration for a purchase of products at lower than prevailing market prices. Under such circumstances, the difference between the present value of the receivable and the cash lent to the supplier is regarded as (a) an additional cost of the purchased goods, and (b) interest income, amortized over the life of the note.

3. When a note is exchanged for property, goods, or services and (a) interest is not stated, or (b) it is stated but is unreasonable, or (c) the stated face amount of the note is materially different from the current cash sale price of goods (or services), the note, the sales price, and the cost of the property (goods or services) should be recorded at their fair value, or at an amount that reasonably approximates the market value of the note, whichever is more clearly determinable.

Any resulting discount or premium should be regarded as interest expense or income and be amortized over the life of the note, in such a way as to result in a constant effective rate of interest when applied to the amount outstanding at the beginning of any given period.

Opinion 21 also provides some general guides for determining an "appropriate" interest rate and the manner of amortization for financial reporting purposes.

IMPUTED INTEREST: When a sale is made for an amount that is collectible at a future time giving rise to an account receivable, the amount is regarded as consisting of a sales price *and* a charge for interest for the period of the payment deferral. APB Opinion 21 requires that in the absence of a stated rate of interest, the present value of the receivable should be determined by reducing the face amount of the receivable by an interest rate that is approximated under the circumstances for the period that payment is deferred.

This rate is the *imputed rate*. It is determined by approximating the rate the supplier pays for financing receivables, or by determining the buyer's credit standing and applying the rate the borrower would have to pay if borrowing the sum from, say, a bank.

The process of arriving at the present value of the receivable is referred to as *discounting* the sum. If the total present value of the receivable (face amount plus the imputed interest) is less than the face amount, the difference between the face value of the receivable and its present value is recognized as a discount. If the present value exceeds the face amount of the receivable, the difference is recognized as a premium.

The sale is recorded as a debit to a receivable account, a credit to a discount on the receivable, and a credit to sales at the present value as reported for the receivable. The discount is amortized as a credit to interest income over the life of the receivable. On the balance sheet any unamortized discount at the end of the accounting period is reported as a direct subtraction from the *face amount* of the receivable.

Example: Seller ships merchandise totaling $10,000 to a customer with payment deferred for five years. Seller and customer agree to impute an interest charge of 10 percent for the $10,000. The journal entries follow.

Accounts Receivable	10,000	
Sales (Present value at 10%)		6,209
Unamortized Discount		3,791
(To record the sale of merchandise		
at the present value of the receivable)		

The *interest method* is applied to amortize the discount.

End of Year 1		
Unamortized Discount	620.90	
Interest Income		620.90
(10% of $6,209.00)		
End of Year 2		
Unamortized Discount	682.99	
Interest Income		682.99
(10% of $6,829.90)		
End of Year 3		
Unamortized Discount	751.29	
Interest Income		751.29
(10% of $7,512.89)		
End of Year 4		
Unamortized Discount	826.42	
Interest Income		826.42
(10% of $8,264.18)		
Unamortized Discount	909.06	
End of Year 5		
Unamortized Discount	909.06	
Interest Income		909.06
(10% of $9,090.60)		

At the end of five years full amortization of the discount has been recorded and the face amount of the receivable results. (*Note*: Opinion No. 21 does not require the imputed interest method when ". . . receivables and payables arising from transactions with customers or suppliers in the normal course of business which are due in customary trade terms not exceeding approximately one year.")

CLASSIFYING AND REPORTING EXTRAORDINARY ITEMS

Income statement presentation requires that the results of *ordinary operations* be reported first, and applicable provision for income taxes provided for.

In order, the following should then be shown:

1. Results of discontinued operations:
   a. Income or loss from the operations discontinued for the portion of the period until discontinuance—shown net of tax, with the tax shown parenthetically;
   b. Loss (or gain) on disposal of the business segments, including provision for phase-out operating losses—also shown net of tax parenthetically.
2. Extraordinary items.

   Should be segregated and shown as the last factor used in arriving at net income for the period. Here, the caption is shown net of applicable income taxes, which are shown parenthetically.

   Note that extraordinary items do *not* include disposal of business segments as such, because they are segregated and shown separately prior thereto (as above).

   An example of the reporting of the above:

	1994		1993
Income from continuing operations before income taxes	$ xxx		$ xxx
Provision for income taxes	xx		xx
Income from continuing operations		$ xxx	xxx
Discontinued operations (Note):			
Income from operations of discontinued Division B (less applicable taxes of $xx)	$ xx		
	1994		1993
Loss on disposal of Division B, including provision for phase-out operating losses of $xx (less applicable income taxes of $xx)	xx	xx	
Income before extraordinary items		xxx	
Extraordinary items (less applicable income taxes of $xx)			
(Note)		xx	
Net Income		$ xxx	$ xxx
Earnings per share:			
Income from continuing operations		$ x.00	$ x.00
Discontinued operations		x.00	x.00
Extraordinary items		x.00	x.00
Net Income		$ x.00	$ x.00

Note that earnings per share should be broken out separately for the factors of discontinued operations and extraordinary items, as well as for income from (continuing) operations.

The criteria for classifying a transaction or event as an "extraordinary item" are as follows:

Extraordinary items are events and transactions that are distinguished by their unusual nature *and* by the infrequency of their occurrence. Thus, *both* of the following criteria should be met to classify an event or transaction as an extraordinary item:

1. *Unusual nature*—the underlying event or transaction should possess a high degree of abnormality and be of a type clearly unrelated to, or only incidentally related to, the ordinary and typical activities of the entity, taking into account the environment in which the entity operates.
2. *Infrequency of occurrence*—the underlying event or transaction should be of a type that would not reasonably be expected to recur in the foreseeable future, taking into account the environment in which the entity operates.

Items which are *not* to be reported as extraordinary, because they may recur or are not unusual, are:

1. Write-downs of receivables, inventories, intangibles, or leased equipment.
2. Effects of strikes.
3. Gains or losses on foreign currency translations.
4. Adjustment of accruals on long-term contracts.
5. Gains or losses on disposal of business segments.
6. Gains or losses from abandonment or sale of property, plant or equipment used in the business.

Note that some highly unusual occurrence might cause one of the above types of gains or losses and should be considered extraordinary, such as those resulting from: major casualties (earthquake), expropriations, and legal restrictions. Disposals of business segments, though not extraordinary in classification, should be shown separately on the income statement, just prior to extraordinary items, but after operations from continuing business.

Miscellaneous data pertaining to extraordinary items:

Bargain sales of stock to stockholders are *not* extraordinary items, but they should be shown separately.

A gain or a loss on sale of coin collections by a bank is *not* an extraordinary item.

PRESENT VALUE COMPUTATION AND APPLICATION

The procedure of computing interest on principal *and interest on interest* underlies the concept of *compounding*. There are a number of accounting procedures (accounting for bonds, accounts receivable, accounts payable, and leases, for example) to which the compound interest formula (and variations) can be applied.

1. The *future value* of a sum of money. If $1,000 (the principal P) is deposited in a bank today, what will be the balance (S) in the account in *n years* (or *periods*) if the bank accumulates interest at the rate of *i* percent per year?
2. The *present value* of a sum of money due at the end of a period of time. What is the value *today* of the amount owed if $1,000 has to be paid, say to a creditor, *n* years from today?
3. The *future value of an annuity* which is a series of *equal* payments made at *equal* intervals. If $1,000 a year is deposited for *n* years, how much will have accumulated at the end of the *n*-years period if the deposits earn interest at the rate of *i* percent per year?
4. The *present value of an annuity* which is a series of *equal* payments made at *equal* intervals. If we are to be paid $1,000 a year for *n* years, how much is this annuity worth today, given *i* percent rate of interest?

The formula for the future value of a sum of money is the familiar compound interest formula. In the four examples to follow let:

S = The future worth of a sum of money invested today.

P = Principal, or the sum of money that will accumulate to S amount of money.

i = The rate of interest (r may be substituted).

n = Number of periods of time.

It is important to understand that a "period of time" is not necessarily one year, even though rates of interest in the United States are always understood to mean the rate for a period of one year. A period can be any length of time—i.e., day, week, month, year, second, minute, hour. Time is a *continuous*, not a *discrete* function.

With compound interest the total amount accumulated (S in the formula) at the end of one period earns interest during the subsequent period, or "interest on interest." The formula is:

$$S = P(1 + i)^n$$

At this point it should be emphasized that the user no longer must do the arithmetic. Not only can the problem types be solved by the use of tables, but now inexpensive hand calculators will perform the computations and give the answers. The user has simply only to enter the numbers that represent the letters in the formula. Users with computers can, of course, program the formulas for permanent storage and simply "call out" whichever formula applies to the problem at hand. With respect to the arithmetic, however, three of the variables in the equation are always known quantities; therefore, finding the value of the fourth and *un*known variable follows.

A word of caution. Computational errors caused by entering the wrong value for *n* are not uncommon. If $i = 12\%$ and the compounding period is every six months, *n* in the formula is 6. If the compounding period is quarterly *n* is 3. If the compounding period is daily (as is the case in many financial institutions savings policies) *n* becomes i/360—360 days in the year are applied in this country for interest calculations instead of 365. This is because the *smaller* the denominator, the bit more interest the *lender* collects. However, if the formula applies to a problem involving U.S. Government bonds, a 365-day year must be assumed because it enables the government to borrow a bit cheaper, relatively.

Annuities

The previous discussion considers the accumulation of interest on a *single* payment, however the single payment may be invested. *Annuities* apply to problems that involve a series of *equal payments* (or investments, savings, etc.,) made at *equal intervals* of time. The period of time between payments is called the *payment period*. The period of time between computation of the interest accumulation is called the *interest-conversion period*. When the payment period exactly equals the interest-conversion period, the annuity is an *ordinary annuity*. The equal payments are termed rents, which are spread over equal periods of time, the first rent payment made at the *start* of the annuity, and the last payment made at the *end* of the annuity.

The *future worth* of the annuity is the sum of the future worths of each of the separate rents. Assuming $100 invested we have $100 at time 1. At time 2 we have the $100 invested that day, plus the $100 invested at time 1, plus the interest earned during the period between time 1 and time 2. At time 3 another $100 is deposited; we now have the $100 deposited that day, the $100 deposited at time 2 plus the interest earned for one period, and the $100 deposited at time 1 plus the interest earned during the period between time 1 and time 2.

The formula for the future worth of an annuity of $1 is:

$$S = \frac{(1 + i)^n - 1}{i}$$

Note that the formula for the accumulation of interest on an ordinary annuity has the same variables as the compounding formula for a single payment.

To obtain S for any amount more than $1, multiply both sides of the equation by the amount invested, by P. In this case multiply both sides of the equation by 100. As above the amount for $1 can be found in tables (or by the use of a hand calculator).

The *present worth* of an annuity concerns the same question as the present worth of a single payment for *n years at i rate of interest*. How much would we pay today for an annuity in order to receive a given number of equal payments at equal intervals for a given number of periods in the future?

The formula for $1 is:

$$S = \frac{1 - (1 + i)^{-n}}{i}$$

The method for accounting for the premium or discount on bonds payable are compound interest procedures. The resultant interest charges are the product of the net balance of bonds payable and the effective interest rate at the time the bonds were issued. For bonds issued at a premium, the computed interest charges will *decrease* each year as the bonds approach maturity because the net balance of the liability decreases each year due to the amortization of the premium. Conversely, for bonds issued at a discount, the computed interest charges will *increase* each year as the bonds approach maturity because of the accumulation of the discount.

A straight-line method is used for the amortization of premiums or accumulation of discounts which involves simply dividing the original premium or discount by the number of years until maturity to determine the constant annual amount of amortization or accumulation.

The most frequent application of the above formula for accounting procedures is the present value formula. For example, when a company issues bonds, cash is debited for the proceeds of the bond issue and a liability account is credited for the amount. The entries will be the present value of the bonds. Assume a bond issue sold at a premium, or for more than the typical $1,000 par value, the present value of which we assume to be $1,200. The entries at the time of the sale of the bonds are:

Cash	$1,200	
Bonds Payable		$1,200

An alternative treatment is permissible by rule:

Cash	$1,200	
Bonds Payable		$1,000 (par)
Premium on Bonds		200

The Premium Account is an adjunct account (an addition) to Bonds Payable. The interest charge each year is computed by multiplying the bond liability *at the end of each year* by the effective rate of interest (see the definition). The adjunct account at the end of each period is debited for the amount of interest which reduces the liability each period. *The interest charge calculation is computed on the reduced amount of the liability that occurs each year as the adjunct account is debited.* At maturity the Premium Account has a zero balance and the liability will be reduced to the maturity, or face amount (the par value of $1,000) of the bond.

Assume the bond is sold at a $200 *discount*, i.e., $200 less than the $1,000 par value. The journal entry is:

Cash	$800	
Bond Discount	200	
Bonds Payable		$1,000

The Bond Discount account is a *contra* account to bonds payable with the liability at time of issue $800. Again, for an amount deposited for the annuity of more than $1 multiply both sides of the equation by that amount. Also, again note the same variables as in the compound interest formula.

SAB 101, *Revenue Recognition in Financial Statements*

This Staff Accounting Bulletin (SAB) summarizes certain of the Securities and Exchange Commission staff's views in applying Generally Accepted Accounting Principles (GAAP) to revenue recognition in financial statements. The staff is providing this guidance due, in part, to the large number of revenue recognition issues that registrants encounter. For example, a March, 1999 report entitled *Fraudulent Financial Reporting 1987-1997: An Analysis of U. S. Public Companies,* sponsored by the Committee of Sponsoring Organizations (COSO) of the Treadway Commission, indicated that over half of financial reporting frauds in the study involved overstating revenue.

During the upcoming 10-K season, the SEC appears to be planning to investigate cases, particularly high profile ones, of improper accounting for premature and excessive revenue recognition.

Because the SEC believes the revenue recognition accounting rules do not cover a number of areas, it is expecting companies to voluntarily correct their improper accounting by the end of the first quarter of 2000. They will then not be subject to enforcement action as long as they have not violated existing generally accepted accounting principles. This correction in most cases will be reported by companies as a one-time accounting change item.

Corrections Required

The corrections the SEC appears to be expecting are exclusion from:

1. Those collections previously included in revenue that were made when acting as an agent for a third party.
2. Revenue recorded in reciprocal barter transactions of similar products or services that do not represent the culmination of the earnings process.
3. Sales recorded before receipt of a written sales agreement.
4. Sales recorded in consignment-like arrangements.
5. Sales where the customer has not taken title and assumed the risks and rewards of ownership.
6. Bill-and-hold sales that do not have a customer business purpose.
7. Sales in situations where returns cannot be reliably estimated, such as "channel stuffing."

Conditions for Recognition

The SEC has stated that a bill-and-hold sale transaction must meet all of the following conditions to qualify for revenue recognition:

1. The risks of ownership must have been passed to the buyer.
2. The customer must commit to purchase the goods.
3. The buyer must substantiate a business purpose for the bill-and-sale transaction.
4. A fixed delivery date must be set.
5. The seller must not have any material performance obligations.
6. The goods must be ready for shipment and not available to meet other orders.

The Effect of SAB 101

Among other responses to SAB 101, some companies will find it necessary to:
1. Exclude from revenues and/or improve the disclosure of amounts collected by the company acting as an agent. One facet of this will involve assessing whether revenue (if recognized) should be reported gross with separate display of cost of sales to arrive at gross profit or on a net basis. In their appraisal, the SEC staff considers whether the registrant:
   a. Acts as principal in the transaction.

    b. Takes title to the products.

    c. Has risks and rewards of ownership, such as the risk of loss for collection, delivery, or returns.

    d. Acts as an agent or broker (including performing services, in substance, as an agent or broker) with compensation on a commission or fee basis.

If the company performs as an agent or broker without assuming the risks and rewards of ownership of the goods, sales should be reported on a net basis.

2. Not recognize revenue from "channel stuffing" and other transactions that make it difficult to estimate product returns.

Registrants and their auditors should carefully analyze all factors, including trends in historical data, that may affect registrants' ability to make reasonable and reliable estimates of product returns.

The staff believes that the following additional factors, among others, may affect or preclude the ability to make reasonable and reliable estimates of product returns:

    a. Significant increases in or excess levels of inventory in a distribution channel (sometimes referred to as "channel stuffing").

    b. Lack of "visibility" into or the inability to determine or observe the levels of inventory in a distribution channel and the current level of sales to end users.

    c. Expected introductions of new products that may result in the technological obsolescence of and larger than expected returns of current products.

    d. The significance of a particular distributor to the registrant's business, sales and marketing.

    e. The newness of a product.

    f. The introduction of competitors' products with superior technology or greater expected market acceptance, and other factors that affect market demand and changing trends in that demand for the registrant's products.

3. Exclude from revenue consignment-like transactions. Products delivered to a consignee pursuant to a consignment arrangement are not sales and do not qualify for revenue recognition until a sale occurs. The staff believes that revenue recognition is not appropriate because the seller retains the risks and rewards of ownership of the product and title usually does not pass to the consignee.

Other situations may exist where title to delivered products passes to a buyer, but the substance of the transaction is that of a *consignment or a financing*. Such arrangements require a careful analysis of the facts and circumstances of the transaction, as well as an understanding of the rights and obligations of the parties, and the seller's customary business practices in such arrangements.

The staff believes that the presence of one or more of the following characteristics in a transaction precludes revenue recognition even if title to the product has passed to the buyer, but the buyer has the right to return the product and:

a. The buyer does not pay the seller at the time of sale, nor is the buyer obligated to pay the seller at a specified date or dates.

b. The buyer does not pay the seller at the time of sale but rather is obligated to pay at a specified date or dates, but the buyer's obligation to pay is contractually or implicitly excused until the buyer resells the product or subsequently consumes or uses the product.

c. The buyer's obligation to the seller would be changed (e.g., the seller would forgive the obligation or grant a refund) in the event of theft or physical destruction or damage of the product.

d. The buyer acquiring the product for resale does not have economic substance apart from that provided by the seller.

e. The seller has significant obligations for future performance to directly bring about resale of the product by the buyer.

4. Only include in revenue those sales backed up by a *binding* written sales agreement. (See discussion in item above.)

5. Exclude from sales all shipments where the customer has not taken title to the goods and thereby not assumed the risks and rewards of ownership. (See 3 above.)

6. Defer revenue recognition of up-front fees until the related earnings process is completed. The staff believes that up-front fees, even if nonrefundable, are normally earned as the products and/or services are delivered and/or performed over the term of the arrangement or the expected period of performance. Therefore, they should generally be deferred and recognized systematically over the periods that the fees are earned.

7. Defer recognition of revenue from refundable membership sales until the end of the refund period, except in limited circumstances when certain rigorous and demanding criteria have been met.

Because reasonable people held, and continue to hold, different views about the application of the accounting literature in this regard, pending further action in this area by the FASB, the SEC staff will not object to the recognition of refundable membership fees, net of estimated refunds, as earned revenue over the membership term in the limited circumstances where *all* of the following criteria have been met:

a. The estimates of terminations or cancellations and refunded revenues are being made for a large pool of homogeneous items (e.g., membership or other service transactions with the same characteristics such as terms, periods, class of customers, nature of service, etc.).

b. Reliable estimates of the expected refunds can be made on a timely basis.

c. There is a sufficient company-specific historical basis upon estimate the refunds, and the company believes that such experience is predictive of future events.

d. The amount of the membership fee specified agreement at the outset of the arrangement is fixed, other customer's right to request a refund.

8. End the practice of including the fair value of free services included as part of a sale transaction as revenue.

The new materiality test is the standard the SEC will use for enforcement purposes in regard to revenue recognition. (See Chapter 18.)

Revenue Recognition Accounting Literature

The accounting literature on revenue recognition includes both broad conceptual discussions as well as certain industry-specific guidance. Examples of existing literature on revenue recognition include:

- Financial Accounting Standards Board (FASB) Statements of Financial Accounting Standards: 13, Accounting for Leases; 45, *Accounting for Franchise Fee Revenue*; 48, *Revenue Recognition When Right of Return Exists*; 49, *Accounting Accounting for Product Financing Arrangements*; 50, *Financial Reporting in the Record and Music Industry*; 51, *Financial Reporting by Cable Television Companies*, and 66, *Accounting for Sales of Real Estate*

- Accounting Principles Board (APB) Opinion 10, *Omnibus Opinion - 1966.*

- Accounting Research Bulletins (ARB) 43 and 45, *Long-Term Construction-Type Contracts.*

- American Institute of Certified Public Accountants (AICPA) Statements of Position (SOP) 81-1, *Accounting for Performance of Construction- Type and Certain Production- Type Contracts*, and 97-2, *Software Revenue Recognition.*

- Emerging Issues Task Force (EITF) Issue 88-18, *Sales of Future Revenues*; 91-9, *Revenue and Expense Recognition for Freight Services in*

Process; 95-1, *Revenue Recognition on Sales with a Guaranteed Minimum Resale Value*, and 95-4, *Revenue Recognition on Equipment Sold and Subsequently Repurchased Subject to an Operating Lease.*

- FASB Statement of Financial Accounting Concepts (SFAC) 5, *Recognition and Measurement in Financial Statements of Business Enterprises.*

If a transaction is within the scope of specific authoritative literature that provides revenue recognition guidance, that literature should be applied. However, in the absence of authoritative literature addressing a specific arrangement or a specific industry, the staff will consider the existing authoritative accounting standards as well as the broad revenue recognition criteria specified in the FASB's conceptual framework that contain basic guidelines for revenue recognition.

Based on these guidelines, revenue should not be recognized until it is realized or realizable and earned. SFAC 5 states that "an entity's revenue-earning activities involve delivering or producing goods, rendering services, or other activities that constitute its ongoing major or central operations, and revenues are considered to have been earned when the entity has substantially accomplished what it must do to be entitled to the benefits represented by the revenues." It continues "the two conditions (being realized or realizable and being earned) are usually met by the time product or merchandise is delivered or services are rendered to customers, and revenues from manufacturing and selling activities and gains and losses from sales of other assets are commonly recognized at time of sale (usually meaning delivery."

If services are rendered or rights to use assets extend continuously over time (for example, interest or rent), reliable measures based on contractual prices established in advance are commonly available, and revenues may be recognized as earned as time passes.

The staff believes that revenue generally is realized or realizable and earned when all of the following criteria are met:

1. Persuasive evidence of an arrangement exists.
2. Delivery has occurred or services have been rendered.
3. The seller's price to the buyer is fixed or determinable.
4. Collectibility is reasonably assured.

Disclosures for Revenue Recognition

Disclosures relating to the recognition of revenue are covered in several different areas of the accounting literature:

1. A registrant should disclose its accounting policy for the recognition of revenue in line with APB Opinion 22, Disclosure of Accounting Policies which states, "…the disclosure should encompass important judgments as to appropriateness of principles relating to recognition of revenue…" Because revenue recognition generally involves some level of judgment, the staff believes that a registrant should always disclose its revenue recognition policy. If a company has different policies for different types of revenue transactions, including barter sales, the policy for each material type of transaction should be disclosed.

2. If sales transactions have multiple elements, such as a product *and* service, the accounting policy should clearly state the accounting policy for each element as well as how multiple elements are determined and valued. In addition, the staff believes that changes in estimated returns recognized in accordance with FASB 48 should be disclosed, if material (e.g., a change in estimate from 2% of sales to 1% of sales).

3. Regulation S-X requires that revenue from the sales of products, services, and other products each be separately disclosed on the face of the income statement. The SEC staff believes that costs relating to each type of revenue similarly should be reported separately on the face of the income statement.

4. Management's Discussion and Analysis (MD&A) requires a discussion of liquidity, capital resources, results of operations and other information necessary to an understanding of a registrant's financial condition, changes in financial condition, and results of operations.

Changes in revenue should not be evaluated solely in terms of volume and price changes, but should also include an analysis of the reasons and factors contributing to the increase or decrease. To go beyond evaluation in terms of volume and price changes, the Commission stated in Financial Reporting Release (FRR) 36 that MD&A should "give investors an opportunity to look at the registrant through the eyes of management by providing a historical and prospective analysis of the registrant's financial condition and results of operations, with a particular emphasis on the registrant's prospects for the future."

Examples of such revenue transactions or events that the staff has asked to be disclosed and discussed in accordance with FRR 36 are:

a. Shipments of product at the end of a reporting period that significantly reduce customer backlog and might be expected to result in lower shipments and revenue in the next period.

b. Granting of extended payment terms that will result in a longer collection period for accounts receivable and slower cash inflows from operations, and the effect on liquidity and capital resources.

c. Changing trends in shipments into, and sales from, a sales channel or separate class of customer that could be expected to have a significant effect on future sales or sales returns.

d. An increasing trend toward sales to a different class of customer, such as a reseller distribution channel with a lower gross profit margin than existing sales to end users.

e. Increasing service revenue that has a higher profit margin than product sales.

f. Seasonal trends or variations in sales.

g. Gain or loss from the sale of an asset(s).

Chapter 3
Stockholders' Equity

"Stockholders' equity" is the most commonly used term to describe the section of the balance sheet encompassing the corporation's capital and retained earnings. Other terms used are "net worth" or "capital and surplus." Stockholders' equity consists of three broad source classifications:

1. Investments made by owners: Capital Stock (Common and/or Preferred)—at par value (legal value) or stated amount. Additional Paid-In Capital—"In Excess of Par," "Capital Surplus," etc.
2. Income (loss) generated by operations: Retained Earnings—the accumulated undistributed annual profits (losses), after taxes and dividends
3. Appraisal Capital—resulting from the revaluation of assets over historical cost (not in conformity with GAAP)

Changes in shareholders' equity, primarily in retained earnings, are caused by:

1. Periodic net income (loss) after taxes
2. Dividends declared
3. Prior period adjustments of retained earnings
4. Contingency reserves (appropriations of retained earnings)
5. Recapitalizations:
   a. Stock dividends and split-ups
   b. Changing par or stated value

    c. Reducing capital
    d. Quasi-reorganizations
    e. Stock reclassifications
    f. Substituting debt for stock
6. Treasury stock dealings
7. Business combinations
8. Certain unrealized gains and losses

CAPITAL STOCK

Capital stock is the capital contributed by the stockholders to the corporation.

Common Stock

The common stockholders are the residual owners of the corporation; that is, they own whatever is left after all preceding claims are paid off. By definition, common stock is "a stock which is subordinate to all other stocks of the issuer."

When a corporation has a single class of stock, it is often called "capital stock" instead of "common stock." The three aspects of stock ownership are (1) dividends, (2) claims against assets on liquidation, and (3) shares in management. As to these aspects of ownership, common stockholders have the following rights: (1) The amount of any/all dividend payments depends upon the profitability of the company. (2) Common stockholders have no fixed rights but, on the other hand, are limited to no maximum payment. (3) Their claim against the assets of the corporation on liquidation is last in the order of priority, following all creditors and all other equity interests. (4) The common stockholders, by statute, must have a voice in management. Their voice is often to the exclusion of all other equity interests, but they may also share their management rights with other classes of stock.

Common stock may be classified:

1. Par and no-par stock. Par stock is stock with a stated, legal dollar value, whereas no-par stock lacks such a given value. The distinction today is largely an academic one. However, state laws regarding stock dividends and split-ups and the adjustments of par value may affect the accounting treatment of such dividends.

2. Classes of common stock. Common stock may be divided into separate classes, e.g., class A, class B, etc. Usually, the class distinction deals with the right to vote for separate directors, or one class may have the right to vote and one class may not. Class stock is a typical technique used where a minority group wishes to maintain control.

Preferred Stock

The second major type of capital stock is preferred stock, that which has some preference with regard to dividend payments or distribution of assets on liquidation. In the usual situation, preferred stock will have a preference on liquidation, to the extent of the par value of the stock. In addition, its right to dividends depends on the following classification:

1. Participating and nonparticipating right.   If the preferred has a right to a fixed dividend each year but has not the right to share in any additional dividends over and above the stated amount, it is nonparticipating preferred. If it is entitled to a share of any dividends over and above those to which it has priority, it is called participating. For example, a preferred may have the right to a 5% annual dividend and then share equally with the common stock in dividends after a dividend (equal to the preferred per-share dividend) has been paid to the common stockholders.

2. Convertible preferred stock.   Convertible preferred is stock which may, at the holder's option, be exchanged for common. The terms of the exchange and the conversion period are set forth on the preferred certificate. Thus one share of $100 par preferred may be convertible beginning one year after issue into two shares of common. The preferred stockholder who converts will own two shares of common at a cost of $50 per share (this assumes the purchase of the preferred at par). A company will issue a convertible security at a time when it needs funds but for one reason or another cannot or does not wish to issue common stock. For example, in a weak stock market, common may be poorly received while a convertible preferred can be privately placed with a large institutional investor. The conversion privilege, from the point of view of the purchaser, is a "sweetener" since it affords the opportunity to take a full equity position in the future if the company prospers. The issuer may be quite satisfied to give the conversion privilege because it means that (assuming earnings rise) the preferred stock, with a prior and fixed dividend claim, will gradually be eliminated in exchange for common shares.

Accounting for a convertible preferred issue follows the usual rules. That is, when the preferred is first issued, a separate capital account will be set up, to which will be credited the par value of the outstanding stock. When conversion takes place, an amount equal to the par of the converted stock is debited to the preferred account. The common stock account will be credited with an amount equal to the par or stated value of the shares issued in exchange for the preferred. Any excess will go to capital surplus.

Both participating 1) and convertible 2) preferred stocks above must be taken into consideration when computing earnings per share.

3. Cumulative and noncumulative. A corporation which lacks earnings or surplus cannot pay dividends on its preferred stock. In that case, the question arises whether the past dividend must be paid in future years. If past dividends do accumulate and must be paid off, the stock is cumulative; otherwise, noncumulative.

The preferred may share voting rights equally with the common stock; it may lack voting rights under any circumstances; or it may have the right to vote only if either one or more dividend is passed. In the latter case, the preferred may have the exclusive right to vote for a certain number of directors to be sure that its interests as a class are protected.

For cumulative stock, the dividends must be accrued each year (even if unpaid), unless issued with an "only as earned" provision. The effect on earnings per share is the extent of the reduction of net income for this accrual.

Par Value, Stated Capital, and Capital Stock Accounts

The money a corporation receives for its stock is in a unique category. It is variously referred to as "a cushion for creditors," "a trust fund," and similar expressions. The point is that in a corporation which gives its stockholders limited liability, the only funds to which the creditors of the corporation can look for repayment of their debts in the event the corporation suffers losses is the money received for stock, which constitutes the stated capital account. Consequently, most state corporation statutes require a number of steps to be taken before a corporation can reduce its stated capital. These steps include approval by the stockholders and the filing of a certificate with the proper state officer, so that creditors may be put on notice of the reduction in capital.

Stated capital is actually divided into separate accounts, each account for a particular class of stock. Thus, a corporation may have outstanding a class A common, a class B common, a first preferred, a second preferred, etc. Each class would have its own account, which would show the number of shares of the class authorized by the certificate of incorporation, the number actually issued and the consideration received by the corporation.

It is at this point that the distinction between par and no-par stock becomes important. Par stock is rarely sold for less than its par value, although it may be sold for more. In many states, it is illegal to sell stock at a discount from par, and even when not illegal, there may be a residual stockholder liability for that original discount to the creditors. In any case, an amount equal to the par value of the stock must be credited to its capital account, with any excess going into a surplus account.

In the case of no-par stock, the corporation, either through its board of directors or at a stockholders' meeting, assigns part of the consideration received as stated capital for the stock and treats the rest as a credit to a capital surplus account. Treating part of the consideration received as stated capital is the equivalent of giving the stock a par value.

Capital Stock Issued for Property

Where capital stock is issued for the acquisition of property in a non-cash transfer, measurement of owners' investment is usually determined by using the fair market value of the assets (and/or the discounted present value of any liabilities transferred).

When the fair value of the assets transferred cannot be measured, the market value of the stock issued may be used instead for establishing the value of the property received.

When the acquisition is an entire business, the principle of "fair value" is extended to cover each and every asset acquired (other than goodwill). If the fair value of the *whole* business is considered to be *more* than the individual values, that excess is considered to be goodwill.

The difference between fair value put on the assets received and the *par value* (stated) of the stock issued goes to the Capital-in-Excess of Par Value account (or Additional Paid-in Capital, etc.) as either a positive or negative (discount) amount. Note that this does *not* pertain to any "negative" goodwill which might have been created; said negative goodwill, if any, should be used to reduce, immediately, the noncurrent assets (except investment securities) proportionately to zero, if necessary, with any remaining excess to be deferred and amortized as favorable goodwill is amortized.

Capital in Excess of Par or Stated Value (Capital Surplus)

The term "capital surplus" is still widely used, although the preferred terminology is "capital in excess of par" or "additional paid-in capital."

The capital in excess of par account is credited with capital received by the corporation which is not part of par value or stated capital. It is primarily the excess of consideration received over par value or the amount of consideration received for no-par stock which is not assigned as stated capital.

In addition, donations of capital to the corporation are credited to this account. If stated capital is ever reduced as permitted by law, the transfer is from the capital stock account to this capital surplus account.

This account is also credited for the excess of market value over par value for stock dividends (which are not split-ups) and for the granting of certain stock options and rights.

RETAINED EARNINGS

Terminology bulletins do not have authoritative status; however, they are issued as useful guides. Accounting Terminology Bulletin No. 1 recommended the following:

1. The abandonment of the term "surplus";
2. The term "earned surplus" be replaced with such terms that indicate the source such as:
   a. Retained Earnings
   b. Retained Income
   c. Accumulated Earnings
   d. Earnings Retained for Use in the Business

Retained earnings are the accumulated undistributed past and current years' earnings, net of taxes and dividends paid and declared.

Portions of retained earnings may be set aside for certain contingencies, appropriated for such purposes as possible future inventory losses, sinking funds, etc. A Statement of Changes in Retained Earnings is one of the basic financial statements *required* for fair presentation of results of operation and financial condition to conform with GAAP. It shows net income, dividends, prior period adjustments. A Statement of Changes in Stockholders' Equity shows additional investments by owners, retirements of owners' interests and similar events (if these are few and simple, they may be put in the notes).

Regardless of how a company displays its undistributed earnings, or the disclosures thereof, for tax purposes, the actual earnings and profits which could have been or are still subject to distribution as "dividends" *under IRS regulations* may, under some circumstances, retain that characteristic for the purpose of ordinary income taxation to the ultimate recipient. There is no requirement for this disclosure other than normal requirement for the "periods presented," which would usually show the activity in retained earnings for only two years and not prior.

PRIOR PERIOD ADJUSTMENTS

Only the following rare types of items should be treated as prior period adjustments and *not* be included in the determination of current period net income:

1. Correction of an error (material) in prior financial statements; and

2. Realization of income tax pre-acquisition operating loss benefits of *purchased* subsidiaries.

Corrections of errors are *not* changes in accounting *estimates*. Error corrections are those resulting from:

1. Mathematical errors;
2. Erroneous application of accounting principles;
3. Misuse of, or oversight of facts existing at a prior statement period.

Changes in accounting *estimates* result from *new* information or developments, which sharpen and improve judgment.

Litigation settlements and income tax adjustments *no longer* meet the definition of prior period adjustments. However, for *interim periods only* (of the current fiscal year), material items of this nature should be treated as prior interim adjustments to the identifiable period of related business activity.

Goodwill cannot be written off as a prior period adjustment.

Retroactive adjustment should be made of all comparative periods presented, reflecting changes to particular items, net income and retained earnings balances. The tax effects should also be reflected and shown. Disclosure of the effects of the restatement should be made.

Prior period adjustments must be charged or credited to the opening balance of retained earnings. They cannot be included in the determination of net income for the current period.

Beginning Retained Earnings		$1,000
Correction Depreciation Error		
$300 x .50 (net of tax)		150
Adjustment Beginning Retained Earnings		1,150
Net Income		400
Ending—Retained Earnings		$1,550
Accumulated Depreciation	$300	
Taxes Payable		150
Retained Earnings		150

CONTINGENCY RESERVES

A "contingency" is defined as "an existing condition, situation, or set of circumstances involving uncertainty as to possible gain or loss to an enterprise that will ultimately be resolved when one or more events occur or fail to occur." Loss contingencies fall into three categories:

1. Probable
2. Reasonably possible
3. Remote

In deciding whether to accrue the estimated loss by charging income or setting aside an appropriation of retained earnings, or merely to make a disclosure of the contingency in the notes to the financial statement, the following standards have been set:

A charge is accrued to income if *both* of the following conditions are met at the date of the financial statements:

1. Information available *before* the issuance of the financial statements indicates that probably the asset will be impaired or a liability incurred; and
2. A *reasonable* estimate of the loss *can* be made.

   (When a contingent loss is probable but the reasonable estimate of the loss can only be made in terms of a range, the amount shall be accrued for the loss. When some amount within the range appears at the time to be a better estimate than any other amount within the range, that amount shall be accrued. When no amount within the range is a better estimate than any other amount, the minimum amount in the range shall be accrued.)

If discovery of the above impairment occurs *after* the date of the statements, disclosure should be made and pro-forma supplementary financial data presented giving effect to the occurrence as of the balance sheet date.

When a contingent loss is only *reasonably possible* or the probable loss cannot be estimated, an estimate of the *range* of loss should be made or a narrative description given to indicate that *no* estimate was possible. Disclosure should be made; but no accrual.

When the contingency is *remote*, disclosure should be made when it is in the nature of a guarantee. Other remote contingencies are not required to be disclosed, but they may be, if desired, for more significant reporting.

General reserves for unspecified business risks are not to be accrued and no disclosure is required.

Appropriations for loss contingencies from retained earnings must be shown with the stockholders' equity section of the balance sheet, and clearly identified as such.

Examples of loss contingencies are:

1. Collectibility of receivables.
2. Obligations related to product warranties and product defects.

3. Risk of loss or damage of enterprise property by fire, explosion, or other hazards.

4. Threat of expropriation of assets.

5. Pending or threatened litigation.

6. Actual or possible claims and assessments.

7. Risk of loss from catastrophes assumed by property and casualty insurance companies including reinsurance companies.

8. Guarantees of indebtedness of others.

9. Obligations of commercial banks under "standby letters of credit."

10. Agreements to repurchase receivables (or to repurchase the related property) that have been sold.

Handling of these loss contingencies depends upon the nature of the loss probability and the reasonableness of estimating the loss. (Gain contingencies are not booked, only footnoted.)

RECAPITALIZATIONS

Essentially, a recapitalization means changing the structure of the capital accounts. It can also mean a reshuffling between equity and debt. A recapitalization may be done voluntarily by the corporation; or it may be part of a reorganization proceeding in a court, pursuant to a bankruptcy or a reorganization petition filed by the corporation or its creditors.

In almost all cases of recapitalizations, stockholder approval is required at some point during the process. This is because a recapitalization may affect the amount of stated capital of the corporation or change the relationships between the stockholders and the corporation or between classes of stockholders. The different categories of recapitalizations are discussed in the following paragraphs.

Stock Split-Ups

A split-up involves dividing the outstanding shares into a larger number, as, for example, two for one in which each stockholder receives a certificate for additional shares equal to the amount of shares already held. The split-up is reflected in the corporate books by reducing the par value or the stated value of the outstanding shares. Thus if shares with a par value of $10 are split two for one, the new par becomes $5. No entry is necessary, other than a memo entry. The stockholder adjusts his or her basis for the unit number of shares.

Reverse split. The opposite of a split-up is a reverse split, which results in a lesser number of outstanding shares. Stockholders turn in their old certificates and receive a new certificate for one-half, for example, of former holdings. The par value or stated value is adjusted to show the higher price per share. A reverse split is sometimes used in order to increase the price of the stock immediately on the open market.

Stock Dividends

As far as the stockholder is concerned, a stock dividend is the same as the stock split; the stockholder receives additional shares, merely changing the unit-basis of holding. But the effect is quite different from the point of view of the corporation. A stock dividend requires a transfer from retained earnings of the *market value* of the shares. Capital stock is credited for the par value and capital in excess of par value is credited for the excess of market price over par. (The stockholder who has the option of receiving cash must report the dividend as ordinary income.)

Stock Split-Up Effected in the Form of a Dividend

Usually, a stock distribution is either a dividend or a split-up. However, there is another type of distribution, which, because of certain state legal requirements pertaining to the minimum requirements for or the changing of par value, necessitates a different nomenclature.

In those instances where the stock dividend materially reduces the market value, it is by nature and AICPA definition a "split-up." However, because certain states require that retained earnings must be capitalized in order to maintain par value, those types of transactions should be described by the corporation as a "split-up effected in the form of a dividend." The entry would then be a reduction of retained earnings and an increase in capital stock for the *par value* of the distribution. For income tax purposes, the corporation may be required to show this reduction of retained earnings as a Schedule M adjustment and may technically still have to consider it as available for ordinary rate ultimate distribution.

CHANGING PAR OR STATED VALUE OF STOCK

This type of recapitalization involves changing from par to no-par or vice versa. This is usually done in conjunction with a reduction of stated capital. A corporation, for example, may decide to change its stock from par stock to no-par stock in order to take advantage of lower franchise fees and transfer taxes.

Or no-par shares may be changed to shares having par value to solve legal problems existing under particular state statutes. A par value stock which is selling in the market at a price lower than its par must be changed if the corporation intends to issue new stock. This is necessary because of some state laws which prohibit a corporation from selling its par value stock for less than par value. In such a case, the corporation may reduce par value or may change the par to no-par; thereby, the new stock can be given a stated value equivalent to the price it can bring in the open market.

Quasi-Reorganizations

Current or future years' charges should be made to the income accounts instead of to capital surplus. An exception to this rule (called "readjustment") occurs when a corporation elects to restate its assets, capital stock and retained earnings and thus avail itself of permission to relieve its future income account or retained earnings account of charges which would otherwise be made. In such an event, the corporation should make a clear report to its shareholders of the restatements proposed to be made, and obtain their formal consent. It should present a fair balance sheet as at the date of the readjustment, in which the readjustments of the carrying amounts are reasonably complete, in order that there may be no continuation of the circumstances which justify charges to capital surplus.

As an example of how this readjustment might occur, suppose that a company has a deficit in its retained earnings (earned surplus) of $100,000. By revaluing its assets upward, it is possible for this company to create a capital surplus account for the write-up to fair value, then write off the deficit in retained earnings to that account. From then on, a new retained earnings account should be established and the fact be disclosed for ten years.

Stock Reclassifications

Another category of stock recapitalization involves reclassifying the existing stock. This means that outstanding stock of a particular class is exchanged for stock of another class. For example, several outstanding issues of preferred stock may be consolidated into a single issue. Or, common stock may be exchanged for preferred stock, or vice versa. The objective in this type of reclassification is to simplify the capital structure, which in many cases is necessary in order to make a public offering or sometimes to eliminate dividend arrearages on preferred stock by offering a new issue of stock in exchange for canceling such arrearages.

SUBSTITUTING DEBT FOR STOCK

One form of recapitalization that has become popular in some areas involves substituting bonds for stock. The advantage to the corporation is the substitution of tax-deductible interest on bonds for nondeductible dividends on preferred stock. Of course, where dealing with a closely held corporation, substituting debt for stock in a manner to give the common stockholders a pro rata portion of the debt may be interpreted for tax purposes as "thin" capitalization, and the bonds may be treated as stock, regardless.

Also, to attract new money into the corporation, it is advantageous to consider the issuance of convertible debt securities bonds—to which are attached the rights (warrants) to buy common stock of the company at a specified price. The advantages of this type of security are:

1. An interest rate which is lower than the issuer could establish for non-convertible debt;
2. An initial conversion price greater than the market value of the common stock;
3. The conversion price which does not decrease.

The portion of proceeds from these securities which can be applied to the warrants should be credited to paid-in capital (based on fair value of both securities) and discounts or premiums should be treated as they would be under conventional bond issuance.

TREASURY STOCK

Treasury stock is stock which has previously been issued by a corporation but is no longer outstanding. It has been reacquired by the corporation and, as its name implies, held in its treasury. Treasury stock is not canceled because cancellation reduces the authorized issue of corporation stock. In some circumstances, it is permissible to show treasury stock as an asset if adequately disclosed.

Treasury Stock Shown at Cost

When a corporation acquires its own stock to be held for future sale or possible use in connection with stock options, or with no plans or uncertainty as to future retirement of that stock, the cost of the acquired stock can be shown separately as a deduction from the total of capital stock, capital surplus and retained earnings. Gains on subsequent sales (over the acquired-cost price) should be credited to capital surplus and losses (to the extent of prior gains) should be charged to that same account, with excess losses going to retained earnings. State law should be followed if in contravention.

Treasury Stock Shown at Par or Stated Value

When treasury stock is acquired for the purpose of *retirement* (or constructive retirement), the stock should be shown at par value or stated value as a reduction in the equity section; the excess of purchase cost over par (stated) value should be charged to capital surplus to the extent of prior gains booked for the same issue, together with pro-rata portions applicable to that stock arising from prior stock dividends, splits, etc. Any remaining excess may be applied pro-rata to either common stock or to retained earnings.

Treasury Stock as an Asset

If adequately disclosed, it is permissible in some circumstances to show stock of a corporation held in its own treasury as an asset. For example, pursuant to a corporation's bonus arrangement with certain employees, treasury stock may be used to pay the bonus, and, in accordance with the concept of a current asset satisfying a current liability, that applicable treasury stock might be shown as current asset. However, dividends on such stock should not be treated as income while the corporation holds the stock.

Treasury stock has neither voting rights nor the right to receive dividends. (Note: treasury stock remains *issued* stock, but not *outstanding* stock). Treasury stock can either be retired or resold. Treasury stock is an owners' equity account and is deducted from the stockholders' equity on the balance sheet.

When a company buys its own stock:		
Treasury Stock	XXX	
Cash		XXX
If the stock is resold:		
Cash	XXX	
Treasury Stock		XXX
(The credit is the amount paid for the stock when purchased by the corporation)		

If there is a difference between the corporation's acquisition of the stock and the resale price, the difference is debited or credited to an account Paid-In Capital from Treasury Stock Transactions for the amount of the difference between the proceeds of the resale and the amount paid by the corporation.

Under the cost method, treasury stock is shown as the last item before arriving at stockholders' equity, while under the par value method treasury stock reduces the common stock account directly under the capital stock section of stockholders' equity.

Chapter 4

Statement of Cash Flows

The term "cash flow" refers to a variety of concepts, but its most common meaning in financial literature is the same as "funds derived from operations." The *concept* of cash flow can be used effectively as one of the major factors in judging the ability to meet debt retirement requirements, to maintain regular dividends, to finance replacement and expansion costs.

In no sense, however, can the amount of cash flow be considered to be a substitute for, or an improvement upon, the net income as an indication of the results of operations or the change in financial position.

IMPORTANCE OF CASH FLOW

The concept of cash flow was originated by security analysts. It has been stated that in evaluating the investment value of a company, cash flow is frequently regarded as more meaningful to them than net income.

Cash flow from operations data in financial summaries shows the liquid or near-liquid resources generated from operations which may be available for the discretionary use of management. Analysts have suggested that this is a useful measure of the ability of the entity to accept new investment opportunities, to maintain its current productive capacity by replacement of fixed assets, and to make distributions to shareholders without drawing on new external sources of capital.

While information about cash flow from operating activities is useful, it should be considered carefully within the framework of the complete statement of cash flows. This statement reflects management's decisions as to the

Basic Cash Cycle

use of these cash flows and the external sources of capital used relating to investing and financing activities. The implication of considering or analyzing only the cash flows generated from the operations portion of a cash flows statement is that its use is entirely at the discretion of management. In fact, certain obligations (e.g., mortgage payments) may exist even if replacement of nondepreciating assets is considered unnecessary.

In using cash flow as an analytic tool, care is required. For example, Corporation X has been capitalized with straight common stock. Corporation Y, the same size as Corporation X and comparable in other respects, has been capitalized 25% with common stock and 75% with debt. A cash flow equivalent to, say, 20% of each corporation's gross sales will seem to be four times as large in relation to Corporation Y's stock when compared with the common stock of Corporation X. Cash flow as a meaningful tool, therefore, will have more significance when related to industries and companies in which long-term debt is limited.

One valid point in using cash flow is to put the profit margin squeeze into proper perspective. One of the most rapidly increasing costs is the depreciation charged against newly acquired plants and equipment. The use of accelerated methods of depreciation has created huge depreciation deductions which reduce profits. At the same time, accelerated depreciation creates additional cash flow and encourages further spending for facilities. In the opinion of some financial authorities, a showing of relatively high cash flow per dollar of capitalization is some compensation for a poor showing of net income per dollar of capitalization.

High cash flow is also the reason that some companies with relatively poor earnings per share are able to continue paying cash dividends per share, sometimes in excess of earnings. The SEC has noted situations where investors were misled by these cash distributions in excess of net income when not accompanied by disclosure indicating clearly that part of the distribution represented a return of capital.

In addition to profits, the extractive industries get cash flow through depletion allowances, drilling write-offs, and amortization of development costs and depreciation.

Cash flow also helps analysts judge whether debt commitments can be met without refinancing, whether the regular cash dividend can be maintained despite ailing earnings, whether the extractive industries (i.e., oils and mining) will be able to continue exploration without raising additional capital, or whether additional facilities can be acquired without increasing debt or present capital.

Relative cash flow is an important factor in deciding whether to buy or lease. But it is not necessarily true that owning property creates funds for use in expansion. The cash made available to a corporation through operations will be similar whether the business property is owned or leased. Owned property acquired by borrowed capital will require periodic payments on the debt which will have to be met before funds are available for expansion.

FASB Statement 95, *Statement of Cash Flows*

Statement 95 was issued in November, 1987. The Statement establishes the standards for reporting cash flows in the financial statements. It. supersedes APB Opinion 19, *Reporting Changes in Financial Position*, and supersedes or amends prior pronouncements.

Specifically, the Statement requires disclosure of cash flows to be included in the full set of financial statements, replacing the *Statement of Changes in Financial Position*.

Business enterprises are encouraged to report cash flows from operating activities *directly* by disclosing the major sources of operating cash receipts and disbursements (the *direct* method). Enterprises can elect not to show operating cash receipts and disbursements, but will be required to disclose the same amount of net cash flow from operating activities *indirectly* by adjusting net income to reconcile the net cash flow from operating activities (the *indirect* reconciliation method) by eliminating the effects of:

1. all deferrals of past operating cash receipts and payments,
2. all accruals of expected future operating cash receipts and payments,
3. all items that are included in net income that do *not* affect operating cash receipts and payments.

It should be noted that if the direct method is applied, a reconciliation of net income and net cash flow from operating activities is required to be provided in a separate schedule.

If a reporting company has foreign business operations, the cash flows statement must disclose the currency equivalent of foreign currency cash flows, applying the current exchange rate at the time of the cash flow. The effect of changes in the exchange rates is disclosed as a separate item in the reconciliation of beginning and ending balances of cash and cash equivalents.

Information about investing and financing activities not resulting in cash receipts or payments is to be disclosed separately.

Terminology.   Precise definitions to clarify the meaning of the terms related specifically to FASB 95 can be helpful to an understanding of the requirements.

Cash. Includes currency on hand, demand deposits with banks, and accounts with financial institutions that have the general characteristics of demand deposits; e.g., a depository that accepts deposits and permits withdrawals without prior notice or penalty.

Cash Equivalent. Short-term, highly liquid investments that are 1) readily convertible into known amounts of cash, and 2) near enough to maturity (see *Original Maturity*) that a change in the interest rate structure presents an insignificant risk of changes in the value of the investment.

Cash Flow. Cash receipts and cash payments resulting from investing, financing, or operating activities.

Direct Method. Shows the principal components to be operating cash receipts and payments; e.g., cash received from accounts receivable; cash paid to suppliers.

Financing Activities. Borrowing money; paying borrowings; long-term credit. In general, transactions to acquire and repay capital.

Indirect Method. Computation starts with net income that is adjusted for revenue and expense items *not* resulting from operating cash transactions (e.g., noncash transactions) to reconcile to net cash flow from operating activities. This method does not disclose operating cash receipts and payments.

Investing Activities. Making loans; collecting loans; acquiring and disposing of debt; acquiring and disposing of equity; acquiring and disposing of productive assets (e.g., plant and equipment).

Net Cash Flow. The arithmetic sum of gross cash receipts and gross cash payments which results in the net cash flow from operating activities.

Noncash and Investing Activities. Investing and financing activities that affect assets or liabilities, but do not result in cash receipts or cash payments.

Operating Activities. All transactions and other events that are not defined as investing or financing activities. Cash flows from activities which generally result from transactions and other events that enter into the determination of net income.

Original Maturity. An investment *purchased* three months from the maturity date.

NOTE: An investment *purchased more than three months from maturity is not* a cash equivalent, even though its remaining maturity on financial statement date is within the three months' rule.)

Summary

The summary that follows brings together in columnar format the significant requirements of the Statement that are scattered throughout the FASB manual.

1. The objective of FASB 95 is to provide detailed information about the cash receipts and cash payments of an enterprise during a specified accounting period.
2. The statement of cash flows reports the cash effects of any enterprise's operations, investing transactions and financing transactions.
3. Related disclosures detail the effects of investing and financing transactions that affect an enterprise's financial position, but do not directly affect cash flows.
4. Net income and net cash flow from operating activities are reconciled to provide information about the *net* effects of operating transactions, other events, and financial activities.
5. The cash flows statement should explain the change during specified accounting period in cash and cash equivalents.
6. FASB 95 requires enterprises with foreign currency transactions (e.g., cash receipts and payments) to report the currency equivalent of foreign currency cash flows applying the exchange rates in effect at the time of the cash flows. (A weighted average exchange rate for the period for translation is permissible as specified in FASB 52, Para. 12.)
7. Noncash transactions have a significant effect on the cash flows of a company and should be disclosed. (Reference APB Opinion 29, *Accounting for Nonmonetary Transactions.*)

CLASSIFICATION OF CASH RECEIPTS AND CASH PAYMENTS

Resulting from Operating Activities

Cash Inflows	*Cash Outflows*
Receipts from sale of goods and services.	Payments to suppliers.
Collections on accounts.	Payments on accounts.
Collections on short- and long-term notes and other credit arrangements.	Principal payments on short- and long-term payables.
Interest and dividend receipts.	Interest payments.
Other cash receipts that do not originate from investment or financing activities.	Other cash payments that do not originate from investment or financing activities.
Generally , the cash effects of transactions that enter into the determination of net income.	Payments to employees, tax payments, etc.

Resulting from Investing Activities

Cash Inflows	*Cash Outflows*
Principal collections on loans	Loans made. Payment for debt instruments of subsidiaries.
Sale of equity securities of other enterprises.	Purchases of equity securities of other enterprises.
Sale of plant, equipment, property, and other productive assets.	Purchases of plant, equipment, property, and other productive assets.

Resulting from Financing Activities

Cash Inflows	*Cash Outflows*
Proceeds from new securities issues.	Repurchase of enterprise's equity securities.
Bonds, mortgages, notes, and other indebtedness.	Debt repayments; dividend payments.

Direct Method—Discussion and Illustration

The direct method requires reporting the three major classes of gross cash receipts and gross cash payments, as well as their arithmetic sum to disclose the *net cash flow* from operating activities.

The Rule allows reporting entities to detail cash receipts and payments to any extent considered to be meaningful. For example, payments to suppliers might be divided between raw material purchases and other major supplies used in the business. Wage and salary payments might be divided between manufacturing, selling, and administrative expenses. Sales receipts could be divided among different sources, with an "other" operating cash receipts, if any.

The reconciliation of net income to net cash flow from operating activities must be provided in a separate schedule.

Statement of Cash Flows
Increase (Decrease) in Cash and Cash Equivalents

(Direct Method)
Year Ended December 31, 19xx

Cash flows from *operating* activities:		
Cash received from customers	$435,000	
Interest received	5,000	
Cash provided by operations		440,000
Cash paid to employees and suppliers	(382,000)	
Interest paid	(13,000)	
Taxes paid	(20,000)	
Cash disbursed by operations		(415,000)
Net cash flow from operations		$ 25,000
Cash flows from *investing* activities:		
Marketable securities purchases	$(32,500)	
Proceeds-marketable securities sales	20,000	
Loans made	(8,500)	
Loan collections	6,000	
Plant purchase	(80,000)	
Proceeds-sale of plant assets	37,500	
Net cash used in investing activities		$(57,500)
Cash flows from *financing* activities:		
Loan proceeds	$ 22,500	
Debt repayment	(27,500)	
Proceeds-Bond issue	50,000	
Proceeds-Common Stock issue	25,000	
Dividends paid	(20,000)	
Net cash provided by financing activities		$50,000
Net increase (decrease) in cash		$17,500

The following is a more comprehensive Statement of Cash Flow from operations applying the *direct* method. This approach includes the disclosure of noncash transactions in a separate schedule formatted beneath the statement.

Statement of Cash Flows
Increase (Decrease) in Cash and Cash Equivalents

(Direct Method)
Year Ended December 31, 19xx

Cash flow from operations:		
Cash from receivables	$10,000,000	
Dividend receipts	700,000	
Cash provided		10,700,000
Cash paid to suppliers	2,000,000	
Wage and salary payments	4,000,000	
Interest payments	750,000	
Taxes	1,000,000	
Cash disbursed		7,750,000
Net cash flow from operations		$2,950,000
Cash flow from investing activities:		
Property and plant purchases	(4,000,000)	
Proceeds from sale of equipment	2,500,000	
Acquisition of Corporation X	(900,000)	
Securities purchases	(4,700,000)	
Securities sales	5,000,000	
Borrowings	(7,500,000)	
Collections on notes receivable	5,800,000	
Net cash outflow from investments		$(3,800,000)
Cash flow from financing activities:		
Increase in customer deposits	1,100,000	
Short-term borrowings (increase)	75,000	
Short-term debt payments	(300,000)	
Long-term debt proceeds	1,250,000	
Lease payments	(125,000)	
Common stock issue	500,000	
Dividends to shareholders	(450,000)	
Net cash provided by financing		$2,050,000
Foreign exchange rate change		100,000
Net increase (decrease) in cash		$1,300,000

Schedule—Noncash Investing and Financing Activities:

Incurred lease obligation	$ 750,000
Acquisition of Corporation X:	
Working capital acquired (except cash)	(100,000)
Property and plant acquired	3,000,000
Assumed long-term debt	(2,000,000)
Cash paid for acquisition	$ 900,000
Common stock issued in payment	
of long-term debt	$ 250,000

INDIRECT METHOD—DISCUSSION AND ILLUSTRATION

The indirect method (also termed the *reconciliation method*) requires *net cash flow* to be reported indirectly with an adjustment of net income to reconcile it to net cash flow from operating activities. The adjustment requires:

1. The removal from net income of the effects of all deferrals of past operating cash receipts and payments.
2. The removal from net income of the effects of all accruals of expected future operating cash receipts and payments.
3. The removal from net income of the effects of items of all investing and financing cash flows.

The reconciliation can be reported *either* within the statement of cash flows *or* in a separate schedule, with the statement of cash flows reporting only the net cash flow from operating activities. However, if the reconciliation is disclosed in the cash flow statement, the adjustments to net income must be identified as reconciling items.

Statement of Cash Flows
Increase (Decrease) in Cash and Cash Equivalents

(Indirect Method)
Year Ended December 31, 19xx

Cash flows from *operating* activities:		
Net cash flow from operating activities*		$ 25,000
Cash flows from *investing* activities:		
Marketable securities purchases	$(32,500)	
Proceeds-marketable securities sales	20,000	
Loans made	(8,500)	
Loan collections	6,000	
Plant purchase**	(80,000)	
Proceeds-sale of plant assets	37,500	
Net cash used in investing activities		$(57,500)
Cash flows from *financing* activities:		
Loan proceeds	$ 22,500	
Debt repayment	(27,500)	
Proceeds-Bond issue	50,000	
Proceeds-Common Stock issue	25,000	
Dividends paid	(20,000)	
Net cash provided by financing activities		$50,000
Net increase (decrease) in cash		$17,500

*See supplemental schedule A. (Details operating activity.)

**See supplemental schedule B. (Details investing and financing activity.)

The following is a more comprehensive Statement of Cash Flow from operations applying the *indirect* method. This approach includes the disclosure of noncash transactions in a separate schedule formatted beneath the statement.

BANKERS' USE OF FINANCIAL STATEMENTS

The accountant needs to know how financial information is used and interpreted by different kinds of statement users who have different needs for credit information. The following review concerns accountants' relationships with banker clients and specific items in financial statements that bankers emphasize in their analysis of financial statements that accompany loan applications.

Of specific concern to a banker are the *trends*, both short-term and long-term, in the prospective borrower's operating results. Sales, liquidity, earnings, and the equity accounts give significant evidence of a company's operating performance since it has been in business and in the near-term trends in those indicators. Banks lend money; a business has inherent risks. The more complete

Statement of Cash Flows

(Indirect Method)		
Year Ended December 31, 19xx		
Net cash flow from operations		$2,950,000
Cash flow from investing activities:		
Property and plant purchases	(4,000,000)	
Proceeds from sale of equipment	2,500,000	
Acquisition of Corporation X	(900,000)	
Securities purchases	(4,700,000)	
Securities sales	5,000,000	
Borrowings	(7,500,000)	
Collections on notes receivable	5,800,000	
Net cash outflow from investments		$(3,800,000)
Cash flow from financing activities:		
Increase in customer deposits	1,100,000	
Short-term borrowings (increase)	75,000	
Short-term debt payments	(300,000)	
Long-term debt proceeds	1,250,000	
Lease payments	(125,000)	
Common stock issue	500,000	
Dividends to shareholders	(450,000)	
Net cash provided by financing		$2,050,000
Foreign exchange rate change		100,000
Net increase (decrease) in cash		$1,300,000
Schedule—Earnings to net cash flow		
reconciliation from operations:		
Net income		$3,000,000
Noncash expenses, revenues, losses, and		
gains included in income:		
Depreciation and amortization		1,500,000

(Indirect Method), *Con't*
Year Ended December 31, 19xx

Deferred taxes	150,000
Net increase in receivables	(350,000)
Net increase in payables	(200,000)
Net increase in inventory	(300,000)
Accrued interest earned	(350,000)
Accrued interest payable	100,000
Gain on sale of equipment	(600,000)
Net cash flow from operations	$2,950,000

Schedule of noncash investing and financing activities:

Incurred lease obligation	$ 750,000

Acquisition of Corporation X:

Working capital acquired (except cash)	$(100,000)
Property and plant acquired	3,000,000
Assumed long-term debt	(2,000,000)
Cash paid for acquisition	$ 900,000
Common stock issued in payment of long-term debt	$ 250,000

and accurate the financial statements of the borrower are, the more acceptable are the borrower's statements in a risk-evaluation examination by a banker.

The acceptability of financial statements and the verifiability of the information in the financial reports that accountants certify give the banker confidence in a borrower's accountant and in the integrity of the financial information furnished by the borrower. There should not be any deficiencies in the auditor's certificate, no violations of accounting principles (GAAP), no AICPA and SEC disclosure deficiencies, and no lack of accuracy and consistency with previous years' reports.

Evaluation of Financial Ratios

While most ratios are valuable in measuring the financial excellence of a business, certain ratios, such as the current ratio, are emphasized for particular purposes. The following discussion covers the more common purposes for which ratios are used by bankers.

With respect to those commonly used by bankers, no one ratio can be said to be the most important, as they are all related to one another. For bank loan officers, one of the particular single items in the balance sheet is the *current ratio*, which is important because the nature of the banking business—deposits available upon demand—requires bank lending activity to be concerned predominantly with furnishing short-term loans, i.e., working capital loans. Banks as creditors attach importance to the *debt-to-net-worth ratio* and the borrower's ability to generate sufficient cash flow to service any current debt load.

Management Evaluation

Management's primary interest is efficient use of the company's assets. Management is particularly interested in the turnover ratios, such as the inventory turnover and the relationship of working capital to total sales. To the extent that assets are not being used efficiently, the company is overinvesting and realizing a smaller return than possible on its equity. On the other hand, excessive turnover is dangerous because it puts the company in a vulnerable position. Bankers are also particularly interested in trend relationships shown in the income statements for the past years. Excessive selling expenses may indicate that commissions or other payments are out of line with the market. Bank creditors will also make a comparison between a loan applicant and its competitors in all areas to indicate where improvements in operations should be expected.

Short-Term Creditors

As was stated earlier, a loan officer making short-term loans is particularly interested in the current ratio, since this is a measure of the borrower's working capital and ability to meet current debt obligations. Also discussed was the importance of the net-worth-to-debt ratio, which shows the relationship of the stockholders' investments to funds furnished by trade creditors and others, and shows a borrower's ability to stand up under pressure of debt. The sales-to-receivables ratio (net annual sales divided by outstanding trade receivables) shows the relationship of sales volume to uncollected receivables and indicates the liquidity of the receivables on the balance sheet. Another ratio important to a short-term lender is cost of sales to inventory, which shows how many times a company turns over its inventory, which shows whether-inventories are fresh and salable and helps evaluate its liquidating value.

Long-Term Creditors

Since the long-term lender is looking far into the future, a banker wants to be convinced that the company's earnings will continue at least at the current level. In addition, a lending officer will study the various working capital ratios to determine if the company will have sufficient cash when needed to amortize the debt. The ratio of total liabilities to the stockholders' equity is important because the long-term lender wants to be sure that the shareholders have a sufficient stake in the business. One ratio which is used virtually solely by long-term lenders is the number of times fixed charges are earned. Fixed charges represent the interest payments on the lender's debt as well as any debt which has priority over it. When total earnings of the company are divided by total fixed charges (including preferred stock dividends, if any) the resulting figure represents the number of times fixed charges are earned.

FASB STATEMENTS AMENDING THE CASH FLOW STATEMENT

FASB 102, *Statement of Cash Flows—Exemption of Certain Enterprises and Classification of Cash Flows from Certain Securities Acquired for Resale*

This amendment of FASB 95 exempts certain entities from the requirement to provide a cash flow statement. Entities that are not required to provide a cash flow statement are as follows:

1. A pension plan classified as a defined benefit plan covered by FASB 35, *Accounting and Reporting by Defined Benefit Pension Plans*, as well as employee benefit plans (other than defined benefit pension plans).
2. Highly liquid investment companies meeting the requirements of the Investment Company Act of 1940, as well as the four conditions listed below, or an investment company that is similar to one that meets these requirements.
3. A fund maintained by an administrator, guardian, or trustee, such as a bank, for the purpose of investing and reinvesting money on a collective basis that meets the four conditions listed below. These could include a trust fund or a variable annuity fund.

An investment company, described in 2 or 3, above, must meet all of the following conditions to be exempt from providing a cash flow statement.

1. Significantly all of the investments held by the company during the accounting period are liquid.
2. Significantly all of the investments held by the company are reported at market value or the lower of cost or market value.
3. As related to average total assets, the company had little, if any debt. Average outstanding debt is used for the comparison.
4. A statement of changes in net assets is provided by the company.

FASB 104, *Statement of Cash Flows—Net Reporting of Certain Cash Receipts and Cash Payments and Classification of Cash Flows from Hedging Transactions*

This amendment of FASB 95, exempts savings institutions, credit unions, and banks from reporting gross cash flows related to customer loans, time deposits, and deposits with other financial institutions.

It also amends FASB 95 to permit cash flows resulting from futures contracts, option contracts, forward contracts, or swap contracts that are accounted for as hedges of identifiable transactions, or events to be classified in the same category as the cash flows from the items being hedged, provided that accounting policy is disclosed.

Concepts Statement 7, *Using Cash Flow Information and Present Value in Accounting Measurements*

This FASB Concepts Statement provides a framework for using future cash flows and present value as the basis for an accounting measurement. The Concepts Statement provides general principles governing the use of present value, especially when the amount of future cash flows, their timing, or both are uncertain. It also provides a common understanding of the objective of present value in accounting measurements.

The release of the Concepts Statement is the result of redeliberation and consideration of comment letters received following the issuance of EDs in 1997 and 1999. It is the first Concepts Statement relating to specific measurements and to articulate a measurement objective. The Statement applies to measurements that use cash flow information:

1. On the initial recognition of assets or liabilities.
2. In fresh-start measurements.
3. In interest methods of allocation.

It does not consider recognition questions, nor does it address when a fresh-start measurement is appropriate. The FASB expects to consider those issues on a project-by-project basis.

The Statement explains that the objective of present value in accounting measurement is to capture, to the extent possible, the economic difference between sets of estimated future cash flows. Without present value, a $1,000 cash flow due tomorrow and a $1,000 cash flow due in 10 years appear the same. Because present value distinguishes between cash flows that might otherwise appear similar, a measurement based on the present value of estimated future cash flows provides more relevant information than a measurement based on the undiscounted sum of those cash flows.

The Board concluded that to be relevant in financial reporting, present value measurements must represent some observable measurement attribute of assets and liabilities. The Board concluded that present value measurements should attempt to capture the elements that taken together would comprise fair value; that is, a market price, if one existed.

The Concepts Statement outlines techniques for:

1. Estimating cash flows and interest rates.
2. The role of risk and uncertainty.
3. The application of present value in the measurement of liabilities.

Chapter 5
Business Combinations

Although the material in the first section of this chapter is the current accounting methodology, it may not be in the near future. In December 1998, the Financial Accounting Standards Board (FASB) issued an invitation to comment by February 15, 1999 on the topic, "Method of Accounting for Business Combinations: Recommendations of the G4+1 for Achieving Convergence." As a result of those comments and further deliberations by the Board, in September 1999, they issued an Exposure Draft, *Business Combinations and Intangible Assets* for comment by December, 1999. In February 1999, the FASB issued an Exposure Draft, *Consolidated Financial Statements: Purpose and Policy.* The comment period on that ED ended in May, 1999.

The latter portion of this chapter is concerned with discussion of points raised in the two Exposure Drafts which are destined to become the basis for new FASB Standards on the topics.

BUSINESS COMBINATIONS AND ACQUISITIONS

This section deals with the *accounting* treatment of dealings involved with the following types of business combinations and acquisitions:

1. Those *combinations* occurring when a corporation and one or more *incorporated* or *unincorporated* businesses *are united into one* accounting entity, with that single entity then carrying on the activities of the prior separate entities. Two methods of accounting are applicable here:

a. The Purchase Method, or

b. The Pooling-of-Interests Method.

2. Those *stock acquisitions* (or stock investments) wherein one corporation *buys the voting common stock* of another corporation—sometimes acquiring voting control, sometimes not—with both entities continuing as separate, individual, distinct operating corporations. Three methods of accounting are applicable here:

a. The Consolidation Method (or the alternate Combining Method),

b. The Equity Method, or

c. The Cost Method.

In each of these methods, the investment in the subsidiary's stock appears on the books of the owning company as an investment asset.

In order to clarify the distinctions involved—as a quick reference—these major points should be considered:

1. Consolidation, the Equity Method and the Cost Method all pertain to the acquisition of *voting stock* by the buying company.

   Pooling and Purchase pertain to the acquisition of *assets* and usually liabilities (inventory, plant, equipment, etc.).

2. How to distinguish between pooling and purchase:

a. With *pooling*, the *acquiring* company uses its *own capital stock* to exchange for the capital stock of the acquired company. For example, a stockholder of Company B (the *acquired* company) will, after pooling, hold stock in Company A, the acquiring company. Company B's stock will have been cancelled. Or, a third Company C might be formed with both A and B companies folding into Company C. Pooling is usually a tax-free combination, provided all requirements are met.

b. With *purchase*, the acquiring company buys the assets (usually net of liabilities), and the acquired company (the one selling the assets) must usually account for gain or loss on the sale of the individual assets, involving the recapture provisions of the tax law.

c. Pooling involves the exchange of stock. Purchase can involve either stock, cash or property.

d. In *purchase*, the assets are valued at *fair value*, usually creating goodwill. In *pooling*, there is no change in asset value, since they are picked up at net *book* value.

e. Under both pooling and purchase, the acquired company is subsequently liquidated.

f. A combination of *both* methods is unacceptable.

3. With *stock acquisitions*, all companies continue separate operations even though under new ownership or managerial control. Accounting records are maintained for each distinct company, and each company prepares financial statements independent of the other company. However, public release of those statements is guided by the rules of consolidation or the equity method.

4. With stock acquisitions:

   a. Use the *cost method* when owning less than 20% of the stock and exercising no effective managerial control.

   b. Use the *equity method* when owning 20% or more (influence is presumed)—or when owning less than 20% *but with substantial managerial* influence. Also, use the equity method when owning *over 50%* and *not using the consolidation method* .

   c. Use the *consolidation method* when ownership is *over 50%* (majority interest), *unless* conditions exist (described later) which constitute exception to the rules of consolidation and permit the use of the equity method.

   d. An acquiring enterprise should account for contingencies that can be reasonably estimated and considered probable as an allocation to the purchase price of the acquired company.

Note that financial accounting (and the SEC) require consolidation for over 50% holdings, with exceptions noted, but the IRS requires a minimum 80% voting control for consolidated tax returns.

Consolidation must also be used for subsidiaries whose principal activity is leasing property or facilities to the parent or other affiliates.

FASB Statement 94, *Consolidation of All Majority-Owned Subsidiaries*, eliminates most of the exceptions from consolidation formerly permitted by Accounting Research Bulletin 51, *Consolidated Financial Statements*. The most significant exception that has been eliminated is the "nonhomogeneity exception," i.e., excluding majority-owned subsidiaries whose business is unrelated to either the business of the parent or of other members of the consolidated group. Essentially, Statement 94 permits only two exceptions: 1) subsidiaries under *temporary* control, and 2) subsidiaries *not* controlled by the majority owner. (Further discussion of FASB 94 appears later in this chapter.)

When *not* using consolidation, and the holdings are over 50%, the equity method must be used for all unconsolidated subsidiaries (foreign as well as domestic).

When holdings are 50% or under, down to 20%, you must use the equity method, since significant managerial voice is presumed (unless you prove the contrary).

Further details of each of these methods are now presented.

THE COST METHOD—STOCK ACQUISITIONS

The cost method: An investor records an investment in the stock of an investee at cost, and recognizes as income dividends received that are distributed from net accumulated earnings of the investee, since the date of acquisition by the investor.

Dividends from the investee's earnings are entered as income;

Dividends in *excess* of investee's earnings after date of investment reduce the cost of the investment;

Losses of the investee (after acquisition) should be recognized under the "marketable security" standards.

For the investor, under the *cost method*, dividends only are to be picked up as income (with cash being debited).

THE EQUITY METHOD—STOCK ACQUISITIONS

The equity method: An investor initially records an investment in the stock of an investee at cost and adjusts the carrying amount of the investment to recognize the investor's share of the earnings or losses of the investee after the date of the acquisition. The amount of the adjustment is included in the determination of net income by the investor, and such amount reflects adjustments similar to those made in preparing consolidated statements including adjustments to eliminate intercompany gains and losses, and to amortize, if appropriate, any difference between investor cost and underlying equity in net assets of the investee at the date of the investment.

Proportionate share of earnings, whether distributed or not, increases the carrying amount of the investment and is recorded as income;

Dividends reduce the carrying amount of the investment and are *not* recorded as income;

After investment, a series of losses by the investee may necessitate additional reduction in the carrying amount.

Under the equity method, the proportionate share of earnings (losses) of the investee (subsidiary) is picked up as income (loss), with the investment asset account being debited (or credited for a loss). Dividends, when received, are thus merely a conversion of part of that increased investment value to cash.

Both the investment and the share of earnings are recorded as single amounts. Market devaluation is *not* applicable.

The Equity Method Should Be Used (for Foreign or Domestic Subsidiaries):

1. When owning *20% or more* of the voting stock of the investee (significant control is presumed); or
2. When owning *less than 20%* and the investor can demonstrate the exercise of significant control; or
3. When not consolidating those investees in which more than 50% is owned; but the equity method should not be used if consolidation is justified; or
4. For participant's share of joint ventures.

The equity method *should not* be used:

1. When consolidation is proper for over 50% control; or
2. When ownership is below 20% and there is *no* demonstrable control (use the cost method); or
3. When the principal business activity of the subsidiary is leasing property or facilities to the parent or other affiliates (consolidate instead).

Voting stock interest is based on the *outstanding* shares without recognition of common stock equivalents.

Applying the Equity Method

1. Follow the rules of intercompany profit and loss eliminations as for consolidations;
2. At purchase of stock, adjust investment to reflect underlying equity and amortize goodwill, if any;
3. Show investment as a single amount, and show income as a single amount, except for (4) below;
4. Show share of extraordinary items separately, net of tax;
5. Any capital structure change of the investee should be accounted for as in consolidations;
6. When stock is sold, account for gain or loss based on the carrying amount then in the investment account;
7. Use the investee's latest financial statement;
8. Recognize non-temporary declines in the value of the investee's stock by adjusting the investment account;
9. Do not write investment account below zero; hold over any losses until future gains offset them;

10. Before picking up share of investee's income, deduct any cumulative preferred dividends (paid or unpaid) not already deducted by the investee;

11. If the level of ownership falls to the point which ordinarily calls for the cost method, stop accruing earnings undistributed, but apply dividends received to the investment account;

12. If changing from the cost method to the equity method for any one investment (because of change in ownership), make the necessary retroactive adjustments;

13. If goodwill is created in (12) above, it should be amortized.

Equity Method: A method of accounting by a parent company for investments in subsidiaries in which the parent's share of subsidiary income (or loss) is recorded in the parent company's accounts.

The accounting procedures for the equity method follow:

Investment—X Co.	275,000	
Cash		275,000
(To record the purchase of 25% of X Co. stock at cost; 25,000 shares @ $11.00)		
Investment—X Co.	40,000	
Goodwill		40,000
(Additional equity in X Co. at date of acquisition)		
Cash	5,000	
Investment—X Co.		5,000
(To record receipt of $20.00 per share cash dividend from X Co.).		
Investment—X Co.	27,500	
Investment from Parent share of X Co. undistributed earnings.		25,000
Income from Parent share of X Co. undistributed extraordinary item.		2,500
(To record 25% of X Co. net income of $100,000 from continuing operations and $10,000 extraordinary income; total income $110,000.)		
Income Tax Expense (on operation)	12,500	
Income Tax Expense (Extra. item)	1,250	
Deferred Taxes		13,750
(To record 50% of reported income as accrued taxes.)		

The following entry is made for the depreciation of the excess of fair value of assets less book value of the acquired assets:

Equity of Earnings of Investee	xxxx	
Investment in Investee		xxxx

Income Taxes

1. Set up a deferred tax based on the investor's proportion of the subsidiary's net income (after tax), based on the investor's rate of tax, *unless*: If it appears that the *undistributed earnings* of the investee meet the *indefinite reversal criteria* (see elsewhere in this text), do *not* accrue taxes, but make disclosure.
2. For dividends received, pull applicable tax out of deferred taxes and put in tax payable account;
3. Disclose applicable timing differences.

(See also Index to Journal Entries in Appendix B, Timing Differences and Disclosures in this text.)

THE CONSOLIDATION METHOD—STOCK ACQUISITIONS

There is a presumption that consolidated statements are more meaningful than separate statements and that they are usually necessary for a fair presentation when one of the companies in the group directly or indirectly has a controlling financial interest in the other companies.

Assets, liabilities, revenues and expenses of the subsidiaries are combined with those of the parent company. Intercompany items are eliminated.

Earned surplus of a subsidiary company from prior to acquisition does not form part of the parent's consolidated earned surplus, and dividends therefrom do not constitute income.

The purpose of consolidated statements is to present the financial data as if it were one single unit.

Rule for Consolidation

The usual condition for a controlling financial interest is ownership of a majority voting interest and, therefore, as a general rule ownership by one company, directly or indirectly, of over 50% of the outstanding voting shares of another company is a condition pointing toward consolidation.

Do *not* consolidate:

1. When control is likely to be temporary; or
2. Where control does *not* rest with the *majority* holder (example: subsidiary is in reorganization or bankruptcy); or
3. Usually, for foreign subsidiaries (See later in this chapter); or
4. Where subsidiary is in a dissimilar business (manufacturer vs. financing); or
5. When the equity method or the cost method is more appropriate for the four conditions named above.

Note that the equity method should *usually* be used for all majority-held subsidiaries which are not consolidated, unless the cost method is necessitated by lack of influential control.

Foreign subsidiaries come under special standards and cost (with proper disclosure) may sometimes be used. (See later in this chapter.)

Other Considerations

A difference in fiscal period is no excuse for *not* consolidating. When the difference is no more than 3 months, use the subsidiary's fiscal-period report. Where greater than 3 months, corresponding period statements should be prepared for the subsidiary.

Intercompany items should be eliminated. (See later in this chapter.)

For partial years:

1. The year of acquisition: Consolidate for the year and, on income statement, deduct preacquisition earnings not applicable to the parent.
2. The year of disposition: do not consolidate income; show only equity of parent in the subsidiary's earnings prior to disposal as a separate line item.

Shares held by the parent should *not* be treated as outstanding stock in the consolidation.

When a subsidiary capitalizes retained earnings for stock dividends or split-ups effected as dividends, such transfer is not required for the consolidated balance sheet which reflects the accumulated earnings and capitalization of the group (not the subsidiary).

Combined Statements

This is the showing of the individual company statements *plus* the combined consolidation, which combination reflects all intercompany eliminations.

Examples of when to use combined statements:

1. Where one individual owns controlling interest in several related corporations; or
2. Where several companies are under common management; or
3. To present the information of a group of unconsolidated subsidiaries; or
4. When it is necessary to show the individual operations of parent as well as subsidiaries, as well as the consolidated results—for creditors usually. This type is also called a "Parent-Company" statement.
5. A subsidiary whose primary business is leasing to a parent should always be consolidated.

Limitations of Consolidated Statements

Along with their advantages, consolidated statements have certain limitations:

1. The separate financial position of each company is not disclosed.
2. The dividend policy of each company cannot be ascertained.
3. Any financial ratios derived from the consolidated statements are only averages and do not represent any particular company.
4. A consolidated income statement does not show which companies have been operating at a profit and which have been losing money.
5. Creditors who are concerned with the financial resources of individual companies would not get the information they desire.
6. Disclosing liens or other particulars of individual companies may require extensive footnotes.

(See Index to Journal Entries, Appendix B, for example of Consolidating Entries.)

THE PURCHASE METHOD

The Purchase Method accounts for a business combination as the acquisition of one company by another. The acquiring company records at its cost the acquired assets less liabilities assumed. A difference between the cost of an acquired company and the sum of the fair values of tangible and intangible assets less liabilities is recorded as goodwill. The reported income of an acquiring corporation includes the operations of the acquired company after acquisition, based on the cost to the acquiring corporation.

The financial statements should be supplemented after purchase with pro forma statements showing:

1. Results of operations for the current period as if the combination had occurred at the beginning of the period; and
2. Results for the immediately preceding period, presented as if they had combined.

The AICPA has listed some general guides for the assigning of values to certain individual items, as follows:

Receivables at present values of amounts to be received, less allowances for uncollectibles.

Marketable securities at net realizable values.

Inventories:

Finished goods at selling prices, less disposal costs and reasonable profit to the acquirer;

Work in process at selling price, less cost to complete, disposal cost and reasonable profit;

Raw materials at current replacement prices.

Plant and equipment at current replacement cost if to be used or, if to be disposed of, at net realizable value.

Intangibles (identifiable, excluding goodwill) at appraised values.

All other assets at appraised values (including land).

Accounts and notes payable, long-term debt and other claims payable at *present values*, using current rates.

Accruals at present values.

Other liabilities and commitments, at present values, determined by using appropriate current interest rates.

Goodwill should be amortized on a straight-line basis over a period not to exceed 40 years, and only to a shorter period if benefit can be pinpointed. Goodwill of the *acquired* company is not brought forward.

THE POOLING-OF-INTERESTS METHOD

The pooling-of-interests method accounts for a business combination as the uniting of ownership interests of two or more companies by exchange of equity securities. No acquisition is recognized because the combination is accomplished without disbursing resources of the constituents. Ownership interests continue and the former bases of accounting are retained. The recorded assets and liabilities of the constituents are carried forward to the combined corporation at their recorded amounts. Income of the combined corporation includes income of the constituents for the entire fiscal period for which the combination occurs. The reported income of the constituents for prior periods is combined and restated as income of the combined corporations.

A pooling involves the combination of two or more stockholder interests which were previously *independent* of each other.

The AICPA has said that a business combination which meets *all* of the following 13 conditions should be accounted for as a pooling:

1. Attributes of the combining companies:
   a. Each is autonomous and has not been a subsidiary or division of any other company for the prior two years; and
   b. Each is independent (10%) of the other combining companies.
2. Manner of combining interests:
   a. Effected within one year in a single transaction per a specified plan; and
   b. The corporation issues only common stock identical with its majority outstanding voting stock in exchange for substantially all (90% or more) of the voting common stock of the acquired company at the date of consummation; and
   c. None of the combining companies changes the equity interest of the voting common stock in contemplation of the combination within two years *before* the plan or between the dates the combination is initiated and it is consummated; and
   d. No company re-acquires more than a normal number of shares and only for purposes other than for business combinations between the dates of initiation and consummation; and
   e. Legal costs of pooling are expensed; and
   f. The ratio of interest remains the same for each common stockholder, with nothing denied or surrendered, with respect to each person's proportion before the combination; and
   g. Stockholder voting rights are neither restricted nor deprived of by the resulting combination; and
   h. The plan is resolved at the planned date and no provisions remain pending or carried over after the combination.
3. There is the absence of the following planned transactions:
   a. The combined corporation does not intend to retire or re-acquire any of the common stock issued to effect the combination; and

b. The combination does not enter any financial arrangements to benefit former stockholders (such as a guaranty of loans secured by stock issued in the combination); and

c. There is no intent or plan to dispose of any of the assets of the combination within two years after the combination other than those in the ordinary course of business or to eliminate duplicate facilities or excess capacity.

Financial statements of the current period, and of any prior period, should be presented as though the companies had been combined at the earliest dates presented and for the periods presented.

Disclosure should cover all the relevant details.

Purchase Method

Accounts Receivable	50,000	
Inventory	40,000	
Building	110,000	
Equipment	30,000	
Investments	5,000	
Goodwill	16,200	
Accounts Payable		25,000
Long-Term Debt		30,000
Unamortized discount on long-term debt		(3,800)
Common Stock (Par $10; 10,000 Shares)		100,000
Additional Paid-In Capital		100,000

Entry to apply the purchase method to account for the purchase of XYZ Co. assets and liabilities for 10,000 shares of common stock. Total purchase price $200,000 based on market price of the stock at date of consummation of $20 per share.

Amortization of Goodwill (1/40)	405	
Goodwill		405
Unamortized discount on long-term debt	760	
Discount Income		760
(Goodwill amortized on straight-line basis.)		

Applying the Pooling-of-Interests Method

It must be recognized that the two methods are not alternatives and it should not be inferred that there is a choice of one or the other method. Rather, the pooling-of-interests method can be applied only when 12 restrictive criteria as set forth in APB Opinion 16, *Accounting for Business*

Combinations are met. GAAP requires *compliance* with *all* 12 of the conditions. If one or more of the criteria is not met, the purchase method of accounting for the combination *must* be applied.

The principal difference between the different methods of business combinations is the resulting corporate entity. In an *acquisition* both the acquired and acquiring companies remain as separate legal entities after the combination, with the acquiring company being the *parent* and the acquired company the *subsidiary*. In a *merger* two or more companies combine and one legal entity results, which can be any one of the combining companies. In a *consolidation*, the combining companies form a new legal entity.

Inventory	43,000	
Cash	5,000	
Accounts Receivable	60,000	
Allowance for Doubtful Accounts		7,000
Building	75,000	
Accu. Depreciation		15,000
Equipment	100,000	
Accu. Depreciation		60,000
Investments	4,000	
Accounts Payable		25,500
Long-Term Debt		30,000
Common Stock (Par, $10; 10,000 shares)		100,000
Additional Paid-In Capital		49,500

(Entries to reflect the pooling of XYZ Co. per the *book* value of the *items* on the date of *consummation*.) Note: *Goodwill cannot* be acquired by the *pooling method*.

APB Opinion 16 prohibits the use of treasury stock transactions for a business combination when a pooling of interest method is used. Treasury stock purchases are restricted to be used for purposes other than for business combinations for a period of two years before and during the period of the combination plan. Treasury shares acquired during this period are "tainted" and only a very small number of treasury shares can be used in a pooling. The restrictions on treasury stock purchased after the start of a plan are to prevent backdoor agreements to buy out certain stockholders.

FOREIGN SUBSIDIARIES

The following are the possible methods of providing information about foreign subsidiaries:

1. Exclude foreign subsidiaries from consolidation. Include a summary of their assets, liabilities, income and losses for the year and the parent's

equity in such foreign subsidiary. The amount of investment in the foreign subsidiary and the basis by which it was arrived at should be shown. If the foreign subsidiary is excluded from consolidation, it is not proper to include intercompany profits (losses) which would have been eliminated by consolidating.

2. Consolidate domestic and foreign subsidiaries, furnishing information of the foreign subsidiaries' assets, liabilities, income and losses, as stated above.

3. Furnish complete consolidated statements:

   a. Including only domestic companies, *and*

   b. Including the foreign subsidiaries.

4. Consolidate domestic and foreign subsidiaries and furnish, in addition, parent company statements showing the investment in and income from foreign subsidiaries separately from those of domestic subsidiaries.

INTERCOMPANY TRANSACTIONS

In Consolidations

Since consolidated statements reflect the position and results of operations of what is considered a single economic entity, all intercompany balances and transactions must be eliminated. Some of these are obvious. Others are not.

Here are some of the items to be eliminated (done on worksheets which combine the company and its subsidiary figures):

1. The investment account in the subsidiary and its corresponding equity offset (capital stock and applicable retained earnings).

2. Intercompany open account balances, such as loans, receivables, payables arising from intercompany sales and purchases.

3. Intercompany security holdings, such as bonds, including related bond discount or premiums.

4. Intercompany profits where goods or services are exchanged for over cost, such as profits on transfers of inventory or fixed assets. Intercompany profits on fixed asset transfers might also involve adjustments to the accumulated depreciation account. Intercompany profits on inventory may affect both opening and closing inventories of raw materials, work in process and finished goods, as well as cost of sales.

5. Intercompany dividends.

6. Intercompany interest, rents, and fees.

7. Intercompany bad debts.

The amount of intercompany profit or loss eliminated is not to be affected by the existence of minority interests. Such items must be eliminated. However, in eliminating them, they may be allocated proportionately between the majority and minority interests.

If "bottom-line" accumulated losses occur to the extent of wiping out the minority interest, any excess losses should then be reflected against the *majority* interest, rather than showing a negative minority interest. However, future earnings should then first be applied to that excessive loss and the positive remaining earnings apportioned between the majority and minority interests.

In the Equity Method

Intercompany gains and losses should be eliminated in the same manner as if the subsidiary were consolidated. It is not necessary to eliminate intercompany gain on sales to such subsidiaries if the gain on the sales does *not* exceed the *unrecorded* equity in the *undistributed* earnings of the unconsolidated subsidiary. However, do *not* eliminate intercompany holdings or debt.

In Combined Statements

Intercompany transactions and intercompany profits and losses should be eliminated following the same manner as for consolidated statements.

GOODWILL

Goodwill arises only from the purchase method; no goodwill is created in the "pooling-of-interests" method of combining businesses, since assets and liabilities are carried forward to the combined corporation at their recorded amounts.

With respect to the purchase method and stock acquisitions treated under either the consolidation method or the equity method, accounting for goodwill requires its amortization over a period not in excess of forty years.

Goodwill is the amount assigned to the excess paid over the fair value of the identifiable net assets acquired.

NEGATIVE GOODWILL

Negative Goodwill: When one company purchases another, negative goodwill arises where there is an excess of the assigned value of identifiable assets over the cost of an acquired company. The goodwill account has a credit balance. When the purchase price is less than the sum of the fair market value of the net assets acquired, the valuation of the noncurrent assets, except investments in Marketable Securities, must be reduced on a proportionate basis until the purchase price for the acquisition equals the adjusted valuation of the fair market value of the net assets acquired. If after the adjusted valuation of noncurrent assets is reduced to zero and the purchase price is still less than the net assets acquired, the difference is disclosed in the balance sheet as negative goodwill (a credit balance) and is amortized to income over a period not to exceed 40 years. (APB Opinion 16)

CONSOLIDATED FINANCIAL STATEMENTS

Consolidated Financial Statements: The combination of the financial positions and earnings reports of the parent company with those of various subsidiaries into an overall statement as if they were a single entity, i.e., the financial statements should reflect a group of affiliated companies as a single business enterprise—a single economic entity. The consolidated statements are in substance summations of the assets, liabilities, revenues, and expenses of the individual affiliates calculated on the basis of transactions with nonaffiliates. Intercompany transactions (transactions among the affiliates), intercompany investments, and account balances must be eliminated to avoid double-counting of resources, account balances, and operating results.

FASB STATEMENT 94, *CONSOLIDATION OF ALL MAJORITY–OWNED SUBSIDIARIES*

FASB Statement 94 is designed to demonstrate the results of operations and the financial position of a parent company and its subsidiaries as if all the component companies were a single company with one or more branches or divisions. This objective is based on the position that, when one of the companies in a group has a controlling financial interest in the other companies, whether directly or indirectly, consolidated statements are more useful to shareholders and creditors than separate statements are necessary for a fair presentation. The normal requirement for a controlling interest revolves around a majority voting interest; in other words, one company claims ownership of more than 50 percent of the outstanding voting shares of the other company.

Statement 94 provisions add substantial amounts of debt on the balance sheets of many companies with unconsolidated subsidiaries in businesses entirely different from the parent. Companies in consumer products, auto, retail, and a number of other businesses have maintained finance, insurance, and real estate subsidiaries that were often more highly leveraged than the parent company.

In the past, this type of subsidiary could keep separate balance sheets when engaged in businesses substantially different from the parent corporation, or when the parent held less than a 50% interest. A real estate subsidiary, therefore, could develop an office building without the mortgage debt appearing on the parent company's balance sheet. However, FASB 94 requires companies to consolidate balance sheets even if the parent owns less than 50% of the subsidiary's stock as long as any degree of control is in the hands of the parent.

Companies can be expected to continue restructuring, repositioning, even divesting, in order to lessen the Rule's effect. Some companies may decide to sell subsidiaries affected by the Rule; other companies may devise more creative strategies than outright selling. They can separate the assets of their subsidiaries into separate and distinct entities over which they do not maintain control. For example, a company planning to develop existing real estate assets can form a partnership wherein it is the limited partner and the developer is the general partner.

Another approach enables a company to loan money to a subsidiary rather than take an equity position through stock ownership. Later the company can convert the debt into equity when the subsidiary's real estate project has been completed. The Rule makes it more difficult, but not impossible, for companies to buy, manage, or develop real estate through subsidiaries. The problem is to devise an approach for investing in real estate or other investments within the limits of the rule, while at the same time keeping as much debt as possible off the balance sheet.

However, these devices should not become so creative that they disguise the true financial status of the various components. The purpose of FASB 94 is to reveal the true picture of the whole. It may have been this type of creativity that made it necessary to adopt FASB 94 in the first place. A possible chance use of the word *heterogeneous* in paragraph 3 of ARB 51, *Consolidated Financial Statements*, resulted in an excuse, if not a valid reason, for avoiding consolidation of majority-owned subsidiaries as being *nonhomogeneous*. Under this paragraph, separate statements or combined statements would be considered preferable for a subsidiary or group of subsidiaries if it was believed that the presentation of financial information concerning the particular activities of such subsidiaries would be more informative to shareholders and creditors of the parent company than would the inclusion of these particular subsidiaries in the consolidation.

For example, separate statements were sometimes required for a subsidiary such as a bank, insurance company, or finance company when the parent and other subsidiaries were manufacturing companies. Nevertheless, abuses resulted and it was deemed necessary to stem the abuses in the interest of the investors and creditors. Therefore, Statement 94 requires companies to consolidate the balance sheets of the parent company and the company's subsidiaries. The Statement is intended to give a complete rundown of companies' assets and liabilities and to prevent corporate abuses in concealing debt through the use of subsidiaries.

The principal exception eliminated is the nonhomogeneity exception mentioned previously. Also eliminated as exceptions are large minority interests and foreign locations.

Only two exceptions remain allowable:

1. Subsidiaries under temporary control.
2. Subsidiaries that the majority owner does not actually control, as in the case of bankruptcy, a legal reorganization, or other governmental restriction.

Also eliminated is the use of only the parent company's financial statements as the primary financial statements of the reporting enterprise. It should be noted further that continuing disclosure of summarized financial information for subsidiaries consolidated as a result of FASB 94 is still required in the consolidated financial statements or notes, either for individual subsidiaries or in groups of similar types of enterprises.

Over a long period of time, business enterprises used nonhomogeneity as a basis for excluding from consolidation majority-owned (and even wholly owned) subsidiaries considered different in character from the parent company and its other affiliates. Subsidiaries most commonly not consolidated on that basis have been finance, insurance, real estate, and leasing subsidiaries of manufacturing and merchandising enterprises. However, some diversified enterprises have consistently consolidated all of their majority owned subsidiaries despite differences in their operations. This resulted in similar enterprises using different consolidation policies. Excluding some subsidiaries from consolidation resulted in the omission of significant amounts of assets, liabilities, revenues, and expenses from the consolidated statements of many enterprises. The omission of large amounts of liabilities, especially those of finance and similar subsidiaries, led to the criticism that not consolidating those subsidiaries is an important factor for what has been termed off-balance-sheet financing.

Statement 94 is important as a solution to the problem of off-balance-sheet financing because unconsolidated majority-owned subsidiaries have been a significant aspect of that problem. The growth in size and importance over the years of finance and other unconsolidated majority-owned subsidiaries and the resulting amounts of assets, liabilities, revenues, and expenses that were not reflected in many consolidated financial statements resulted in it being almost impossible to compare the economic health, or the lack of it, of what should have been readily comparable companies.

Not only would this aspect of the "noncomparability" picture be of interest to the investor or creditor, but also the internal user of the enterprise's financial statements has been affected. What useful information could be obtained relating to differences in operational methods over a given period of time, or to financial status at comparison dates, if there were no basis for comparison? Information that is most relevant to investors, creditors, and other external and internal users of financial statements revolves around consolidated statements that are presented in a manner that clearly demonstrates the result of operations and the financial position of a parent company and its subsidiaries as if the group were a single company with one or more branches or divisions. Therefore, consolidated financial statements that include all majority-owned subsidiaries are significantly more informative than statements that exclude significant parts of an enterprise. Excluded parts would presumably be the weak or atrophied parts that could actually be evidence of a company's deteriorating financial condition.

Basic analytical tools are affected by whether a subsidiary was consolidated or accounted for by the equity method. One example is the debt-equity ratio, which is much lower if finance or other highly leveraged subsidiaries were reported by the equity method rather than consolidated. Consolidation of majority-owned subsidiaries results in significantly higher debt-equity ratios for many companies and may have, or may still require, renegotiation of loan covenants to avoid possible defaults. Affected companies can expect to spend time reeducating creditors and examining alternatives for meaningful financial statement presentation. To encourage experimentation, FASB does not outline specific rules for implementation, but leaves room for the aforementioned creativity.

Use of the equity method for majority-owned subsidiaries that were significant parts of an enterprise provided less information about the enterprise. Consolidation of all majority owned subsidiaries greatly improves comparability between enterprises with similar information, especially quantitative information.

Consolidated financial statements that include all majority-owned subsidiaries result in more relevant information and comparable statements of cash flow. Although the equity method and consolidation may report the same net income and net assets, they do not report the same cash receipts and payments related to operating, investing, and financing activities. It is possible for significant information about how an enterprise generated cash to be omitted or obscured if subsidiaries are not consolidated.

EXPOSURE DRAFT, *CONSOLIDATED FINANCIAL STATEMENTS: PURPOSE AND POLICY*

The FASB decided to delay the issuance of its new consolidated statement Standard. The new Standard, if adopted as now proposed, will require some companies to fully consolidate some of their less than 50% plus owned entities that the parent effectively controls. In effect, the new standard substitutes a qualitative control criterion for the current 50% plus ownership criterion. The result—more affiliated entities will be consolidated.

The proposed Statement does not apply to financial statements of certain reporting entities, such as pension plans and investment companies. In accordance with generally accepted accounting practices, these organizations carry substantially all of their assets, including investments in controlled entities, at fair value with all changes in value reported in a statement of net income or financial performance.

Control is defined as the ability to direct the ongoing policies and management that guide the activities of another entity to increase the benefits and limit losses from directing those activities, and this decision-making ability is not shared with others. The definition also includes an explicit condition that the decision-making powers must provide the controlling entity with the ability to increase the benefits and limit the losses that it can derive from that decision-making power. (This is similar to the explicit condition included in definitions of control adopted in the UK and by the IASC.)

The proposed Statement requires a controlling entity to consolidate all entities that it controls unless control is temporary when acquired. The current rule is that 50% plus owned entities be fully consolidated unless control is temporary. Full consolidation results—after adjusting for inter-company activities—in combining all of the controlled entity's assets, liabilities, revenues, expenses, gains and losses, and cash flows into the reporting entity's consolidated financial statements.

Business enterprises and not-for-profit organizations often carry out and finance a significant part of their economic activity through subsidiaries, joint ventures and complex strategic arrangements. The Board believes that this Statement fills a significant need by providing a framework for assessing and determining whether a particular relationship between two entities involves control of one entity by the other entity or not.

Resolving Questions of Control

The proposed Statement provides the basis for resolving several issues not addressed by FASB 94, *Consolidation of All Majority-Owned Subsidiaries*. FASB 94 eliminated certain exceptions to consolidation that existed prior to 1987, but did not resolve:

1. When control exists through means other than a majority voting interest.
2. When control does not rest with the owner of a majority voting interest.

3. When control is temporary.

The proposed Statement provides guidances for applying its definition of control. That guidance includes certain situations that lead to rebuttable presumptions of control. As presently written, when and if, this rule is adopted it could be expected that it would result in full consolidation of entities where the reporting company can be said to have:

1. A majority voting interest in the election of a corporation's governing body.
2. A right to appoint a majority of its governing body.
3. If not a majority, a large minority voting interest in the election of a corporation's governing body. (And no other minority group has a significant voting interest.)
4. A unilateral ability to *obtain* a majority voting interest in the election of a corporation's governing body.
5. A unilateral ability to *obtain a right to appoint* a majority of the corporation's governing body through the present ownership of convertible securities or other rights that are currently exercisable at the option of the holder.
6. Is the only general partner in a limited partnership and no other partner or organized group of partners has the current ability to dissolve the limited partnership or otherwise remove the general partner.

It is expected that the proposed standard would result in a number of now unconsolidated controlled entities being included in the controlling entity's consolidated statements on a fully consolidated basis. As a result, financial statements would provide a better understanding of some companies' business and financing risks and a clearer understanding of their actual net income.

Lessening the Gap

This proposal moves U.S. consolidation policy closer to that of many other countries that have also adopted similar objectives, similar definitions of control, and other requirements relating to consolidated financial statements. However, one rather important difference does exist.

Many other countries base their consolidation accounting on the *entity* approach. The consolidated financial statements are prepared from the *consolidated entity's point of view*. Minority interest is included in consolidated owners' equity and consolidated net income. The FASB's proposal continues the U.S. practice of basing consolidation accounting on the *parent company point of view*. Minority interest is shown outside of consolidated owners' equity and is deducted in the measurement of consolidated net income.

AN INVITATION TO COMMENT ON BUSINESS COMBINATIONS

The FASB, the G4+1 (standard setters from Australia, Canada, New Zealand, United Kingdom and the United States) and the International Accounting Standards Committee (IASC), published an Invitation to Comment on certain issues that they expect to deliberate in their projects on business combinations. The content of the document reflects the conclusions of the *individuals* participating in its development, not the standard-setting bodies themselves. It states that one method of accounting should be used for all business combinations and that *the purchase method, rather than the pooling of interests or fresh start methods*, is the appropriate method.

The FASB felt that the comments received on the Invitation to Comment were helpful to the Board in deliberating the issues in its own project on business combinations. They emphasized the point that this is the first time this international group has issued a joint position paper. Since there are currently significant differences internationally in the accounting standards on this important and controversial issue, the FASB hopes to reach convergence among the countries involved and the IASC so that the accounting standards, and the resulting financial reporting, are similar. (Where these standard setters go, the rest of the accounting world is very apt to follow.)

This is not a sudden decision by the Board. It has been researching business combinations issues since 1996. The issues surrounding the project are particularly important because the increasing growth of mergers has brought greater attention to perceived flaws and deficiencies in existing accounting standards. The rapidly accelerating movement of capital flows globally continues to point up the need for standards to be comparable internationally. Evidently the comments resulting from this invitation left little doubt about the demerits of "pooling."

EXPOSURE DRAFT, *BUSINESS COMBINATIONS AND INTANGIBLE ASSETS*

As was expected, the FASB issued the Exposure Draft of its proposed Standard to eliminate the pooling-of-interests method and shorten the write-off period of goodwill and many other intangible assets.

The FASB's business combinations project along with the attendant doing away with pooling-of-interests, and reducing the life expectancy of goodwill, is raising concern in many quarters. This can be attested to by the fact that representatives of the FASB testified concerning the plan in March, 2000 before the Senate Committee on Banking, Housing, and Urban Affairs.

They pointed out that there are few areas of accounting that need improvement more than the accounting for business combinations: at present accounting literature allows two economically similar business combinations to be accounted for using different accounting methods. These methods produce dramatically different financial results, causing confusion for investors trying to evaluate the combined companies.

The hearing focused on the FASB's plan to eliminate the pooling method of accounting for business combinations in favor of the purchase method of accounting. The point was made that in a pooling, the book values of the combining companies are simply added together, giving *no recognition at all to the price one company actually paid to acquire the other*. The true cost of the transaction is never revealed to investors, who have no ability to track the company's investment over time. The purchase method, on the other hand, shows the *real cost* of the transaction and gives investors the valuable information they need to make investment and capital allocation decisions.

The FASB's proposal on business combinations is the result of years of research and public deliberation. The Board completed the public comment process during which they received about 200 comment letters and heard from more than 40 individuals during four days of public hearings. The next step involves evaluation of the comments and public hearing testimony, including the testimony in the Senate hearing.

Because of the extensive input from many areas of the business and political world, this evaluation may be a rather lengthy process.

The Board will not make a final decision about the ED or issuing a final Standard before considering the substantive issues raised by all constituents, including members of Congress. While the Board members expect to complete their redeliberations by the end of 2000, they have no "deadline" for completing the project.

Elimination of Pooling-of-Interests Accounting

The Board earlier announced that it would eliminate pooling of interests as a method of accounting for business combinations. In a unanimous vote, the Board tentatively decided that using the purchase method is preferable to allowing more than one method to be used when businesses combine. The change would be effective for business combinations initiated after the FASB issues a final Standard on the issues.

Merits of Purchase Method Accounting

The Board has come to the conclusion that it is difficult for investors to make sound decisions about combining companies when two different accounting treatments exist for what is essentially the same transaction. They decided that the *purchase method* of accounting gives investors a better idea of the initial cost of a transaction and the investment's performance over time than does the pooling of interests method.

With the *purchase method*, one company is identified as the buyer and records the company being acquired at the price it actually paid. With the *pooling of interests method*, the two companies just add together the old book values of their net assets. As a result, the shareholders and investors have a difficult time discovering just what did occur in the transaction.

Using the purchase method in a business combination is consistent with how other acquired assets are accounted for because all assets, whether a piece of inventory, a building, or a whole company, are recorded on the balance sheet at their cost (the current market value at that date) when they are initially acquired.

Under this method, the excess of the purchase price over the fair market value of the acquired company's net assets is known as *goodwill*. Goodwill is charged to the buyer's earnings over time.

The FASB decided that all acquisitions should be recorded in the same way based on the value of what is given up for them and that the purchase method reflects these values while the pooling-of-interests method does not.

Widespread use of the pooling-of-interests method is largely an American phenomenon. The U.S. not only is out of step with other countries on the pooling versus purchase issue, but domestically the accounting treatment shows a great deal of diversity in practice as well. Pooling of interests is the exception almost everywhere else in the world, and some countries, including Australia actually ban its use altogether; New Zealand is planning to eliminate it.

The Board's decisions to date do not affect combinations of companies under control of nonprofit organizations.

Results of Eliminating Pooling-of-Interests

The increasing likelihood of the elimination of pooling could result in some interesting maneuvers:

1. Some companies in an acquisitive mode may be spurred to action if they perceive advantages in acquiring other companies *before* they cannot use the pooling-of-interests method.

2. Companies that might be less attractive acquisitions if they had to be accounted for as a purchase could include pharmaceutical, financial and service enterprises, as well as the frequently sought-after software, high-tech, bio-med and Internet companies.

3. Acquirers may be tempted to overpay to obtain targeted acquisitions immediately in order to use the old accounting methods. The "signing bonus" could be kept out of future operating earnings by using pooling of interests.

4. Those companies willing to be or wanting to be acquired may also be motivated to accelerate their plans to be acquired. Their attitude might result from a desire to capture any beat-the-deadline premium for their shareholders, and avoid the adverse earnings effects of revised goodwill accounting for the combined acquirer and acquiree company.

Regardless of the reasoning of the acquirers and the acquirees, the FASB's proposals are expected to accelerate corporate takeovers as companies race to find partners before the accounting changes can take effect. As an indication of the popularity of the pooling-of-interest accounting method, 9 of the 10 largest acquisitions in 1998 were accounted for in this manner.

Other Considerations

The decision to eliminate pooling-of-interests accounting is one of a number of decisions the FASB made as part of its business combination and intangible assets agenda. The FASB's other related decisions include a whole new approach to goodwill to get more in step with the recently adopted IASs and the rest of the accounting world.

Goodwill

1. When allocating the cost of an acquired entity to the assets acquired and liabilities assumed, every effort should be made to recognize all of the net assets acquired (including intangible assets), and measure them at their fair values.
2. If the fair value of the acquired net assets exceeds the fair value of the purchase, consideration (negative goodwill) would be allocated on a pro rata basis:
   a. First to reduce the valuation of acquired intangible assets for which there is no observable market.
   b. Second, if an excess still remained, to acquired depreciable nonfinancial assets and any other acquired intangible assets.
   c. If any excess remains after these allocations, it is recognized as an extraordinary gain.

(Current accounting requires the excess to be used to reduce the values assigned to the acquiree's noncurrent assets, except marketable securities. If any remains after reducing these values to zero, the residual is amortized systematically as a credit to income over a period not to exceed 40 years.)

3. If the fair value of the purchase consideration exceeds the fair value of the net assets acquired (positive goodwill), it would be amortized

on a straight line basis over its useful economic life, which may not exceed 20 years.

4. Goodwill charges (including goodwill impairment costs) would be presented in the income statement as a separate line item on a net-of-tax basis.

5. A separate line item, income before goodwill charges, would be shown on the income statement.

6. Per share amounts would be presented on the face of the income statement for income before goodwill charges and goodwill.

7. At the time the final Standard is issued, previously acquired goodwill being accounted for under Accounting Research Bulletin 43, Chapter 5, would be written off as the cumulative effect of an accounting change. The manner in which previously acquired goodwill was accounted for under Opinion 17, and previously recognized intangible assets other than goodwill were accounted for under ARB 43 or Opinion 17, would be grandfathered.

Other Purchased Intangible Assets

Intangible assets that are reliably measurable should be recognized separately as assets. Intangible assets should be presumed to have a useful economic life of 20 years or less and generally should be amortized over their useful economic lives. The existing rule permits a maximum amortization period of 40 years.

Intangible assets that are separable or potentially exchangeable, and that have (a) either an observable market value, or (b) are based on rights conveyed by law or contract that extend beyond 20 years may be amortized over longer periods. They may not be amortized at all if they have indefinite lives. If this is the case, they should be reviewed for impairment on a fair value basis.

Chapter 6

International Federation of Accountants

Founded in 1977, the International Federation of Accountants (IFAC) with headquarters in New York, consists of 153 national accountancy bodies from 113 countries with well over two million members.

IFAC seems not to command the notice in the business press that the International Accounting Standards Committee receives, and decidedly not that of the SEC, FASB, and GASB in this country. However, it does appear to be doing a workman-like job of seeing to it that the global spread of the business community does not damage the justified respect accorded the accounting profession.

IFAC AND IASC RELATIONSHIP

By 1982, it became obvious to the leadership of IFAC and the International Accounting Standards Committee (IASC), located on Fleet Street in London, that their particular bailiwicks needed to be clearly established in order to avoid confusion concerning their respective roles. It was agreed that the IASC should be the sole international body to set *financial accounting and reporting standards*. IFAC, on behalf of the accountancy profession, also agreed to contribute a certain portion of the IASC budget. Thus, the IASC primarily through the IASC Board, develops, issues and promotes worldwide acceptance of international standards on financial accounting and reporting.

At the same time, IASC agreed to IFAC's role as the worldwide *organization for the accountancy profession* and accepted IFAC member bodies into the IASC. It was further established that IFAC would nominate 13 countries

116

to sit on the IASC Board, with four other seats to be selected at IASC's discretion. Since 1995, IFAC has also funded the cost of one Board seat so that certain emerging market nations, otherwise unable to afford the cost, could participate in the IASC Board.

The Board of IFAC considers the following to be among their most important tasks:

1. Develop auditing initiatives.
2. Develop guidance and standards relating to education, ethics, management accounting, information technology and the public sector.
3. Give consideration to professional issues such as accountant's liability and the liberalization of professional services.
4. Act as primary spokesman on professional accountancy issues.

Two Separate International Organizations

IFAC emphasizes that the international accountancy profession could be considered to have two primary standard-setting bodies: IFAC and the IASC. The organizations have common memberships in that the 153 national accountancy bodies from 113 countries that are full members of IFAC are *ipso facto* members of IASC (the associate and affiliate IFAC members are not officially IASC members). However, as pointed out above, they are two separate and distinct organizations with two agendas.

Associate members are national organizations whose members work in a support role to the accountancy professions and newly formed accountancy bodies that have not yet met the full membership criteria.

Affiliate members are international organizations that represent a particular area of interest or a group of professionals who frequently interact with accountants.

There is considerable mutual support for one another's objectives. IFAC member bodies, in addition to their responsibility to promote and use IFAC guidance, are committed to promote and implement IASC pronouncements. There is also regular contact and coordination between the two organizations at the leadership level.

This arrangement has worked for the last 15 years or so. In addition, both organizations appear to believe that it provides, on the one hand, the necessary degree of independence for the IASC Board to set accounting standards but also ensures the commitment of the accountancy profession in helping to see that these standards are actually implemented in international practice.

Comparison to U.S. Organizations

The IFAC likens their and the IASC's roles on the international scene to those of the AICPA (with a nod to the Institute of Management Accountants (IMA) and the Institute of Internal Auditors (IIA)) and the FASB, respectively. The FASB is completely independent of the profession and sets accounting standards. AICPA, etc., are the professional accountancy bodies and set standards and guidelines for accountants. They also comment on FASB pronouncements and support the FASB by providing representation to the Financial Accounting Foundation (FAF) Board of Trustees, but there is no control by the profession over the FASB.

IFAC and International Firms Combine Efforts

At a meeting in London in January, 2000, IFAC and several large international firms launched a major initiative designed to raise standards of financial reporting and auditing globally. Their aim is to protect the interests of cross-border investors and promote international flows of capital.

The firms are working closely with IFAC in developing and encouraging implementation of international accounting and auditing standards. Their work provides for independent oversight of IFAC's public interest activities.

Participation in the new IFAC grouping of firms will be open to any firms that have transnational clients, and are willing to comply with certain requirements which include:

1. Firm policies and practices in compliance with International Standards on Auditing (ISAs) and the IFAC Code of Ethics.
2. Maintenance of appropriate internal control procedures including intrafirm practice review.
3. Agreement to implement training on international accounting and auditing standards including the Code of Ethics.
4. Agreement to subject assurance work to periodic external quality assurance.
5. Agreement to support the development of the professional bodies and implementation of international standards of accounting and auditing in developing countries.

IFAC sees this as a significant step towards the achievement of global harmonization of financial reporting and auditing. The organization considers the willingness of international firms to work with IFAC on these terms will:

1. Promote transparency, reliability, and comparability of financial information across national borders.
2. Facilitate the international transfer of public and private capital.
3. Strengthen business transactions.
4. Ultimately contribute to the broader public interest through wealth creation and the strengthening of civil societies.

Much of the funding for the group is provided by participating firms, who will also contribute additional resources to strengthen IFAC's audit standards setting and monitoring work.

ORGANIZATIONAL STRUCTURE

The organization of IFAC is based on the Assembly, which is made up of one representative from each membership accounting body. The Assembly elects the Council which, in turn, selects an Executive Committee to advance the organization's policies and to appoint and oversee special task forces and seven standing committees.

The IFAC Council expanded its agenda by appointing task forces to work in specific areas: anti-corruption, small- and medium-sized enterprises, quality assurance, and structure and organization. As their work is completed, the committees are disbanded and new groups are formed to consider current problems and needs.

Anti-Corruption

This task force has now been disbanded and a discussion of its completed guidance paper, *The Accountancy Profession and the Fight Against Corruption,* is found later in this chapter.

Small-and Medium-Sized Enterprises (SME)

Recognizing that the growth of small businesses contributes to the economic well-being of many countries, IFAC is focusing greater attention on this constituency. Plans are to identify the unique needs of small- and medium-sized enterprises, available resources, and how the international accountancy profession can best help this group.

Therefore, the task force is charged with:

1. Evaluating the extent of the IFAC membership that works in the area of SME and the programs and practice that provide support for this constituency.

2. Publicizing the availability of relevant programs and materials.
3. Developing, as appropriate, guidance for those working in the SME area, whether as public practitioners or as management employees.
4. Recommending to IFAC committees and IASC that they make their standards and guidance relevant to those practitioners in the SME area. A task force will recommend the development of guidance for both practitioners and SME advisors and owners.

Quality Assurance

IFAC has released an International Professional Practice Statement, *Assuring the Quality of Professional Services*, calling for the world's accountants to implement widespread quality control systems. The new statement requires firms of professional accountants to have a system of quality control that covers all of their professional work, and to provide access to continuing professional education programs focusing on quality control polices and procedures.

Additionally, it provides that each firm of professional accountants should be the subject of an external review, either by their professional body or by another firm of accountants. The review should cover the firm's quality control system and the quality of the work carried out for assurance engagements.

IFAC feels that the extension of their former guidance on quality assurance beyond the traditional audit to cover all professional services provided by practicing firms is a further demonstration of their commitment to the achievement of a profession that operates with the highest professional standards worldwide and that meets the expectations of clients, regulators, and the public at large.

Money Laundering

In May, 1999, the council appointed a task force to look at the special issue of anti-money laundering, the accountant's responsibility with respect to this form of corruption, and guidance that may be needed to help accountants meet this responsibility.

Technical Activities

Technical activities of the IFAC are carried on by several committees in addition to the special task forces.

Ethics Committee

As a result of the work of this committee, a revision of the *Code of Ethics for Professional Accountants* was recently issued. However, because of the growing acceptance of the code as fundamental guidance for accountants practicing worldwide, and as a model for national accounting and auditing framework, IFAC considers revision and further guidance to be an ongoing process.

Committee Agenda. Among numerous measures that have been in the revision and exposure drafts (EDs) are the following:

a. Clarification of rules affecting confidentiality. Emphasis is placed on the belief that the rules of confidentiality must be balanced by the public's need to know certain information. It is agreed that professional accountants must respect the confidentiality of a client's or employer's affairs. However, instances may arise in which professional, legal or ethical considerations overrule the need for confidentiality. An effort is being made to clarify when public interest may take precedence over the confidentiality of specific information.

b. Guidance for accountants who employ nonaccountants. Taking the stand that accountants are ultimately responsible for any service performed for their client, whether by a lawyer, actuary or appraiser, the IFAC is suggesting guidance on the applicability of the code to nonaccountants.

c. Separation of ethical issues into sections relating to:

- all accountants,
- those in public practice, and
- those employed in commerce, industry, the public sector
- and education.

d. Guidance when accountants are asked to give a second opinion. The code requires that they contact the original or existing accountant to obtain all relevant facts and information about the client. The assumption is that the objectivity of the second opinion could be open to question if it were not based on thorough research and investigation.

e. Guidance relating to auditor independence and rotation concerns. The code cautions that accountants in public practice should rotate senior personnel when retained on long-term engagements. Otherwise, the use of the same auditor over an extended period could lead to the appearance of a lack of independence.

f. Stipulation that the *quality* of an audit must not suffer because an accountant has drastically underbid a competitor in order to gain a client.

g. Recommendation that IFAC member bodies and professional accounting institutes provide support, and hotlines to answer queries relating to ethical dilemmas.

Auditor Independence. Maintaining independence in today's complex and competitive business environment has become increasingly challenging for auditors. Around the globe, accountancy organizations and those responsible for the regulation of auditors are focusing on the issue. IFAC, as part of its ongoing effort to work in the public interest, is participating in this effort.

Members of the committee are now participating on an international team that is discussing auditor independence with the European Commission and also participating in the on-going work of the Independence Standards Board in the U.S. In addition, the committee is reviewing the section of the rules relating to auditor independence contained in the Code of Ethics.

Plans are to change from the current "rules based" approach to a new conceptual framework under which independence matters can be addressed. Although the independence rules now relate primarily to accountants in public practice, whatever changes take place could have wider applicability, as the idea of a broader assurance services concept begins to take hold.

Public Sector Committee (PSC)

Eight International Public Sector Accounting Standards (IPSASs) designed to improve the accountability and financial management of governments worldwide have been released. IPSASs 1-8 introduce a set of accrual-based accounting standards based on International Accounting Standards (IASs). These Standards have been adapted to reflect their application to the public sector.

In addition, the Public Sector Committee realizes that many governments may not yet be able to adopt the accrual-based IPSASs. To assist them, the PSC has developed an exposure draft ED 9, *Financial Reporting under the Cash Basis of Accounting*, prescribing the requirements for the presentation of the primary financial statement under the cash basis of accounting.

IPSAS 1, *Presentation of Financial Statements* prescribes the overall considerations for presentation of financial statements, guidance for the structure, and minimum requirements for the content of financial statements prepared under the accrual basis of accounting.

IPSAS 2, *Cash Flow Statements* requires information about historical changes in cash and cash equivalents of an entity in a cash flow statement which classifies cash flows during the period from operating, investing, and financing activities.

IPSAS 3, *Net Surplus or Deficit for the Period, Fundamental Errors and Changes in Accounting Policies* requires the classification and disclosure of extraordinary items and separate disclosure of certain items in the financial statements. It also specifies the accounting treatment for changes in accounting estimates, changes in accounting policies and correction of fundamental errors.

IPSAS 4, *The Effect of Changes in Foreign Exchange Rates* deals with accounting for foreign currency transactions and foreign operations. It specifies requirements for determining which exchange rate is appropriate and how to recognize in the financial statements the financial effect of changes in exchange rates.

IPSAS 5, *Borrowing Costs* prescribes the accounting treatment and generally requires the immediate expensing of borrowing costs. However, the Standard permits, as an allowed alternative treatment, the capitalization of borrowing costs that are directly attributable to the acquisition, construction, or production of a qualifying asset.

IPSAS 6, *Consolidated Financial Statements and Accounting for Controlled Entities* requires all controlling entities to prepare consolidated financial statements which consolidate all controlled entities on a line by line basis. It also contains a detailed discussion of *control* within the public sector and guidance on determining whether control exists for financial reporting purposes.

IPSAS 7, *Accounting for Investments in Associates* requires that all of these investments be accounted for in consolidated financial statements using the equity method, except when the investment is acquired and held exclusively for disposal in the near future. In that case, the cost method is required.

IPSAS 8, *Financial Reporting of Interests in Joint Ventures* specifies proportionate consolidation as the benchmark treatment for accounting for joint venturers entered into by public sector entities. It also permits, as an allowed alternative, joint ventures to be accounted for using the equity method of accounting.

ED 9, *Financial Reporting under the Cash Basis of Accounting* sets out the overall considerations for the presentation of the financial statement under the cash basis of accounting, guidelines for their structure, and minimum requirements for their content.

Financial and Management Accounting Committee (FMAC)

Annually, this committee publishes *Articles of Merit*, award winning articles selected from IFAC member body journals. Articles are chosen by a panel of three judges, members of the FMAC, in a "blind" selection process. Articles submitted are judged on the basis of having made, or having the potential to make "a distinct and valuable contribution to the advancement of management accounting."

In addition, the committee publishes special studies, guidance and the results of research in the area of management accounting. It also disseminates information through international forums and seminars on these issues.

Intellectual Capital. A recent study issued by this committee, *The Accountant's Role In Intellectual Capital Management*, highlights the key issues surrounding the management and measurement of *intellectual capital* and the accountant's role in this process. It refers to key research demonstrating the importance of intellectual capital in positioning a company for growth and focuses on how management accountants can contribute to an entity's overall success by identifying, valuing, reporting on, and participating in the management of the intellectual capital of the firm.

Significantly, the study recognizes that accounting for intellectual capital will ultimately require the invention of new financial and management accounting concepts and practices.

International Auditing Practices Committee (IAPC)

This committee's task is to upgrade auditing and related services standards globally by developing benchmark statements on varied auditing and attest functions to increase the credibility of financial statements. This endeavor is centered around the IFAC's codification of International Standards on Auditing (ISAs) and Related Practices.

Going Concern, ISA 570. In June, 1999, the IAPC approved a revision to ISA 570, *Going Concern*, dealing with the auditor's responsibility in the audit of financial statements with respect to this assumption used in the preparation of financial statements.

Since this assumption is a fundamental principle in preparation of the statements, the ISA recognizes that management has a responsibility to assess the entity's ability to continue as a going concern, even if this is not explicitly required within the financial reporting framework. The organization realizes that management's assessment may not always involve detailed analysis, particularly when the entity has a history of profitable operations and a ready access to financial resources.

Nevertheless, they believe that such an assessment should be an integral part of the auditor's consideration of the assumption, and that he or she should consider whether there are material uncertainties about the entity's ability to continue as a going concern which should be disclosed in the financial statement.

Of course, the auditor cannot predict future events or conditions that may cause an entity to cease operations. Accordingly, the absence of any reference to going concern uncertainty in an auditor's report cannot be viewed as a guarantee that the entity will continue as a going concern.

However, the new ISA recommends that, in planning the audit, the auditor should *consider* whether there are events or conditions which may cast significant doubt on the entity's ability to continue as a going concern. If so, the auditor takes them into account when making preliminary assessments of the components of audit risk and in planning audit procedures. The auditor must also remain alert throughout the audit for indications of such events and/or conditions.

As noted above, management's input is important and the auditor evaluates their assessment by considering:

1. The process management followed.
2. The assumptions made.

3. Management's plans for future action.

The auditor also considers whether management has taken into account all relevant information that has been identified as a result of his or her audit procedures.

The auditor should review the same assessment period as that used by management with the minimum period being twelve months from the balance sheet date. If management's assessment period covered a shorter period, the auditor should ask management to extend their assessment.

The auditor also needs to inquire about events or conditions beyond the period of assessment, and may ask management to determine the potential significance of any identified event or condition on their going concern assessment. If, as a result of the above procedures, an event or condition is identified that may cast significant doubt on the entity's ability to continue as a going concern, the auditor is to review management's plans for future action and request written evidence relating to questions raised by the auditor about whether or not a material uncertainty may, in fact, exist.

The auditor's report should include either a matter of emphasis paragraph, or a qualified or adverse opinion, depending upon whether or not the financial statements fully disclose the event and condition as well as the material uncertainty about the entity's ability to continue as a going concern.

If the going concern basis has been used to prepare the financial statements when it is not appropriate, the auditor should express an *adverse opinion*. At various times, the auditor may find it necessary to ask management to make or extend its assessment. If management is unwilling to do so, it is not the auditor's responsibility to rectify management's lack of analysis and the auditor must consider the need to modify the report because of insufficient appropriate evidence. Guidance is also provided on additional considerations if there has been a significant delay in signing or approving the financial statements.

The revised ISA will become effective for audits of financial statements for periods ending on or after December 31, 2000.

Assurance. Another of the committee's most important tasks involves assuring the credibility of information. As trade in goods and services spreads over the globe, the demand for reliable information spreads even faster. The changing information needs of businesses and consumers are resulting in increased demands for the audit to extend beyond the traditional attest function into assurance services. The IAPC is taking a leadership role in supporting the accountant as a provider of these services by developing standards and guidance in areas where the opinion of the independent auditor can add value and credibility to the information provided by directors and management.

Through this committee, IFAC is attempting to provide guidance on assuring the credibility of financial information with accountants assuming the role as the "primary care" providers. Building on the framework of existing auditing procedures and practices, the aim is to examine how and when these practices are effective in reporting on the reliability of information and how these practices can be improved and expanded.

As a result, IAPC released ISA 100 providing guidance in this area. The International Standard entitled *Assurance Engagements* is designed to help accountants meet the demand for services that increase the value of information for decision making.

The Standard describes the elements of an assurance engagement and the requirements for professional accountants undertaking such an engagement. In addition to providing the professional benchmark for these types of engagements, the Standard outlines the framework and general principles to be applied in developing specific standards for particular types of assurance engagements.

The proposed Standard takes into consideration comments that were received relating to an ED released in 1997, *Reporting on the Credibility of Information*, as well as another published in 1999. There was a strong view at the earlier time that although the proposal allowing for a range of assurance was conceptually sound, it appeared to pose implementation issues. The primary cause of that concern was the perceived difficulty in being able to communicate *different levels of assurance* to report users.

As a result, the later exposure draft took this into consideration. The ISA provides that:

1. Engagements should be limited to providing two levels of assurance, high and moderate.
2. Outlines the factors that would determine the appropriate level of assurance.
3. Provides guidance on reporting on the two levels of assurance.
4. Recommends that the conclusion for an assurance engagement providing a high level of assurance will generally be expressed in the form of an opinion.

Communications of Audit Matters. In June, 1999, the committee approved a new ISA, *Communications of Audit Matters with Those Charged with Governance*. It establishes standards and provides guidance on communication of audit matters arising from the audit of financial statements between the auditor and those charged with governance of an entity.

The affected personnel are those responsible for:

1. Ensuring that the entity achieves its objectives.
2. Supervising financial reporting.
3. Reporting pertinent information to interested parties.

The focus on the quality of corporate governance is sharpening as deregulated financial markets, enhanced global competition and technological progress increasingly influence corporate behavior. The auditors who should present an independent, objective view, play an important role in contributing to the achievement of the entity's objectives, particularly in relation to financial reporting.

In connection with a financial statement audit, the auditor contributes by expressing an opinion on the fairness of the financial statements in conformity with an accounting framework.

The structures of governance vary from country to country reflecting cultural and legal backgrounds. The new ISA provides guidance to the auditor who faces unfamiliar situations in attempting to determine:

1. The relevant persons charged with governance.
2. With whom audit matters should be communicated.
3. Which matters arising from the audit of the financial statements would be both important and relevant to those charged with governance in overseeing the financial reporting and disclosure process.
4. Which are audit matters of governance interest that need to be communicated and to whom.

This ISA is effective for audits of financial statements for periods ending on or after December 31, 2000.

New Projects. The IAPC has agreed to develop a new statement on auditing derivatives. The project will be put on a fast track so that a Statement can be issued as quickly as possible because of the importance of derivatives in global finance.

In addition, IAPC and the Information Technology Committee are in the process of developing a proposal on e-commerce. The proposal is being developed from the perspective of all technical committees, as e-commerce impacts all of their work.

Information Technology Committee (ITC)

This group is charged with keeping the worldwide accounting community abreast of the latest developments and applications relating to information technology (IT). It encourages member bodies to keep up-to-date on available hardware and software and the relationship between IT and the accounting profession.

At a recent international meeting, the committee focused on the use of IT in developing countries and approved a research program and budget. Research will involve determination of the current usage of IT in these countries and identification of the type and level of assistance which would be appropriate in developing economies.

Since being formed in 1995, the committee has begun formulating a series of guidelines to help management cope with rapidly expanding technological developments. The first guideline to be approved was *Managing Security in Information and Communications*. It emphasized the growing importance of closely managing the risks related to information technology. The other earlier guideline is *Managing Information Technology Planning for Business Impact*.

Three additional guidelines being finalized for issuance in 2000 include: *Acquiring Information Technology, Implementation of Information Technology Solutions, and IT Delivery and Support*. The expressed aim is to help executives maximize IT investments and minimize IT risks.

It becomes increasingly evident that the development, management, and delivery of IT solutions is critical to business success today. The committee's guidelines are designed to help executives integrate IT into business strategy, increase understanding of the core principles involved in developing and managing a technology infrastructure, and keep costs under control. The three EDs specifically address the following:

1. *Acquiring Information Technology* provides executives with a framework for a structured acquisition process to help them generate sufficient support for the acquisition and to ensure that there are no major omissions from a business, technical or legal standpoint.
2. *The Implementation of Information Technology Solutions* outlines the key factors pertaining to successful IT implementation and defines the roles and responsibilities of management in maintaining control over the quality and cost of the project throughout its implementation life cycle.
3. *IT Delivery and Support* focuses on how to build a technology infrastructure that is responsive to the needs of both management and customers. It also points out how management and staff functions can be structured to ensure the effective delivery of IT services.

Education Committee

In the effort to bring about global accounting standards and mutual recognition agreements related to professional accounting services, this committee recommends the necessary elements for the education and training of all accounting professionals. Further, emphasis is placed on the importance and quality of continuing professional education (CPE) programs.

Recognizing the significant impact of the Internet and distributed learning on both requalification and continuing education of accountants, the committee has developed a discussion paper entitled *Quality Issues for Internet and Distributed Learning in Accounting Education.*

In addition to undertaking a project that will outline various competence-based approaches to the development of professional accountants, the committee is also addressing the following issues:

1. Teaching innovations.
2. Assessment methodologies.
3. Reciprocity guidance from an educational perspective.

Membership Committee

IFAC increases its membership through this committee by checking on the accountancy profession in various countries, particularly those with developing economies. It provides guidance and assistance to groups that are attempting to increase the professional level of their members to attain the level of competency to meet IFAC membership requirements.

IFAC FORMS COALITION TO ADVANCE ACCOUNTANCY DEVELOPMENT

The organization is leading a worldwide coalition seeking to get developing and emerging national economies off to the right start in establishing accountability in the public interest through building a responsible, organized accountancy profession.

Early in 1999, IFAC, the World Bank, the International Monetary Fund, various international lending and development agencies, the regional accountancy organizations, the international financial institutions, the regulators, and the Big 5 firms agreed to create the International Forum on Accountancy Development (IFAD). The aim of the new Forum is to bring the accounting profession and International Financial Institutions (IFIs) together to develop programs to establish accountability, transparency, and general accounting know-how in those countries with the greatest needs.

With the increasing interconnectedness of countries doing business on a global scale, financial instability in one nation can very quickly bring about the same in another, as was graphically demonstrated in the recent past during the Southeast Asian financial crisis.

IFAC views the Forum's role as a helpmeet in formulating a comprehensive plan, establishing a common frame of reference and determining priorities and projects most likely to succeed in building the accounting capacity needed for both the public and private sectors in developing countries.

Plan of Action

Specifically, the Forum intends to:

1. Promote understanding by national governments of developing countries about the value to them of transparent financial reporting by a strong accounting profession.
2. Help harness funds and expertise to build accounting capacity in developing and transitional economies.
3. Assist in defining expectations relating to the manner in which the accounting profession should carry out its responsibilities to support the public interest in these countries.
4. Bring pressure on governments to focus more directly on the needs of developing countries.
5. Promote cooperation between governments, the profession, the international financial institutions, regulators, standard-setters, capital providers, and issuers.
6. Contribute to a common strategy or framework of reference for accountancy development.

To meet these goals, the Forum will initially concentrate on developing guidance that focuses on:

1. The "cultural" issues, setting out some of the basic misunderstandings that often surround the need for transparent financial reporting and accountability.
2. Regulatory infrastructures that are likely to achieve a proper balance between the rights and responsibilities of government, shareholders, directors, and auditors.
3. Programs to enable developing economies to structure their own national standards to conform to IFAC, IASC, and other appropriate international guidance.

IFAC knows it can't meet these goals alone. Only by working together with the other members of the Forum, who have the ability to reach their own unique constituencies, can anyone hope to overcome tremendous obstacles and achieve positive and lasting changes.

Emphasis on Developing Countries

In countries where it does not yet exist, legislative and regulatory agencies must become aware of the need to reflect the proper balance of responsibilities between government, enterprise leadership, and accountants and auditors. Transparency must be improved through better financial reporting, more accountable control environments, and management of financial risk. If all of this progresses, governments of developing nations could gain improved access to more efficient local and international financial markets for themselves and their countries' public and private sector enterprises.

The Forum will be comprised of approximately 30 organizations representing the entities most heavily involved in accountancy-capacity building projects. The initial membership of the Forum will include the following:

1. International financial institutions (IFIs), providing the greater part of funding of all aid disbursed for projects within the scope of the Forum; e.g., World Bank, United Nations Development Project, the European Union, the Regional Development Banks, and very large bilateral donors, notably from the Group of Seven Countries (U.S., UK, Canada, Germany, France, Italy and Japan).

2. Multilateral development agencies and institutions primarily concerned with improving financial management throughout the international community, notably the International Monetary Fund, the International Organization of Supreme Audit Institutions, the United Nations Conference on Trade and Development, the Organization for Economic Development, the Basle Committee for Banking Supervision, and the International Organization of Securities Commissions.

3. The international accountancy profession, represented by IFAC, the International Accounting Standards Committee (IASC), IFAC's four "recognized" Regional Organizations, and the major firms working across the largest number of countries and undertaking projects on behalf of the development agencies and their clients.

The four regional groups are the Confederation of Asian and Pacific Accountants, Eastern Central and Southern African Federation of Accountants (ECSAFA), Fédération des Experts Comptables Européens (FEE) and the Interamerican Accounting Association (IAA). These are independent bodies which, in many cases, share IFAC's membership and have similar objectives. IFAC considers them especially effective in accomplishing their objectives because of the more intimate knowledge of the needs and resources of particular regions of the world.

Given the magnitude of the goals, it is unrealistic to expect rapid solutions. However, IFAC hopes that the Forum can help its participants bring an effective and shared focus to an essential building block of stability and growth—relevant, accurate and credible accounting information.

ACCOUNTANCY'S FIGHT AGAINST CORRUPTION

IFAC has published a discussion paper, *The Accountancy Profession and the Fight Against Corruption,* aimed at promoting debate at the national and global levels on the issue of corruption. The paper points out that while there is corruption worldwide, both public and private, it is more pervasive in some places than others.

The paper suggests that corruption has a negative impact on everyone:

1. Economic development is hampered.
2. Investors lose confidence.
3. Entrepreneurs suffer increased costs of doing business and face higher risks.
4. Country credit ratings drop.
5. Professionals, businesspersons, and government officials lose credibility.

Society at large becomes quite cynical. And the impact could be felt most deeply in developing and emerging countries where a resulting drop in aid and investment can certainly have a significant impact on economic development, and create social hardships for peoples attempting to build a better life.

Legal and Governmental Support

The IFAC may be tilting at windmills, but the organization feels that combating corruption must be carried on by all and at all levels of society. They call for a commitment by governments and the existence of a solid framework of laws, regulations, control systems and disciplinary measures that proscribe corrupt acts and prescribe strong penalties for those found guilty of them, as well as adequate protection for whistle blowers.

Just what is the accountant's role in all of this? The profession cannot carry on this battle alone but, as an integral part of society and a major player in the business world, IFAC believes it must be and is ready to play its part if there is appropriate infrastructure and public support.

The Many Faces of Corruption

Bribery, fraud, illegal payments, money laundering, smuggling, and as many other forms as criminal minds may devise, IFAC finds lurking everywhere. The paper points out that often corruption takes place not only involving money, but also involving special favors or influence. Economic growth, globalization, and new developments in technology provide a changing scenario in which corrupt individuals devise ever-changing forms of corruption. Thus, it concludes, it is impossible to provide an all-purpose rule book on how to contain corruption. The problem is too complex—and never-ending—but the fight must go on.

Coordinated Responsibilities

IFAC concedes that in the business world, management has a critical role in the battle against corruption. It is the management of an organization that will set the parameters by developing and enforcing systems of proper corporate governance. In the public sector, similar governance codes have been or need to be developed.

Since accountants have long been commended for high integrity, objectivity and service to the public interest, IFAC feels that their key internal positions in the public and private sectors, as well as their external responsibilities as auditors or advisors, make them essential in the efforts to reduce corruption.

In addition, the paper cites other aids to tightening the reins on corruption:

1. Most national organizations of accountants, as well as the International Federation of Accountants, have developed standards that are designed to combat corruption.
2. Ethics codes, which apply to all accountants, be they in public practice, business, industry or government, require them to follow the highest standards of objectivity and professional care.
3. Auditing standards alert practitioners to the possibility of fraud and require them to document such possibility in planning audits and to report their findings to management.
4. Codes of corporate governance and appropriate financial and other internal controls should ensure that those accountants in business or in government are aware of their responsibilities to report corruption in a similar manner.

IFAC Proposals

But where is all of this background leading? IFAC states its wish to contribute to the global and national debates which it believes should be developed to ensure that the fight against corruption moves forward. To this end:

1. It has developed the paper on corruption to raise awareness of the issues and contribute to the debate.

2. It is proposing to its 153 member bodies in 113 countries that they:

   a. Develop programs that build collaborative relationships with legislative and regulatory authorities, the legal profession, and other groups interested in strengthening the framework for good governance, transparency, and accountability, as well as the legal framework, so as to minimize corrupt practices, propose solutions based on model legislation and regulations introduced in other countries, and point out where swift action may be required.

   b. Work with government to ensure that the requisite definition of corruption is in place, the legislation proscribing corrupt acts is prepared and appropriate means of protection are developed for those who may "blow the whistle."

   c. Initiate education programs for accountants and the public to create awareness of the detrimental effects of corruption, thereby motivating public action toward its elimination, through press articles, seminars, continuing professional education courses, and speeches by leaders of the profession.

   d. Encourage the national media to make corruption a public issue by devoting attention to the types and hazards of corrupt activities, by publishing studies of the harm caused by corruption, and by enumerating various steps that can be taken to prevent or expose such harm.

   e. Provide assistance, including technical support, to national and international organizations fighting corruption by publicizing their activities, offering assistance in their research, and promoting their proposals.

   f. Encourage practicing firms, their clients and governments to adopt codes of conduct setting the "tone at the top" by establishing sound principles of corporate governance that expressly prohibit corrupt activity, and that provide the benefits flowing from the implementation of internal control systems that help expose corrupt activities.

   g. Encourage audit committees expressly to consider whether appropriate policies are in place to prohibit corrupt acts and to require that any such act be reported to them.

   h. Promote a tax system that is efficient and equitable so as to discourage the disparity and burden that leads to corruption, and that does not allow corrupt payments to be deductible from income for tax purposes.

3. It will use its influence with organizations such as the World Bank, the IMF, the Organisation of Economic Co-operation and Development (OECD) and the United Nations to encourage the development of proper legislation in all member states.

4. It will establish and maintain links with organizations such as Transparency International and the Financial Action Task Force to ensure that the profession is represented in their governing councils and periodic conferences as a means to increase its profile in the fight against corruption.

In the Final Analysis

The organization calls upon the individual accountant to carry out his or her responsibility in the anticorruption campaign. Professional skepticism is necessary when establishing business relationships, and in the review of transactions between related parties, especially when they appear to have questionable business sense. Corrupt entities and individuals must realize that accountants constitute a barrier against corruption. Above all, each individual accountant must ensure that his or her own behavior reflects an unswerving commitment to truth and honesty in financial reporting.

Chapter 7

The International Accounting Standards Committee

The International Accounting Standards Committee (IASC) was established in 1973 by professional accountancy bodies (including the AICPA) from nine countries to attempt to bring some degree of order, uniformity, and reliability to accounting practices and procedures in developing market countries. The IASC has delivered to the International Organization of Securities Commissions (IOSCO) a set of core accounting standards suitable for use in cross-border listings. It has also approved a new constitution for the restructured IASC.

The original group has increased to 153 accounting organizations in 113 countries representing 2,000,000 accountants worldwide.

With the adoption of International Accounting Standards (IAS) 40, *Accounting for Investments,* and 39, *Financial Instruments: Recognition and Measurement,* the IASC completed the core set of Standards identified in an agreement with the IOSCO in 1993. IASC feels confident that it has a comprehensive set of Standards covering all of the major areas of importance to general businesses.

THE CHANGING WORLD ECONOMY

The position of accounting standard setters has changed enormously since IASC's formation. Not the least important of these positions is the attitude toward IASC. The tide has turned from a rather grudging tolerance of their activities to a realization that it's important to offer input or you may find the rest of the accounting world leaving you behind.

At the time of its inception, many countries, even some with highly developed economies, had no official accounting standards or only rudimentary ones. As the IASC points out, the explosion of demand for global accounting standards had been set in motion. The investing public had been made aware, by headline events in the financial newspapers, of the enormous flexibility in measuring a company's results or assets and liabilities under the existing rules. In the U.S., the Securities and Exchange Commission, in particular, had embarked upon a program to tighten up the rules relating to financial statement preparation.

These problems have not *all* been fully resolved nor are they likely to be as long as there is anyone capable of painting a corporate picture in a rosier hue than it deserves. But it's up to the standard makers—nationally and internationally—to keep trying.

The Securities and Exchange Commission publicly criticized U.S. business managers for continuing to use means available to them to disguise the pattern of income or profits over time, from what it would be with unbiased measurement, to produce the appearance of a smoother trend.

The international organization reasoned that accounting standards can limit the opportunities for earnings management, and they believe the Standards finalized by IASC do so, along with those of the many national standard setters. However, they realize that strong and independent behavior by auditors and regulators can also contribute to resolving this problem to limit the degree of judgment in applying accounting Standards and their focus is likely to shift towards enforcement activities.

Evidently, they believe the SEC concern is having a beneficial effect upon progress in standard setting and enforcement by reminding one and all that these problems continue *even in the most financially sophisticated countries of the world.*

THE IMPORTANCE OF GLOBAL ACCOUNTING STANDARDS

The need for global accounting standards, or at a minimum for less diversity in national standards, became painfully evident in 1998. The economic difficulties that began in Asia and spread to other regions of the world rather graphically demonstrated the interdependencies of different nations in the modern global economy.

It has been suggested that part of the blame should be placed on "accounting"—or lack of it. The IASC felt that international investors lacked confidence in the accounting of the countries where the difficulties originated. They felt that the lack of confidence made capital more expensive than it needed to be and added to the threat of serious worldwide economic recession.

As a result, the IASC is as committed as the SEC and the FASB to the belief that "comparability" and "transparency" are key words in healthy financial markets. They acknowledge that:

1. An important emphasis in the demand for global accounting standards is *comparability* among businesses in different countries to serve the demands of international capital markets.
2. Accounting standards are needed to bring about greater *transparency* and openness in financial reporting by individual countries and their business corporations and financial institutions.

The European Union

Another important current development in the demand for International Accounting Standards is taking place in Europe. A key current objective of the European Union (EU) is the development of a single economic market. The introduction of the euro on January 1,1999 was an important step in that direction. The single economic market would almost necessitate a single capital market with companies from the different countries competing for capital on equal terms.

Those putting up the capital must be able to assess the performance of different companies with full comparability. Said comparability is not attainable if different accounting standards are used by different companies—even if they are reporting in a common currency. IASs are crucial to this process.

From the beginning, rather than establish a separate European Accounting Standards Board, the European Commission (EC) planned to work with the IASC to standardize accounting practices for multinational companies within the European Union. The EC's preferred option for the future development of accounting in the EU is to "oblige" listed companies to follow International Accounting Standards. Other companies would follow national codes within the framework of the European directives.

The European Commission concluded that there are no significant conflicts between the EC Accounting Directives and those International Accounting Standards and interpretations of the Standing Interpretations Committee (SIC) that are applicable to accounting periods beginning before July 1, 1998.

Completing the Core Standards

The main focus of IASC's technical work had been the completion of the core set of Standards agreed upon with IOSCO. The work program to complete the core Standards was comprised of 40 topics classified into twelve major projects. (See later in this chapter.) In that they are now completed, the emphasis has shifted to enforcement of the Standards and reorganization of the Commission.

THE STANDING INTERPRETATIONS COMMITTEE

In 1997, faced with an ever-growing list of Standards to be revised, adopted, applied, interpreted, the IASC Board set up a Standing Interpretations Committee (SIC) to consider, on a timely basis, accounting issues that are likely to receive divergent or unacceptable treatment in the absence of authoritative guidance. The SIC reviews accounting issues within the context of existing International Accounting Standards and the IASC Framework. In developing Interpretations, the SIC works closely with similar national committees. It also seeks public input before reaching a final consensus. When consensus is reached, the SIC publishes authoritative pronouncements on the application of IAS and recommends solutions for situations not covered by existing standards. Its function is similar to that of the FASB's Emerging Issues Task Force (EITF). Its form and function remain the same under the new constitution.

Standard-setting requires some type of committee to provide guidance on the application of Standards. IASC considers it vital that this task be undertaken at the international level, rather than being left to national groups that could undoubtedly develop conclusions that differed from country to country, even when exemplary translations are available.

As an indication of the area covered by this committee, the three initial interpretations focused on the following topics:

1. SIC-1. A company should use the same cost formula for all inventories having similar nature and use. Different cost formulas may be justified for inventories with different nature and use but, for example, a difference in geographic location of inventories, in itself, should not be construed to justify the use of a different cost formula.
2. SIC-2. A company capitalizing borrowing costs directly attributable to the acquisition, construction, or production of qualifying assets, should apply that policy consistently for all qualifying assets and periods.
3. SIC-3. Unrealized gains and losses from transactions between an investor and associates should be eliminated in consolidated financial statements to the extent of the investor's interest in the associate. Unrealized losses should not be eliminated to the extent that the transaction provides evidence of an impairment.

SIC Draft Interpretations have dealt with numerous topics. Under 20 have been ratified thus far.

The Role of IOSCO

In May 2000, IOSCO announced completion of its assessment of the accounting standards issued by the International Accounting Standards Committee (IASC). It recommended that its members allow multinational issuers to use 30 IASC standards, as supplemented by *reconciliation, disclosure*, and *interpretation* where necessary to address outstanding substantive issues at a national or regional level. These are labeled "the IASC 2000 standards."

IOSCO believes that use of these standards by multinational enterprises in preparing their financial statements will facilitate cross-border offerings and listings, and will promote the further development of internationally accepted accounting standards.

The members of IOSCO (including the U.S. Securities and Exchange Commission) undertake their own review process before they accept financial reports prepared in accordance with International Accounting Standards for cross-border listings in their own countries. Many countries have already accepted the complete list of IASs. The other members (including the SEC) are in an advanced stage of the evaluation process.

Merger Accounting Differences

Existing Standards of IASC and national standard setters contain wide differences on merger accounting with very important consequences for the comparability of financial statements. The G4+1 group of standard setters (the national standard setters of Australia, Canada, New Zealand, the United Kingdom and the United States, together with IASC) have agreed to work on a project to eliminate existing differences in members' standards on merger accounting. This involves a review of the existing Standard on business combinations, as regards the relative roles of "purchase accounting" and "pooling accounting."

The Group supported a paper put forward by the U.S. FASB proposing the elimination of "pooling accounting." IASC, along with the members of G4+1, has published this proposal as a consultative paper. (For information on FASB proposed elimination of "pooling of interests," see Chapter 5.)

Accounting for Developing Economies and Emerging Markets

Increasingly, emerging market countries and their regulatory authorities have adopted, indicated their intention to adopt, and/or based their own standards on IAS.

The IASC is working on accounting systems in developing countries and countries with emerging markets. The organization is emphasizing its commitment to help these countries with the development of their accounting standards. In many of the countries, International Accounting Standards are already used as national standards. Some extra Standards, modifications and/or additional guidance may be needed to assist in applying IASs in countries that are only now developing market economies.

When one considers that U.S. GAAP is based upon almost 140 FASB Standards, well over 300 opinions by the FASB's Emerging Issues Task Force, APB Opinions, SEC accounting and financial reporting requirements, AICPA Position papers and Industry Accounting Guides, plus assorted other documents—40 IAS Standards and fewer than 20 SICs might provide rather thin coverage for international accounting regulation.

However, it is apparent that U.S. and non-U.S. investors, exchanges, accountants, corporate managers, CEOs, CFOs and others in international business should become knowledgeable about the IAS and the activities of the IASC because they will soon play a very important part in capital formation and financial accounting worldwide.

Authorized Translations

The official language of IASC is English. It is the only language in which International Accounting Standards are approved by the Board, but they are aware that it is imperative to have reliable translations available in other languages. It is quite reasonable to assume that accounting standards will not receive effective application if they are not understood. To assure the quality of any translation, IASC has developed processes for making high quality "authorized" translations of its Standards. A poor translation could nullify the benefits of the very carefully worded original English language Standard. German, Russian and Spanish translation have been made with other widely used languages to follow.

PROVISIONS OF THE NEW IASC CONSTITUTION

The IASC Board unanimously approved a new Constitution in a key step in the implementation of the new structure through which the IASC is expected to play an even more central role in developing high quality global accounting standards, and to bring about international convergence to those standards.

The new structure has the following main features:

1. The IASC is to be established as an independent organization such as a foundation.
2. The organization will have two main bodies, the Trustees and the Board, as well as a Standing Interpretations Committee and Standards Advisory Council.

3. The Trustees appoint the Board Members, exercise oversight and raise the funds needed.

4. The Board has sole responsibility for setting accounting standards.

Additional key features are:

Trustees

The Trustees are a group of nineteen individuals from diverse geographic and functional backgrounds. They have the authority to replace membership until their terms expire.

The Trustees are responsible for appointing the Members of the Board, the Standing Interpretations Committee and the Standards Advisory Council. In addition to monitoring IASC's effectiveness and raising its funds, the Trustees approve IASC's budget and have responsibility for constitutional changes. All Trustees are committed to acting in the public interest in all matters.

Trustees are to be appointed so that initially there are six from North America, six from Europe, four from Asia Pacific, and three others from any area, as long as geographic balance is maintained.

The International Federation of Accountants (IFAC) has the right to suggest candidates to fill five of the nineteen Trustee seats and international organizations of preparers, users, and academics each suggest one candidate. The remaining eleven Trustees are "at-large" in that they are not selected through the constituency nomination process; they should be individuals with strong public interest experiences and backgrounds.

Now that the initial Trustees have been selected, the existing Trustees are responsible for the selection of subsequent Trustees to fill vacancies as they arise. The same procedures are to be followed as for the initial Trustee appointments, including consultation with the relevant constituency organization(s) where the vacancy arose on the retirement of a Trustee appointed as a result of such consultation.

The Board

The current Board is replaced by a new Board of fourteen individuals, twelve full-time Members and two part-time Members. The foremost qualification for Board membership is technical expertise. The Trustees are expected to exercise their best judgment to ensure that the Board is not dominated by any particular constituency or regional interest.

To achieve a balance of perspectives and experience, a minimum of five Board Members are to have a background as practicing auditors; a minimum of three are to have a background in the preparation of financial statements;

a minimum of three, are to be users of financial statements; at least one Member is to be from academia. Seven of the fourteen Board Members are expected to have direct liaison responsibility with one or more national standard setters. The publication of a Standard, Exposure Draft, or final SIC Interpretation requires approval by eight of the Board's fourteen members.

The Standards Advisory Council

A new Standards Advisory Council is to provide a formal vehicle for other groups and individuals having diverse geographic and functional backgrounds to give advice to the Board and Trustees.

The Standing Interpretations Committee

The SIC continues in its present form.

THE GROWING ACCEPTANCE OF INTERNATIONAL STANDARDS

As mentioned above, many countries base their standards to a great extent directly on IASs as their national standards or develop national standards based primarily upon them. In some cases, the national standards indicate the relationship or comparison between the national standard and the relevant IAS.

In fewer than one dozen countries are national standards developed primarily with little reliance upon IASs. A number of those countries (highly developed economic powers) have moved toward meshing their national standards with the IASC Standards.

Examples include:

1. The FASB-IASC development of the Earnings per Share Standard.
2. IASC revision of the Standard on Segment Reporting to harmonize with the Standards developed jointly by FASB and Canadian standard setters.
3. The UK-IASC cooperation on their Standards on Impairment of Assets and also on Provisions, Contingent Liabilities, and Contingent Assets.
4. The current joining of forces by the G4+1 and the IASC to work on merger accounting.

Many foreign companies appear willing to adopt IAS Standards while being loath to abide by U.S. GAAP. Now that many of the international standards have been tightened and more of the U.S. requirements have been adjusted to move closer to other national standards and the IASs, the more obvious advantages to complying only with the international standards may disappear.

What originally concerned much of the regulatory hierarchy in the U.S. might be dubbed the "either/or" mentality of the IASC in its attempt to provide something for everyone. (Some have suggested that this occurred primarily because of the attempt to keep both the U.S. and the UK happy when their Standards were often at odds.) But subsequently the differences in these accounting systems have been reduced.

But what about the attitude of various interested groups and organizations in the U.S.?

THE NYSE AND SECURITIES DEALERS

The New York Stock Exchange and securities dealers are in favor of permitting foreign corporations that have adopted the international standards to be listed on U.S. exchanges even if this means having to educate the investor on remaining discrepancies between GAAP and IAS. Many of the largest 500 corporations worldwide are not listed here principally because of what the companies have considered the too onerous U.S. GAAP requirements. Listing all of those foreign corporations would result in much greater volume; even adding two or three dozen of the largest foreign firms to the NYSE listings could certainly result in a marked increase in its market capitalization.

THE FASB'S ATTITUDE

The FASB's growing involvement with the IASC (after a very tentative, if not altogether hostile, appraisal of this outside influence) is smoothing the way toward the time when both IAS and U.S. GAAP will be regarded as being acceptable and practicable global accounting standards. Understandably, the FASB is zealously guarding its power over U.S. accounting standards. It appears that the group realizes the inevitability of compromise and cooperation inasmuch as many U.S. firms and institutions had become disenchanted with some of the gyrations necessary to meet existing or proposed requirements relating to earnings per share, derivatives, hedging.

The FASB's and the IASC's efforts toward a common goal appears to have begun in earnest with the earnings per share and segment Standards. That this cooperation became a two-way street was made easier since even the FASB admitted that the IASC's—and much of the rest of the world's—approach to figuring EPS was superior to and far less convoluted than previous U.S. requirements.

Close cooperation between the two bodies has moved IAS closer to U.S. GAAP and, at the same time, U.S. GAAP is closing the gap with international accounting standards. All along, the FASB has undoubtedly had reservations about the breadth and depth of the IASC representation actively engaged in the standard-setting process. They may have worried that what could turn out to be good enough for a foreign firm would fall short of being good enough for a U.S. firm to file in the U.S.

At least this had been the perception-that the U.S. would protect GAAP regardless. Not so. The FASB has taken steps to change or nullify several of the more divergent provisions to bring them closer to IAS requirements. And now the FASB has come out explicitly in favor of the IASC's aim of establishing a single set of Standards.

Support for the New Structure

The Board believes the restructuring when completed will create an organization that is independent, objective, and structured to operate in an open, due process environment.

These were points that the FASB has emphasized all along. They had made it evident that they could not support any structure that did not embody these principles. The FASB had taken quite seriously an attempt to show how the earlier proposed structure of the revamped IASC was too full of pitfalls. Rather than merely criticize, the Board came up with a well-thought-out list of points that needed reconsideration and/or revision.

There had been informal talks (even rumors) of the FASB becoming the *de facto* international standard setter simply by default—and by the power of the U.S. economy. The Board sincerely did not want that role, and whole-heartedly pushed for an acceptable organization coming out of the IASC. "Acceptable," to the FASB, essentially meant independent. The board did not want to see an international standard-setting committee that was subject to veto or excessive power by a board of directors, nor did it want a board of part-time individuals who might feel beholden to a corporation, accounting firm, or other organization.

On their part, IASC's decision follows a global debate over what organizational structure would maximize independence while considering the needs of large and small economies as well as those of the preparers and users of financial information. The FASB, while agreeing that such an organization must be created, as mentioned above, was rather critical of the earlier proposal.

The FASB's fears were somewhat ameliorated when many of their suggestions were incorporated in the last version of the plan. While admitting that the result is a compromise, the FASB considers it at least a step forward.

The SEC's Cautious Appraisal

From the very beginning, the Securities and Exchange Commission displayed cautious interest in the IASC, and as a member of IOSCO supported development of international standards. But, of course, the SEC's stated purpose is to safeguard the U.S. investor—whether naive or sophisticated, but particularly the former.

The more sophisticated investor and his adviser are aware of the fact that a foreign stock or bond is not the bargain it appears to be if insufficient data has been reported to permit an intelligent analysis of the offering. Therefore, the market drives the price of the securities down and the issuing company discovers that capital raising is more costly than necessary if management is coy about revealing the full picture of the financial status of the company. (And, of course, formal adoption of the IASs will not guarantee that an entity is actually following them.)

This truth was made abundantly clear when the SEC reported situations where a registrant prepares its financial statements in accordance with home country GAAP and in its footnotes asserts that the financial statements comply in all material respects with, or are consistent with International Accounting Standards. In some of these situations, the registrant may have applied only certain International Accounting Standards or omitted certain information without giving any explanation of why the information was excluded. The SEC routinely challenges these assertions. Where the assertion cannot be sustained, the Commission requires either changes to the financial statements to conform with International Accounting Standards, or removal of the assertion of compliance with International Accounting Standards.

Reaction to the Restructuring Plan

SEC officials and staff members have pinpointed several of the advantages of the restructuring to establish a single set of accounting standards for global use.

1. It supports an approach that focuses on the public interest, especially the interests of investors in capital markets, as the linchpin for its restructuring.
2. The IASC Board and its Strategy Working Party endeavored to understand and evaluate the many views (including those of the SEC and FASB) offered about the IASC's future structure.
3. It positions the IASC to be the international focal point for the development and convergence of accounting standards to meet the needs of global capital markets.

4. The proposal balances needs for a structure based upon *geographic representation* and those based on *technical competence* and *independence*.
5. It recognizes the need for Board members to be selected based on expertise, so that the Board can have the best possible combination of technical skills and relevant experience.
6. Representation would also be provided by the geographic distribution of the Trustees, who are essential to ensuring the effectiveness and independence of the Board.

SEC officials emphasize that ultimately, acceptance of the restructured IASC will depend on the selection of high quality Trustees and Board members. At this point the proposed structure appears to them to represent the best opportunity to realize the goal of approving a single set of standards for global use.

THE ADOPTION OF IAS 40, *INVESTMENT PROPERTY*

With the adoption of IAS 40, *Investment Property*, to become effective on or after January 1, 2001, all of the basic core topics listed by IOSCO have now been covered.

IAS 40 concerns investment property held by all enterprises and will not be limited to enterprises whose main activities are in this area. Investment property is property (land or a building—or part of a building—or both) held (by the owner or by the lessee under a finance lease) to earn rentals or for capital appreciation or both. Investment property does not include:

1. Property held for use in the production or supply of goods or services or for administrative purposes.
2. Property being constructed for third parties.
3. Property held for sale in the ordinary course of business.
4. An interest held under an operating lease if the interest was a long-term interest acquired in exchange for a large up-front payment.

Under IAS 40, an enterprise must choose either:

1. A fair value model in which investment property should be recognized in the income statement.
2. A cost model, the same as the benchmark treatment in IAS 16, *Property, Plant, and Equipment*. Investment property should be measured at depreciated cost (less any accumulated impairment losses). An enterprise that chooses the cost model should disclose the fair value of its investment property.

The Standard requires an enterprise to apply the model chosen to all its investment property. A change from one model to the other model to the other model should be made only if the change will result in a more appropriate presentation. The Standard states that this is highly unlikely to be the case for a change from the fair value model to the cost model.

In exceptional cases, an enterprise that has chosen the fair value model may conclude that it cannot determine the fair value of an investment property. In such cases the enterprise measures that investment property using the benchmark treatment in IAS 16 until the disposal of the investment property. The residual value of the investment property should be assumed to be zero. The enterprise measures all of its other investment property at fair value.

SELECTED IASC STANDARDS WITH COMPARISONS TO U.S. GAAP

The following are recently adopted international standards, several of which have been prepared in cooperation with the U.S. or other English-speaking standard setting bodies. Each of them covers an important aspect of accounting that has been uppermost in the minds of concerned standard-setters. Each of these discussions pinpoints the relationship between the international standard and the relevant GAAP accounting treatment.

IAS 33, EARNINGS PER SHARE

The objective of the FASB and IASC earnings per share standards is to prescribe principles for the determination and presentation of earnings per share that will lead to global harmonization of earnings per share measurements and disclosures. To this end, both standard setters have concluded where appropriate two earnings per share figures should be presented, namely,

1. Basic Earnings Per Share, which is computed by dividing income available to stockholders by the weighted average number of common shares outstanding during the period. Shares issued during the period and shares reacquired during the period should be weighted for the portion of the period they were outstanding.

2. Diluted Earnings Per Share, which is computed in a similar manner to basic earnings per share after adjusting the numerator and denominator of the calculation for the effects of all potential dilutive common shares that were outstanding during the period. One difference between FASB 128, *Earnings per Share*, and IAS 33 is a matter of degree. FASB 128 requires disclosure of per-share figures for income from continuing operations on the face of the income statement and for extraordinary

items, accounting changes and discontinued operations. The international standard requires only net profit per-share amounts on the face of the income statement but also encourages other disclosures.

The IASC and FASB also differ in their view of the objective of a diluted earnings per share presentation. The IASC views the figures as an early warning to investors of possible reductions in the value of EPS while the FASB sees it as a measure of performance rather than an indicator of the future. However, except for some language differences, the basic provisions of IAS 33 are substantially the same as those of FASB 128. (These provisions are discussed more fully in connection with FASB 128 in Chapter 1.)

Global Adoption

It is anticipated that IAS 33 will be adopted by:

1. Many countries as a national standard.
2. Stock exchanges for listing purposes.
3. Corporations with a global stock ownership.

These adoptions will be a significant contribution to facilitating global investing in common stocks.

IAS 34, *INTERIM FINANCIAL REPORTING*

IAS 34 *Interim Financial Reporting* requires that companies that prepare interim reports apply the same accounting recognition and measurement principles used in their last annual statements. This requirement will tend to make interim earnings more volatile for non-U.S. companies that heretofore had followed U.S.-style interim reporting rules. U.S. rulings permit some interim income smoothing recognition and measurement practices. The statement also specifies that measurements in interim financial statements should be made on a financial year-to-date basis.

It does not mandate that interim reports be published in the first place, who should publish them, how often they should be prepared, or how soon they should appear after the end of an interim reporting period, if they are prepared. The IASC decided these matters were better left to the discretion of the national governments, securities regulators, stock exchanges, and accounting organizations. At present, in at least 30 countries, the securities regulators and stock exchanges do, in fact, require interim reporting. Interim reports are used by investors and creditors to check for any signs of weakness—or strength, for that matter.

IAS 34 applies to recognizing, measuring, and disclosing assets, liabilities, income, and expenses for quarterly, biannual, or any other type of interim report.

The United Kingdom's Accounting Standards Board (ASB) recently issued a nonmandatory "best practice" statement on interim reporting that is almost identical to the IASC standard. Both use the discrete method for interim reporting. Under this method, as amplified below, the interim period is treated as an accounting period distinct from the annual period. Incomplete transactions are reported, using the same principles that are used for the annual reports.

This statement will get close scrutiny from many sources including U.S. investors and creditors with worldwide interests. Interim financial reports issued by foreign companies do not conform to APB 28, *Interim Financial Reporting*. This new standard also differs in a number of significant areas from U.S. GAAP. However, U.S. accountants, investors, and financial advisors are already aware of the fact that the accounting used for interim financial reporting purposes in many countries outside of the U.S. is considerably different from U.S. GAAP. The foreign standards are similar in many respects to IAS 34.

Below is a comparison of a few of the provisions to U.S. GAAP governing interim financial reports included in Accounting Principles Board APB 28. (A discussion of other information relating to U.S. GAAP can be found in Appendix E.)

Independent Theory

IAS 34 for the most part adopts the independent theory of interim reporting. This approach regards each interim period as a discrete or "standalone" reporting period. That is, the events and transactions within each accounting period are to be reported in the accounting period, regardless of its length. Under the independent view, the results of operations for each interim period should be determined basically in the same manner as if the interim period were an annual accounting period. Under this approach, deferrals, accruals, and estimations at the end of each interim period are determined by following basically the same approach as in the annual reports. Thus, if an expenditure is expensed in the annual statement, it should be expensed in any interim report, regardless of the amount of the expenditure and the relationship to the annual amount or the revenues of other interim periods for that year.

Dependent Approach

APB 28 generally follows the dependent theory of interim period reporting. This approach regards each interim period as an integral part of the annual period. According to the dependent view, interim financial data are an integral part of the annual period, and it is essential to provide investors with timely information on the progress the entity is making in realizing its annual results of operations. Therefore, the usefulness of interim data rests on the predictive relationship that it has to the annual report. Thus, each interim period should be regarded as an integral part of the annual period rather than a discrete period standing on its own.

Under this approach, deferrals, accruals, and estimations at the end of each interim period are affected by predictions about the results of operations for the remainder of the year. Thus, for example, a portion of an estimated annual expenditure that might be expensed for the entire annual period might be accrued or deferred at the end of an interim period as management allocates the estimated annual expense between interim periods on a basis that reflects time, sales volume, or production activity.

Other Differences

If fully aware of the important differences between the two alternative interim financial reporting approaches, the user of the financial reports should be able to make an intelligent analysis of the information presented. Some of those differences are presented below:

Dependent/independent.   Because the dependent approach gives accounting flexibility in managing interim earnings to minimize any possibility that the figures might give a misleading picture of the company's current and future performance, company management probably prefers it.

Some users believe that the dependent approach properly applied gives a better indication of a company's annual results, earnings volatility, and risks when the company is geared to such things as seasonal ups and downs of irregular sales, income and expenses. Here the independent approach may result in interim financial reports that overstate the level of risk and volatility associated with the company's actual annual earnings picture.

On the other hand, there are others who are quite sure that the independent approach produces a clearer and more timely picture of coming events in a company's financial prospects.

Mandated/suggested.   The new Statement does not require companies complying with IAS in their annual reports to publish interim financial reports. The IASC, however, has indicated that it intends to strongly encourage governments, security regulators, stock exchanges, international bodies, and accounting standard setters to require companies whose debt or equity securities are publicly traded to provide interim financial reports that conform to IAS 34 principles. The IASC will also encourage publicly traded companies to provide interim reports complying with the Statement's principles at least at the end of the first six months of their financial year.

U.S. GAAP does not mandate publication of interim financial reports; however, the Securities and Exchange Commission and the stock exchanges do require listed companies to publish them for the first three quarters of the fiscal year.

When interim financial reports are published, both IAS 34 and U.S. practice require that they include:

1. Condensed balance sheet.
2. Condensed income statement.
3. Condensed cash flow statement.
4. Footnote disclosures focusing on changes since the last annual report in accounting principles or estimates, unusual events, trends, and turning points.

Costs. According to APB 28, costs and expenses that are not allocated or associated directly with product and service revenues may be expensed as incurred or allocated among interim periods based on an estimate of time expired, benefit received, or other activity associated with the period.

IAS 34 requires costs that are incurred unevenly during a company's financial year be anticipated or deferred for interim reporting only if it is appropriate to anticipate or defer those costs at the end of the financial year. An example of costs that often fall into this category are periodic major maintenance or retooling projects.

Comparability. In the final analysis, even though the interim financial statements may look alike, the operating results for the period under the IASC proposal of a discrete approach and the U.S. GAAP integral approach will not be comparable because of the different concepts. At the same time, comparison of operating results among U.S. companies is not always possible because of discretionary accounting differences permitted for certain items under APB 28.

IAS 35, DISCONTINUING OPERATIONS

This Standard's objectives are to establish a basis for segregating information about a major operation that an enterprise is discontinuing from information about its continuing operations and to specify minimum disclosures about a discontinuing operation.

IAS 35 is a presentation and disclosure Standard that focuses on how to present a discontinuing operation in an enterprise's financial statements and what information to disclose. It does not establish any new principles for deciding when and how to recognize and measure the income, expenses, cash flows, and changes to assets and liabilities relating to a discontinuing operation. Instead, it requires that enterprises follow the recognition and measurement principles in other International Accounting Standards.

Definition of a Discontinuing Operation

A discontinuing operation is considered in IAS 35 to be a component of an enterprise:

1. That the enterprise, pursuant to a single plan, is:
    a. disposing of substantially in its entirety,
    b. disposing of piecemeal, or
    c. terminating through abandonment.
2. That represents a separate major line of business or geographical area of operations.
3. That can be distinguished operationally and for financial reporting purposes.

Thus, a discontinuing operation is a relatively large component of an enterprise—such as a business or geographical segment under IAS 14, *Segment Reporting*—that the enterprise, pursuant to a single plan, is disposing of substantially in its entirety or is terminating through abandonment or piecemeal sale.

The new Standard requires that disclosures about a discontinuing operation begin earlier, after the *earlier* of the following:

1. An enterprise has entered into an agreement to sell substantially all of the assets of the discontinuing operation.
2. The board of directors or other similar governing body has both approved and announced a detailed plan for discontinuance.

Disclosure Requirements

Required disclosures include:

1. Description of the discontinuing operation.
2. The business or geographical segment(s) in which it is reported in accordance with IAS 14, *Segment Reporting*.
3. The date that the plan for discontinuance was announced.

4. The timing of expected completion (date or period), if known or determinable.

5. The carrying amounts of the total assets and the total liabilities to be disposed of.

6. The amounts of revenue, expenses, and pretax profit or loss from ordinary activities attributable to the discontinuing operation during that specific reporting period, and the related income tax expense.

7. The amount of any gain or loss that is recognized on the disposal of assets or settlement of liabilities attributable to the discontinuing operation, and related income tax expense.

8. The net cash flows attributable to the operating, investing, and financing activities of the discontinuing operation.

9. The net selling prices received or expected from the sale of those net assets for which the enterprise has entered into one or more binding sale agreements, and the expected timing thereof, and the carrying amounts of those net assets.

Further Considerations

Financial statements for periods after initial disclosure must update those disclosures, including a description of any significant changes in the amount or timing of cash flows relating to the assets and liabilities to be disposed of or settled and the causes of those changes.

The disclosures would be made if a plan for disposal is approved and publicly announced after the end of an enterprise's financial reporting period but before the financial statements for that period are approved. The disclosures continue until completion of the disposal.

To improve the ability of users of financial statements to make projections, comparative information for prior periods presented in financial statements prepared after initial disclosure must be restated to segregate the continuing and discontinuing assets, liabilities, income, expenses, and cash flows.

Comparison to U.S. GAAP

IAS 35 brings another of IASC's accounting standards closer to U.S. GAAP in that the IASC's standards now actually include a discontinuing operation standard—similar in many respects to the comparable U.S. GAAP standard, Accounting Principles Board Opinion 30 (APB 30).

However, as in most instances, this standard does vary slightly from GAAP. Two examples follow:

1. APB 30 requires the results of discontinuing operations to be reported on the face of the financial statements while IAS 35 only recommends this approach to disclosure.

2. While IASC emphasizes the timeliness of its required initial disclosure event, APB's requirement would very probably occur earlier than IAS 35's requirement. The initial disclosure event specified in IAS 35 is a *binding sales agreement* or board of director's approval of a *detailed discontinuing operations plan* and a formal announcement of that plan. On the other hand, APB 30 specifies that the initial disclosure event is the date on which management having authority to approve the discontinuance commits to a formal plan to dispose of a segment of the business.

More Uniform Approach

Since many developing economies (as well as other more advanced ones) do not have specific guidance relating to discontinuing operations accounting, it is probable that the issuance of IAS 35 will inspire a number of them to adopt it outright or to develop their own national standard which will closely follow the requirements of IAS 35. Regardless, a more uniform approach to reporting discontinuing operations should result. As an additional inducement to use the principles of this Standard, appendices to IAS 35 provide illustrative disclosures and guidance on how prior period information should be restated to conform to the presentation requirements of IAS 35.

IAS 36, *IMPAIRMENT OF ASSETS*

International Accounting Standard 36, *Impairment of Assets*, prescribes the accounting and disclosure requirements specifically for impairment of:

1. Goodwill.
2. Intangible assets and property.
3. Plant and equipment.

The Standard includes requirements for identifying an impaired asset, measuring its recoverable amount, recognizing or reversing any resulting impairment loss, and disclosing information on impairment losses or reversals of impairment losses.

It prescribes how an enterprise should test its assets for impairment; that is:

1. The procedures that an enterprise should apply to ensure that its assets are not overstated in the financial statements.
2. How an enterprise should assess the amount to be recovered from an asset (the "recoverable amount").
3. When an enterprise should account for an impairment loss identified by this assessment.

The Standard does *not* cover accounting and disclosure requirements for:

1. Inventories.
2. Deferred tax assets.
3. Assets arising from construction contracts.
4. Assets arising from employee benefits.
5. Most financial assets.

Requirements of IAS 36

According to this IAS, an impairment loss should be recognized whenever the recoverable amount of an asset is less than its carrying amount (sometimes called "book value"). The Standard spells out in detail the procedures to follow when this occurs:

1. The recoverable amount of an asset is defined as the higher of:
   a. Net selling price as measured by the amount obtainable from the sale of the asset in an arm's length transaction between knowledgeable, willing parties, less the cost of disposal.
   b. Value in use as measured by the present value of the asset's estimated future cash flows including disposable cash flows, if any, expected to arise from its continuing use and eventual disposal. The discount rate should be a pretax rate that reflects current market assessments of the time value of money and the risks specific to the asset.
2. An impairment loss should be recognized as an expense in the income statement for assets carried at cost and treated as a revaluation decrease for assets carried at revalued amount.
3. An impairment loss should be reversed and income recognized when there has been a *change* in the estimates used to determine an asset's recoverable amount after the last impairment loss was recognized.

4. The recoverable amount of an asset should be estimated whenever there is an indication that the asset may be impaired. IAS 36 includes a list of indicators of impairment to be considered at each balance sheet date. In some cases, the IAS applicable to an asset may include requirements for additional reviews.

5. In determining value in use, an enterprise should use:

   a. Cash flow projections based on reasonable and supportable assumptions that reflect the asset in its current condition and represent management's best estimate of the set of economic conditions that will exist over the remaining useful life of the asset.

   b. Estimates of future cash flows should include all estimated future cash inflows and cash outflows except for cash flows from financing activities and income tax receipts and payments.

   c. A pretax discount rate that reflects current market assessments of the time value of money and the risks specific to the asset. The discount rate should not reflect risks for which the future cash flows have been adjusted.

6. If an asset does not generate cash inflows that are largely independent from the cash inflows from other assets, an enterprise should determine the recoverable amount of the cash-generating unit to which the asset belongs. IAS 36 provides explicit directions concerning these cash-generating units:

   a. "Cash-generating unit" refers to the smallest identifiable group of assets that generates cash inflows which are largely independent of the cash inflows from other assets or group of assets.

   b. The requirements for recognizing and reversing impairment losses for a cash-generating unit are the same as those for an individual asset.

   c. The concept of cash-generating units should often be used in testing assets for impairment because, in many cases, assets work together rather than in isolation.

   d. In addition, IAS 36 provides information on how to identify the cash-generating unit to which an asset belongs and further requirements on how to measure an impairment loss for a cash-generating unit and then allocate the loss between the assets of the unit.

7. Reversal of impairment losses also comes in for extensive consideration:

   a. An impairment loss recognized in prior years should be reversed if, and only if, there has been a change in the estimates used to determine recoverable amount since the last impairment loss was recognized.

   b. An impairment loss should only be reversed to the extent the reversal does not increase the carrying amount of the asset above the carrying amount that would have been determined for the asset (net of amortization or depreciation) had no impairment loss been recognized.

   c. An impairment loss for *goodwill* should be reversed only if the specific external event that caused the recognition of the impairment loss reverses.

   d. A reversal of an impairment loss should be recognized as income in the income statement for assets carried at cost and treated as a revaluation increase for assets carried at revalued amount.

8. When impairment losses are recognized or reversed, an enterprise should disclose certain information by *class of assets* and by *reportable segments*. Further disclosure is required if impairment losses recognized or reversed are *material* to the financial statements of the reporting enterprise as a whole.

Upon first adoption of IAS 36, its requirements should be applied *prospectively* only; that is, prior periods will *not* be restated.

IASC-UK Cooperation

IAS 36 differs materially in a number of instances from U.S. Generally Accepted Accounting Principles (U.S. GAAP) and the asset impairment rules of a number of other countries. On the other hand, there are aspects of the international standard that are closer to the provisions of other established national standards.

For example, in developing IAS 36, proposals of the Accounting Standard Board (ASB) in the United Kingdom for a Financial Reporting Standard (FRS) on impairment of assets were closely monitored by the international body. The ASB and the IASC shared the same objectives for their project, and many of their views regarding requirements coincided. Therefore, the resulting standards are very similar.

Furthermore, IAS 36 provides a standard approach to the recognition, measurement, and disclosure of asset impairments by non-U.S. companies that use IAS in financial statements and also furnishes a model for the many developing economies which have not yet adopted an asset impairment standard of their own, but look often to IASC for guidance.

The IASC considers this an important step forward from the requirements and guidance for impairment losses that were previously included in their Standards. They point out that it provides more details on how to perform an impairment test and it eliminates certain alternatives, such as the option not to use discounting in measuring recoverable amount. (The "options" in many of the older IASs have been particularly worrisome to the SEC, the FASB and other standard-setting bodies.)

Differences from GAAP

As mentioned above there are a number of significant differences between IAS 36 and U.S. GAAP specified in FASB 121, *Accounting for the Impairment of Long-Lived Assets and for Long-Lived Assets to Be Disposed Of.*

Differences between the two Standards include:

1. Probably most significantly, FASB 121 *does not permit reversal* of asset impairment losses as does IAS 36—along with much of the rest of the accounting world. (It might be pointed out here that there seems to be little global consensus yet about how to account for asset impairment. Some countries have rulings similar to GAAP, others to the new IAS, others to the old IAS. Still others have standards relating to assessment of recoverability, not valuation; many have no standard at all on impairment. On the other hand, many of the emerging nations will undoubtedly adopt IAS 36.)

2. GAAP requires a *quantitative test* of asset impairment before the measurement and recognition of an asset impairment loss is necessitated. This involves figuring the expected cumulative net cash flows from continuing use of the asset, not including interest and not to be discounted less than the asset's carrying amount. IAS 36 does not include this type of test.

3. IAS 36 does not distinguish between assets to be held and used and assets to be disposed of when measuring impairment loss; FASB 121 has different impairment loss measurement approaches for the two categories.
    a. FASB 121's measurement of the impairment loss of an asset *to be used* is the difference between the asset's carrying amount and its fair value.
    b. FASB 121 measurement of the impairment loss of an asset *to be disposed of* is the asset's carrying amount less its net realizable value.
    c. IAS 36's measurement of *either* impairment loss is the asset's carrying amount less the higher of its value in use or its net realizable value (fair value minus disposal costs).

4. FASB 121 relies on *management judgment* to determine the appropriate future cash flow period and cash flows to determine the equivalent of IAS 36's value in use. Unless management can justify otherwise, IAS 36

limits the maximum future cash flow period to five years and specifies the growth rate in cash flows.

IAS 37, PROVISIONS, CONTINGENT LIABILITIES AND CONTINGENT ASSETS

IAS 37, *Provisions, Contingent Liabilities and Contingent Assets* requires that:

1. Provisions should be recognized in the balance sheet only when:
    a. An enterprise has a present obligation (either legal or constructive) as a result of a past event;
    b. More likely than not a transfer of economic benefits will be required to settle the obligation;
    c. The amount of the obligation can be measured reliably.
2. Provisions should be measured in the balance sheet at the best estimate of the expenditure required to settle the present obligation at the balance sheet date. This is the amount that an enterprise would rationally pay to settle the obligation, or to transfer it to a third party, at that date. When measuring provisions, an enterprise should take into account any risks and uncertainties. However, uncertainty does not justify the creation of excessive provisions or a deliberate overstatement of liabilities—in other words, the "big bath."

    An enterprise should discount a provision where the effect of the time value of money is material and should take future events, such as changes in the law and technological changes, into account where there is sufficient objective evidence that they will occur.
3. The amount of a provision should not be reduced by gains from the expected disposal of assets (even if the expected disposal is closely linked to the event giving rise to the provision) or by expected reimbursements—from insurance contracts, indemnity clauses, suppliers' warranties and the like. When it is virtually certain the reimbursement will be received if the enterprise settles the obligation, the reimbursement should be recognized as a separate asset.
4. A provision should be used only for expenditures for which the provision was originally recognized and should be reversed if an outflow of resources is no longer probable.

IAS 37 sets out three specific applications of these general requirements:

1. A provision *should not be recognized* for future operating losses.

2. A provision *should be recognized* for an onerous contract in which the unavoidable costs of meeting the obligations under the contract are greater than the expected economic benefits.

3. A provision for restructuring costs *should be recognized only* when an enterprise has a detailed formal plan for the restructuring and has raised a valid expectation in those affected that it will carry out the restructuring by starting to implement that plan or announcing its main features to those affected by it; for this purpose, a management or board decision is not enough.

A restructuring provision should exclude costs—such as retraining or relocating continuing staff, marketing or investment in new systems and distribution networks—that are not necessarily entailed by the restructuring or that are not associated with the enterprise's ongoing activities.

IAS 37 replaces part of IAS 10, *Contingencies and Events Occurring After the Balance Sheet Date*. It prohibits the recognition of contingent liabilities and contingent assets. An enterprise should disclose a contingent liability, unless the possibility of an outflow of resources embodying economic benefits is remote, and disclose a contingent asset if an inflow of economic benefits is probable.

UK-IASC Cooperative Effort

Here again, the IASC and the UK's Accounting Standards Board worked in close conjunction to develop virtually identical accounting standards. Their aim is to eliminate many of the questionable accounting practices that have been developing.

One of the most obvious is the "big bath" mentioned above and included in the "hocus pocus" practices that the SEC feels has been sullying the financial reporting process here—as well as globally. (The ploy is to report excessive liabilities currently to make future profits look even rosier at the time the liabilities are actually being incurred.)

Global Aspects

On the global front, the Standards should help to lessen the diversity of provision recognition and measurement practices that have evolved along with varying accounting regulations and tax treatment of provisions. Not only do these Standards cut down on the welter of provisions that were previously provided for in financial statements prepared according to UK and IAS principles, but they also move much closer to U.S. GAAP (contained in FASB 5, *Accounting for Contingencies*).

Some technical differences between GAAP and the two Standards are slight enough that they should pose no problem in doing comparative valuations of U.S. and non-U.S. companies. Since provisions can significantly affect a company's balance sheet and net income, reducing the divergence in the handling of "provisions" should be considered an important step in harmonization of global accounting practices, particularly when considering the fact that many countries that have no established procedure for handling provisions and contingencies—or very haphazard ones—will now adopt IAS 37.

IAS 38, *INTANGIBLE ASSETS*

IAS 38 applies to all intangible assets that are not specifically handled in other IASs. Included in the lists of things it does deal with are the accounting for expenditures on advertising, training, start-up activities, research and development activities (R&D), mortgage servicing rights, customer lists, licensing agreements, motion picture patents, and copyrights. It also covers expenditures for computer software that is an integral part of a tangible asset.

The Standard does *not* apply to intangible assets covered by other IASs; financial instruments; mineral rights and expenditures for the exploration, development, and extraction of minerals, oil, natural gas—nonregenerative resources; insurance contracts.

Among those intangible assets covered by another IAS are deferred tax assets, intangible assets held for sale in the ordinary course of business, leases, employee benefits, and goodwill arising from a business transaction.

IAS 38 includes transitional provisions that clarify when the Standard should be applied retrospectively and when it should be applied prospectively.

Requirements of IAS 38

The basic features of IAS 38 include:

1. An intangible asset should be recognized initially, at cost, in the financial statement whether it has been acquired externally or generated internally, if, and only if:
   a. it is probable that the future economic benefits attributable to the asset will flow to the enterprise;
   b. cost of the asset can be measured reliably;
   c. the asset falls within the classification of an *intangible* asset; that is, it is *an identifiable nonmonetary asset without physical substance held for use in the production or supply of goods or services, for rental to others, or for administrative purposes.*

2. If an intangible item does not meet both the definition and the criteria for the recognition of an intangible asset, IAS 38 requires the expenditure on this item to be recognized as an *expense* when it is incurred. An enterprise is not permitted to include this expenditure in the cost of an intangible asset at a later date.

3. Therefore, it becomes evident from the recognition criteria that all expenditures on research should be recognized as an expense. The same treatment applies to start-up costs, training costs, and advertising costs. IAS 38 also specifically prohibits the recognition as assets of internally generated goodwill, brands, mastheads, publishing titles, customer lists and such. However, as mentioned above, occasionally developmental expenditure may result in the recognition of an intangible asset—some internally developed computer software, for example.

4. In accounting for a business combination that is an acquisition, IAS 38 works in combination with IAS 22, *Business Combinations*. This reinforces the stipulation that if an intangible item does not meet both the *definition* and the *criteria* for the recognition as an intangible asset, the expenditure for this item which was included in the cost of acquisition should form part of the amount attributed to goodwill at the date of acquisition.

   Therefore, according to this Standard, purchased R&D-in-process should not be recognized as an expense immediately at the date of acquisition, but it should be recognized as part of the goodwill recognized at the date of acquisition and amortized under IAS 22 (rev.), unless it meets the criteria for separate recognition as an intangible asset.

   IAS 22 (rev.) provides that if there is sufficient evidence that the useful life of goodwill will exceed 20 years, an enterprise should amortize the goodwill over its estimated useful life and:

   a. Test goodwill for impairment at least annually in accordance with IAS 36, *Impairment of Assets*.

   b. Disclose the reasoning behind the presumption in the initial recognition that the useful life of goodwill would not exceed 20 years, and specify the factor(s) that were significant later in determining the useful life of goodwill.

   IAS 22 (rev.) does not permit an enterprise to assign an infinite useful life to goodwill.

5. Requires that after initial recognition in the financial statement, an intangible asset be measured under either the *benchmark treatment* or the allowed *alternative treatment*.

   a. The benchmark treatment is historical cost less any amortization and impairment losses. It is consistent with the GAAP approach.

b. The allowed alternative treatment is the revalued amount based on fair value minus any subsequent amortization and impairment losses. However, this treatment is permitted if, and only if, fair value can be determined by reference to an active market for the intangible asset—which is fairly unlikely for *intangible* assets.

The Standard defines fair value of an asset as the amount for which that asset could be exchanged between knowledgeable, willing parties in an arm's-length transaction.

Comparison to GAAP

IAS 38 and the comparable GAAP are similar in many respects. There are some major differences, but even here the FASB and the SEC are looking into revisions in some areas. Current differences include:

1. Here again, an international standard differs from U.S. GAAP on the revaluation issue: IAS 38 permits revaluation; GAAP does not.
2. GAAP requires that an intangible asset's amortization period not exceed forty years. IAS 38 specifies a maximum twenty-year amortization period. This is rebuttable if a longer amortization period can be justified. (The FASB has now voted to cut to twenty years the write-off time for goodwill from an acquisition.)
3. GAAP does not require an active market-based valuation for internally generated intangible assets; IAS does.
4. Except for computer software development, GAAP does not permit capitalization of development costs. On the other hand, IAS 38 requires capitalization of development costs in certain cases.

IAS 39, *FINANCIAL INSTRUMENTS: RECOGNITION AND MEASUREMENT*

In March, 1999, IASC announced that it had published a comprehensive standard on accounting for financial instruments after nine years' effort and four public comment documents. This new Standard, IAS 39, *Financial Instruments: Recognition and Measurement*, will take effect for annual financial statements covering periods beginning on or after January 1, 2001. Earlier application is permitted as of the beginning of a fiscal year that ends after March 15,1999. Retrospective application is not permitted.

Financial instruments include conventional financial assets and liabilities, such as cash, trade receivables and payables, investments in debt and equity securities, and notes, bonds, and loans payable. Financial instruments also include derivatives such as futures, forwards, swaps, and option contracts.

Background

IAS 39 had been in development by IASC since 1989. Its "final" form was preceded by exposure drafts in 1991, 1994, and 1998 and by a steering committee discussion paper in 1997. In 1996, IASC adopted *Financial Instruments: Disclosure and Presentation* (IAS 32) pending completion of a standard on recognition and measurement. IAS 39 expands those disclosures and resolves the accounting questions, including the important area of accounting for hedging transactions.

IASC officials emphasized their belief that IAS 39 fills the biggest void in global accounting standards. They pointed out that of their 104 member countries only the United States has adopted a truly comprehensive standard on recognition and measurement of financial instruments and hedge accounting (FASB 133).

Need for Greater Uniformity

With the phenomenal growth of global trading (and the equally amazing growth of imaginative derivatives which are often not recognized in the financial statements), IASC suggests that investors sometimes get very unwelcome surprises when losses surface.

The IASC is aware that current accounting practices for financial instruments vary widely around the world, with the result being noncomparability and investor confusion. Even when financial assets such as investments have been recognized on the balance sheet, some companies have measured them at cost, others at lower of cost or market, and still others at fair value.

Further, in the absence of hedge accounting standards, companies often have postponed recognizing any changes in the fair values of financial instruments or, if recognized, companies have deferred the profit-or-loss effects of such changes in the balance sheet. IAS 39 addresses these and other shortcomings of current practice.

Many developing economies are adopting the International Accounting Standards outright or using them as a basis for developing their own national standards. It is probable that not only they, but also many of the developed economies, will progress to more comprehensive accounting standards for financial instruments, including derivatives. After all, both the FASB and the IASC have spent years going over the ground trying to find an effective solution to satisfy all segments of the business and financial world.

IAS 39 does not go as far in accounting for certain financial instruments as U.S. GAAP, but it does move the international standards closer. It should also reduce the global diversity of financial instrument accounting practices, particularly those dealing with debt and equity security instruments, derivatives, and hedges.

Principal Requirements

IAS 39 requires that all financial assets and all financial liabilities, including all derivatives, be recognized on the balance sheet. This means that derivatives can no longer be off-balance-sheet items.

Initially, financial assets and liabilities will be measured at cost, including transaction costs. After initial recognition, most financial assets must be remeasured at fair value; however, the following will be carried at amortized cost subject to a test for impairment:

1. Loans and receivables originated by the enterprise and not held for trading.
2. Other fixed maturity investments, such as debt securities and mandatorily redeemable preferred shares, that the enterprise intends and is able to hold to maturity.
3. Financial assets whose fair value cannot be reliably measured (limited to some equity instruments with no quoted market price and some derivatives that are linked to and must be settled by delivery of such unquoted equity instruments).

After acquisition, most liabilities will be measured at original recorded amount less principal repayments and amortization. Only derivatives and liabilities held for trading (such as short sales of securities) will be remeasured to fair value.

To record the complete amount of periodic unrealized fair value changes an enterprise will have a single, enterprise-wide option to either:

1. Recognize the entire amount in income; or
2. Recognize in income only those changes in fair value relating to financial assets and liabilities held for trading, with the value changes for nontrading instruments reported in equity until the financial asset is sold, at which time the realized gain or loss is reported in net profit or loss. For this purpose, derivatives are always deemed held for trading unless they are part of a hedging relationship that qualifies for hedge accounting.

Hedge Accounting

The IASC considers hedging, for accounting purposes, as designating the change in value of a derivative, or in limited circumstances a nonderivative financial instrument, as an offset, in whole or in part, to the change in fair value or cash flows of a hedged item. A hedged item can be an asset, liability, firm commitment, or forecasted future transaction that is exposed to risk of change in value or changes in future cash flows. Hedge accounting recognizes the offsetting effects on net profit or loss symmetrically.

Thus, hedge accounting is permitted under IAS 39 in certain circumstances, provided that the hedging relationship is *clearly defined, measurable, and actually effective.*

IAS 39, like FASB 133, recognizes and defines three types of hedges although they are not identical.

1. Fair value hedge: a hedge of the exposure to changes in the fair value of a recognized asset or liability (such as a hedge of exposure to changes in the fair value of fixed rate debt as a result of changes in interest rates). To the extent that the hedge is effective, the gain or loss from remeasuring the hedging instrument at fair value is recognized immediately in net profit or loss.

   At the same time, the gain or loss on the hedged item adjusts the carrying amount of the hedged item and is recognized immediately in net profit or loss.

2. Cash flow hedge: a hedge of the exposure to variability in cash flows attributable to a recognized asset or liability (such as all or some future interest payments on variable rate debt) or a forecasted transaction (such as an anticipated purchase or sale). A hedge of an unrecognized firm commitment to buy or sell an asset at a fixed price in the enterprise's reporting currency is accounted for as a cash flow hedge even though it has a fair value exposure. To the extent that the gain or loss on the effective portion of the hedging instrument is recognized initially, it is recorded directly in equity. Subsequently, that amount is included in net profit or loss in the same period or periods during which the hedged item affects net profit or loss (for example, through cost of sales, depreciation, or amortization). For hedges of forecasted transactions, the gain or loss on the hedging instrument will adjust the basis (carrying amount) of the acquired asset or liability.

3. A hedge of a net investment in a foreign entity (as defined in IAS 21, *The Effects of Changes in Foreign Exchange Rates*): These are accounted for as cash flow hedges.

As we have seen above, hedge accounting is permitted when the hedging relationship is clearly defined, measurable, and actually effective. The enterprise must designate a specific hedging instrument as a hedge of a change in value or cash flow of a specific hedged item, rather than as a hedge of an overall net balance sheet position. However, the approximate income statement effect of hedge accounting for an overall net position can be achieved, in some cases, by designating part of one of the underlying items as the hedged position.

Derecognition

In addition, IAS 39 establishes conditions for determining when control over a financial asset or liability has been transferred to another party. For financial assets a transfer normally would be accounted for as a sale (derecognized) when:

1. The transferee has the right to sell or pledge the asset.
2. The transferor does not have the right to reacquire the transferred assets unless either the asset is readily obtainable in the market or the reacquisition price is fair value at the time of reacquisition.

With respect to derecognition of liabilities, the debtor must be legally released from primary responsibility for all or part of the liability either judicially or by the creditor. If part of a financial asset or liability is sold or extinguished, the carrying amount is split based on relative fair values. If fair values are not determinable, a cost recovery approach to profit recognition is taken.

Additional Disclosure Requirements

IAS 39 moves international requirements a big step in the direction of greater transparency. The principal disclosure requirements for financial instruments include:

1. Description of methods and assumptions used in estimating fair values.
2. Disclosure of whether purchases of financial assets are accounted for at trade date or settlement date.
3. Description of the enterprise's financial risk management objectives and policies.
4. For each category of hedge: a description of the hedge; which financial instruments are designated as hedging instruments; and the nature of the risks being hedged.
5. Disclosure of significant items of income and expense and gains and losses resulting from financial assets and financial liabilities, and whether they are included in net profit or loss or as a separate component of equity and, if in equity, a reconciliation of movements in and out of equity;
6. Explanation of details of securitization and repurchase agreements.
7. Description of the nature, effect, and reasons for reclassifications of financial assets from amortized cost to fair value.
8. Explanation of the nature and amount of any impairment loss or reversal of an impairment loss.

A Stop-Gap Solution

Even though IAS 39 goes a long way toward fair value accounting, the IASC considers it only a partial step. The Board decided not to require fair value measurement for the originated loans and receivables or for held-to-maturity investments at this time for a number of reasons:

1. Too drastic a change from current practice would be required in many jurisdictions.
2. The existence of portfolio linkage of those assets, in many industries, to liabilities that, under IAS 39, will continue to be measured at their amortized original amount. Banks, for example, say that they manage their depositor liabilities in tandem with their portfolios of mortgage and commercial loans.
3. Some question the relevance of fair values for financial assets intended to be held until maturity, particularly if fair value changes enter into measuring net profit or loss.

The resulting standard should probably be considered a stop-gap measure published to meet the deadline the IASC had set to submit the core set of standards to IOSCO. As noted, it also serves, at least to a certain extent, to answer the urgent need in many countries for a comprehensive financial instruments standard. While it is similar in many respects to U.S. GAAP, IAS 39 needs more work to raise it to the level of quality the IASC seeks in its standards. (As a matter of fact, there is still considerable debate about whether FASB 133 is the final word on financial instrument accounting and disclosure in this country.)

THE CORE STANDARDS

Following is a list of the IASC Standards covering what is considered to be the core group of international standards necessary for cross-border filings. Some of the core group have been rather extensively revised; some have just recently been written; others may be considered for slight modification. A few are not actually a part of the "core."

IAS 1 (rev.), *Presentation of Financial Statements*
IAS 2, *Inventories*
IAS 3, Replaced by IAS 27
IAS 4, *Depreciation*
IAS 5, Superseded by IAS 1 (rev.)

IAS 6, Replaced by IAS 15

IAS 7, *Cash Flow Statements*

IAS 8, *Net Profit or Loss for the Period, Fundamental Errors and Changes in Accounting Policies*

IAS 9, Superseded by IAS 1 (rev.)

IAS 10 (rev.), *Contingencies and Events Occurring After the Balance Sheet Date* (Partly superseded by IAS 37)

IAS 11, *Construction Contracts*

IAS 12 (rev.), *Income Taxes*

IAS 13, Superseded by IAS 1 (rev.)

IAS 14 (rev.), *Segment Reporting*

IAS 15, *Information Reflecting the Effects of Changing Prices* (not a core IAS)

IAS 16, *Property, Plant and Equipment* (Not mandatory; impairment provisions revised in IAS 36)

IAS 17 (rev.), *Accounting for Leases*

IAS 18, *Revenue*

IAS 19 (rev.), *Employee Benefits*

IAS 20, *Accounting for Government Grants and Disclosure of Government Assistance*

IAS 21, *The Effects of Changes in Foreign Exchange Rates*

IAS 22 (rev.), *Business Combinations*

IAS 23, *Borrowing Costs*

IAS 24, *Related Party Disclosures*

IAS 25, *Accounting for Investments* (superseded by IAS 40)

IAS 26, *Accounting and Reporting by Retirement Benefit Plans* (not a core IAS)

IAS 27, *Consolidated Financial Statements and Accounting for Investments in Subsidiaries*

IAS 28, *Accounting for Investments in Associates*

IAS 29, *Financial Reporting in Hyperinflationary Economies*

IAS 30, *Disclosures in the Financial Statement of Banks and Similar Financial Institutions* (not a core IAS)

IAS 31, *Financial Reporting of Interests in Joint Ventures*

IAS 32, *Financial Instruments: Disclosures and Presentation*

IAS 33, *Earnings Per Share*

IAS 34, *Interim Financial Reporting*

IAS 35, *Discontinuing Operations*

IAS 36, *Impairment of Assets*

IAS 37, *Provisions, Contingent Liabilities and Contingent Assets*
IAS 38, *Intangible Assets*
IAS 39, *Financial Instruments: Recognition and Measurement*
IAS 40, *Investment Properties*

Chapter 8

The G4+1: Representatives of National Accounting Standard-Setting Bodies

G4+1 stands for "The Group of Four Plus One." It is made up of representatives of national accounting standard-setting bodies from Australia, Canada, New Zealand, the United Kingdom, and the United States, and observers from the International Accounting Standards Committee (IASC).

OBJECTIVES OF G4+1

The Group's *Memorandum of Understanding on Objectives* which was revised in March, 1999 lists the following objectives shared by G4+1 organizations:

1. Providing high-quality financial standards for the primary purpose of providing information useful to capital market participants.
2. Seeking common solutions to financial reporting issues. A single, quality financial reporting approach is more useful to capital market participants than multiple approaches.
3. Financial reporting standards should be based on a conceptual framework. It follows that membership of the Group requires acceptance of a conceptual framework similar to that of other members.
4. Seeking common solutions to financial reporting issues requires members to have the willingness and ability to commit resources to the resolution of those issues within the context of a conceptual framework.

G4+1 organizations seek to:

1. Further their shared objectives through analyses and discussions of financial reporting issues. Those analyses and discussions help participants from member organizations develop a common understanding of the issue, a common language and tools for discussing and analyzing the issues, and an understanding of the views and constraints in each others' jurisdictions.
2. Learn more about the timing and approach of standard-setting agenda projects in other jurisdictions. That knowledge can help them identify and take advantage of opportunities to coordinate their efforts and thereby further their shared objectives.
3. Further their shared objectives by exchanging new ideas and approaches to financial reporting issues and standard-setting processes that can be applied in their own jurisdictions.
4. Seek to further their shared objectives by pursuing projects that have the potential to bring about convergence of financial reporting standards across member jurisdictions at a high level of quality. The ultimate goal of this convergence would be global.

Changes Being Considered

At a recent meeting, the Group discussed a number of matters relating to the pursuit of joint projects with the objective of identifying potential changes that could facilitate the efficient development of Group projects, including:

1. Alignment of due process.
2. Alignment of work programs.
3. Scope and resourcing of joint projects.
4. Style of exposure drafts and standards.
5. Interaction among member organizations at both board member and staff levels.

Open Meetings

The G4+1 decided that, beginning with meetings in the year 2000, the discussions of technical issues in their meetings should generally be open to public observation when such arrangements are possible, and appropriate meeting facilities are available in the host country. The host country would be responsible for making meeting details and the current meeting agenda available to the public.

ORGANIZATIONAL STRUCTURE

The organization appears to be rather amorphous: There is no headquarters; chairmanship is on a rotating basis; a staff person from one of the participating organizations heads up each individual project, and that person prepares and distributes papers for the meetings.

TIE-IN WITH MEMBER ORGANIZATIONS

G4+1 projects characteristically tie in with Exposure Drafts and studies going on more-or-less independently in one or more of the member groups.

ACCOUNTING FOR CONTRIBUTIONS RECEIVED

In January, 2000 the G4+1 published a Discussion Paper on the accounting treatment of contributions received, entitled *Accounting by Recipients for Nonreciprocal Transfers, Excluding Contributions by Owners: Their Definition, Recognition and Measurement.*

This is the tenth in the series of papers resulting from discussions of the G4+1 aimed at developing solutions to accounting problems based on the bodies' common conceptual frameworks. The purpose of the Discussion Paper is to establish principles that will lead to consistent accounting treatments by recipients of nonreciprocal transfers, often referred to as "contributions."

Contributions are essentially transfers of resources from one party to another where the transferors do not directly receive approximately equal value in return. These include everyday transfers such as gifts, donations, government grants, and taxes. They may be received as cash, or as other assets, or as reductions in liabilities (for example, forgiven loans), and may or may not have conditions or restrictions attached. Nonreciprocal transfers are a major source of funding for government and other not-for-profit organizations.

Suggested Accounting Treatment

In practice, the accounting treatment of contributions by recipients varies greatly and it is often debated whether they should be reported by recipients as revenues, as reductions in expenses or in the cost of assets, as liabilities, or as direct additions to equity. The Discussion Paper takes the position that many recipients should report contributions as revenues in the periods the transfers are made, rather than over several periods in line with how the transferred assets are consumed by the recipients.

Important issues dealt with in the Discussion Paper include:

1. In what circumstances contributions include promises to give and whether these promises should be recognized by promisees.
2. Whether liability recognition is appropriate in the case of contributions received with conditions.
3. How go-between entities should account for receipts of contributions (go-between entities, which are often charities, are entities that receive contributions and distribute them on behalf of the transferors to other organizations).
4. How specified beneficiaries of go-betweens should account for contributions held on their behalf by the go-betweens.
5. When donated services should be recognized by recipient entities.

Leases: Proposals for Change

A Discussion Paper published in December, 1999 entitled *Leases: Implementation of a New Approach.* presents a Position Paper that was developed by the G4+1. This paper set out an agreed-upon approach to the treatment in financial reporting of leases, which differs in fundamental respects from what is required by existing standards of members of the G4+1.

Accounting for leases was the subject of a previous Special Report of the G4+1 entitled *Accounting for Leases: A New Approach,* published in 1996. That report, dealing mainly with accounting by lessees, concluded that the distinction between operating leases and finance leases required by present standards is arbitrary and unsatisfactory. The main deficiency of these standards noted in the report is that they do not provide for the recognition in lessees' balance sheets of material assets and liabilities arising from operating leases.

Classification of Leases

How leases are classified has important implications; for example, for:

1. Reported levels of indebtedness
2. Gearing ratios
3. Return on assets employed
4. Interest cover

The report suggested that the comparability (and hence usefulness) of financial statements would be enhanced if the present treatment of operating leases and finance leases were replaced by an approach that applied the same requirements to all leases.

The Position Paper develops this approach. It explores the principles that should determine the extent of the assets and liabilities that lessees and lessors would recognize under leases, and how those principles might be applied in new accounting standards to account for many of the complex features (such as options, contingent rentals, and residual value guarantees) that are found in lease contracts.

Recommendations for Change

The main recommendations are as follows:

1. For lessees, the objective should be to record, at the beginning of the lease term, the fair value of the rights and obligations that are conveyed by the lease.

Leases that are at present characterized as operating leases (and, therefore, not included in the balance sheet) would give rise to assets and liabilities—but only to the extent of the fair values of the rights and obligations that are conveyed by the lease. Thus, where a lease is for a small part of an asset's economic life, only that part would be reflected in the lessee's balance sheet.

2. The fair value of the rights obtained by a lessee would, in general, be measured as the present value of the minimum payments required by the lease, plus any other liabilities incurred.

3. Lessors should report financial assets (representing amounts receivable from the lessee) and residual interests as separate assets, since they are subject to quite different risks. The amounts reported as financial assets by lessors would, in general, be the converse of the amounts reported as liabilities by lessees.

Some members of G4+1 feel that a powerful case for change is made in the paper, and that the approach it sets out merits serious consideration as a basis for new accounting standards. To some, a particularly persuasive factor is the common and growing practice by investment analysts of recasting financial statements on a basis that is similar to that proposed.

All the organizations that participate in the G4+1 have agreed to publish the Position Paper in their own jurisdictions. They will consider, in the light of comments received in response to the Position Paper, whether its proposals should form a basis for developing new accounting standards.

Additional Points Considered

Other facets of leases considered by the Group include the following:

1. The distinction between executory or service contracts and leases in which the leased asset is not made available to the lessee on a continuous, uninterrupted basis, as for example, in the lease of a time-share.

2. The impact of contingent rentals, price changes, cancellation and renewal options, and residual value guarantees on the measurement of the lessee's assets and liabilities under the contract.

3. Subsequent measurement of lessee guarantees to the lessor. The Group discussed whether changes in the fair value of residual value guarantees should be expensed or reflected in the carrying amount of the lessee's asset.

4. The assets that should be separately identified in the lessor's balance sheet, including assets arising from future lease payments, residual values, and residual value guarantees. The Group also considered the extent to which contingent rentals, price changes, and cancellation and renewal options should be included in the lessor's assets arising from the lease contract and three possible methods of accounting for the lessor's residual interest in the asset at the end of the lease.

5. Leases of land or buildings in circumstances in which the land or building is reported at fair value under existing accounting practice.

6. Methods for recognition of gain or loss on sale-leaseback transactions.

SPECIAL REPORT ON JOINT VENTURES

The IASC published a Special Report in October, 1999, developed by the individual members of the G4+1. The report addresses accounting for investments in joint ventures.

The Special Report, entitled *Reporting Interests in Joint Ventures and Similar Arrangements*, identifies the wide diversity of standards and practices that currently exist among the G4+1 members. For example, under IAS 31, *Financial Reporting of Interests in Joint Ventures*, both the equity method and proportionate consolidation are allowed.

1. Under the equity method, the investor reports its share of the joint venture's net profit or loss on one line in its income statement and its investment on one line in its balance sheet.

2. Under proportionate consolidation, the investor adds its percentage share of each item in the joint venture's income statement and balance sheet to each similar item in the investor's income statement and balance sheet.

Proposed Accounting Treatment

The paper proposes:

1. A definition of joint venture for accounting purposes: No one party alone has the power to control its strategic operating, investing, and financing decisions, but two or more parties together can do so, and each of the parties sharing control (joint venturers) must consent.
2. That a joint venturer should use the equity method of accounting (proportionate consolidation would not be permitted).
3. Disclosures for interests in a joint venture and other forms of joint arrangements.

IASC does not currently have on its agenda a project on accounting for interests in joint ventures. The IASC Secretariat intends to review the comments on the Special Report that are received by the G4+1 members and will make a recommendation to the IASC Board as to whether IAS 31 should be reconsidered.

REPORTING FINANCIAL PERFORMANCE

In September, 1999, IASC issued a discussion paper that invites comment on certain proposals for Reporting Financial Performance that were developed by the G4+1.

Comments were considered on the following:

1. Financial performance should be presented in one financial statement rather than two or more statements.
2. The single statement of financial performance should be divided into three components:
   a. The results of operating (or trading) activities.
   b. The results of financing and other treasury activities.
   c. Other gains and losses.
3. "Recycling" should not generally be permitted. (Recycling is reporting the same item of income, expense, gain, or loss in two different periods in two different types of performance measures. For example, it might show up first in *other gains and losses* and subsequently in the *results of operating activities).*
4. The category of *extraordinary items* should be abolished, and abnormal or exceptional items should not be reported as a separate category of revenue or expenses.

5. Results of *continuing* and *discontinued* operations should be segregated.
6. Changes in accounting policy should be reported by retrospectively applying the new policy with restatement of prior periods.

It was pointed out that traditionally, the income statement has been the main vehicle a company uses to report its financial performance for a period. However, today some gains and losses are reported directly in equity *outside* the income statement. These instances may include, for example:

1. Revaluations of land and buildings.
2. Changes in fair values of certain financial instruments.
3. Some foreign currency translation gains and losses.

In IASC's current projects on investment properties and agriculture, the Board is wrestling with the question of how best to report changes in values of real estate held for investment and agricultural assets.

At present, practice is not consistent:

1. Some aspects of performance are reported in the notes; for example, disclosure of operating results by line of business and geographical area.
2. Others may be reported by subtotals in the income statement, for example, by segregating continuing and discontinuing operations or by highlighting unusual items.

The challenge is to bring greater consistency to reporting practice without destroying the usefulness of existing practice.

To further complicate the problem, practice varies among the G4+1 member standard-setters. Therefore, all of them are publishing the same proposals for comment. IASC intends to review carefully the responses it and the other G4+1 members receive to determine whether modification of IAS 1, *Presentation of Financial Statements*, or other Standards is warranted.

METHODS OF ACCOUNTING FOR BUSINESS COMBINATIONS

A Discussion Paper containing the text of a Position Paper prepared by the G4+1 was published by IASC in December, 1998. Each of the member organizations has agreed to issue the Paper, *Convergence on the Methods of Accounting for Business Combinations* for public comment in their own constituencies.

The Position Paper has not been considered by the Board of IASC and does not necessarily represent its views. The Staff of the IASC is issuing the

Discussion Paper to enable participation of the IAS constituency in the international debate on the methods of accounting for business combinations. International practice on accounting for business combinations is diverse, particularly in the allowed methods of accounting and criteria identifying when it is appropriate to apply a particular method.

The G4+1 Position Paper indicates that "achieving convergence on the method(s) of accounting for business combinations would eliminate the cause of one of the most significant reconciling items." Thus. the international debate on the methods of accounting for business combinations is highly relevant to the goal of IASC in promoting the harmonization of accounting standards.

Purchase Method Selected

The G4+ 1 Position Paper is solely concerned with the topic of convergence on the methods of accounting for business combinations and does not address detailed points of application of those methods. In considering the methods of accounting for business combinations, the following fundamental issues are addressed by the Paper:

1. Whether a single method of accounting for business combinations is preferable to two (or more) methods.
2. If so, which method of accounting should be applied to all business combinations?
3. If not, which methods should be applied and to which combinations should they be applied?

The G4+1 Position Paper concludes that the use of a single method of accounting is preferable, and that the *purchase method* is the appropriate method. A Steering Committee was established to review comments received in response to the Paper.

"Pooling of Interests" Abandoned

Of course, what this means is that, if the proposals in the Paper are implemented, all combinations would be accounted for as the acquisition by one entity of another. Purchase accounting requires the assets and liabilities of the acquired entity to be restated at their fair values and goodwill to be recognized on the consolidated balance sheet.

The effect normally increases the charges to the profit and loss accounts of subsequent periods with higher depreciation and any amortization of goodwill. The alternative approach, "pooling" makes no adjustments to the values of assets and liabilities but to add them together as though the two entities had always been combined.

Because of the perceived advantages of lower subsequent charges to a profit and loss account, pooling is often the preferred method for a merger.

As noted above, international practice in accounting for business combinations is diverse. In the U.S., as is quite evident at present, although pooling is supposedly applied only when specific conditions are met, no size test is involved, and in practice the method is used for many large mergers. At this point, the FASB has reiterated the decision to do away with "pooling of interests," but it will not actually happen without a great deal of resistance.

The potential for differences between the two methods of accounting is so great and the effects are so long-lasting that there are obvious advantages if common standards could apply to business combinations internationally.

Chapter 9

Insurance Accounting

THE IASC PAPER ON INSURANCE ACCOUNTING

As one of the final steps to fill out their core of basic standards for financial reporting, the International Accounting Standards Committee (IASC) published an Issues Paper on Insurance in December, 1999. The Issues Paper developed by IASC's Steering Committee on Insurance is the first step in this project.

It includes the following topics:

1. The different forms of insurance contract and specific characteristics that are relevant in determining the appropriate accounting treatment.
2. Accounting and disclosure issues and arguments for and against possible solutions to those issues.
3. The tentative views of the Steering Committee at this early stage of the project.

It was published together with an accompanying booklet that contains the following:

1. Illustrative examples; 82 are shown.
2. Summaries of relevant national standards and requirements in 17 countries.
3. Summaries of the main features of the principal contracts found in 8 countries.

4. A glossary of terms used in the paper.

5. Summaries of the tentative views expressed in the paper.

It seems obvious from the scope of the booklet that there is a need to bring about at least partial convergence of accounting treatment for insurance.

The chairman of IASC's steering committee on insurance pointed out that the industry is becoming increasingly important as an international industry.

This takes on particular significance when considering the diversity in accounting practices for insurers. Not only are insurance industry accounting practices significantly different in a number of countries, but even within the same country, accounting practices for insurance varies.

It follows that this makes it difficult for users to compare financial statements issued by insurers in different countries, and even by insurers within the same country.

With the worldwide emphasis on the need for transparency and comparability in financial reporting, it becomes apparent that accounting for insurance needs serious attention. Insurers need to provide more relevant and reliable information that the users of their financial statements can rely upon as a basis for economic decisions.

The information disclosed by insurers should enable users to compare the financial position and financial performance of insurers in different countries. That information should also be comparable with information disclosed about similar transactions by enterprises that are not insurers.

Insurance Contracts

The project addresses accounting for insurance contracts (or groups of contracts), rather than all aspects of accounting by insurance enterprises.

An insurance contract is a contract under which one party (the insurer) accepts an insurance risk by agreeing with another party (the policyholder) to make payment if a specified uncertain future event occurs.

Exceptions are an event that is only a change in a specified variable:

1. Interest rate.
2. Security price.
3. Commodity price.
4. Foreign exchange rate.
5. Index of prices or rates.
6. Credit rating or credit index.
7. Similar variable.

The following are examples of contracts that meet the definition of an insurance contract:

1. Insurance against damage to property.
2. Insurance against product liability, professional liability, civil liability or legal expenses.
3. Life insurance (although death is certain, it is uncertain when death will occur or, for some types of life insurance, whether death will occur at all within the period covered by the insurance).
4. Annuities and pensions (for annuities, the uncertain future event is the survival of the annuitant)
5. Disability and medical coverage.
6. Performance bonds and bid bonds (under which an enterprise undertakes to make a payment if another party fails to perform a contractual obligation, for example, an obligation to construct a building).
7. Product warranties issued either directly by a manufacturer or dealer or indirectly by an insurer.
8. Financial guarantees; for example, of a loan.
9. Title insurance (insurance against the discovery of defects in title to land that were not apparent when the insurance contract was written. In this case, the uncertain future event is the discovery of a defect in the title, not the defect itself).
10. Travel assistance (compensation in cash or in kind to policyholders for losses suffered while they are traveling).
11. Catastrophe bonds (bonds that provide for reduced payments of principal and/or interest if a specified event occurs).
12. Contracts that require a payment based on climatic, geological, or other physical variables (referred to as weather derivatives).
13. Reinsurance (insurance contracts between a direct insurer and a reinsurer, or between two reinsurers, in order to limit the risk exposure of the first insurer).

Types of Insurance Risk

The Steering Committee believes that the feature that distinguishes insurance contracts from other financial instruments is the risk that the insurer will need to make payment to another party if a specified uncertain future event occurs. They also believe that a contract that transfers only price risk (i.e. a derivative) should not be included in the definition of an insurance contract and should fall within the scope of the financial instruments project. Therefore, the Committee proposes that the definition of insurance contract should exclude contracts where the only uncertain future event that triggers payment is *a change in one of the seven variables* listed above.

This is consistent with IAS 39, *Financial Instruments: Recognition and Measurement*. Thus it is appropriate to describe the risk that is present in an insurance contract as *insurance risk* and the risk that is present in a derivative financial instrument as *price risk*.

Insurance risk covers a number of different types of risk, including:

1. Occurrence risk: the possibility that the number of insured events will differ from those expected.
2. Severity risk: the possibility that the cost of events will differ from expected cost.
3. Development risk: a residual category. It refers generally to changes in the amount of an insurer's obligation after the end of a contract period. Such changes may result from the late identification of insured events that occurred during the contract period; the possibility that claims will settle more quickly or in amounts greater than expected; that courts may interpret the insurer's liability differently than expected; other factors that may change the insurer's initial estimate of costs to settle incurred claims.

Recognition and Measurement

The objective should be to measure the assets and liabilities that arise from insurance contracts (an asset-and-liability measurement approach), rather than to defer income and expense so that they can be matched with each other (a deferral-and-matching approach).

Insurance liabilities (both general insurance and life insurance) should be discounted.

The measurement of insurance liabilities should be based on current estimates of future cash flows from the current contract. Estimated future cash flows from renewals are:

1. Included if the current contract commits the insurer to pricing for those renewals.
2. Excluded if the insurer retains full discretion to change pricing.

In the view of a majority of the Steering Committee, catastrophe and equalization reserves are not liabilities under IASC's framework. There may be a need for specific disclosures about low-frequency, high-severity risks, perhaps by segregating a separate component of equity.

The measurement of insurance liabilities should reflect risk to the extent that risk would be reflected in the price of an arm's length transaction between knowledgeable, willing parties. It follows that the sale of a long-term insurance contract may lead in some cases to the immediate recognition of income. The Steering Committee recognizes that some may have reservations about changing current practice in this way.

1. Overstatement of insurance liabilities should not be used to impose implicit solvency or capital adequacy requirements.
2. Acquisition costs should not be deferred as an asset.
3. All changes in the carrying amount of insurance liabilities should be recognized as they arise. In deciding what components of these changes should be presented or disclosed separately, the Steering Committee will monitor progress by the Joint Working Group on Financial Instruments.

Anticipated Requirement of Full Fair Value Accounting

The Steering Committee is working on the assumption that IAS 39, *Financial Instruments: Recognition and Measurement* will be replaced before the end of the Insurance project by a new IAS that will require full fair value accounting for the substantial majority of financial assets and liabilities

The Committee believes that:

1. If such a standard exists, portfolios of insurance contracts should also be measured at fair value. IASC defines fair value as "the amount for which an asset could be exchanged or a liability settled between knowledgeable, willing parties in an arm's length transaction."
2. In a fair value accounting model, the liability under a life insurance contract that has an explicit or implicit account balance may be less than the account balance.
3. Determining the fair value of insurance liabilities on a reliable, objective and verifiable basis poses difficult conceptual and practical issues, because there is generally no liquid and active secondary market in liabilities and assets arising from insurance contracts.

General Discussion of Measurement Issues

To avoid excessive detail, the Issues Paper discusses measurement issues in fairly general terms. The Steering Committee will develop more specific guidance on measurement issues at a later stage in the project.

Pending further discussion, the Steering Committee is evenly divided on the effect of future investment margins. Some members believe that future investment margins should be reflected in determining the fair value of insurance liabilities. Other members believe that they should not.

For participating and with-profits policies:

1. Where the insurer does not control allocation of the surplus, unallocated surplus should be classified as a liability.

2. Where the insurer controls allocation of the surplus, unallocated surplus should be classified as equity (except to the extent that the insurer has a legal or constructive obligation to allocate part of the surplus to policy-holders).

Liability classification is the default to be used unless there is clear evidence that the insurer controls allocation of the surplus.

For investment-linked insurance contracts, premiums received may need to be split into a risk component (revenue) and an investment component (deposit).

The accounting for reinsurance by a reinsurer should be the same as the accounting for direct insurance by a direct insurer.

Presentation and Disclosure

These proposals include the following:

1. Amounts due from reinsurers should not be offset against related insurance liabilities.
2. Most of the disclosures required by IAS 32, *Financial Instruments: Disclosure and Presentation*, and IAS 37, *Provisions, Contingent Liabilities and Contingent Assets*, are likely to be relevant for insurance contracts. Some of the disclosures required by IAS 39 may not be needed in a fair value context.
3. Other items that may require disclosure are regulatory solvency margins, key performance indicators (such as sum insured in life, retention / lapse rates, level of new business) information about risk adjustments and information about value-at-risk and sensitivity.

FINANCIAL ACCOUNTING STANDARDS BOARD STATEMENTS THAT COVER ACCOUNTING AND REPORTING BY INSURANCE ENTERPRISES

Four statements apply to insurance entities. The basic document is FASB 60, *Accounting and Reporting by Insurance Enterprises*. It has been amended and amplified by the three other statements in the following discussions.

FASB 97, *Accounting and Reporting by Insurance Enterprises for Certain Long–Duration Contracts and for Realized Gains and Losses from the Sale of Investments*

FASB Statement 97 amends Statement 60 by concluding that the accounting methods required by Statement 60 are not appropriate for insurance contracts in which the insurer can vary amounts charged or credited to the policyholder's account or the policyholder can vary the amount of premium paid.

The Statement outlines the accounting methods for three different classifications of long-duration life and annuity products. These classifications are:

1. Universal life-type policies
2. Limited payment policies
3. Policies not covering significant mortality or morbidity risks

Universal life-type policies.   Universal life-type policies must utilize a retrospective deposit method. The liability for this type of policy will be equal to the gross account balances before deduction of surrender charges. Revenues reported will be made up of charges assessed against the policy for mortality, expenses, and surrenders. These charges are presumed to be earned in the period during which they were assessed; however, charges, such as front-end fees, for example, assessed a limited number of times are deferred as unearned revenue.

For universal life-type policies, acquisition costs will be deferred and amortized in relation to present value of estimated future gross profits. Interest accrues to the unamortized balance of the deferred acquisition costs. The estimated gross profits are computed from estimated future mortality charges minus the estimated benefit claims exceeding:

1. The related account balances.
2. Expense charges minus the policy's estimated administration costs.
3. Estimated surrender charges.
4. Estimated future earnings based on investment yields of the policyholder's account balances, minus the estimated interest to be credited to account balances.

When the estimates of future gross profits are reevaluated, the amortization of deferred acquisition costs accrued to date must be adjusted and recognized in current operations. Any deferred revenues, including deferred front-end fees, are recognized as income on the same basis as the amortization of deferred acquisition costs.

Limited-payment policies.   Limited-payment policies consist of life insurance and annuity policies with fixed and guaranteed terms having premiums that are payable over a period shorter than the period during which benefits are paid. The premiums for this type of policy are reported as revenues (reserves are computed in accordance with rulings set forth in Statement 60). However, the accumulated profit, formerly shown as a percentage of premiums, is deferred. The amount of coverage must be related to life insurance in force or expected future annuity benefit payments.

Policies not covering significant mortality or morbidity risk. Policies not covering significant mortality or morbidity risks, such as *guaranteed investment contracts* (GICs) and some types of annuities, are shown as interest-bearing or other financial instruments, rather than as insurance contracts. Therefore, the accounting for these policies would show the account balance as a liability, and premiums as deposits rather than as revenues. Deferred acquisition costs would primarily be amortized in relation to future interest margins.

Policies including accident and health insurance not falling under one of these three classifications remain within the requirements of Statement 60.

Statement 97 also requires that property/casualty and stock life insurance companies must provide one-step income statements for realized investment gains or losses instead of the currently required two-step statement. The latter shows operating income after taxes but before net realized investment gains or losses. The one-step income statement presents realized investment gains or losses on a pretax basis with revenues, investment income, and expenses to show income before taxes.

FASB 113, *Accounting and Reporting for Reinsurance of Short-Duration and Long-Duration Contracts*

Definitions. The following definitions of terms relate to this Statement. They will be helpful in understanding their exact meaning in this Statement.

Amortization—The act or process of extinguishing a debt, usually by equal payments over a specific period of time. The liquidation of a financial obligation on an installment basis.

Assuming Enterprise—The receiving company in a reinsurance contract. The assuming enterprise (or reinsurer) receives a reinsurance premium and, in turn, accepts an obligation to reimburse a ceding enterprise under specified terms; reinsures on a risk or exposure.

Ceding Enterprise—The company seeking a reinsurance contract. The ceding enterprise exchanges a reinsurance premium for the right to reimbursement from the assuming enterprise under specified terms. The insurer that cedes all or part of the insurance or reinsurance it has written to another insurer. Also known as the *direct writer.*

Contract Period—The length of time over which the specified terms are covered by the reinsured contracts.

Covered Period—Same as contract period (above).

Fronting Arrangements—Reinsurance provisions in which the ceding enterprise issues a policy to the assuming enterprise to reinsure all or substantially all of the insurance risk.

Incurred but Not Reported (IBNR) —Refers to losses that have occurred but have not been reported to the insurer or reinsurer.

Indemnification—Action of compensating for the actual loss or damage sustained; the fact of being compensated; the payment made for loss or damage.

Insurance Risk—The risk caused by the uncertain nature of the under-writing risk relating to the amount of net cash flows from premiums, commissions, claims, and claim settlement expenses paid as a result of contract specifications and the equally uncertain nature of the timing risk, which involves the timing of the receipt and payment of those cash flows. Actual or imputed investment returns are not an element of insurance risk. An insurance risk encompasses the possibility of adverse events occurring outside the control of the insured.

Long-Duration Contract—A contract expected to cover a prolonged period of time; in contrast to a short-duration contract (*see* Short-Duration Contract). While the time element is obvious from the long/short descriptive terms applied, the nature of the services rendered and the degree of control by the insurance company also differ. Along with insurance coverage, the long-duration carrier provides additional services and functions for the policyholder, including loans secured by the insurance policy, various options for payment of benefits, etc. The contract is usually not unilaterally controlled as is the short-duration type. It is customarily noncancellable, guaranteed renewable, and has fixed contract terms.

Most life and title insurance policies are considered long-duration contracts, while accident and health insurance policies depend on the expected term of coverage for the determination of long- or short-duration.

Offsetting—Showing a recognized asset and a recognized liability as a net amount on a financial statement. As a result of offsetting the assets and liabilities in reinsurance contracts, pertinent information could be lost and financial statement relationships altered.

Prospective Reinsurance—Reinsurance in which an assuming enterprise agrees to reimburse a ceding enterprise for losses that may be incurred as a result of future insurable events covered under contracts subject to the reinsurance. A reinsurance contract may include both prospective and retroactive reinsurance provisions.

Reinsurance—A device whereby an insurance company lessens the catastrophic hazard in the operation of the insurance mechanism; insurance for the insurer.

Reinsurance Receivables—All amounts recoverable from reinsurers for past and unpaid claims and claim settlement expenses, including estimated amounts receivable for unsettled claims, claims incurred but not reported, or policy benefits.

Reinsurer—*See* Assuming Enterprise.

Retroactive Reinsurance—Reinsurance in which an assuming enterprise agrees to reimburse a ceding enterprise for liabilities incurred as a result of past insurable events covered under contracts subject to reinsurance. A reinsurance contract may include both prospective and retroactive reinsurance provisions.

Retrocession—The process by which the reinsurer, or assuming enterprise, in turn, becomes a party in a reinsurance contract with still other reinsurers.

Settlement Period—The estimated period over which a ceding enterprise expects to recover substantially all amounts due from the reinsurer under the specified terms of the reinsurance contract.

Short-Duration Contract—An insurance policy not expected to cover an extended period of time. A carrier primarily provides insurance for a short, fixed period. The insurance carrier has more one-way control than in the long-duration contract *(see* Long-Duration Contract). The various specified terms of the contract, including amount of premiums and coverage, may be altered or canceled at the end of any contract period by the insurance company. Short-duration contracts include most property and liability policies and, to a lesser extent, some short-term life policies.

Statutory Accounting—The accounting system followed by insurance companies as required by the statutes of the various states. These procedures are geared to the National Association of Insurance Commissioners' (NAIC's) standardized reporting format. Differs in some instances from GAAP, but because the principal emphasis is on reflecting the ability of the insurer to meet its contract commitments, tends to be conservative.

General Provisions of the Statement. FASB Statement 113, *Accounting and Reporting for Reinsurance of Short-Duration and Long-Duration Contracts* amends FASB Statement 60, *Accounting and Reporting by Insurance Companies,* and was effective for fiscal years starting after December 15, 1992. This rule eliminated the former practice of reporting assets and liabilities related to insurance contracts net of the effects of reinsurance. Statement 60, which is the basic document dealing with specialized insurance accounting and reporting practices, had continued the statutory accounting practice of offsetting reinsurance assets and liabilities. However, this procedure is now considered inconsistent with the generally accepted criteria for offsetting. Under this rule, the practice is eliminated for general-purpose financial statements.

Beginning in 1993, reinsurance receivables and prepaid reinsurance premiums are reported as assets. Reinsurance receivables include amounts related to (a) claims incurred but not reported and (b) liabilities for future policy benefits. Estimated reinsurance receivables are recognized in a manner consistent with the related liabilities.

Statement 113 set up a method of determining whether a specific contract qualified for reinsurance accounting. The accounting standard revolves around determination of whether the reinsurance is long-duration or short-duration, and, if short-duration, whether it is prospective or retroactive insurance. A contract must result in a reasonable possibility that the reinsurer may realize a significant loss from assuming insurance risk, or the contract does not qualify for reinsurance accounting, but must be accounted for as a deposit. All reinsurance contracts prohibit the reinsurance from recognizing immediately a gain if there remains a chance of liability to the policyholder by the ceding enterprise.

To further clarify the financial picture, the reinsurer is required to provide footnote disclosures explaining all facets of the terms, nature, purpose, and effect of ceded reinsurance transactions. In addition, disclosures of concentrations of credit risk associated with reinsurance receivables and prepaid premiums are also required under the provisions of FASB 105, *Disclosures of Information About Financial Instruments with Off-Balance-Sheet Risk and Financial Instruments with Concentrations of Credit Risk.*

Cause for Concern. A portion of the impetus for consideration, or reconsideration, of the accounting and reporting for reinsurance has evolved from the general concern about the highly visible failure of some insurance companies. Risk relating to reinsurance has been considered germane to some of the failed enterprises.

Among the concerns voiced in regard to reinsurance have been:

1. The effect of reinsurance accounting relating to contracts that did not provide indemnification for the ceding party against loss or liability.
2. The fact that FASB Statement 60 did not provide sufficient guidance relating to reinsurance accounting. Among other weaknesses, this led to acceleration of the recognition of income relating to reinsurance contracts.
3. The absence of requirements for disclosure of reinsurance transactions. The policyholder was seldom aware of any reinsurance arrangement.
4. The inconsistency between the widespread use of *net* accounting for reinsurance-related assets and liabilities in spite of not meeting the established criteria for offsetting.

Therefore, the thrust of the Statement is: (a) as already noted, to address these perceived problems; (b) to provide guidance in the determination of whether specific reinsurance contracts actually make provision for indemnification of the ceding enterprise to qualify for reinsurance accounting; and (c) to establish the necessary accounting methods.

Statement 113 did *not* change practice in accounting for reinsurance *assumed* other than to require certain disclosures relating to reinsurance by all insurance companies.

For short-duration contracts to qualify for reinsurance accounting, there should be a positive answer to the following questions:

1. Does the reinsurer assume significant insurance risk under the reinsurance provisions of the underlying insurance contracts?
2. Is there a reasonable possibility that the assuming enterprise may be faced with a significant loss as a result of this contract?
3. Is there a possibility of a significant variation in the amount or timing of payments by the reinsurer?

A ceding company's evaluation of whether it is reasonably possible for a reinsurer to realize a significant loss should be based on a present value analysis of cash flows between the ceding and assuming enterprises under reasonably possible outcomes. When the ceding company reaches the conclusion that the reinsurer is not exposed to the possibility of significant loss, the ceding company can decide that it is indemnified against loss or liability related to insurance risk only if *substantially all* of the insurance risk relating to the reinsured portion of the specific underlying insurance policy has been assumed by the reinsurer. Thus, any insurance risk remaining with the ceding company must be of little or no importance or of a trivial nature if the ceding company decides to consider itself indemnified against loss or liability.

For a long-duration contract to qualify for reinsurance accounting, there must be a reasonable probability that the reinsurer may realize significant loss from assuming the insurance risk. FASB Statement 97, *Accounting and Reporting by Insurance Enterprises for Certain Long-Duration Contracts and for Realized Gains and Losses from the Sale of Investments*, defines long-duration contracts that do not subject the insurer to mortality or morbidity risks as investment contracts. Consistent with that definition, if a contract does not subject the reinsurer to the reasonable possibility of significant loss from the events insured by the underlying insurance contracts, it does not indemnify the ceding enterprise against insurance risk.

FASB 113 mandates that reinsurance contracts can lead to recognition of immediate gains only if the reinsurance contract is a legal replacement of one insurer by another and the ceding company's liability to the policyholder is extinguished.

Amounts paid for prospective reinsurance of short-duration insurance contracts must be accounted for as prepaid reinsurance premiums. They are to be amortized over the remaining contract period in proportion to the amount of insurance protection provided.

Amounts paid for retroactive reinsurance of short-duration insurance contracts must be reported as insurance receivables to the extent those amounts do not exceed the recorded liabilities relating to the reinsured contracts. If the recorded liabilities exceed the amount paid, reinsurance receivables should be increased to reflect the difference and the resulting gain should be deferred. The deferred gain is to be amortized over the estimated remaining settlement period. If the amount paid for retroactive reinsurance exceeds the recorded related liabilities, the ceding company must increase the related liabilities or reduce the reinsurance receivable, or both, at the time the reinsurance contract is entered into. The excess is charged to earnings.

If, when both prospective and retroactive provisions are included in a single short-duration reinsurance transaction and it is deemed impracticable to account for every provision separately, retroactive short-duration reinsurance contract accounting must be used. Amortization of the estimated costs of insuring long-duration insurance contracts depends on whether the reinsurance contract is long- or short-duration. These costs should be amortized over the remaining life of the underlying insured contracts if the contract is long-duration, or over the reinsurance contract period if the reinsurance contract is short-duration. Determining whether a contract that reinsures a long-duration insurance contract is long- or short-duration is a matter of judgment.

Disclosure Requirements.   The financial statements of all insurance companies must now disclose the following information:

1. The nature, purpose, and effect of ceding and reinsurance transactions on the insurance company's operations.
2. The ceding company must disclose the amount of earned premiums ceded and recoveries recognized under reinsurance contracts in footnotes to the financial statement, unless these are reported separately in the statement of earnings.
3. Premiums from direct business, reinsurance assumed, and reinsurance ceded, on both a written and earned basis, must be disclosed for short-duration contracts.
4. For long-duration contracts, premiums and amounts assessed against policyholders from direct business, reinsurance assumed and ceded, and premiums and amounts earned must be disclosed.
5. Companies must detail the methods used for income recognition on their reinsurance contracts.

FASB 120, *Accounting and Reporting by Mutual Life Insurance Enterprises and by Insurance Enterprises for Certain Long–Duration Participating Contracts*

FASB 120 is the result of considerable cooperation between the Financial Accounting Standards Board and the American Institute of CPAs to provide guidance in accounting, reporting, and disclosure procedures to mutual life insurance companies. Prior to the enactment of this standard and those rulings cited below, these companies reported financial information to their creditors and policyholders primarily following the statutory provisions of various state insurance regulatory bodies. The companies are now to report insurance and reinsurance activities according to GAAP.

The thrust of this Statement is to apply the provisions of FASB 60, *Accounting and Reporting by Insurance Enterprises*; FASB 97, *Accounting and Reporting by Insurance Enterprises for Certain Long-Duration Contracts and for Realized Gains and Losses from the Sale of Investments*, and FASB 113, *Accounting and Reporting for Reinsurance of Short-Duration and Long-Duration Contracts*, to mutual life insurance enterprises, assessment enterprises and to fraternal benefit societies. Certain participating life insurance contracts of those same enterprises have also been addressed in the AICPA's Statement of Position 95-1, *Accounting for Certain Activities of Mutual Life Insurance Enterprises*. Both become effective for financial statements for fiscal years beginning after December 15, 1995.

The three earlier FASB Statements had specifically exempted mutual life insurance enterprises from their requirements. FASB Interpretation 40, *Applicability of Generally Accepted Accounting Principles to Mutual Life Insurance and Other Enterprises*, did not address or change the exemption of mutual life insurance companies from these Statements. Interpretation 40 had been scheduled to become effective earlier but the date was changed to permit simultaneous application with FASB 120 and SOP 95-1.

It was because there seemed to be little authoritative accounting guidance relative to the insurance and reinsurance activities of mutual life insurance enterprises that the FASB, along with the AICPA, decided to extend the requirements of the above mentioned standards to them. The AICPA's Statement of Position 95-1 sets guidelines for participating insurance contracts of mutual life insurance companies when:

1. They are long-duration participating contracts that are expected to pay dividends to policyholders based on the actual experience of the insurer.
2. The annual policyholder dividends are paid in a way that identifies divisible surplus, then distributes that surplus in approximately the same proportion that the contracts are estimated to have contributed to that surplus. Otherwise, accounting and reporting for these contracts are covered by the four basic FASB insurance enterprise standards listed above.

The effect of initially applying FASB 120 was reported retroactively through restatement of all previously issued annual financial statements presented for comparative purposes for fiscal years beginning after December 15, 1992.

Chapter 10

Derivatives

There is little doubt that Derivatives was the '90s buzz word in the areas of accounting, finance, banking, and investments. The SEC, the AICPA, the FASB, the GASB, the GAO, the FEI, the AIMR, the IASC, IOSCO, CBOT and myriad other worthy organizations all jumped into the fray to attempt to prevent another Orange County, California-type debacle from occurring. The losses of Procter and Gamble, other large companies, and banks had raised concern, but the fiasco of a public body so obviously misusing derivatives—and being caught—called for drastic action. How best to guard against anything like this happening again?

The Financial Accounting Standard Board's FASB 119, *Disclosures About Derivative Financial Instruments and Fair Value of Financial Instruments,* was a giant step in the right direction as far as disclosure was concerned, but it was not enough. After 10 years of wresting with the derivatives problem, the Board adopted FASB 133, *Accounting for Derivative Instruments and Hedging Activities.* This new Standard supersedes FASBs 80, 105, and 119 and also amends FASBs 52 and 107.

Various private sector entities highlighted, pinpointed, and underlined problems associated with disclosures about these market risk sensitive instruments, as identified by users of financial reports. The Securities and Exchange Commission's study, preceding the release (in March, 1996) of their proposals for amendments to regulations governing disclosure information about derivatives and other financial instruments and the issuance in February, 1997 of amendments to SEC rules, took into consideration concerns by many organizations. For example, the Association for Investment Management and Research (AIMR), an organization of financial analysts, in a paper discussing financial reporting in the 1990s and on into the next century, noted that users are confounded by the complexity of financial instruments.

After considerable investigation into the needs of investors and creditors, the American Institute of Certified Public Accountants' (AICPA) Special Committee on Financial Reporting confirmed in a study completed in 1994 that users are confused. The users complained that business reporting is not meeting their needs in answering difficult but important questions about innovative financial instruments that companies may have entered into. They felt they needed more specific information about how companies account for those instruments, how that accounting affects the financial statements, and how risk is handled.

Other organizations have made recommendations about how to improve such disclosures on market risk sensitive instruments. These organizations include regulators, such as the Group of Ten Central Bankers, the Federal Reserve Bank of New York, the Basle Committee and the Technical Committee of the International Organization of Securities Commissions (IOSCO), and private sector bodies, such as the Group of Thirty and a task force of the Financial Executives Institute (FEI).

The SEC study found that, in general, these organizations have stressed the need to make more understandable the risks inherent in market risk sensitive instruments. In particular, they have called for additional quantitative and qualitative disclosures about market risk. For example, the Federal Reserve Bank of New York recommended a new financial statement providing quantitative information about the overall market risk of an entity. In addition, the FEI task force recommended that companies disclose some type of information that conveys overall exposure to market risk. In this regard, the FEI task force suggested two distinct approaches. One approach is to provide a high-level summary of relevant statistics about outstanding activity at period end. The second approach is to communicate the potential loss which could occur under specified conditions using either a value at risk or another comprehensive model to measure market risk.

FASB STATEMENT 119

FASB 119 prescribed, among other things, disclosures in the financial statements about the policies used to account for derivative financial instruments, and a discussion of the nature, terms, and cash requirements of derivative financial instruments. It also encouraged, but did not require, disclosure of quantitative information about an entity's overall market risk. As mentioned earlier, this was a first decisive step in the right direction, but further standards, particularly relating to *accounting* for derivatives and hedging, were considered necessary.

Standards similar to FASB 119 have been adopted by the International Accounting Standards Committee, IAS 32; the Canadian Institute of Chartered Accountants; and the Australian Accounting Standards Board. Whether all of these bodies will endeavor to expand upon the requirements in these standards remains to be seen. However, the IASC has adopted IAS 39, *Financial Instruments: Recognition and Measurement* to become effective on or after January 1, 2001. A more long-range Standard relating to financial instruments including derivatives is also under consideration.

During 1994, in response, in part, to the concerns of investors, regulators, and private sector entities, the SEC staff reviewed the annual reports of approximately 500 registrants. In addition, during 1995, annual reports were reviewed by the SEC staff to assess the effect of FASB 119 on disclosures about market risk sensitive instruments. As a result of these reviews, the SEC staff observed that FASB 119 did have a positive effect on the quality of disclosures about derivative financial instruments. However, the SEC staff also concluded there was a need to improve disclosures about them, other financial instruments, and derivative commodity instruments. In particular, the SEC staff had identified the following three primary disclosure issues which should be considered when following the new rules.

FURTHER DISCLOSURE MEASURES NEEDED

1. Footnote disclosures of accounting policies for derivatives often are too general to convey adequately the diversity in accounting that exists for derivatives. As a result, it is often difficult to determine the impact of derivatives on registrants' statements of financial position, cash flows, and results of operations.

2. Disclosures frequently focus on derivatives and other financial instruments only in isolation. For this reason, it may be difficult to assess whether these instruments increase or decrease the net market risk exposure of a registrant.

3. Disclosure about financial instruments, commodity positions, firm commitments, and other anticipated transactions, *reported items*, in the footnotes to the financial statements, Management's Discussion and Analysis (MD&A), schedules, and selected financial data may not reflect adequately the effect of derivatives on such reported items. Without disclosure about the *effects* of derivatives, information about the reported items may be incomplete or perhaps misleading.

For Study and Consideration

For one and one-half years, members of the SEC staff researched derivatives, related risk management activities, and alternative disclosure approaches to make these activities less a mystery to investors, the general public, and even many professionals who actually deal with these activities in one capacity or another, before drawing up proposals for consideration. In addition, during this period, the SEC and its staff developed a list of guiding principles to provide a foundation for proposed amendments and recommendations.

1. Disclosures should make it possible for investors to understand better how derivatives affect a registrant's statements of financial position, cash flows, and results of operations.
2. Disclosures should provide information about market risk.
3. Disclosures should clearly explain for the investor how market risk sensitive instruments are used in the registrant's business.
4. Disclosures about market risk should not focus on derivatives in isolation, but rather should point out the "opportunity" for loss inherent in all market risk sensitive instruments.
5. Disclosure requirements about market risk should be flexible enough to accommodate different types of registrants, different degrees of market risk exposure, and different ways of measuring market risk.
6. Disclosures about market risk should highlight, where appropriate, special risks relating to leverage, option, or prepayment features.
7. New disclosure requirements should build on existing disclosure requirements, where possible, to simplify the learning process for additional procedures and to minimize compliance costs to registrants.

Derivatives—Good and Bad

During the last several years, there has been substantial growth in the use of derivative financial instruments, other financial instruments, and derivative commodity instruments. The SEC agrees that these instruments can be effective tools for managing registrants' exposures to market risk. After all, grain futures, hedging, and the commodity market are all good heartland, conservative agricultural measures undertaken as risk prevention, not as flyers in a volatile market. However, what was an ordered, conservative approach to hedging in the 1800s began developing rapidly and spectacularly in some areas as wild speculation in the late 1900s. During 1994, some investors and registrants experienced significant, and sometimes unexpected, losses in market risk sensitive instruments due to, among other things, changes in interest rates, foreign currency exchange rates, and commodity prices. In light of these losses and the substantial growth in the use of market risk sensitive instruments, public disclosure about these instruments has emerged as an important issue in financial markets.

As mentioned, a portion of the SEC study on derivatives during 1994 and 1995 was a review of annual reports filed by approximately 500 registrants. The avowed purpose was to assess the quality of disclosures relating to market risk sensitive instruments and to determine what, if any, additional information was needed to improve disclosures about derivatives. They determined that partly because of FASB 119, disclosures reviewed in 1995 were more informative than those reviewed in 1994.

THREE BASIC PROPOSALS

It was the opinion of those reviewing the situation that the three aforementioned significant disclosure issues remain as problems. To address these specific disclosure issues, the SEC proposed guidance reminders and amendments to their basic regulations, and it is these specific proposals that have led to the new amendments to the SEC regulations:

1. Amendments to Regulation S-X requiring enhanced descriptions in the footnotes to the financial statements of accounting policies for derivative financial instruments and derivative commodity instruments. These disclosures would be required unless the registrant's derivative activities are not material. The materiality of derivatives activities would be measured by the fair values of derivative financial instruments and derivative commodity instruments at the end of each reporting period and the fair value of those instruments during each reporting period.

2. Amendments creating a new item within Regulation S-K requiring disclosure outside the financial statements of qualitative and quantitative information about derivative financial instruments, other financial instruments, and derivative commodity instruments. These disclosures would be required if the fair values of market risk sensitive instruments outstanding at the end of the current reporting period were material or the potential loss in future earnings, fair values, or cash flows of market risk sensitive instruments from reasonably possible market movements appeared likely to be material.

3. Reminders to registrants that when they provide disclosure about financial instruments, commodity positions, firm commitments, and other anticipated transactions, such disclosure must include information about derivatives that affect directly or indirectly such reported items, to the extent the effects of such information is material and

necessary to prevent the disclosure about the reported item from being misleading. For example, when information is required to be disclosed in the footnotes to the financial statements about interest rates and repricing characteristics of debt obligations, registrants should include, when material, disclosure of the effects of derivatives. Similarly, summary information and disclosures in MD&A about the cost of debt obligations should include, when material, disclosure of the effects of derivatives.

THE SEC TAKES ACTION

Disclosure of Accounting Policies for Derivative Financial Instruments and Derivative Commodity Instruments and Disclosure of Quantitative and Qualitative Information About Market Risk Inherent in Derivative Financial Instruments, Other Financial Instruments, and Derivative Commodity Instruments

From the title of the rules released on February 3, 1997, it would almost appear that the Securities and Exchange Commission feels the ills of the "derivatives problem" can be solved if someone can just come up with the right disclosure and accounting policy formulas to make everything clear to the naive, as well as the sophisticated, investor and end user. At least they tried very hard to find that formula for the disclosure part, and appeared to have faith that the FASB would soon come up with the accounting part.

Thus, the Commission has amended rules and forms for domestic and foreign issuers to clarify and expand existing disclosure requirements for "market risk sensitive instruments." The amendments require enhanced disclosure of accounting policies for derivative financial instruments and derivative commodity instruments (derivatives) in the *footnotes* to the financial statements. In addition, the amendments expand existing disclosure requirements to include quantitative and qualitative information about market risk inherent in market risk sensitive instruments. The required quantitative and qualitative information should be disclosed *outside the financial statements and footnotes*. In addition, the quantitative and qualitative information will be provided safe harbor protection under a new Commission rule.

Disclosures about financial instruments, commodity positions, firm commitments, and anticipated transactions (reported items) must include disclosures about derivatives that *directly* or *indirectly* affect such reported items, to the extent such information is material and necessary to prevent the disclosures from being misleading. The amendments are designed to provide additional information about market risk sensitive instruments, which investors can use to better understand and evaluate the market risk exposures of a registrant.

Planned Reconsideration

The Commission recognizes the evolving nature of market risk sensitive instruments, market risk measurement systems, and market risk management strategies and, thus, intends to continue considering how best to meet the information needs of investors. In this regard, the Commission expects to monitor continuously the effectiveness of these new rules and final disclosure items, as well as the need for additional proposals.

Specifically, the Commission expects to reconsider these amendments after each of the following:

1. The FASB issues a new accounting standard for improving accounting recognition, measurement, and related discoveries for derivatives. (This should be underway with the adoption of FASB 133.)
2. Development in the marketplace of new generally accepted methods for measuring market risk.
3. A period of three years from the initial effective date of Item 305 of Regulation S-K and Item 9A of Form 20-F.

Effective Dates

The amendments became effective over a period of several months to provide registrants with time to respond to the new disclosure requirements. Some compliance dates were staggered depending upon the type of entity and its capitalization. For registrants that were likely to have experience with measuring market risk, less lead time was provided.

Provisions of Items 305 and 9A

The amendments to Regulation S-K to add Item 305, and Form 20F to add Item 9A, require disclosure of *quantitative* and *qualitative* information about market risk for derivatives and other financial instruments, and require that those disclosures be presented *outside the financial statements*. Items 305 and 9A do not pertain solely to derivatives, but also to other financial instruments. Thus, disclosures under those Items are required for registrants that have material amounts of other financial instruments, even when they have no derivatives.

These Items also *encourage* registrants to include other market risk sensitive instruments, positions, and transactions (such as commodity positions, derivative commodity instruments that are not permitted by contract or business custom to be settled in cash or with another financial instrument, and cash flows from anticipated transactions) within the scope of their quantitative and qualitative disclosures about market risk. Registrants that select the sensitivity analysis or value at risk disclosure alternatives and voluntarily include those other market risk sensitive instruments, positions, and transactions within their quantitative disclosures about market risk are permitted to present comprehensive market risk disclosures, which reflect the combined effect of both the required and voluntarily selected instruments, positions, and transactions.

Finally, if those other market risk sensitive instruments, positions, and transactions are not voluntarily included in the quantitative disclosures about market risk and, as a result, the disclosures do not fully reflect the net market risk exposures of the registrant, Items 305(a) and 9A(a) require that registrants discuss the absence of those items as a limitation of the disclosed market risk information.

Quantitative Information

Items 305(a) and 9A(a) require registrants to disclose quantitative information about market risk sensitive instruments using one or more of the following alternatives:

1. Tabular presentation of fair value information and contract terms relevant to determining future cash flows, categorized by expected maturity dates.
2. Sensitivity analysis expressing the potential loss in future earnings, fair values, or cash flows from selected hypothetical changes in market rates and prices.
3. Value at risk disclosures expressing the potential loss in future earnings, fair values, or cash flows from market movements over a selected period of time and with a selected likelihood of occurrence.

Preparation of this quantitative information also requires the registrants to categorize market risk sensitive instruments into instruments entered into for trading purposes, and instruments entered into for purposes other than trading. Within both the trading and other than trading portfolios, separate quantitative information should be presented for each market risk exposure category (i.e., interest rate risk, foreign currency exchange rate risk, commodity price risk, and other relevant market risks, such as equity price risk), to the extent material.

Registrants may use different disclosure alternatives for each of the separate disclosures.

Qualitative Information

In addition to the quantitative information, Items 305(b) and 9A(b) also require registrants to disclose qualitative information about market risk. These items require disclosure of:

1. A registrant's primary market risk exposures at the end of the current reporting period.
2. How the registrant manages those exposures (such as a description of the objectives, general strategies, and instruments, if any, used to manage those exposures).
3. Changes in either the registrant's primary market risk exposures or how those exposures are managed, when compared to the most recent reporting period and what is known or expected in future periods.

Requirements for Small Business Issuers

Small companies and registered investment companies are exempt from a portion of the new requirements. The amendments in Rule 4–08(n) of Regulation S-X and Item 310 of Regulation S-B, relating to accounting policy disclosures, apply to registered investment companies and small business issuers, along with other registrants. However, Item 305 and Item 9A do not apply to registered investment companies and small business issuers.

The Commission believes that because of the evolving nature of the disclosures and the relative costs of compliance for small business issuers, it is appropriate, at this time, to exempt them from disclosing quantitative and qualitative information about market risk. Furthermore, they will not be required to provide these market risk disclosures whether or not they file on specially designated small business forms. In addition, the Commission has extended the safe harbor for forward-looking information to Item 305 disclosures that are made voluntarily by small business issuers.

Accordingly, at this time, the Commission is not adopting amendments to Regulation S-B to incorporate an item similar to Item 305. Small business issuers, however, are required to comply with the amendment regarding accounting policies disclosures for derivatives, to comply with Rule 12b-20 under the Exchange Act and Rule 408 under the Securities Act. These rules require registrants to provide additional information about the material effects of derivatives on other information expressly required to be filed with the Commission, and to the extent market risk represents a known trend, event, or uncertainty, to discuss the impact of market risk on past and future financial condition and results of operations, pursuant to Item 303 of Regulation S-B.

Application to Foreign Private Issuers

As the interest in international securities and investment grows, it is important to keep in mind that the SEC also is charged with the responsibility of seeing that the investor has adequate information about the financial status of foreign entities.

Item 9A of Form 20-F requires disclosure by all foreign private issuers of quantitative and qualitative information about market risk. In addition, foreign private issuers that prepare financial statements in accordance with Item 18 of Form 20-F are required to provide all information required by U.S. GAAP and Regulation S-X, including descriptions in the footnotes to the financial statements of the policies used to account for derivatives.

Lack of Direction Noted

The SEC study revealed that in the absence of comprehensive requirements for accounting for derivatives, registrants had been developing accounting practices for options and complex derivatives by piecemeal application of the various APB Opinions, FASB Statements, EITF Issues, and the limited amount of such literature that did exist.

The varied applications were complicated because existing derivative literature referred to at least three distinctly different methods of accounting for derivatives: fair value accounting, deferral accounting, and accrual accounting. Further, the underlying concepts and criteria used in determining the applicability of these accounting methods were not consistent.

To illustrate: Under the fair value method, derivatives were carried on the balance sheet at fair value with changes in that value recognized in earnings or stockholders' equity. Under the deferral method, gains and losses from derivatives were deferred on the balance sheet and recognized in earnings in conjunction with earnings of designated items. Under the accrual method, each net payment or receipt due or owed under the derivative was recognized in earnings during the period to which the payment or receipt related; there was no recognition on the balance sheet for changes in the derivative's fair value.

All that is now so much history. All derivative instruments are subject to fair value accounting. And hedging rules have been clearly spelled out so that there is no longer the tug-of-war between accounting applications suggested in FASB 52, *Foreign Currency Translation* (amended by FASB 133), and FASB 80, *Accounting for Futures Contracts* (superseded by FASB 133). Various other interpretations and opinions have also been superseded in an attempt to bring uniformity to accounting for derivatives.

As a result of lack of consistent direction during its 1994–1995 reviews of filings, the SEC staff observed that registrants, in attempting to interpret the literature, were accounting for the same type of derivative in many different ways. (We assume that it remained a moot question as to whether the interpretation was based on evidence of advantage to the registrant.) Thus, it was difficult to compare the financial statement effects of derivatives across registrants.

Building on FASB 119

In order to provide a better understanding of the accounting for derivative financial instruments, FASB 119 required disclosure of the policies used to account for such instruments, in line with the requirements of APB 22. Specifically, FASB 119 emphasized the disclosure of policies for recognizing, or not recognizing, and measuring derivative financial instruments. When recognized, the location of where those instruments and related gains and losses were reported in the statements of financial position and income must be clearly indicated.

However, FASB 119 did not provide explicit instruction concerning what must be disclosed in accounting policies footnotes to make more understandable the effects of derivatives on the statements of financial position, cash flows, and results of operations; and it does not address disclosure of accounting policies for derivative commodity instruments. Thus, to facilitate a more informed assessment of the effects of derivatives on financial statements, the amendments make explicit the items to be disclosed in the accounting policies footnotes for derivative financial instruments and derivative commodity instruments. At this time, the SEC was still very hopeful that the FASB would come up with a more effective answer to the *accounting* problem as they attempted to deal with the disclosure problem. Possibly their faith will be justified by results from FASB 133.

Disclosure Rule in Regulation S-X

The SEC's amendments to Regulation S-X require enhanced descriptions in the footnotes to the financial statements of accounting policies for derivative financial instruments and derivative commodity instruments. These disclosures are required unless the registrant's derivative activities are not material. The materiality of derivatives' activities is to be measured by the fair values of derivative financial instruments and derivative commodity instruments at the end of each reporting period, and the fair value of those instruments during each reporting period.

The amendments pertaining to accounting policies add a new paragraph to Regulation S-X to require disclosure in the footnotes to the financial statements relating:

1. Each method used to account for derivatives.
2. Types of derivatives accounted for under each method.
3. The criteria required to be met for each accounting method used (e.g., the manner in which risk reduction, correlation, designation, and/or effectiveness tests are applied).

4. The accounting method used if the specified criteria are not met.
5. The accounting for the termination of derivatives designated as hedges or used to affect directly or indirectly the terms, fair values, or cash flows of a designated item.
6. The accounting for derivatives if the designated item matures, or is sold, extinguished, terminated, or, if related to an anticipated transaction, is no longer likely to occur.
7. Where and when derivatives and their related gains and losses are reported in the statements of financial position, cash flows, and results of operations.

The amendments require registrants to distinguish between accounting policies used for derivatives entered into for trading purposes, and those that are entered into for purposes other than trading.

Disclosure of accounting policies for derivatives are required unless the registrant's derivative activities are not material. The materiality of derivatives activities is to be measured by the fair values of derivative financial instruments and derivative commodity instruments at the end of each reporting period, and the fair value of those instruments during each reporting period. In essence, the amendments clarified the application of the accounting policy disclosure requirements that had been set forth in FASB 119 for derivative financial instruments. They also extended those requirements to the disclosure of accounting policies for derivative commodity instruments.

Disclosure of Quantitative and Qualitative Information About Market Risk in Regulation S-K and Elsewhere

The amendments create a new item in Regulation S-K, requiring disclosure outside the financial statements of *quantitative* and *qualitative* information about derivative financial instruments, other financial instruments, and derivative commodity instruments. If any of the following items are material, these disclosures are required:

1. The fair values of market risk sensitive instruments outstanding at the end of the current reporting period.
2. The potential loss in future earnings, fair values, or cash flows of market risk sensitive instruments from reasonably possible market movements.

In complying with the proposed amendments requiring disclosure of quantitative information about market risk, registrants would be permitted to select any one of the three disclosure alternatives listed above as well as the necessary qualitative information. However, it must be remembered that market risk is inherent in *both derivative and nonderivative* instruments, including:

1. Other financial instruments, comprised of nonderivative financial instruments such as investments, loans, structured notes, mortgage-backed securities, indexed instruments, interest-only and principal-only obligations, deposits, and other debt obligations.
2. Derivative financial instruments—futures, forwards, swaps, options, and other financial instruments with similar characteristics.
3. Derivative commodity instruments that are reasonably possible to be settled in cash or with another financial instrument including commodity futures, commodity forwards, commodity swaps, commodity options, and other commodity instruments with similar characteristics, to the extent such instruments are not derivative financial instruments.

Generally accepted accounting principles (GAAP) and SEC rules require disclosure of certain *quantitative* information about some of these derivative financial instruments. For example, registrants are currently required to disclose notional amounts of derivative financial instruments and the nature and terms of debt obligations. However, this information is often abbreviated, is presented piecemeal in different parts of the financial statements, and does not apply to all market risk sensitive instruments. Thus, investors often are unable to determine whether, if, or how particular financial and commodity instruments actually affect a registrant's net market risk exposure. FASB 119 encouraged, but did not require, disclosure of quantitative information about the overall market risk inherent in derivative financial instruments and other instruments subject to market risk. Therefore, implementation of this portion of the amendments is spelled out in detail for both quantitative and qualitative disclosure.

General Considerations on Quantitative Disclosure

In addition to selecting and using one of the three alternative quantitative market risk disclosure methods, registrants are required to discuss material limitations that could cause that information not to reflect the overall market risk of the entity. This discussion necessarily includes descriptions of each limitation, and if applicable, the instruments' features that are not reflected fully within the selected quantitative market risk disclosure alternative.

Registrants are also required to summarize information for the preceding fiscal year, and discuss the reasons for any material changes in quantitative information about market risk when compared to the information reported in the previous period. Provision is made for companies to change their method of presentation of the quantitative information from one to another of the three alternatives. However, if they do change, they should explain why they changed, and summarize comparable information under the new method for the year preceding the year of the change.

Qualitative Information About Market Risk

A *qualitative* discussion of a registrant's market risk exposures, and how those exposures are managed, is important to an understanding of a registrant's market risk. Such qualitative disclosures help place market risk management activities in the context of the business and, therefore, are a useful complement to quantitative information about market risk. FASB 119 required that certain qualitative disclosures be provided about market risk management activities associated with derivative financial instruments held or issued for purposes other than trading. In particular, it required disclosure of the entity's objectives for holding or issuing the derivative financial instruments, the context needed to understand those objectives, and its general strategies for achieving those objectives. In addition, Statement 119 required separate disclosures about derivative financial instruments used as hedges of anticipated transactions. As indicated above, these requirements applied only to certain derivatives held or issued for purposes other than trading.

In essence, the qualitative disclosure requirements created a new requirement in Regulation S-K, which expanded certain FASB 119 disclosures to:

1. Encompass derivative commodity instruments, other financial instruments, and derivative financial instruments entered into for trading purposes.
2. Require registrants to evaluate and describe material changes in their primary risk exposures, and material changes in how those exposures are managed.

In particular, the amendments require narrative disclosure outside the financial statements of:

1. A registrant's primary market risk exposures.
2. How those exposures are managed; e.g., a description of the objectives, general strategies, and instruments, if any, used to manage those exposures.

In preparing the qualitative disclosures about market risk, the Commission expects registrants to describe their primary market risk exposures as they exist at the end of the current reporting period, and how those risks currently are being managed. Registrants also are asked to describe material changes in their primary market risk exposures and material changes in how these risks are managed as compared to what was in effect during the most recent reporting period, and what is known or expected to be in effect in future reporting periods.

These qualitative disclosure requirements apply to derivative financial instruments, other financial instruments, and derivative commodity instruments. As in the case with respect to the quantitative disclosures about market risk, the qualitative disclosures are presented separately for market risk sensitive instruments that are entered into for trading purposes, and those that are entered into for purposes other than trading. In addition, qualitative information about market risk is presented separately for those instruments used to manage risks inherent in anticipated transactions.

Finally, to help make disclosures about market risk more comprehensive, as is the case with the quantitative disclosures, the Commission also is encouraging registrants to disclose qualitative information about market risk relating to other items, such as derivative commodity instruments not reasonably possible to be settled in cash or with another financial instrument, commodity position, cash flows from anticipated transactions, and operating cash flows from nonfinancial and noncommodity instruments, e.g., cash flows generated by manufacturing activities.

Chapter 11

Foreign Currency Translations and Derivative Disclosure

FASB Statement 52, *Foreign Currency Translation*

FASB 52 covers accounting for the translation of foreign currency statements and the gain and loss on foreign currency transactions. Foreign currency transactions and financial statements of foreign entities include branches, subsidiaries, partnerships and joint ventures, which are consolidated, combined, or reported under the equity method in financial statements prepared in accordance with U.S. generally accepted financial principles.

Why is translation necessary? It is not arithmetically possible to combine, add, or subtract measurements expressed in different currencies. It is necessary, therefore, to translate assets, liabilities, revenues, expenses, gains, and losses that are measured or denominated in a foreign currency.

Definitions

An understanding of this rather complex accounting rule can be aided by becoming familiar with the terms used in the Statement. The following list of definitions will enable the accountant to apply the accounting procedures and methods outlined below.

Attribute—For accounting purposes, the quantifiable element of an item.

Conversion—Exchanging one currency for another.

Currency Exchange Rate—The rate at which one unit of a currency can be exchanged or converted into another currency. For purposes of translation of financial statements, the current exchange rate is the rate at the end of the

211

period covered by the financial statements, or the dates of recognition in the statements for revenues, expenses, gains and losses.

Currency Swap—An exchange between enterprises of the currencies of two different countries with a binding commitment to reverse the exchange of the two currencies at the same rate of exchange on a specified future date.

Current Rate Method—All assets and liabilities are translated at the exchange rate in effect on the balance sheet date. Capital accounts are translated at *historical exchange rates*.

Discount or Premium on a Forward Contract—The foreign currency amount of a contract multiplied by the difference between the contracted forward rate and the spot rate at the date of inception of the contract.

Economic Environment—The nature of the business climate in which an entity *primarily* generates and expends cash.

Entity—In this instance, a party to a transaction which produces a monetary asset or liability denominated in a currency other than its functional currency.

Exchange Rate—The ratio between a unit of one currency and the amount of another currency for which that unit can be exchanged at a particular time. The appropriate exchange rate for the translation of income statement accounts is the rate for the date on which those elements are recognized during the period.

Foreign Currency—A currency other than the functional currency of the entity being referred to. For example, the dollar could be a foreign currency for a foreign entity. Composites of currencies, such as the Special Drawing Rights (SDRs), used to set prices or denominate amounts of loans, etc., have the characteristics of foreign currency for purposes of applying Statement 52.

Foreign Currency Transaction—A transaction in which the terms are denominated in a currency other than an entity's functional currency. Foreign currency transactions arise when an enterprise buys or sells goods or services on credit at prices which are denominated in foreign currency; when an entity borrows or lends funds and the amounts payable or receivable are denominated in foreign currency; acquires or disposes of assets, or incurs or settles liabilities denominated in a foreign currency.

Foreign Currency Translation—Amounts that are expressed in the reporting currency of an enterprise that are denominated in a foreign currency. An example is the translation of the financial statements of a U.S. company from the foreign currency to U.S. dollars.

In the translation of balance sheets, the assets and liabilities are translated at the *current exchange rate*, e.g., rate at the balance sheet date. Income statement items are translated at the *weighted-average exchange rate* for the year.

There are two steps in translating the foreign country's financial statements into U.S. reporting requirements:

1. Conform the foreign country's financial statements to GAAP.
2. Convert the foreign currency into U.S. dollars, the reporting currency.

Foreign Entity—An operation (subsidiary, division, branch, joint venture, etc.) whose financial statements are prepared in a currency other than the currency of the reporting enterprise. The financial statements are combined and accounted for on the equity basis in the financial statements of the reporting enterprise.

Foreign Exchange Contract—An agreement to exchange, at a specified future date, currencies of different countries at a specified rate, which is the *forward rate.*

Functional Currency—The currency of the primary economic environment in which an entity operates; that is, the currency of the environment in which an entity primarily generates and expends cash.

Hedging—An effort by management to minimize the effect of exchange rate fluctuations on reported income, either directly by entering into an exchange contract to buy or sell one currency for another, or indirectly by managing exposed net assets or liabilities' positions by borrowing or billing in dollars rather than the local currency. An agreement to exchange different currencies at a specified future date and at a specified rate is referred to as *the forward rate.*

Highly Inflationary Economy—Economies of countries in which the *cumulative* local inflation rate over a three-year period exceeds approximately 100 per cent, or more.

Historical Exchange Rate—A rate, other than the current or a forward rate, at which a foreign transaction took place.

Inflation—Not defined by specific reference to a commonly quoted economic index. Management can select an appropriate method for measuring inflation. An annual inflation rate of about 20% for three consecutive years would result in a cumulative rate of about 100%.

Intercompany Balance—The foreign currency transactions of the parent, the subsidiary, or both. An intercompany account denominated in the local foreign currency is a foreign currency transaction of the parent. An intercompany account denominated in dollars is a foreign currency transaction of a foreign entity whose functional currency is a currency *other than* the U.S. dollar.

Local Currency—The currency of a particular country.

Measurement—Measurement is the process of measuring transactions denominated in a unit of currency (e.g., purchases payable in British pounds).

Remeasurement—Measurement of the functional currency financial statement amounts in other than the currency in which the transactions are denominated.

Reporting Currency—The currency used by an enterprise in the preparation of its financial statements.

Reporting Enterprise—An entity or group whose financial statements are being referenced. In Statement 52, those financial statements reflect a) the financial statements of one or more foreign operations by combination, consolidation, or equity accounting; b) foreign currency transactions; c) both a) and b).

Self-Contained Operations—Operations which are integrated with the local economic environment, and other operations which are primarily a direct or integral component or extension of a parent company's operations.

Speculative Contracts—A contract that is intended to produce an investment gain (not to hedge a foreign currency exposure).

Spot Rate—An exchange for *immediate delivery* of the currencies exchanged.

Transaction Date—The date at which a transaction, such as a purchase of merchandise or services, is recorded in accounting records in conformity with GAAP. A long-term commitment may have more than one transaction date; for example, the due date of each progress payment under a construction contract is an *anticipated transaction date* credited to shareholders' equity.

Transaction Gain or Loss—Gains or losses from a change in exchange rates between the functional currency and the currency in which a foreign transaction is denominated.

Translation Adjustment—Translation adjustments translate financial statements from the entity's functional currency into the reporting currency. The amount necessary to balance the financial statements after completing the translation process. The amount is charged or credited to shareholder's equity.

Unit of Measure—The currency in which assets, liabilities, revenues, expenses, gains and losses are measured.

Weighted Average Rates—Determined on a monthly basis by an arithmetic average of daily closing rates, and on a quarterly and an annual basis by an arithmetic average of average monthly rates.

Discussion of FASB Statement 52

Statement 52 applies to the financial reports of most companies with foreign operations. The essential requirements of the Statements are:

1. Transaction adjustments arising from consolidating a foreign operation which do not affect cash flows are *not* included in net income. Adjustments should be disclosed separately and accumulated in a separate classification of the equity section of the balance sheet.

2. Exchange rate changes on a foreign operation which directly affect the parent's cash flows must be included in net income.

3. Hedges of foreign exchange risks are accounted for as hedges without regard to their form.

4. Transaction gains and losses result from exchange rate changes on transactions denominated in currencies other than the functional currency.

5. The balance sheet translation uses the exchange rate prevailing as of the date of the balance sheet.

6. The exchange rate used for revenues, expenses, gains and losses is the rate on the date those items are recognized.

7. Upon sale (or liquidation) of an investment in a foreign entity, the amount accumulated in the equity component is removed and reported as a gain (or loss) on the disposal of the entity.

8. Intercompany transactions of a long-term investment nature are not included in net income.

9. Financial statements for fiscal years before the effective date of this Statement may be restated. If restatements are provided, they must conform to requirements of the Statement.

10. The financial statements of a foreign entity in a highly inflationary economy must be remeasured as if the functional currency were the reporting currency. A "highly inflationary economy" is defined in the Statement to be an economy that has had a cumulative inflation rate of 100%, or more, over a three-year period.

11. If material change in an exchange rate has occurred between year-end and the audit report date, the change should be reported as a subsequent event.

Background. The rapid expansion of international business activities of U.S. companies and dramatic changes in the world monetary system created the need to reconsider the accounting and reporting for foreign currency translation. In considering this topic, the FASB issued FASB Statement 52, which related to the following four areas:

1. Foreign currency transactions including buying or selling on credit goods or services whose prices are denominated in a foreign currency; i.e., currency other than the currency of the reporting entity's country.

2. Being a party to an unperformed foreign exchange contract.

3. Borrowing or lending funds denominated in a foreign currency.

4. For other reasons, acquiring assets or incurring liabilities denominated in foreign currency.

Statement 52 also applies to a foreign enterprise which reports in its currency in conformity with U.S. generally accepted accounting principles. For example, a French subsidiary of a U.S. parent should translate the foreign currency financial statements of its Italian subsidiary in accordance with Statement 52. The objective of translation is to measure and express in dollars, and in conformity with U.S. generally accepted accounting principles, the assets, liabilities, revenues, or expenses that are measured or denominated in foreign currency. In achieving this objective, translation should remeasure these amounts in dollars without changing accounting principles. For example, if an asset was originally measured in a foreign currency under the historical cost concept, translation should remeasure the carrying amount of the asset in dollars at historical cost, not replacement cost or market value.

The most common foreign currency transactions result from the import or export of goods or services, foreign borrowing or lending, and forward exchange contracts. Import or export transactions can be viewed as being composed of two elements—a sale or purchase and the settlement of the related receivable or payable. Changes in the exchange rate, which occur between the time of sale or purchase and the settlement of the receivable or payable, should not affect the measurement of revenues from exports or the cost of imported goods or services.

Foreign currency statements should be translated based on the exchange rate at the end of the reporting year. Translation gains and losses are presented in the stockholders' equity section. Also important is the accounting treatment of gains and losses resulting from transactions denominated in a foreign currency. These are shown in the current year's income statement.

Because of the proliferation of multinational companies, expanding international trade, business involvement with foreign subsidiaries, and joint ventures, FASB 52 was established, in effect, by popular demand. The stated aims of Statement 52 are to (a) provide information that is generally compatible with the expected effects of a rate change on an enterprise's cash flows and equity, and (b) reflect in consolidated statements the financial results and relationships of the individual consolidated entities as measured in their functional currencies, whether the U.S. dollar or a specified foreign currency, in conformity with U.S. generally accepted accounting principles.

The method adopted to achieve these aims is termed the *functional currency approach* which is the currency of the primary economic environment in which the entity carries on its business; in substance, where it generates and expends cash. The Statement permits a multiple measurement basis in consolidated financial statements (depending upon the country in which the subsidiary operates) because business enterprises made up of a multinational enterprise operate and generate cash flows in diverse economic environments, each with its own functional currency. When an enterprise operates in several of these environments, the results of business transactions are measured in the functional currency of the particular environment. "Measured in the functional currency" has the specific meaning that gains and losses comprising income are determined only in relation to accounts denominated in the functional currency.

Mechanically, the functional currency approach calls for eventual translation of all functional currency assets and liabilities into dollars at the current exchange rate. Under Statement 52, use of the current rate for all accounts resolves both the economically compatible results and operating margins distortions. In the past, these distortions came about with the translation of non-monetary accounts at historical rates. The volatility of earnings distortions is alleviated by recording the translation adjustments directly into shareholders' equity.

The functional currency approach presumes the following:

1. Many business enterprises operate and generate cash flows in a number of different countries (different economic environments).
2. Each of these operations can usually be identified as operating in a single economic environment: the local environment or the parent company's environment. The currency of the principal economic environment becomes the functional currency for those operations.
3. The enterprise may be committed to a long-term position in a specific economic environment and have no plans to liquidate that position in the foreseeable future.

Because measurements are made in multiple functional currencies, decisions relating to the choice of the functional currency of a specific foreign operation will in all likelihood have a significant effect upon reported income. Even though the management of the business enterprise is entitled to a degree of latitude in its weighing of specific facts, the thinking behind adoption of this Statement is that the functional currency is to be determined based on the true nature of the enterprise and not upon some arbitrary selection which management feels might be of particular advantage to the reporting entity.

Determining the functional currency. Multinational companies are involved with foreign business interests either through transactions or investments in foreign entities operating in a number of different economic environments. Each of these endeavors may be associated with one primary economic environment whose currency then becomes the functional currency for that operation. On the other hand, in a foreign country where the economic and/or political environment is so unstable that a highly inflationary economy is likely, it may be deemed wise to carry on the enterprise with the dollar as the functional currency. If the operations in situations of this nature are remeasured on a dollar basis, further erosion of nonmonetary accounts may be avoided.

When there is a reasonably stable economic situation, the national environment of each operation should be considered as the primary economic environment of the particular operation since national sovereignty is a primary consideration in relation to currency control.

Industry practice, on the other hand, may in some instances be instrumental in the determination of a primary economic environment and functional currency. If it is an industry-wide practice that pricing or other transaction attributes are calculated in a specific currency, such as prices set in dollars on a worldwide basis, that fact may be more of a determinant than local currency considerations.

The actual decisions in determining a functional currency depend to a large extent upon the operating policy adopted by the reporting company. Two broad classes of foreign operations are to be considered:

1. Those in which a foreign currency is the functional currency. This designation will have been made after receiving the facts and determining that this particular aspect of foreign business operations is largely autonomous and confined to a specific foreign economic environment. That is, ordinary operations are not dependent upon the economic environment of the parent company's functional currency, nor does the foreign operation primarily generate or expend the parent's functional currency.

2. When the workaday business of the foreign operation is deemed to be in actuality just an extension of the parent company's operation and dependent upon the economic environment of the parent company, the dollar may be designated as the functional currency. In substance, most transactions can reasonably be in dollars, thus obviating the need for foreign currency translation.

One of the objectives of Statement 52 is to provide information that is generally compatible with the expected economic effects of a rate change on an enterprise's cash flow and equity in a readily understood manner. If a foreign operation's policy is to convert available funds into dollars for current or nearterm distribution to the parent, selection of a dollar functional currency may be expedient.

Therefore, reporting for investments expected to be of short-term duration, such as construction or development joint ventures, the dollar should probably be designated the functional currency. If the nature of an investment changes over a period of time, future redetermination of the appropriate functional currency may become necessary. Such redetermination is permissible only when, in actual fact, significant changes in economic facts and/or circumstances have occurred. The operative functional currency cannot be redetermined merely because management has "changed its collective mind." It becomes evident that functional currency determination should be carefully considered with the decision weighted in favor of the long-term picture rather than short-term expectations.

In the event that redetermination is necessary, three procedures should be kept in mind:

1. When the functional currency has been changed, Statement 52 provides that the prior year's financial statement need not be restated for a change in functional currency.
2. When the functional currency change is from the local currency to the dollar, historical costs and exchange rates are to be determined from translated dollar amounts immediately prior to the change.
3. When the functional currency change is from the dollar to the local currency, nonmonetary assets are to be translated at current exchange rates, charging the initial translation adjustment to equity similar to that produced when Statement 52 was adopted.

Translation.   Translation is the process of converting financial statements expressed in one unit of currency to a different unit of currency (the reporting currency). In short, translation as used in Statement 52 is the restatement into the reporting currency (the U.S. dollar) of any/all foreign currency financial statements utilized in preparing the consolidated financial statements of the U.S. parent company.

Thus, the focus for the preparation and subsequent translation of the financial statements of individual components of an organization is, as previously stated, to:

1. Provide information that is generally compatible with the expected economic effects of a rate change on the enterprise's cash flows and equity, and
2. Reflect in consolidated statements the financial results and relationships of the individual consolidated entities as measured in their functional currencies in conformity with U.S. generally accepted accounting principles.

Measurement is the process of stating the monetary value of transactions denominated in a particular unit of currency (e.g., purchases payable in British pounds). These transactions may also be figured in a unit of currency other than that in which they are denominated. This process then becomes remeasurement and is accomplished by assuming that an exchange of currencies will occur at the exchange rate in effect at the time of the remeasurement. As is evident, should the exchange rate fluctuate between the date of the original transaction and the date of the exchange, a foreign exchange gain or loss will result. The gains or losses so recorded vary little from other trading activities and are, therefore, included in income.

It is important to note that while translations were formerly based on the premise that financial statements of a U.S. enterprise should be measured in a single unit of currency—the U.S. dollar—translation was under FASB 80, *Accounting for Futures Contracts*, a one-step process that included both remeasurement and reporting in dollars. In the newer context of the functional approach, multiple units of measure are permitted so that remeasurement is required only when (1) the accounts of an entity are maintained in a currency other than its own functional currency, or (2) an enterprise is invoiced in a transaction which produces a monetary asset or liability not denominated in its functional currency.

The subsequent translation to dollars under FASB 52 is the second step of a two-step process necessary to prepare U.S. dollar financial statements.

Foreign currency transactions. Foreign currency transactions are those denominated in a currency other than the entity's functional currency. These transactions include:

1. Buying or selling goods priced in a currency other than the entity's functional currency.
2. Borrowing or lending funds (including intercompany balances) denominated in a different currency.
3. Engaging in an unperformed forward exchange contract.

As becomes evident, companies with foreign subsidiaries can readily become engaged in foreign currency transactions which must be considered when financial statements are prepared. But, in addition, companies which have no foreign branches may also in the everyday course of business become involved in foreign currency transactions.

Regardless of whether the company is entirely domestic-based or not at the transaction date, each resulting asset, liability, revenue, expense, gain, or loss not already denominated in the entity's functional currency must be so measured and recorded. At the close of each subsequent accounting period, all unsettled monetary balances are to be remeasured using the exchange rates in effect on the balance-sheet date. Gains and losses from remeasuring or settling foreign currency transactions are accounted for as current income.

FASB STATEMENT 107, *DISCLOSURE ABOUT FAIR VALUE OF FINANCIAL INSTRUMENTS*

Statement 107, *Disclosure About Fair Value of Financial Instruments*, defines fair value to mean the amount at which a financial instrument could be exchanged in a current transaction between willing parties, other than a forced or liquidation sale.

The rule is a broad approach to help issuers of financial statements understand what is required of them in meeting the newer, improved disclosure requirements, as well as to help minimize the costs of providing that information. Of course, the reasoning behind the stipulations in this Statement is to ensure a clearer, better defined picture of the fair value of financial instruments than has been provided in the past. This truer picture of an entity's financial activities should be of value to creditors, current and potential investors, and others in making informed decisions concerning granting credit to, investing in, or investigating more thoroughly, a particular entity.

Other impetus for enactment of this rule comes from a desire to provide another useful indicator of the solvency of a financial institution. A recent report issued by the U.S. Treasury Department has suggested that further market value information about various financial institutions could be of aid in regulatory supervision.

Since in many instances generally accepted accounting principles already necessitate disclosure, the term *fair value* use in FASB 107 in no way supersedes or modifies the set of figures obtained using *current value, mark-to-market,* or simply *market value*. It is simply an attempt to get more accurate information about financial instruments—both their assets and liabilities whether on or off the balance sheet—available for easy access.

For the purposes of this Statement, a financial instrument is cash, an ownership interest in an entity, or a contract that imposes on one entity a contractual obligation to deliver cash or another financial instrument to a second entity, or to exchange other financial instruments on potentially unfavorable terms with the second entity. The agreement gives the second entity a contractual right to receive cash or another financial instrument from the first entity, or to exchange other financial instruments on potentially favorable terms with the first entity.

If available, open-market prices are the best and easiest to obtain a measure of fair value of financial instruments. If quoted market prices or other established values are not available, estimates of fair value can be based on the quoted market price of a financial instrument with similar characteristics. Estimates can also be based on valuation techniques, such as the present value of estimated future cash flows using a discount rate commensurate with the risks involved, or using option pricing models. If it is not practicable to estimate the fair value of a particular financial instrument, reasons why it is not practicable must be thoroughly explained.

In all instances, descriptive material must be included detailing the method(s) and the basis for assumptions utilized in arriving at a stated fair value or in the failure to do so. In any event, failure to do so is not to be considered final. A continuing effort to arrive at a practicable (without incurring excessive cost) fair value should be carried out. Because the Board realizes that the cost of attempting to compute fair value in some instances would become excessive, certain types of financial instruments have been excepted from the requirements of Statement 107. These are:

1. Extinguished debt and assets held in trust in connection with a defeasance of that debt.
2. Insurance contracts, other than financial guarantees and investment contracts.
3. Lease contracts as defined in FASB Statement 13.
4. Warrant obligations and rights.
5. Unconditional purchase obligations.
6. Investments accounted for under the equity method.
7. Minority interests in consolidated subsidiaries.
8. Equity investments in consolidated subsidiaries.
9. Equity instruments issued by the entity and classified in stockholders' equity in the statement of financial position.
10. Obligations of employers and plans for pension benefits, other postretirement benefits including health care and life insurance benefits, employee stock option, and stock purchase plans.

FASB STATEMENT 133, ACCOUNTING FOR DERIVATIVE INSTRUMENTS AND HEDGING ACTIVITIES

The derivatives standard was adopted by a unanimous vote on June 1, 1998, after more than 10 years of painstaking effort by the FASB. Unquestionably, this Standard will be one of the most far-reaching accounting standards yet produced. It will also be the one that has raised the most hue and cry in every segment of the economy.

The FASB repeatedly made it clear that they would not back down on certain requirements, regardless of "special interest" objections. The Board pointed out that trillions of dollars' worth of derivative transactions are occurring in the marketplace and they believe "investors have little, if any, information about them." They believe that the new Standard will give the investor further information about an entity so that they can make more knowledgeable decisions.

The U.S. Senate, the House of Representatives, the Federal Reserve, the American Bankers Association, and assorted others entered the fray over derivatives with very little success. On the other hand, the Board had modified some of the earlier positions in response to user requests, as in the Chicago Board of Trade's concern about some of the provisions relating to hedging.

One of the most important concessions was to the projected timing of the effective date. The Standard was to have become effective June 15, 1999. This meant that for calendar-year companies it would be effective January 1, 2000. Many segments had complained that the extra time and money being expended on trying to solve Y2K problems, coping with a new derivatives Standard of such proposed magnitude by December 15, 1998, was expecting too much.

FASB Statement 137, *Accounting for Derivative Instruments and Hedging Activities—Deferral of the Effective Date of FASB Statement 133—* delayed for a year the required application of FASB 133 to June 15, 2000. However, entities that had already issued interim or annual financial statements according to the requirements of Statement 133 could not return to their previous method of accounting for derivatives or hedging activities.

FASB 137 does not change any of the requirements; it merely postpones the inevitable to give the issuers additional time to cope with Y2K considerations and digest the ramifications of the new requirements.

The FASB has also appointed a special task force to aid with implementation issues on derivatives. Among the comments received from users were many related to the complicated provisions of the proposed Standard— admittedly covering very complicated financial instruments. The Board agreed with the constituents that it should be prepared to provide assistance and guidance on a timely basis: thus, the task force. It will help in identifying implementation issues and recommending conclusions to the Board.

ED Modified Somewhat, Not Substantially

FASB Standard 133 retained most of the provisions that were issued in the ED of September, 1997. All derivatives are to be reported as assets or liabilities in financial statements at their fair value. New approaches to hedge accounting are outlined. As a result, more detailed, useful disclosures of derivatives, hedging activities, and related accounting practices should furnish the investor, creditor, and user with a better picture of an entity's true financial condition. In effect, the new derivative accounting practices should then reveal the economic realities of derivative transactions to the financial statement reader.

The requirements to record all derivatives on the face of the balance sheet at fair value, and some of the new hedge accounting requirements, may very well increase the assets reported by some companies and change their return on assets. On the other hand, the result may be an increase of the liabilities reported by some companies, resulting in a change in their liabilities-to-owners' equity ratio.

Hedge Accounting

Under certain conditions, the new derivative Standard will permit management to designate a derivative as one of the following hedges—a fair value, cash flow, or foreign exchange hedge.

1. A *fair value hedge* is a hedge of the exposure to changes in the fair value of an asset or liability recognized on the balance sheet or of a firm commitment. The exposure to change must be attributable to a specific risk.

   For this type of hedge, the gain or loss is recognized in current income. This amount is offset by the gain or loss in the fair value of the hedged item. The carrying amount is adjusted to reflect the fair value gain or loss. If the hedge is working as it is intended, the adjustment to the carrying amount of the hedged item recognized in income will equal the offsetting gain or loss on the hedging derivative and there will be no net effect on earnings. If the hedge, on the other hand, is not operating as it should, earnings will be affected to the extent that the hedge is ineffective. Assessment of effectiveness is required.

2. A *cash flow hedge* is a hedge of an exposure to variability in the cash flows of an asset or liability recognized on the balance sheet, or of a forecasted transaction, that is attributable to a particular risk. Forecasted transactions include forecasted sales and purchases for which no firm commitment has been made, and interest payments on variable rate debt reported as a liability.

   The effective part of a gain or loss on a derivative designated as a cash flow hedge is initially recognized in owners' equity as part of other comprehensive income and then in earnings in the same period in which the hedged forecasted transaction affects earnings. The ineffective aspect of the gain or loss is recognized in earnings.

3. A *foreign currency exposure hedge* is a hedge of the foreign currency exposure of:

   a. A firm commitment which is a foreign currency fair value hedge.

b. An available-for-sale debt security, a foreign currency fair value hedge.

c. A foreign currency-denominated forecasted transaction which is a foreign currency cash flow hedge.

d. A net investment in a foreign operation.

The gain or loss on a derivative or nonderivative financial instrument designated as a foreign currency hedge is accounted for depending upon its designations as a fair value or cash flow hedge in the same way as outlined above for those types of hedges.

Thus, the gain or loss on a derivative financial instrument designated and qualifying as a foreign currency hedging instrument is to be accounted for as follows:

a. The gain or loss on the hedging instrument in a hedge of a firm commitment is to be recognized in current earnings along with the loss or gain on the hedged firm commitment.

b. The gain or loss on the hedging derivative in a hedge of an available-for-sale security is to be recognized in current earnings along with the loss or gain on the hedged available-for-sale security.

c. In general, the effective aspect of the gain or loss on the hedging instrument in a hedge of a foreign-currency denominated forecasted transaction is to be reported as a component of other comprehensive income, outside of earnings. It is to be recognized in earnings in the same period or periods during which the hedged forecasted transaction affects earnings. The ineffective aspect of the gain or loss on the hedging instrument and any other remaining gain or loss on the hedging instrument is to be recognized in current earnings.

d. The foreign currency transaction gain or loss on the hedging instrument in a hedge of a net investment in a foreign operation is to be reported in other comprehensive income as part of the cumulative translation adjustment. The remainder of the gain or loss on the hedging instrument is to be recognized in current earnings.

Derivatives

A derivative is a financial instrument or other contract with several distinguishing characteristics:

1. It has one or more *underlyings* and one or more *notional amounts* or payment provisions or both. Those terms determine the amount of the settlement or settlements, and in some cases, whether or not a settlement is required.

2. It requires no initial net investment or one that is smaller than would be required for other types of contracts expected to have a similar response to changes in market factors.

3. The terms require or permit net settlement; it can readily be settled net by a means outside the contract, or it provides for delivery of an asset that puts the recipient in a position not substantially different from net settlement.

An "underlying" may be one of a number of variables that is applied to the notional amount to determine the cash flows or other exchanges required by the contract—a commodity price, a per-share price, an interest rate, a foreign exchange rate, or some other variable.

"Notional amount" refers to an amount of money, a number of shares, a number of bushels, pounds, or whatever can be dreamed up to create a more exotic derivative. A contract with these characteristics is a derivative instrument according to the Statement if, by the terms at its inception or upon the occurrence of a specified event, the entire contract meets the conditions delineated above.

FASB 133 specifically states that the following transactions do not constitute derivatives for the purpose of this Statement:

1. Regular security trades.
2. Normal purchases and sales.
3. Contingent consideration from a business combination.
4. Traditional life insurance contracts.
5. Traditional property and casualty contracts.
6. Most financial guarantee contracts.

The new Statement also points out that some contracts may be accounted for as derivatives by the holder but not by the user. These would include:

1. Contracts that are both indexed to the entity's own stock and classified in stockholders' equity on their balance sheets.
2. Contracts issued in connection with stock-based compensation arrangements covered in FASB 123, *Accounting for Stock-Based Compensation.*

How FASB 133 Affects Other Accounting Literature

FASB 133 supersedes and amends several other Statements. It supersedes:

1. FASB 80, *Accounting for Futures Contracts.*
2. FASB 105, *Disclosure of Information About Financial Instruments with Off-Balance-Sheet Risk and Financial Instruments with Concentrations of Credit Risk.*
3. FASB 119, *Disclosure About Derivative Financial Instruments and Fair Value of Financial Instruments.*

It amends:

1. FASB 52, *Foreign Currency Translation,* to permit special accounting for a hedge of a foreign currency forecasted transaction with a derivative.
2. FASB 107, *Disclosures About Fair Value of Financial Instruments,* to include in Statement 107 the disclosure provisions about concentrations of credit risk from FASB 105.

FASB 133 also nullifies or modifies the consensuses reached in a number of issued addressed by the Emerging Issues Task Force.

Application to Not-for-Profit Organizations

Since the Statement applies to all entities, not-for-profit organizations should recognize the change in fair value of all derivatives as a change in net assets in the period of change. In a fair value hedge, the changes in the fair value of the hedged item attributable to the risk being hedged also are recognized.

However, because of the format of their statement of financial performance, not-for-profit organizations may *not* apply special hedge accounting for derivatives used to hedge forecasted transactions. In addition, FASB 133 does not consider how a not-for-profit organization should determine the components of an operating measure if one is presented.

Another Amendment

The Financial Accounting Standards Board issued Statement 138, *Accounting for Certain Derivative Instruments and Certain Hedging Activities—an Amendment of FASB Statement 133* in June, 2000. The Statement addresses a limited number of issues causing implementation difficulties for a large number of entities getting ready to apply Statement 133.

The Board points out that FASB 133, *Accounting for Derivative Instruments and Hedging Activities,* establishes accounting and reporting standards for derivative instruments, including certain derivative instruments embedded in other contracts, (collectively referred to as derivatives) and for hedging activities. Because of difficulties in application and interpretations, the Statement amends FASB 133 so that:

1. The normal purchases and normal sales exception is expanded.
2. The specific risks that can be identified as the hedged risk are redefined so that in a hedge of interest rate risk, the risk of changes in a benchmark interest rate would be the hedged risk.
3. Recognized foreign-currency-denominated debt instruments may be the hedged item in fair value hedges or cash flow hedges.
4. Intercompany derivatives may be designated as the hedging instruments in cash flow hedges of foreign currency risk in the consolidated financial statements even if those intercompany derivatives are offset by unrelated third-party contracts on a net basis.

Certain Board decisions based on recommendations of the Derivatives Implementation Group (DIG) to clarify Statement 133 also have been incorporated in the Statement. Statement 138 is the result of the Board's decision, after listening to its constituents, to address a limited number of issues using the following criteria:

1. Implementation difficulties would be eased for a large number of entities.
2. There would be no conflict with or modifications to the basic model of Statement 133.
3. There would be no delay in the effective date of Statement 133.

Chapter 12

Governmental Fund Accounting

DIFFERENCES BETWEEN GOVERNMENTAL AND COMMERCIAL ACCOUNTING

While both types of entities use double-entry bookkeeping procedures and either cash or accrual methods, and both prepare balance sheets and operating statements, there are many differences between commercial and governmental systems.

Governmental accounting is associated with: (1) an absence of a profit; (2) compliance with statutory and/or legal requirements; (3) a fundamental difference in the treatment of net worth. Commercial accounting provides accounting for preferred and common stock and retained earnings, with a paid-in capital account where appropriate. Governmental accounting treats "net worth" under account classifications *Reserve for Encumbrances or Unappropriated Surplus*; (4) characteristically, government accounts will include a *Reserve for Contingencies* account since the projected (budgeted) reserve may not materialize as the accounting year progresses.

As will be evident in the next chapter, "New Governmental Accounting," accounting for state and local governments is in a transitional stage. Over the next several years, these entities will be adding more "business-like" requirements to their financial reporting. At the same time, the government accountant will still need to draw upon his or her knowledge of fund accounting.

The new Government Accounting Board Statement 34, *Basic Financial Statements—and Management's Discussion and Analysis—for State and Local*

Governments establishes new financial reporting requirements for state and local governments. However, these entities are to continue to present financial statements that provide fund information. The focus of these fund statements has been sharpened to require governments to report information about their major funds, including the general fund. In current annual reports, fund information is reported in the aggregate by fund type. This has often made it difficult for users to assess accountability.

Fund statements will continue to measure and report the "operating results" of many funds by measuring cash on hand and other assets that can easily be converted to cash. These statements show the performance, in the short-term, of individual funds using the same measures that governments use when financing their current operations.

LEGAL PROVISIONS

In governmental accounting, legal provisions relate to budgeting and to the disposition of assets. The preparation and implementation of the projected budget and related accounting procedures are governed by certain legal provisions expressed specifically in legislation (statutory) or restrictions imposed by a nonlegislative (regulatory) authority. The accounting system must have built-in safeguards that expenditures will comply with both types of restrictions. Governmental accounting must also include revenue and expense data which facilitates the preparation of budgets for the future.

As will be seen, certain *funds* are considered less flexible in their accounting treatment. The least flexible type is the one created by a state constitution or by legislation, because the accountant must keep the books as determined by law. The most flexible is the type established by executive authority, since such authority can make changes in a fund without prior legislative approval.

In fund accounting *estimated and actual revenues* and *expenditures* are compared on an ongoing basis, e.g., reviewed by the governing bodies approving the initial budget and the appropriation for the fund. Comparisons reveal the extent to which the "actuals" are in line with the estimates (the budget) and will show significant deviations, if any, during the fiscal year of actual revenues and expenditures from the budgeted amounts.

Assets and liabilities incurred by a fund are similar to those in a commercial enterprise. Asset accounts, for example, will include cash, accounts receivable, etc., while liabilities will show accounts or vouchers payable, notes payable, bonds payable, etc.

A separate *general ledger* must be maintained for each fund related to the governmental entity's budget. Each general ledger has a self-balancing account that brings the revenue and appropriation accounts into balance at the end of the fiscal year.

As a general rule independent auditors will insist on the entity using an *accrual* system, unless the financial authorities for that specific fund can demonstrate that the financial reports would not *materially* differ if a cash accounting system is used.

Is Governmental Accounting Complex? No!

While fund accounting is perceived to be complicated, it is not any more difficult than commercial accounting. Why then is it thought to be complicated? The answer is for the same reason that we initially think any totally new and unfamiliar discipline appears difficult—the *terminology* is the culprit. It is well-settled that learning the terminology of a new discipline is 50% or more of the learning battle of anything new that one endeavors to learn. Governmental accounting terminology is indeed entirely different from commercial accounting terminology; it has a vocabulary that is totally unique to governmental accounting; no governmental accounting term can be found in any other system of accounting, whether commercial, industrial, or otherwise.

The first step, then, to acquire an understanding of fund accounting procedures is to review and become familiar with the terms. The following list of definitions will enable the user to easily apply the accounting methods for the various types of funds which are covered in the material following the definitions.

Terminology

Here is a listing of definitions applicable only to fund accounting:

Abatement. Cancellation of amounts levied or of charges made for services.

Accrued Assets. Assets arising from revenues earned but not yet due.

Accrued Expenses. Expenses resulting in liabilities which are either due or are not payable until some future time.

Accrued Revenues. Levies made or other revenue earned and not collected.

Allotment Ledger. A subsidiary ledger which contains an account for each allotment showing the amount allotted, expenditures, encumbrances, the net balance, and other related information.

Appropriation. An authorization granted by the legislative body to make expenditures and to incur obligations for specific purposes.

Appropriation Expenditure. An expenditure chargeable to an appropriation.

Appropriation Ledger. A subsidiary ledger containing an account with each appropriation.

Assessment. The process of making an official valuation of property for the purpose of taxation.

Authority Bonds. Bonds payable from the revenues of a specific public authority.

Betterment. An addition or change made in a fixed asset which prolongs its life or increases its efficiency.

Budget. A plan of financial operation embodying an estimate of proposed expenditures for a given period or purpose, and the proposed means of financing them.

Budgetary Accounts. The accounts necessary to reflect budget operations and condition, such as estimated revenues, appropriations, and encumbrances.

Capital Budget. An improvement program and the methods for the financing.

Clearing Account. An account used to accumulate total charges or credits for the purpose of distributing them among the accounts to which they are allocable, or for the purpose of transferring the net difference to the proper account.

Current Special Assessment. Assessments levied and due during the current fiscal period.

Current Taxes. Taxes levied and becoming due during the current fiscal period—from the time the amount of the tax levy is first established, to the date on which a penalty for nonpayment is attached.

Debt Limit. The maximum amount of gross or net debt legally permitted.

Debt Service Requirement. The amount of money necessary periodically to pay the interest on the outstanding debt and the principal of maturing bonded debt not payable from a sinking fund.

Deficit. The excess of the liabilities of a fund over its assets.

Delinquent Taxes. Taxes remaining unpaid on and after the date on which a penalty for nonpayment is attached.

Direct Debt. The debt which a governmental unit has incurred in its own name, or assumed through the annexation of territory.

Encumbrances. Obligations in the form of purchase orders, contracts, or salary commitments which are chargeable to an appropriation, and for which a part of the appropriation is reserved.

Endowment Fund. A fund whose principal must be maintained inviolate, but whose income may be expended.

Expendable Fund. A fund whose resources, including both principal and earnings, may be expended.

Expenditures. If the fund accounts are kept on the accrual basis, expenditures are the total charges incurred, whether paid or unpaid, including expenses, provision for retirement of debt not reported as a liability of the fund from which retired, and capital outlays.

Franchise. A special privilege granted by a government permitting the continuing use of public property.

Full Faith and Credit. A pledge of the general taxing body for the payment of obligations.

Fund Accounts. All accounts necessary to set forth the financial operations and financial condition of a fund.

Fund Group. A group of related funds.

Governmental Accounting. The preparation, reporting, and interpretation of accounts for governmental bodies.

Grant. A contribution by one governmental unit to another unit.

Gross Bonded Debt. The total amount of direct debt of a governmental unit, represented by outstanding bonds before deduction of sinking fund assets.

Indeterminate Appropriation. An appropriation which is not limited either to any definite period of time, or to any definite amount, or to both time and amount.

Inter-Fund Accounts. Accounts in which transactions between funds are reflected.

Inter-Fund Loans. Loans made by one fund to another fund.

Inter-Fund Transfers. Amounts transferred from one fund to another.

Judgment. An amount to be paid or collected by a governmental unit as the result of a court decision, including a condemnation award in payment for private property taken for public use.

Lapse. As applied to appropriations, this term denotes the automatic termination of an appropriation.

Levy. To impose taxes or special assessments.

Lump-Sum Appropriation. An appropriation made for a stated purpose, or for a named department, without specifying further the amounts that can be spent for specific activities or for particular expenditures.

Municipal. An adjective applying to any governmental unit below or subordinate to the state.

Municipal Corporation. A body or corporate politic established pursuant to state authorization, as evidenced by a charter.

Net Bonded Debt. Gross bonded debt less applicable cash or other assets.

Non-Expendable Fund. A fund the principal, and sometimes the earnings, of which may not be expended.

Non-Operating Income. Income of municipal utilities and other governmental enterprises of a business character, which is not derived from the operation of such enterprise.

Operating Expenses. As used in the accounts of municipal utilities and other governmental enterprises of a business character, the term means the costs necessary to the maintenance of the enterprise, or the rendering of services for which the enterprise is operated.

Operating Revenues. Revenues derived from the operation of municipal utilities or other governmental enterprises of a business character.

Operating Statement. A statement summarizing the financial operations of a municipality.

Ordinance. A bylaw of a municipality enacted by the governing body of the governmental entity.

Overlapping Debt. The proportionate share of the debts of local governmental units, located wholly or in part within the limits of the reporting government, which must be borne by property within such government.

Prepaid Taxes. The deposit of money with a governmental unit on condition that the amount deposited is to be applied against the tax liability of the taxpayer.

Proprietary Accounts. Accounts which show actual financial condition and operations such as actual assets, liabilities, reserves, surplus, revenues, and expenditures as distinguished from budgetary accounts.

Public Authority. A public agency created to perform a single function, which is financed from tolls or fees charged those using the facilities operated by the agency.

Public Trust Fund. A trust fund whose principal, earnings, or both, must be used for a public purpose.

Quasi-Municipal Corporation. An agency established by the state primarily for the purpose of helping the state to carry out its functions.

Refunding Bonds. Bonds issued to retire bonds already outstanding. The refunding bonds may be sold for cash and outstanding bonds redeemed in cash, or the refunding bonds may be exchanged with holders of outstanding bonds.

Related Funds. Funds of a similar character which are brought together for administrative and reporting purposes.

Reserve for Encumbrances. A reserve representing the segregation of surplus to provide for unliquidated encumbrances.

Revenue Bonds. Bonds the principal and interest on which are to be paid solely from earnings, usually the earnings of a municipally owned utility or other public service enterprise.

Revolving Fund. A fund provided to carry out a cycle of operations.

Special Assessment. A compulsory levy made by a local government against certain properties, to defray part or all of the cost of a specific improvement or service, which is presumed to be of general benefit to the public and of special benefit to the owners of such properties.

Special District Bonds. Bonds of a local taxing district, which has been organized for a special purpose—such as road, sewer, and other special districts—to render unique services to the public.

Suspense Account. An account which carries charges or credits temporarily pending the determination of the proper account or accounts to which they are to be posted.

Tax Anticipation Notes. Notes issued in anticipation of collection of taxes, usually retired only from tax collections as they come due.

Tax Levy. An ordinance or resolution by means of which taxes are levied.

Tax Liens. Claims which governmental units have upon properties until taxes levied against them have been paid.

Tax Rate. The amount of tax stated in terms of a unit of the tax base.

Trust Fund. A fund consisting of resources received and held by the governmental unit as trustee, to be expended or invested in accordance with the conditions of the trust.

Unencumbered Appropriation. An appropriation or allotment, or a part thereof, not yet expended or encumbered.

Utility Fund. A fund established to finance the construction, operation, and maintenance of municipally owned utilities.

Warrant. An order drawn by a legislative body, or an officer of a governmental unit, upon its treasurer, directing the treasurer to pay a specified amount to the person named, or to the bearer.

GOVERNMENTAL ACCOUNTING SYSTEMS

Governmental Accounting Standards Board (GASB)

The GASB was established in 1984, under the oversight of the Financial Accounting Foundation which, in turn, oversees the Financial Accounting

Standards Board (FASB). Before the establishment of the GASB, the reports of governmental entities were criticized by the accounting community because they could not be interpreted in a manner consistent with the financial reports of private business organizations. The primary purpose of the GASB is to develop standards of reporting for state and local government entities; its organizational and operational structure is similar to that of the FASB, and its objective is to make the combined general purpose financial reports of governmental entities as comparable as possible to those of private business.

As a general rule the GASB will promulgate standards that parallel GAAP. However, there are instances that require a governmental entity to comply with a state law or regulatory accounting requirement that is in non-compliance with GAAP. Such reports are classified as *Special Reports or Supplemental Schedules*, which are not a part of the general purpose statements. In these cases governmental units can publish two sets of statements, one in compliance with legal requirements and one in compliance with GAAP. (An example of this problem is that it is not uncommon for some governmental entities to be required by law to apply the cash basis of accounting.)

Governmental accounting systems are developed on a *fund basis*. A fund is defined as an independent fiscal and accounting entity with a self-balancing set of accounts recording cash and other resources together with all related liabilities, obligations, reserves, and equities that are segregated for the purpose of carrying on specific activities or attaining specified objectives in accordance with applicable regulations, restrictions, and other statutory and regulatory limitations.

In addition to each fund's transactions within the fund itself, each fund in a governmental unit can have financial transactions with other funds in the same entity. The financial statements must reflect interfund transactions which result from services rendered by one fund to another.

The accrual basis of accounting is recommended for matching revenues and expenditures during a designated period of time which refers specifically to the time when revenues and expenditures are recorded as such in the accounting records.

Governmental revenues should be classified by fund and source. Expenditures should be classified by fund, function, organization unit, activity, character, and principal classes of objectives in accordance with standard recognized classifications. Common terminology and classifications should be used consistently throughout (1) the budget; (2) the accounts; and (3) the financial reports. These three elements of governmental financial administration are inseparable and can be thought of as the "cycle" of governmental financial transactions and final product of the accounting system.

Seven Types of Funds

1. The *General Fund* which accounts for all transactions not accounted for in any other fund.
2. *Special Revenue Fund* which accounts for revenues from specific sources or to finance specific projects.
3. *Debt Service Fund* which accounts for the payment of interest and principal on longterm debt.
4. *Capital Project Fund* which accounts for the receipt and disbursement of funds used for the acquisition of capital facilities.
5. *Enterprise Funds* which account for the financing of services to the public paid for by the users of the services.
6. *Fiduciary Funds: Trust and Agency Funds* which account for assets held by a governmental unit as trustee or agent for individuals, private organizations, or other governmental units.
7. *Internal Service Funds* which account for the financing of special projects and services performed by one governmental entity for an organization unit within the same governmental entity.

The accountant should:

- Maintain complete and adequate files for the initial documentation which established or restricted the fund, together with any special reporting requirements demanded.
- Keep separate detailed books of entry for each fund, separate bank account for that fund, separate identification of all property and securities.
- Under *no* circumstances should assets of separate funds be commingled. Transfers between funds should not be permitted without documentary authorization, and inter-fund receivables and payables should, in contra-effect, be equal and clearly identified, always maintaining the original integrity of each fund.
- Interest accruals, cooperative-share funding (example: government 80%—college 20% in Work Study Program), expense allowances or allocations—all should be made timely.
- Federal, state and local reporting requirements should be studied, met and reported as due to avoid stringent penalties, interest and possible loss of tax-exempt status. Options may exist regarding the handling of payroll and unemployment taxes; they should be studied and explored for money-saving possibilities.

- Independently audited annual financial statements by fund are usually required both by organizational charter and governmental departments (especially where grant-participation is involved). Publication of the availability of these statements is sometimes mandatory (foundations).

- One area of discussion and dispute is the "compliance" feature of audits involving certain governmental agency grants. Here, the independent auditor is called upon to measure the agency's compliance with certain non-accounting rules, such as eligibility of money-recipients, internal controls and other matters not ordinarily associated with a financial audit. The integrity of the auditor's financial opinion should never be compromised by peripheral compliance requirements. In most cases, the auditor should qualify any opinion indicating the results and *extent of tests* made for compliance. The AICPA, to some extent, has spelled out guidelines for "compliance" opinions in Section 9641 of its "Statements on Auditing Standards."

- Municipal accounting techniques, procedures, format and demands are not discussed here. Their overall application involves the use of fund accounting. The main distinction is the entering of the budget—the anticipated revenues and the appropriations thereof—directly on and as part of the books of account. Progress reports then show how actual compares with anticipated. The estimates are then zeroed out at year-end. The meaning and use of "encumbrances" should also be understood. Reports for some local subdivisions, such as school boards, usually involve a strict accounting of each receipt and disbursement, including the detailing of outstanding checks.

Accounting for the General Fund (GF).   The General Fund is the type most frequently used as it accounts for revenues not allocated to specified activities by law or by contract. Every governmental entity *must* have a General Fund; none of the other types of funds are required, but are established as needed.

Entries in the GF system originally are made to Estimated Revenues and Appropriations and simultaneously a debit or credit, whichever is the case, is recorded in the Fund Balance account. For proper controls the encumbrance system is used with entries recorded when commitments are made or orders placed. This procedure has the effect of setting aside the money for the payment of future purchase orders and payment vouchers. When a purchase is actually made, the entries to an Encumbrances and Reserve for Encumbrances are reversed and those accounts cleared. (The later expenditure is not always the same as the encumbrance.) Simultaneously, the actual expenditure is recorded by a Debit to an Expenditures account and a credit to Vouchers Payable.

Taxes and service charges are budgeted in a Taxes-Receivable—Current Account. The estimated amounts should be recorded after the estimate and posting of uncollectibles, so the entries are a credit to Revenues and a credit to Estimated Uncollectible Taxes. When collections are actually received during the fiscal year, they are recorded with a debit to cash and a credit to Taxes Receivable—Current. Subsequently, it is determined that a certain amount of taxes will become delinquent as the year progresses. These amounts are recorded in a Taxes Receivable—Delinquent account (debit) and a credit to Taxes Receivable-Current. At this point an Interest and Penalties account should be opened for fees, penalties and other charges associated with the collection of delinquent taxes.

Taxes Receivable—Delinquent	xxx	
Estimated Uncollectible Current Taxes	xxx	
Taxes Receivable—Current		xxx
Estimated Uncollectible Delinquent Taxes		xxx
Interest and Penalties	xxx	
Estimated Uncollectible Interest and		
Penalties		xxx

At the end of the fiscal year, the accounts of the General Fund are closed out. Any differences are recorded for or against the Fund Balance.

Accounting for Special Revenue Funds (SRF). Special Revenue Funds account for revenues obtained via specific taxes or other designated revenue sources. They are usually mandated by statute, charter, or local ordinance to fund specific functions or activities. Examples are parks, museums, highway construction, street maintenance, business licensing.

Revenue Funds resources cannot be used for any purpose other than the purpose for which the bonds were sold.

Journal entries:		
Encumbrances	xxx	
Reserve for Encumbrances		xxx
Reserve for Encumbrances	xxx	
Encumbrances		xxx
Expenditures	xxx	
Vouchers Payable		xxx
Vouchers Payable	xxx	
Cash		xxx

Taxes and service charges are budgeted in a Taxes-Receivable—Current account. The estimated amounts should be recorded after the estimate and posting of uncollectibles, so the entries are a credit to Revenues and a credit to Estimated Uncollectible Taxes; e.g.,

Taxes Receivable—Current	xxx	
Estimated Uncollectible Current Taxes		xxx
Revenues		xxx

When collections are actually received during the fiscal year they are recorded with a debit to Cash and a credit to Taxes Receivable—Current.

Accounting for Debt Service Funds (DSF).   Debt Service Fund accounts for the payment of interest and principal on long-term debt resulting from the sale of general obligation bonds. This fund does not include the accounting for special assessments and service debts of governmental enterprises.

There are three types of long-term debt:

- Term or sinking fund bonds.
- Serial bonds.
- Notes and time warrants having a maturity of *more than one year* after issuance.

The first entry in the accounting cycle for a bond fund is to record the bond authorization:

Bonds Authorized—unissued	xxx	
Appropriations		xxx
The bonds are sold:		
Cash	xxx	
Bonds Authorized—unissued		xxx

If the bonds are sold at a premium, a Premium on Bonds account is credited. If sold at a discount, a Discount on Bonds account is debited.

Accounting for the Capital Projects Fund (CPF).   Capital Projects Funds are a set of accounts for all resources used to acquire *capital* facilities (except funds financed by special assessment and enterprise funds). There must be Capital Project Funds for each authorized project to ensure that the proceeds of a bond issue, for example, are expended only as authorized. There is also a separate budget for the CPF, usually labeled the Capital Budget.

The accounting process begins with project authorization which is in memorandum form; no entry is necessary. Assuming the project is financed by the proceeds of a bond issue (as most projects are), the proceeds of the borrowing is an entry to the Cash account and a credit to Revenues for the *par value* of the bonds. If the bonds were sold at a premium, there is a credit to a Premium on Bonds account for the amount of the premium. Since GAAP requires bond premiums to be treated as an adjustment to the interest costs, the premiums are transferred *to* the Debt Service Fund established to service the debt. The entry to record the transfer is:

Premium on Bonds	xxx	
Cash		xxx

If the bonds are sold at a discount, the discount is eliminated by a transfer of the amount of the discount *from* the Debt Service Fund *to* the Capital Projects Fund.

Accounting for Enterprise Funds (EF).   Enterprise Funds finance self-supporting (not taxpayers') activities of governmental units that render services on a user charge basis to the general public. Common enterprises are water companies, electricity, natural gas, airports, transportation systems, hospitals, port authority, and a variety of recreational facilities.

In most jurisdictions, utilities and other enterprises are required to adopt and operate under budgets in the same manner as non-enterprise operations of governmental units. A budget is essential for control of each enterprise's operating results and to ensure that the resources of one enterprise are not illegally or improperly utilized by another.

The accrual basis of accounting is the required method for Enterprise Funds. As customers are billed, Accounts Receivable accounts are debited and revenue accounts *by sources* are credited.

Four financial statements are required to disclose fully the financial position and results of operations of an Enterprise Fund:

- Balance Sheet
- Revenue and Expenses
- Changes in Financial Position
- Analysis of Changes in Retained Earnings

Accounting for Trust and Agency Funds (TAF).   Trust and Agency Funds are similar; the primary difference is that a Trust Fund is usually in existence for a long period of time, even permanently. Both have fiduciary responsibilities for funds and assets that are not owned outright by the funds.

There are two types of Trust Funds, i.e., expendable and nonexpendable funds. The former allows the principal and income to be spent on designated operations, while nonexpendable funds must be preserved intact. Pension and various retirement funds are examples of expendable funds; a loan fund from which loans are made for specific purposes and must be paid back, which requires maintaining the *original amount* of the fund, is a nonexpendable fund.

Trust Funds are operated as required by statutes and governmental regulations established for their existence. Accounting for Trust Funds consists primarily of the proper recording of receipts and disbursements. Additions are credited directly to the Fund Balance account and expenditures charged directly against the Fund Balance.

An Agency Fund can be thought of as sort of a clearinghouse fund established to account for assets received for and paid to others; the main asset is cash which is held only for a brief period of time, so is seldom invested because cash is usually paid out shortly after receipt.

An Agency Fund simplifies the complexities that can result from the use of numerous fund accounting entities; e.g., instances in which a single transaction affects several different funds. All Agency Fund assets are owed to another fund, a person, or an organization. The entries for receipts and disbursements in Agency Funds are easy:

Upon receipt:		
Cash	xxx	
Fund Balance		xxx
Upon disbursement:		
Fund Balance	xxx	
Cash		xxx

Accounting for Intergovernmental Service Funds (ISF).   ISF, also referenced as Working Capital Funds and Internal Service Funds, finances and provides accountability for services and commodities provided by a designated agency of a governmental unit to other departments, agencies, etc., of the same governmental entity. Examples are motor pools, centralized garages, central purchasing, storage, facilities, and central printing services.

Funds for the establishment of ISF usually originate from three sources:

- Contributions from another operating fund—e.g., the General Fund or an Enterprise Fund.
- The sale of general obligation bonds.
- Long-term advances from other funds, which are to be repaid over a specific period of time from the earnings of a revolving fund.

As cash is expended for the benefit of other fund-users, the users are charged with the cost of the materials or services furnished by the ISF and the ISF is then reimbursed by interdepartmental cash transfers from the departments of other funds to which materials or services have been furnished.

The accounting for ISF should include all accounts necessary to compile an accurate statement of the outcome of its financial operations, and of its financial position at any given time. These accounts will usually include the fixed assets owned by the fund, accounts for buildings financed from capital Project Funds, depreciation recorded on fixed assets to obtain an accurate computation of costs and to preclude depletion of the fund's capital. The accrual basis must be used for all ISF accounting, with all charges to departments of various funds billed at the time materials or services are rendered and expenditures are recorded when incurred. Encumbrances may or may not be formally recorded in the books of account; if they are the entries would be:

Encumbrances	xxx	
Reserve for Encumbrances		xxx

If encumbrances are not recorded in the accounts, memorandum records of orders and commitments should be maintained to preclude over-obligation of cash and other fund resources.

When an ISF is established, the entry to be made will depend upon the service the fund is to provide. If the fund's capital is obtained from the General Fund, the entry would be:

Cash	xxx	
Contribution from General Fund		xxx

If a general obligation bond issue is a source of the fund's capital:

Cash	xxx	
Contribution from		
General Obligation Bonds		xxx

If fund capital is obtained from another fund of the same governmental unit the entry is:

Cash	xxx	
Advance from (name of fund)		xxx

Accounting for the General Fixed Assets Account Group (GFA). The fixed asset accounts are maintained on the basis of original cost, or the estimated cost if the original cost is not available, as in the case of gifts. The appraised value at the time of receipt of the asset is an acceptable valuation. Otherwise, initial costs of fixed assets are obtainable from contracts, purchase vouchers, and other transaction documents generated at the time of acquisition or construction.

Depreciation on fixed assets should not be recorded in the general accounting records. Depreciation charges are computed for unit cost purposes, provided such charges are recorded in memorandum form and do not appear in the fund accounts.

Different from depreciation accounting for commercial enterprises, the depreciation of fixed assets is not recorded as an expense because there is no purpose in doing so. Property records should be kept, however, for each piece of property and equipment owned by the fund. The sum of the cost value of the properties—buildings, improvements, machinery, and equipment—should equal the corresponding balances of those accounts carried in the general ledger.

Accounting for the Long-Term Debt Group (LTD). General Obligation Bonds and other types of long-term debt supported by general revenues are obligations of the governmental unit as a whole, not of any of the entity's constituent funds individually. Additionally, the monies from such debt can be expended on facilities that are used in the operation of several funds. Accordingly, the total of long-term indebtedness backed by the "full faith and credit" of the government should be recorded and accounted for in a separate self-balancing group of accounts titled General Long-Term Debt Group of Accounts. Included in this debt group are general obligation bonds, time warrants, and notes that have a maturity date of *more than one year* from the date of issuance.

Long-term debt is recorded in the self-balancing accounts, so do not affect the liabilities of any other fund. The reason for these accounts is to record a governmental unit's long-term debt at any point in time from the date the debt is incurred until it is finally paid. Under GAAP the proper valuation for the long-term debt liability is the sum of (1) the present discounted value of the principal payable at the stipulated maturity date in the future and (2) the present discounted value of the periodic interest payments to the maturity date.

The entries to be made at the time the bonds are sold are:

Amounts to be Provided for the Payment of Term Bonds	xxx	
Term Bonds Payable		xxx

The proceeds of the bond issue are entered in a Capital Projects Fund account to be expended as authorized in the Authorized Capital Outlay account.

(Note: Not-for-profit accounting for other than governmental entities uses the accrual basis of accounting—e.g., colleges and universities, voluntary hospitals, health and welfare organizations, and so on.)

OBJECTIVES OF FINANCIAL REPORTING BY NONBUSINESS ORGANIZATIONS

The main distinguishing characteristics of nonbusiness organizations include:

1. Receipts of significant amounts of resources from resource providers who do not expect to receive either repayment or economic benefits commensurate with the resources provided.
2. Operating purposes for objectives other than to provide goods or services at a profit.
3. Absence of defined ownership interests that can be sold, transferred, or redeemed, or that convey entitlement to a share of a residual distribution of resources in the event of liquidation of the organization.

These characteristics result in certain types of transactions that are largely, although not entirely, absent in business enterprises, such as contributions and grants, and in the absence of transactions with owners, such as issuing and redeeming stock and paying dividends. General purpose financial reporting by nonbusiness organizations does not attempt to meet all the information needed by those interested parties or to furnish all of the different types of information that financial reporting can provide. It is not intended to meet specialized needs of regulatory bodies, donors or grantors, or others having the authority to obtain the information they need. The most important users in the nonbusiness environment are resource providers, such as members, taxpayers, contributors, and creditors. A full set of financial statements for a period should show:

1. Financial position at the end of the period.
2. Earnings for the period.
3. Comprehensive income for the period.
4. Cash flows during the period.
5. Investments by and distributions to owners during the period.

Financial statements result from simplifying, condensing, and aggregating masses of data. As a result, they convey information that would be obscured if great detail were provided.

Chapter 13
"New" Governmental Accounting

The Governmental Accounting Standards Board unanimously adopted the long-awaited comprehensive changes for state and local government financial reporting throughout the country in June 1999. GASB 34, *Basic Financial Statements—and Management's Discussion and Analysis—for State and Local Governments*, provides a new look and focus in reporting public finance in the U.S. The Board's action may be a response to the oft-voiced complaint, "...if only they'd run the government more like a business!" Now "they" must, at least from an accounting standpoint. Many big "businesses" and even more mid-size and small "businesses"—states, cities, counties, towns—adding up to a total of 87,000 in 1999, according to the GASB, will be adopting the new measures.

GOVERNMENTAL ACCOUNTING STANDARDS BOARD GAINS STATURE

This Statement can certainly be considered the most significant change in the history of governmental accounting and should signal the "coming of age" of the GASB. It represents a dramatic shift in the manner and comprehensiveness in which state and local governments present financial information to the public. When implemented, it will create new information and will restructure much of the fund information that governments have presented in the past.

The new requirements were developed to make annual reports more comprehensive and easier to understand and use. Now, anyone with an interest (vested or otherwise) in public finance—citizens, the media, bond raters,

246

creditors, investors, legislators, investment bankers and others—will have readily available information about the respective governmental bodies.

Thousands of preparers, auditors, academics, and users of governmental financial statements participated during the past decade and a half in the research, consideration, and deliberations that preceded the publication of GASB 34. Members of various task forces began work on this and related projects as early as 1985.

PROVISIONS OF GASB 34

Among the major innovations of Statement 34, governments will be required to:

1. Report on the *overall* state of the government's financial health, not just its individual funds as has been the case.
2. Provide the most complete information ever made available about the cost of providing services to the citizens.
3. Prepare an introductory narrative section (the Management's Discussion and Analysis—MD&A) to the basic report analyzing the government's financial performance.
4. Provide enhanced fund reporting.
5. Include information about the government's public infrastructure assets. The Statement explains these assets as long-lived assets that are normally stationary and capable of being preserved longer than most capital assets. Bridges, roads, storm sewers, tunnels, drainage systems, dams, lighting systems, and swimming pools are among those mentioned (This is certainly the most innovative requirement introduced to governmental financial reporting.)

BACKGROUND INFORMATION

The GASB's first concepts Statement, *Objectives of Financial Reporting*, issued in 1987, identified what the Board believes are the most important objectives of financial reporting by governments. Some of those objectives reaffirm the importance of information that governmental units have historically included in their annual reports. To cover more of the original objectives, the Board felt it necessary to provide for a much broader range of information.

As a result, Statement 34 is a dual-perspective report requiring governmental bodies to retain much of the information they currently report, but also requiring them to go further in revealing their operations. The first perspective focuses on the traditional funds with some additional information required for major funds. The second perspective is government-wide to provide an entirely new look at a government's financial activities

The Board feels that adding new material will result in reports that will accomplish more of the objectives emphasized in the original concepts Statement.

THE TIME FOR ACCOUNTABILITY IS NOW

According to the GASB, state and local governments in the U.S. invest approximately $140-$150 billion annually in the construction, improvement, and rehabilitation of capital assets, including infrastructure assets like bridges, highways, and sewers. Since these expenditures represent more than 10% of the monies spent by those governments, it would appear quite natural for them to be accounted for in financial documents readily available to the public.

The majority of this infrastructure investment is financed by borrowing—selling municipal bonds and using the proceeds to pay for construction. (Enter the investor.)

The need for public accountability arises when such sums are spent and when current and future generations are committed to repay such debts. The public should know how much governments spend on infrastructure construction and how much they borrow to finance it. (Enter the taxpayer.)

The public also wants to know if government officials subsequently are caring for the infrastructure they have built with public resources. (Enter the voter.)

Although the need for information about infrastructure should be fairly obvious, the primary instruments for demonstrating fiscal accountability (the government's annual financial statements) have not previously been required to provide this information. The accounting method for preparing state and local government financial statements has focused on short-term financial resources like cash and investments. Infrastructures have been left off the balance sheet and no charge was included on the income statement for the cost of using the infrastructure assets to provide services. Because of the significant share of government spending devoted to capital assets, this has been a major omission. But with the advent of GASB 34, all of that is changing.

Opportunities for Government Consulting

Considering the number of affected governmental bodies—regardless of the considerable lead time provided—the present supply of government accountants will certainly be stretched to the limit. In addition, many have had little experience in the newly required more "corporate-style" accounting. Even though the smaller governments have the longest time to make the necessary changes, they face a rather daunting task as they will have few, if any, accounting professionals on their staff.

Thus, the Statement opens up business opportunities for interested accountants. It should be fairly obvious that many governments will need help in complying with these new requirements that mandate the dramatic shift in the way state and local governments present their financial information.

RETENTION OF FUND ACCOUNTING

Annual reports currently provide information about funds. Most funds are established by governing bodies (such as state legislatures, city councils, or school boards) to show restrictions on the planned use of resources or to measure, *in the short term*, the revenues and expenditures arising from certain activities. GASB 1 noted that annual reports should allow users to assess a government's accountability by assisting them in determining compliance with finance-related laws, rules, and regulations.

This new Statement requires governments to continue to present financial statements that provide fund information. The focus of these statements has been sharpened to require governments to report information about their major funds, including the general fund. In current annual reports, fund information is reported in the aggregate by fund type. This has often made it difficult for users to assess accountability of any "public servants."

Fund statements will continue to measure and report the "operating results" of many funds by measuring cash on hand and other assets that can be easily converted to cash. These statements show the performance, in the short term, of individual funds using the same measures that many governments use when financing their current operations. The Board points out that if a government issues fifteen-year debt to build a school, it does not collect taxes in the first year sufficient to repay the *entire* debt; it levies and collects what is needed to make that year's required payments. On the other hand, when governments charge a fee to users for services—as is done for most water or electric utilities—fund information will continue to be based on accrual accounting to ensure all costs of providing services are being measured.

THE ALL-IMPORTANT GOVERNMENTAL BUDGET

Showing budgetary compliance is an important component of government's accountability. (At the national level, with which GASB 34 has no connection, of course, THE BUDGET is undoubtedly the most widely recognized financial document.) At the state and local levels, diverse citizen groups, special interest groups, and individuals participate in the process of establishing the original annual operating budgets of state and local governments.

Governments will be required to continue to provide budgetary comparison information in their annual reports. An important change that should certainly make the comparison more meaningful is the requirement to add the government's *original* budget to that comparison. Many governments revise their original budgets during the year for various reasons. Requiring governments to report that original document in addition to their *revised* budget adds a new analytical dimension and should increase the usefulness of the budgetary comparison.

Presumably, the original budget was the "best thought" of the adopting body at the time. Subsequent "revised" budgets could be the result of political pressures or personal preferences. The GASB concedes that budgetary changes are not necessarily undesirable. However, the Board decided that in the interest of accountability to those who were aware of, and may have made decisions based upon the original budget, inclusion of its contents could deter ill-considered changes. The comparison would also give the user a look at any changes that had been made. The Board suggested that this would be an additional method of assessing the governmental body's ability to estimate and manage its general resources—without too many detours.

Thus, the original budget, the final appropriated budgets and the actual inflows, outflows and balances stated on the government's budgetary basis are mandated as required supplemental information (RSI) for the general fund and for each major special revenue fund that has a legally adopted annual budget. Rather than include this information in RSI, a government may elect to report these comparisons in a budgetary comparison statement as part of the basic financial statements.

New Information Is Readily Available

For the first time, government financial managers will be required to introduce the financial report by sharing their attitude toward and understanding of the transactions, events, and conditions reflected in the government's report and of the fiscal policies that govern its operations. The required management's discussion and analysis (MD&A) should give the users an easily readable analysis of the government's *financial* performance for the year. Users will thus have information they need to help them gauge the government's state of financial health as a result of the year's operations.

Additionally, financial managers themselves will be in a better position to provide this analysis because, for the first, time the annual report will also include new government-wide financial statements prepared using accrual accounting for all of the government's activities. Most governmental utilities and private-sector companies use accrual accounting. With GASB 34, state and local governments will join most of the rest of the world in using it. The reason for the change is that accrual accounting measures not just current assets and liabilities, but also long-term assets and liabilities (such as capital assets, including infrastructure, and general obligation debt). It also reports all revenues and *all* costs of providing services each year, not just those received or paid in the current year or soon after year-end. After all, government is an ongoing endeavor; officials elected or appointed come and go.

Users Will Benefit

These government-wide financial statements will help users:

1. Assess the finances of a government in its entirety, including the year's operating results.
2. Determine whether a government's overall financial position improved or deteriorated.
3. Evaluate whether a government's current-year revenues were sufficient to pay for current-year services.
4. Be aware of the cost of providing services to the citizenry.
5. Become cognizant of the way in which a government finances its programs—through user fees and other program revenues, or general tax revenues.
6. Understand the extent to which a government has invested in capital assets, including roads, bridges, and other infrastructure assets.
7. Make better comparisons between governments.

REQUIRED INFORMATION AND FORMAT

GASB 34 sets financial reporting standards for state and local governments, including states, cities, towns, villages, and special-purpose governments such as school districts and public utilities. It establishes that the basic financial statements and required supplementary information for general purpose governments should consist of:

1. ***Management's Discussion and Analysis (MD&A).*** MD&A introduces the basic financial statements and provides an analytical overview of the government's financial activities. Although it is required supplementary information (RSI) and one would expect to find it in the final portion of the report, governments are required to present MD&A *before* the basic

financial statements. Presumably the belief is that a clearly written—plain English, perhaps—introduction will provide a link between the two perspectives (fund and government-wide) to prepare the reader for a better understanding of the financial statements.

2. **Basic Financial Statements.** The basic financial statements are to include:

   a. *Government-wide financial statements,* consisting of a statement of net assets and a statement of activities. Prepared using the economic resources measurement focus and the accrual basis of accounting, these statements should report all of the assets, liabilities, revenues, expenses, and gains and losses of the government. Each statement should distinguish between the *governmental* and *business-type activities* of the primary government and between the total primary government and the separately presented component units by reporting each in separate columns. (*Fiduciary activities*, with resources not available to finance the government's programs, are not included in the government-wide statements.)

   b. *Fund financial statements* consisting of a series of statements that focus on information about the government's major governmental and enterprise funds, including blended component units. Fund financial statements also should report information about a government's fiduciary funds and component units that are fiduciary in nature.

   c. *Governmental* fund financial statements (including financial data for the general fund and special revenue, capital projects, debt service, and permanent funds). These are to be prepared using the current financial resources measurement focus and the modified accrual basis of accounting.

   d. *Proprietary* fund financial statements (including financial data for enterprise and internal service funds) and *fiduciary* fund financial statements (including financial data for fiduciary funds and similar component units). This group is to be prepared using the economic resources measurement focus and the accrual basis of accounting.

   e. *Notes to the financial statements* are notes and explanations that provide information which is *essential* to a user's understanding of the basic financial statements.

3. **Required Supplementary Information (RSI).** In addition to MD&A, this Statement requires *budgetary comparison schedules* to be presented as RSI along with other types of data as required by previous GASB pronouncements. This Statement also requires RSI for governments that use the modified approach for reporting infrastructure assets.

Special-purpose governments engaged in only governmental activities (such as some library districts) or engaged in both governmental and business-type activities (such as some school districts) should normally be reported in the same manner as general purpose governments. Special-purpose governments engaged only in business-type activities (such as utilities) should present the financial statements required for enterprise funds, including MD&A and other RSI.

CONTENT OF MD&A

MD&A should provide an objective and easily readable analysis of the government's financial activities based on currently known facts, decisions, or conditions. It should be emphasized that this section is a preparation for the casual reader who is less skilled in reading financial statements as well as the more experienced "user" to understand fully the implications of the basic report.

MD&A should include:

1. Comparisons of the current year to the prior year based on the government-wide information
2. An analysis of the government's overall financial position and results of operations to assist users in assessing whether that financial position has improved or deteriorated as a result of the year's activities.
3. An analysis of balances and transactions of individual funds and significant budget variances.
4. A description of capital asset and long-term debt activity during the period.
5. A conclusion with a description of currently known facts, decisions, or conditions that could be expected to have a significant effect upon the financial position or results of operations.

GOVERNMENT-WIDE FINANCIAL STATEMENTS

The new annual reports will contain much more comprehensive financial information. Government-wide statements are to display information about the reporting government as a whole, except for its fiduciary activities. These statements will include separate columns for the governmental and business-type activities of the primary government and its component parts. Government-wide statements are to be prepared using the economic resources measurement focus and the accrual basis of accounting. This latter requirement is a fairly dramatic step forward since heretofore governmental accounting followed only the modified-accrual basis. The statement will have to include a statement of net assets as well as all of the government's activities, not just those that cover costs by charging a fee for services as currently required.

Governments should report all *capital assets*, including infrastructure assets, in the government-wide statement of net assets and generally should report depreciation expenses in the statement of activities. Infrastructure assets that are part of a network or subsystem of a network are not required to be depreciated as long as the government manages those assets using an asset management system that has certain characteristics and the government can document that the assets are being preserved approximately at (or above) a condition level established and disclosed by the government in the RSI.

To qualify for a qualified asset management system, the government must:

1. Have an up-to-date inventory of the eligible infrastructure assets.
2. Perform condition assessments of the eligible assets and summarize the results using a measurement scale.
3. Estimate each year the annual amounts necessary to maintain and preserve the assets at the established and disclosed condition level. Condition assessments are to be documented so that they can be replicated. The assessments may be performed by the government itself or by contract with an outside source.

The net assets of a government should be reported in three categories—*invested in capital assets net of related debt, restricted, and unrestricted*. Net assets are considered "restricted" when constraints are placed on their use by:

1. External sources such as creditors, grantors or contributors.
2. Laws or regulations of other governments.
3. Legal or constitutional provisions or enabling legislation.

Permanent endowments or permanent fund principal amounts included in restricted net assets should be displayed in two additional components—*expendable and nonexpendable*.

The government-wide *statement of activities* should be presented in a format that reports expenses minus program revenues, to obtain a measurement of "net (expense) revenue" for each of the government's functions. Program expenses should include all direct expenses. General revenues, such as taxes, and special and extraordinary items should be reported separately to arrive at the change in net assets for the period.

Special and extraordinary items are both significant transactions or other events, either unusual or infrequent, over which management has control. Both types should be reported separately at the bottom of the statement of activities with special items listed prior to any extraordinary items. These types of transactions or events over which a government does not have control should be disclosed in the notes to financial statements.

FUND FINANCIAL STATEMENTS

To report additional and detailed information about the primary government, separate fund financial statements should be presented for each fund category: governmental, proprietary and fiduciary.

1. *Governmental funds* report on the basic activities of the government, including general fund accounts and special revenue, capital projects, debt service, and permanent funds.
2. *Proprietary funds* cover activities that are generally financed and operated like private businesses such as enterprise (fees charged to outside users) and internal service funds.
3. *Fiduciary funds* include pension and other employee benefit and private purpose trust funds that cannot be used to support the government's own programs.

Required *governmental fund* statements are:

1. A balance sheet.
2. A statement of revenues, expenditures, and changes in fund balances.

Required *proprietary fund* statements are:

1. A statement of net assets.
2. A statement of revenues, expenses, and changes in fund net assets.
3. A statement of cash flows.

To allow users to assess the relationship between fund and government-wide financial statements, governments should present a summary reconciliation to the government-wide financial statements at the bottom of the fund financial statements or in an accompanying schedule.

Each of the fund statements should report separate columns for the *general fund* and for *other major governmental and enterprise funds.*

1. *Major funds* are funds in which revenues, expenditures/expenses, assets, or liabilities (excluding extraordinary items) are at least 10% of corresponding totals for all governmental or enterprise funds and at least 5% of the aggregate amount for all governmental and enterprise funds. Any other fund may be reported as a major fund if the government's officials consider it to be particularly important to financial statement users.
2. *Nonmajor funds* should be reported in the aggregate in a separate column.
3. *Internal service funds* also should be reported in the aggregate in a separate column on the proprietary fund statements.

Fund balances for governmental funds should also be segregated into *reserved* and *unreserved* categories. Proprietary fund net assets should be reported in the same categories required for the government-wide financial statements. Proprietary fund statements of net assets should distinguish between current and noncurrent assets and liabilities and should display restricted assets.

Proprietary fund statements of revenues, expenses, and changes in fund net assets should distinguish between operating and nonoperating revenues and expenses. These statements should also report capital contributions, contributions to permanent and term endowments, special and extraordinary items, and transfers separately at the bottom of the statement to arrive at the all-inclusive change in fund net assets. Cash flow statements should be prepared using the direct method.

Separate fiduciary fund statements (including component units that are fiduciary in nature) also should be presented as part of the fund financial statements. Fiduciary funds should be used to report assets that are held in a trustee or agency capacity for others and that cannot be used to support the government's own programs.

Required *fiduciary fund* statements are:

1. A statement of fiduciary net assets.
2. A statement of changes in fiduciary net assets.

Interfund activity includes interfund loans, interfund services provided and used, and interfund transfers. This activity should be reported separately in the fund financial statements and generally should be eliminated in the aggregated government-wide financial statements.

REQUIRED SUPPLEMENTARY INFORMATION (RSI)

To demonstrate whether resources were obtained and used in accordance with the government's legally adopted budget, RSI should include budgetary comparison schedules for the general fund and for each major special revenue fund that has a legally adopted annual budget.

The budgetary comparison schedules should include:

1. The original budget.
2. The final appropriated budgets for the reporting period.
3. Actual inflows, outflows, and balances, stated on the government's budgetary basis.

As pointed out above, the Statement also requires certain disclosures in RSI for governments that use the modified approach for reporting infrastructure assets and data currently required by earlier Statements.

EFFECTIVE DATE AND TRANSITION

The requirements of this Statement are effective in three phases based on a government's total annual revenues in the first fiscal year ending after June 15, 1999. Governments with total annual revenues (excluding extraordinary items) of $100 million or more (phase 1) should apply this Statement for fiscal years beginning after June 15, 2001. Medium-size governments with at least $10 million but less than $100 million in revenues (phase 2) should apply this Statement for fiscal years beginning after June 15, 2002. Smaller governments with less than $10 million in revenues (phase 3) should apply this Statement for periods beginning after June 15, 2003. Earlier application is encouraged.

Governments that elect early implementation of this Statement for periods beginning before June 15, 2000, should also implement GASB Statement 33, *Accounting and Financial Reporting for Nonexchange Transactions*, at the same time. (See below.)

If a primary government chooses early implementation of this Statement, all of its component units should also implement this standard early in order to provide the necessary financial information required for the government-wide financial statements.

REQUIREMENTS FOR PROSPECTIVE AND RETROSPECTIVE REPORTING

Prospective reporting of general infrastructure assets is required at the effective dates of this Statement. Retroactive reporting of all existing major general governmental infrastructure assets is encouraged at that date.

For phase 1 and phase 2 governments, retroactive reporting is *required four years after* the effective date on the basic provisions for all major general infrastructure assets that were acquired or significantly reconstructed, or that received significant improvements, in fiscal years ending after June 30, 1980. Thus, larger governments will have to report retroactively all major general infrastructure assets for all fiscal years beginning after June 15, 2005 and medium-size governments have until fiscal years beginning after June 15, 2006.

Phase 3 governments are encouraged to report infrastructure retroactively, but may elect to report general infrastructure prospectively only.

GUIDANCE ON MODIFIED ACCRUAL STANDARDS

The Governmental Accounting Standards Board issued Interpretation 6, *Recognition and Measurement of Certain Liabilities and Expenditures in Governmental Fund Financial Statements.* This Interpretation clarifies the application of standards for modified accrual recognition of fund liabilities and expenditures in governmental fund financial statements.

In GASB 34, the Board concluded that traditional governmental fund financial statements continue to provide useful information for assessing a government's fiscal accountability and should continue to be prepared with a current financial resources measurement focus and modified accrual basis of accounting. This Interpretation clarifies undefined terms and reduces differences in the ways that financial statement preparers, auditors, and others interpret and apply the standard.

The goal is to provide an interpretation that will promote more consistent and comparable reporting. The Board pointed out that the effect of the Interpretation may include both increases and decreases in accruals for governments that have applied the standards differently.

The effective date of the proposed Interpretation should coincide with the effective date of Statement 34 for the reporting government. Earlier application is encouraged, provided that this Interpretation and Statement 34 are simultaneously adopted.

GASB STATEMENT 35 FOR PUBLIC COLLEGES AND UNIVERSITIES

After an earlier decision by the Governmental Accounting Standards Board not to require a separate financial reporting model for public colleges and universities in order to make it easier for state and local governments to include these institutions in their financial statements, the GASB issued a proposal in July, 1999 to provide accounting and financial reporting guidance for public colleges and universities in their separately issued financial statements. That proposal became GASB 35.

This Statement amends GASB 34, *Basic Financial Statements—and Management's Discussion and Analysis—for State and Local Governments*, to include public colleges and universities within its guidance for general purpose external financial reporting.

It is anticipated that this step will make it easier to compare public institutions and their private counterparts. Such a step had been requested by GASB constituents.

Under the new guidance, public colleges and universities can report their finances as public institutions:

1. Engaged only in business-type activities.
2. Engaged only in governmental activities.
3. Engaged in both governmental and business-type activities.

A public institution is also required to include the following in separately issued financial reports, regardless of whether or not they are legally separate entities:

1. Management's discussion and analysis (MD&A).
2. Basic financial statements, as appropriate for the category of special-purpose government reporting.
3. Notes to the financial statements.
4. Required supplementary information other than MD&A.

The requirements of the Statement are effective in three phases for public institutions that are not part of another reporting entity, beginning with fiscal years beginning after June 15, 2001. All public institutions that are part of (or are component units of) a primary government are required to implement this standard at least by the same time as its primary government, regardless of the phase-in guidance contained in GASB 34.

Public colleges and universities are required to report infrastructure assets as follows:

1. Public institutions that are not part of another primary government and report as either special-purpose governments engaged only in governmental activities or engaged in both governmental and business-type activities must report infrastructure in accordance with the phase-in guidance of GASB 34 beginning with fiscal years ending after June 15, 2005.

2. Public institutions that report as special-purpose governments engaged only in business-type activities are required to report infrastructure upon implementation, without regard to the phase-in periods included in Statement 34.

GASB Statement 33 on Nonexchange Transactions

Late in 1998, the Governmental Accounting Standards Board issued GASB Statement 33, *Accounting and Financial Reporting for Nonexchange Transactions*, which specifies the accounting and reporting for nonexchange transactions involving financial or capital resources. These transactions include most taxes, grants, and donations. The Statement is effective for periods beginning after June 15, 2000.

In a nonexchange transaction, the government gives or receives value without directly receiving or giving equal value in exchange. When there isn't an exchange, it can be difficult to decide *when* a transaction should be recognized in the financial statements. Statement 33 attempts to simplify the problem.

The timing of financial statement recognition will depend on the nature of the nonexchange transaction as well as the basis of accounting (accrual or modified accrual). The GASB has identified four classes of nonexchange transactions:

1. Derived tax revenues, such as sales and income taxes. These will be recognized when the underlying exchange on which the government imposes the tax actually occurs. An example would be when a customer buys a washing machine or refrigerator that is subject to a sales tax.
2. Imposed nonexchange revenues, such as property taxes and fines. These are to be recognized as assets when the government has an enforceable legal claim. For example, property taxes receivable generally will be recognized on the lien date, even though a lien may not be formally placed on the property at that date. Revenues will be recognized in the period in which the resources are required to be used.
3. Government-mandated nonexchange transactions, such as federal or state programs that state or local governments are required to provide. These will be recognized when all eligibility requirements are met, as specified in Statement 33. For example, when a recipient is required to incur allowable costs before reimbursement is made, the incurring of allowable costs is an eligibility requirement.
4. Voluntary nonexchange transactions, such as most grants, appropriations, donations, and endowments. These will also be recognized when the Statement 33 eligibility requirements are met. These requirements include contingencies. For example, to qualify for a grant, a recipient may be required to provide matching resources.

For revenue recognition on the modified accrual basis, resources also should be "available," as defined in existing standards. Statement 33 goes hand in hand with the Board's standards on the governmental and the college and university financial reporting models under GASB 34. Until these new models become effective, GASB 33 should be implemented under the existing models. The Board believed it was important to have a separate Statement on nonexchange transactions inasmuch as they are a large proportion of most governments' transactions in addition to presenting some special accounting problems. For that reason, the Board also decided not to delay issuance of Statement 33 pending completion of the new reporting models required by Statement 34. The Board feels that GASB 33 will improve consistency in how governments report nonexchange transactions.

GASB Statement on Symmetry Between Recipients and Providers in Accounting for Certain Shared Revenues

GASB 36 amends GASB 33, *Accounting and Financial Reporting for Nonexchange Transactions*, which required recipients of shared derived tax or imposed nonexchange revenue to account for it differently from the provider government. This practice could have resulted in the two governments recognizing the sharing at different times.

The new Statement provides symmetrical accounting treatment for both the giver and the receiver of the shared revenue. Statement 36 eliminates the timing difference by requiring recipients to account for the sharing in the same way as provider governments.

It should be implemented simultaneously with Statement 33, which becomes mandatory for periods beginning after June 15, 2000. Governments that have implemented Statement 33 early should apply Statement 36 in the next GAAP report that is issued.

GASB Guide for Implementing New Financial Statements

The Governmental Accounting Standards Board has issued an Implementation Guide to help the preparers and auditors of state and local government financial statements understand and apply the provisions of GASB 34. The guide includes nearly 300 questions and answers developed by the GASB staff with the assistance of a 36-member advisory group. The guide also includes more than 50 illustrative financial statement exhibits, how-to exercises on ten of the more difficult requirements, and the complete standards section of Statement 34.

Also included are sample financial statements for a state government, a municipal government, and an independent school district. The municipal statements include a complete illustrative management's discussion and analysis and selected note disclosures.

Chapter 14

Not-For-Profit or Exempt Organizations

Accounting for nonbusiness organizations such as not-for-profit and exempt organizations has many of the same characteristics as accounting for business entities; however, there are also wide differences. Among the foremost of these are differing objectives of financial reporting by nonbusiness entities.

The main distinguishing characteristics of nonbusiness organizations include:

1. Receipts of significant amounts of resources from resource providers who do not expect to receive either repayment or economic benefits commensurate with the resources provided.
2. Operating purposes for objectives other than to provide goods or services at a profit.
3. Absence of defined ownership interests that can be sold, transferred, or redeemed, or that convey entitlement to a share of a residual distribution of resources in the event of liquidation of the organization.

These characteristics result in certain types of transactions that are largely, although not entirely, absent in business enterprises, such as contributions and grants, and in the absence of transactions with owners, such as issuing and redeeming stock and paying dividends. General purpose financial reporting by nonbusiness organizations does not attempt to meet all the information needed by those interested parties or to furnish all of the different types of information that financial reporting can provide. It is not intended to meet specialized needs of regulatory bodies, donors or grantors, or others having the authority to obtain the information they need. The most important users in the nonbusiness environment are resource providers, such as members, tax-payers, contributors, and creditors. A full set of financial statements for a period should show:

1. Financial position at the end of the period.
2. Earnings for the period.
3. Comprehensive income for the period.
4. Cash flows during the period.
5. Investments by and distributions to owners during the period.

Financial statements result from simplifying, condensing, and aggregating masses of data. As a result, they convey information that would be obscured if great detail were provided.

Following are FASB Statements, legislation, and IRS regulations relating specifically to not-for-profit organizations.

FASB 136, TRANSFERS OF ASSETS TO A NOT–FOR–PROFIT ORGANIZATION OR CHARITABLE TRUST THAT RAISES OR HOLDS CONTRIBUTIONS FOR OTHERS

FASB Statement 136, the most recent FASB pronouncement on not for profit organizations (NPOs) establishes standards for transactions in which a donor makes a contribution by transferring assets to a not-for-profit organization or charitable trust—the recipient organization.

The not-for-profit organization accepts the assets from the donor and agrees to do one of the following:

1. Use those assets on behalf of a beneficiary specified by the donor.
2. Transfer those assets to said beneficiary.
3. Transfer the return on investment of those assets to that beneficiary.
4. Transfer both the assets and the return on investments to the specified beneficiary.

It also establishes standards for transactions that take place in a similar manner but are not contributions because the transfers are any of the following:

1. Revocable.
2. Repayable.
3. Reciprocal.

It follows that the Statement requires a recipient organization that is willing to accept cash or other financial assets from a donor and to agree to abide by the stipulations spelled out above in the interest of that specified unaffiliated beneficiary. In doing so, it also agrees to recognize the fair value of those assets as a liability to the specified beneficiary concurrent with recognition of the assets received from the donor.

However, if the donor explicitly grants the recipient organization variance power, or if the recipient organization and the specified beneficiary are financially *interrelated* organizations, the recipient organization is required to recognize the fair value of any assets it receives as a contribution received.

Not-for-profit organizations are financially interrelated if:

1. One organization has the ability to influence the operating and financial decisions of the other.
2. One organization has an ongoing economic interest in the net assets of the other.

The Statement does not establish standards for a trustee's reporting of assets held on behalf of specified beneficiaries, but it does establish standards for a beneficiary's reporting of its rights to assets held in a charitable trust.

Further, it requires that a specified beneficiary recognize its rights to the assets held by a recipient organization as an asset unless the donor has explicitly granted the recipient organization variance power. Those rights are one of the following:

1. An interest in the net assets of the recipient organization.
2. A beneficial interest.
3. A receivable.

If the beneficiary and the recipient organization are financially interrelated organizations, the beneficiary is required to recognize its interest in the net assets of the recipient organization and adjust that interest for its share of the change in net assets of the recipient organization.

If the beneficiary has an unconditional right to receive all or a portion of the specified cash flows from a charitable trust or other identifiable pool of assets, the beneficiary is required to recognize that beneficial interest, measuring and subsequently remeasuring it at fair value, using a valuation technique such as the present value of the estimated expected future cash flows.

If the recipient organization is explicitly granted variance power, the specified beneficiary does not recognize its potential for future distributions from the assets held by the recipient organization. In all other cases, a beneficiary recognizes its rights as a receivable.

FASB 136 covers four conditions under which a transfer of assets to a recipient organization is accounted for as *a liability* by the recipient organization and as *an asset* by the resource provider because the transfer is revocable or reciprocal.

The four circumstances occur when:

1. The transfer is subject to the resource provider's unilateral right to redirect the use of the assets to another beneficiary.
2. The transfer is accompanied by the resource provider's conditional promise to give or is otherwise revocable or repayable.
3. The resource provider controls the recipient organization and specifies an unaffiliated beneficiary.
4. The resource provider specifies itself or its affiliate as the beneficiary and the *transfer is not an equity transaction.*
   - When the transfer is an equity transaction and the resource provider specifies itself as beneficiary, it records an interest in the net assets of the recipient organization (or an increase in a previously recognized interest).
   - When the resource provider specifies an affiliate as beneficiary, the resource provider records an equity transaction as a separate line item in its statement of activities, and the affiliate named as beneficiary records an interest in the net assets of the recipient organization. The recipient organization records an equity transaction as a separate line item in its statement of activities.

Certain disclosures are required when a not-for-profit organization transfers assets to a recipient organization and specifies itself or its affiliate as the beneficiary or if it includes in its financial statements a ratio of fundraising expenses to amounts raised.

The Statement incorporates without reconsideration the guidance in FASB Interpretation 42, *Accounting for Transfers of Assets in Which a Not-for-Profit Organization Is Granted Variance Power,* and supersedes that Interpretation. (It states that an NPO should be considered both a *donee* and a *donor* when it receives assets from a resource provider, *and* has received explicit unilateral authority to redistribute the assets and income from the assets to a beneficiary.)

FASB 136 became effective for financial statements issued for fiscal periods beginning after December 15, 1999, except for the provisions incorporated from Interpretation 42, which continue to be effective for fiscal years ending after September 15, 1996. Earlier application was encouraged. This Statement was applicable either by restating the financial statements of all years presented or by recognizing the cumulative effect of the change in accounting principle in the year of the change.

IRS RULINGS AND LEGISLATION RELATING TO DISCLOSURE

At the same time that the Financial Accounting Standards Board was adopting FASB 136, the Internal Revenue Service was issuing new rulings relating to the availability to the public of financial documents revealing the details of the operations of not-for-profit (or in the parlance of the IRS, *exempt*) organizations. The new regulations increase the disclosure burden of exempt organizations—and their accountants.

These exempt organizations are entities described in Sections 501(c) and 501(d) of the Internal Revenue Code and exempt from taxation under Section 501(a). They include charitable, educational, scientific, literary, and medical organizations, trade and professional associations, sports leagues, social welfare organizations, public radio and television stations, trade and professional associations, social clubs, cemeteries, and fraternal beneficiary societies. The rules do not apply to disclosure requirements of private foundations.

Other Disclosure Requirements

Considering the huge sums of money that many of these NPOs handle, it is not surprising that in addition to other FASB Standards discussed later in this chapter, Congress has seen fit to set up some rules relating to disclosure by not-for-profits. Legislation has included the Omnibus Budget Reconciliation Act of 1987 and the Taxpayer Bill of Rights 2, passed in 1996.

The former required exempt organizations, including public foundations, to provide access for public inspection of their tax exemption applications. It also required that they (other than private foundations) allow public inspection at their principal offices of the last three years' annual reports. The Taxpayer Bill of Rights 2 provided for additional public disclosures which have been finalized in these IRS rulings.

Specific Documents for Inspection

Not only do the most recent rulings specify *what* should be disclosed, but they are very specific about *how* and *where* applicable documents are made available by the exempt organization (other than a private foundation).

The documents that must be available upon request for inspection if they apply to the particular organization include:

1. Form 990, *Return of Organization Exempt from Income Tax.*

2. Form 990BL, *Information and Initial Excise Tax Return for Black Lung Benefit Trusts and Certain Related Persons.*

3. Form 990EZ, *Short Form Return for Organization Exempt from Income Tax.*

4. Form 1023, *Application for Recognition of Exemption Under Section 501(c)(3) of the Internal Revenue Code.*

5. Form 1024, *Application for Recognition of Exemption Under Section 501(a) for Determination Under Section 120 of the Internal Revenue Code.*

6. Form 1065, *U.S. Partnership Return of Income.*

In addition to the documents themselves, other relevant information must also be made available:

For Forms 1023 or 1024, all supporting documents filed by, or on behalf of the organization in connection with that application, as well as any correspondence with the IRS should be available. If the application was filed before July 15, 1987, the organization need not supply the document unless the organization possessed a copy of the application on that date.

For Forms 990, 990-EZ, 990-BL or Form 1065, including all schedules and attachments filed with the IRS, the organization must make available its three most recent returns. However, in the interest of confidentiality, the organization should *not* including the portions of the returns that give the names and addresses of contributors.

The exempt organization must also copy documents, or portions thereof, when requested either in writing or in person.

Procedures

The ruling is quite specific about establishing the various procedures for making these documents available for public inspection.

1. It specifies the amount of fees for copying and postage the organization may charge. The organization may charge a reasonable amount for copying and mailing as long as it does not exceed the IRS fees for copies of documents (currently $1 for the first page and 15 cents for each subsequent page). They can charge for the actual cost of postage.

2. It gives instructions on *where* the documents must be available for inspection. In general, the documents must be made available at the organization's principal office, and at larger regional or district offices.

3. It sets limitations an organization may put on requests for copies of documents. Copies of documents should normally be available upon personal request the same day at the place where the documents are avail-

able for inspection. Under unusual circumstances, the organization may respond on the next business day, or on the business day following the day the unusual circumstances occurred, as long as the delay does not exceed 5 business days. Written requests must be honored within 30 days of receipt.

4. It outlines how an organization can avoid having to respond to individual requests for copies. Rather than furnish copies, an organization may put the documents on its Web page or another Internet site where there is a database of similar information. Placing the specified documents on the Internet covers the requirement to provide copies, but the organization must still allow public inspection. The regulations specify a number of criteria for posting documents on the Internet.

   a. The documents must be posted so that the public can view, download, and print them in the same format as the original document.

   b. The documents must be accessible without a fee and without having any specialized computer hardware or software.

5. It furnishes guidance to organizations that believe they are the victims of harassment campaigns. If an exempt organization has sufficient cause based on facts and circumstances to believe it is the victim of a harassment campaign, it may take certain steps:

   a. Demonstrate that a group of apparently unreasonable requests aims to disrupt the organization's operations rather than to obtain information.

   b. Refuse to respond to those requests.

   c. Request the IRS district director for a determination.

   d. While a determination is pending, the organization need not respond to the apparently frivolous requests.

   e. Comply on a timely basis with any seemingly valid requests.

Noncompliance

The IRS has set rather stiff penalties for noncompliance:

1. An *individual* whose duty it is to make the required disclosures, but fails to comply without reasonable cause with his or her obligations on behalf of the exempt organization is subject to a penalty of $20 per return or exemption application for each day the failure continues. The maximum penalty for failure to disclose is $10,000 per return. No maximum is specified for the exemption application.

2. An exempt *organization* that willfully fails to comply with the requirement to allow public inspection or to provide copies of returns or

exemption applications upon proper request is liable for a $5,000 penalty (per return or application).

3. Criminal penalties may be applied to any person or exempt organization that willfully furnishes false or fraudulent information.

FASB Statement 93, Recognition of Depreciation by Not–for–Profit Organizations

FASB Statement 93 provides that all not-for-profit organizations must recognize depreciation on all long-lived, tangible assets in general-purpose external financial statements. Thus, the Statement eliminates previously allowed exemptions from depreciation accounting for landmarks, monuments, cathedrals, certain historical treasures, and structures such as churches or temples used primarily as houses of worship.

However, rare works of art and historical treasures that have exceptionally long lives will continue to be exempt from depreciation accounting; but to be in line for this exemption, these assets must have recognized cultural, aesthetic, or historical value, and normally will already have had a long existence, and be expected to retain this value far into the future. Statement 93 also requires not-for-profit organizations to disclose depreciation expense periodically. The financial statement is to include:

1. Depreciation expense for the current reporting period.
2. Balance of major classes reported by nature or function.
3. Accumulated depreciation by major class or in total.
4. Description of accounting methods employed in figuring depreciation.

FASB Statement 116, Accounting for Contributions Received and Contributions Made

FASB Statement 117, Financial Statements of Not–for–Profit Organizations

In the past, differing requirements, or deficient guidelines, have led divergent forms of not-for-profit enterprises to abide by various rulings promulgated for their particular type of organization, to follow lines of least resistance, or merely to perpetuate custom. This was true whether or not the organization or the external users were gaining insightful information from the various accounting and reporting procedures. The new rules supersede any/all inconsistencies or discrepancies with previous guides, announcements, or statements.

Statement 116 specifically addresses accounting standards for contributions of cash, assets, services or unconditional promises to provide these at some future time, made or received by any organization, whether it be a not-for-profit or a for-profit business concern:

1. Contributions *received*, including unconditional promises to give, are recognized at fair market value in the period received.
2. Contributions *made*, including unconditional promises to give, are recognized as expenses at fair market value in the period when given.
3. Conditional promises to give (whether received or made) are appropriately recognized when the conditions are substantially met.

This Statement acts to tighten some of the provisions relating to measurement and recognition of volunteer services and their relevancy. It specifies that before these services can be included in revenue, they must create or enhance nonfinancial assets, be of a specialized nature, and be provided by skilled individuals contributing services that would otherwise be purchased. Therefore, the services requiring little skill or training provided by the average volunteer will not be considered as revenue or gains. On the other hand, volunteer work by trained professionals and tradesmen, such as nurses, teachers, carpenters, plumbers may be measured at fair value and recognized in the financial report with explanatory notes describing the value of service rendered to various aspects of particular programs. Recognition of these services must also be deemed to be clearly relevant and clearly measurable. If practicable, the fair value of the ordinary volunteer services contributed but not recognized as revenue should also be disclosed even though not recognized as revenue.

Both Statements 116 and 117 take into consideration three classes of contributions:

1. Permanently restricted net assets.
2. Temporarily restricted net assets.
3. Unrestricted net assets.

Statement 116 also requires accounting for the expiration of donor-imposed restrictions if/when said restrictions expire. It also establishes standards for accounting for disclosures relating to works of art, historical treasures, rare books and manuscripts—collections whether capitalized or not.

To be considered a "collection," the assets must be:

1. For the purpose of public exhibition, education or research, not an investment for financial gain.
2. Conserved, cared for, and remain unencumbered.
3. Protected by an organizational policy requiring that proceeds from the sale of any collection items be used to acquire other items for collections.

An organization is not required to recognize contributions if they are added to collections which meet the above criteria. However, when applying FASB 116, organizations are encouraged to capitalize previously acquired collections retroactively or to capitalize them on a prospective basis. One stipulation is that capitalization of selected collections or items is *not* permitted. If capitalized retroactively, these assets may be stated at their cost, at fair value at the time of acquisition, current cost or current market value.

When collections have been capitalized, additional contributed items are to be recognized as revenue or gains; if the collections have not been capitalized, these items are not recognized. There is, however, additional disclosure information required for them and for collections which have been capitalized prospectively.

1. On the face of the statement of activities, apart from revenues, expenses, gains and losses an organization that has not capitalized must report the cost of items purchased as a decrease in the appropriate class of net assets; or proceeds resulting from the sale of items; or from insurance recoveries as an increase in the appropriate class of net assets.
2. An organization that capitalizes prospectively must report proceeds from sales or insurance recoveries of items not previously capitalized separately.
3. Both those organizations that do not capitalize, or do so prospectively, must describe the collections and their significance, and the accounting conservatorship policies relating to them.
4. They must also describe and report the fair value of items lost or removed from collections for whatever reason.
5. A line in the body of the financial statement must refer directly to the note on collections.

In addition to the accounting functions which these stipulations provide, they would appear to help ensure the integrity of important collections.

The intent and purpose of FASB 117 is to begin to bring a measure of uniformity to the financial statements of NPOs, particularly for the benefit of external users. Emphasis is upon relevance and significance of the information provided, the ease with which it can be understood and interpreted, and the readiness with which financial reports can be compared with those of other not-for-profit entities.

FASB 117 stipulates that three financial statements with appropriate notes be included in all NPO financial reports:

1. Statement of financial position.
2. Statement of activities.
3. Statement of cash flows.

This latter requirement is new for not-for-profit entities and thus amends FASB 95, *Statement of Cash Flows*, in which the requirements had previously applied only to business entities. Statement 117 also *requires* Voluntary Health and Welfare Organizations (*encourages* other NPOs) to prepare an additional financial statement showing expenses in natural classifications as well as the functional classifications required of all NPOs. Organizations may continue to present other financial reports if they have found them to be beneficial in demonstrating the handling of the service aspects of the particular type of NPO.

Most organizations probably found that their accounting and reporting activities had not become more complicated and restrictive, but simplified, and at the same time, more meaningful once the initial changeover had been completed. This is particularly true if the organization carried fund accounting to the extreme and attempted to fit everything into the pattern whether or not this proved to be appropriate or useful. Statement 117 does not tamper with fund accounting *per se* but does require that the emphasis on financial reporting be placed on the entity as a whole. Thus, organizations may continue to prepare their statement of financial position showing fund groups, but the groups must be aggregated into net asset classes.

In line with the aim to give a clear picture of an NPO's liquidity, FASB 117 requires that an organization must break down its net assets into the three classes mentioned above. Further, information about the amounts and/or conditions of the two restricted categories can be made in the statement itself if this is deemed sufficient, or it may be necessary to give detailed explanations in the notes. The latter could be more frequently necessary than not, since the restrictions could range from a wealthy donor's desire to aid a "pet project" to a government grant funding a Congressional bill.

Much of the impetus for these statements was to bring about more readily usable full disclosure. Requirements will now make it more important than ever to distinguish between program and support activities and expenses. FASB 117 separates expenses into three classes:

1. Managements and general.

2. Fund-raising.
3. Membership development.

It is important for the preparer of the financial statement to be reminded that the focus should be on the *service* aspect of the NPO and how well this is being accomplished. Since it is doubtful if this information can be conveyed adequately in the body of the financial statement, the accompanying notes will be of particular relevance.

Below are some important points to keep in mind relating to the purpose of the three basic financial reports of not-for-profit entities.

Statement of Financial Position

- Present assets, liabilities and net asset figures for the organization as a whole.
- Demonstrate credit status, liquidity, ability to meet service and financial obligations, need for outside financial aid.
- Distinguish between permanently restricted assets, temporarily restricted assets, unrestricted assets.
- Disclose donor-imposed restrictions and internally imposed restrictions relating to both time and purpose.

Statement of Activities (Operating Statement for NPOs)

- Report the changes in total net assets (equities).
- Present the changes in each of the three net asset classes (not fund balances): permanently restricted, temporarily restricted, unrestricted.
- Indicate total changes in net assets.
- Disclose expenditures by functional and/or natural classification as required/recommended for a particular type of NPO.

Statement of Cash Flows

- Amends FASB 95 to require *all* NPOs to include a cash flow statement in their external financial reports.
- Present changes in cash and cash equivalents including certain donor-restricted cash used on a long-term basis.
- Present cash flow information utilizing either direct or indirect method.

FASB STATEMENT 124, ACCOUNTING FOR CERTAIN INVESTMENTS HELD BY NOT–FOR–PROFIT ORGANIZATIONS

FASB 124 is another step in the process of bringing reason, conformity, consistency, and comparability in accounting and financial reporting to the world of not-for-profit entities.

This statement is reminiscent of FASB 115, *Accounting for Certain Investments in Debt and Equity Securities*, to the extent that it covers the same securities; however, accounting treatment for NPOs is markedly different from that applied to for-profit businesses.

Fair Value Requirements

Statement 124 requires that certain equity securities and all investments in debt securities be reported at fair value. The specific equity securities are those with readily determined fair value which are not accounted for by the equity method or as investments in consolidated subsidiaries. Gains and losses are to be reported in the statement of activities. This Statement also requires specific disclosures about all investments, including the return on the investments.

Readily determinable fair value of an equity security is considered to have been met if one of the following criteria applies:

1. Sale prices or bid or asked quotations are available on an SEC registered exchange.
2. Sales prices or bid or asked prices on OTC markets if they are reported by NASDAQ or the National Quotation Bureau.
3. If the equity security is traded only on a foreign market, that market is comparable to one of those given above.
4. If a mutual fund investment, fair value per share or unit has been determined and published as the basis for ongoing transactions.

Although many NPOs have been reporting all of their investments at fair value, it has not been required; therefore, there has been a considerable degree of diversity in the various organizations' accounting and financial reporting. The FASB believes that fair value will give a truer picture of the resources available for the further growth of the program of a not-for-profit organization. In addition, not only the staff and administrators, but also the donors will have improved information to assist them in allocating their efforts and resources.

Accounting Procedures

Application of this Statement may be made in either of two ways:

1. Restating of all financial statements presented for prior years.
2. Recognizing the cumulative effect of the change in the year of adoption.

Accounting and reporting for investments by various types of not-for-profit organizations has heretofore been provided by several AICPA guides. Any guidance in those sources which is inconsistent with the provisions of FASB 124 are superseded by these new requirements in this Statement.

In addition to the accounting principles set forth in this pronouncement, any additional disclosure and accounting requirements not discussed here but included in other Statements may apply to investments held by not-for-profit entities as well as to for-profit companies. They are:

1. FASB 107, *Disclosure about Fair Value of Financial Instruments* (amended).
2. FASB 133, *Accounting for Derivative Instruments and Hedging Activities.*

Disclosure and Reporting

The Statement of Activities for each reporting period for an NPO must include the following specific items:

1. Investment income from dividends, interest, etc.
2. Net gains or losses on investments reported at other than fair value.
3. Net gains or losses on those reported at fair value.
4. Reconciliation of investment return if separated into operating and nonoperating amounts.
5. Description of the policy used to decide what items should be included in determining operating costs.
6. Discussion for so doing if there is a change in that policy.

The Statement of Financial Position for each reporting period for an NPO must include the following:

1. Aggregate carrying amount of investments by major type.
2. Basis on which carrying amounts were determined for investments other than equity securities with readily determinable fair value and all debt securities.

3. Procedures used in determining fair values of investments other than financial instruments if carried at fair value. (Financial instruments are covered by the same requirement in FASB 107.)

4. Aggregate amount of any deficiencies in donor-related funds in which fair value of the assets has fallen below the level necessary to abide by donor stipulation or legal requirements.

For the most recent period, a not-for-profit organization must disclose in the Statement of Financial Position the nature of and carrying amount of any investments that represent a significant concentration of market risk.

FASB Project on NFPO Combinations

Not-for-profit (NFP) organizations had been included in the scope of the FASB's business combinations project since its inception in August 1996. However, at its meeting on March 1999, the Board decided to consider issues associated with combinations of NFP organizations in a separate project. For that reason, NFPO combinations are excluded from the scope of Part I of the September 1999 FASB Exposure Draft, *Business Combinations and Intangible Assets*.

The provisions of the business combinations ED and those of APB Opinion 16, *Business Combinations* (as it would be amended by that ED) were developed in the context of transactions between *business* enterprises, and would prohibit use of the pooling-of-interests method of accounting for business combinations.

NFP organizations actively engage in combination transactions, many of which are accounted for using the pooling method. Many of these mergers, however, possess characteristics that distinguish them from business combinations. For example, unlike business combinations, many NFPO combinations do not include an exchange of cash nor other assets as consideration. In addition, NFP organizations possess characteristics that distinguish them from business enterprises.

1. No equity ownership interests exist.
2. Operation is for purposes other than to provide goods and services at a profit.
3. Significant resources are obtained from donors who do not expect to receive monetary repayment of or a return on resources provided.

Thus, the Board has undertaken an on-going project to develop accounting and reporting guidance for NFPOs that takes into consideration the unique characteristics of the combinations and the financial reporting objectives of NFP organizations.

Chapter 15

Budgeting for Profit Planning and Budgetary Control

A budget in its simplest terms is an estimate of future events A budget is not a purely random guess, but a forecast which is computed from historical data that has been verified and assumed with some degree of credibility. The volume of sales for the following year, for example, may be estimated by using data from past experience, present-day market conditions, buying power of the consumer and other related factors.

Merely preparing the annual budget, then leaving it unaltered for the remainder of the budget period, is not the purpose. Preparation is only the first step. The second step is for management to control the operations of the firm and to adhere to the budget. Budgetary control is the tool of management for carrying out and controlling business operations. It establishes predetermined objectives and provides bases for measuring performance against these objectives. If variations between performance and objective arise, management should alter the situation by either correcting the weakness in performance or modifying the budget. Firms that adopt budgetary control have a better control of operations and are better able to modify them to meet expectations.

In addition to a review of the rolling budgets based on previous years' expenditures and operations, two management tools related to budgeting will also be discussed: break-even analysis (BE) and zero-base budgeting (ZBB).

The objective of break-even analysis is to determine an approximation as close as possible to the changes in costs generated by changes in the volume of production. Determining the BE point is a technique that can be applied to the control of costs, in the evaluation of alternatives, in the allocations of a firm's resources, and in making decisions in virtually every phase of a company's business.

The value to budgeting in break-even analysis is that the approach can be applied to sales, profits, costs, and selling prices, to help make sound decisions for the utilization of idle plant capacity, for proposed advertising expenditures, and for proposed expansion in production levels.

ZBB is a logical process, combining many elements of management. The key components of ZBB are:

1. Identifying objectives.
2. Determining value of accomplishing each activity.
3. Evaluating alternative funding levels.
4. Establishing priorities.
5. Evaluating workload and performance measures.

What ZBB does is to recognize that the budgeting process is a management process, a decision-making process and a driving force.

TYPES OF BUDGETS

There are two principal types of annual profit budgets: the operating or earnings budget, and the financial or cash budget. The earnings budget, as its name implies, is an attempt to forecast the earnings of a company for a future period. To make such forecast, other estimates must be made. Consequently, organizations have sales budgets, production budgets (which include labor budgets, materials budgets, manufacturing expense budgets), capital expenditure budgets, administrative expense budgets, distribution expense budgets and appropriation-type budgets (e.g., advertising, research). The accuracy of each of these budgets determines the accuracy of the earnings forecast.

The cash budget, on the other hand, tries to forecast the utilization of the company's cash resources. It estimates the company's anticipated cash expenditures and resources for a period of operation. Cash budget forecasts, like the earnings forecast, depend heavily on sales forecasts. The amount of sales determines the amount of cash the company has for purposes of its operation.

THE SALES BUDGET

The foundation of the entire budget program is the sales budget. If anticipated sales of a particular product (or project) do not exceed the cost to produce and market it by an amount sufficient to reward the investors and to compensate for the risks involved, the product (project) should not be undertaken. Sales forecasting must be continuous. Conditions change rapidly; in order to direct one's efforts into the most profitable channels, there must be a continuous review and revision of the methods employed.

Forecasting Sales

A sales forecast represents the revenue side of the earnings forecast. It is a prediction as to the sales quantity and sales revenue. Sales forecasts are made for both short and long periods.

Forecasting sales with any degree of accuracy is not an easy task. For example, a firm which estimates sales with the expectation that a patent which it holds will not become obsolete may be disappointed.

In general, the business forecaster has two situations: 1) those which he or she can to some extent control, and 2) those where conditions created by others can only be observed, recorded, interpreted and applied to his or her own situation. A firm that has a monopoly due to an important patent which it owns is an example of a company which controls the situation. Forecasts made by such a company may be very accurate. In most cases, however, a company has no such control. It must attempt to interpret general conditions, the situation in its own industry, and future sales of its particular company before making forecasts.

Making the forecast is the responsibility of the sales manager, who, with the help of the district managers and the individual salespersons, determines the primary sales objectives for the year. Corrections of the forecast are made by the heads of the firm so that sales estimates will better reflect expected economic conditions. Before an estimate of sales is made, there must be a reasonable expectation that the projection is attainable. It must be based on the best evidence available. As conditions change, the forecast is revised.

If a firm desires to sell more than in the past, an analysis of past sales performances must be supplemented by other analyses. Consideration must be given to general business conditions. The effects of political and economic changes throughout the world are quickly reflected on individual business communities. Some of these factors which affect sales are wars, government regulations, and technological developments. This information should be used in appraising the probable effect of these changes on the sales of the firm for the budget period.

Market Analysis

A sales manager needs to know if the firm is getting its full share of potential customer demand as indicated by a market analysis.

The questionnaire is a popular method of reaching consumers, retailers and jobbers. Data collected give the firm valuable information, essential in arriving at a forecast of sales possibilities.

A market analysis at a given time gives a picture of the present and potential consumption of a product. This picture provides only half the significant information. The other half can be obtained by continuing the survey over a period of time to discover market trends.

Pricing Policy

The sales budget is not complete until the firm decides on a practical policy as to what price can be secured for its product(s). Generally, estimates should be made to conform with the market prices during the budget period.

The next step is to formulate the sales policies of the firm. These policies should be established relative to such considerations as territorial expansion and selection, customer selection, types and quality of products and service, prices, terms of sales, and sales organization and responsibility.

Only after a firm has thoroughly analyzed past sales experience, general business conditions, market potentials, the product to be sold, determined the prices to be charged and formulated its sales policies is it ready to develop the sales program.

Measuring Individual Performance

As a basis for measuring individual performance, a rewarding-merit sales standard could be established. A sales standard is an opinion of the best qualified judgment of performance which may reasonably be achieved under ideal conditions. By comparing this standard with the budget estimate (the figure expected) under normal conditions, management has provided the most important tool of sales control.

An example of how a comparison between the standard and budget estimate may serve as a basis for reward is the following: A saleswoman may be told to produce sales of $150,000 (standard), but the firm may expect her to produce sales of only $125,000 (budget estimate). The saleswoman does not have to be told what the firm's budget figures are. In an endeavor to reach $150,000, she is trying to better what she believes is the budget figure. Depending on how close she comes to the $150,000, the firm may devise a method of rewarding her It should be kept in mind, however, that the standard should not be set too high, since it may have a reverse effect if the sales personnel feel it is unreachable.

THE PRODUCTION BUDGET

After the sales budget has been prepared, the next step is to prepare the production budget which specifies the quantity and timing of production requirements.

While the sales budget is prepared in anticipation of seasonal fluctuations, the production budget endeavors to smooth out the fluctuations and thus make most effective use of productive capacity. This is accomplished by manufacturing for stock over the slow periods and using the stock to cover sales during busy periods.

There are different problems for a firm that sells stock products and one that produces special-order goods. The objective for a stock-order-type firm is to coordinate sales and production to prevent excessive inventories, but at the same time to have enough stock to meet sales. A forecast of production in such a firm should enable the executive to arrange to lay out the factory so as to handle the anticipated volume most conveniently. Production in such a firm must be as evenly distributed as possible over the year. It is uneconomical to manufacture the whole period's requirements within a relatively short time at the beginning of the budget period. This involves unduly heavy capital costs of carrying the large inventory. Also, distributing the work over the entire period spreads the labor costs.

With special-order items, the production department must be prepared at all times to manufacture the goods as soon as possible after receiving the order. Production in this case has to be arranged for the best possible utilization of equipment and labor, so that idle time is reduced to a minimum.

Budgeting Production Costs

Production budgets should be rigid as long as conditions remain the same, but they should be capable of prompt adjustment when circumstances change. For example, if a company operates at 70 percent of capacity in a period and the budget was based on a production volume of 80 percent, the budget is of little use. The budget will have to be altered to show what production costs will be at the 70 percent level. It is prudent when planning production at a particular anticipated percentage level to indicate in the budget the estimates of possible production costs at different levels.

Preparing the Production Budget

The production budget period may vary in length. However, it is common practice among large corporations to use what is known as a "product year." As an example, the automobile industry will usually start with the introduction of new models. The budget year should include at least one complete cycle of operations so that money tied up in raw materials and work-in-process materials may undergo one complete liquidation. Another factor influencing the budget period is the stability of general business conditions. It is more difficult to budget operations during an unstable period, and it is advisable at these times to shorten the budget period.

The production budget should be expressed in terms of physical units. To compute the physical quantities is simple. For example, a simple computation to estimate production required is:

	Units
Estimated sales	250,000
Less opening inventory	150,000
Total requirements	100,000
Add: Closing inventory	100,000
Production required	200,000

Before computing the quantity to be produced, it is necessary to decide quantities to be in the inventory at the end of the period. This decision should be based on factors such as:

a. Adequate inventory to meet sales demands
b. Evenly distributed production to prevent shortage of material and labor
c. Danger of obsolescence
d. High costs of storing large inventories.

Available Facilities.   The production program must conform with the plant facilities available and should determine the most economical use of these facilities. The capacity of the plant is measured in two ways: optimum plant capacity and normal plant capacity. All other measurements are in percentages of optimum or normal capacity. Optimum capacity of course, can never actually be attained. There are many unavoidable interruptions, such as waiting for setup of machines; time to repair machines; lack of help, tools, materials; holidays; inefficiency; etc. However, these interruptions should be looked into to determine how they can be minimized.

Management should also consider whether additional equipment is needed just to meet temporary sales demands. Later, such equipment may be idle. The replacement of old machinery with new high-speed equipment should also be considered. A careful study should help determine which step would be more profitable in the long run.

Records for each product showing the manufacturing operations necessary and a record of each machine's capability and capacity, should be maintained. Estimates must be made of material to be used, number of labor hours and quantities of service (power) required for each product. These estimates are called "standards of production performance." The establishment of these standards is an engineering rather than an accounting task. In this respect, these standards are similar to those used in standard cost accounting.

Cost of Production.   The following illustrates how cost of production is determined: Assume a concern has a normal capacity of 100 units of product. Current production budget calls for 80 units. Only one product is made; and its production requires two operations, A and B. The standard costs are: variable costs per unit of product, one unit of direct material, $2; operation A (direct labor and overhead), $3; operation B (direct labor and overhead), $5; total $10. Fixed production costs for the budget period are $500, or $5 per unit based on normal capacity. This production cost budget would then be expressed as follows:

Variable cost (80 units @ $10)	$ 800
Fixed costs (80 units @ $5)	400
Costs chargeable to production	1,200
Cost of idle capacity (500 less 400)	100
Total budgeted costs	$1,300

There is a tie-in here between estimated costs, standard costs, and production budgets.

THE LABOR BUDGET

The labor budget deals only with direct labor. Indirect labor is included in the manufacturing expense budget. (The manufacturing expense budget includes the group of expenses in addition to indirect labor, expenses such as indirect material, repairs and maintenance, depreciation and insurance.)

The purpose of the labor budget is to ascertain the number and kind of workers needed to execute the production program during the budget period. The labor budget should indicate the necessary worker-hours and the cost of labor required for the manufacture of the products in the quantities shown by the production budget.

Preparation of the Labor Budget

The preparation of a labor budget begins with an estimate of the number of labor hours required for the anticipated quantity of products. Before this can be done, it is necessary to know the quantity of items to be produced, as in the production budget. If the products are uniform and standard labor time allowances have been established, it is just a matter of multiplying the production called for by the standards to determine the labor hours required.

If the products are *not* uniform but there is uniformity of operations, it is first necessary to translate production into operation requirements. Operation standards then should be established in terms of worker- or machine-hours to ascertain the quantity of labor required. The next step in preparing the labor budget is to estimate the cost of direct labor. These estimates are computed by multiplying the number of units to be produced by the labor costs per unit. The problem then is to predetermine the unit labor costs. Some of the methods of determining these costs are:

1. Day rate system
2. Piece rate system.
3. Bonus system.

In firms where standard labor costs have been established for the products manufactured, it is necessary only to multiply the units of the product called for in the production budget by the standard labor costs.

A detailed analysis should frequently be made of the differences between actual and estimated labor costs to determine whether they are justified. An investigation may reveal inefficient workers, wasted time, defective materials, idle time, poor working conditions, high-priced workers, etc. Responsibility must be definitely placed and immediate action taken to correct those factors which are capable of being controlled.

The budgets for direct labor and manufacturing expenses are not complete until schedules of the final estimates are prepared. The form will vary, depending on the needs of the firm. The following is an example of a schedule of estimated direct labor costs where estimates are shown for each department of the firm:

X Corporation

Estimated Direct Labor Costs
for the Period 1/1/xx to 12/31/xx

Dept.	Quantity to Be Produced	Standard Labor Cost Per Unit	Total Estimated Labor Cost
1	127,600	$ .90	$115,000
2	127,600	1.60	204,000
3	127,600	1.12	143,000
		$3.62	$462,000

MATERIALS BUDGET

The purpose of the materials budget is to be sure that there are sufficient materials to meet the requirements of the production budget. This budget deals with the purchase of raw materials and finished parts and controls the inventory. How to estimate the material required depends on the nature of the individual company. A company manufacturing standard articles can estimate fairly accurately the amount of raw materials and the purchases required for the production program. Even where the articles are not standard, there is usually a reliable relationship between the volume of business handled and the requirements for the principal raw materials.

Tie-in to Standard Costs

In the preparation of the material budget, there is a tie-in to standard costs. Here is an example of how purchase requirements are computed:

Quantity required for production	300,000 units
Desired inventory at end of budget period	75,000 units
Total requirements	375,000 units
Less: Inventory at beginning of period	80,000 units
Purchase requirements	295,000 units

The next step is to express material requirements in terms of prices. Some firms establish standard prices based on what are considered normal prices. Differences between standard and actual purchase prices are recorded as price variance.

Factors Affecting Policy

These are:

1. The time it takes the material to be delivered after the purchase order is issued.
2. The rate of consumption of material as indicated by the production budget.
3. The amount of stock that should be on hand to cover possible delays in inventory of raw materials.

On the basis of these factors, the purchasing department working with the production department can establish figures of minimum stocks and order quantities of raw materials and parts for each product handled. Purchases in large quantities are advisable if price advantages can be obtained. Bulk purchases are advisable during periods of rising prices but not during periods of declining prices. The unavoidable time lag between order and delivery of the material is also a reason to buy in advance.

Buying in advance does not necessarily involve immediate delivery. The deliveries may be spread over the budget period in order to coordinate purchases with production and to control inventory. To control inventory, it is desirable to establish minimum and maximum quantities for each material to be carried. The lower limit is the smallest amount which can be carried without risk of production delays. If materials can be obtained quickly, the inventory can be held near the lower limit. The advantage of keeping inventory at this lower limit is that it minimizes the cost of storage and possible obsolescence. If materials cannot be obtained quickly, there is the possibility of a rise in prices, as well as an unforeseen delay in delivery which could hold up production and so it is advisable to carry more than minimum inventory.

Goods in Process

The time it takes for material to enter the factory and emerge as a finished product is frequently much longer than necessary for efficient production. Comparisons with other companies may reveal that a firm allows its goods to remain in process much longer than other firms. Investigations should be made to determine the causes of such delays and formulate remedies. These investigations are usually made in connection with the production budget.

Finished Goods

The budget of finished goods inventory is based on the sales budget. For example, if 100 units of an item are expected to be sold during the budget period, the problem is to determine how much must be kept in stock to support such a sales program. Since it is difficult to determine the exact quantity customers will demand each day, the finished goods inventory must maintain a margin of safety so that satisfactory deliveries can be made. Once this margin is established, the production and purchasing programs can be developed to replenish the stock as needed.

MANUFACTURING EXPENSE BUDGET

In preparing the manufacturing expense budget, estimates and probable expenses should be prepared by persons responsible to authorize expenditures. The general responsibility for variable expenses lies with the production manager. But the immediate responsibility for many of these expenses lies with the supervisors of the several departments. Generally, expenses are estimated by those who control them. Each person who prepares a portion of the manufacturing expense budget is furnished with data of prior periods and any plans for the budget period which may affect the amount of expenses. With these data decisions can be made about:

1. Which, if any, present expenses can be eliminated.
2. Probable effect of the sales and production forecasts on those expenses which must be incurred.

No plans for the elimination or reduction of variable expenses should be made unless it is certain that the plan can be enforced.

The responsibility for many fixed manufacturing expenses is with the general executives. Such fixed expenses include long-term leases, pension plans, patents, amortization, salaries of major production executives, etc.

In preparing the budget estimates of manufacturing expenses, a common practice is to use percentages. Each expense is taken as a percent of sales or production costs. For example, if a certain expense is estimated to be 5 percent of sales, this percentage is applied to the sales estimate to obtain the amount of this expense. The fallacy with this method is that all expenses do not vary proportionately with sales or production. A sounder method of estimating manufacturing expenses is to give individual expenses separate treatment.

In estimating the indirect labor expense, it is important to first analyze the expense for the period preceding the budget period. The requirements for additional help, or the possibility of eliminating some of the help, should be considered along with plans for increasing or decreasing any rates of compensation. Detailed schedules should be prepared, showing the nature of each job and the amount to be paid. By summarizing these schedules, an aggregate estimate can be determined.

Indirect materials expense should be estimated by first analyzing the amount consumed in prior periods. This, together with the production budget showing the proposed volume for the budget period, serves as a basis for estimating the quantities of the indirect material requirements. The probable cost of such requirements estimated by the purchasing department is the amount to be shown in the manufacturing expense budget.

Repairs and maintenance estimates are based on past experience data, supplemented by a report on the condition of the present equipment. If any additional equipment is to be installed during the budget period, recognition must be given to the prospect of additional repairs and maintenance charges. Electric power expense is in direct proportion to the production volume. The charges for depreciation of equipment can be estimated with considerable accuracy.

Insurance expense for the budget period is estimated on the basis of the insurance in force charged to production with adjustments made for contemplated changes in equipment, inventories, or coverage of hazard incident to manufacturing.

To budget manufacturing expenses effectively it is important to establish standard overhead rates.

At frequent intervals during the budget period, comparison should be made between the actual expenses in each department and the amount estimated to be spent for actual production during the period. Variations should be investigated and steps taken to correct weaknesses in the production program.

A distinction should be made between controllable and uncontrollable expenses so that the responsibility of individuals can be more closely determined. To facilitate the estimating of expenses, a further distinction is made between fixed and variable expenses. Fixed expenses are those which remain the same regardless of the variations in sales or production. Variable expenses are those which increase or decrease proportionally with changes in volume, sales or production. Maintenance is seldom treated in a separate budget. It is usually regarded as part of the manufacturing expense budget.

Following is an example of a Schedule of Estimated Manufacturing Expenses for each operation of a particular product:

Y Corporation
for the Year Ended 12/31/xx

	Total	Operation 1	Operation 2	Operation 3
Variable expenses:				
Indirect materials	$ 20,000	$ 5,000	$ 10,000	$ 5,000
Indirect labor	100,000	10,000	15,000	75,000
Light and power	30,000	5,000	13,000	12,000
Telephone	5,000	3,000	—0—	2,000

	Total	Operation 1	Operation 2	Operation 3
Fixed and semi-variable:				
Factory rent	50,000	14,000	18,000	18,000
Superintendence	100,000	30,000	35,000	35,000
Depreciation	100,000	20,000	60,000	20,000
General and				
administrative expense	50,000	12,000	17,000	21,000
Total	$455,000	$ 99,000	$168,000	$188,000

After estimates of materials, direct labor and manufacturing expenses have been prepared, a Schedule of Estimated Cost of Production may be prepared as follows:

Z Corporation
for the Year Ended 12/31/xx

	Total	Product A	Product B	Product C
Cost Element:				
Materials	$200,000	$ 80,000	$ 50,000	$ 70,000
Labor	340,000	100,000	80,000	160,000
Manufacturing expenses	70,000	30,000	30,000	10,000
Total	$610,000	$210,000	$160,000	$240,000

CAPITAL EXPENDITURES BUDGET

Since capital expenditures represent a large part of the total investment of a manufacturing concern, the capital expense budget is of great importance. Unwise capital expenditures can seldom be corrected without serious loss to stockholders. The purpose of the capital expenditures budget is to subject such expenditures to careful examination and so avoid mistakes that cannot easily be corrected.

A carefully prepared capital expenditures budget should point out the effect of such expenditures on the cash position of the company and on future earnings. For example, too large a portion of total assets invested in fixed plant and equipment sooner or later may result in an unhealthy financial condition because of the lack of necessary working capital.

Preparation of Capital Expenditures Budget

In preparing the capital expenditures budget, the following information is recorded:

1. The amount of machinery, equipment, etc., on hand at the beginning of the budget period;
2. Additions planned for the period;
3. Withdrawals expected for the period;
4. The amount of machinery, equipment, etc., expected at the end of the budget period.

Consideration should be given to estimates of additions planned for the period. Additions will be justified if they increase the volume of production and earnings, will reduce unit costs, and the money needed can be spared. Consideration should also be given to the percentage of investment for fixed assets as compared with net worth of the firm for a number of years. Various business authorities have realized that an active business enterprise with a tangible net worth between $50,000 and $250,000 should have as a maximum not more than two-thirds of its tangible net worth in fixed assets. Where the tangible net worth is in excess of $250,000, not more than 75% of the tangible net worth should be represented by fixed assets. When these percentages are greatly exceeded, annual depreciation charges tend to be too heavy, the net working capital too moderate, and liabilities expand too rapidly for the good health of the business; alternative leasing should be considered.

The capital expenditures budget should include estimates not only for the budget period, but long-range estimates covering a period of many years. The ideal situation occurs when machinery is purchased at a time when prices are low. A long-range capital expenditures budget will indicate what machinery will be of use in the future; then, machinery may be acquired when prices are considered low. Inefficient or obsolete machines can sometimes be made into satisfactory units by rebuilding. If it is estimated that gains derived from rebuilding machinery will exceed the costs, then provision should be made in the capital expenditures budget to incur these expenses. Such expenditures are frequently called betterments and prolong the useful life of the machines. The preparation of detailed and accurate records is an essential part of the capital expenditures budget. The following information should be included in such a record:

1. Description of machines;
2. Date of requisition;
3. Cost for depreciation rate.

From the above information, it is a simple matter to complete the depreciation for the budget period.

As with other budgets, actual expenditures should be compared with the estimates, and any variation should be analyzed. In addition, a statement should be prepared showing the extent to which actual results obtained from the use of certain capital expenditures are in line with expectations. This is particularly important where substantial investments are made in labor-saving equipment, new processes or new machines.

THE CASH BUDGET

The cash budget is a composite reflection of all the operating budgets in terms of cash receipts and disbursements. Its purpose is to determine the cash resources that will be available during the entire budget program so that the company will know in advance whether it can carry out its program without borrowing or obtaining new capital or whether it will need to obtain additional capital from these sources. Thus, the company can arrange in advance for any necessary borrowing, avoiding emergencies and, more important, a cash crisis caused by a shortage.

A knowledgeable financial person goes into the market to borrow money when there is the cheapest rate. The cash budget will tell the manager when there is the need to borrow so he or she can plan accordingly. In a like manner, the manager can foresee when there will be sufficient funds to repay loans.

A cash budget is very important to a firm which does installment selling. Installment selling ties up cash resources, and a careful analysis of estimated future collections is needed to forecast the cash position of the company.

Other purposes of the cash budget are: (1) to provide for seasonal fluctuations in business which make heavy demands on funds to carry large inventories and receivables; (2) to assist the financial executive in having funds available to meet maturing obligations; (3) to aid in securing credit from commercial banks (a bank is more likely to lend funds for a definite plan that has been prepared, indicating when and how the funds will be repaid) and 4) to indicate the amount of funds available for investments, when available and for what duration.

Preparation of the Cash Budget

The main difference between a cash budget and other budgets is that in the cash budget all estimates are based on the dates when it is expected cash will be received or paid. Other budgets are prepared on the basis of the accrual of the different items (for accrual-basis companies). Therefore, in the cash budget, the budget executive cannot base the estimate of cash receipts directly on the sales budget for the obvious reason that all the cash will not be received from such sales in the same month in which they are billed. This is not true in the case of a business on a strictly cash basis.

Depreciation is another item handled differently in the cash budget. Depreciation is a cost of doing business; it increases expenses and reduces net income for financial reporting purposes. It is not, however, a cash item and is ignored in preparing the cash budget, but the amount paid for a new plant or equipment in a single year or budget period is included in full in the cash budget.

Cash receipts of a typical firm come from cash sales, collections on accounts and notes receivable, interest, dividends, rent, sale of capital assets and loans. The cash sale estimate is taken from the sales budget. The estimate of collections on accounts should be based on the sales budget and company experience in making collections. With concerns whose sales are made largely on account, the collection experience should be ascertained with considerable care. As an illustration, assume the March account sales have actually been collected as follows:

Month	%
March	6.4
April	80.1
May	8.5
June	3.6
Cash Discount Taken	1.1
Bad Debts Loss	.3
Total	100.00

If the same experience is recorded for each month of the year, it is possible to resolve the sales estimates into a collection budget. It is sometimes desirable to develop the experience separately for different classes of customers for different geographical areas. Once these figures are ascertained, they should be tested from time to time.

Cash disbursements in a typical firm are made for payroll, materials, operating expenses, taxes, interest, purchases of equipment, repayment of loans, payment of dividends, etc. With a complete operating budget on hand, there is little difficulty in estimating the amount of cash that will be required and when it will be required. Wages and salaries are usually paid in cash and on definite dates. For purchases of material (from the materials budget), the purchasing department can readily indicate the time allowed for payments. Operating expenses must be considered individually. Some items, such as insurance, are prepaid. Others, such as commissions, are accrued. So, cash payments may not coincide with charges on the operating budget.

ZERO-BASE BUDGETING

A different approach to budgeting adopted by some industrial organizations as well as not-for-profit entities and governmental units is appropriately termed *Zero-Base Budgeting*. Whether adopted wholeheartedly on a yearly basis, as a review every few years, or merely as a mind-set tool, its precepts can be of value in the budgeting process.

Expenses for industrial organizations can be divided into two categories:

1. Direct manufacturing expense, for materials, labor, and overhead.
2. Support expense, for everything else.

It is the "everything else" that causes problems at budget time, when, for example, management is beset by rising costs and must decide between decreasing the budgetary allocation for a research and development project or cutting funds for executive development. Traditionally, problems like these boil down to one question: How should the company shift its allocations around? Rather than tinker with their existing budget, many companies have implemented this budgeting method that starts at base-zero.

This approach requires that the company view all of its discretionary activities and priorities afresh, and create a different and hopefully better set of allocations for the ensuring budget year. The base-zero procedure gives management a firm grip on support allocations of all kinds, a procedure for describing all support expense minutely, classifying the alternatives to each, and sorting them all according to their importance and priority.

This technique in budgeting differentiates between the basic and necessary operations and those of a more discretionary character, thus enabling management to focus specific attention on the optional group. The basic steps for effective zero-base budgeting require justification of every dollar spent on discretionary costs, and a prescribed order of approach to the final allocation of funds:

1. Describe each optional activity in a "decision" package.
2. Evaluate and rank these decision packages by cost/benefit analysis.
3. Allocate resources based on this analysis.

Where to Use Zero-Base Budgeting

Zero-base budgeting is best applied to service and support areas of company activity rather than to the basic manufacturing operation. Since a corporation's level of manufacturing activity is determined by its sales volume, the production level, in turn, determines how much the company should spend on labor, materials, and overhead. Hence, there is not the same simple relationship between costs and benefits here as there is in the service and support areas where management can trade off a level of expenditures on a given project against the direct returns on investment. Cost benefit analysis, which is crucial to zero-base budgeting, cannot be applied directly to decisions to increase or decrease expenditures in the manufacturing areas.

The main use of zero-base budgeting occurs when management has discretion to choose between different activities having different direct costs and benefits. Such areas normally include marketing, finance, quality control, personnel, engineering and other non-production areas of company activity.

Decision Package Concept

When implementing ZBB, a company must explain the "decision package concept" to all levels of management and then present guidelines for the individual manager to use in breaking the specific activities into workable packages. Next, higher management must establish a ranking, consolidation and elimination process. The decision package is the document that identifies and describes a specific activity in such a manner that management can (1) evaluate and rank that activity against other activities competing for limited resources, (2) decide whether to approve or disapprove expenditures in that area.

The specifications in each package must provide management with the information needed to evaluate the activity. Included should be (1) a statement of the goals of the activity; (2) the program by which the goals are to be attained; (3) the benefits expected from the program and methods of determining whether they have been attained; (4) suggested alternatives to the program; (5) possible consequences of not approving the package and expenditure of funds; (6) designation of personnel required to carry out the program.

There are two basic types of decision packages:

1. Mutually exclusive packages identify alternative means of performing the same function. The best alternative is chosen and the other packages are discarded.
2. Incremental packages reflect different levels of effort that may be expended on a specific function or program. One package, the "base package," may establish a minimum level of activity, and others identify increased activity or expenditure levels.

A logical starting point for determining next year's needs is the current year's operations. Each ground level manager who has the ultimate responsibility takes the areas's forecasted expense level for the current year, identifies the activities creating this expense, and calculates the cost for each activity. At this stage, the manager identifies each activity at its current level and method of operation and does not attempt to identify alternatives or increments.

After current operations have been separated into preliminary decision packages, the manager looks at requirements for the upcoming year. To aid in specifying these requirements, upper management should issue a formal set of assumptions on the activity levels, billings, and wage and salary increases for the upcoming year. These formal assumptions provide all managers with uniform benchmarks for estimating purposes.

At the conclusion of the formulation stage, the manager will have identified all of the proposed activities as follows:

1. Business-as-usual packages.
2. Decision packages for other ongoing activities.
3. Decision packages for new activities.

The ranking process forces management to face squarely the most basic decision: How much money is available and where should it be spent to obtain the greatest good? Management arrives at the decisions by listing, and then studying all the packages identified in order of decreasing benefit to the company, and eliminating those of least value.

It is possible for one ranking of decision packages to be obtained for an entire company and judged by its top management. While this one, single ranking would identify the best allocation of resources, ranking and judging the high volume of packages created by describing all of the activities of a large company would result in an unwieldy task for top management.

This problem can be resolved by grouping decision units which may correspond to a budget unit in organizations with detailed cost-center structures, or they can be defined on a project basis.

The initial ranking should occur at the cost-center or project level so that each manager can evaluate the relative importance of the segments and rank the packages accordingly.

The manager at the next level up the ladder then reviews these rankings with the appropriate managers and uses the resulting rankings as guides to produce a single consolidated ranking for all packages presented from below.

At higher levels of a large organization, the expertise necessary to rank packages is best obtained by committee. The committee membership should consist of all managers whose packages are being ranked with their supervisor serving as chairperson.

Each committee produces its consolidated ranking by voting on the decision packages presented by its members. As at the cost-center level, the most beneficial packages are ranked highest and the least important ranked lowest.

It is best to establish the cutoff line at the highest consolidation level first, and then for the lower levels. The most effective way to establish the first cutoff is for management at the highest consolidation level to estimate the expense that will be approved at the top level and then to set the cutoff line far enough below to allow trading off between the divisions whose packages are being ranked.

The ability to achieve a list of ranked packages at any given organization level allows management to evaluate the desirability of various expenditure levels throughout the budgeting process. This ranked list also provides management with a reference point to be used during the year to identify activities to be reduced or expanded if allowable expenditure levels change.

Zero-base budgeting can be a flexible and useful tool in simplifying the budgeting process and in bringing about better resource allocation by forcing meaningful consideration of varying priorities for available funds.

Break-Even Point Analysis

Definition. The break-even point (BE) is that amount of sales necessary to yield neither income nor loss.

If sales should be less than indicated by the BE point, a loss results. If the total cost of goods sold and other expenses is less than sales, and if this total varied in direct proportion to sales, operations would result in net income. BE analysis is not a budget, in itself, but is an approach in the budgeting process for dealing intelligently with the uncertainty of estimates for future operations that are based on statistical data. Breakeven analysis can be applied to sales, profit, costs, and selling price problems, and it can be used to help make sound decisions for employing idle plant capacity, planning advertising, granting credit, and expanding production. BE is a tool, and a useful one, with which to begin to approach decision problems.

BE Analysis, is an inexpensive method for analyzing the possible effects of decisions. Discounted cash flow techniques require large amounts of data expensive to develop. BE can help with the decision whether or not it is worthwhile to do more intensive, costly analysis.

BE provides a means for designing product specifications, which permits a comparison of different designs and their costs before the specifications for a specific product are accepted as the best choice cost-wise. For example, a new product with an uncertain volume is considered to be feasible if it's made with hand tools rather than with expensive capital equipment. The first method typically has higher variable costs, but lower fixed costs. This often results in a lower breakeven point for the project, and lower risks and potential profits. The fixed capital equipment approach raises the BE, but also raises the risks and profit potential for the manufacturer. BE helps to examine these trade-offs.

An important factor when using BE analysis is the nature of the user's cost structure. Some firms have a flexible labor force and standard cost analysis works well. In other businesses, however, management must treat labor costs differently. Certain skilled workers cannot be laid off when business is slow. BE analysis assumes a realistic definition of costs, both in amount and type. While fixed costs will not change with changes in revenue, variable and semi-variable costs do change with changes in sales, up or down. Product pricing can be significantly aided by using variations of breakeven analysis.

Break-Even Chart. A break-even chart presents a visual representation of sales volume, capacity, or output when expenses and revenues are equal, i.e., a volume level at which income equals expenses. A BE chart provides a projection of the impact of output upon expenses, income, and profits which makes the chart a useful tool for profit planning and control.

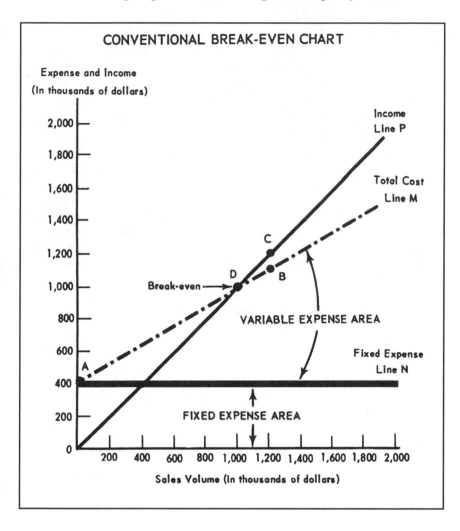

The BE chart assumes that selling prices do not change, total fixed expenses remain the same at all levels of output, and variable costs increase or decrease in direct proportion to sales. The N line remains the same regardless of sales volume; the point B on the chart is the total of the fixed and variable expenses on the list on the vertical axis. The area between line M and the fixed expense line N is the amount of variable expenses at different volumes of sales. The area between line M and the horizontal axis represents the total costs at various levels of sales. Line M can be considered a total cost line, since total costs for various volumes of sales can be readily determined from it. This can be done by starting at any point on the horizontal scale and measuring upward to line M and across to the vertical scale.

The income line P starts at zero and extends through point C, which is the point at which total sales and total income are shown on both scales, about $1,200. The profit area lies to the right of break-even point D where the revenue line P crosses the total cost line M. Revenue is greater than costs above—to the right—of the break-even point D; the loss area is below—to the left—of the break-even point D.

Break-Even is an inexpensive technique to determine whether or not it would be advisable to do more intensive and costly analysis of a proposed project. It provides a method for designing product specifications. Each design has costs which affect price and marketing feasibility by providing comparison of possible designs before the specifications are frozen by cash commitments. BE serves as a substitute for estimating an unknown factor in making project decisions. In deciding whether to go ahead with a project or to disband it, there are always variables to be considered such as costs, price, demand, and other miscellaneous factors. When most expenses associated with a proposed project can be determined, only two variables need be considered as variable items—profits (cash flow) and demand (sales). Demand is usually more difficult to estimate. By deciding that profit must at least be zero, the BE point, the demand is more easily estimated by determining what sales levels are needed to make the project a worthwhile undertaking. BE provides a way to attack uncertainty, to at least develop marketing targets for desired levels of income. One of the major problems of BE analysis is that no product exists in isolation; there are always alternative uses for an organization's funds. BE analysis helps decision makers to consider not only the value of an individual project, but how it compares to other uses of the funds and facilities.

Another problem is that BE analysis does not permit proper examination of cash flows. In considering financial commitments, the appropriate way to make investment or capital decisions is to consider the value of a proposed project's anticipated cash flows. If the discounted value of the cash flows exceeds the required investment outlay in cash, the project is acceptable. BE analysis makes restrictive assumptions about cost-revenue relationships; it is basically a negative technique defining constraints rather than looking at benefits; it is essentially a static tool for analyzing income and outflow for a single period of time.

The BE technique requires a realistic definition of costs, both in amount and type. A BE approach, therefore, should not be considered a technique to be used to make *final* investment decisions. It is a supplemental tool among the many factors a business decision maker must consider; it is an approach helpful to apply at the beginning of an analysis of a proposed solution of a business problem.

Although a complete and adequate budget may be developed without using a break-even analysis, its use adds to the understanding of estimates as shown in the following example.

Where the total cost of goods sold and other expenses is less than sales and if this total varied in direct proportion to sales, operations would always result in net income. For example, in a company in which the cost of goods sold and expenses amount to $1.80 per unit sold and the sale price is $2, on the first unit there would be net income of 20¢. On a million items, the net income would amount to $200,000.

As a practical matter, the simple example cited above is not realistic. Although some expenses may vary with volume of sales (e.g., salesperson's commissions, traveling expenses, advertising, telephone, delivery costs, postage, supplies, etc.), there are many other types of expenses which are not affected by the variations in sales. These expenses are the fixed expenses. Examples are depreciation, rent, insurance, heat, and so on.

If, going back to the above illustration, it is assumed that fixed costs and expenses amount to $40,000, at least $40,000 of costs and expenses are incurred before even one unit is sold. If a million units are sold, however, income before deducting fixed expenses is $200,000. After fixed expenses, net income is $160,000. So, the income picture goes from a loss of $40,000 (where no units are produced) to a profit of $160,000 (where one million units are produced). Somewhere between these, however, is a point represented by a certain number of units at which there will be neither income nor loss—the break-even point.

How to Compute the Break-Even Point

To determine the break-even point, let S equal the sales at the break-even point. Since sales at this point are equal to the total fixed costs and expenses ($40,000) plus variable costs and expenses ($1.80 per unit or 90 percent of sales):

$$
\begin{aligned}
S &= \$\ 40,000 + .9S \\
S - .9S &= \$\ 40,000 \\
.1S &= \$\ 40,000 \\
S &= \$400,000
\end{aligned}
$$

Even the above illustration oversimplifies the problem. It makes the assumption that all costs and expenses can be classified as either fixed or *variable*. However, in actual operations, expenses classified as fixed expenses may become variable where sales increase beyond a certain point, and some variable expenses may not vary in direct proportion to the sales.

Rent expense, for example, may not always be a fixed expense. A substantial increase in sales may create a need for additional showroom or salesroom space or, perhaps, expenses for salesperson's offices, or salesperson's commissions may rise unexpectedly when they have gone above a certain quota.

Then, there are types of hybrid expenses which may be classified as *semifixed*. For example, executives' salaries, association dues, subscriptions to periodicals and many other expenses are not in proportion to sales. Another unreality in the above problem is that as sales increase, there is a likelihood that sale prices will decrease because of larger orders. Now let's take a look at another situation:

Net sales		$2,500,000
Costs and expenses:		
Fixed	$250,000	
Variable	$1,500,000	1,750,000
Net income		$750,000

This company currently has under consideration an investment in a new plant which will cause an increase in its fixed expenses of $200,000.

The present break-even point is as follows:

$$S = \$250,000 + .6S$$
$$S-.6S = \$250,000$$
$$.4S = \$250,000$$
$$S = \$625,000$$

If the company builds the plant, the break-even calculation will be:

$$S = \$450,000 + .6S$$
$$S-.6S = \$450,000$$
$$.4S = \$450,000$$
$$S = \$1,125,000$$

If the plant expansion is undertaken, then the sales must be increased by $500,000 for the company to maintain its net income of $750,000, as follows:

$$S = \$450,000 + .6S + \$750,000$$
$$S - .6S = \$1,200,000$$
$$.4S = \$1,200,000$$
$$S = \$3,000,000$$
Increase $= \$500,000$ ($3,000,000 less $2,500,000)

The situation can be analyzed using two alternatives. The maximum production with the present plant is 1,500,000 units. At an average sale price of $2 per unit, sales would be $3,000,000. With the new plant, sales are estimated to hit $5,000,000 (2,500,000 units @ $2 per unit).

	Without New Plant	With New Plant
Net Sales	$3,000,000	$5,000,000
Less: Fixed costs and expenses	250,000	450,000
	2,750,000	4,550,000
Less: Variable costs		
and expenses (60% of sales)	1,800,000	3,000,000
Net income	$950,000	$1,550,000

If sales do not increase, the increase in fixed costs and expenses of $200,000 would cut the net income to $550.000. The break-even point will have been boosted $500,000, and the sales will have to be increased by this amount to produce the current $750,000 of income. Alternatively, the net income can be increased by $600,000 if the sales figure is increased by $2,000,000. Although these figures are based on an assumption that all costs and expenses are fixed or variable, the break-even analysis focuses attention on the factors involved in costs and income and provides a basis for consideration of various problems.

Chapter 16

Change in Accounting Methods and Consideration of Accounting Periods

To simplify the procedures to obtain IRS consent for taxpayers to change methods of accounting for federal income tax purposes, the IRS has modified and/or eliminated a number of the complicated rules governing changes in these accounting methods. The purpose of the new procedures is to provide incentives to encourage prompt, voluntary compliance with proper tax accounting principles. Under this approach, a taxpayer usually receives more favorable terms and conditions by filing a request for a change in method before the IRS contacts the taxpayer for an examination. A taxpayer who is contacted for an examination and required by the IRS to change his or her method of accounting generally receives less favorable terms and conditions and may also be subject to penalties.

SIGNIFICANT CHANGES

Probably the single most important change for the taxpayer is that Form 3115 requesting a change in method may now be filed any time during the year. Other new rules reduce or eliminate many of the complex provisions of the previous procedure including:

1. The Category A and Category B, and Designated A and Designated B have been eliminated.
2. The 90-day window at the *beginning* of an examination has been eliminated.

302

3. The 30-day window for taxpayers under *continuous examination* has been increased to 90 days.

4. The number of consecutive months the taxpayer is required to be under examination has been reduced from 18 to 12.

5. The definition of "under examination" has been clarified.

6. The consent requirement for taxpayers before an appeals officer or a federal court has been replaced with a notification procedure.

7. The various adjustment periods have been replaced with a single 4-year adjustment period for both positive and negative adjustments.

8. Several of the terms and conditions relating to the adjustment have been eliminated.

CHANGE IN METHOD OF ACCOUNTING DEFINED

A change in method of accounting includes a change in the overall plan of accounting for gross income or deductions, or a change in the treatment of any material item. A *material item* is any item that involves the proper time for the inclusion of the item in income or the taking of the item as a deduction.

In determining whether a taxpayer's accounting practice for an item involves timing, the relevant question is whether the practice permanently changes the amount of the taxpayer's lifetime income. If the practice does not permanently affect the taxpayer's lifetime income, but does or could change the taxable year in which income is reported, it involves timing and is, therefore, a method of accounting.

Consistency: Although a method of accounting may exist under this definition without a pattern of consistent treatment of an item, a method of accounting is not adopted in most instances without consistent treatment. The treatment of a material item in the same way in determining the gross income or deductions in two or more consecutively filed tax returns, without regard to any change in status of the method as permissible or not permissible, represents consistent treatment of that item. If a taxpayer treats an item properly in the first return that reflects the item, however, it is not necessary for the taxpayer to treat the item consistently in two or more consecutive tax returns to have adopted a method of accounting. If a taxpayer has adopted a method of accounting under the rules, the taxpayer cannot change the method by amending prior income tax returns.

Classification: A change in the classification of an item can constitute a change in the method of accounting if the change has the effect of shifting income from one period to another. A change in method of accounting does not include correction of mathematical or posting errors, or errors in the computation of a tax liability.

FILING FORM 3115

Except as otherwise provided, a taxpayer must secure the consent of the Commissioner before changing a method of accounting for federal income tax purposes. In order to obtain the Commissioner's consent for a method change, a taxpayer must file a Form 3115, *Application for Change in Accounting Method* during the taxable year in which the taxpayer wants to make the proposed change.

The Commissioner can prescribe administrative procedures setting forth the limitations, terms, and conditions deemed necessary to permit a taxpayer to obtain consent to change a method of accounting. The terms and conditions the Commissioner can prescribe include the year of change, whether the change is to be made with an adjustment or on a cutoff basis, and the adjustment period.

Unless specifically authorized by the Commissioner, a taxpayer cannot request, or otherwise make, a retroactive change in method, regardless of whether the change is from a permissible or an impermissible method.

METHOD CHANGE WITH ADJUSTMENT

Adjustments necessary to prevent amounts from being duplicated or omitted must be taken into account when the taxpayer's taxable income is computed under a method of accounting different from the method used to compute taxable income of the preceding tax year. When a change in method is applied, income for the taxable year preceding the year of change must be determined under the method of accounting that was then employed. Income for the year of change and the following taxable years must be determined under the new method as if the new method had always been used.

Required adjustments can be taken into account in determining taxable income in the manner and subject to the conditions agreed to by the Commissioner and the taxpayer. In the absence of an agreement, the adjustment is taken into account completely in the year of change, which limits the amount of tax where the adjustment is substantial. However, under the Commissioner's authority to prescribe terms and conditions for changes in method, specific adjustment periods are permitted that are intended to achieve an appropriate balance between mitigating distortions of income that result from accounting method changes and providing appropriate incentives for voluntary compliance.

METHOD CHANGE USING A CUTOFF METHOD

Certain changes can be made in a method and without an adjustment, using a cutoff method. Under a cutoff method, only the items arising on or after the beginning of the year of change are accounted for under the new method. Certain changes, such as changes in the last-in first-out (LIFO) inventory method, *must* be made using the cutoff method. Any items arising before the year of change or other operative date continue to be accounted for under the taxpayer's former method of accounting. Because no items are duplicated or omitted from income when a cutoff method is used to make a change, no adjustment is necessary.

INITIAL METHOD

A taxpayer can generally choose any permitted accounting method when filing the first tax return. IRS approval is not needed for the choice of the method. The method chosen must be used consistently from year to year and clearly show the taxpayer's income. A change in an accounting method includes a change not only in an overall system of accounting, but also in the treatment of any material item. Although an accounting method can exist without treating an item the same all the time, an accounting method is not established for an item, in most cases, unless the item is treated the same every time.

IRS APPROVAL

After a taxpayer's first return has been filed, the taxpayer must get IRS approval to change the accounting method. If the current method clearly shows the income, the IRS will consider the need for consistency when evaluating the reason for changing the method used. The following changes require IRS approval:

1. A change from the cash method to an accrual method or vice versa unless this is an automatic change to an accrual method.
2. A change in the method or basis used to value inventory.
3. A change in the method of figuring depreciation, except certain permitted changes to the straight-line method for property placed in service before 1981.

   Approval is not required in the following instances:

1. Correction of a math or posting error.
2. Correction of an error in computing tax liability.
3. An adjustment of any item of income or deduction that does not involve the proper time for including it in income or deducting it.
4. An adjustment in the useful life of a depreciable asset.

REFLECTIONS OF INCOME

The important point to remember is that methods of accounting should clearly reflect income on a continuing basis, and that the IRS exercises its discretion and in a manner that generally minimizes distortion of income across taxable years on an annual basis. Therefore, if a taxpayer asks to change from a method of accounting that clearly reflects income, the IRS, in determining whether to consent to the taxpayer's request, will weigh the need for consistency against the taxpayer's reason for desiring to change the method of accounting.

NEED FOR ADJUSTMENT

The adjustment period is the applicable period for taking into account an adjustment, whether positive (an increase in income) or negative (a decrease in income), required for the change in method of accounting. Adjustments necessary to prevent amounts from being duplicated or omitted are taken into account when the taxpayer's taxable income is computed under a method of accounting different from the method used to compute taxable income for the preceding taxable year. When there is a change in method of accounting, income for the year preceding the year of change must be determined under the method of accounting that was then employed, and income for the year of change and the following years must be determined under the new method of accounting.

90-DAY AND 120-DAY WINDOW PERIODS

A taxpayer under examination cannot file a Form 3115 to request a change in accounting methods except as provided in the 90-day window and 120-day window periods, and the consent of the district director. A taxpayer filing a Form 3115 beyond the time periods provided by the 90-day and 120-day windows will not be granted an extension of time to file except in unusual and compelling circumstances.

A taxpayer can file a Form 3115 during the first 90 days of any taxable year if the taxpayer has been under examination for at least 12 consecutive months as of the first day of the taxable year. The 90-day window is not available if the method of accounting the taxpayer is requesting to change is an issue under consideration at the time the Form 3115 is filed, or is an issue the examining agent has placed in suspense at the time.

A taxpayer requesting a change under the 90-day window must provide a copy of the Form 3115 to the examining agent at the same time the original form is filed with the IRS. The form must contain the name and telephone number of the examining agent, and the taxpayer must attach to the form a separate statement signed by the taxpayer certifying that, to the best of his or her knowledge, the same method of accounting is not an issue under consideration or an issue placed in suspense by the examining agent.

A taxpayer can file a Form 3115 to request a change in accounting method during the 120-day period following the date an examination ends regardless of whether a subsequent examination has commenced. The 120-day window is not available if the method of accounting the taxpayer is requesting to change is an issue under consideration at the time the form is filed or is an issue the examining agent has placed in suspense at the time of the filing.

A taxpayer requesting a change under the 120-day window rule must provide a copy of the Form 3115 to the examining agent for any examination that is in process at the same time the original form is filed with the IRS. The form must contain the name and telephone number of the examining agent, and must have a separate signed statement attached certifying that, to the best of the taxpayer's knowledge, the same method of accounting is not an issue under consideration or an issue placed in suspense by the examining agent.

UNDER EXAMINATION

A taxpayer is "under examination" if the taxpayer has been contacted in any manner by a representative of the IRS for the purpose of scheduling any type of examination of any of its federal income tax returns. If a consolidated return is being examined, each member of the consolidated group will be considered under examination for purposes of the accounting method change requirements.

However, according to the 1997 ruling, on the date a new subsidiary becomes affiliated with a consolidated group, a 90-day window period can be provided within which the parent of the group may request a method change on behalf of the new member, unless the subsidiary itself is already under examination. Previously, if a consolidated group was being examined, each member of the consolidated group was considered under examination regardless of the tax year under examination.

An examination of a taxpayer, or consolidated group of which the taxpayer is a member, is considered to end at the earliest of the date:

1. The taxpayer or consolidated group of which the taxpayer is a member receives a "no-change" letter.
2. The taxpayer or consolidated group of which the taxpayer is a member pays the deficiency—or proposed deficiency.
3. The taxpayer or consolidated group requests consideration by an appeals officer.

4. The taxpayer requests consideration by a federal court.
5. The date on which a deficiency, jeopardy, termination, bankruptcy, or receivership assessment is made.

A taxpayer under examination cannot ask to change an impermissible method of accounting if under examination for the year in which the taxpayer adopted the method, and it was an impermissible method of accounting in the year of adoption. A taxpayer under examination cannot ask to change a method to which it changed without permission if under examination for the year in which the unauthorized change was made. Under any other circumstance, a taxpayer under examination can change an accounting method only if the taxpayer requests the change under the applicable procedures, terms, and conditions set forth in the regulation.

APPLICATION PROCEDURES

The IRS can decline to process any Form 3115 filed in situations in which it would not be in the best interest of sound tax administration to permit the requested change. In this regard, the IRS will consider whether the change in method of accounting would clearly and directly interfere with compliance efforts of the IRS to administer the income tax laws.

A change in the method of accounting filed must be made pursuant to the terms and conditions provided in the regulations. The rule notwithstanding, the IRS can determine, based on the unique facts of a particular case, terms and conditions more appropriate for a change different from the changes provided in the regulations.

In processing an application for a change in an accounting method, the IRS will consider all the facts and circumstances, including whether:

1. The method of accounting requested is consistent with the Tax Code regulations, revenue rulings, revenue procedures, and decisions of the United States Supreme Court.
2. The use of the method requested will clearly reflect income.
3. The present method of accounting clearly reflects income.
4. The request meets the need for consistency in the accounting area.
5. The taxpayer's reasons for the change are valid.
6. The tax effect of the adjustment is appropriate.
7. The taxpayer's books and records and financial statements will conform to the proposed method of accounting.
8. The taxpayer previously requested a change in the method of accounting for the same item but did not make the change.

If the taxpayer has changed the method of accounting for the same item within the four taxable years preceding the year of requesting a change for that item, an explanation must be furnished stating why the taxpayer is again requesting a change in the method for the same item. The IRS will consider the explanation in determining whether the subsequent request for change in method will be granted.

Consolidated Groups

Separate methods of accounting can be used by each member of a consolidated group. In considering whether to grant accounting method changes to group members, the IRS will consider the effects of the changes on the income of the group. A parent requesting a change in method on behalf of the consolidated group must submit any information necessary to permit the IRS to evaluate the effect of the requested change on the income of the consolidated group. A Form 3115 must be submitted for each member of the group for which a change in accounting method is requested. A parent can request an identical accounting method change on a single Form 3115 for more than one member of a consolidated group.

Separate Trades or Businesses

When a taxpayer has two or more separate and distinct trades or businesses, a different method of accounting may be used for each trade or business, provided the method of accounting used for each trade or business clearly reflects the overall income of the taxpayer as well as that of each particular trade or business. No trade or business is separate and distinct unless a complete and separate set of books and records is kept for that trade or business. If the reason for maintaining different methods of accounting creates or shifts profits or losses between the trades or businesses of the taxpayer so that income is not clearly reflected, the trades or businesses of the taxpayer are not separate and distinct.

Resolving Timing Issues: Appeals and Counsel Discretion

An appeals officer or counsel for the government may resolve a timing issue when it is in the interest of the government to do so. To reflect the hazards of litigation, they are authorized to resolve a timing issue by changing the taxpayer's method of accounting using compromise terms and conditions or they may use a nonaccounting method change basis using either an alternative-timing or a time-value-of-money resolution.

Requirement to Apply the Law to the Facts

An appeals officer or counsel for the government resolving a timing issue must treat the issue as a change in method of accounting. The law must be applied without taking into account the hazards of litigation when determining the new method of accounting. An appeals officer or government official can change a taxpayer's method of accounting by agreeing to terms and conditions that differ from those applicable to an "examination-initiated" accounting method change.

The appeals officer may compromise on several points:

1. The year of change (by agreeing to a later year of change).
2. The amount of the adjustment (a reduced adjustment).
3. The adjustment period (a longer adjustment period).

If an appeals officer agrees to compromise the *amount* of an adjustment, the agreement must be in writing.

A change in a taxpayer's method of accounting ordinarily will *not defer the year of change* to later than the most recent taxable year under examination on the date of the agreement finalizing the change, and in no event will the year of change be deferred to later than the taxable year that includes the date of the agreement finalizing the change.

Alternative Timing

An appeals officer can resolve a timing issue by not changing the taxpayer's method of accounting, and by the IRS and the taxpayer agreeing to alternative timing for all or some of the items arising during/prior to and during, the taxable years before appeals or a federal court. The resolution of a timing issue on an alternative-timing basis for certain items will not affect the taxpayer's method of accounting for any items not covered by the resolution.

Time-Value-of-Money

An appeals officer or government counsel may resolve a timing issue by not changing the taxpayer's method of accounting, and by the IRS and the taxpayer agreeing that the taxpayer will pay the government a specified amount that approximates the time-value-of-money benefit the taxpayer derived from using its method of accounting for the taxable years before appeals or a federal court. This approach is instead of the method of accounting determined by the appeals officer to be the proper method of accounting. The "specified amount" is reduced by an appropriate factor to reflect the expense of litigation. The specified amount is not interest and cannot be deducted or capitalized under any provision of the law. An appeals officer may use any reasonable manner to compute the specified amount.

Taxpayer's Advantage

As outlined above, these IRS requirements, which are part of the "new" IRS image, cover timing problems that have been resolved by the IRS on a nonaccounting-method change basis. They provide terms and conditions for IRS-initiated changes that are intended to encourage taxpayers to *voluntarily request a change from an impermissible method of accounting* rather than being contacted by an agent for examination. Under this approach, a taxpayer who is contacted for *examination* and required to change methods of accounting by the IRS generally receives less favorable terms and conditions than if the taxpayer had filed a request to change before being contacted for examination.

The new regulations may be consistent with the policy of encouraging prompt voluntary compliance with proper tax accounting principles, but they appear to have some limitations. It is now easier for the taxpayer to change an accounting method, but the IRS ordinarily will not initiate an accounting method change if the change will place the taxpayer in a more favorable position than if the taxpayer had been contacted for examination. An examining agent will not initiate a change from an impermissible method that results in a negative adjustment. If the IRS declines to initiate such an accounting method change, the district director will consent to the taxpayer requesting a voluntary change.

RESOLVING TIMING ISSUES: DISCRETION OF EXAMINING AGENT

An examining agent proposing an adjustment on a timing issue will treat the issue as a change in method of accounting. In changing the taxpayer's method of accounting, the agent will properly apply the law to the facts without taking into account the hazards of litigation when determining the new method of accounting. An examining agent changing a taxpayer's method of accounting will impose an adjustment.

The change can be made using a cutoff method only in rare and unusual circumstances when the examining agent determines that the taxpayer's books and records do not contain sufficient information to compute the adjustment and the adjustment is not susceptible to reasonable estimation. An examining agent changing a taxpayer's method of accounting will effect the change in the earliest taxable year under examination (or, if later, the first taxable year the method is considered impermissible) with a one-year adjustment period.

METHOD CHANGES INITIATED BY THE IRS

If a taxpayer does not regularly employ a method of accounting that clearly reflects his or her income, the computation of taxable income must be made in a manner that, in the opinion of the Commissioner, does clearly reflect income. The Commissioner has broad discretion in determining whether a taxpayer's method of accounting clearly reflects income, and the Commissioner's determination must be upheld unless it is clearly unlawful.

The Commissioner has broad discretion in selecting a method of accounting that properly reflects the income of a taxpayer once it has been determined that the taxpayer's method of accounting does not clearly reflect income. The selection can be challenged only upon showing an abuse of discretion by the Commissioner.

The Commissioner has the discretion to change a method of accounting even though the IRS had previously changed the taxpayer to that method if it is determined that the method of accounting does not clearly reflect the taxpayer's income. The discretionary power does not extend to requiring a taxpayer to change from a method of accounting that clearly reflects income to a method that, in the Commissioner's view, more clearly reflects income.

The accounting method of a taxpayer that is under examination, before an appeals office, or before a federal court, can be changed except as otherwise provided in published guidance. The service is generally precluded from changing a taxpayer's method of accounting for an item for prior taxable years if the taxpayer timely files a request to change the method of accounting for the item.

Retroactive Method Change

Although the Commissioner is authorized to consent to a retroactive accounting method change, the taxpayer does not have a right to a retroactive change, regardless of whether the change is from a permissible or impermissible method.

Except under unusual circumstances, if a taxpayer who changes the method of accounting is subsequently required to change or modify that method of accounting, the required change or modification will not be applied retroactively provided that:

1. The taxpayer complied with all the applicable provisions of the consent agreement.
2. There has been no misstatement nor omission of material facts.
3. There has been no change in the material facts on which the consent was based.

4. There has been no change in the applicable law.
5. The taxpayer to whom consent was granted acted in good faith in relying on the consent, and applying the change or modification retroactively would be to the taxpayer's detriment.

New Method Established

An IRS-initiated change that is final establishes a new method of accounting. As a result, a taxpayer is required to use the new method of accounting for the year of change and for all subsequent taxable years unless the taxpayer obtains the consent of the commissioner to change from the new method or the IRS changes the taxpayer from the new method on subsequent examination. As indicated above, the IRS is not precluded from changing a taxpayer from the new method of accounting if the IRS determined that the new method does not clearly reflect the taxpayer's income. A taxpayer who executes a closing agreement finalizing an IRS initiated accounting method change will not be required to change or modify the new method for any taxable year for which a federal income tax return has been filed as of the date of the closing agreement, provided that:

1. The taxpayer has complied with all the applicable provisions of the closing agreement.
2. There has been no taxpayer fraud, malfeasance, or misrepresentation of a material fact.
3. There has been no change in the material facts on which the closing agreement was based.
4. There has been no change in the applicable law on which the closing agreement was based.

Required Change or Modification of New Method

The IRS may require a taxpayer to change or modify the new method in the earliest open taxable year if the taxpayer fails to comply with the applicable provisions of the closing agreement, or upon a showing of taxpayer's fraud, malfeasance, or misrepresentation of a material fact. The taxpayer can be required to change or modify the new method in the earliest open taxable year in which the material facts have changed, and can also be required to change or modify the new method in the earliest open taxable year in which the applicable law has changed. For this purpose, a change in the applicable law includes:

1. A decision of the U.S. Supreme Court.
2. The enactment of legislation.

3. The issuance of temporary or final regulations.

4. The issuance of a revenue ruling, revenue procedure, notice, or other guidance published in the Internal Revenue Bulletin.

Except in rare and unusual circumstances, a retroactive change in applicable law is deemed to occur when one of the events described in the preceding sentence occurs and not when the change in law is effective.

ACCOUNTING PERIODS

Taxable income must be figured on the basis of a tax year. A *tax year* is an annual accounting period for keeping records and reporting income and expenses. The tax years usable are:

1. A calendar year.
2. A fiscal year.

The tax year is adopted in the first year that an income tax return is filed. The tax year must be adopted by the due date, not including extensions, for filing a return for that year. The due date for individual and partnership returns is the 15th day of the 4th month after the end of the tax year. "Individuals" include sole proprietorships, partners, and S corporation shareholders. The due date for filing returns for corporations and S corporations is the 15th day of the 3rd month after the end of the tax year. If the 15th day of the month falls on a Saturday, Sunday, or legal holiday, the due date is the next business day.

Calendar Year

If a calendar year is chosen, the taxpayer must maintain books and records and report income and expenses from January 1 through December 31 of each year. If the first tax return uses the calendar year and the taxpayer later begins business as a sole proprietor, becomes a partner in a partnership, or becomes a shareholder in an S corporation, the calendar year must continue to be used unless the IRS approves a change. Anyone can adopt the calendar year. However, if any of the following apply, the calendar year must be used:

1. The taxpayer does not keep adequate records.
2. The taxpayer has no annual accounting period.
3. The taxpayer's tax year does not qualify as a fiscal year.

Fiscal Year

A fiscal year is 12 consecutive months ending on the last day of any month except December. A 52–53-week tax year is a fiscal year that varies from 52 to 53 weeks. If a fiscal year is adopted, books and records must be maintained, and income and expenses reported using the same tax year.

A 52–53-week tax year may be elected if books and records are kept, and income and expenses are reported on that basis. If this election is chosen, the tax year will be 52 or 53 weeks long, and will always end on the same day of the week. The tax year can end only on the same day of the week that:

1. Last occurs in a particular month.
2. Occurs nearest to the last day of a particular calendar month.

To make the choice, a statement with the following information is attached to the tax return for the 52–53-week tax year:

1. The month in which the new 52–53-week tax year ends.
2. The day of the week on which the tax year always ends.
3. The date the tax year ends. It can be either of the following dates on which the chosen day:
   a. Last occurs in the month in (1).
   b. Occurs nearest to the last day of the month in (1).

When depreciation or amortization is figured, a 52–53-week tax year is considered a year of 12 calendar months unless another practice is consistently used. To determine an effective date, or apply provisions of any law, expressed in terms of tax years beginning, including, or ending on the first or last day of a specified calendar month, a 52–53-week tax year is considered to:

1. Begin on the first day of the calendar month beginning nearest to the first day of the 52–53-week tax year.
2. End on the last day of the calendar month ending nearest to the last day of the 52–53-week tax year.

If the month in which a 52–53-week tax year ends is changed, a return must be filed for the short tax year if it covers more than 6 but less than 359 days. If the short period created by the change is 359 days or more, it should be treated as a full tax year. If the short period created is 6 days or less, it is not a separate tax year. It is to be treated as part of the following year.

A corporation figures tax for a short year under the general rules described for individuals. There is no adjustment for personal exemptions.

Improper Tax Year

A calendar year is a tax year of 12 months that ends on December 31, and a fiscal year is a tax year of 12 months that ends on the last day of any month except December, including a 52–53-week tax year. If business operations start on a day other than the last day of a calendar month and adopt a tax year of exactly 12 months from the date operations began, the taxpayer has adopted an *improper* tax year. The requirements for a calendar or fiscal tax year, including a 52–53-week tax year, have not been met. To change to a proper tax year, one of the following requirements must be met:

1. An amended tax return should be based on a calendar year.
2. IRS approval should be sought to change to a tax year, other than a calendar year.

Business Purpose Tax Year

A business purpose tax year is an accounting period that has a substantial business purpose for its existence.

In considering whether there is a business purpose for a tax year, significant weight is given to tax factors. A prime consideration is whether the change would create a substantial distortion of income. The following are examples of distortions of income:

1. Deferring substantial income or shifting substantial deductions from one year to another to reduce tax liability.
2. Causing a similar deferral or shifting for any other person, such as a partner or shareholder.
3. Creating a short period in which there is a substantial net operating loss.

The following nontax factors, based on convenience for the taxpayer, are generally not sufficient to establish a business purpose for a particular year:

1. Using a particular year for regulatory or financial accounting purposes.
2. Using a particular pattern, such as typically hiring staff during certain times of the year.
3. Using a particular year for administration purposes, such as:

    a. Admission or retirement of partners or shareholders.

    b. Promotion of staff.

    c. Compensation or retirement arrangements with staff, partners, or shareholders.

4. Using a price list, model year, or other item that changes on an annual basis.

5. Deferring income to partners or shareholders.

Natural Business Year

One nontax factor that may be sufficient to establish a business purpose for a tax year is an annual cycle of business, called a "natural business year." A natural business year exists when business has a peak and a nonpeak period. The natural business year is considered to end at or soon after the end of the peak period. A business whose income is steady from month-to-month all year would not have a natural business year as such. A natural business year is considered a substantial business purpose for an entity changing its accounting period. The IRS will ordinarily approve this change unless it results in a substantial deferral of income or another tax advantage.

The IRS provides a procedure for a partnership, an S corporation, or a personal service corporation to retain or automatically change to a natural business year as determined by the 25% test. It also allows an S corporation to adopt, retain, or change to a fiscal year that satisfies the "ownership tax year test." The 25% test uses the method of accounting used for the tax returns for each year involved. To figure the 25% test:

1. The gross sales and services receipts for the most recent 12-month period that includes the last month of the requested fiscal year are totaled for the 12-month period that ends before the filing of the request. Gross sales and services receipts for the last 2 months of that 12-month period are then totaled.

2. The percentage of the receipts for the 2-month period is then determined by dividing the total of the 2-month period by the total for the 12-month period. The percentage should be carried to two decimal places.

3. The percentage following steps 1 and 2 should then be figured for the two 12-month periods just preceding the 12-month period used in 1.

If the percentage determined for each of the three years equals or exceeds 25%, the requested fiscal year is the *natural business year*. If the partnership, S corporation, or personal service corporation qualifies for more than one natural business year, the fiscal year producing the higher average of the three percentages is the natural business year. If the partnership, S corporation, or personal service corporation does not have at least 47 months of gross receipts—which may include a predecessor organization's gross receipts—it cannot use this automatic procedure to obtain permission to use a fiscal year.

If the requested tax year is a 52–53-week tax year, the calendar month ending nearest the last day of the 52–53-week tax year is treated as the last month of the requested tax year for purposes of computing the 25% test.

An S corporation or corporation electing to be an S corporation qualifies for automatic approval if it meets the ownership tax year test. The test is met if the corporation is adopting, retaining, or changing to a tax year and shareholders holding more than 50% of the issued and outstanding shares of stock on the first day of the requested tax year have, or are all changing to, the same tax year.

Change in Tax Year

A tax year change must be approved by the IRS. A current Form 1128 must be filed by the 15th day of the end calendar month after the close of the short tax year to get IRS approval. The *short tax year* begins on the first day after the end of the present tax year and ends on the day before the first day of the new tax year. If the short tax year required to effect a change in tax years is a year in which the taxpayer has a net operating loss (NOL), the NOL must be deducted ratably over a 6-year period from the first tax year after the short period.

A husband and wife who have different tax years cannot file a joint return. There is an exception to this rule if their tax years began on the same date and ended on different dates because of the death of either or both. If a husband and wife want to use the same tax year so they can file a joint return, the method of changing a tax year depends on whether they are newly married. A newly married husband and wife with different tax years who wish to file a joint return can change the tax year of one spouse without first getting IRS approval.

The correct user fee must be included, if any. The IRS charges a user fee for certain requests to change an accounting period or method, certain tax rulings, and determination letters. The fee is reduced in certain situations and for certain requests, such as a request for substantially identical rulings for related entities.

Year of Change

While this heading and the one above are similar, the connotation is somewhat different. The year of change is the taxable year for which a change in the method of accounting is effective, that is, the first taxable year the new method is used even if no affected items are taken into account for that year. The year of change is also the first taxable year for taking an adjustment and complying with all the terms and conditions accompanying the change.

Partnership

A partnership must conform its tax year to its partners' tax years unless the partnership can establish a business purpose for a different period. The rules for the required tax year for partnerships are:

1. If one or more partners having the same tax year own a majority interest—more than 5%—in partnership profits and capital, the partnership must use the tax year of those partners.
2. If there is no majority interest tax year, the partnership must use the tax year of its principal partners. A principal partner is one who has a 5% or more interest in the profits or capital of the partnership.
3. If there is no majority interest tax year and the principal partners do not have the same tax year, the partnership generally must use a tax year that results in the least aggregate deferral of income to the partners.

If a partnership changes to a required tax year because of these rules, the change is considered to be initiated by the partnership with IRS approval. No formal application for change in the tax year is needed. Any partnership that changes to a required tax year must notify the IRS by writing at the top of the first page of its tax return for its first required tax year: *Filed Under Section 806 of the Tax Reform Act of 1986.*

The tax year that results in the least aggregate deferral of income is determined by:

1. Figuring the number of months of deferral for each partner using one partner's tax year. The months of deferral are found by counting the months from the end of that tax year forward to the end of each other partner's tax year.
2. Each partner's months of deferral figured in step (1) are multiplied by that partner's share of interest in the partnership profits for the year used in step (1).

3. The amounts in step (2) are added to get the aggregate (total) deferral for the tax year used in step (1).
4. Steps (1) through (3) are repeated for each partner's tax year that is different from the other partners' years.

The partners' tax year that results in the lowest aggregate—total—number is the tax year that must be used by the partnership. If more than one year qualifies as the tax year that has the least aggregate deferral of income, the partnership can choose any year that qualifies. If one of the tax years that qualifies is the partnership's existing tax year, the partnership must retain that tax year.

S Corporations

If a business meets the requirements of a small business corporation, it can elect to be an S corporation. All S corporations, regardless of when they became an S corporation, must use a *permitted tax year.* A permitted tax year is the calendar year or any other tax year for which the corporation establishes a business purpose.

Personal Service Corporations

A personal service corporation must use a calendar year unless it can establish a business purpose for a different period or it makes a Section 444 election (discussed below). For this purpose, a corporation is a personal service corporation if all of the following conditions are met:

1. The corporation is a C corporation.
2. The corporation's principal activity during the testing period is the performance of personal services.
3. Employee-owners of the corporation perform a substantial part of the services during the testing period.
4. Employee-owners own more than 10% of the corporation's stock on the last day of the testing period.

The principal activity of a corporation is considered to be the performance of personal services if, during the testing period, the corporation's compensation costs for personal service activities is more than 50% of its total compensation costs.

Generally, the *testing period for a tax year is the prior tax year.* The testing period for the first tax year of a new corporation starts with the first day of the tax year and ends on the earlier of the following dates:

1. The last day of its tax year.
2. The last day of the calendar year in which the tax year begins.

The *performance of personal services* involves any activity in the fields of health, veterinary services, law, engineering, architecture, accounting, actuarial science, performing arts, or certain consulting services.

An employee-owner of a corporation is a person who:

1. Is an employee of the corporation on any day of the testing period.
2. Owns any outstanding stock of the corporation on any day of the testing period.

A further clarification of the definition of an independent contractor by the 1997 Act states, "A person who owns any outstanding stock of the corporation and who performs personal services for or on behalf of the corporation is treated as an *employee* of the corporation. This rule applies even if the legal form of the person's relationship to the corporation is such that the person would be considered an independent contractor for other purposes."

Section 444 Election

A partnership, S corporation, or personal service corporation can elect under Section 444 of the Internal Revenue Code to use a tax year different from its required tax year. Certain restrictions apply to the election. In addition, a partnership or S corporation may have to make a payment for the deferral period. The Section 444 election does not apply to any partnership, S corporation, or personal service corporation that establishes a business purpose for a different period.

A partnership, S corporation, or personal service corporation can make a Section 444 election if it meets all the following requirements:

1. It is not a member of a tiered structure.
2. It has not previously had a Section 444 election in effect.
3. It elects a year that meets the deferral period requirement.

The determination of the *deferral period* depends on whether the partnership, corporation, or personal service corporation is retaining its current tax year or adopting or changing its tax year with a Section 444 election.

A partnership, S corporation, or personal service corporation can make a Section 444 election to *retain* its tax year only if the deferral period of the new tax year is three months or less. The deferral period is the number of months between the beginning of the retained year and the close of the first required tax year.

If the partnership, S corporation, or personal service corporation is *changing* to a tax year other than its required year, the deferral period is the number of months from the end of the new tax year to the end of the required tax year. The IRS will allow a Section 444 election only if the deferral period of the new tax year is less than the shorter of:

1. Three months.
2. The deferral period of the tax year being changed. This is the tax year for which the partnership, S corporation, or personal service corporation wishes to make the Section 444 election.

If the tax year is the same as the required tax year, the deferral period is zero.

A Section 444 election is made by filing a form with the IRS by the earlier of:

1. The due date of the income tax return resulting from the 444 election.
2. The 15th day of the 6th month of the tax year for which the election will be effective. For this purpose, the month in which the tax year begins is counted, even if it begins after the first day of that month. The Section 444 election stays in effect until it is terminated. If the election is terminated, another Section 444 election cannot be made for any tax year. The election ends when any of the three corporations does any of the following:

1. Changes its tax year to a required tax year.
2. Liquidates.
3. Willfully fails to comply with the required payments or distributions.
4. Becomes a member of a tiered structure.

The election also ends if:

1. An S corporation's election is terminated. However, if the S corporation immediately becomes a personal service corporation, it can continue the Section 444 election of the S corporation.
2. A personal service corporation ceases to be a personal service corporation. If the personal service corporation elects to be an S corporation, it can continue the election of the personal service corporation.

Corporations

A new corporation establishes its tax year when it files its first return. A newly reactivated corporation that has been inactive for a number of years is treated as a new taxpayer for the purpose of adopting a tax year. A corporation other than an S corporation, a personal service corporation, or a domestic international sales corporation (C-DISC) can change its tax year without getting IRS approval if all the following conditions are met:

1. It must not have changed its tax year within the 10 calendar years ending with the calendar year in which the short tax year resulting from the change begins.
2. Its short tax year must not be a tax year in which it has a net operating loss.
3. Its taxable income for the whole tax year, if figured on an annual basis, is 80% or more of its taxable income for the tax year before the short tax year.
4. If a corporation is one of the following for either the short tax year or the tax year before the short tax year, it must have the same status for both the short tax year and the prior tax year.
    a. Personal holding company.
    b. Foreign personal holding company.
    c. Exempt organization.
    d. Foreign corporation not engaged in a trade or business within the United States.
5. It must not apply to become an S corporation for the tax year that would immediately follow the short tax year required to effect the change.

The corporation must file a statement with the IRS office where it files its tax return. The statement must be filed by the due date for the short tax year required by the change. It must indicate the corporation is changing its annual accounting period, and show that all the preceding conditions have been met. If the corporation does not meet all the conditions because of later adjustments in establishing tax liability, the statement will be considered a timely application to change the corporation's annual accounting period to the tax year indicated in the statement.

The IRS will waive conditions (1) and (5) above, as well as conditions (2) and (3)(c) outlining automatic approval criteria for a corporation that:

1. Meets all the other conditions.

2. Elected to be an S corporation for the tax year beginning January 1, 1997.
3. It must:
   a. Write "Filed" at the top of the forms required.
   b. Write "Attention, Entity Control" on the envelope.
   c. Mail the forms to the IRS where the corporation files its return.

Corporations can automatically change their tax year if it cannot meet the five conditions and has not changed its annual accounting period within 6 calendar years or in any of the calendar years of existence, and if the corporation is *not any of the following*:

1. A member of a partnership.
2. A beneficiary of a trust or an estate.
3. An S corporation.
4. An interest-charging DISC or a foreign sales corporation (FSC).
5. A personal service corporation.
6. A controlled foreign corporation.
7. A cooperative association.
8. Certain tax-exempt organizations.

CHANGES DURING THE TAX YEAR

A corporation, other than an S corporation, a personal service corporation, or a domestic international sales corporation (IC-DISC) can change its tax year without getting IRS approval if all the following conditions are met:

1. It must not have changed its tax year within the 10 calendar years in which the short tax year resulting from the change begins.
2. Its short tax year must not be a tax year in which it has a net operating loss (NOL).
3. Its taxable income for the short tax year, when figured on an annual basis, annualized, is 80% or more of its taxable income for the tax year before the short tax year.
4. If a corporation is one of the following for either the short tax year or the tax year before the short tax year, it must have the same status for both the short tax and the prior tax year.
5. It must not apply to become an S corporation for the tax year that would immediately follow the short tax year required to effect the change.

The corporation must file a statement with the IRS office where it files its tax return. The statement must be filed by the due date, including extensions, for the short tax year required by the change. It must indicate the corporation is changing its annual accounting period, and that all the preceding conditions have been met.

Certain corporations can *automatically* change their tax year by meeting all the following criteria:

1. It cannot meet the conditions listed earlier.
2. It has not changed its annual accounting period within 6 calendar years of existence, or in any of the calendar years of existence, if less than 6 years.

Chapter 17

The Securities and Exchange Commission— Organization and the Acts

In today's world of regulated business, it is important for accountants to have a working knowledge of the rules and regulations influencing SEC accounting.

In the late 1920s there was widespread speculation in the stock market. When the market crashed in 1929, the public demanded protective action by their legislators. Congressional committees held hearings into all phases of the securities industry, investment banking, and commercial banking activities prior to the market crash. As a result of these hearings, eight Federal statutes were enacted between 1933 and 1940 (with a ninth in 1970), bringing the securities markets and the securities business under federal jurisdiction. These laws are referenced as the "truth in securities" statutes. They include the Securities Act of 1933, the Securities Exchange Act of 1934, the Public Utility Holding Company Act of 1935, the Maloney Amendment to the Securities Exchange Act of 1934, and the Federal Bankruptcy Code. Also included are the Trustee Indenture Act of 1939, the Investment Company Act of 1940, the Investment Advisers Act of 1940, the Securities Investor Protection Act (SPIC) of 1970, and the Securities Act Amendments of 1975.

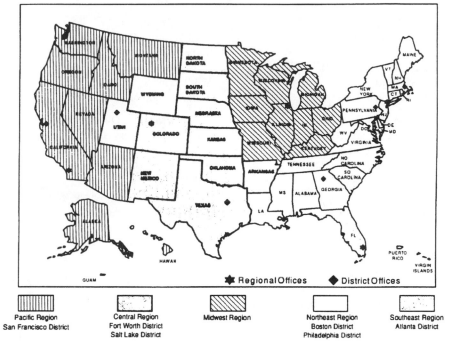

Pacific Region	Central Region	Midwest Region	Northeast Region	Southeast Region
San Francisco District	Fort Worth District		Boston District	Atlanta District
	Salt Lake District		Philadelphia District	

PREPARED BY THE SECURITIES AND EXCHANGE COMMISSION

REGION 1

Northeast Regional Office
7 World Trade Center
Suite 1300
New York, NY 10048
212-748-8000
e-mail: newyork@sec.gov

   Boston District Office
   73 Tremont Street
   Suite 600
   Boston , MA 02108-3912
   617-424-5900
   e-mail: boston@sec.gov

   Philadelphia District Office
   The Curtis Center, Suite 1005 E.
   601 Walnut Street
   Philadelphia , PA 19106-3322
   215-597-3100
   e-mail: philadelphia@sec.gov

REGION 2

Southeast Regional Office
1401 Brickell Avenue
Suite 200
Miami, FL 33131
305-536-4700
e-mail: miami@sec.gov

   Atlanta District Office
   3475 Lenox Road, N.E.
   Suite 1000
   Atlanta, GA 30326-1232
   e-mail: atlanta@sec.gov

REGION 3

Midwest Regional Office
Citicorp Center
500 W. Madison Street, Suite 1400
Chicago, IL 60661-2511
312-533-7390
e-mail: chicago@sec.gov

REGION 4

Central Regional Office
1801 California Street
Suite 4800
Denver, CO 80202-2648
303-391-6800
e-mail: denver@sec.gov

    Fort Worth District Office
    801 Cherry Street
    Suite 1900 Fort Worth, TX 76102
    817-334-3821
    e-mail: dfw@sec.gov

    Salt Lake District Office
    500 Key Bank Town
    50 South Main Street, Suite 500
    Salt Lake City, UT 84144-0402
    801-524-5796
    e-mail: saltlake@sec.gov

REGION 5

Pacific Reginal Office
5670 Wilshire Boulevard
Suite 1100
Los Angeles, CA 90036-3648
323-965-3998
e-mail: losangeles@sec.gov

    San Francisco District Office
    44 Montgomery Street
    Suite 110
    San Francisco, CA 94104
    415-705-2500
    e-mail: sanfrancisco@sec.gov

THE SECURITIES AND EXCHANGE COMMISSION

The Commission is composed of five members: a Chairman and four Commissioners. Commission members are appointed by the President, with the advice and consent of the Senate, for five-year terms. The Chairman is designated by the President. Terms are staggered; one expires on June 5th of every year. Not more than three members can be of the same political party.

Under the direction of the Chairman and Commissioners, the SEC staff ensures that publicly held entities, broker-dealers in securities, investment companies and advisers, and other participants in the securities markets comply with federal securities laws. These laws are designed to facilitate informed investment analyses and decisions by the investment public, primarily by ensuring adequate disclosure of material significant information. Conformance with federal securities laws and regulations does not imply merit of securities. If information essential to informed investment analysis is properly disclosed, the Commission cannot bar the sale of securities which analysis may show to be of questionable value. Investors, not the Commission, must make the ultimate judgment of the worth of securities offered for sale.

The Commission's staff is composed of lawyers, accountants, financial analysts and examiners, engineers, investigators, economists, and other professionals. The staff is divided into divisions and offices, including eleven regional and district offices, each directed by officials appointed by the Chairman.

GLOSSARY OF SECURITY AND EXCHANGE COMMISSION TERMINOLOGY

The Securities and Exchange Commission in Article 1, Rule 1-02, Title 17, Code of Federal Regulations (which is Accounting Regulation S-X), defines the meaning of terms used by the SEC in its Accounting Rules and Regulations. Also, many of the terms are defined as they appear in the Securities Act of 1933, the Securities Exchange Act of 1934, in Regulations S-K and D, and in the various Forms which publicly held corporations must file periodically with the SEC.

Occasionally, the Commission will use a term in a rule which in context will have a meaning somewhat different from its commonly understood meaning. Many of the definitions as they are written in the statutes and accounting regulations are lengthy and legalistic in style. The objective here is to "delegalize" the "legalese" in the interests both of clarity and brevity. The definitions are not, therefore, verbatim as developed by the Commission.

Accountant's Report. In regard to financial statements, a document in which an independent public accountant or certified public accountant indicates the scope of the audit (or examination) which has been made and sets forth an opinion regarding the financial statements taken as a whole, or an assertion to the effect that an overall opinion cannot be expressed. When an overall opinion cannot be expressed, the reasons therefore should be stated.

Accounting Principle, Change In. Results from changing one acceptable principle to another principle. A change in practice, or in the method of applying an accounting principle, or practice, is also considered a change in accounting principle.

Affiliate. One that directly or indirectly, through one or more intermediaries, controls or is controlled by, or is under common control with, the person specified (see **Person** below).

Amicus Curiae ("Friend of the Court"). An SEC advisory upon request of a court which assists a court in the interpretation of some matter concerning a securities law or accounting regulation.

Amount. When used to reference securities means:
a. The principal amount of a debt obligation if "amount" relates to evidence of indebtedness.
b. The number of shares if "amount" relates to shares.
c. The number of units if "amount" relates to any other type of securities.

Application for Listing. A detailed questionnaire filed with a national securities exchange providing information concerning the corporation's history and current status.

Assets Subject to Lien. Assets mortgaged, pledged, or otherwise subject to lien, and the approximate amounts of each.

Associate. When used to indicate a relationship with any person (see **Person** below), any corporation or organization, any trust or other estate, and any relative or spouse of such person, or any relative of such spouse.

Audit (or **examination**). When used in regard to financial statements, an examination of the statements by an accountant in accordance with generally accepted auditing standards for the purpose of expressing an opinion.

Audit Committee. A special committee of the board composed of directors who are *not* (if possible) officers of the company. The SEC wants the Audit Committee to assume the responsibility for arranging the details of the audit. In addition, an audit committee's major responsibilities include dealing with the company's financial reports, its external audit, and the company's system of internal accounting control and internal audit. The duties and responsibilities of audit committee members should be reasonably specific, but broad enough to allow the committee to pursue matters believed to have important accounting, reporting and auditing consequences.

Balance Sheet. Includes statements of assets and liabilities as well as statements of net assets unless the context clearly indicates the contrary.

Bank Holding Company. A person who is engaged, either directly or indirectly, primarily in the business of owning securities of one or more banks for the purpose, and with the effect of exercising control.

Blue Sky Laws. Terminology for State securities laws.

Broker. A person in the business of buying and selling securities, for a commission, on behalf of other parties.

Call. (see **Option** below.)

Censure. A formal reprimand by the SEC for improper professional behavior by a party to a filing.

Certificate. A document of an independent public accountant, or independent certified public accountant, that is dated, reasonably comprehensive as to the scope of the audit made, and states clearly the opinion of the accountant in respect to the financial statements and the accounting principles and procedures followed by the registrant (see **Registrant** below).

Certification. It is the accountant's responsibility to make a reasonably unqualified certification of the financial statements. It is important for the auditor to incorporate in the certificate an adequate explanation of the scope (see **Scope** below) of the audit.

Certified. When used in regard to financial statements, examined and reported upon with an opinion expressed by an independent public or certified public accountant.

Certiorari, Writ of. An order issued by a superior court directing an inferior court to deliver its record for review.

Chapter X Bankruptcy. Voluntary or involuntary reorganization of a corporation with publicly held securities.

Chapter XI Bankruptcy. Deals with individuals, partnerships and with corporations whose securities are not publicly held. Affects only voluntary arrangements of unsecured debts.

Charter. Includes articles of incorporation, declarations of trust, articles of association or partnership, or any similar instrument, as amended, affecting the organization of an incorporated or unincorporated person.

Civil Actions. Involves the private rights and remedies of the parties to a suit; actions arising out of a contract.

Class of Securities. A group of similar securities that give shareholders similar rights.

Closed-End Investment Company. A corporation in the business of investing its funds in securities of other corporations for income and profit. Investors wishing to "cash out" of the investment company do so by selling their shares on the open market, as with any other stock.

Closing Date. Effective date (see **Effective Date** below) of a registration statement.

Comment Letters (see **Deficiency Letter** below.)

Common Equity. Any class of common stock or an equivalent interest, including but not limited to a unit of beneficial interest in a trust or a limited partnership interest.

Compensating Balance. Restricted deposits of a borrower required by banks to be maintained against short-term loans. A portion of any demand, time, or certificate of deposit, maintained by a corporation, or by any person on behalf of the corporation, which constitutes support for existing borrowing arrangements of the corporation, or any other person, with a lending institution. Such arrangements include both outstanding borrowings and the assurance of future credit availability.

Consent Action. Issued when a person agrees to the terms of an SEC disciplinary action without admitting to the allegations in the complaint.

Consolidated Statements. Include the operating results of a corporation's subsidiary(ies) with inter-company transactions eliminated.

Control. (including the terms "controlling," "controlled by," "under common control with"). The possession, direct or indirect, of the power to direct or cause the direction of the management and policies of a person, whether through the ownership of voting shares, by contract, or otherwise.

Cooling-Off Period. The period between the filing and effective date (see **Effective Date** below) of a registration statement.

Criminal Action. Suits initiated for the alleged violation of a public law.

Dealer. A person in the business of buying and selling securities for his or her own account.

Deficiency Letter. A letter from the SEC to the registrant setting forth the needed corrections and amendments to the issuing corporations' registration statement.

Delisting. Permanent removal of a listed security from a national securities exchange.

Depositary Share. A security evidenced by an American Depositary Receipt that represents a foreign security or a multiple of or fraction thereof deposited with a depositary.

Development Stage Company. A company is considered to be in the development stage if it is devoting substantially all of its efforts to establishing a new business and either of the following conditions exists.

1. Planned principal operations have not commenced.
2. Planned principal operations have commenced, but there has been no significant revenue therefrom.

Disbarment. Permanent removal of a professional's privilege to represent clients before the SEC.

Disclosure. The identification of accounting policies and principles that materially affect the determination of financial position, changes in financial position, and results of operations.

Domiciled Corporation. A corporation doing business in the state in which its corporate charter was guaranteed.

Due Diligence Meeting. A meeting of all parties in the preparation of a registration statement to assure that a high degree of care in investigation and independent verification of the company's representations has been made.

Effective Date. The twentieth (20th) day after the filing date of a registration statement or amendment unless the Commission shortens or extends that time period.

Employee. Any employee, general partner, or consultant or advisor, insurance agents who are exclusive agents of the registrant, its subsidiaries or parents. It also includes former employees as well as executors, administrators or beneficiaries of the estates of deceased employees, guardians or members of a committee for incompetent former employees, or similar persons duly authorized by law to administer the estate or assets of former employees.

Equity Security. Any stock or similar security; or any security convertible, with or without consideration, into such a security, or carrying any warrant or right to subscribe to or purchase such a security, or any such warrant or right.

Examination. (See **Audit** above).

Exchange. An organized association providing a market place for bringing together buyers and sellers of securities through brokers.

Exempt Security. One that is not required to be registered with the SEC.

Exempt Transaction. A transaction in securities that does not require registration with the SEC.

Expert. Any specialist, accountant, attorney, engineer, appraiser, etc., who participates in the preparation of a registration statement. Broadly, any signatory to the registration statement is assumed to be an expert.

Fifty-Percent-Owned-Person. A person whose outstanding voting shares are approximately 50 percent owned by another specified person directly, or indirectly, through one or more intermediaries.

Filing. The process of completing and submitting a registration statement to the SEC.

Filing Date. The date a registration statement is received by the SEC.

Financial Statement. Includes all notes to the statements and all related schedules.

Fiscal Year. The annual accounting period or, if no closing date has been adopted, the calendar year ending on December 31.

Float. The difference on a bank's ledger and a depositor's books caused by presentation of checks and deposits in transit.

Footnote. Appended to financial statements as supplemental information for specific items in a statement.

Foreign Currency. Any currency other than the currency used by the enterprise in its financial statements.

Forms. Statements of standards with which registration statements and other filings must comply. Essentially, SEC forms are a set of instructions to guide the registrant in the preparation of the SEC reports to be filed; the forms are not required to be precisely copied.

Form S-1. A registration statement (see **Registration Statement** below) is filed on Form S-1 for companies issuing securities to the public. This form incorporates specified standards for financial statements and auditor's report.

Form 8-K. A report which is filed only when a reportable event occurs which may have a significant effect on the future of a company and on the value of its securities. Form 8-K must be filed not later than 15 days after the date on which the specified event occurs.

Form 10-K. The annual report to the SEC which covers substantially all of the information required in Form S-1. Form 10-K is due 90 days after a company's December 31 fiscal year, or by March 31 of each year.

Form 10-Q. A quarterly report containing *unaudited* financial statements. If certain types of events occur during the period, they must be reported on the Form. The 10-Q is due 45 days after the end of the first three fiscal quarters.

Going Private. The term commonly used to describe those transactions having as their objective the complete termination or substantial reduction of public ownership of an equity's securities.

Going Public. Registering a new issue of securities with the SEC. *Going public* is closely related to the process of applying for listed status on one or more of the exchanges, or registering for trading in the over-the-counter market.

Indemnification Provision. An agreement protecting one party from liability arising from the occurrence of an unforeseeable event.

Independent Accountants *(CPA).* Accountants who certify financial statements filed with the SEC. Accountants must maintain strict independence of attitude and judgment in planning and conducting and audit and in expressing an opinion on financial statements. The SEC will not recognize any public accountant or certified public accountant that is not independent.

Information Statement. A statement on any pending corporate matters furnished by the registrant to every shareholder who is entitled to vote when a proxy is not solicited.

Initial Margin Percentage. The percentage of the purchase price (or the percentage of a short sale; see **Short Selling** below), that an investor must deposit with his/her broker in compliance with Federal Reserve Board margin requirements.

Injunction. A court order directing a person to stop alleged violations of a securities law or regulation.

Insurance Holding Company. A person who is engaged, either directly or indirectly, primarily in the business of owning securities of one or more insurance companies for the purpose, and with the effect, of exercising control.

Integrated Disclosure System (IDS). An extensive revision of the mandatory business and financial disclosure requirements applicable to publicly-held companies. It establishes a uniform and integrated disclosure system under the securities laws. The IDS adopted major changes in its disclosure systems under the Securities Act of 1933, and the Securities Exchange Act of 1934. The changes include amendments to Form 10-K and 10-Q, amendments to the proxy rules, amendments to Regulation S-K which governs the non-financial statement disclosure rules (see **Regulation S-K** below), uniform financial statement instructions, a general revision of Regulation S-X which governs the form, content, and requirements of financial statements (see **Regulation S-X** below), and a new simplified form for the registration of securities issued in business combinations.

Issuer. Any corporation that sells a security in a public offering.

Letter-of-Consent. Written permission from participating experts to include their names and signatures in a registration statement.

Line-of-Business Reporting. Registrants must report financial information regarding segments of their operations. The SEC does not define the term "line-of-business." Rather, the responsibility of determining meaningful segments that reflect the particular company's operations and organizational concepts is the responsibility of management. No more than ten classes of business are required to be reported.

Listed Status. Condition under which a security has been accepted by an exchange for full trading privileges. As long as a corporation remains listed on an exchange, it must file periodic reports to its stockholders.

Listing. A corporation applying to list its securities on an exchange must file a registration statement and a copy of the application for listing with the SEC.

Majority-Owned Subsidiary. A subsidiary more than 50 percent of whose outstanding voting shares is owned by its parent and/or the parent's other majority-owned subsidiaries.

Managing Underwriter. Underwriter(s) who, by contract or otherwise, deals with the registrant; organizes the selling effort; receives some benefit directly or indirectly in which all other underwriters similarly situated do not share in proportion to their respective interests in the underwriting; or represents any other underwriters in such matters as maintaining the records of the distribution, arranging the allotments of securities offered or arranging for appropriate stabilization activities, if any.

Margin Call. The demand by a broker that an investor deposit additional cash (or acceptable collateral) for securities purchased on credit when the price of the securities declines to a value below the minimum shareholder's equity required by the stock exchange.

Material. Information regarding any subject that limits the information required to those matters about which an average prudent investor ought reasonably to be informed.

Mutual Fund. Not legal terminology. It is a financial term commonly used in street jargon to mean an open-end investment company (see **Open-End Investment Company** below) as defined in the Investment Company Act of 1940.

National Association of Securities Dealers, Inc. (NASD). An association of brokers/dealers who are in the business of trading over-the-counter securities.

Net Sales. Income or loss from continuing operations before extraordinary items and cumulative effect of a change in accounting principle.

New York Stock Exchange (and **Regional Exchanges**). An association organized to provide physical, mechanical, and logistical facilities for the purchase and sale of securities by investors through brokers and dealers.

No-Action Letter. The SEC's written reply to a corporate issuer of securities stating its position regarding a specific filing matter.

Notification. Filing with the SEC the terms of an offering of securities that are exempt from registration.

Offering Date. The date a new security can be offered to the public.

Open-End Investment Company. A corporation in the business of investing its funds in securities of other corporations for income and profit. An open-end company continuously offers new shares for sales and redeems shares previously issued to investors who want to cash out.

Opinion. A required statement in the certification that the auditor believes the audit correctly reflects the organization's financial condition and results of operation.

Option. The contractual privilege of purchasing a security (Call) for a specified price, or delivering a security (Put) at a specified price.

Over-the-Counter Securities. Corporate and government securities that are not listed for trading on a national stock exchange.

Parent. A "parent" of a specified person(s) is an affiliate controlling such person(s) directly or indirectly through one or more intermediaries.

Pension Plan. An arrangement whereby a company undertakes to provide its retired employees with benefits that can be determined or estimated in advance.

Person. An individual, corporation, partnership, association, joint-stock company, business trust, or unincorporated organization.

Predecessor. A person from whom another person acquired the major portion of the business and assets in a single succession or in a series of related successions. In each succession the acquiring person acquired the major portion of the business and assets of the acquired person.

Prefiling Conference. A meeting of corporate officers and experts outlining the SEC requirements for the filing of a registration statement. Occasionally an SEC staff member will attend.

Previously Filed or Reported. Previously filed with, or reported in a definitive proxy statement or information statement, or a registration statement. Information contained in any such document will be assumed to have been previously filed with the exchange.

Principal Holder of Equity Securities. Used in respect of a registrant or other person named in a particular statement or report, a holder of record or a known beneficial owner of more than 10 percent of any class of securities of the registrant or other person, respectively, and of the date of the related balance sheet filed.

Promoter. Any person who, acting alone or in conjunction with one or more other persons, directly or indirectly takes initiative in founding and organizing the business or enterprise of an issuer. Any person is a promoter who, in connection with the founding and organizing of the business or enterprise of an issuer, directly or indirectly receives in consideration of services or property, or both services and property, 10 percent or more of any class of securities of the issuer or 10 percent or more of the proceeds from the sale of any class of securities. However, a person who receives such securities or proceeds either solely as underwriting commissions or solely in consideration of property shall not be deemed a promoter within the meaning of this paragraph if such person does not otherwise take part in founding and organizing the enterprise.

Prospectus. Document consisting of Part 1 of the registration statement filed with the SEC by the issuing corporation that must be delivered to all purchasers of newly issued securities.

Proxy. A power of attorney whereby a stockholder authorizes another person, or group of persons, to act (vote) for that stockholder at a shareholders' meeting.

Proxy Statement. Information furnished in conjunction with a formal solicitation in the proxy for the power to vote a stockholder's shares.

Put. (See **Option** above.)

Red-Herring Prospectus. Preliminary prospectus with a statement (in red ink) on each page indicating that the security described has not become effective, that the information is subject to correction and change without notice, and is not an offer to buy or sell that security.

Refusal. SEC action prohibiting a filing (see **Filing** above) from becoming effective.

Regional Exchanges. (See **New York Stock Exchange** above.)

Registrant. An issuer of securities for which an application, a report, or a registration statement has been filed.

Registration. Act of filing with the SEC the required information concerning the issuing corporation and the security to be issued.

Registration Statement. The document filed with the SEC containing legal, commercial, technical, and financial information concerning a new security issue.

Regulation S-K. An authoritative statement of disclosure standards under all securities acts. Regulation S-K establishes the standards of disclosure for non-financial information not included in financial statements, footnotes or schedules.

Regulation S-X. The principal document reporting for financial statements, footnotes and schedules' standards under all securities acts. No filing can be made without reference to Regulation S-X. It integrates all accounting requirements prior to February 21, 1940, into a single regulation.

Related Party. One that can exercise control or significant influence over the management and/or operating policies of another party, to the extent that one of the parties may be prevented from fully pursuing its own separate interests. Related parties consist of all affiliates of an enterprise, including its management and their immediate families, its principal owners and their immediate families, its investments accounted for by the equity method, beneficial employee trusts that are managed by the management of the enterprise, and any party that may, or does, deal with the enterprise and has ownership of, control over, or can significantly influence the management or operating policies of another party to the extent that an arms-length transaction may not be achieved. Transactions between related parties are generally accounted for on the same basis as if the parties were not related, unless the substance of the transaction is not arm's length. Substance over form is an important consideration when accounting for transactions involving related parties.

Replacement Cost. The lowest amount that would have to be paid in the normal course of business to obtain a new asset of equivalent operating or productive capability.

Restricted Security. Private offering of an issue that cannot be resold to the public without prior registration. Also called "investment letter" securities for the letter that the purchaser of such securities must submit to the SEC stating that the securities are being acquired for investment purposes, not for immediate resale.

Right. Provides current security holders the privilege of participating on a pro rata basis in a new offering of securities.

Roll-Up Transaction. Any transaction or series of transactions that, directly or indirectly through acquisition or otherwise, involves the combination or reorganization of one or more partnerships. The term includes the offer or sale of securities by a successor entity, whether newly formed or previously existing, to one or more limited partners of the partnership to be combined or reorganized, or the acquisition of the successor entity's securities by the partnerships being combined or reorganized.

Rules of Practice. Establishes standards of conduct for professionals practicing before the SEC.

Sale. Every contract of sale, disposition, or offer of a security for value (see **Security** below).

Schedule. Detailed financial information presented in a form prescribed by the SEC in Regulation S-X.

Scienter. Intent to deceive, manipulate, or defraud. Requires proof that defendant knew of material mistatements or omissions; that defendant acted willfully and knowingly.

Scope (of an Audit). A complete, detailed audit. The auditor includes in the certificate an adequate explanation of the extent of the audit.

Securities Act of 1933. Requires the disclosure of financial data for issues not exempted from registration and prohibits fraudulent acts and misrepresentations and omission of material (see **Material** above) facts in the issue of securities.

Securities Exchange Act of 1934 (The **Exchange Act**). Covers the regulation of stock market activities and the public trading of securities. The regulations covered are the disclosure of significant financial data, the regulation of securities market practices and operation, and control of credit (margin requirements) extended for the purchase and short sales of securities.

Security. Any instrument representing a debt obligation, an equity interest in a corporation, or any instrument commonly known as a security. In the Securities Act, security is defined to include by name or description many documents in which there is common trading for investment or speculation. Some, such as notes, bonds and stocks, are standardized and the name alone carries well settled meaning. Others are of a more variable character and were necessarily designated by more descriptive terms, such as transferable share, investment contract, and in general any interest or instrument commonly known as a security.

Selling Group. Several broker/dealers who distribute a new issue of securities at retail.

Share. A share of stock in a corporation or unit of interest in an unincorporated person.

Short-Selling. Selling a security that is not owned with the expectation of buying that specific security later at a lower market price.

Significant Subsidiary. A subsidiary (including its subsidiaries) in which the registrant's (and its other subsidiaries') investments in and advances to exceed 10% of the total assets of the registrant and its subsidiaries consolidated as of the end of the most recently completed fiscal year. For a proposed business combination to be accounted for as a pooling of interests, this requirement is also met when the number of common shares exchanged by the registrant exceeds 10% of its total common shares outstanding at the date the combination is initiated, or the registrant's (and its other subsidiaries') proportionate share of the total assets, after intercompany eliminations, of the subsidiary exceeds 10% of the total assets of the registrant and its subsidiaries consolidated as of the end of the most recently completed fiscal year.

Small Business Issuer. An entity that (a) has revenues of less than $25,000,000; (b) is a U.S. or Canadian issuer; (c) is not an investment company; (d) if a majority-owned subsidiary, the parent corporation is also a small business issuer.

Solicitation. Any request for a proxy or other similar communication to security holders.

Sponsor. The person proposing the roll-up transaction. (See **Roll-Up Transaction** above.)

Spread. The difference between the price paid for a security by the underwriter and the selling price of that security.

Stockholders' Meeting, Regular. The annual meeting of stockholders for the election of directors and for action on other corporate matters.

Stockholders' Meeting, Special. A meeting in which only specified items can be considered.

Stop Order. An SEC order stopping the issue or listing of a security on a stock exchange.

Subsidiary. An affiliate controlled by a specified person directly, or indirectly, through one or more intermediaries.

Substantial Authoritative Support. FASB principles, standards and practices published in Statements and Interpretations, AICPA Accounting Research Bulletins, and AICPA Opinions, except to the extent altered, amended, supplemented, revoked or superseded by an FASB Statement.

Succession. The direct acquisition of the assets comprising a going business, whether by merger, consolidation, or other direct transfer. This term does not include the acquisition of control of a business unless followed by the direct acquisition of its assets.

Successor. The surviving entity after completion of the roll-up transaction, or the entity whose securities are being offered or sold to, or acquired by, limited partners of the partnerships or the limited partnerships to be combined or reorganized.

Summary Prospectus. A prospectus containing specific items of information which subsequently will be included in the registration statement.

Suspension. An SEC order temporarily prohibiting the trading of a security on the stock exchange, usually invoked by the SEC when a news release is pending which may cause a disorderly market in that security. Trading is usually resumed shortly after the information has been publicly disseminated.

Totally Held Subsidiary. A subsidiary substantially all of whose outstanding securities are owned by its parent and/or the parent's other totally held subsidiaries. The subsidiary is not indebted to any person other than its parent and/or the parent's other totally held subsidiaries in an amount which is material in relation to the particular subsidiary, excepting indebtedness incurred in the ordinary course of business which is not overdue and which matures within one year from the date of its creation, whether evidenced by securities or not.

Underwriter. (See **Managing Underwriter** above.)

Unlisted Trading Privileges. A security issue authorized by the SEC for trading on an exchange without requiring the corporation to complete a formal listing application.

Voting Securities. Securities whose holders are presently entitled to vote for the election of directors.

Warrant. A security that grants the holder the right to purchase a specific number of shares of the security to which the warrant is attached at a specified price and usually within a stated period of time.

Wholly Owned Subsidiary. A subsidiary substantially all of whose outstanding voting securities are owned by its parent and/or the parent's other wholly owned subsidiaries.

SECURITIES ACT OF 1933

The *truth in securities* law has two main objectives:

1. To require that investors are provided with material information concerning securities offered for sale to the public.
2. To prevent misrepresentation, deceit, and other fault in the sale of securities.

The primary means of accomplishing these objectives is by requiring full disclosure of financial information by registering offerings and sales of securities. Securities transactions subject to registration are mostly offerings of debt and equity securities issued by corporations, limited partnerships, trusts and other issuers. Federal and certain other government debt securities are not. Certain securities and transactions qualify for exemptions from registration provisions. They are included in the discussion that follows.

REGISTRATION

Registration is intended to provide adequate and accurate disclosure of material facts concerning the company and the securities it proposes to sell. This enables investors to make a thorough appraisal of the merits of the securities and exercise informed judgment in determining whether or not to purchase them.

Registration requires, but does not guarantee, the accuracy of the facts represented in the registration statement and prospectus. However, the law does prohibit false and misleading statements under penalty of fine, imprisonment, or both. Investors who purchases securities and suffer losses have important recovery rights under the law if they can prove that there was incomplete or inaccurate disclosure of material facts in the registration statement or prospectus. If such misstatements are proven, the following could be liable for investor losses sustained in the securities purchase:

1. The issuing company.
2. Its responsible directors and officers.
3. The underwriters.
4. The controlling interests.
5. The sellers of the securities.
6. Others that are affiliated with the securities of the issuer.

Registration of securities does not preclude the sale of stock in risky, poorly managed, or unprofitable companies. Nor does the Commission *approve or disapprove* securities on their merits; and it is unlawful to represent otherwise in the sale of securities. The only standard which must be met when registering securities is adequate and accurate *disclosure* of required material facts concerning the company and the securities it proposes to sell. The fairness of the terms, the issuing company's prospects for successful operation, and other factors affecting the merits of investing in the securities have no bearing on the question of whether or not securities can be qualified for registration.

The Registration Process

To facilitate registration by different types of enterprises, the Commission has special forms that vary in their disclosure requirements, but generally provide essential facts while minimizing the burden and expense of complying with the law. In general, registration forms call for disclosure of information such as:

1. Description of the registrant's properties and business.
2. Description of the significant provisions of the security to be offered for sale and its relationship to the registrant's other capital securities.
3. Information about the management of the registrant.
4. Financial statements certified by independent public accountants.

Registration statements become public immediately upon filing with the SEC. After the registration statement is filed, securities can be *offered* orally or by summaries of the information in the registration statement, but it is unlawful to *sell* the securities until the *effective date* which is on the 20th day after filing the registration statement, or on the 20th day after filing the last amendment, if any. The SEC can issue a *stop order* to refuse or suspend the effectiveness of the statement if the Commission concludes that material deficiencies in a registration statement appear to result from a deliberate attempt to conceal or mislead. A stop order is not a permanent prohibition to the effectiveness of the registration statement, or to the sale of the securities, and can be lifted and the statement declared effective when amendments are filed correcting the statement in accordance with the requirements in the stop order decision.

There are exemptions to the registration requirements:

1. Private offerings to a limited number of persons or institutions who have access to the kind of information that registration would disclose and who do not propose to redistribute the securities.
2. Offerings restricted to residents of the state in which the issuing company is organized and doing business.
3. Securities of municipal, state, federal and other governmental instrumentalities, such as charitable institutions and banks.
4. Offerings not exceeding certain specified amounts made in compliance with regulations of the Commission.
5. Offerings of small business investment companies made in accordance with the rules and regulations of the Commission.

Regardless of whether or not the securities are exempt from registration, anti-fraud provisions apply to all sales of securities involving interstate commerce or the mails.

The small business exemption from registration provides that offerings of securities under $5 million can be exempt from full registration, subject to conditions the SEC prescribes to protect investors. Certain Canadian and domestic companies are permitted to make exempt offerings.

UNITED STATES
SECURITIES AND EXCHANGE COMMISSION
Washington, D.C. 20549

FORM 10

GENERAL FORM FOR REGISTRATION OF SECURITIES
Pursuant to Section 12(b) or (g) of The Securities Exchange Act of 1934

_____

(Exact name of registrant as specified in its charter)

_____

(State or other jurisdiction of incorporation or organization)   (I.R.S. Employer Identification No.)

_____

(Address of principal executive offices)   (Zip Code)

Registrant's telephone number, including area code _____

Securities to be registered pursuant to Section 12(b) of the Act:

Title of each class to be so registered	Name of each exchange on which each class is to be registered

Securities to be registered pursuant to Section 12(g) of the Act:

_____

(Title of class)

_____

(Title of class)

INFORMATION REQUIRED IN REGISTRATION STATEMENT

Item 1. Business.
Furnish the information required by Item 101 of Regulation S-K (§229.101 of this chapter).

Item 2. Financial Information.
Furnish the information required by Items 301 and 303 of Regulation S-K (§§229.301 and 229.303 of this chapter).

Item 3. Properties.
Furnish the information required by Item 102 of Regulation S-K (§229.102 of this chapter).

Item 4. Security Ownership of Certain Beneficial Owners and Management.
Furnish the information required by Item 403 of Regulation S-K (§229.403 of this chapter).

Item 5. Directors and Executive Officers.
Furnish the information required by Item 401 of Regulation S-K (§229.401 of this chapter).

Item 6. Executive Compensation.
Furnish the information required by Item 402 of Regulation S-K (§229.402 of this chapter).

Item 7. Certain Relationships and Related Transactions.
Furnish the information required by Item 404 of Regulation S-K (§229.404 of this chapter).

Item 8. Legal Proceedings.
Furnish the information required by Item 103 of Regulation S-K (§229.103 of this chapter).

Item 9. Market Price of and Dividends on the Registrant's Common Equity and Related Stockholder Matters.
Furnish the information required by Item 201 of Regulation S-K (§229.201 of this chapter).

Item 10. Recent Sales of Unregistered Securities.
Furnish the information required by item 701 of Regulation S-K (§229.701 of this chapter).

Item 11. Description of Registrant's Securities to be Registered.
Furnish the information required by Item 202 of Regulation S-K (§229.202 of this chapter).

Item 12. Indemnification of Directors and Officers.
Furnish the information required by Item 702 of Regulation S-K (§229.702 of this chapter).

Item 13. Financial Statements and Supplementary Data.
Furnish all financial statements required by Regulation S-X and the supplementary financial information required by Item 302 of Regulation S-K (§229.302 of this chapter).

Item 14. Changes in and Disagreements with Accountants on Accounting and Financial Disclosure.
Furnish the information required by Item 304 of Regulation S-K (§229.304 of this chapter).

Item 15. Financial Statements and Exhibits.
(a) List separately all financial statements filed as part of the registration statement.
(b) Furnish the exhibits required by Item 601 of Regulation S-K (§229.601 of this chapter).

SIGNATURES

Pursuant to the requirements of Section 12 of the Securities Exchange Act of 1934, the registrant has duly caused this registration statement to be signed on its behalf by the undersigned, thereunto duly authorized.

_____

(Registrant)

Date _____   By _____

(Signature)*

_____

*Print name and title of the signing officer under his signature.

GENERAL INSTRUCTIONS

A. Rule as to Use of Form 10.

Form 10 shall be used for registration pursuant to Section 12(b) or (g) of the Securities Exchange Act of 1934 of classes of securities of issuers for which no other form is prescribed.

B. Application of General Rules and Regulations.

(a) The General Rules and Regulations under the Act contain certain general requirements which are applicable to registration on any form. These general requirements should be carefully read and observed in the preparation and filing of registration statements on this form.

(b) Particular attention is directed to Regulation 12B [17 CFR 240.12b-1–240.12b-36] which contains general requirements regarding matters such as the kind and size of paper to be used, the legibility of the registration statement, the information to be given whenever the title of securities is required to be stated, and the filing of the registration statement. The definitions contained in Rule 12b-2 [17 CFR 240.12b-2] should be especially noted.

C. Preparation of Registration Statement.

(a) This form is not to be used as a blank form to be filled in, but only as a guide in the preparation of the registration statement on paper meeting the requirements of Rule 12b-12 [17 CFR 240.12b-12]. The registration statement shall contain the item numbers and captions, but the text of the items may be omitted. The answers to the items shall be prepared in the manner specified in Rule 12b-13 [17 CFR 240.12b-13].

(b) Unless otherwise stated, the information required shall be given as of a date reasonably close to the date of filing the registration statement.

(c) Attention is directed to Rule 12b-20 [17 CFR 240.12b-20] which states: "In addition to the information expressly required to be included in a statement or report, there shall be added such further material information, if any, as may be necessary to make the required statements, in light of the circumstances under which they are made, not misleading."

D. Signature and Filing of Registration Statement.

Three complete copies of the registration statement, including financial statements, exhibits and all other papers and documents filed as a part thereof, and five additional copies which need not include exhibits, shall be filed with the Commission. At least one complete copy of the registration statement, including financial statements, exhibits and all other papers and documents filed as a part thereof, shall be filed with each exchange on which any class of securities is to be registered. At least one complete copy of the registration statement filed with the Commission and one such copy filed with each exchange shall be manually signed. Copies not manually signed shall bear typed or printed signatures.

E. Omission of Information Regarding Foreign Subsidiaries.

Information required by any item or other requirement of this form with respect to any foreign subsidiary may be omitted to the extent that the required disclosure would be detrimental to the registrant. However, financial statements, otherwise required, shall not be omitted pursuant to this instruction. Where information is omitted pursuant to this instruction, a statement shall be made that such information has been omitted and the names of the subsidiaries involved shall be separately furnished to the Commission. The Commission may, in its discretion, call for justification that the required disclosure would be detrimental.

F. Incorporation by Reference.

Attention is directed to Rule 12b-23 [17 CFR 240.12b-23 which provides for the incorporation by reference of information contained in certain documents in answer or partial answer to any item of a registration statement.

SECURITIES EXCHANGE ACT OF 1934

The 1934 Act extends the disclosure doctrine of investor protection to securities that are listed and registered for public trading on U.S. national securities exchanges. In 1964 the SEC was authorized by Congress to include disclosure and reporting requirements to equity securities in the over-the-counter market. The object of the 1934 Act is to ensure *fair and orderly securities markets* by prohibiting certain types of activities and by setting forth rules regarding the operation of the markets and the participants.

Companies wanting to have their securities registered and listed or publicly traded on an exchange must file a registration application with the exchange and the SEC. Companies whose equity securities are traded over-the-counter must file a similar registration form. SEC rules prescribe the content of registration statements and require certified financial statements. After a company's securities have become registered, annual and other periodic reports to update information contained in the original registration statement must be filed.

The 1934 Act governs the solicitation of proxies (votes) from holders of registered securities, both listed and over-the-counter, for the election of directors and for approval of other corporate action. All material facts concerning matters on which shareholders are asked to vote must be disclosed. In 1970 Congress amended the Exchange Act to extend its reporting and disclosure provisions to situations where control of a company is sought through a tender offer to other planned stock acquisitions of over five percent of a company's equity securities by direct purchase or by a tender offer. Disclosure provisions are supplemented by other provisions to help ensure investor protection in tender offers.

INSIDER TRADING

Insider trader prohibitions are designed to curb misuse of material confidential information not available to the general public. Examples of such misuse are buying or selling securities to make profits or avoid losses based on material nonpublic information, or by telling others of the information before such information is generally available to all shareholders. The *Insider Trading Sanctions Act of 1984* allows imposing fines up to three times to profit gained or losses avoided by use of material nonpublic information. All officers and directors of a company and beneficial owners of more than ten percent of its registered equity securities must file an initial report with the SEC and with the exchange on which the stock is listed, showing their holdings of each of the company's equity securities. Thereafter, they must file reports for any month during which there was any change in those holdings, and any profits obtained by them from purchases and sales, or sales and purchases, of such equity securities within any six-month period can be recovered by the company or by any security holder on its behalf. Insiders are also prohibited from making short sales of their company's equity securities.

Margin Trading

The 1934 Act authorizes the Board of Governors of the Federal Reserve System to set limits on the amount of credit which can be extended for the purpose of purchasing or carrying securities. The objective is to restrict excessive use of credit in the securities markets. While the credit restrictions are set by the Board of Governors, investigation and enforcement is the responsibility of the SEC.

Division of Corporation Finance

Corporation Finance has the overall responsibility of ensuring that disclosure requirements are met by publicly held companies registered with the SEC. Its work includes: reviewing registration statements for new securities; proxy material and annual reports the Commission requires from publicly held companies; documents concerning tender offers, and mergers and acquisitions in general.

This Division renders administrative interpretations to the public of the Securities Act and the Securities Exchange Act, and to prospective registrants, and others. It is also responsible for certain statutes and regulations pertaining to small businesses and for the Trust Indenture Act of 1939. Applications for qualification of trust indentures are examined for compliance with the applicable requirements of the law and the Commission's rules. Corporation Finance works closely with the Office of the Chief Accountant in drafting rules and regulations which prescribe requirements for financial statements.

Truth in Securities Laws

The objectives of the laws are twofold. First is the protection of investors and the public against fraudulent acts and practices in the purchase and sale of securities. The second objective is to regulate trading in the national securities markets. For example:

1. "To provide full and fair disclosure of the character of securities sold in interstate and foreign commerce and through the mails, and to prevent fraud in the sale thereof, and for other purposes." (Securities Act of 1933.)

2. "To provide for the regulation of securities exchanges and the over-the-counter markets operating in interstate and foreign commerce and through the mails, to prevent inequitable and unfair practices on such exchanges and markets, and for other purposes." (Securities Exchange Act of 1934.)

3. "To provide for the registration and regulation of investment companies and investment advisers, and for other purposes." (Investment Company Act of 1940 and the Investment Advisers Act of 1940.)

DEVELOPMENT OF DISCLOSURE: 1933 AND 1934 ACTS

Two separate disclosure systems developed under the two principal securities laws. Generally, the Securities Act of 1933 regulates the *initial* public distribution of securities. The disclosure system developed under the 1933 Act emphasizes the comprehensive information about the issuer, because it was developed primarily for companies going public for the *first time* and about which the public had very little information.

The Securities Exchange Act of 1934 regulates the trading of securities in *publicly held companies* which are traded both on the exchanges and in the over-the-counter markets. The dual disclosure system developed under the 1933 and 1934 Acts deals primarily with the form and content of financial and business data in the annual reports to the SEC and to shareholders, and concerns proxy statements as well as the dissemination of interim data. The emphasis of this disclosure system is on periodic information concerning issuers already known to security holders, and the purpose is to keep the data up-to-date.

The dual system generated a large number of registration and periodic reporting forms, each with its own set of instructions. Many publicly-held companies filed numerous registration statements and distributed related reports to the public containing the same information produced several times in slightly different forms, repeating much information that was already available within the financial community.

In addition, the audited primary financial statements prepared in conformity with GAAP that were included in the annual reports to shareholders, were not explicitly covered by the very detailed disclosure requirements in S-X. These mandated the form and content of the audited primary financial statements that were included in documents filed with the SEC and in prospectuses. However, since the financial statements had to be in conformity with GAAP there were no essential differences between the two.

Financial statements that conformed to S-X included numerous additional technical disclosures to satisfy the needs of professional financial analysts and the SEC staff. Uniform financial disclosure requirements for virtually all documents covered by either the 1933 or the 1934 Acts as well as for nonfinancial disclosures under the 1934 Act and for a major portion of those required under the 1933 Act have been formulated. To reach the objective, where identical disclosures are included both in documents filed with the Commission and distributed to security holders in prospectuses, proxy statements and annual reports, the Commission has two basic regulations. These are Regulation S-X (See Chapter 16) which covers the requirements for audited primary financial statements, and Regulation S-K which covers most of the other business, analytical, and unaudited financial disclosures.

Regulation S-K covers analytical and unaudited supplementary financial disclosures under the 1934 Act and most disclosures under the 1933 Act. One of the key requirements in Regulation S-K is the *Management's Discussion and Analysis of Financial Condition and Results of Operations*. The discussion must cover the three years presented in the audited financials and treat not only results of operations, but also financial condition and changes in financial condition. Although the requirement is for three years, the SEC suggests that when trends are being discussed, references to five years of selected financial data are appropriate.

The discussion and analysis is filed under the Securities Acts, as well as included in all annual reports and prospectuses. Accordingly, companies should document the adequacy of their systems and procedures for analyzing past results to be sure that there is an adequate and reliable information base for the management discussion and analysis, including decisions as to scope and content. Since future plans and expectations, such as capital expenditure commitments, are important in formulating management's discussion and analysis, it may be prudent to reappraise internal financial forecasting procedures periodically.

Although forward-looking information is not mandated, the specifically required information is such that financial analysts will be able to work out a forecast of future operating results. As practice develops, managements may find it preferable simply to include formal financial forecasts and comply with the safe harbor rules, rather than rely solely on the forecasts analysts will make based on data presumed to be reliable.

Form S-15. When a company acquires a business that is relatively minor when compared to the acquiring company, a process that was difficult because of the complexity and cost of registration requirements is greatly simplified by the use of Form S-15 for the registration requirements. Form S-15 enables an issuer to provide an abbreviated prospectus accompanied by the issuer's latest annual report to shareholders instead of larger documents. This procedure is limited to cases where the acquiring company's key financial indices as specified in the regulations are not affected by more than 10% by the acquired company, and where State law applicable to the merger does not require a vote by the security holders of the company being acquired. There are other restrictions, however, and it is likely this simplified procedure will be most usable for mergers where the company to be acquired is closely-held and will not become a significant part of the combined company.

Three copies of Forms-15 must be filed with the SEC. One copy must be signed manually by an officer of the registrant, or by counsel, or by any other authorized person. The name and title of the person signing Forms-15 should be typed or printed under that person's signature.

Synopsis: The Securities Act of 1933

In 1933, the first Federal legislative act designed to regulate the securities business on an interstate basis was passed. Its expressed purpose was:

"To provide full and fair disclosure of the character of securities . . . and to prevent frauds in the sale thereof, and for other purposes." There are four things to note:

1. It related to newly-issued securities, not to those already in the hands of the public.
2. It called for full and fair disclosure of all the facts necessary for an intelligent appraisal of the value of a security.
3. It was designed to prevent fraud in the sale of securities.
4. This legislation led to the Securities Exchange Act of 1934 establishing the Securities and Exchange Commission which would administer both acts.

There are 26 sections to the Act:

Section 1. "This title may be cited as the Securities Act of 1933." Various court decisions have very liberally interpreted the meaning of "securities" as covered by the Act. One decision contains the following: ". . . that this statute was not a penal statute but was a remedial enactment . . . A remedial enactment is one that seeks to give a remedy for an ill. It is to be liberally construed so that its purpose may be realized." (SEC v Starmont, (1940) 31 F. Supp. 264.)

Section 2. Definitions. This section defines many of the terms used throughout the other sections of the Act. Importantly, it contains definitions of "security," "person," "sale," "offer to sell," and "prospectus," among many others. Several important Rules of the SEC are directly derived from this section, including Rule 134 (discussed in Section 5).

Section 3. Exempted Securities. Some securities, such as those issued or guaranteed by the United States, are exempted from the provisions of the Act.

Section 4. Exempted Transactions. Describes the transactions for which Section 5 does not apply.

Section 5. Prohibitions Relating to Intrastate Commerce and the Mails. It is unlawful to offer any security for sale "by any means or instruments of transportation or communication in interstate commerce or of the mails," unless a registration statement is in effect as to that security. It also prohibits the transportation by any means of interstate commerce or the mails of such a security for the purpose of sale or delivery after sale.

This Section further requires that any security that is registered cannot be sold without prior or concurrent delivery of an effective prospectus that meets the requirements of Section 10(a) of the Act.

There have been two important Rules promulgated by the SEC under this Section. The first, Rule 134, defines the types of advertising and of letters or other communications that can be used without prior or concurrent delivery of a prospectus. This Rule is frequently violated in letter form and also in telephone conversations. SEC Release 3844 of October 8, 1957, shows the importance of delivering a prospectus either before or at the same time that an attempt to sell is made. This Release states that a prospectus is defined to include any notice, circular, advertisement, letter, or communication, written or by radio or by television, which offers any security for sale except that any communication sent or given after the effective date of a registration statement shall not be deemed a prospectus if, prior to or at the same time with such a communication, a written prospectus meeting the requirements of Section 10 of the Act was sent or given.

Thus, any letter that gives more information than that allowed by Rule 134 becomes itself a prospectus, unless it is preceded or accompanied by the actual prospectus. A letter prospectus is in violation of Section 5 since it could not possibly comply with the requirements of Section 10.

The second, Rule 433, deals with the so-called "red-herring" prospectus which cannot be used as an offer to sell, but merely to disseminate information prior to the delivery of a regular prospectus which does offer the security for sale.

Section 6. Registration of Securities and Signing of Registration Statement. This Section details what securities may be registered and how such registration is to be done.

Section 7. Information Required on Registration Statement. This Section gives the SEC broad powers in regulating what must appear in a registration statement. In part, the section reads:

"Any such registration statement shall contain such other information, and be accompanied by such other documents, as the Commission may by rules or regulations require as being necessary or appropriate in the public interest or for the protection of investors."

Section 8. Taking Effect of Registration Statements and Amendments Thereto. Registration statements normally become effective on the twentieth day after filing, under this section. However, the SEC is empowered to determine whether or not the statement complies with the Act as to completeness and may refuse to allow the statement to become effective unless amended. If it appears to the SEC that untrue statements have been included, the Commission may issue a stop order.

Section 9. Court Review of Orders. As with any other act of Congress, provision is made so that any person who is aggrieved by an order of the administrative body (in this case the SEC) may obtain a review of the order in the Federal courts.

Section 10. Information Required in Prospectus. A prospectus must contain the same information as that contained in the registration statement. In addition, the SEC is given the authority to define the requirements for any additional material which that body considers necessary in the public interest. "Red herring" requirements and the manner of use of this type of preliminary prospectus are also detailed in this Section.

Note the application of Rule 134, discussed under Section 5, with respect to an "incomplete" prospectus.

One part of the Section, 10(3), relates to the length of time a prospectus may be used (that is, be considered an effective prospectus).

Under this Section of the Act, the SEC issued Rule 425, which requires the statement at the bottom of the first page of all prospectuses "These securities have not been approved or disapproved by the Securities and Exchange Commission nor has the commission passed upon the accuracy or adequacy of this prospectus. Any representation to the contrary is a criminal offense."

Section 11. Civil Liabilities on Account of False Registration Statement. Anyone directly connected with a company or signing the registration statement is subject to suit at law or in equity should the registration statement contain an untrue statement or fail to include a material fact necessary to make the statement not misleading.

Section 12. Civil Liabilities. If any person offers to sell or does sell a security in violation of Section 5, or uses any fraudulent means to sell a security, he or she is liable to civil suit for damages. This liability is in addition to any criminal liability arising under the Act.

Section 13. Limitation of Actions. Specified are the time limits within which civil suits may be instituted under Sections 11 and 12.

Section 14. Contrary Stipulations Void. Any provision in the sale of a security that binds the purchaser to waive the provisions of this Act or of the rules and regulations of the SEC is void. In other words, no one buying a security can relieve the seller from complying with the Act and with the rules issued under the Act.

Section 15. Liability of Controlling Persons. A dealer or broker is liable under Section 11 or 12.

Section 16. Additional Remedies. "The rights and remedies provided by this title (the Act) shall be in addition to any and all other rights and remedies that may exist at law or in equity."

Section 17. Fraudulent Interstate Transactions. As interpreted by the SEC, this section might be referred to as a "catch-all" section.

(a) "It shall be unlawful for any person in the offer or sale of any securities by the use of any means or instruments of transportation or communication in interstate commerce or by the use of the mails, directly or indirectly.

1. to employ any device, scheme or artifice to defraud, or
2. to obtain money or property by means of any untrue statement of a material fact or any omission to state a material fact necessary in order to make the statements made, in the light of the circumstances under which they were made, not misleading, or
3. to engage in any transaction, practice or course of business that operates or would operate as a fraud or deceit upon the purchaser."

Both TV and radio have been included by the SEC as "communication in interstate commerce" because it is impossible to control their area of reception.

While Section 17(a) refers only to the criminal courts in the term "unlawful," a court decision makes it clear that civil liability, in addition to criminal liability is incurred by violation of the section.

Court decisions also implement and amplify the language of the Act itself, with respect to the phrase "or by use of the mails." It would appear that Section 17 only applies to interstate mailings. However, the courts have ruled that if one used the mails *within one State* on an *intrastate* offering, and violated any provision in Section 17(a), that person is as guilty as if he or she had mailed across a state line.

Subparagraph (b) of Section 17 makes it illegal for anyone to publish descriptions of securities when the publisher is paid for such publicity, without also publishing the fact that compensation has been, or will be, received.

Section 17(c) makes the Section applicable to those securities exempted under Section 3. In other words, fraud is fraud whether in connection with exempt or other securities.

Section 18. State Control of Securities. "Nothing in this title (the Act) shall affect the jurisdiction of the Securities Commission . . . of any State . . . ." In other words, all the provisions of the Federal act *and* all the laws of the State in which business is being conducted must be complied with.

Section 19. Special Powers of Commission. The Commission has the authority to make, amend, and rescind such rules and regulations as may be necessary to carry out the provisions of the Act. Commissioners or their representatives are also empowered to subpoena witnesses and to administer oaths.

Section 20. Injunctions and Prosecution of Offenses. The SEC is empowered to make investigations and to bring criminal actions at law against persons deemed to have violated the Act. The wording of the section is interesting in that it gives the Commission power to act "whenever it shall appear . . . that the provisions of this title (the Act) . . . have been *or are about to be* violated . . . ."

Section 21. Hearings by Commission. "All hearings shall be public and may be held before the Commission or an officer or officers of the Commission designated by it, and appropriate records shall be kept."

Section 22. Jurisdiction of Offenses and Suits. Jurisdiction of offenses and violations and certain rules in connection with them, are defined in this section. Jurisdiction is given to the District Courts of the United States, the U.S. Court of any Territory, and the U.S. District Court of the District of Columbia.

Section 23. Unlawful Representations. The fact that the registration statement for a security has been filed or is in effect does not mean that the statement is true and accurate, or that the Commission has in any way passed upon the merits of the security. It is unlawful to make any representations to the contrary.

In short, the words in the registration statement (*and* the prospectus) have been made under the penalties of fraud. The registrants are liable, even though the Commission has not certified the truth and accuracy of the statements or of the worth of the security.

Section 24. Penalties. "Any person who willfully violates any of the provisions of this title (the Act), or the rules and regulations promulgated by the Commission under authority thereof . . . shall upon conviction be fined not more than $10,000.00 or imprisoned not more than five years, or both."

Section 25. Jurisdiction of Other Government Agencies Over Securities. Nothing in the Act shall relieve any person from submitting to other U.S. Government supervisory units information required by any provision of law.

Section 26. Separability of Provisions. If any one section of the Act is invalidated, such findings will not affect other sections.

Schedule A. Sets forth the requirements for the registration of securities.

Schedule B. Sets for the registration requirements for securities issued by a foreign government or political subdivision thereof.

SYNOPSIS: THE SECURITIES EXCHANGE ACT OF 1934

The Securities Act of 1933 protects investors in the purchase of newly-issued securities. The Securities Exchange Act of 1934 concerns the regulation of trading in already issued securities.

The stated purpose of the 1934 Act is "to provide for the regulation of securities exchanges and of over-the-counter markets operating in interstate and foreign commerce and through the mails, to prevent inequitable and unfair practices on such exchanges and markets, and for other purposes."

The Act has been of importance in prohibiting abuses and manipulations through its creation of the SEC and later of the self-regulatory National Association of Securities Dealers, Inc.

The Act has 34 sections:

Section 1. Short Title. "This Act may be cited as the Securities Exchange Act of 1934."

Section 2. Necessity of Regulation. Citing that transactions in securities are affected with a national public interest, this section states that it is necessary to regulate and control such transactions and other matters in order to protect interstate commerce, the national credit, the Federal taxing power, to protect and make more effective the national banking system and Federal Reserve System, and to insure the maintenance of fair and honest markets in such transactions.

Parts of Sections 2(3) and 2(4) explain the effects of "rigged" markets and manipulative practices:

Section 2(3). Frequently, the prices of securities on such exchanges and markets are susceptible to manipulation and control, and the dissemination of such prices gives rise to excessive speculation, resulting in sudden and unreasonable fluctuations in the prices of securities which (a) cause alternately unreasonable expansion and unreasonable contraction of the volume of credit available for trade, transportation, and industry in interstate commerce . . . (c) prevent the fair valuation of collateral for bank loans and/or obstruct the effective operation of the national banking system and Federal Reserve System.

Section 2(4). "National emergencies, which produce widespread unemployment and the dislocation of trade, transportation, and industry, and which burden interstate commerce and adversely affect the general welfare, are precipitated, intensified, and prolonged by manipulation and sudden and unreasonable fluctuations of security prices and by excessive speculation on such exchanges and markets, and to meet such emergencies the Federal Government is put to such great expense as to burden the national credit."

Section 3. Definitions. In addition to defining 38 technical terms used in the Act, this Section gave the Securities Exchange Commission and the

Federal Reserve System the authority to define technical, trade, and accounting terms so long as such definitions are not inconsistent with the provisions of the Act itself.

Section 4. This Section established the Securities and Exchange Commission. Prior to the Commissioners' taking office, the Securities Act of 1933 was administered by the Federal Trade Commission.

Section 5. Transactions on Unregistered Exchanges. Under this Section, it became illegal for transactions to be effected by brokers, dealers, or exchanges on an exchange unless the exchange was registered under Section 6 of the Act.

Section 6. Registration of Exchanges. Combined with Section 5, this Section sets forth the requirements for exchanges to be registered and the method of registration. Exchanges file their rules and regulations with the SEC and must agree to take disciplinary action against any member who violates the Act or violates any of the rules and regulations issued by the SEC under the Act.

Section 7. Margin Requirements. The Board of Governors of the Federal Reserve System is given the power to set margin requirements for any securities, which requirements may be changed from time to time at the discretion of the Board. Under this authority, the Board issued Regulation T and Regulation U. Regulation T governs the extension and maintenance of credit by brokers, dealers, and members of national securities exchanges. Regulation U governs loans by banks for the purpose of purchasing or carrying stocks registered on a national securities exchange.

Section 8. Restrictions on Borrowing. In four parts, this Section (a) details from whom brokers or dealers may borrow money on listed securities, (b) lays the foundation for the SEC's "net capital rule," (c) deals with pledging and co-mingling of customers' securities, and (d) states no broker or dealer may lend or arrange for the lending of any securities carried for the account of a customer without the written consent of the customer.

Section 9. Prohibition Against Manipulation. Both this Section and Section 10 deal with manipulative practices that are intended to make money for those in the Securities business at the expense of the general public.

Section 9 makes it unlawful to do certain things that constitute manipulation, such as: (a) creating a false or misleading appearance of active trading in a security, (b) giving of information to potential investors as to the likelihood of a rise or fall in price solely for the purpose of causing the market price to react to purchases or sales by such potential investors, (c) making false or misleading statements about a security, (d) "pegging" or "fixing" prices, (e) improper use of puts, calls, straddles, or other options to buy or sell. Transactions in which there is no real change in ownership are also specifically prohibited.

Section 10. Regulation of Manipulative and Deceptive Devices. Section 10 first forbids the use of short sales or stop-loss orders that violate any rules or regulations the Commission may set to protect investors. Its wording, then, becomes much more inclusive than Section 9 or the first part of Section 10, since it forbids in general "any manipulative or deceptive device or contrivance . . . ."

Section 11. Trading by Members of Exchanges, Brokers, and Dealers. Authority is given to the Commission to set rules and regulations as to floor trading by members, brokers, or dealers for their own accounts and to prevent excessive trading off the floor of the exchanges. A part of this Section deals with the roles of the odd-lot dealers and the specialist on the floor of the exchange. Further, the Section places a limitation on certain customer credit extension in connection with underwritings.

Section 11A. National Market System for Securities; Securities Information Processors. Concerns the planning, developing, operating, or regulating of a national market system.

Section 12. Registration Requirements for Securities. It is unlawful for any broker or dealer to effect transactions in a security or a national securities exchange unless a registration statement is effective for that security. Information stating how such registration is to be accomplished is given here. The SEC is given authority to allow trading on one exchange in securities that are listed on another exchange (such securities are said to have "unlisted trading privileges").

Section 13. Reports. All companies whose securities are listed on a national securities exchange must file reports at such intervals and in such form as the SEC may require. The purpose of requiring such reports was to ensure that enough information was available on any company to enable an investor to make an intelligent decision concerning the worth of its securities.

Section 14. Proxies. Paragraph (a) of this Section gives the SEC the authority to make rules and regulations as to the solicitation of proxies and makes it illegal to solicit proxies other than in accord with such rules and regulations. Several rules have been issued under this Section which detail the manner in which proxies may be solicited and the information that must be given to shareholders whose proxies are being solicited. All of these rules are designated to ensure that the recipient of a proxy solicitation will understand what it is that he or she is being asked to sign and to give enough background on the matter in question so that the shareholder can make an intelligent decision about how to vote.

Paragraph (b) relates to the giving of proxies by broker or dealers in connection with securities held for the accounts of customers. It is standard practice for broker/dealers to vote proxies for shares held in their names for customers directly in accord with the wishes of the customers themselves.

Section 15. Over-The-Counter Markets. It is mandatory that all brokers and dealers who deal in the over-the-counter market (on other than an intrastate basis) be registered with the SEC. Further, the Section states that registration will be in accord with rules and regulations issued by the Commission. "Intrastate" means that the broker or dealer deals in intrastate securities as well as doing business only within his state. Here, as elsewhere in the Act,the "use of mails," even if within one State, places the user under the Act.

Section 15 also defines the grounds for denial of registration, for suspension, or for revocation of registration. Basically, these grounds are:

1. Making false or misleading statements in the application for registration.
2. Having been convicted within the last ten years of a felony or misdemeanor involving the purchase or sale of any security or arising out of the business of a broker or dealer.
3. Being enjoined by a court from engaging in the securities business.
4. Having willfully violated any of the provisions of the 1933 Act or of the 1934 Act. (After passage of the Investment Advisers Act of 1940 and the Investment Company Act of 1940, violation of those Acts also became grounds for suspension or revocation.)

Sections 9 and 10 dealt with manipulation with respect to securities listed on a national exchange. Section 15 adds a prohibition against over-the-counter manipulation as defined by the Commission. Some of the practices that have been so defined are:

1. Excessive prices that are not fairly related to the market.
2. False representations to customers.
3. Taking of secret profits.
4. Failure to disclose control of a market.
5. Creating false impression of activity by dummy sales.
6. "Churning," or unnecessary purchases and sales in a customer's account.

Another important rule of the SEC under Section 15 seeks to protect investors by forbidding certain practices in connection with pledging or comingling of securities held for the accounts of customers. This rule specifically applies to over-the-counter broker/dealers; a similar rule, under Section 8, applies to broker/dealers who are members of or do business through members of a national exchange.

Section 15A. Registration of National Securities Associations. Aided by the Maloney Act of 1938, which amended the original Act by adding this

Section, the formation of associations, such as the National Association of Securities Dealers, was authorized.

Section 15B. Concerns municipal securities dealers and transactions in municipal securities.

Section 15(c)(3) requires financial responsibility on the part of broker/dealers.

Sections 12 and 13 deal with registration and report requirements for listed securities. Section 15(d) is a corresponding list of requirements with respect to unlisted securities.

Section 16. Directors, Officers, and Principal Stockholders. Requires statements of ownership of stocks by "insiders" and other related information.

Section 17. Accounts and Records. Not only does this Section require that all brokers and dealers maintain records in accord with such rules and regulations as the SEC may set forth, but it also authorizes the SEC to make examinations of any broker's or dealer's accounts, correspondence, memoranda, papers, books, and other records whenever the Commission deems it in the public interest. Rules and regulations issued by the SEC under this Section state the types of records that must be kept. In practice, an SEC examiner may walk into a broker/dealer's office and ask that all files and books be opened for inspection. Under the law, no broker/dealer may refuse the examiner access to any and all correspondence and records. A broker/dealer can have his or her registration suspended or revoked by failure to keep copies of all correspondence or to keep books and records as required by the SEC.

Section 17A. Settlement of Securities Transactions. Concerns the clearance and settlement of securities transactions, transfer of ownership, and safeguarding of securities and funds. Congress directed the SEC to facilitate the establishment of a national system for securities clearings.

Section 18. Liability for Misleading Statements. In a rather unusual statement of law, this Section makes a person both criminally and civilly liable for any misleading statements made in connection with the requirements of Section 15 of this Act.

Section 19. Registration, Responsibilities, and Oversight of Self-Regulatory Organizations. The SEC has the power to suspend for 12 months or revoke the registration of any national securities exchange or of any security, if the Commission is of the opinion that such action is necessary or appropriate for the protection of investors. Further, authority is granted the SEC to suspend or expel from an exchange any member or officer who has violated any of the provisions of this Act.

Other provisions of this Section give the SEC broad powers in supervising the rules of national securities exchanges, which the Commission may require to be changed or amended. In other words, the SEC supervises the members of an exchange through the exchange itself as well as on an individual basis.

Section 20. Liabilities of Controlling Persons. In effect, this Section states that if A commits an illegal act under the direction of B, who controls A, then both A and B are equally liable under the law. Section 20 also makes it illegal for any "controlling person" to "hinder, delay, or obstruct" the filing of any information required by the SEC under this Act.

Section 21. Investigations; Injunctions and Prosecution. In the Securities Act of 1933, Sections 19 and 20 gave the SEC special powers in the areas of investigation, subpoenaing of witnesses, prosecutions of offenses and the like. Section 21 of this Act is similar in its provisions.

Section 22. Hearings. It is interesting to note the difference in wording with respect to hearings in the 1933 Act and in this Act. Section 21 of the 1933 Act states that "All hearings *shall* be public . . . ." Section 22 of the 1934 Act states "Hearings *may* be public . . . ."

Section 23. Rules and Regulations. Power to make rules and regulations under this Act is specifically given the SEC and the Board of Governors of the Federal Reserve System by this Section. Both bodies are required to make annual reports to Congress.

Section 24. Public Availability of Information. To protect those required to file under this Act, this Section makes it possible for certain information, such as trade secrets, to be made confidential and not a matter of public record. This Section also forbids any member or employee of the Commission to use information that is not public for personal benefit.

Section 25. Court Review of Orders and Rules. Like Section 9 of the 1933 Act, this Section reserves final judgment on any issue to the courts, rather than to the Commission itself.

Section 26. Unlawful Representations. It is unlawful to make any representation to the effect that the SEC or the Federal Reserve Board has passed on the merits of any issue. Also, the failure of either body to take action against any person cannot be construed to mean that that person is not in violation of the law.

Section 27. Jurisdiction of Offenses and Suits. Jurisdiction of violations of this Act is given to the district courts of the United States.

Section 28. Effect on Existing Law. "The rights and remedies provided by this title (the Act) shall be in addition to any and all other rights and remedies that may exist in law or at equity . . . ." The Section also leaves jurisdiction of offenses against a State law with the State.

Section 29. Validity of Contracts. No one can avoid compliance with the provisions of this Act by getting someone else to waive the requirements in any contract. Any contract that seeks to avoid the provisions of this Act are automatically void.

Section 30. Foreign Securities Exchange. It is unlawful to deal in securities whose issuers are within the jurisdiction of the United States on a foreign exchange in any manner other than that in which dealing in such securities would have to be handled in this country. In other words, the laws of the U.S. exchanges cannot be circumvented by placing business through a foreign exchange.

Section 31. Transaction Fees. Each national securities exchange is required to pay an annual fee to the Commission.

Section 32. Penalties. Individuals may be fined a maximum of $1,000,000 or sentenced to a maximum term of imprisonment of 10 years, or both, for violations of the Act.

Section 33. Separability of Provisions. An escape section that states that if any one section of the Act is found to be invalid, such findings shall have no effect on the other sections.

Section 34. Effective Date. July 1, 1934.

PUBLIC UTILITY HOLDING COMPANY ACT OF 1935

Interstate holding companies engaged through subsidiaries in the electric utility business or in the retail distribution of natural or manufactured gas are subject to regulation under the Act. These systems must register with the SEC and file initial and periodic reports. Detailed information concerning the organization, financial structure, and operations of the holding company and its subsidiaries is contained in these reports. If a holding company or its subsidiary meets certain specifications, the Commission can exempt it from part or all of the duties and obligations otherwise imposed by statute. Holding companies are subject to SEC regulations on matters such as structure of the system, acquisitions, combinations, and issues and sales of securities.

The most important provisions of the Act are the requirements for physical integration and corporation simplification of holding company systems. Integration standards restrict a holding company's operations to an *integrated utility system*. An integrated system is defined as one:

1. Capable of economical operation as a single coordinated system.
2. Confined to a single area or region in one or more states.
3. Not so large that it negates the advantages of localized management, efficient operation, and effective regulation.

The original structure and continued existence of any company in a holding company system must not necessarily complicate the corporate structure of the system or result in the distribution of voting power inequitably among security holders of the system.

The SEC can determine what action, if any, must be taken by registered holding companies and their subsidiaries to comply with Act requirements. The SEC can apply to federal courts for orders compelling compliance with Commission directives.

Acquisitions

To be authorized by the SEC, the acquisition of securities and utility assets by holding companies and their subsidiaries must meet the following standards:

1. The acquisition must not tend toward interlocking relations or concentrating control to an extent detrimental to investors or the public interest.
2. Any consideration paid for the acquisition, including fees, commissions, and remuneration, must not be unreasonable.
3. The acquisition must not complicate the capital structure of the holding company systems or have a detrimental effect on system functions.
4. The acquisition must tend toward economical and efficient development of an integrated public utility system.

Issuance and Sale of Securities

Proposed security issues by any holding company must be analyzed and evaluated by the SEC staff and approved by the Commission to ensure that the issues meet the following tests under prescribed standards of the law:

1. The security must be reasonably adapted to the security structure of the issuer, and of other companies in the same holding company system.
2. The security must be reasonably adapted to the earning power of the company.
3. The proposed issue must be necessary and appropriate to the economical and efficient operation of the company's business.
4. The fees, commissions, and other remuneration paid in connection with the issue must not be unreasonable.
5. The terms and conditions of the issue or sale of the security must not be detrimental to the public or investor interest.

Other provisions of the Act concern regulating dividend payments, inter-company loans, solicitations of proxies, consents and other authorizations, and insider trading.

TRUST INDENTURE ACT OF 1939

This Act applies to bonds, debentures, notes, and similar debt securities offered for public sale and issued under trust indentures with more than $7.5 million of securities outstanding at any one time. Even though such securities are registered under the Securities Act, they cannot be offered for sale to the public unless the trust indenture conforms to statutory standards of this Act. Designed to safeguard the rights and interests of the investors, the Act also:

1. Prohibits the indenture trustee from conflicting interests which might interfere with exercising its duties on behalf of the securities purchasers.
2. Requires the trustee to be a corporation with minimum combined capital and surplus.
3. Imposes high standards of conduct and responsibility on the trustee.
4. Precludes, in the event of default, preferential collection of certain claims owing to the trustee by the issuer.
5. Provides that the issuer supply to the trustee evidence of compliance with indenture terms and conditions.
6. Requires the trustee to provide reports and notices to security holders.

Other provisions of the Act prohibit impairing the security holders' right to sue individually for principal and interest, except under certain circumstances. It also requires maintaining a list of security holders for their use in communicating with each other regarding their rights as security holders.

In 1987 the Commission sent a legislative proposal to Congress which would modernize procedures under the Act to meet the public's need in view of novel debt instruments and modern financing techniques. This legislative proposal was adopted and enacted into law in 1990.

INVESTMENT ADVISERS ACT OF 1940

This law establishes a pattern of regulating investment advisers. In some respects, it has provisions similar to the Securities Exchange Act provisions governing the conduct of brokers and dealers. This Act requires that persons or firms compensated for advising others about securities investment must register with the SEC and conform to the statutory standards designed to protect investors.

The Commission can deny, suspend, or revoke investment adviser registrations if, after notice and hearings, it finds that grounds for a statutory disqualification exist and that the action is in the public interest. Grounds for disqualification include conviction for certain financial crimes or securities law violations, injunctions based on such activities, conviction for violating the mail fraud statute, willfully filing false reports with the SEC, and willfully violating the Advisers Act, the Securities Act, the Securities Exchange Act, the Investment Company Act, or the rules of the Municipal Securities Rulemaking Board. The SEC can recommend criminal prosecution by the Department of Justice for violations of the laws, fraudulent misconduct or willful violation of Commission rules.

The law contains antifraud provisions and empowers the Commission to adopt rules defining fraudulent, deceptive, or manipulative acts and practices. It requires that investment advisers:

1. Disclose the nature of their interest in transactions executed for their clients.
2. Maintain books and records according to SEC rules.
3. Make books and records available to the SEC for inspections.

TRUST INVESTMENT COMPANY ACT OF 1940

Activities of companies engaged primarily in investing, reinvesting, and trading in securities, and whose own securities are offered to the public, are subject to statutory prohibitions and to SEC regulations under this Act. Public offerings of investment company securities must be registered under the Securities Act of 1933. It is important that investors understand that the SEC does not supervise the investment activities of these companies and that regulation by the Commission does not imply safety of investment in them.

In addition to the registration requirement for investment companies, the law requires that they disclose their financial condition and investment policies to provide investors complete information about their activities. This Act also:

1. Prohibits investment companies from substantially changing the nature of their business or investment policies without stockholder approval.
2. Prohibits persons guilty of securities fraud from serving as officers and directors.
3. Prevents underwriters, investment bankers, or brokers from constituting more than a minority of the directors of the companies.
4. Requires that management contracts and material changes be submitted to security holders for their approval.
5. Prohibits transactions between companies and their directors, officers, or affiliated companies or persons, except when approved by the SEC.

6. Forbids investment companies to issue senior securities except under specific conditions and upon specified terms.
7. Prohibits pyramiding of such companies and cross-ownership of their securities.

Other provisions of the Act involve advisory fees, nonconformance of an adviser's fiduciary duty, sales and repurchases of securities issued by investment companies, exchange offers, and other activities of investment companies, including special provisions for periodic payment plans and face-amount certificate companies.

Investment companies must register securities under the Securities Act, and also must file periodic reports and are subject to the SEC proxy and insider trading rules.

CORPORATION REORGANIZATION

Reorganization proceedings in the U.S. Courts under Chapter 11 of the Bankruptcy Code are begun by a debtor voluntarily, or by its creditors. Federal bankruptcy law allows a debtor in reorganization to continue operating under the court's protection while the debtor attempts to rehabilitate its business and work out a plan to pay its debts. If a debtor corporation has publicly issued securities outstanding, the reorganization process may raise many issues that materially affect the rights of public investors.

Chapter 11 authorizes the SEC to appear in any reorganization case and to present its views on any issue. Although Chapter 11 applies to all types of business reorganizations, the SEC generally limits its participation to proceedings involving significant public investor interest, i.e., protecting public investors holding the debtor's securities, and participating in legal and policy issues of concern to public investors. The SEC also continues to address matters of traditional Commission expertise and interest relating to securities. When appropriate, the SEC comments on the adequacy of reorganization plan disclosure statements and participates where there is a Commission law enforcement interest.

Under Chapter 11, the debtor, official committees, and institutional creditors negotiate the terms of a reorganization plan. The court can confirm a reorganization plan if it is accepted by creditors for:

1. At least two-thirds of the amounts of allowed claims.
2. More than one-half the number of allowed claims.
3. At least two-thirds in amount of the allowed shareholder interest.

The principal safeguard for public investors is the requirement that a disclosure statement containing adequate information be transmitted by the debtor or plan proponent in connection with soliciting votes on the plan. In addition, reorganization plans involving publicly-held debt usually provide for issuing new securities to creditors and shareholders which are exempt from registration under Section 5 of the Securities Act of 1933.

Chapter 18

The Securities and Exchange Commission—Materiality

SEC STAFF ACCOUNTING BULLETIN 99

The Securities and Exchange Staff Accounting Bulletin (SAB) 99, *Materiality*, issued in August, 1999 delineates the staff's views concerning reliance on certain quantitative benchmarks to assess materiality in preparing financial statements and performing audits of those financial statements. The SEC has decided that the practice of adopting an arbitrary margin of error is inappropriate. SAB 99 concludes that misstatements are not immaterial simply because they fall beneath a numerical threshold.

The SEC is quick to point out that statements in the staff accounting bulletins are not rules or interpretations of the Commission, nor are they published as bearing the Commission's official approval. However, they do represent interpretations and practices followed by the Division of Corporation Finance and the Office of the Chief Accountant in *administering the disclosure requirements of the federal securities laws.* To put it bluntly, anyone ignoring this SAB, is putting himself, herself and/or their company at risk: this new materiality test is the standard the SEC will use for enforcement purposes.

It should be emphasized that SAB 99 does not constitute a new approach to the consideration of "materiality," but is an attempt to "shore up" the definition of the concept and in so doing reemphasize the Commission's foremost goal—the protection of the investor. Therefore, it provides guidance in applying materiality thresholds to the *preparation of financial statements filed with the Commission and the performance of audits of those financial statements.*

367

Misusing the "Rule of Thumb"

The SEC staff has been cognizant of the fact that many registrants gradually adopted as "rules of thumb" a 5% quantitative margin of error in preparing their financial statements, and that auditors also have used these thresholds in their evaluation of whether items might be considered material to users of a registrant's financial statements. One rule of thumb in particular suggests that the *misstatement* or *omission* of an item that falls under a 5% threshold is not material in the absence of particularly "egregious circumstances, such as self-dealing or misappropriation by senior management." (In this SAB, "misstatement" or "omission" refers to a financial statement assertion that would not be in conformity with GAAP.)

The staff reminds registrants and the auditors of their financial statements that exclusive reliance on this or any percentage or numerical threshold has no basis in the *accounting literature* or the *law*.

The use of a percentage as a numerical threshold, such as 5%, may provide the basis for a *preliminary* assumption that, without considering all relevant circumstances, a deviation of less than the specified percentage with respect to a particular item on the registrant's financial statements is unlikely to be material. The staff has no objection to such a "rule of thumb" as an *initial* step in assessing materiality. But the bulletin cautions that quantifying the magnitude of a misstatement in percentage terms can be only the beginning of an analysis of materiality; it cannot be used as a substitute for a *full analysis* of all relevant considerations.

DEFINING MATERIALITY

Materiality concerns the significance of an item to users of a registrant's financial statements. A matter is "material" if there is a substantial likelihood that a reasonable person would consider it important. Early in its existence, the Financial Accounting Standards Board made this clear. In its Statement of Financial Accounting Concepts 2, the FASB stated the essence of the concept of materiality as follows: *The omission or misstatement of an item in a financial report is material if, in the light of surrounding circumstances, the magnitude of the item is such that it is probable that the judgment of a reasonable person relying upon the report would have been changed or influenced by the inclusion or correction of the item.*

This Statement is almost identical to that expressed by the courts in interpreting the federal securities laws. In 1976, the Supreme Court held that a fact is material if there is "a substantial likelihood that the fact would have been viewed by the reasonable investor as having significantly altered the 'total mix' of information made available."

Thus, we see that an assessment of materiality requires that the facts be considered in the context of the "surrounding circumstances," according to accounting literature, or the "total mix" of information, in the opinion of the Supreme Court.

QUALITATIVE AND QUANTITATIVE FACTORS ARE IMPORTANT

In the context of a misstatement of a financial statement item, while the "total mix" includes the *size* in numerical or percentage terms of the misstatement, it also includes the *factual context* in which the user of financial statements appraises the financial statement item. Therefore, financial management and the auditor must consider both "quantitative" and "qualitative" factors in assessing an item's materiality. Court decisions, Commission rules and enforcement actions, and accounting and auditing literature have all considered "qualitative" factors in various contexts.

The FASB has repeatedly emphasized that materiality cannot be reduced to a numerical formula. In FASB Statement 2, the FASB noted that some commenters had urged it to promulgate quantitative materiality guides for use in various situations. The FASB decided against a blanket approach as representing only a "minority view" and went on to explain, "The predominant view is that materiality judgments can properly be made only by those who have all the facts."

According to FASB 2, an additional factor in making materiality judgments revolves around the *degree of precision* that can be attained in *estimating* the judgment item. The amount of deviation that is considered immaterial may increase as the attainable degree of precision decreases. As an example, the SAB points out that *accounts payable* usually can be estimated more accurately than can *contingent liabilities* arising from litigation or threats of it. Therefore, a deviation considered to be material in figuring accounts payable may be quite trivial when considering contingent liabilities.

FASB CONSIDERATIONS AND OPINION

The FASB's present position is that no general standards of materiality can be formulated to take into account all the considerations that enter into an experienced human judgment. The Board noted that, in certain limited circumstances, the SEC and other authoritative bodies have issued quantitative materiality guidance, citing as examples guidelines ranging from 1 to 10% with respect to a variety of disclosures. They looked at contradictory studies: one showing a lack of uniformity among auditors on materiality judgments; another suggesting widespread use of a "rule of thumb" of 5 to 10% of net income. They also considered whether an evaluation of materiality could be based solely on anticipating the market's reaction to accounting information.

In the end, the FASB rejected any simplified approach to discharging "the onerous duty of making materiality decisions" in favor of an approach that takes into account *all relevant considerations*. In so doing, it made clear that, "Magnitude by itself, without regard to the nature of the item and the circumstances in which the judgment has to be made, will not generally be a sufficient basis for a materiality judgment."

SMALL FIGURES MAY CAUSE BIG MISSTATEMENTS

Evaluation of materiality requires a registrant and its auditor to consider all the relevant circumstances, and the staff believes that there are numerous circumstances in which misstatements below 5% could well be material. As does the SEC Chairman who pointed out that given the attitude of investors in the stock market today, *everything* matters when "...missing an earnings projection by a penny can result in a loss of millions of dollars in market capitalization."

SAB 99 takes into consideration this concern that *qualitative factors* may cause misstatements of quantitatively extremely small amounts to be material. Thus, the bulletin, in effect, cautions the auditor that as a result of the interaction of quantitative and qualitative considerations in materiality judgments, misstatements of relatively small amounts that come to the auditor's attention *could* have a material effect upon the financial statements. Among those considerations that may well render material a quantitatively small misstatement of a financial statement item are whether the misstatement:

1. Results from an item capable of precise measurement or from an estimate and, if so, the degree of imprecision inherent in the estimate.
2. Masks a change in earnings or other trends.
3. Hides a failure to meet analysts' consensus expectations for the enterprise.
4. Actually changes a loss into income or vice versa.
5. Concerns a *segment* or other portion of the registrant's business that has been identified as playing a *significant role* in the registrant's operations or profitability.
6. Affects the registrant's compliance with regulatory requirements.
7. Affects the registrant's compliance with loan covenants or other contractual requirements.
8. Has the effect of increasing management's compensation, for example, by satisfying requirements for the award of bonuses or other forms of incentive compensation.

9. Involves concealment of an unlawful transaction.
10. Aims toward smoothing earnings artificially to give a false impression of stability.

The bulletin does not claim this to be an exhaustive list of the circumstances that may affect the materiality of a quantitatively small misstatement, but it certainly makes the decision process a little more exhausting than merely adhering to some predetermined "percentage."

OTHER CONSIDERATIONS

Other factors and situations may bring to question the materiality of a quantitatively small misstatement of a financial statement item:

1. The demonstrated volatility of the price of a registrant's securities in response to certain types of disclosures may provide guidance as to whether *investors* regard quantitatively small misstatements as material.
2. Consideration of potential market reaction to disclosure of a misstatement is by itself "too blunt an instrument to be depended on" in considering whether a fact is material. However, when management or the independent auditor expects (based, for example, on a pattern of market performance) that a known misstatement *may* result in a significant positive or negative market reaction, that expected reaction should be taken into account when considering whether a misstatement is material.

Even if management does not expect a significant market reaction, a misstatement still may be material and should be evaluated under the criteria discussed in this SAB.

"MANAGED" EARNINGS—HERE, THERE, AND EVERYWHERE

For the reasons noted above, the staff believes that a registrant and the auditors of its financial statements should *not* assume that even small intentional misstatements in financial statements—for example those pursuant to actions to "manage" earnings—are immaterial. (Intentional management of earnings and intentional misstatements, as used in SAB 99, do not include insignificant errors and omissions that may occur in systems and recurring processes in the normal course of business.)

While the *intent* of management does not render a misstatement material, it may provide significant evidence of materiality. The evidence may be particularly revealing when management has intentionally misstated items in the financial statements to "manage" reported earnings.

In such an instance, management has presumably done so believing that the resulting amounts and trends *would be significant* to users of the registrant's financial statements. Or have the earnings been "managed" just enough to meet or marginally exceed the expectations of securities analysts who appear to be very significant players in today's volatile markets?

SAB 99 mentions that assessment of materiality should occur not only in annual financial reports, but also during the preparation of each quarterly or interim financial statement. After all, savvy investors and even less well informed ones are known to research these statements.

Consider the Investor

The staff believes that investors generally would regard as significant a management practice to overstate or understate earnings up to an amount just short of a percentage threshold in order to "manage" earnings. Investors presumably also would regard with a jaundiced eye an accounting practice that, in essence, rendered all earnings figures subject to a management-directed margin of misstatement.

The materiality of a misstatement may be judged based upon where it appears in the financial statements. For example, if a misstatement involves a segment of the registrant's operations, in assessing materiality of a misstatement to the financial statements taken as a whole, registrants and their auditors should consider:

1. The *size* of the misstatement.
2. The *significance* of that particular segment information to the financial statements as a whole.

A misstatement of the revenue and operating profit of a relatively small segment which management indicates is important to the future profitability of the entity is more likely to be material to investors than a misstatement in a segment that management has not identified as especially important. In assessing the materiality of misstatements in segment information, as with materiality generally, situations may arise in practice where the auditor will conclude that a matter relating to segment information is *qualitatively material* even though, in his or her judgment, it is *quantitatively immaterial* to the financial statements as a whole.

AGGREGATING AND NETTING MISSTATEMENTS

In determining whether multiple misstatements cause the financial statements to be materially misstated, registrants and the auditors of their financial statements should consider the effect of each misstatement separately, and in the aggregate.

Obviously, the concept of materiality takes into consideration that some information, whether viewed individually or as a part of the whole report, may be required for fair presentation of financial statements in conformity with GAAP in one context or the other. Furthermore, it is necessary to evaluate misstatements in light of quantitative and qualitative factors. It is also necessary to consider whether the following can materially misstate the financial statements taken as a whole:

1. Individual line item amounts
2. Subtotals
3. Totals

This requires consideration of:

1. The significance of an item to a particular type of business enterprise; for example, inventories to a manufacturing company. (An adjustment to inventory seen as immaterial to pretax or net income could be material to the financial statements because it could affect a working capital ratio or cause the registrant to be in default of a loan covenant.)
2. The pervasiveness of the misstatement—whether it affects the presentation of numerous financial statement items.
3. The effect of the misstatement on the financial statements taken as a whole.

Accountants and auditors should consider whether each misstatement is material, regardless of its effect when combined with other misstatements. The literature notes that the analysis should consider whether the misstatement of "individual amounts" causes a material misstatement of the financial statements taken as a whole. As with materiality generally, this analysis requires consideration of both quantitative and qualitative factors.

If the misstatement of an individual amount causes the financial statements as a whole to be materially misstated, that effect cannot be eliminated by other misstatements whose effect may be to diminish the impact of the misstatement on other financial statement items.

Quantitative materiality assessments often are made by comparing adjustments to revenues, gross profit, pretax and net income, total assets, stockholders' equity, or individual line items in the financial statements. The particular items in the financial statements to be considered as a basis for the materiality determination depend on the proposed adjustment to be made and other factors, such as those identified in this SAB. For example, an adjustment to inventory that is immaterial to pretax income or net income may be material to the financial statements because it may affect a working capital ratio or cause the registrant to be in default of loan covenants.

Aggregation May Lead to Aggravation

If a registrant's revenues are a material financial statement item and if they are materially overstated, the financial statements taken as a whole will be materially misleading even if the effect on earnings is completely offset by an equivalent overstatement of expenses. Even though *one misstatement* of an individual amount may not cause the financial statements taken as a whole to be materially misstated, it may nonetheless, when *aggregated with other mis-statements*, render the financial statements taken as a whole to be materially misleading.

Registrants and the auditors of their financial statements should consider the effect of the misstatement on *subtotals* or *totals*. The auditor should aggregate all misstatements that affect each subtotal or total and consider whether the misstatements in the aggregate affect the subtotal or total in a way that causes the registrant's financial statements taken as a whole to be materially misleading.

The staff believes that, in considering the aggregate effect of multiple misstatements on a subtotal or total, accountants and auditors should exercise particular care when considering misstatement of an estimated amount with a misstatement of an item capable of precise measurement. As noted above, *assessments of materiality should never be purely mechanical*; given the imprecision inherent in estimates, there is by definition a corresponding imprecision in the aggregation of misstatements involving estimates with those that do not involve an estimate.

Registrants and auditors also should consider the effect of misstatements from prior periods on the current financial statements. For example, the auditing literature states that matters underlying adjustments proposed by the auditor but not recorded by the entity could potentially cause future financial statements to be materially misstated, even though the auditor has concluded that the adjustments are not material to the current financial statements. This may particularly be the case where immaterial misstatements recur in several years and the cumulative effect becomes material in the current year.

INTENTIONAL IMMATERIAL MISSTATEMENTS

The SEC reemphasizes their caution that a registrant may *not* make intentional immaterial misstatements in its financial statements. A registrant's management may never intentionally make adjustments to various financial statement items in a manner inconsistent with GAAP.

In any accounting period in which such actions might be taken, it could be that none of the individual adjustments would be considered material, nor would the aggregate effect on the financial statements taken as a whole be material *for the period.*

The adjustments could even be considered irrelevant; however at the same time, they could actually be unlawful. In the books and records provisions under the Exchange Act, even if misstatements are immaterial, registrants must comply with the law. Under these provisions, each registrant with securities registered pursuant to the Act, or required to file reports pursuant to it, must:

1. Make and keep books, records, and accounts, which, in *reasonable detail*, accurately, and fairly reflect the transactions and dispositions of assets of the registrant.

2. Maintain internal accounting controls that are sufficient to provide *reasonable assurances* that, among other things, transactions are recorded as necessary to permit the preparation of financial statements in conformity with GAAP.

FASB Statements of Financial Accounting Standards generally include the statement: "The provisions of this Statement need not be applied to immaterial items." This SAB does not countermand that provision of the Statements. However, it does vanquish the 5% of net income quantitative test often applied in the past. The SEC admits that, in theory, this language in the FASBs is subject to interpretation that a registrant may intentionally record immaterial items in a manner that would unquestionably be contrary to GAAP if the misstatement were considered material. It should be carefully noted, however, that the staff believes the FASB did not intend such a conclusion. Regardless, some companies have in the past apparently interpreted the sentence in just that fashion. They evidently felt they could ignore certain immaterial transactions and misapply GAAP to so-called immaterial transactions with impunity. No more!

Both the U.S. Code and the Securities Exchange Act indicate that criminal liability may be imposed if a person knowingly circumvents or knowingly fails to implement a system of internal accounting controls or knowingly falsifies books, records, or accounts. This should make it perfectly clear that any degree of "cooking the books," setting up "cookie jar reserves," "managing," or otherwise obfuscating may result in violations of the securities laws.

THE PRUDENT MAN CONCEPT

In this context, determinations of what constitutes "reasonable assurance" and "reasonable detail" are based not on a "materiality" analysis but on the level of detail and degree of assurance that would satisfy *prudent* officials in the conduct of their own affairs. The books and records provisions of the Exchange Act, in which this is developed, originally were passed as part of the Foreign Corrupt Practices Act (FCPA). In the conference committee report regarding the 1988 amendments to the FCPA, the report stated, "The conference committee adopted the prudent man qualification in order to clarify that the current standard does not connote an unrealistic degree of exactitude or precision. The concept of reasonableness contemplates the weighing of a number of relevant factors, including the costs of compliance."

"REASONABLENESS" SHOULD NOT BE UNREASONABLE

The SEC staff is well aware of the fact that there is little authoritative guidance regarding the "reasonableness" standard in the Exchange Act. A principal statement of the Commission's policy in this area was set forth in a 1981 address by the SEC Chairman who noted that, like materiality, "reasonableness" is not an "absolute standard of exactitude for corporate records."

Unlike materiality, however, "reasonableness" is not solely a measure of the significance of a financial statement item to investors. "Reasonableness," here reflects a judgment as to whether an issuer's failure to correct a known misstatement brings into question the purposes underlying the accounting provisions of the Exchange Act. In assessing whether a misstatement results in a violation of a registrant's obligation to keep books and records that are accurate "in reasonable detail," registrants and their auditors should consider, in addition to the factors discussed above concerning an evaluation of a misstatement's potential materiality, the following factors.

1. *The significance of the misstatement.* Though the staff does not believe that registrants need to make in-depth determination of significance regarding all immaterial items, it is "reasonable" to treat misstatements whose effects are clearly inconsequential differently from possibly more significant ones.

2. *How the misstatement arose.* It is undoubtedly never "reasonable" for registrants to record misstatements or not to correct known misstatements, even immaterial ones, as part of an ongoing effort directed by or known to senior management for the purposes of "managing" earnings. On the other hand, insignificant misstatements that arise from the operation of systems or recurring processes in the normal course of business generally will not cause a registrant's books to be inaccurate "in reasonable detail."

   To carry it a step further, the SEC appears to be emphasizing the caution that criminal penalties *will be imposed* where acts of commission or omission in keeping books or records or administering accounting controls *are deliberately aimed at* falsification, or circumvention of the accounting controls set forth in the Exchange Act. (This would also include the deliberate falsification of books and records and other conduct calculated to evade the *internal accounting controls requirement* which is about to come under close scrutiny by the Commission. See below.)

3. *The cost of correcting the misstatement.* The books and records provisions of the Exchange Act do not require registrants to make major expenditures to correct small misstatements. (To put it succinctly, thousands of dollars should ordinarily not be spent conserving hundreds.) Conversely, where there is little cost or delay involved in correcting a misstatement, failure to do so is unlikely to be "reasonable."

4. *The clarity of authoritative accounting guidance with respect to the misstatement.* In instances where reasonable individuals could differ about the appropriate accounting treatment of a financial statement item, a failure to correct it may not render the registrant's financial statements inaccurate "in reasonable detail." On the other hand, when there is little basis for reasonable disagreement, the case for leaving a misstatement uncorrected is decidedly weaker.

The SEC acknowledges that there may be additional indicators of "reasonableness" that registrants, their accountants and auditors may take into consideration. Because the judgment is seldom unanimous, the staff will be inclined to continue to defer to judgments that "allow a business, acting in good faith, to comply with the Act's accounting provisions in an innovative and cost-effective way."

THE AUDITOR'S RESPONSE TO INTENTIONAL MISSTATEMENTS

The Exchange Act requires auditors to consider several courses of action when discovering an illegal act which is defined as "...an act or omission that violates any law, or any rule or regulation having the force of law."

The statute specifies among other things that:

1. These obligations are triggered regardless of whether or not the illegal acts are considered to have a material effect upon the financial statements of the issuer.

2. The auditor is required to inform the appropriate level of management of an illegal act unless it is clearly "inconsequential."

3. When an auditor discovers an intentional misstatement of immaterial items in a registrant's financial statements which violates the Exchange

Act and thus is an illegal act, the auditor must take steps to see that the registrant's audit committee is "adequately informed" about the illegal act. (Since the provisions of the Act are triggered regardless of whether an illegal act has a material effect on the registrant's financial statements, when the illegal act is a misstatement in the registrant's financial statements, the auditor is required to report that illegal act to the audit committee irrespective of any "netting" of the misstatements with other financial statement items.)

Auditors who become aware of intentional misstatements may also be required to:

1. Reevaluate the degree of audit risk involved in the audit engagement.
2. Determine whether to revise the nature, timing, and extent of audit procedures accordingly.
3. Consider whether to resign.

Cases of intentional misstatements may serve as a signal of the existence of reportable conditions or material weaknesses in the registrant's system of internal accounting control that should have been designed to detect and deter improper accounting and financial reporting.

Management's Role

As stated by the National Commission on Fraudulent Financial Reporting (also known as the Treadway Commission) in its 1987 report, the *tone* set by top management, the corporate environment, or the culture within which financial reporting occurs is the most important factor contributing to the integrity of the financial reporting process. Even if there is an in-depth set of written rules and procedures, if this tone is lax or permissive, fraudulent financial reporting is more likely to occur.

Here again, it is up to the auditor to report to a registrant's audit committee any *reportable conditions or material weaknesses* in a registrant's system of internal accounting control that he or she uncovers in the course of the examination of the registrant's financial statements.

GAAP Takes Precedence Over Industry Practice

It has been argued that registrants should be permitted to continue to follow an *industry* accounting practice even though that practice is—or has become—inconsistent with authoritative accounting literature. Such a situation might occur:

1. If a practice is developed when there are few transactions.
2. The accounting results are clearly inconsequential.
3. That particular industry practice never changed despite a subsequent growth in the number or materiality of such transactions.

Regardless of how or why the practice had developed, this may *not* be considered a valid argument for its continued use. Authoritative literature *always* takes precedence over industry practice that is contrary to GAAP.

Determining Appropriate Accounting Treatment

As pointed out above, SAB 99 is not intended to change current law or guidance in the accounting or auditing literature. This SAB and the authoritative accounting literature cannot specifically address all of the novel and complex business transactions and events that may occur. Accordingly, registrants may at times account for, and make disclosures about these transactions and events based on analogies to similar situations or other factors.

The SEC staff may not, however, always be convinced that a registrant's determination is the most appropriate under the circumstances. When disagreements occur after a transaction or an event has been reported, the consequences may be severe for registrants, auditors, and, most important, for the *users of financial statements* who have a right to expect consistent accounting and reporting for, and disclosure of, similar transactions and events.

The SEC, therefore, encourages registrants, their accountants and auditors to discuss on a timely basis with the staff proposed accounting treatments for, and disclosures about, transactions or events not specifically covered by the existing accounting literature. This caution should also apply in instances where there is any question in the mind of any of the entity's "team" concerning the appropriateness of a particular procedure. In more forceful terms, "Don't let creative accounting get you or your firm into trouble."

Chapter 19

The Securities and Exchange Commission: Private Securities Litigation Reform Act of 1995

To reduce the number of frivolous class action lawsuits, Congress passed the Private Securities Litigation Reform Act of 1995 (the Act). The Act revises the securities laws that professional investors and class action lawyers have used against corporations, accountants, and securities underwriters to win billions of dollars in damages. A safe harbor provision now protects companies from the legal liability for forecasts that subsequently proved to be incorrect, as well as for statements that were inaccurate when they were made. Key personnel of a large number of national CPA firms and various state CPA associations urged members of Congress to support reforms in the bill; the passage of the bill is considered to be significantly helpful to business corporations and the accounting and investment banking professions. The law encourages the dissemination of forward-looking information and forecasts, using easily understood language that lessens the possibility of frivolous lawsuits by the users of financial statements. The Act's fundamental purpose is to address concerns, raised in a number of Congressional hearings over a four-year period, that the securities litigation system was misaligned in a way that overcompensated weak cases to the detriment of strong cases, and that served investor interests poorly.

PROVISIONS OF THE ACT

The following are some of the Act's provisions:

1. The Act implements a system of proportionate liability in which peripheral defendants pay only their fair share of a judgment. Less ac-

380

countable defendants will pay a proportionate share of the damages, but parties that knowingly engage in fraudulent actions are still subject to the fullest extent of joint and several liability. Proponents of the bill argued that joint and several liability in the previous law caused plaintiffs' lawyers to target rich defendants.

The proportionate liability of proportionately liable defendants can exceed their percentage of responsibility in two respects. First, if the liability share of any codefendant is found to be uncollectible within six months of entry of the judgment, proportionately liable defendants will be liable for the uncollectible portion in proportion to their share of responsibility, up to 50 % of each covered person's proportionate share. Second, plaintiffs with net worth of under $200,000 and who incur damages equal to more than 10% of their net worth could still enforce their judgment against all defendants jointly and severally.

The Act also clarifies a number of open issues concerning the operation of rights of contribution among codefendants. A defendant who settles a private action is discharged from all claims of contribution brought by other persons, and any subsequent judgment in the action is reduced by the greater of the percentage of responsibility of the settling defendant or the amount paid to the plaintiff by the settling defendant. A defendant against whom a judgment is not collectible is subject to contribution and to continuing liability to the plaintiff. A proportionate share of responsibility has a contribution claim against other defendants, except settling defendants, or any other person responsible for the conduct. All claims for contribution are to be determined based on the percentage of responsibility of the claimant and of each person who would have been liable if joined in the original action. Contribution claims are subject to a six-month statute of limitations.

2. A significant part of the Act for the various professions is its system of proportionate liability which the professions had urged Congress to adopt as part of the legislation. For example, a defendant who is found only to have acted carelessly, and did not *knowingly* commit fraud, would be responsible for a proportionate amount of the damages instead of for the fullest amount of money possible as under the old law.

3. All defendants involved in the action remain jointly and severally liable to investors with a net worth under $200,000 who lost more than 10% of their net worth. Defendants liable for their proportionate share are also liable for up to an additional 50% of their share to help pay for insolvent codefendants.

4. The Act encourages voluntary disclosure of forward-looking information to investors by establishing a carefully designed safe harbor rule.

The safe harbor protects statements made and meaningful cautionary risk disclosures that identify factors that could alter actual results.

5. Language was added to the safe harbor provision to make certain that forward-looking information has meaningful support behind it. The safe harbor does not protect those who knowingly make a false or misleading statement.

6. The 1995 Act requires that auditors immediately disclose illegal acts discovered in the course of an audit. Auditors must notify the SEC of illegal acts ignored or improperly considered by management. This puts a time limit on when illegal acts must be reported to the SEC. The board of directors has *one* business day to report to the SEC that the independent auditor has reported a material illegal act, and the auditor has determined that senior management and the board of directors have not taken appropriate actions, or are not expected to take appropriate action. If the independent auditor does not receive a copy of the board of directors' report to the SEC within the one business day period, the independent auditor must resign from the engagement or furnish the SEC with a copy of the original fraud report. This requirement ensures immediate reporting of illegal acts.

7. The Act gives the SEC the power to sue people or companies for aiding and abetting others who commit fraud. The provision is designed to ensure the SEC's enforcement authority which prevents aiding and abetting from not being considered an actionable offense in private securities fraud lawsuits.

8. The law does not require the loser of a case to pay all attorneys' fees, but it does impose sanctions against attorneys who file frivolous lawsuits. If a court finds that either the plaintiff's or the defendant's attorneys made arguments that were legally irrelevant or lacking evidentiary support, the court must impose sanctions unless it is a trifling violation. Reasonable attorneys' costs and fees are presumed to be adequate reimbursement. The statute of limitations is not changed with respect to the three-year time limit for filing securities fraud lawsuits. Current law permits actions to be brought within one year after discovery of an alleged violation, and no more than three years after the alleged violation occurred.

CERTIFICATION FILED WITH COMPLAINT

Each plaintiff seeking to serve as a representative party on behalf of a class must provide a sworn certification, which shall be personally signed by the plaintiff and filed with the complaint, that states that the plaintiff has reviewed the complaint and authorized this filing, and states that the plaintiff did not purchase the security that is the subject of the complaint at the direction of plaintiff's counsel or in order to participate in any private action.

Nonwaiver of Attorney Privilege

The certification filed shall not be construed to be a waiver of the attorney-client privilege.

Appointment of Lead Plaintiff

No later than 20 days after the date on which the complaint is filed, the plaintiff or plaintiffs shall cause to be published, in a widely circulated national business-oriented publication or wire service, a notice advising members of the purported plaintiff class of the action, and the claims asserted therein. Not later than 60 days after the date on which the notice is published, any member of the purported class may move the court to serve as lead plaintiff of the purported class.

No later than 90 days after the date on which a notice is published, the court shall consider any motion made by a class member who is not individually named as a plaintiff in the complaint or complaints, and shall appoint as lead plaintiff the member or members of the purported plaintiff class that the court determines to be most capable of adequately representing the interests of class members who is referred to as the *most adequate plaintiff.*

Additional Notices Required Under Federal Rules

Notice required under the early notice requirement should be in addition to any other required notice.

Consolidated Actions

If more than one action on behalf of a class asserts substantially the same claim or claims for pretrial purposes or trial, the court will appoint the most adequate plaintiff as lead plaintiff for the consolidated actions.

Rebuttable Presumption

The court shall adopt a presumption that the most adequate plaintiff in any private action is the person or group of persons who has either filed the complaint, or made a motion in response to a notice in the determination of the court, and has the largest financial interest in the relief sought by the class.

DISCOVERY

Discovery relating to whether a member or members of the purported plaintiff class is the most adequate plaintiff can be conducted by a plaintiff only if the plaintiff first demonstrates a reasonable basis for a finding that the presumptively most adequate plaintiff is incapable of adequately representing the class.

SELECTION OF LEAD COUNSEL

The most adequate plaintiff will, subject to the approval of the court, select and retain counsel to represent the class.

RESTRICTIONS ON PROFESSIONAL PLAINTIFFS

A person may be a lead plaintiff, or an officer, director, or fiduciary of a lead plaintiff, in no more than five securities class actions brought as plaintiff class actions.

RECOVERY BY PLAINTIFFS

The share of any final judgment or of any settlement that is awarded to a representative party serving on behalf of a class shall be equal, on a per share basis, to the portion of the final judgment or settlement awarded to all members of the class. However, the court may permit lead plaintiffs to recover reasonable costs and expenses, including lost wages.

RESTRICTIONS ON SETTLEMENTS UNDER SEAL

The terms and provisions of any settlement of a class action should not be filed under seal, except that on motion of any party to the settlement, the court can order filing under seal for those portions of a settlement agreement as to which good cause is shown for a filing under seal.

RESTRICTIONS ON PAYMENT OF ATTORNEYS' FEES AND EXPENSES

Total attorneys' fees and expenses awarded by the court to counsel for the plaintiff class shall not exceed a reasonable percentage of the amount of any damage and prejudgment interest actually paid to the class.

DISCLOSURE OF SETTLEMENT TERMS TO CLASS MEMBERS

Any proposed or final settlement agreement that is published or otherwise disseminated to the class will include a cover page summarizing the information contained in the following statements:

Statement of plaintiff recovery. The amount of the settlement proposed to be distributed to the parties to the action, is determined in the aggregate and on an average per share basis.

Agreement of the amount of damages. If the settling parties agree on the average amount of damages per share that would be recoverable if the plaintiff prevailed on each claim alleged, a statement concerning the average amount of such potential damages per share, and a statement from each settling party should be made.

Disagreement on the amount of damages. If the parties do not agree on the average amount of damages per share that would be recoverable if the plaintiff prevailed on each claim alleged, a statement from each settling party must be made concerning the issue or issues on which the parties disagree.

Inadmissibility for certain purposes. A statement made concerning the amount of damages shall not be admissible in any federal or state judicial action or administrative proceeding, other than an action or proceeding arising out of such statement.

Statement of attorneys' fees or costs sought. If any of the settling parties or their counsel intend to apply to the court for an award of attorneys' fees or costs from any fund established as part of the settlement, a statement indicating which parties or counsel intend to make such an application, the amount of such fees and costs determined on an average per share basis, and a brief explanation supporting the fees and costs sought is required. Such information will be clearly summarized on the cover page of any notice to a party of any proposed or final settlement agreement.

Identification of lawyers' representatives. The name, telephone number, and address of one or more representatives of counsel for the plaintiff class who will be reasonably available to answer questions from the class.

Reasons for settlement. A brief statement explaining the reasons why the parties are proposing the settlement must be made.

Other information. Information that might be required by the court.

ATTORNEY CONFLICT OF INTEREST

If a plaintiff class is represented by an attorney who directly owns or otherwise has a beneficial interest in the securities that are the subject of a litigation, the court shall make a determination of whether such ownership or other interest constitutes a conflict of interest sufficient to disqualify the attorney from representing the plaintiff class.

SECURITY FOR PAYMENT OF COSTS IN CLASS ACTIONS

In any private action that is certified as a class action, the court may require an undertaking from the attorneys for the plaintiff class, the plaintiffs' class, or both, in such proportions and at such times as the court determines are just and equitable for the payment of fees and expenses that may be awarded.

The Act does permit a court to require plaintiffs, defendants, or their attorneys to post a bond for the payment of fees and expenses that may be awarded.

MISLEADING STATEMENTS AND OMISSIONS

In actions in which the plaintiff alleges that the defendant made an untrue statement of a material fact, or omitted a material fact necessary to prevent the statements from being misleading, the complaint must specify the following:

1. Each statement alleged to have been misleading,
2. The reason or reasons why the statement is misleading, and
3. If an allegation regarding the statement or omission is made on information and belief, the complaint should state the specific facts on which that belief is based.

REQUIRED STATE OF MIND

In any private action in which the plaintiff may recover money damages only on proof that the defendant acted with a particular state of mind, the complaint shall state specifically which facts give rise to a strong inference that the defendant acted with the required state of mind.

SANCTION FOR WILLFUL VIOLATION

A party aggrieved by the willful failure of an opposing party to comply with this Act may apply to the court for an order awarding appropriate sanctions.

CAUSATION OF LOSS

In any private action, the plaintiff shall have the burden of proving that the act or omission of the defendant alleged to violate this Act caused the loss for which the plaintiff seeks to recover damages.

LIMITATION ON DAMAGES

Stock prices frequently have a tendency to recover part of their market price after the initial price adjustment to adverse news about a company. If a security recovers some or all of its market price during the 90-day period after the dissemination of information correcting the misstatement or omission that is the basis for the action, damages will be capped at the difference between the price paid for the security and the mean trading price of the security during the 90-day period.

If the plaintiff sells or repurchases the subject security prior to the expiration of the 90-day period, the plaintiff's damages shall not exceed the difference between the purchase or sale price paid or received, as appropriate, by the plaintiff for the security and the mean trading price of the security during the period beginning immediately after dissemination of information correcting the misstatement or omission and ending on the date on which the plaintiff sells or repurchases the security. For the purposes of this rule, the *mean trading price* of a security shall be an average of the daily trading price of that security, determined as of the close of the market each day during the 90-day period.

PRIVATE CLASS ACTIONS

The provisions of this Act shall apply in each private action arising that is brought as a plaintiff class action.

MULTIPLE ACTIONS

If more than one action is filed on behalf of a class asserting substantially the same claim or claims, only the plaintiff or plaintiffs in the first filed action will be required to cause notice to be published.

Presumption in Favor of Attorneys' Fees and Costs for Abusive Litigation

The court shall adopt a presumption that the appropriate sanction for failure of any responsive pleading, or dispositive motion to comply with any requirement of the court, is an award to the opposing party of the reasonable attorneys' fees and other expenses incurred as a direct violation.

Rebuttal Evidence for Sanctions Against Abusive Litigation

The presumption may be rebutted only upon proof by the party, or attorney against whom sanctions are to be imposed, that the award of attorneys' fees and other expenses will impose an unreasonable burden on that party or attorney and would be unjust, and the failure to make such an award would not impose a greater burden on the party in whose favor sanctions are to be imposed. If the party or attorney against whom sanctions are to be imposed meets its burden, the court shall award the sanctions that the court deems appropriate.

Availability of Documents

Any document filed with the Commission or generally disseminated shall be deemed to be readily available.

Stay Pending Decision on Motion Exemption Authority

In any private action, the court shall stay discovery, other than discovery that is specifically directed to the application of an exemption, during the tendency of any motion by a defendant for summary judgment that is based on the ground that the statement or omission upon which the complaint is used is a forward-looking statement, and the exemption provided precludes a claim for relief.

Exemption Authority

The Commission may provide presumptions from any provision of this Act that is consistent with the public interest and the protection of investors as determined by the Commission.

EFFECT ON OTHER AUTHORITY OF THE COMMISSION

Nothing in the Act limits, either expressly or by implication, the authority of the Commission to exercise similar authority or to adopt similar rules and regulations with respect to forward-looking statements under any other statute under which the Commission exercises rule-making authority.

DEFINITION OF FORWARD-LOOKING STATEMENTS

Forward-Looking Statement. The term means a statement containing a projection of revenues, income including income loss, earnings including earnings loss per share, capital expenditures, dividends, capital structure, or other financial items. These could include, but are not limited to, the following:

- A statement of the plans and objectives of management for future operations, including plans or objectives relating to the products or services of the issuer.
- A statement of future economic performance, including any such statement contained in a discussion and analysis of financial condition by the management or in results of operations included pursuant to the rules and regulations of the Commission.
- Any statement of the admissions underlying or relating to any other statement.
- Any report issued by an outside reviewer retained by an issuer, to the extent that the report assesses a forward-looking statement made by the issuer.
- A statement containing a projection or estimate of such other items as may be specified by rule or regulation of the Commission.

SAFE HARBOR FOR FORWARD-LOOKING STATEMENTS

Liability for forward-looking statements such as earnings or sales forecasts has had the undesirable effect of discouraging companies from sharing such information with investors, despite keen market interest in this information. This has become a particular concern for high technology and biotech companies which tend to have volatile stock prices, and therefore are frequent targets of class action lawsuits when projections are not realized. While the primary beneficiaries of the safe harbor are issuers and their officers, the Act also offers useful protection to broker-dealers in their roles as underwriters and analysts. The safe harbor is offered to:

1. An issuer who, at the time that the statement is made, is subject to the reporting requirements of the Exchange Act.
2. A person acting on behalf of such issuer.
3. An outside reviewer retained by such issuer making a statement on behalf of such issuer.
4. An underwriter, with respect to information provided by such issuer or information derived from information provided by the issuer.

In addition, the safe harbor excludes certain categories of issuers and transactions, most notably issuers who have been subject to criminal or SEC enforcement sanctions within the preceding three years, issuers that are investment companies, and statements made in connection with a tender offer or initial public offering, or that are included in an audited financial statement. The safe harbor generally applies to a forward-looking statement if it is identified as a forward-looking statement, and is accompanied by meaningful cautionary statements identifying important factors that could cause actual results to differ materially from those in the forward-looking statement; or is immaterial; or the plaintiff fails to prove the forward-looking statement was made with actual knowledge; or if made by a business entity was made by and with the approval of an executive officer of that entity, and made or approved by such officer with actual knowledge by that officer that the statement was false or misleading.

Oral statements made by an issuer, or by a person acting on behalf of such issuer, can also be covered under a corollary formulation of the safe harbor. Under the corollary, an oral statement qualifies for the safe harbor if the oral statement is accompanied by a cautionary statement pointing out that the oral statement is a forward-looking statement, that actual results may vary, and identifying an available written document setting out the meaningful cautionary statements identifying important factors that could cause actual results to differ that are required by the primary safe harbor.

The safe harbor was drafted in such a way that even if a forward-looking projection or estimate did not contain adequate cautionary language, a plaintiff would still have to prove that the speaker had actual knowledge that the statement was false or misleading. The safe harbor directs courts to stay all discovery, except for discovery directed at the applicability of the safe harbor, while a motion to dismiss based on the safe harbor is pending.

CLASS ACTION REFORMS

The Act creates a procedure for the court to appoint as lead plaintiff the plaintiff with the largest financial interest. The Act also adopts other class action reforms, such as prohibiting the payment of referral fees to securities brokers.

PROPORTIONATE LIABILITY AND CONTRIBUTIONS

The Act generally limits joint and several liability to persons who knowingly commit a violation of the securities laws. The Act requires a defendant to pay 50% more than its proportionate share of damages in certain cases where other defendants' shares are uncollectible, and preserves joint and several liability for plaintiffs with a net worth under $200,000 whose damages exceed 10% of their net worth. The Act clarifies certain issues regarding the operation of rights of contribution.

REDUCTION OF DAMAGE

The Act provides that a defendant can reduce damages by proving that all or part of the decline in the value of the securities was caused by factors other than the alleged misstatement or material omission in the prospectus.

RIGHT OF RESCISSION

The Act provides a right of rescission to the buyer of a security if the security was sold in violation of the registration or prospectus delivery requirements, or if it was offered or sold by means of a prospectus or oral communication which included an untrue statement of a material fact or omitted to state a material fact.

AIDING AND ABETTING

The Act gives the SEC (but not private plaintiffs) authority to bring civil injunctive actions and to seek civil money penalties against any person who knowingly provides substantial assistance to another person in violation of the Exchange Act to the same extent as the person to whom such assistance is provided.

STAY OF DISCOVERY AND PRESERVATION OF EVIDENCE

A stay of discovery is required while a motion to dismiss is pending, other than a particular discovery needed to preserve evidence. Any party to the action with actual notice of the allegations contained in the complaint shall treat all documents, data compilation, and tangible objects that are in the custody or control of such person and that are relevant to the allegations, as if they were the subject of a continuing request for production of documents from an opposing party. A party aggrieved by the willful failure of an opposing party to comply with this requirement may apply to the court for sanctions. The use of the term *willful failure* should give protection from liability for inadvertent violations.

PROTECTIONS FOR SENIOR CITIZENS AND QUALIFIED INVESTMENT RETIREMENT PLANS

The SEC must determine whether senior citizens or qualified retirement plans have been adversely impacted by abusive securities fraud litigation and whether they are adequately protected from such litigation by the Act. If the SEC finds any such adverse impact or lack of adequate protection, it is to submit to Congress a report containing recommendations for protection from securities fraud, or for protection from abusive litigation.

RACKETEER INFLUENCED AND CORRUPT ORGANIZATION ACT (RICO)

The Act eliminates private RICO liability, with its accompanying exposure to treble damages, for conduct that would have been actionable as fraud in the purchase or sale of securities. This does not apply to an action against any person who is criminally convicted in connection with the fraud, in which case the statute of limitations will begin to run from the date the conviction becomes final.

PROPORTIONATE LIABILITY

Major accounting firms argued that joint and several liability under the anti-fraud provisions of the securities laws had created an unjustifiable liability exposure in cases where their role was relatively peripheral, but their potential deep-pocket liability for the more culpable conduct of others was enormous. Accounting firms argued that this disproportionate liability exposure was forcing them to curtail audit services for companies that were regarded as high risks for potential litigation, particularly start-up firms and firms with volatile stock prices in the high technology and biotech sectors. In place of joint and several liability, accounting firms sought a limited system of proportionate liability, so that the liability of less culpable defendants would bear some relationship to their degree of responsibility for the damages incurred.

The Act provides that a defendant in an action is jointly and severally liable only if the person who tries the facts specifically finds that the defendant *knowingly committed* a violation of the securities laws. The provision provides an extensive clarification of the term, which essentially requires that the defendant engaged in conduct with actual knowledge of the facts and circumstances that make the conduct a violation of the securities laws. The Act also expressly provides that *reckless conduct* will not be construed to constitute a knowing commission of a violation of the securities laws. The Act also takes pains to avoid supporting the argument that recklessness is a sufficient standard for anti-fraud liability by providing that nothing in the Act should be construed to create, affect, or in any manner modify, the standard of liability associated with any action arising under the securities laws. For defendants who are not found to have committed a knowing violation of the securities laws, the Act offers a qualified form of proportionate liability. Such a defendant is only liable for the portion of the judgment that corresponds to its percentage of responsibility.

In determining the percentage of responsibility for each defendant, the person examining the facts must consider:

1. The nature of the conduct of each covered person found to have caused or contributed to the loss incurred by the plaintiff or plaintiffs.
2. The nature and extent of the causal relationship between the conduct of each such person and the damages incurred by the plaintiff or plaintiffs.

INDEMNIFICATION AGREEMENTS

The indemnification agreement expressly permits a defendant to recover attorneys' fees and costs incurred in connection with an action in which the defendant prevails. The Act does not change the enforceability of indemnification contracts in the event of settlement.

RULE OF CONSTRUCTION

The Act clarifies two points:

1. Nothing in the Act is to be deemed to prevent the SEC from restricting or otherwise regulating private actions under the Exchange Act.
2. Nothing in the Act is to be deemed to create or ratify any implied right of action.

THE ACT'S EXCEPTION PROVISION

The Act's exception for material of little value could alleviate a concern about the Act's use of the term *substantial* in relation to complaints. The word *substantial* might be used to argue that plaintiffs' complaints are to be subjected to a less rigorous scrutiny than papers filed by other parties. The ability to rebut any finding of a violation by showing that the finding was of little value suggests that the standard probably will be the same for both plaintiffs and defendants. Although it is not clear whether there is some distinction intended between substantial and irrelevancy, *the exception provision* in the Act was not the intention of Congress to hold defendants to a more stringent standard than plaintiffs.

CONCLUSION

The Act reforms many of the procedures that govern private class actions. It is intended to address a number of concerns about securities class actions, such as the race to the courthouse to file cases within days or even hours of a sharp stock price decline; the ability of attorneys to select plaintiffs with nominal holdings to bring a class action case; the lack of opportunities for institutional investors to participate in litigation brought on their behalf; and the lack of effective notice to investors of the terms of class action settlements. Institutional investors are encouraged to take a more active role in securities class action lawsuits. Within 20 days of filing a class action lawsuit, the plaintiff must provide notice to members of the purported class. The notice is to identify the claims alleged in the lawsuit and indicate that potential members have 60 days from publication to file a motion to seek to serve as lead plaintiff. If more than one action is filed, only the plaintiff in the first action is required to file the notice. The notice must be filed in a widely circulated business publication.

Once designated by the court, the lead plaintiff is authorized to select and retain counsel for the class. It is unclear whether this provision would encompass other related powers, such as to replace counsel, to direct litigation strategy, or to reject or give preliminary approval to settlements. The amount of autonomy that courts actually give to lead plaintiffs to manage the case could have a significant impact on whether institutional investors will avail themselves of this new procedure.

Chapter 20

Segment Reporting

FASB Statement 131, *Disclosures About Segments of an Enterprise and Related Information*

Continuing the newfound path of developing Standards with other standard setting bodies, the FASB issued Statement 131, *Disclosures About Segments of an Enterprise and Related Information* in conjunction with the Accounting Standards Board (AcSB) of the Canadian Institute of Chartered Accountants. Simultaneously, the two bodies published almost identical statements that became effective in 1998. FASB 131 supersedes FASB 14, *Financial Reporting for Segments of a Business Enterprise.*

At the same time as the U.S. and Canadian groups were working together, the International Accounting Standards Committee (IASC) was also working closely with them to revise International Accounting Standard (IAS)14, *Reporting Financial Information by Segment.* However, after the many discussions to minimize differences that did effectively reduce the gap, the international organization still decided to publish its own Standard. That group declined to go as far in requiring increased disclosure in IAS 14 (rev.), *Segment Reporting*, as the U.S.and Canadian pronouncements required.

Reporting Requirements

FASB 131 sets forth stricter requirements than previously for the way a business reports financial and related information about reportable operating segments in annual and interim reports. The Statement does not apply to non-public business enterprises nor to not-for-profit organizations.

The requirements went into effect for the first annual statement after December 15, 1997, but quarterly interim statements were not due until after the first annual disclosure. Thus, the interim statements did not begin until 1999. Then, comparative information for interim periods in the first year was to be reported in financial statements for the second year.

FASB 131 establishes new standards for related financial and other disclosures in relation to:

1. Products and services.
2. Geographical areas.
3. Major customers.

This information must be reported whether the business actually uses it in making operating decisions or not—unless preparing information that is not used internally would be impracticable. The enterprise must also:

1. Provide background information about the manner in which the operating segments were established.
2. Describe the particular products and/or services provided by each segment.
3. Explain any differences between the measurements used in reporting segment information and those used in their general-purpose financial statements.
4. Explain any changes in the measurement of segments from one reporting period to another.

Objectives of the Standard

It would appear that the FASB considers this a refinement of the general principles of good general-purpose financial reporting. The Board apparently feels that providing the required segment information will better the financial statement user's ability to:

1. Understand the enterprise's performance.
2. Estimate the enterprise's prospects relating to future cash flows.
3. Arrive at better informed judgments about the enterprise as a whole.

Information from Within

Generally, this Standard requires that the information be reported on the same basis as the enterprise uses *internally* for evaluating segment performance and deciding how to allocate resources to segments. This leads to new data being disclosed by companies and should be useful to investment analysts and informed investors. They become privy to much of the operations information that goes to upper management to assist them in their decision making.

Reporting financial information under FASB 131 is based on the *management approach* in contrast to the *industry approach* that was used in FASB 14. While this Standard required reporting of information about major customers, and some data was provided on related product and service groups, it was felt that the industry approach was too subjective. So much discretion was left to the reporting company in the application of FASB 14 that unfavorable earnings figures could be hidden (by switching industry groupings around, for example).

Management Approach

The management approach is based on the way management organizes the segments within a company for making operating decisions and assessing performance. Because of this, the segments should be evident from the structure of the company's organization. Therefore, financial statement preparers should be able to provide the additional required information without a great amount of additional time and effort.

The management approach should result in consistent descriptions of a company in its annual report since it focuses on financial information that an enterprise's decision makers have been using to make their decisions regarding company operations. The components that management establishes for that purpose are referred to in FASB 131 as operating segments.

According to the FASB, if management were to change the internal structure of their organization to the extent that the operating segment lines were altered, the changed reporting may be handled in one of two ways:

1. By restating segment information for earlier periods, including interim periods.
2. By disclosing segment information for the current period under both the old and the new bases of segmentation unless it is impracticable to do so.

IASC's Revised Segment Reporting Standard

As mentioned, the release of the IASC's revised Standard on segment reporting was delayed while efforts were made to synchronize it with the new segment disclosure Standards developed by the FASB and Canadian standard setters. The original IAS 14 was revised to bring it into line with the common disaggregated disclosure requirements agreed upon by the IASC and the FASB, and embodied in FASB 131.

The IASC went along with the FASB/Canadian measures as far as to adopt the management approach in which a company's internal structure and its system of internal financial reporting to senior management is normally the basis for identifying reportable segments and, thus, for its segment disclosures. Unlike the two North American Standards, IAS 14 (rev.) does allow management under some circumstances to depart from the management approach.

It also differs from them in another respect. The IASC Standard requires that segment data disclosures be prepared using the accounting policies adopted for the company's consolidated financial statements. In contrast, FASB 131 requires the same accounting as management uses internally to be used in its segment data disclosures.

Operating Segments Defined

FASB 131 defines an operating segment as a component of an enterprise:

1. That engages in business activities from which it may earn revenues and incur expenses.
2. Whose operating results are regularly reviewed by the enterprise's chief operating decision maker regarding decisions about resources to be allocated to the segment and to assess its performance.
3. For which discrete financial information is available.

   (The term "chief operating decision maker" identifies a function, not a person with that title. The person's or persons' function is to allocate resources to and assess the performance of the company's segments. A chief operating decision maker is frequently a company's chief executive officer or chief operating officer, but it also could be a group of decision makers, for example, the company's president, executive vice presidents, and others.)

No More Secrets

As with other recent exposure drafts and standards, there was a storm of protest raised about the requirements. Most of the complaints were leveled at the increased disclosure requirements that respondents felt would result in competitive harm. They felt that the specificity of the required reporting would place them at a disadvantage by giving competitors and suppliers sufficient information to figure out their profit margins on particular products.

Strangely enough, when the SEC requested comment on whether the proposed revisions, if adopted, would have an adverse effect on competition, or would impose a burden on competition that was neither necessary nor appropriate in furthering the purposes of the Securities Act and the Exchange Act, no commenter addressed the issue. Therefore, based upon this apparent lack of concern and further study, the Commission determined that there would be no adverse effect on competition, and that the rule changes would not impose any unnecessary burden on competition that is not appropriate in furthering the purposes of the federal securities laws.

Segment Quantitative Thresholds

A company must report separately information about an operating segment that meets any of the following quantitative thresholds:

1. Its reported revenue, including both sales to external customers and intersegment sales or transfers, is 10% or more of the combined revenue, internal and external, of all reported operating segments. (The *revenue* test.)
2. The absolute amount of its reported profit or loss is 10% or more of the greater, in absolute amount, of one of the following:
   a. The combined reported profit of all operating segments that did not report a loss.
   b. The combined reported loss of all operating segments that did report a loss. (The *profitability* test.)
3. Its assets are 10% or more of the combined assets of all operating segments. (The *asset* test.)

Information about operating segments that do not meet any of the quantitative thresholds may be disclosed separately.

FASB 131 permits combining information about operating segments that do not meet the quantitative thresholds with information about other operating segments that do not meet the quantitative thresholds to produce a reportable segment only if the operating segments have similar economic characteristics and share a majority of the following aggregation criteria:

1. The nature of the products and services.
2. The nature of the production process.
3. The type or class of customers for their products and services.
4. The methods used to distribute their products or provide their services.
5. If applicable, the nature of the regulatory environment (banking, insurance, or public utilities, for example).

If the total of external revenue reported by operating segments is less than 75% of the enterprise's total consolidated revenue, additional operating segments must be identified as reportable segments. This must be done even if the segments do not meet the quantitative threshold criteria until at least 75% of total consolidated revenue is included in reportable segments.

Finally, an "all other" category is to be set up for disclosure about other business activities and operating segments that are not reportable under the previously mentioned quantitative threshold criteria. Sources of the revenue included in this category must be revealed.

Rules for Single Segment Entities

FASB 131 includes disaggregated disclosure requirements for companies that have a single reportable segment and whose business activities are not organized on the basis of differences in related products and services or differences in geographical areas of operations. Disclosures about products and services, geographical areas, and major customers are required of these companies. As a result:

1. The expanded disclosure of operating segment income statements and asset data should enhance investors' understanding of an operating segment's performance, cash flows, and investment requirements.
2. The operating segment data presentation should be more consistent with other parts of a company's annual report.

Other Aspects

Under FASB 131, the following take effect.

1. Disclosures about different parts of a business are required, but the basic income statement and balance sheet are not changed.
2. Entities may no longer claim that their business consists of only one segment if, in fact, it does not.
3. Operating segment data will be reported quarterly.
4. Reporting geographic operating data by countries should aid in the evaluation of performance and risk resulting from the global nature of present day business and commerce. The cultural, economic, political, and social data resulting from this disclosure and reporting should better serve top management as well as creditors and investors in evaluating a company as a whole—not just particular segments.
5. The FASB has taken the first big step in its consolidations projects. Consolidations policy and procedure, and unconsolidated entities are still to come.

In the final analysis, FASB 131 attempts to provide information for the user of financial statements about the different types of business activity in which a company engages, the different environments in which it operates, and the nature of its client base.

SECURITY AND EXCHANGE COMMISSION RESPONSE TO FASB 131

As a result of the promulgation of FASB 131, the Security and Exchange Commission adopted technical amendments to Regulations S-X, S-K, and Schedule 14A in order to bring SEC reporting requirements in line with new disclosures relating to a business enterprise's operating segments. These steps also required consistent changes to Form 20-F and a section of the Codification of Financial Reporting Policies (CFRP).

Since FASB 14 had required corporations to disclose certain financial information by "industry segment" as defined in that statement and by geographic area, the SEC had adopted amendments to their rules to integrate that information to be furnished under FASB 14 with the narrative and financial disclosures required in various SEC disclosure forms.

The SEC agreed to adopt the rules in FASB 131 essentially as proposed. They believe that this is in keeping with their long-standing policy to rely upon the private sector for the promulgation of generally accepted accounting principles (GAAP). The Commission felt this step was also in line with their goal of integrating existing accounting information into the narrative disclosure in documents mandated by the federal securities laws. However, as frequently happens, the SEC retains some of their more stringent requirements while adopting the FASB rules.

Operating Segment Disclosure Rules Change

FASB 14 required (and the Commission's rules and forms have required) disclosure along industry segment lines. An "industry segment," as defined by FASB 14, is "a component of an enterprise engaged in providing a product or service or a group of related products and services primarily to unaffiliated customers . . . for a profit."

Recognizing that businesses often evaluate their operations using criteria not necessarily related to the products or services offered to the public, the FASB replaced the industry segment reporting standard with one that requires businesses to report financial information on the basis of "operating segments." Under FASB 131, an operating segment is a component of a business, for which separate financial information is available, that management regularly evaluates in deciding how to allocate resources and subsequently assess performance thereof.

Although FASB 131 did not adopt any new accounting principles relating to measurement or recognition, it did change how a business should identify its segments. It also changed the types of information to be disclosed for each segment.

FASB 14 required an issuer to report its revenues, operating profit (loss), and identifiable assets if a segment's revenues, operating profit, or identifiable assets were 10% or more of all the industry segments' revenues, operating profits, or assets, respectively. The entity was to reconcile these three items to the consolidated amounts in the financial statements. In addition, FASB 14 required each segment to report depreciation, depletion, amortization, capital expenditures, equity in net income of unconsolidated subsidiary or equity-method investee, and the effect of a change in accounting principle on operating profit (loss).

By contrast, FASB 131 requires that a company provide for each reportable segment quantitative disclosure of two basic items—total assets and a measure of profit or loss. The newer standard defines neither segment profit (loss) nor assets. Instead, as stated above, management is required to determine what is reportable based on how they operate their business. In addition, companies must disclose the following items for each segment, but only if management includes them in measuring segment profit or loss:

1. Revenues from external customers.
2. Revenues from other operating segments.
3. Interest income.
4. Interest expense.
5. Depreciation, depletion, and amortization.
6. Unusual items.
7. Equity in net income of equity method investees.
8. Income taxes.
9. Extraordinary items.
10. Significant noncash items other than depreciation, depletion, and amortization.

A company must also disclose for each segment the amount of investment in equity-method investees and total expenditures for additions to long-lived assets if it includes the amount in its determination of segment assets.

The company must reconcile the totals of the reportable segments' amounts for all of these listed items to consolidated amounts.

The FASB required more items to be disclosed per segment under the new Standard because analysts have long wanted more information and, as mentioned above, most of the items required were already available in management reports.

The SEC, therefore, amended their narrative and financial reporting rules to conform their segment reporting requirements to the FASB's revised accounting standards. However, the Commission retained certain requirements relating to disclosure of principal products or services and major customers that traditionally have differed from the FASB Standards.

Description of Business—Item 101

In the past, Regulation S-K had required issuers to disclose in the "business description" sections of documents that they filed with the Commission, pertinent financial information based on GAAP's old "industry segment" standard. Now, registrants report segment information in accordance with GAAP's operating segment standard.

Principal Products or Services.   Historically, the SEC has required a discussion, by segment, of the principal markets for and methods of distribution of each segment's products and services. On the other hand, GAAP required, and continues to require, only disclosure of the types of products and services from which each segment derives its revenues, without reference to principle markets and distribution methods. The SEC continues to believe such information is also useful to investors; consequently, the provision is retained in their rules.

The SEC also requires registrants to disclose the amounts of revenues from each class of similar products and services based on quantitative thresholds. Specifically, the issuer must state the amount or percentage of total revenue contributed by any class of similar products or services that accounted for 10% or more of consolidated revenue in any of the last three fiscal years, or if total revenue did not exceed $50,000,000 during any of those three fiscal years, 15% or more of consolidated revenue. The Commission amended their rules to conform with FASB 131 requirements, but retained some of their own previous provisions.

FASB 131 requires disclosure of revenues from external customers for each product and service or each group of similar products and services, regardless of amount, unless it is impracticable to do so. It appears, then, to require more disclosure than SEC rules. FASB 131 provisions result in *disclosure of a range of amounts of products and services, depending upon how a company defines a class of related products or services.* In fact, the SEC decided that Statement 131 could well require disclosure of amounts below the existing 10% threshold of SEC requirements.

However, the Commission believes that a clearly stated minimum threshold for disclosure is desirable. Such a measure should eliminate any possible ambiguity resulting from attempts to apply an unwritten materiality threshold to small amounts of reportable revenues. The SEC, therefore, decided to retain the thresholds.

Retroactive Restatement of Information. The SEC has required issuers to restate retroactively previously reported financial information when there has been a material change in the way they group products or services into industry segments and that change affects the reported segment information. FASB 131 provides that if an issuer changes the structure of its internal organization in a manner that causes the composition of its reportable segments to change, the issuer must restate the corresponding information for earlier periods unless it is impracticable to do so. In their final rule, the SEC conforms the language of Item 101 with the language of FASB 131 regarding when a company must restate information.

Property—Item 102

Regulation S-K Item 102 requires descriptions of an issuer's principal plants, mines, and other "materially important" physical properties. Companies must identify the industry segment(s) that use the described properties. An updating of the item reflects FASB 131 financial statement reporting requirements.

Management's Discussion and Analysis

Regulation S-K Item 303, which requires management to include a discussion and analysis of an issuer's financial condition and results of operations, provides:

"Where in the registrant's judgment a discussion of segment information or other subdivisions of the registrant's business would be appropriate to an understanding of such business, the discussion shall focus on each relevant, reportable segment or other subdivision of the business and on the registrant as a whole."

The Commission has in the past relied on the FASB's definition for segment disclosure in Management's Discussion and Analysis (MD&A), and intends to continue to rely on the FASB's standards, thereby allowing issuers to use the management approach under FASB 131. No rule change is necessary.

Under the language in Item 303, a multi-segment registrant preparing a full fiscal year MD&A should analyze revenues, profitability (or losses) and total assets of each significant segment in formulating a judgment as to whether a discussion of segment information is necessary to an understanding of the business.

Although the SEC did not adopt changes to the language of Item 303, they did amend the CFRP which provides informal guidance about MD&A. (See later in this chapter.) The revisions in Item 303 conform the Codification's language with that of FASB 131, and add a new footnote, that reads:

"Where consistent with the registrant's internal management reports, FASB 131 permits measures of segment profitability that differ from consolidated operating profit as defined by GAAP, or that exclude items included in the determination of the registrant's net income. Under FASB 131, a registrant also must reconcile key segment amounts to the corresponding items reported in the consolidated financial statements in a note to the financial statements. Similarly, the Commission expects that the discussion of a segment whose profitability is determined on a basis that differs from consolidated operating profit as defined by GAAP or that excludes the effects of items attributable to the segment also will address the applicable reconciling items in Management's Discussion and Analysis.

"For example, if a material charge for restructuring or impairment included in management's measure of the segment's operating profit or loss, registrants would be expected to discuss in Management's Discussion and Analysis the applicable portion of the charge, the segment to which it relates and the circumstances of its incurrence. Likewise, the Commission expects that the effects of management's use of non-GAAP measures, either on a consolidated or segment basis, will be explained in a balanced and informative manner, and the disclosure will include a discussion of how that segment's performance has affected the registrant's GAAP financial statements."

In short, SEC wants to make it clear that they expect a narrative discussion in MD&A of items that affect the operating results of a segment but that are not included in segment operating profit defined by management.

Where consistent with the registrant's internal management reports, FASB 131 permits measures of segment profitability that differ from consolidated operating profit as defined by GAAP, or that exclude items included in the determination of the registrant's net income. Under FASB 131, a registrant also must reconcile key segment amounts to the corresponding items reported in the consolidated financial statements in a note to the financial statements.

Similarly, the Commission expects that the discussion of a segment whose profitability is determined on a basis that differs from consolidated operating profit as defined by GAAP, or that excludes the effects of items attributable to the segment, will also explain the applicable reconciling items in MD&A.

For example, if a material charge for restructuring or impairment relates to a specific segment, but is not included in management's measure of the segment's operating profit or loss, registrants would be expected to discuss in MD&A:

1. The applicable portion of the charge.
2. The segment to which it relates.
3. The circumstances relating to how and why the charge was incurred.

The Commission expects that the effects of management's use of non-GAAP measures, either on a consolidated or segment basis, will be explained in a balanced and informative manner, and the disclosure will include a discussion of how that segment's performance has affected the registrant's GAAP financial statements.

Form 20-F

Form 20-F is the registration statement and annual report for foreign private issuers promulgated under the Securities Exchange Act of 1934. Form 20-F has permitted a foreign registrant that presents financial statements according to United States GAAP to omit FASB 14 disclosures if it provides the information required by Item 1 of the form. A reference to FASB 131 replaces that to FASB 14.

Much of the material required by the FASB Standards is supplied in Item 1, which requires registrants to disclose sales and revenues by categories of activity and geographical areas, as well as to discuss each category of activities that provides a disproportionate contribution to total "operating profit" of the registrant.

Other Reporting Requirements

Geographic Areas.   Now companies must disclose revenues from external customers deriving from:

a.   Their country of domicile.
b.   All foreign countries in total from which the company derives revenues.
c.   An individual foreign country, if material.

A company must also disclose the basis for attributing revenues from external customers to individual countries.

The Standard requires an issuer to disclose long-lived assets other than financial instruments, long-term customer relationships of a financial institution, mortgage and other servicing rights, and deferred policy acquisition costs. It is also necessary to include deferred tax assets located in its country of domicile and in all foreign countries, in total, in which the enterprise holds assets. If assets in an individual foreign country are material, an issuer must disclose those assets separately.

Even those companies whose segments were defined by geography, continue to report designated information based on geographic areas, unless the information is already provided as part of the reportable operating segment information required by the accounting standards. Consistent with FASB 131, rules no longer will require companies to disclose geographic information relating to profitability, unless their segments are defined by geographic areas, or export sales.

Major Customers. Since the adoption of FASB 14, GAAP has required disclosure of revenues from major customers. FASB 131 now requires issuers to disclose the amount of revenues from each external customer that amounts to 10% or more of an enterprise's revenue as well as the identity of the segment(s) reporting the revenues.

The accounting standards had never before required issuers to identify major customers. On the other hand, the SEC has historically required naming a major customer if sales to that customer equal 10% or more of the issuer's consolidated revenues and if the loss of the customer would have a material adverse effect on the issuer and its subsidiaries. The Commission believes that the identity of major customers is material information to investors.

This disclosure improves a reader's ability to assess risks associated with a particular customer. Additionally, material concentrations of revenues related to a particular customer may be judged more accurately. Consequently, the SEC continues to require this information.

SEGMENT INFORMATION ADDED TO INTERIM REPORTS

GAAP historically has not required segment reporting in interim financial statements. In FASB 131, the FASB changed its position. Under the new accounting standards, issuers must include in condensed financial statements for interim periods the following information about each reportable segment:

1. Revenues from external customers.
2. Intersegment revenues.
3. A measure of segment profit or loss.
4. Total assets for which there has been a material change from the amount disclosed in the last annual report.
5. A description of differences from the last annual report in the basis of segmentation or in the basis of measurement of segment profit or loss.
6. A reconciliation of the total of the reportable segments measures of profit or loss to the enterprise's consolidated income before income taxes, extraordinary items, discontinued operations, and the cumulative effect of changes in accounting principles.

Thus, issuers must now disclose in interim financial statements, including those filed with the Commission, condensed financial information about the segments identified as reportable segments for purposes of their annual reports.

CODIFICATION UPDATE, REVISED SECTION 501.06

The Codification of Financial Reporting Policies (CFRP) contains current Commission interpretive guidance relating to financial reporting and is updated whenever it is deemed necessary. In this case the new guidance information results from the technical amendments to Regulations S-X and S-K.

Segment Analysis

In formulating a judgment as to whether a discussion of segment information is necessary to an understanding of the business, a multi-segment registrant preparing a full fiscal year MD&A should analyze revenues, profitability, and the cash needs of its significant segments.

To the extent any segment contributes in a *materially disproportionate* way to those items, or where discussion on a consolidated basis would present an incomplete and misleading picture of the enterprise, *segment discussion* should be included.

Examples could include:

1. When there are legal or other restrictions upon the free flow of funds from one segment, subsidiary, or division of the registrant to others.
2. When known trends, demands, commitments, events, or uncertainties within a segment are reasonably likely to have a material effect on the business as a whole.
3. When the ability to dispose of identified assets of a segment may be relevant to the financial flexibility of the registrant.
4. Other circumstances in which the registrant concludes that segment analysis is appropriate to an understanding of its business.

The following example illustrates segment disclosure for a manufacturer with two segments. The two segments contributed to segment profit amounts that were disproportionate to their respective revenues. The registrant should discuss:

1. Sales and segment profit trends.
2. Factors explaining such trends.
3. Where applicable, known events that will impact future results of operations of the segment.

Financial Information About Segments.

Each segment must report, as defined by GAAP, revenues from external customers, a measure of profit or loss and total assets. A registrant must report this information for each of the last three fiscal years or for as long as it has been in business, whichever period is shorter. If the information provided in response to *this* paragraph conforms with GAAP, a registrant may include in its financial statements a cross reference to this data instead of presenting duplicate information in the financial statements; conversely, a registrant may cross reference to the financial statements.

If a registrant changes the structure of its internal organization in a manner that causes the composition of its reportable segments to change, the registrant must restate the corresponding information for earlier periods, including interim periods, unless it is impracticable to do so.

Following a change in the composition of its reportable segments, a registrant must disclose whether it has restated the corresponding items of segment information for earlier periods. If it has not restated the items from earlier periods, the registrant is to disclose, in the year in which the change occurs, the segment information for the current period under both the old basis and the new basis of segmentation, unless it is impracticable to do so.

Financial Information About Geographic Areas

1. The registrant must state the following for the last three fiscal years, or for each fiscal year the registrant has been engaged in business, whichever period is shorter:
   a. Revenues from external customers attributed to:
      - The registrant's country of domicile.
      - All foreign countries, in total, from which the registrant derives revenues.
      - Any individual foreign country, if material. The registrant must disclose the basis for attributing revenues from external customers to individual countries.
   b. Long-lived assets, other than financial instruments, long-term customer relationships of a financial institution, mortgage and other servicing rights, deferred policy acquisition costs, and deferred tax assets, located in:
      - The registrant's country of domicile.
      - All foreign countries, in total, in which the registrant holds assets.
      - Any individual foreign country, if material.
2. A registrant must report the amounts based on the financial information that it uses to produce the general-purpose financial statements. If pro-

viding the geographic information is impracticable, the registrant must disclose that fact. A registrant may wish to provide, in addition to the information required by this Section, subtotals of geographic information about groups of countries. If the disclosed information conforms with GAAP, the registrant may include a cross reference to this data instead of presenting duplicate data that is in its financial statements; conversely, a registrant may cross-reference to the financial statements.

3. A registrant is required to describe any risks attendant to the foreign operations and any dependence on one or more of the registrant's segments upon its foreign operations. Or the registrant might consider it more appropriate to discuss this information in connection with one or more of the segments in an individual foreign country.

A Parting Thought

The SEC has been concerned about the sometimes dubious manner in which some companies have been interpreting these segment disclosure rules. They point out that it should not be too difficult a task. After all, the disclosures are supposed to be based upon how management evaluates performance and makes decisions about allocating resources to segments.

Chapter 21
Plain English Disclosure Rule

The Securities and Exchange Commission has adopted a Plain English Disclosure rule incorporating changes made as a result of comments received and the lessons learned from participants in the plain English pilot program. The rule requires issuers to write the *cover page, summary*, and *risk factors section* of prospectuses in plain English. The previous requirements for those sections have been changed to the extent they conflicted with the plain English rule. In conjunction with this rule, the SEC also provides issuers more specific guidance on how to make the entire prospectus clear, concise, and understandable.

The Commission believes that using plain English in prospectuses will lead to a better informed securities market in which investors can more easily understand the disclosure required by the federal securities laws. The rule became effective on October 1, 1998, with the compliance date being the same.

INVESTOR PROTECTION

Obviously, the intended purpose of financial reporting should be full and fair disclosure. In fact this is one of the cornerstones of investor protection under federal securities laws. The SEC points out that if a prospectus fails to communicate information clearly, investors do not receive the basic protection intended.

Yet prospectuses have often employed complex, legalistic language, confounding all but the most erudite lawyers, accountants or financial experts. The Commission emphasizes that the proliferation of complex transactions and securities (including all manner of derivatives) has only magnified this problem. A major challenge facing the securities industry and its regulators is the assurance that financial and business information reaches investors in a form they can read *and understand*.

The SEC anticipates, and many public comment letters concur, that implementation of the plain English rule will:

1. Allow investors to make better-informed assessments of the risks and rewards of investment opportunities.
2. Reduce the likelihood that investors make investment mistakes because of incomprehensible disclosure documents.
3. Reduce investors' costs of investing by lowering the time required to read and understand information.
4. Increase consumers' interest in investing by giving them greater confidence in their understanding of investments.
5. Reduce the number of costly legal disputes because investors are more likely to understand disclosure documents better.
6. Lower offering costs because investors will ask issuers fewer questions about the offering.

All well and good, but how is all of this expected to happen?

PROSPECTUS SIMPLIFICATION

The Commission stated that the new rules will change the face of every prospectus used in registered public offerings of securities. They expect these prospectuses will be simpler, clearer, more useful, and hopefully, more widely read and understood when clarity prevails:

1. The new rules require issuers to write and design the cover page, summary, and risk factors section of their prospectuses in plain English. Issuers will also have to design these sections to make them inviting to the reader. The new rules will *not* require issuers to limit the length of the summary, limit the number of risk factors, or prioritize risk factors.
2. The SEC is also providing guidance to issuers on how to comply with the current rule that requires the entire prospectus to be clear, concise, and understandable. The goal is to dispense with legalese and repetitions that tend to blur the pertinent information (and facts) that investors actually need in making informed decisions.

With that in mind, the Office of Investor Education and Assistance produced a handbook with practical tips on document presentation. A *Plain English Handbook: How to Create Clear SEC Disclosure Documents*, outlining methods and techniques on how to apply plain English principles to the disclosure documents, is the resulting publication.

PLAIN ENGLISH PILOT PROGRAM

To test plain English in disclosure documents, the Division of Corporation Finance experimented with a pilot program in 1996 for public companies willing to file plain English documents under either the Securities Act of 1933 or the Securities Exchange Act of 1934. More than 75 companies volunteered to participate in the pilot program. Many participants got into the spirit of the project to the extent that they even prepared disclosure documents that are not subject to the plain English rule: proxy statements, footnotes to financial statements, management's discussion and analysis of financial condition and results of operations.

Assessment of the results of the pilot program affirmed the SEC's belief that preparing documents in plain English increases investors' understanding and helps them make informed investment decisions. Thus, the package of rules adopted, as well as the handbook, should enable issuers to improve dramatically the clarity of their disclosure documents.

RULE 421(D), THE PLAIN ENGLISH RULE

Basic rules outline how prospectuses must be prepared. This new ruling requires preparation of the front portion of the prospectus in plain English. The plain English principles apply to the organization, language, and design of the front and back cover pages, the summary, and the risk factors section. Also, when drafting the language in these front parts of the prospectus, the preparer must comply substantially with six basic principles:

1. Short sentences.
2. Definite, concrete, everyday language.
3. Active voice.
4. Tabular presentation or bulleted lists for complex material, whenever possible.
5. No legal jargon or highly technical business terms.
6. No multiple negatives.

Does this all sound very reminiscent of your high school English teacher preparing you to write term papers? It should. And it does seem strange that it takes a Final Rule of the Securities and Exchange Commission to remind prospectus preparers of these basic rules for written communication. (Unless obfuscation is their objective.)

A number of comment letters noted that the rule *dictates* how to write the front of the prospectus. The SEC observed marked improvement in the clarity of disclosure when pilot participants used these recognized, basic principles of clear writing. They decided that the benefits to investors supported *mandating* the use of the principles for the front of the prospectus.

In addition, the cover page, summary, and risk factors section must be easy to read. The text and design of the document must highlight important information for investors. The rule permits the issuer to use pictures, charts, graphics, and other design features to make the prospectus easier to understand.

RULE 421(B), CLEAR, CONCISE, UNDERSTANDABLE PROSPECTUSES

This ruling currently requires that the entire prospectus be clear, concise, and understandable. These stipulations are in addition to the plain English rule, which applies only to the front of the prospectus.

Amendments to Rule 421(b) also provide guidance on how to prepare a prospectus that is actually clear, concise, and understandable. The amendments set out four general writing techniques and list four conventions to *avoid* when drafting the prospectus. In effect, these amendments codify earlier interpretive advice.

Amended Rule 421(b) requires use of the the following techniques when writing the entire prospectus:

1. Presentation of information in clear, concise sections, paragraphs, and sentences. Whenever possible, the use of short explanatory sentences and bullet lists.
2. Use of descriptive headings and subheadings.
3. Avoidance of frequent reliance on glossaries or defined terms as the primary means of explaining information in the prospectus. Definition of terms in a glossary or other section of the document only if the meaning is unclear from the context. Use of a glossary only if it facilitates understanding of the disclosure.
4. Avoidance of legal and highly technical business terminology.

How to Comply

The new note to Rule 421(b) provides further guidance on how to comply with the rule's general requirements. Because they make the document harder to read, the note lists the following tactics to *avoid*:

1. Legalistic or overly complex presentations that make the substance of the disclosure difficult to understand.
2. Vague boilerplate explanations that are readily subject to differing interpretations.
3. Complex information copied directly from legal documents without any clear and concise explanation or interpretation of the provision(s).
4. Repetitive disclosure that increases the bulk of the document, but fails to further clarify the information.

Technical Terminology

Several comment letters stated that the SEC should permit public companies to use legal and technical business terminology. The argument was that high tech companies must use technical terms to distinguish their products or services from others in the industry. The Commission agreed that certain business terms may be necessary to describe operations properly, but cautioned against using excessive technical jargon that only competitors or industry specialists could understand.

The focus of the Plain English Rule is that the disclosure in the prospectus is for the benefit of the *investors*. When too many highly technical terms are employed, the investor soon becomes bogged down in a welter of verbiage and little if anything is "disclosed." If technical terms are unavoidable, the preparer must attempt to make their meaning perfectly clear at the onset.

Legal Documents

Several comment letters noted that some investors, particularly institutional investors, want to read the specific terms of contracts or of the securities offered. For example, the SEC concedes an investor may want to read the specific language of a loan agreement's financial covenants or an indenture's default provisions.

The current rule permits summarizing an exhibit's key provisions in the prospectus. The issuer is also required to file material contracts and any instruments that define the rights of security holders. The SEC believes this approach generally serves the needs of all investors in the market.

If the language from an exhibit in the prospectus cannot be summarized adequately, then the explicit language may be included, but it must be presented clearly and its meaning to the investor explained precisely.

REVISIONS TO REGULATIONS S-K AND S-B

The following revisions to Regulation S-K and S-B, covering requirements applicable to nonfinancial portions of the registration statements, annual and interim reports to stockholders, proxy, and other information statements, are addresses to specific sections of the narrative portions of the disclosure documents. Evidently the SEC hopes that prospective customers and stockholders will be given a better opportunity to understand the written portions of a prospectus and other relevant documents whether they really grasp the financial import of the documents or not. (Regulation S-B applies specifically to "small" businesses.)

Item 501—Forepart of Registration Statement and Outside Front Cover Page of Prospectus

The formal design requirements for the prospectus cover page have been eliminated but the issuer is required to limit the front cover of the prospectus to one page. It is expected that the revisions will result in a cover page written and designed to focus investors on *key information* about the offering and encourage them to read the important information in the prospectus. The SEC also expects the amendments to give the flexibility needed to design a cover page tailored to the specific company and the offering.

Under the revised disclosure item, the issuer is free to use pictures, graphs, charts, and other designs that accurately depict the company, business products, and financial condition; however, design features and font types that make the disclosure difficult to read or understand are taboo.

The formalized requirements on how to present the mandatory legends on the cover page have been amended. The only restrictions on presentation of these legends are:

1. The legends must be prominent.
2. The print type must be easy to read.

The Commission has amended Item 501 to provide two plain English examples of the legend that state the Commission has not approved the offering. The item also provides a plain English example of the legend that states the prospectus is not yet complete. It is commonly printed in red ink and referred to as the "red herring" legend.

The Commission has amended the requirements detailing information that must always be included on the prospectus cover page. The goal is to have the cover page focus only on *key information* about the offering. The issuing company is cautioned to avoid moving unnecessary information to this page.

Original plans were to eliminate the requirement to refer to the risk factors on the cover page; however, comment letters suggested the mandate be retained. Therefore, the cover page must now not only reference the risk factors section but must also cite the page number on which the risk factors begin.

Cover Page Format

Retained on the cover page from previous requirements are:

1. Company name.
2. Title, amount, and description of securities offered.
3. Selling securities holder's offering.
4. Bona fide estimate of range of maximum offering price, and numbers of securities.
5. If price not set, indication of how price will be determined.
6. State-required legends.
7. Date of prospectus.

Adopted changes to Regulation S-K—Item 501 to the prospectus cover page include:

1. Cross reference to risk factors *must include page number.*
2. Bullet list or other design that highlights the information showing *price, underwriting commission, and proceeds of the offering* replaces formatted distribution table.
3. Bullet list or other design that highlights the *best efforts disclosure* replaces the formatted distribution table.
4. Commission legend retained in plain English. Reference to *state securities commissions* to be included.
5. Information concerning *underwriters' over-allotment option and the number of shares* retained on the cover page. Expenses of the offering, the number of shares, commissions paid by others, and other non-cash consideration and finder's fees *moved* to the plan of distribution section.
6. Identification of market for securities, trading symbol, underwriters, and type of underwriting arrangements.

7. Prospectus "Subject to Completion" legend retained in plain English.
8. Cover limited to one page.

Limited Partnership Offerings Risk

Several comment letters suggested that the plain English rule and the revised disclosure requirements should replace earlier interpretive advice on cover page disclosure for *limited partnership* offerings.

The SEC acknowledges that under existing advice, the cover page must list the offering's key risks, resulting in repetitious disclosure of those risks. However, they feel that the unique nature of limited partnership offerings and the risks they present to investors warrant requiring the issuer to highlight these risks on the cover page. Of course, the cover page, summary, and risk factors section must otherwise comply with the plain English rule and the revised disclosure requirements being adopted.

Item 502—Inside Front and Outside Back Cover Pages

Item 502's amended requirements for the inside front cover page and outside back cover page of the prospectus now significantly limit the information required on these pages. The hope is that this will give further freedom to the issuer to arrange the information in the prospectus from the *investor's viewpoint.*

The Commission prefers that the required table of contents immediately follow the cover page, but the ruling permits the preparer to have the flexibility to include it on either the inside front or outside back cover page of the prospectus. However, if a prospectus is delivered to investors electronically, the table of contents must come immediately after the cover page so that investors need not scroll to the end of the prospectus to see how it is organized.

Although some comment letters recommended elimination of the requirement to disclose the dealer's prospectus delivery obligations, the SEC decided to retain this disclosure on the outside back cover page. They suggest this disclosure is helpful to dealers in reminding them of their legal obligation to deliver the prospectus

Following are disclosures *previously required* on the inside front or outside back cover pages and their *new location* adopted under Regulation S-K—Item 502:

1. Availability of Exchange Act reports generally—moved to description of business section or, for short-form registration statements, to the incorporation by reference disclosure.
2. Identification of market for securities—moved to cover page.

3. Availability of annual reports to shareholders with financial statements for foreign issuers and others not subject to proxy rules—moved to description of business section.
4. Availability of Exchange Act reports incorporated by reference in short-form registration statements—moved to incorporation by reference disclosure.
5. Stabilization legend—moved to plan of distribution section.
6. Passive market-making activities legend—deleted. Disclosure retained in plan of distribution section.
7. Dealer prospectus delivery page—retained on outside back cover as noted above.
8. Enforceability of civil liability provisions of federal securities laws against foreign persons—moved to description of business section.
9. As mentioned above, the table of contents may still be located on either the inside front cover or the outside back cover unless it is sent electronically. Then it must be on the inside front cover.

In line with other changes, Forms S-2, S-3, S-4, F-2, F-3, and F-4 are also being amended.

Along with the list of reports incorporated by reference, the issuer must include information on:

1. How investors may obtain a copy of these reports.
2. How investors may obtain copies of the other reports filed with the SEC.

Item 503—Summary Information, Risk Factors, and Ratio of Earnings to Fixed Charges

Summary Information. If a summary is included, it must be brief and in plain English. Further, if a summary description of the company's business operations or financial condition is included, the information must be written in plain English even if not identified as a "summary."

Length of the summary is not mandated, but the SEC emphasizes that this section should *highlight the most important features* of the offering. It *should not* include a lengthy description of the company's business and business strategy. They suggest this detailed information is better included in the disclosure in the body of the prospectus.

Although there is no list of items that must be in a summary (if there is one), since the financial statements are an important part of the disclosures made by public companies, the SEC believes the issuer should continue to *highlight financial information* in the summary in a manner readily understood by the user.

Risk Factors. When a risk factors section is included in the prospectus, the risk factors must be detailed in plain English avoiding trite "boilerplate" risk factors. Any risk factors must be explained in context so investors can understand the specific risk applicable to that particular company and its operations.

Ratio of Earnings to Fixed Charges. Where a summary or similar section is included in the prospectus, amended Item 503 requires showing the ratio of earnings to fixed charges as part of the summarized financial data.

Issuers offering debt securities must show a *ratio of earnings to fixed charges*. Those registering preference equity securities must show the *ratio of combined fixed charges and preference dividends to earnings*. The issuer must present the ratio for each of the last five fiscal years and the latest interim period for which financial statements are presented in the document.

If the proceeds from the sale of debt or preference securities are used to repay any outstanding debt or to retire other securities, and the change in the ratio would be ten percent or greater, a ratio showing the application of the proceeds, the *pro forma ratio*, must be used. If a ratio indicates less than one-to-one coverage, the dollar amount of the deficiency is to be disclosed. The pro forma ratio may be shown only for the most recent fiscal year and the latest interim period. The net change in interest or dividends from the refinancing should be used to calculate the pro forma ratio.

COMMENTS ON THE PLAIN ENGLISH REQUIREMENTS

Forty-five comment letters on the plain English proposals generally favored requiring plain English for the front of prospectuses—the cover page, summary, and risk factors section—to ensure that investors receive clear information. They believe that requiring plain English will focus all parties involved in the offering process—issuers, underwriters, trustees, and counsel—on clear and readable disclosure.

Other comment letters raised the following general concerns about the rule:

1. Will the plain English rule increase a registrant's liability?
2. How will the staff review and comment on plain English filings?
3. Will the Commission deny acceleration of a filing if it does not comply with the plain English rule?

After studying these questions, the SEC has concluded that issuers really have little, if any cause, for concern: *following the new rulings* should not alter established procedures and practices for handling relevant matters.

Cost Factors

While project participants who responded to benefit-cost questions had incurred some additional document preparation costs, the majority estimated them to be low and predicted that they would fall over time. The participants anticipated little added, and perhaps even lower, overall cost. Some even predicted they might save money on printing and distribution costs and on the amount of time spent on answering investors' questions. Based on the experiences of pilot program participants, the SEC believes that the substantial benefits to investors of plain English—and the probable ongoing cost savings to issuers—justify the short-term cost to public companies of learning to prepare documents in plain English.

Updated Staff Legal Bulletin 7

In June, 1999, The SEC updated Staff Legal Bulletin 7 relating to the Plain English requirements for registration statements filed on or after October 1, 1998, with the Division of Corporation Finance. This bulletin is not a rule, regulation, or statement of the Securities and Exchange Commission, nor have its contents been approved or disapproved by the agency.

Risk Factor Guidance

According to the staff members responsible for reviewing the filings, the most vexing problem for most issuers involved risk factor disclosures. Amended Item 503(c) of Regulation S-K specifies that issuers should not present risks that could apply to any issuer or any offering. Further, the subheadings must adequately describe the risk that follows.

Item 503(c) seems to be the least understood of the plain English requirements. For this reason, the SEC has provided additional information as well as sample risk factor disclosures and subheadings to help preparers comply with Rule 421(d) of Regulation C and Item 503(c) of Regulation S-K.

Types of Risk

Risk factors loosely fall into three broad categories:

1. *Industry Risk*—risks companies face by virtue of the industry they're in. For example, many REITs run the risk that, despite due diligence, they will acquire properties with significant environmental issues.
2. *Company Risk*—risks that are specific to the company. For example, a REIT owns four properties with significant environmental issues and cleaning up these properties will be a serious financial drain.

3. **Investment Risk**—risks that are specifically tied to a security. For example, in a debt offering, the debt being offered is the most junior subordinated debt of the company.

When drafting risk factors, the issuer should specifically link each risk to the specific industry, company, or investment, as applicable.

Cautions and Suggestions Relating to Risk Disclosure

After the staff had gained several months' experience issuing plain English comments under the new rule and amendments, they thought it would be helpful to list some of the comments that had been recorded most frequently. By alerting filers to these comments before they file subsequent registration statements, the SEC hopes filers will be able to avoid making these types of mistakes in the future.

Of course, the following selected, abridged comments do not encompass all of the varied plain English comments that were issued. Each prospectus is different and many of the comments issued are unique to the organization of and disclosure in individual prospectuses.

Following are several of the types of cautions made relative to risk disclosure:

1. More than one risk factor should not be "bundled" under one subheading. In order to give the proper prominence and weight to each risk presented, it should be given its own descriptive subheading.
2. Risks should be presented in concrete terms. For example, a reference to "risks due to the 'costs' associated with the benefit plans" is too vague. A better understanding of the risks would be gained by a statement that the "costs" are not expenses of running the plans, but result from the added compensation expense that stems from the shares purchased by or granted to employees and executives under those plans.
3. In each risk factor, the risk should be clearly and succinctly stated as quickly as possible without undue introductory background material and extensive detailed discussion.
4. The issuer should provide the information investors need to assess the magnitude of the risk. For example, a statement that "increases in short-term interest rates could have a material adverse effect" on XYZ Bank's profitability raises more questions than it provides information.

   Why? Are a substantial percentage of XYZ's interest-earning assets in long-term investments that pay fixed rates while the interest paid to depositors fluctuates? If so, what percentage of interest-earning assets are in long-term investments? Explain.

5. Item 503(c) of Regulation S-K states that issuers should not "present risk factors that could apply to any issuer or to any offering."

   For example, a risk disclosed under "Dependence on Key Personnel" could apply to nearly any issuer in an industry or in almost any industry. If general risk factors are retained in a prospectus, they must be clearly explained. How do they apply to a particular industry, company, or offering? Why is there a concern about losing key personnel? Are they about to retire? Are they not bound by employment contracts?

6. If the subheadings in the risk factors section are too vague and generic they will not adequately describe the risk that follows as is required in Item 503(c) of Regulation S-K.

   For example, the subheading "Competition" is certainly not descriptive because all companies operating in a free market economy are subject to competition.

7. To the extent possible, generic conclusions about the risk should be avoided. Statements like "...would have a material adverse effect on..." operations, financial condition, or business are too imprecise. Instead, there should be specific disclosure of *how* operations, financial condition or business would be affected *by what* specific risk.

8. In an introductory paragraph to the risk factors section, the issuer should not "hedge" against noncompliance by stating that there might be risks not considered material at the time that could become material. Or by making a blanket statement that there might be unidentified risks. The issuer must disclose all risks considered material at the time.

Glossaries and Defined Terms

Rule 421(b) specifies that the issuer "must avoid frequent reliance on glossaries or defined terms as the primary means of explaining information in the prospectus. Define terms in a glossary or other section of the prospectus only if the meaning is unclear from the context. Use a glossary only if it facilitates understanding of the disclosure."

Obviously, then, there are times when a glossary should be used. The bulletin suggests the following:

1. Terms used in a prospectus which are understood only by industry experts should be included in a glossary.

2. If the meanings of terms cannot be made clear from the context or explained concisely where they are first used, then the glossary is appropriate.

3. It is not necessary to use a glossary to define commonly understood abbreviations, like SEC, or acronyms, like NASDAQ.

4. A glossary should not be used to define terms that have been created solely for the purpose of the registration statement. In fact, with the exception of brand or trade names used to identify the type of security being offered, new terms should not be created.

Creating terms that exist only for use in a prospectus forces investors to learn a new vocabulary before they can begin to understand the disclosure. The issuer should eliminate over-reliance on defined terms as a primary means of explaining information in the prospectus, and instead, disclose material information in a clear, concise, and understandable manner.

Documents Incorporated by Reference

Some, but not all of the documents incorporated by reference into registration statements are subject to the plain English rule and amendments.

1. The information incorporated by reference in response to a general requirement need not comply with the plain English rule. For example, Item 12 on Form S-3 requires incorporation by reference of the issuer's recent Exchange Act reports in their entirety. The reports need not be rewritten.

2. However, any information incorporated by reference to satisfy a specific disclosure requirement must comply with the applicable plain English rule and amendments. For example, on Form S-3, if the filer incorporates by reference risk factors from a Form 10-K to satisfy Item 3, the risk factors must comply with Rule 421(d).

Post-Effective Amendments to Registration Statements

A post-effective amendment to a Form S-3 that, when first filed, was not subject to plain English will trigger the plain English requirements in two instances. A post-effective amendment must be rewritten to comply if:

1. It incorporates by reference audited financials that are more recent than those incorporated in any earlier post-effective amendment or the original registration statement.

2. Enough time has elapsed since the last post-effective amendment or the original registration statement that the issuer is required to post-effectively amend the prospectus under Section 10(a)(3) of the Securities Act of 1933.

Use of Legal Documents in Prospectus

Under Rule 421(b) of Regulation C, the issuer must avoid copying complex information directly from legal documents without any clear and concise explanation of the information. Language in the body of the prospectus should not be taken directly from the underlying indenture, shareholder agreements, rights plan, merger agreement, statute on dissenters rights, employment agreement, or similar document. The disclosure relating to such documents should be revised so that it is clear, concise, and understandable.

In the event that the issuer feels the language as it appears in the underlying legal documents is indispensable to a prospectus, it is necessary to:

1. Present it clearly, using bullet lists and concise sections and paragraphs.
2. Explain how that particular document affects investors.

Highly Technical Business Description in Plain English

Under the plain English rule, an issuer with a highly technical business should provide a brief, general description of the business with, if necessary, concrete examples to illustrate the description.

By comparing the following two descriptions of Computational Systems, Inc., it is obvious that it is possible to describe a tech-business effectively in plain English. The first example is from CSI's 1996 10-K, prior to the adoption of the plain English rules. The second is from the summary of a merger proxy that CSI filed during the company's participation in the Division's plain English pilot program:

1. *Computational Systems, Inc. 10-K*

   "The Company primarily designs, produces and markets an integrated family of advanced predictive maintenance products and services for use in large scale, continuous run manufacturing facilities. The Company's Reliability-Based Maintenance products and services help customers detect potentially disruptive conditions in the operation of their machinery before damage or complete mechanical failure occurs, thereby allowing maintenance to be scheduled at the most appropriate time."

2. *Computational Systems, Inc./Emerson Electric Company's merger proxy*

   "CSI's primary business is the design manufacture, and sale of a family of high-tech instruments that help companies determine when their industrial machines are in need of repair or adjustment. CSI also offers services to help its customers better manage the maintenance of their equipment. CSI's products and services help its customers keep their production lines running and maintain the quality of their products which may be adversely affected by an improperly functioning production line machine. CSI's customers are primarily large manufacturing, processing or power generating companies."

If the issuer must include technical terms that are understood only by industry experts, every effort must be made to explain these terms where they are first used. Where this is simply not possible, a glossary is acceptable.

In addition, technical terms and industry jargon are not appropriate for concise explanations.

Clarity, Not Brevity, Is the Goal

The goal of plain English is clarity, not brevity. Writing disclosure in plain English can sometimes actually increase the length of particular sections of a prospectus. The aim should be to reduce the length of a prospectus by writing concisely and eliminating redundancies—not by eliminating substance.

Electronic Filers Selected for Review

The Division of Corporation Finance has announced that, because issuers are required to file their registration statements electronically on EDGAR, the staff did not want them to send paper copies of their filings. However, in the plain English adopting release, if a registration statement that is subject to the new plain English rule is selected for review, the staff will need paper copies.

When issuers file their registration statements electronically on the EDGAR system, the document's layout is lost. Because the plain English rule is intended to enhance the readability of the prospectus through language *and design*, the staff needs to see the layout of the plain English sections as they are delivered to investors.

At present, the staff member assigned to a filing will call to request paper copies of the prospectus. The SEC is working to upgrade the EDGAR system to give issuers the option of filing an exact duplicate of the paper copy sent to investors, but this may not occur for some time.

Plain English and Acceleration Requests

The staff may ask the Commission to deny acceleration of a registration statement where the issuer has not made a good faith effort to comply with the plain English rule and amendments. The issuer must make a bona fide effort to make the prospectus reasonably concise, readable, and in compliance with the plain English requirements.

Cover Page Reminders

1. If the cover page exceeds the one page limit imposed by the rule, much of the information included is probably too detailed. The information that is not required by Item 501 of Regulation S-K and other information that is not key to an investment decision should be moved off the cover page. More in-depth information should be in the summary.

   Superfluous information such as the par value of common stock, highly technical explanations of industry operations, and minute details about the mechanics of a possible merger obscure the information that is key to potential investors' decisions.

2. Using all capital letters, cascading margins, narrow margins and dense text all impede readability of the text on the cover page. Since requirements limit this page to information that is key to an investment decision, it is very important that it be readable and visually inviting. The layout must highlight the information required by Item 501 and encourage investors to read the prospectus.

3. Item 501(a)(5) of Regulation S-K requires the issuer to highlight the cross reference to the risk factors section by using prominent type or in another manner. In other words, the cross reference should be visually distinctive from the other text on the cover page. Highlighting this cross reference using bold-faced and italicized type is suggested. Placing the cross reference in all capital letters is not recommended.

Comments Relating to the Summary

1. *Like information* should be grouped together. For example, if in a summary the items that discuss how a transaction directly affects shareholders are mixed with information on other topics, a naive investor could very easily become confused. If the exchange ratio, the tax consequences for payments on fractional shares, discussions of regulatory matters, termination fees, conditions to the merger, and such are not organized in a logical order, even a sophisticated investor would be at a loss.

2. In the summary, the issuer should carefully consider and identify those aspects of an offering that are the *most significant* and determine how best to highlight them in clear, plain language. It is not necessary to explain at length technical steps a company must take, such as creating a

merger subsidiary, directors' reasons for the merger, or the conflicts of interest that may result. This type of information would not be helpful for a shareholder making an investment decision.

3. The summary should not contain a lengthy description of the company's business and business strategy. Disclosure of this nature appears later in the prospectus. Detailed information is better suited for the body of the prospectus. If the issuer feels it important to highlight key aspects of the entity's business strategy, listing these in a bullet-point format, with one sentence per bullet point, is acceptable.

Sample Cautions for the Entire Prospectus

1. Long sentences make it difficult to understand on the first reading, particularly if there are embedded lists of information in paragraph form. Rather than including lists in paragraph form, they should be broken out, and each item marked with a bullet point, a number, or a letter.

2. Sentences containing parenthetical phrases disrupt the flow of information and make the sentences very long. As a result, investors may have to read them several times to understand the disclosure. Possible ways to eliminate parenthetical phrases are:
   a. If the information in the parenthetical phrase is part of the sentence, it may be set off by commas.
   b. If the parenthetical phrase does not fit as part of the sentence, it should be a separate sentence.

3. The use of footnotes should be avoided where possible. Some suggestions are:
   a. If the text in a footnote applies to an entire financial table, the footnoted material could be included in the narrative discussion that precedes the table.
   b. If a number of footnotes repeat the same text of a table, the information could be moved to the introductory paragraph.
   c. The footnoted material could be included in a column in the table.

4. A prospectus should be organized from the shareholders' perspectives. Information about the mechanics of a merger, for instance, is not important to investors. How the proposed transactions will affect their investments is important to them.

5. Redundancy should be consciously avoided. The only type of repetition that is appropriate in the prospectus would be:
   a. Introduction of topics on the cover page.
   b. Expansion of those topics in a summary fashion while summarizing other key aspects of the transaction in the summary.

    c. Discussion of those and the remaining topics in greater detail in the body of the prospectus.

6. Informative subheadings provide readers with helpful navigational cues. They should be descriptive and specific to a particular prospectus. If subheadings would work equally well in any other company's disclosure document, they are probably too vague to be helpful.

7. A prospectus should never be written from the perspective of someone who is already quite familiar with the transaction and the entities involved. For example, references to "certain circumstances," "certain matters," "certain amendments," "certain persons," and "certain extraordinary matters" would make sense to someone who is already familiar with these transactions. But, would the shareholders be? Probably not. The term "certain" should be replaced with a brief description of what makes the information qualify as "certain."

8. Legalese and industry jargon should not be used in a prospectus. Instead, concepts should be explained in concrete, everyday language. As always, any industry terms should be used in context so those potential investors who do not work in the industry can understand the disclosure.

Chapter 22

E-Commerce and E-Communication

Forecasts of Internet business—variously called e-commerce, e-business, EC, e-tail, cyber-business or virtual markets—are so astronomical that they strain credibility. Internet commerce is growing in exponential leaps and bounds.

It is estimated that e-business will reach $1.3 trillion by 2003 in this country alone. And according to the SEC, e-trading is there already, "In today's hot-wired financial markets, modern technology allows traders to move money anywhere in the world at lightning speed, more than $1.5 trillion every-day—a sum equal to world trade for four months."

Web-based technologies and their support structures are changing on an average of every four to eight months. Along the way, e-commerce is creating new ways to sell, to advertise, and to communicate with customers, suppliers, employees and shareholders. And the accountant is faced with attempting to determine how to account for these evolving technologies.

Properly reporting the acquisition and then disposal of technology (with its rapid turnover) will be only one of the many new issues organizations will have to deal with.

The accounting issues raised by e-commerce factors will undoubtedly call for new accounting and auditing standards that haven't even been thought of yet. Some of the older ones will require very careful consideration.

In effect, the Net is not only creating new business, it is creating new ways to do business and to be in business. And therein lies the work for the accountant.

ACCOUNTING ISSUES

A study "Electronic Commerce Trends, Technology and the Security, Control and Audit Implications" was prepared for the Institute of Internal Auditors (IIA) with partial funding from the International Federation of Accountants (IFAC). That report emphasized the need for accountants and auditors of an organization to work closely with management in setting up and developing their e-business and e-communication systems. The study identifies many accounting issues that must be considered.

TOPICS FOR CONSIDERATION

The following is a discussion of some of these accounting problems and considerations relating to them.

Software

The considerable software infrastructure needed to implement an ecommerce strategy will be obtained from software vendors or developed internally. Existing U.S. software related accounting rules governing these transactions are expected to remain unchanged.

Vendor Software. *Software Revenue Recognition* (SOP 97-2) requires that revenue should be recognized on software or software systems arrangements that do not require significant production, modification, or customization of software when delivery has occurred and all of the following tests are met:

1. Persuasive evidence that a sale or lease arrangement exists.
2. Delivery of the product or service has occurred.
3. The seller must not retain any specific performance obligation.
4. The vendor's fee is fixed or determinable.
5. Appropriate recognition is given to the likelihood of returns.
6. Collectibility is probable.

Revenue from software or software system arrangements that require significant production, modification, or customization of software should be accounted for using long-term construction-type contract accounting.

The vendor fee in software arrangements that consist of multiple elements, such as upgrades, must be allocated to the various elements. The portion of a fee allocated to an element should be recognized when the revenue is earned and realized.

Internally Developed Software.   *Accounting for the Cost of Computer Software Developed for Internal Uses* (SOP 98-1) requires the costs associated with the acquisition and development of software for internal use to be *capitalized* when both of the following occur:

1. Management authorizes and commits to funding a computer software project and believes that it is probable that the project will be completed and the software will be used to perform the function intended.
2. Conceptual formulation, design, and testing of possible software project alternatives have been completed.

Capitalization of costs should cease when the computer software development project is substantially completed and ready for its intended use. This point occurs when substantially all testing is complete.

Thus, companies developing their e-commerce software internally, will find it necessary to:

1. Capitalize the direct costs of the development.
2. Amortize the capitalized cost over the software's useful life.

A high level of uncertainty typically accompanies the introduction of new software applications, such as e-commerce. How reliable are the decisions to commence capitalization of e-commerce development costs and the choice of their related amortization periods?

If there is a question of application for U.S. companies, the issue is of even more concern when dealing with non-U.S. companies. Many of them rely heavily on local accounting standards which may or may not make provision for accounting for software.

Acquisitions and Mergers

Growth through mergers and acquisitions has become a popular e-commerce strategy. E-commerce companies are seeking to benefit from economies of scale by rapidly expanding their share of existing markets and entering new markets. In nearly all of these business combinations, the accounting for in-process research and development and goodwill could be major issues because of the large amount of money involved and the level of uncertainty associated with potential benefits. An acquired company could present a sizable goodwill factor involving market share, software, and people not on the balance sheet.

As detailed in Chapter 5, new accounting rules are being formulated to cover these business combination transactions. To recap briefly, the FASB plans to:

1. Eliminate pooling-of-interests accounting
2. Require goodwill to be written off over ten years with a possible maximum period of twenty years.
3. Require capitalization of acquired in-process research and development. Similar changes in business combination accounting are also being planned outside of the U.S.

Contingency Losses

There is a high level of uncertainties associated with e-commerce related contingency losses. Transactions often involve purchases of products and services where the purchaser does not physically inspect the product purchased or interview the service provider directly.

This is not a new phenomenon. Catalog sales companies have operated in this way for many years. The change that the expansion of e-commerce brings is that many companies without any experience in this type of transaction are now engaged in it.

The e-commerce accounting issue that this development raises for these inexperienced companies is:

How do you estimate reliably such contingency losses as returns, volume discounts, and other sales allowances when you do not have an historical record on which to base your estimates of future losses and adjustments?

This uncertainty issue is more important to companies in the U.S. and those other countries, such as the UK, that have contingency losses recognition rules that require reasonable estimates of contingency losses and strictly prohibit the establishment of general reserves.

Start-Up Activities

E-commerce is not a single technology, but rather a sophisticated combination of technologies and consumer-based services integrated to form a new way of conducting business. This new form, however, is still itself in a start-up mode. The future of e-commerce is bright and viable; the application, however, has not been fully integrated into the business mainstream. For many companies, the introduction of e-commerce sales activities could be considered a start-up activity.

Start-up activities are defined broadly as those one-time activities related to opening a new facility, introducing a new product or service, conducting business in a new territory, conducting business with a new class of customer or beneficiary, initiating a new process in an existing facility, or commencing some new operation. Start-up activities include activities related to organizing a new entity.

According to generally accepted accounting practices (GAAP), start-up activity costs must be expensed as incurred. For U.S. companies that add e-commerce sales activities to their traditional business practices, the question will be: Is this a start-up activity?

If it is not, the costs may be capitalized. Again, this raises the issue of the level of uncertainty associated with the amortization period selected. Outside of the U.S., entities and their investors are confronted with a variety of different accounting treatments of e-commerce start-up sales activities.

Since these e-commerce start-up costs can be very material, management, their shareholders and potential investors need to be aware of the costs and the accounting for them.

Nondisclosure

In many companies, e-commerce activities are not carried out by a specific organizational unit. Often these activities will spread throughout the operating activities of many organizational units.

Under U.S. operating segment disclosure rules, as well as those of many other countries, only the organizational unit's operating results need be disclosed. If a company chooses to stick by the rules, investors may not be given the company's e-commerce-related operating results. Since, as noted above, e-commerce start-up activities are often unprofitable, nondisclosure may be detrimental to the interests of investors at least in the short run.

Credit Losses

Electronic payment systems are often an integral part of e-commerce activities. From the accounting point of view, this can be good news and bad news.

From the vendor's point of view, it can be good news since often the buyer's payment is guaranteed by a third party, such as a credit card issuer, that absorbs the bad debt risk. This reduces the uncertainty associated with establishing bad debt reserves.

On the other hand, it can be bad news for the party absorbing the credit risk. With the expansion of e-commerce, many products, customers, sellers, and services outside of the prior experience of the credit grantor will be paid for electronically. Again, the lack of a historical record raises the level of uncertainty associated with making estimates about future events, which in this case is the appropriate level of the bad debt reserve.

Asset Impairments

Radical changes in the way business is conducted have always led to asset impairments. Therefore, it should be expected that the growth of e-commerce may lead to the impairment of some asset groups. In some cases, asset groups used in traditional business activities may be made obsolete by the introduction of e-commerce. In fact, the rapid evolution of e-commerce and its associated technologies will define technical obsolescence in terms of months, not years. The "new" assets may be impaired very quickly. In other circumstances, some asset groups devoted to e-commerce may become impaired as a result of the inability of the company to implement its e-commerce strategy successfully.

Historically, management has been slow to recognize asset impairment losses. This attitude will probably not change; therefore, balance sheets of companies engaging in e-commerce could very possibly include overvalued assets.

Customer Solicitation Costs

Many of the companies engaged in e-commerce will have to spend considerable sums of money to build their e-commerce customer base. Some may capitalize part of these customer solicitation costs.

U.S. accounting standards generally require these customer solicitation costs to be expensed as incurred. The only exception is the cost of direct mail advertising. It can be capitalized only if the company can base the amortization period choice on a reasonable estimate of the direct mailings' response rate. Since for many companies, e-commerce will be a new business activity, they will not have a historical record of response rates upon which to base their estimate of future response rates.

Outside of the U.S., advertising costs are generally accounted for under the local intangible assets rules, which may permit capitalization of advertising costs. Companies with limited e-commerce experience that capitalize direct mail advertising costs must be very cautious since their historical response-rate record may be inadequate.

Materiality

Under generous interpretations of what is *material*, the sales, costs, assets, and liabilities of a company's e-commerce start-up activities may be regarded as *immaterial*. This could be a problem. In recent years, some managers have adopted the point of view that since U.S. GAAP does not apply to immaterial items, they can account for immaterial items in any way they choose.

As shown in Chapter 18 *Materiality*, the SEC has changed all of this. A cavalier attitude toward materiality is unacceptable practice. The new definition of materiality in essence says, "if it's material to investors, it's material." Under this test, relatively small amounts can be material in a high price-earnings ratio-valued stock situation.

Uncertainty

E-commerce is a new form of business and, like many new business forms, there can often be a high level of uncertainty associated with the future prospects of many of those engaging in it. Since accounting involves many estimates of future events, this uncertainty can create major accounting problems involving contingency loss estimates, recognition of intangibles, asset impairment loss recognition, and amortization period choices. Consequently, the reliability of management estimates will be crucial to the welfare of the entity.

TAXING PROBLEMS

What of the tax accountant? The accounting for e-commerce will require organizations to review current policies and procedures. Accounting concerns such as recording multiple tax payments, which might not be an issue in a paper-based trading environment, could quickly become a major concern. Very possibly, other tax concerns will develop with many more questions than answers:

1. How soon will the federal government decide that it really should get its share from all of these Web sites?
2. Will there be a flat electronic tax applied to every e-business transaction?
3. How will an organization account for and respond to different tax regulations governing commerce as they vary by country, by state, by county, by city?
4. Will there be some form of interstate or intercountry tax?
5. How would these taxes (if forthcoming) affect the cost of doing e-business?
6. Who will collect the appropriate taxes, and how will the taxes be submitted to the proper taxing authority?
7. Will electronic transactions be taxed in their city/state/country of origin or at some other destination (or all of the above)?
8. What new procedures will be designed to account for varying tax revenue, which will be transferred to organizations in distant countries and various states?

These and many additional questions, that affect tax accounting for Web-based commerce, will need to be addressed on an international level. In the meantime, they are being considered here on a national level.

Commission on Electronic Commerce

Even discounting the global aspects of Internet taxation, there are more than enough questions relating to domestic taxes. "The Internet Tax Freedom Act," enacted by Congress in October 1998 established a three-year moratorium on "new Internet tax" and set up the Advisory Commission on Electronic Commerce. It is made up of 19 members—13 representatives from governmental and nonprofit entities and 6 from private-sector industry.

They are assigned the task of conducting a thorough study of "Federal, state and local and international taxation and tariff treatment of transactions using the Internet and Internet access and other comparable intrastate, interstate or international sales activities."

Consensus appears to be growing to extend the ban on levying "new" taxes on the Internet for as much as three-to-five years beyond the present cutoff date of October 22, 2001. But what of the "old" taxes? Yes, there are some and there could be more, regardless of a moratorium.

1. Consumers in some areas are supposed to pay use taxes on those purchases on the Internet for which no sales tax was paid. (In fact, some states include the appropriate tax form in their income tax package as a reminder.)
2. Sales tax must be paid if the buyer lives in a state in which the e-business has a facility such as a retail store, warehouse, or factory in that state. (Therefore, many e-retailers that actually do have a physical site of any variety have located them in the states that have no retail sales tax— Alaska, Delaware, Montana, New Hampshire, and Oregon.)
3. Then there is the distinction between "new" and "old." If the state and local governments begin losing too much tax revenue from e-commerce, they might decide that sales tax is an "old" tax and just extend it to e-commerce.

CAUTIONS FOR E-COMMUNICATION WEB SITE USE

With the Internet now playing an increasingly important role in investing and financial reporting, the Securities and Exchange Commission Private Securities Litigation Reform Act of 1995 (see Chapter 19) may be cited frequently. It is important that companies be aware of pitfalls that could lead to a new wave of litigation.

Following are several cautions that could reduce the legal risks from electronic disclosures, particularly for those associated with company Web sites:

1. Meaningful, obvious, clearly worded cautionary disclaimers must accompany any and all "forward-looking" statements.

2. Some of these forward-looking statements may appear in varied guises: transcripts of speeches, press conferences, and quotes should be treated as written disclosures and must include an appropriate written disclaimer situated as closely as possible to the statement.

3. A full set of financial statements and notes should always be included. "Selected" portions, summations, "fractured" financial statements, even a complete set without the footnotes, could be an invitation for litigation.

4. A company should not commit to update disclosures and should include on its Web site disclaimers regarding the absence of any obligation to do so. However, the site should be monitored very closely for any information that is outdated or misleading.

5. Management should be wary of any "selectivity" relating to analysts. Do not frame, inline, or link to analysts' sites or include analysts' comments on the company's site. If a list of analysts covering the company is provided, the names of *all* analysts must be included, not just those with favorable comments.

6. Probably the most cogent advice relating to "chat rooms" (for the company as well as the investor) has come from the chairman of the SEC in a much publicized speech:

   "Chat rooms, which increasingly have become a source of information and misinformation for many investors, have been compared to a high-tech version of morning gossip or advice at the company water cooler. But, at least you knew your co-workers at the water cooler. For the future sake of this medium, I encourage investors to take what they see over chat rooms—not with a grain of salt—but with a rock of salt."

   Obviously, it is in the best interest of the company to establish well-defined policies for employee participation in chat room discussions about their jobs and their organization.

7. Keeping in mind the seemingly never-ending abilities of the "hackers" to access a mainframe and compromise a Web site, it is paramount that there should be continuing reevaluation of a system's security measures.

THE IASC STUDY: BUSINESS REPORTING ON THE INTERNET

The International Accounting Standards Committee published a study of business and financial reporting on the Internet in November, 1999 as the first step in a possible project to develop accounting standards in that area.

The study examines:

1. The current technologies available for electronic business reporting.
2. What companies around the world are actually doing (this involved a detailed analysis of the Web sites of the 30 largest companies in each of 22 countries, 660 companies in all).
3. The sort of standards for electronic business reporting that are needed now, within the constraint of today's technologies.
4. The shortcomings of financial reporting on the Internet within current technologies.
5. The technological changes that are on the horizon and how they can improve electronic reporting.

Changes in Paper Financial Reports

Technology has altered irreversibly not only the physical medium of corporate financial reporting, but also its traditional boundaries. The Committee realized that paper reports are being supplemented—and, for many users, replaced—by electronic business reporting, primarily via the Internet. They became aware that investors and lenders had moved far beyond traditional financial statements and related note disclosures.

Four experts from the academic world authored the IASC study, *Business Reporting on the Internet*. It illustrates to accounting policy makers the nature of changes occurring in business reporting and explains how those changes are affecting the dissemination of accounting and financial information.

The study also identifies the effects those changes may have on accounting standard-setting in the future. The report charts a course of IASC—and, in fact, the rest of the accounting world—to follow in helping to ensure that high-quality electronic data is available for the users of business and financial information.

A Code of Conduct for Web-Based Business Reporting

Among other recommendations, the study urges IASC to adopt a Code of Conduct for Web-based business reporting. The report is designed to enhance the quality of business reporting information provided on the Web by corporations. The authors of the suggested Code are quick to point out that it is not intended to be a permanent solution to resolving the issues related to business reporting online since technology will continue to change and develop, and user expectations and demands will change. A complete draft of a proposed Code is included in the report.

E-Business Reporting Language

The study recommends that a global electronic business reporting language (BRL) be developed to meet the needs of those who look to the Internet for financial and operating information.

Those represented in the consortium should include:

1. The IASC.
2. Global information distributors.
3. Software developers.
4. Securities regulators.
5. National accounting standard setters.
6. International accounting firms.
7. Others. (Presumably "others" will become evident as e-business and e-communication become better defined!)

FASB's Business Reporting Research Project

Many organizations are interested in this new information technology and do in-depth studies to discover the advantages as well as the pitfalls of its use. The FASB is one of the most recent to publish a very comprehensive study.

The Three Part Study

The report, *Electronic Distribution of Business Reporting Information*, published in January 2000, is the first section of a broader study—the Business Reporting Research Project. The objective of the FASB is to determine the kind of business information corporations are reporting outside of financial statements.

The first portion describes the electronic distribution of business information and investigates the possibilities and problems of the Internet on the reporting process.

The second will deal with the redundancies between SEC and FASB reporting requirements, thus helping to eliminate overlapping and duplication.

A third portion will discuss the results of 10 selected industries' business reporting practices.

Objectives of the First Study

Growth of the Internet as a medium for delivering business reporting information has altered the way that information flows from companies to investors and creditors. The structure will continue to change as companies bring new technologies to the process and as information users find new ways to access and analyze information.

The stated objectives of the first FASB study were to:

1. Survey the state of reporting information over the Internet.
2. Identify notable practices.

Financial Information Online

More and more companies are using the Internet to disseminate information about themselves. This includes stock quotes and the latest annual report, as well as forward-looking information, detailed plans about new products and services, and other material from outside the financial statements.

The Internet offers vast amounts of financial information available to the nonspecialist investor and allows delivery of that information instantaneously and at very low cost. Any investor with a computer and a modem can obtain information that was previously available, as a practical matter, only to a limited range of company officials, professional investment analysts, and the financial press.

Some of the present practices observed in the report include:

1. Transcripts of management presentations.
2. Analysts' reports on the company.
3. Traditional financial information.
4. Live and archived audio-visual versions of meetings that were previously open only to selected analysts.

The FASB report discusses legal and other issues that are of interest to companies using or thinking about using the Internet for distributing business information.

THE SEC ON REPORTING IN THE NEW ECONOMY

As the Securities and Exchange Commission makes quite evident, they are not about to let e-communication and e-trading progress too far without adequate protection for the investor. New industries, spurred by new services and new technologies, are creating new questions and challenges that must be addressed.

Rules for valuation of manufacturing inventory or assessing what a factory is worth are well established. But what of the value of R&D invested in a software program, or the value of a user base on an Internet shopping site? As intangible assets continue to grow in size and scope, more and more people are questioning whether the true value—and the drivers of that value—is being reflected in a timely manner in publicly available disclosure.

To look into these questions, a group of leaders from the business community, academia, the accounting profession, standard-setting bodies, and corporate America is being formed to examine whether the current business reporting framework can more effectively handle these changes in our economy.

As always, the SEC embraces free market principles to foster greater competition, while ensuring effective regulatory oversight to protect investor interest. To that effect, they are simultaneously taking a very close look at the many complaints about online trading.

ELECTRONIC DATA INTERCHANGE (EDI)

Electronic commerce involves individuals as well as organizations engaging in a variety of electronic business transactions (without paper documents) using computer and telecommunication networks. These networks can be either private or public, or a combination of the two. Actually the big leap in e-business has been in conducting business over the Internet (specifically the Web).

This is due to the Web's surge in popularity and the acceptance of the Internet as a viable transport mechanism for business information. The use of a public network-based infrastructure like the Internet can reduce costs and make it feasible for small as well as large companies to extend their services and products to a broad customer base.

Electronic commerce has been defined as a means of conducting business electronically via online transactions *between merchants and consumers*; traditionally, the definition of electronic commerce had focused on Electronic Data Interchange (EDI) as the primary means of conducting business electronically *between entities having a preestablished contractual relationship.*

EDI involves computer application-to-computer application transmission of business documents in a predetermined, standard format. While e-commerce is targeted for global trading and is suited to anyone interested in online commerce, EDI is best suited for a selected group of trading partners.

EDI improves business operations dealing with high volumes of transactions by providing electronic information exchange between those trading partners. Such an established electronic connection reduces data entry errors by eliminating repetitive tasks and lowers administrative overhead costs associated with paper-based processing methods.

E-commerce and EDI, whatever its nature, will require accounting professionals of those organizations using the new technology to reexamine the nature of the entity's business practices and the manner in which transactions are recorded. This might be especially true for organizations which, up until their entrance into e-commerce, had only domestic trading partners and never sold directly to the consumer. E-commerce is changing the conduct of business, as most organizations have known it.

THE CPA WEBTRUST AND SMALL BUSINESS

WebTrust is a comprehensive seal of assurance for e-commerce sites developed jointly by the American Institute of Certified Public Accountants (AICPA) and the Canadian Institute of Chartered Accountants (CICA). The designers believe that WebTrust can help small businesses build consumer confidence necessary for electronic commerce to reach its full potential.

Testimony Before the House

In testimony before the House Committee on Small Business, one AICPA official suggested that small Web-based businesses rely upon the accounting profession to provide assurance services like CPA WebTrust which are designed to make cyberspace a safer place to shop. Another of the AICPA officials identified their goal, as trusted CPAs, to raise awareness of WebTrust to the point where consumers around the world seek out small business Web sites with WebTrust seals as the safest, most secure place to shop on the Internet.

Advantages of Assurance Services

The AICPA considers WebTrust a way to level the playing field for small, online businesses. Although they do not benefit from nationally recognized brand names, they still may assure their customers that the Web site has met the most comprehensive e-commerce standards to protect consumers online.

These standards, known as the *WebTrust Principles and Criteria*, ensure that the site:

1. Discloses its business practices for e-commerce transactions to Web site visitors.
2. Follows these business practices.
3. Has appropriate controls so that transactions executed at the site are completed as ordered.
4. Protects the privacy of customer information and financial data.

The program licenses CPAs to certify the sites to ensure that electronic transactions meet high standards. Those that do will display the CPA WebTrust "seal," assuring consumers that these sites are trustworthy and reliable, and that consumer information will remain confidential.

Handling Consumer Complaints

WebTrust provides a consumer complaint mechanism that allows consumers to resolve problems about product quality and customer service. This mechanism enhances the assurance service with binding third-party arbitration. Consumers or businesses that have problems with a WebTrust certified company can file a claim online with the independent third party, the National Arbitration Forum, through a link provided on the CPA WebTrust site.

The designers anticipate that giving credibility to small business Web sites through WebTrust can help an entity to:

1. Build a worldwide customer base.
2. Develop global electronic commerce.
3. Deliver on their sales promises.
4. Build a loyal, online customer base.
5. Build consumer confidence.
6. Help reduce risk of online fraud.

AICPA officials testified that they believe WebTrust, CPAs and their international counterparts to be uniquely qualified to examine online businesses to determine:

1. If the business is legitimate.
2. Its transactions are secure.
3. The information it collects from consumers is kept private.

Chapter 23

Employee Benefits: Savings Plans

With the wealth of savings plans, pension plans, medical savings plans, education savings plans, it is important for the individual as well as the small and larger business owners to heed the considered advise of a knowledgeable accountant. Only after considerable study and comparison is it possible to select the best alternatives for a specific situation.

THE TRADITIONAL IRA

The original or "traditional" individual retirement arrangement (IRA) is a personal savings plan that offers individual tax advantages when setting aside money for retirement. (The term traditional IRA does not refer to a Roth IRA, a SIMPLE IRA or to an education IRA.)

Two advantages of an IRA are:

1. Most contributions may be deducted in whole or in part, depending on the type of IRA and the circumstances surrounding the contribution.
2. Generally, the amounts in the IRA, including earnings and gains, are not taxed until distributed, or, in some cases, are not taxed at all if distributed according to the rules.

To set up and make contributions to a traditional IRA, an individual (or, if a joint return is filed, an individual and a spouse) must receive taxable compensation during the year and neither individual has reached the age $70\frac{1}{2}$ by the end of the year. A traditional IRA may be established, whether or not the individual is covered by any other retirement plan. However, it may not be possible to deduct all of the contributions if either individual is covered by an employer retirement plan.

Setting Up a Traditional IRA

A traditional IRA may be set up at any time. However, the time for making contributions for any year is limited. There are a variety of IRAs available through different financial organizations. An IRA can be set up at a bank or other financial institution or with a mutual fund or life insurance company. An IRA may also be set up through a stockbroker. However, any IRA must meet Internal Revenue Code requirements.

A traditional IRA can be an individual retirement account or an annuity. It can be part of either a simplified employee pension (SEP) or a part of an employer or employee association trust account.

Individual Retirement Account.   An individual retirement account is a trust or custodial account set up for the exclusive benefit of an individual or his or her beneficiaries. The account is created by a written document that shows that the account meets the following requirements.

1. The trustee or custodian must be a bank, a federally insured credit union, a savings and loan association, or an entity approved by the IRS to act as trustee or custodian.
2. The trustee or custodian generally cannot accept contributions of more than $2,000 a year.
3. Contributions, except for rollover contributions, must be in cash.
4. The amount in the account must be fully vested (the individual must have a nonforfeitable right to the amount) at all times.
5. Money in the account cannot be used to buy a life insurance policy.
6. Assets in the account cannot be combined with other property, except in a common trust fund or common investment fund.
7. An individual is required to start receiving distributions by April 1 of the year following the year in which he or she reaches age 70$\frac{1}{2}$.

Individual Retirement Annuity.   An individual may set up an individual retirement annuity by purchasing an annuity contract or an endowment contract from a life insurance company. An individual retirement annuity must be issued in a specific name as the owner, and only the named individual or his or her surviving beneficiaries can receive the benefits or payments. An individual retirement annuity must meet all the following requirements.

1. The entire interest in the contract must be nonforfeitable.
2. The contract must provide that no portion may be transferred to any person other than the issuer.
3. There must be flexible premiums so that if the individual's compensation changes, payments can also change. This provision applies to contracts issued after November 6, 1978.
4. The contract must provide that contributions cannot be more than $2,000 in any year, and that the individual must use any refunded premiums to pay for future premiums or to buy more benefits before the end of the calendar year after the year the refund is received.
5. Distributions must begin by April 1 of the year following the year in which the individual reaches age 70½.

Individual Retirement Bonds.   The sale of individual retirement bonds issued by the federal government was suspended after April 30, 1982. The bonds have the following features.

1. Interest is paid on them only when they are cashed in.
2. No further interest is paid on them after the individual reaches age 70½. If the individual dies, interest will stop five years after his or her death, or on the date the individual would have reached age 70½, whichever is earlier.
3. The bonds cannot be transferred. If the bonds are redeemed before the year in which the individual reaches age 59½, the money may be subject to a 10% additional tax. Redemption proceeds may be rolled into IRAs.

Employer and Employee Association Trust Accounts.   An employer, labor union, or other employee association can set up a trust to provide individual retirement accounts for its employees or members. The requirements for individual retirement accounts apply to these employer or union-established traditional IRAs.

Simplified Employee Pension (SEP).   A simplified employee pension (SEP) is a written arrangement that allows an employer to make deductible contributions to a traditional IRA (a SEP-IRA) set up for an employee to receive such contributions.

Inherited IRAs.   If a spouse inherits a traditional IRA, the survivor can choose to treat it as his or her own by making contributions to it. If, however, someone other than a spouse inherits a traditional IRA he or she cannot contribute to it.

The inheritor generally will not owe tax on the assets in the IRA until he or she receives distributions from it. A surviving spouse can elect to treat a traditional IRA inherited from a spouse as his or her own. The surviving spouse will be treated as having made this election if:

1. Contributions (including rollover contributions) are made to the inherited IRA.
2. Required distributions are not made from it.

Required Disclosures.   The trustee or issuer (sometimes called the sponsor) of the traditional IRA generally must give the individual a disclosure statement at least seven days before an IRA is set up. However, the sponsor does not have to give the individual the statement until the set up date, provided the individual is given at least seven days from that date to revoke the IRA. If the individual chooses to revoke the IRA within the revocation period, the sponsor must return the entire amount.

Disclosure statement.   The disclosure statement given by the plan sponsor must explain certain items in plain language. For example, the statement should explain when and how the IRA can be revoked, and include the name, address, and telephone number of the person to receive the notice of cancellation. This explanation must appear at the beginning of the disclosure statement.

Making Contributions

As soon as a traditional IRA is established, contributions can be made to it through a chosen sponsor (trustee or other administrator). Contributions must be in the form of money (cash, check or money order). Property cannot be contributed. However, certain property may be transferred or rolled over from one retirement plan to another. Contributions can be made to a traditional IRA for each year that the individual has received compensation and has not reached age 70½ during the year.

For any year in which the individual does not work, contributions cannot be made to an IRA unless he or she receives alimony or files a joint return with a spouse who has compensation. Even if contributions cannot be made for the current year, the amounts contributed for years in which the individual did qualify can remain in the IRA. Contributions can resume for any years that the individual does qualify.

Limits on Contributions

There are limits that affect the amount that can be contributed:

1. The most that can be contributed for any year to a traditional IRA is the smaller of the following amounts:

   a. Compensation that must be included in income for the year, or

   b. $2,000.

   This is the most that can be contributed regardless of whether the contributions are to one or more traditional IRAs or whether all or part of the contributions are nondeductible. Contributions on an individual's behalf to a traditional IRA reduce the limit for contributions to a Roth IRA.

2. If an individual files a joint return and the taxable compensation is less than that of the spouse, the most that can be contributed for the year to the IRA is the smaller of the following two amounts:

   a. $2,000, or

   b. The total compensation includable in the gross income of the individual and the spouse for the year, reduced by the spouse's IRA contribution for the year and any contributions for the year to a Roth IRA on behalf of the spouse. This means that the total combined contributions that can be made for the year to the IRA and the spouse's IRA can be as much as $4,000.

3. Generally, filing status has no effect on the amount of allowable contributions to a traditional IRA. However, if during the year either an individual or spouse was covered by a retirement plan at work, a deduction may be reduced or eliminated, depending on the filing status and income.

4. Usually each spouse figures his or her limit separately, using his or her own compensation. This is the rule even in states with community property laws.

5. An individual does not have to contribute to a traditional IRA for every tax year, regardless of ability to do so. However, if contributions to a traditional IRA for a year were less than the limit, it is not possible to contribute more in a later year to make up the difference. On the other hand, if contributions to an IRA for a year were more than the limit, it is possible to apply the excess contribution in one year to a later year if the contributions for that later year are less than the maximum allowed for that year.

6. If an individual has more than one IRA, the limit applies to the total contributions made on his or her behalf to all of his or her traditional IRAs for the year. The limit for contributions to Roth IRAs is reduced by contributions made on the individual's behalf to a traditional IRA.

7. Brokers' commissions paid in connection with a traditional IRA are subject to the contribution limit; trustees' administrative fees are not sub-

ject to the contribution limit. However, trustees' administrative fees that are billed separately and paid in connection with a traditional IRA are deductible.

General Rules

1. Contributions cannot be made to a traditional IRA for the year the individual reaches age 70½ or any later year.
2. If spouses both have compensation and are under age 70½, each can set up an IRA. Spouses cannot both participate in the same IRA.
3. If an individual invests in an annuity or endowment contract under an individual retirement annuity, no more than $2,000 can be contributed toward its cost for the tax year, including the cost of life insurance coverage. If more than $2,000 is contributed, the annuity or endowment contract is disqualified.
4. Contributions can be made to a traditional IRA for a year at any time during the year or by the due date for filing the individual's return for that year, not including extensions. For most people, this means that contributions for 1999 must have been made by April 17, 2000.

A claim can be filed for a traditional IRA contribution before the contribution is actually made. However, the contribution must be made by the due date of the return, not including extensions.

Deduction Limits

The deduction taken for contributions made to a traditional IRA depends on whether an individual or a spouse was covered for any part of the year by an employer retirement plan. The deduction is also affected by income and filing status.

Usually, if neither spouse was covered for any part of the year by an employer retirement plan, a deduction can be taken for a total contribution to one or more traditional IRA of up to $2,000, or 100% of compensation, whichever is less.

In the case of a married couple with unequal compensation who file a joint return, the deduction for contributions to the traditional IRA of the spouse with less compensation is limited to the smaller of the following two amounts:

1. $2,000, or
2. The total compensation includable in the gross income of both spouses for the year reduced by the following two amounts:

a. A spouse's IRA deduction for the year.

b. Any contributions for the year to a Roth IRA on behalf of a spouse.

If either spouse is covered by an employer retirement plan, they may be entitled to only a partial (reduced) deduction or no deduction at all, depending on income and filing status. The deduction begins to decrease when income rises above a certain amount and is eliminated altogether when it reaches a higher amount. The amounts vary depending on filing status.

If an individual is covered by an employer retirement plan, the IRA deduction is reduced or eliminated entirely depending on filing status.

Income from IRA Distributions

If distributions were received in a calendar year from one or more traditional IRAs and the traditional IRAs include only deductible contributions, the distributions are fully taxable.

If contributions to a traditional IRA for the calendar year appear to be nondeductible contributions, the distributions may be partly tax-free and partly taxable.

Moving Retirement Plan Assets

Traditional IRA rules permit the transfer (tax free) of assets from other retirement programs to a traditional IRA. The rules permit the following kinds of transfers:

1. Transfers from one trustee to another.
2. Rollovers.
3. Transfers incident to a divorce.

Withdrawing or Using IRA Assets

Because a traditional IRA is a tax-favored means of saving for retirement, there are rules limiting the withdrawal and use of IRA assets. Violation of the rules generally results in additional taxes in the year of violation.

Generally, if an individual is under age 59½ and assets are withdrawn from a traditional IRA, there is a 10% additional tax. Withdrawals before age 59½ are called premature distributions or early withdrawals. This tax is 10% of the part of the distribution that must be included in gross income. This is in addition to any regular income tax on the amount that has to be included in gross income. There may be a 25%, rather than 10%, additional tax if money is withdrawn from a SIMPLE IRA before age 59½.

After age 59½, assets can be withdrawn from traditional IRA without having to pay the 10% additional tax. Although withdrawals can be made after the age 59½, withdrawals are not required until age 70½.

Exceptions

There are several exceptions to the age 59½ rule. An individual may qualify for an exception if he or she is in one of the following situations.

1. An individual has unreimbursed medical expenses that are more than 7.5% of his or her adjusted gross income.
2. The distributions are not more than the cost of the medical insurance.
3. An individual is disabled.
4. An individual is the beneficiary of a deceased IRA owner.
5. An individual is receiving distributions in the form of an annuity.
6. The distributions are not more than qualified higher education expenses.
7. An individual uses the distributions to buy, build, or rebuild a first home.
8. The distribution is of contributions returned before the due date of an individual's tax return.
9. The distribution is due to an IRS levy of the qualified plan.

Distributions that are timely and properly rolled over, as discussed earlier, are not subject to either regular income tax or the 10% additional tax. Certain withdrawals of excess contributions after the due date of an individual's return are also tax free and not subject to the 10% additional tax. This also may apply to transfers incident to divorce.

The 10% additional tax on withdrawals made before age 59½ does not apply to these tax-free withdrawals.

Required Distribution

Funds may not be kept in a traditional IRA indefinitely. Eventually they must be withdrawn. If an individual does not make any withdrawals, or not enough is withdrawn, there may be a 50% excise tax on the amount not withdrawn as required. The requirements for withdrawing IRA funds differ.

The owner of a traditional IRA must withdraw the entire balance in the IRA or start receiving periodic distributions from the IRA by April 1 of the year following the year in which he or she reaches age 70½. This date is referred to as the required beginning date.

Periodic distributions.   If the entire balance in a traditional IRA is not withdrawn by the required beginning date, the individual must start to withdraw periodic distributions over one of the following periods:

1. The individual's life.
2. The lives of the individual and the designated beneficiary.
3. A period that does not extend beyond the individual's life expectancy.
4. A period that does not extend beyond the joint life and last survivor expectancy of the individual and his or her designated beneficiary.

Penalties for Rule Infractions

The tax advantages of using traditional IRAs for retirement savings can be offset by additional taxes and penalties if the rules are not followed. For example, there are additions to the regular tax for using the IRA funds in prohibited transactions. There are also additional taxes for, but not limited to, the following activities.

1. Investing in collectibles.
2. Making excess contributions.
3. Making early withdrawals.
4. Failing to make required withdrawals.

Prohibited Transactions

If there is a prohibited transaction in connection with a traditional IRA account at any time during the year, the account generally stops being an IRA as of the first day of that year. A prohibited transaction is any improper use of a traditional IRA account or annuity. The following are examples of prohibited transactions with a traditional IRA.

1. Borrowing money from it.
2. Selling property to it.
3. Receiving unreasonable compensation for managing it.
4. Using it as security for a loan.
5. Buying property for personal use (present or future) with IRA funds.

ROTH IRAs

Regardless of age, an individual may be able to establish and make nondeductible contributions to an individual retirement plan called a Roth IRA. A

Roth IRA is an individual retirement plan that has slightly different rules than those that apply to a traditional IRA. It can be either an account or an annuity.

To be a Roth IRA, the account or annuity must be designated as a Roth IRA when it is set up. Neither a SEP-IRA nor a SIMPLE IRA can be designated as a Roth IRA. Unlike a traditional IRA, contributions to a Roth IRA cannot be deducted. But, per requirements, qualified distributions are tax free. Contributions can be made to a Roth IRA regardless of age and these amounts may be left in a Roth IRA for life.

Contributions and Conversions

The contribution limit for Roth IRAs depends on whether a contribution is made only to Roth IRAs or to both traditional IRAs and Roth IRAs. If a contribution is made only to Roth IRAs, the maximum contribution limit is the lesser of $2,000 or an individual's taxable compensation. Under special circumstances, a contribution limit may be reduced.

It is possible to convert amounts from a traditional, SEP, or SIMPLE IRA into a Roth IRA. It is also possible to recharacterize contributions made to one IRA as having been made directly to a different IRA and to roll amounts over from one Roth IRA to another Roth IRA.

A traditional IRA may be converted to a Roth IRA. The conversion is treated as a rollover, regardless of the conversion method used. Amounts from a traditional IRA may be converted to a Roth IRA in any of the following three ways:

1. Rollover. A distribution from a traditional IRA may be rolled over (contribute it) to a Roth IRA within 60 days after the distribution.
2. Trustee-to-trustee transfer. A trustee of the traditional IRA may transfer an amount from the traditional IRA to the trustee of the Roth IRA.
3. Same trustee transfer. If the trustee of the traditional IRA also maintains the Roth IRA, the trustee can be directed to transfer an amount from the traditional IRA to the Roth IRA. Conversions made with the same trustee can be made by redesignating the traditional IRA as a Roth IRA, rather than opening a new account or issuing a new contract.

Distributions from Roth IRAs.

Qualified distributions or distributions that are a return of regular contributions from Roth IRAs are not included in gross income, nor are distributions from a Roth IRA that is rolled over tax free into another Roth IRA.

This generally includes any payment or distribution from a Roth IRA made after the five-taxable-year period beginning with the first taxable year for which a contribution was made to a Roth IRA if the payment or distribution is:

1. Made on or after the date an individual reaches age 59½.
2. Made because the individual is disabled.
3. Made to a beneficiary or to the estate after an individual's death.
4. Meets the "first home" requirements.

A distribution is not a qualified distribution if it is:

1. Made within the five-year period beginning with the first year for which either a regular or a conversion contribution was made to a Roth IRA set up for the individual's benefit.
2. Made after the five-year period described in (1), but the individual does not meet any of the following requirements.
   a. The individual has not reached age 59½.
   b. The individual is not disabled.
   c. The distribution is not made to a beneficiary or to the individual's estate after his or her death.
   d. The individual does not use the distribution to pay certain qualified first-time home buyer amounts.
3. The withdrawal of contributions and earnings on or before the due date of a return (including extensions) for the year in which the individual made the contributions.

Generally, there is a 10% additional tax on premature distributions of funds from Roth IRAs.

THE SIMPLIFIED EMPLOYEE PENSION (SEP)

A simplified employee pension (SEP) is a written plan that allows a self-employed individual to make contributions toward his or her own retirement or to an employee's retirement without getting involved in a more complex qualified plan.

Under a SEP, the employer makes contributions to a traditional individual retirement arrangement (called a SEP-IRA) set up by or for each eligible employee. SEP-IRAs are owned and controlled by the employee, and the employer makes contributions to the financial institution where the SEP-IRA is maintained.

Employees eligible for the plan must be at least 21 years of age; must have worked for the employer at least three of the last five years, and must have received at least $400 in compensation in the immediate past year.

If an employer desires to reward a hard worker, less restrictive participation requirements than those above may be used—but the employer may not use more restrictive ones for those who work less hard.

Employees who may be excluded from coverage under a SEP include those who are covered by a union agreement and whose retirement benefits were bargained for in good faith by their union and the employer; or employees who are nonresident aliens and received no earned income from sources within the United States.

Setting Up a SEP

There are three basic steps in setting up a SEP.

1. The employer must execute a formal written agreement to provide benefits to all eligible employees.
2. The employer must give each eligible employee the appropriate IRS forms and instructions.
3. A SEP-IRA must be set up by or for each eligible employee with an appropriate bank, insurance company, or other qualified financial institution.

SEP Deadline. SEPs may be set up as late as the due date (including extensions) of the SEP receiver's income tax return for that year. To deduct contributions, the participant must make the contribution by the due date (including extensions) of the tax return for the year.

Contribution Amount

The SEP rules permit contributions of a limited amount of money each year to each employee's SEP-IRA. A self-employed individual may contribute to his own SEP-IRA. Contributions must be in the form of money (cash, check, or money order). Property cannot be contributed to a SEP-IRA. However, participants may be able to transfer or roll over certain property from one retirement plan to another. Contributions do not have to be made every year, but if a contribution is made it must be based on a written allocation formula and must not discriminate in favor of highly compensated employees. Contributions must be made for all participants who actually performed personal services during the year for which the contributions are made—even employees who die or terminate employment before the contributions are made.

Contributions made under a SEP are treated as if made to a qualified pension, stock bonus, profit-sharing, or annuity plan. Consequently, contributions are deductible within limits and generally are not taxable to the plan participants.

A SEP-IRA cannot be designated as a Roth IRA; however, employer contributions to a SEP-IRA do not affect the amount that an individual can contribute to a Roth IRA.

Contribution Limits

Contributions made for a year to a common-law employee's SEP-IRA cannot be more than the smaller of 15% of the employee's compensation or $30,000. A common-law employee is a person who performs services for an employer and the employer has the right to control and direct both the results of the work and the way in which it is done. By this definition, a leased employee can be a common-law employee.

The annual limits on a contribution to a common-law employee's SEP-IRA also apply to contributions an employer makes to his own SEP-IRA. However, special rules apply when figuring the self-employed's maximum deductible contribution.

An employee's compensation that is over $160,000 may not be included when figuring the contribution limit for that employee. Therefore, $24,000 is the maximum contribution amount for an eligible employee whose compensation is $160,000 or more.

If the employee also contributes to a defined contribution plan, annual additions to an account are limited to the lesser of $30,000 or 25 % of the participant's compensation. When figuring this limit, contributions to all defined contribution plans must be added. Because a SEP is considered a defined contribution plan for this limit, the contributions to a SEP must be added to the contributions to other defined contribution plans.

Tax treatment of excess contributions. Excess contributions are contributions to an employee's SEP-IRA (or to a self-employed SEP-IRA) for a year that are more than the lesser of the following amounts.

1. 15% of the employee's compensation (or 13.0435% of net earnings from self-employment).
2. $30,000.

Excess contributions are included in the employee's income for the year.

Deduction Limit for Contributions on Behalf of Employees

The most an employer can deduct for contributions for participants is the lesser of the following amounts.

1. Contributions (including any elective deferrals and excess contributions carryover), or
2. 15% of the compensation (compensation limited to $160,000 per participant) paid by the business to the individual during the year.

Deduction Limit for Self-Employed Individuals

If a self-employed individual contributes to his or her own SEP-IRA, a special computation is needed to figure the maximum deduction allowed. Compensation is considered net earnings and takes into account both of the following deductions.

1. The deduction for one-half of the self-employment tax.
2. The deduction for contributions to the self-employed individual's SEP-IRA.

The deduction for contributions to a self-employed individual's own SEP-IRA and the net earnings depend upon each other.

Deduction Limits for Multiple Plans

For the deduction limits, all qualified defined contribution plans are treated as a single plan and all of the qualified defined benefit plans as a single plan. If an individual has both types of plans, a SEP is treated as a separate profit-sharing plan.

SEP and profit-sharing plans. If an individual also contributes to a qualified profit-sharing plan, the 15 % deduction limit for that profit-sharing plan must be reduced by the allowable deduction for contributions to the SEP-IRAs of those participating in both the SEP plan and the profit-sharing plan.

Carryover of Excess SEP Contributions

If SEP contributions are made in excess of the deduction limit (nondeductible contributions), the excess may be carried over and deducted in later years. However, the excess contributions carryover, when combined with the contribution for the later year, cannot be more than the deduction limit for that year. Nondeductible (excess) contributions to a SEP, may be subject to a 10% excise tax.

When to Deduct Contributions

The time for deducting contributions made for a year depends on the tax year on which the SEP is maintained.

1. If the SEP is maintained on a calendar year, contributions made for a year are deducted on a tax return for the year with or within which the calendar year ends.
2. If a tax return is filed and the SEP is maintained using a fiscal year or short tax year, contributions made for a year are deducted on the tax return for that year.

Distributions

An employer cannot prohibit distributions from a SEP-IRA. Nor can an employer make contributions on the condition that any part of the contribution must be kept in the account.

Additional Taxes

The tax advantages of using SEP-IRAs for retirement savings can be offset by additional taxes. There are additional taxes for all the following actions.

1. Making excess contributions.
2. Making early withdrawals.
3. Not making required withdrawals.
4. Being involved in a prohibited transaction.

An individual's SEP-IRA may be disqualified, or an excise tax may apply, if the account is involved in a prohibited transaction. If an employee improperly uses a SEP-IRA, such as by borrowing money from it, the employee has engaged in a prohibited transaction. In that case, his or her SEP-IRA will no longer qualify as an IRA.

If a SEP-IRA is disqualified because of a prohibited transaction, the assets in the account will be treated as having been distributed to the employee of that SEP-IRA on the first day of the year in which the transaction occurred. The employee must include in income the assets' fair market value (on the first day of the year) that is more than any cost basis in the account. Also, the employee may have to pay the additional tax for making early withdrawals.

SIMPLE PLANS

A Savings Incentive Match Plan for Employees (SIMPLE plan) is a written arrangement that provides the employer and employees with a simplified way to make contributions to provide retirement income. A SIMPLE plan can be set up by an employer who had 100 or fewer employees who earned at least $5,000 in compensation for the preceding calendar year and meets certain other requirements.

Under a SIMPLE plan, employees can choose to make salary reduction contributions to the plan rather than receiving these amounts as part of their regular pay. In addition, the employer will contribute matching or nonelective contributions. SIMPLE plans can only be maintained on a calendar-year basis. A SIMPLE plan can be set up in either of the following ways:

1. Using SIMPLE IRAs (SIMPLE IRA plan).
2. As part of a 401(k) plan (SIMPLE 401(k) plan).

The SIMPLE IRA Plan

A SIMPLE IRA plan is a retirement plan that requires SIMPLE IRAs to be set up for each eligible employee. No other qualified plan may be maintained unless the other plan is for collective bargaining employees.

Employee limit.   A SIMPLE IRA plan may be set up for only 100 or fewer employees who earned $5,000 or more in compensation during the preceding year. Under this rule, all employees must be taken into account, including those employed at any time during the calendar year regardless of whether they are eligible to participate. Employees include leased employees and also self-employed individuals who received earned income. Once a SIMPLE IRA plan is set up, the business must continue to meet the 100-employee limit each year that the plan is maintained.

Other qualified plan.   The SIMPLE IRA plan generally must be the only retirement plan to which contributions are made, or benefits accrue, for service in any year beginning with the year the SIMPLE IRA plan becomes effective. If a qualified plan is maintained for collective bargaining employees, it is permitted to maintain a SIMPLE IRA plan for other employees.

Participation in a SIMPLE IRA

Any employee who received at least $5,000 in compensation during any two years preceding the current calendar year and is reasonably expected to earn at least $5,000 during the current calendar year is eligible to participate. The term "employee" includes a self-employed individual who received earned income. Less restrictive eligibility requirements may be used (but not more restrictive ones) by eliminating or reducing the prior year compensation requirements, the current year compensation requirements, or both. For example, participation for employees who received at least $3,000 in compensation during any preceding calendar year is allowed. However, no additional conditions on participating in a SIMPLE IRA plan may be imposed.

Excludable employees.   The following employees do not need to be covered under a SIMPLE IRA plan.

1. Employees who are covered by a union agreement and whose retirement benefits were bargained for in good faith by their union and their employer.
2. Employees who are nonresident aliens and received no earned income from sources within the United States.

Compensation.   Compensation for employees is the total amount of wages required to be reported on Form W-2, including elective deferrals (deferred amounts elected under any 401(k) plans, 403(b) plans, government (section 457(b)) plans, SEP plans, and SIMPLE IRA plans). If an individual is self-employed, compensation is the net earnings from self-employment before subtracting any contributions made to the SIMPLE IRA plan for the employer.

Notification Requirements

An employee must be given specific information if a SIMPLE IRA plan is adopted. This information includes:

1. The employee's opportunity to make or change a salary reduction choice under a SIMPLE IRA plan.
2. The employer's choice to make either reduced matching contributions or nonelective contributions.
3. A summary description and the location of the plan. The financial institution should provide this information.
4. Written notice that the employee's balance can be transferred without cost or penalty if a designated financial institution is used.

Contributions

Contributions are made up of salary reduction contributions and employer contributions. The employer must make either matching contributions or nonelective contributions. No other contributions can be made to the SIMPLE IRA plan. These deductible contributions must be made timely.

The employee cannot contribute more than the amount set for a particular year. Restrictions cannot be placed on the contribution amount (such as limiting the contribution percentage), except to comply with the dollar limit. If an employee is a participant in any other employer plan during the year and has elective salary reductions or deferred compensation under those plans, the salary reduction contributions under a SIMPLE IRA plan also are an elective deferral that counts toward the overall annual limit on exclusion of salary reductions and other elective deferrals. If the other plan is a deferred compensation plan of a state or local government or a tax-exempt organization, the limit on elective deferrals is also established.

An employer is generally required to match each employee's salary reduction contributions on a dollar-for-dollar basis up to 3% of the employee's compensation. This requirement does not apply if nonelective contributions are made.

Instead of matching contributions, the employer can choose to make nonelective contributions of 2% of compensation on behalf of each eligible employee who has at least $5,000 of compensation for the year. Only a certain amount of the employee's compensation can be taken into account to figure the contribution limit. If the employer chooses this 2% contribution formula, the employees must be notified within a reasonable period of time.

When to Deduct Contributions

Contributions may be deducted for a particular tax year if they are made for that tax year and are made by the due date (including extensions) of the federal income tax return for that year.

Tax Treatment of Contributions

The employer can deduct contributions, and the employees can exclude these contributions from their gross income. SIMPLE IRA contributions are not subject to federal income tax withholding. However, salary reduction contributions are subject to social security, Medicare, and federal unemployment (FUTA) taxes. Matching and nonelective contributions are not subject to these taxes.

Distributions

Distributions from a SIMPLE IRA are subject to IRA rules and generally are includable in income for the year received. Tax-free rollovers can be made from one SIMPLE IRA into another SIMPLE IRA. A rollover from a SIMPLE IRA to another IRA can be made tax free only after a two-year participation in the SIMPLE IRA plan.

Early withdrawals generally are subject to a 10 % additional tax. However, the additional tax is increased to 25 % if funds are withdrawn within two years of beginning participation.

The SIMPLE 401(k) Plan

A SIMPLE plan may be adopted as part of a 401(k) plan if the 100-employee limit is met. A SIMPLE 401(k) plan generally must satisfy the rules that apply to a 401(k) plan. However, contributions and benefits under a SIMPLE 401(k) plan will be considered not to discriminate in favor of highly compensated employees provided the plan meets the conditions listed below.

1. Under the plan, an employee can choose to have salary reduction contributions made for the year to a trust in an amount expressed as a percentage of the employee's compensation, but not more than $6,000 for 1999.
2. The employer must make either matching contributions up to 3% of compensation for the year, or nonelective contributions of 2% of compensation on behalf of each eligible employee who has at least $5,000 of compensation for the year.
3. No other contributions can be made to the trust.
4. No contributions are made, and no benefits accrue, for services during the year under any other qualified retirement plan of the employer on behalf of any employee eligible to participate in the SIMPLE 401(k) plan.
5. The employee's rights to any contributions are nonforfeitable.

No more than $160,000 of the employee's compensation can be taken into account in figuring salary reduction contributions, matching contributions, and nonelective contributions. The notification rules that apply to SIMPLE IRA plans also apply to SIMPLE 401(k) plans.

QUALIFIED PLANS (KEOGH PLANS)

A qualified employer plan set up by a self-employed individual is sometimes called a Keogh or HR-10 plan. A sole proprietor or a partnership can set up a qualified plan. A common-law employee or a partner cannot set up a qualified plan. The plans described here can also be set up and maintained by employers that are corporations. All the rules discussed here apply to corporations except where specifically limited to the self-employed. The plan must be for the exclusive benefit of employees or their beneficiaries. A qualified plan can include coverage for a self-employed individual.

A self-employed individual is treated as both an employer and an employee. As an employer, if is possible to deduct contributions made to a qualified plan, including those made for the employer's own retirement. The contributions (plus earnings and gains on them) are generally tax free until distributed by the plan.

The qualified plan rules are more complex than the SEP and SIMPLE plan rules. However, there are some advantages available to qualified plans, such as the special tax treatment that may apply to qualified plan lump-sum distributions.

Kinds of Plans

There are two basic kinds of qualified plans—defined contribution plans and defined benefit plans—and different rules apply to each. It is possible to have more than one qualified plan, but contributions to all the plans must not total more than the overall limits.

Defined Contribution Plan

A defined contribution plan provides an individual account for each participant in the plan. It provides benefits to a participant largely based on the amount contributed to that participant's account. Benefits are also affected by any income, expenses, gains, losses, and forfeitures of other accounts that may be allocated to an account. A defined contribution plan can be either a profit-sharing plan or a money purchase pension plan.

A profit-sharing plan is a plan for sharing business profits with employees. However, contributions do not have to be made out of net profits to have a profit-sharing plan. The plan does not need to provide a definite formula for figuring the profits to be shared. But, if there is no formula, there must be systematic and substantial contributions. The plan must provide a definite formula for allocating the contribution among the participants and for distributing the accumulated funds to the employees after they reach a certain age, after a fixed number of years, or upon certain other occurrences.

Forfeitures under a profit-sharing plan can be allocated to the accounts of remaining participants in a nondiscriminatory way or they can be used to reduce contributions.

Contributions to a money purchase pension plan are fixed and are not based on business profits. If a plan requires that contributions be 10% of the participants' compensation without regard to company profits (or the self-employed person's earned income), the plan is a money purchase pension plan. This applies even though the compensation of a self-employed individual as a participant is based on earned income derived from business profits.

Defined Benefit Plan

A defined benefit plan is any plan that is not a defined contribution plan. Contributions to a defined benefit plan are based on what is needed to provide definitely determinable benefits to plan participants. Actuarial assumptions and computations are required to figure these contributions. Generally, professional help is required to have a defined benefit plan. Forfeitures under a defined benefit plan cannot be used to increase the benefits any employee would otherwise receive under the plan. Forfeitures must be used instead to reduce employer contributions.

Setting Up a Qualified Plan

There are two basic steps in setting up a qualified plan: First, a written plan must be adopted; then, the plan assets must be invested. The employer is responsible for setting up and maintaining the plan. A self-employed individual is not required to have other employees to sponsor and set up a qualified plan.

To take a deduction for contributions for a tax year, a plan must be set up (adopted) by the last day of that year (December 31 for calendar-year employers).

To qualify a plan, it must be in writing and must be communicated to all employees.

The following organizations generally can provide IRS-approved master or prototype plans:

1. Banks (including some savings and loan associations and federally insured credit unions).
2. Trade or professional organizations.
3. Insurance companies.
4. Mutual funds.

Investing Plan Assets

There are several ways to establish how the plan's funds will be used to build its assets:

1. Establish a trust or custodial account to invest the funds.
2. Buy an annuity contract from an insurance company. Life insurance can be included only if it is incidental to the retirement benefits.
3. Buy face-amount certificates from an insurance company. These certificates are treated like annuity contracts.

A trust is set up professionally by a legal document. A custodial account may be established with a bank, savings and loan association, credit union, or other person who can act as the plan trustee.

A trust or custodial account is not needed to invest the plan's funds in annuity contracts or face-amount certificates. If anyone other than a trustee holds them, however, the contracts or certificates must state that they are not transferable.

Eligible Employees

An employee must be allowed to participate in the plan if he or she has:

1. Reached age 21.
2. At least one year of service (two years if the plan is not a 401(k) plan and provides that, after not more than two years of service, the employee has a nonforfeitable right to all of his or her accrued benefit).

Minimum Funding Requirements

In general, if a plan is a money purchase pension plan or a defined benefit plan, sufficient funds must be paid into the plan to satisfy the minimum funding standard for each year. Determining the amount needed to satisfy the minimum funding standard is complicated. The amount is based on what should be contributed under the plan formula using actuarial assumptions and formulas.

A defined benefit plan is subject to the minimum funding requirements; quarterly installment payments must be made of the required contributions. If the full installments are not timely, interest payments may have to be made on any underpayment for the period of the underpayment.

The due dates for the installments are 15 days after the end of each quarter. For a calendar-year plan, the installments are due on April 15, July 15, October 15, and January 15 (of the following year).

Each quarterly installment must be 25% of the required annual payment.

Additional contributions required to satisfy the minimum funding requirement for a plan year will be considered timely if made by 8½ months after the end of that year.

Contributions

A qualified plan is generally funded by an employer's contributions. However, employees participating in the plan may be permitted to make contributions.

Deductible contributions may be made for a tax year up to the date that returns are due (plus extensions) for that year.

A self-employed individual can make contributions on behalf of himself only if he has net earnings (compensation) from self-employment in the trade or business for which the plan was set up. The net earnings must be from personal services, not from investments. If there is a net loss from self-employment, contributions may not be made for the year, even if the employer can contribute for common-law employees based on their compensation.

When Contributions Are Considered Made

Plan contributions are generally applied to the year in which they are made. They can be applied to the previous year if all the following requirements are met.

1. The contributions are made by the due date of the individual's tax return for the previous year (plus extensions).
2. The plan was established by the end of the previous year.
3. The plan treats the contributions as though it had received them on the last day of the previous year.
4. It is specified in writing to the plan administrator or trustee that the contributions apply to the previous year; or the contributions are deducted on the individual's tax return for the previous year.

Employer Contributions

There are certain limits on the contributions and other annual additions allowed each year for plan participants. There are also limits on the amount the employer can deduct. The limits differ depending on whether the plan is a defined contribution plan or a defined benefit plan.

Defined benefit plan.   The annual benefit for a participant under a defined benefit plan could not be more than the lesser of the following amounts:

1. The dollar limit set for that year.
2. 100% of the participant's average compensation for his or her highest three consecutive calendar years.

Defined contribution plan.   A defined contribution plan's annual contributions and other additions (excluding earnings) to the account of a participant could not be more than the lesser of the following amounts:

1. The dollar limit set for the year.
2. 25% of the compensation actually paid to the participant.

The maximum compensation that can be taken into account for this limit is also established and changes periodically.

Excess annual additions. Excess annual additions are the amounts contributed that are more than the limits discussed previously. A plan can correct excess annual additions caused by any of the following actions:

1. A reasonable error in estimating a participant's compensation.
2. A reasonable error in determining the amount of elective deferrals permitted.
3. Forfeitures allocated to participants' accounts.

Employee Contributions

Participants may be permitted to make nondeductible contributions to a plan in addition to the employer's contributions. Even though these employee contributions are not deductible, the earnings on them are tax free until distributed in later years.

Employer Deduction

The employer can usually deduct, subject to limits, contributions made to a qualified plan, including those made for the employer's own retirement. The contributions (and earnings and gains on them) are generally tax free until distributed by the plan.

The deduction limit for the contributions to a qualified plan depends on the kind of plan. The deduction limit for a defined contribution plan depends on whether it is a profit-sharing plan or a money purchase pension plan.

An employer's deductions for contributions to a profit-sharing plan cannot be more than 15% of the compensation paid (or accrued) during the year to the eligible employees participating in the plan.

An employer's deduction for contributions to a money purchase pension plan is generally limited to 25% of the compensation paid (or accrued) during the year to the eligible employees.

The deduction for contributions to a defined benefit plan is based on actuarial assumptions and computations. Consequently, an actuary must figure the deduction limit.

If an employer contributes to both a defined contribution plan and a defined benefit plan and at least one employee is covered by both plans, the employer's deduction for those contributions is limited. The deduction cannot be more than the greater of the following amounts.

1. 25% of the compensation paid (or accrued) during the year to the eligible employees participating in the plan. The employer must reduce this 25% limit in figuring the deduction for contributions made to the employer's account.
2. The employer's contributions to the defined benefit plans, but not more than the amount needed to meet the year's minimum funding standard for any of these plans.

ELECTIVE DEFERRALS (401(K) PLANS)

A qualified plan can include a cash or deferred arrangement (401(k) plan) under which participants can choose to have the employer contribute part of their before-tax compensation to the plan rather than receive the compensation in cash. (As a participant in the plan, the employer can contribute part of the before-tax net earnings from the business.) This contribution and any earnings on it remain tax free until distributed by the plan. A partnership also may have a 401(k) plan.

In general, a qualified plan can include a 401(k) plan only if the qualified plan is a profit-sharing plan or a money purchase pension plan in existence on June 27, 1974, that included a salary reduction arrangement on that date.

There are certain other limitations that apply to setting up a 401(k) plan:

1. The plan may not require, as a condition of participation, that an employee complete more than one year of service.
2. If permitted by the plan, an employer can make matching contributions for an employee who makes an elective deferral to the 401(k) plan.
3. Under a qualified 401(k) plan it is possible to make contributions (other than matching contributions) for the participating employees without giving them the choice to take cash instead.
4. No more than a periodically established dollar amount of the employee's compensation can be taken into account when figuring contributions.

Limit on Elective Deferrals

The plan must provide that the employees cannot defer more than the limit that applies for a particular year. This limit applies without regard to community property laws. This limit is subject to annual increases to reflect inflation (as measured by the Consumer Price Index). If, in conjunction with other plans, the deferral limit is exceeded, the excess is included in the employee's gross income.

Matching contributions to a 401(k) plan on behalf of a self-employed individual are not subject to the limit on elective deferrals. These matching contributions receive the same treatment as the matching contributions for other employees.

The contributions to a 401(k) plan are generally deductible by the employer and tax free to participating employees until distributed. Participating employees have a nonforfeitable right to the accrued benefit resulting from these contributions. Deferrals are included in wages for social security, Medicare, and federal unemployment (FUTA) tax.

Treatment of Excess Deferrals

If the total of an employee's deferrals is more than the limit for the year, the employee can have the difference (called an excess deferral) paid out of any of the plans that permit these distributions. The employee must notify the plan by March 1 of the amount to be paid from each plan. The plan must then pay the employee that amount by April 15.

If the employee takes out the excess deferral by April 15, it is not reported again by including it in the employee's gross income for the year. However, any income earned on the excess deferral taken out is taxable in the tax year in which it is taken out. The distribution is not subject to the additional 10% tax on early distributions.

If the employee takes out part of the excess deferral and the income on it, the distribution is treated as made proportionately from the excess deferral and the income.

Distributions

Distributions from a qualified plan may be nonperiodic, such as lump-sum distributions, or periodic, such as annuity payments. Also, certain loans may be treated as distributions.

A qualified plan must provide that each participant will either:

1. Receive his or her entire interest (benefits) in the plan by the required beginning date (defined later), or
2. Begin receiving regular periodic distributions by the required beginning date in annual amounts calculated to distribute the participant's entire interest (benefits) over his or her life expectancy or over the joint life expectancy of the participant and the designated beneficiary.

These distribution rules apply individually to each qualified plan. The requirement for one plan cannot be satisfied by taking a distribution from another. These rules may be incorporated in the plan by reference. The plan must provide that these rules override any inconsistent distribution options previously offered.

If the account balance of a qualified plan participant is to be distributed (other than as an annuity), the plan administrator must figure the minimum amount required to be distributed each distribution calendar year. This amount is figured by dividing the account balance by the applicable life expectancy.

Minimum distributions must also meet the minimum distribution incidental benefit requirement. This requirement ensures that the plan is used primarily to provide retirement benefits to the employee. After the employee's death, only "incidental" benefits are expected to remain for distribution to the employee's beneficiary (or beneficiaries).

Distributions from 401(k) Plans

Generally, a distribution may not be made until one of the following occurs.

1. The employee retires, dies, becomes disabled, or otherwise separates from service.
2. The plan ends and no other defined contribution plan is established or continued.
3. In the case of a 401(k) plan that is part of a profit-sharing plan, when the employee reaches age 59 1/2 or suffers financial hardship.

Some of the above distributions may be subject to the tax on early distributions discussed later.

Tax Treatment of Distributions

Distributions from a qualified plan minus a prorated part of any cost basis are subject to income tax in the year they are distributed. Since most recipients have no cost basis, a distribution is generally fully taxable. An exception is a distribution that is properly rolled over. The recipient of an eligible rollover distribution from a qualified plan can defer the tax on it by rolling it over into an IRA or another eligible retirement plan. However, it may be subject to withholding. The tax treatment of distributions depends on whether they are made periodically over several years or life.

Eligible rollover distribution.   This is a distribution of all (such as a lump-sum distribution) or any part of an employee's balance in a qualified retirement plan that is not any of the following:

1. A required minimum distribution.
2. An annual (or more frequent) payment under a long-term (10 years or more) annuity contract or as part of a similar long-term series of substantially equal periodic distributions.
3. A hardship distribution.
4. The portion of a distribution that represents the return of an employee's nondeductible contributions to the plan.
5. A corrective distribution of excess contributions or deferrals under a 401(k) plan and any income allocable to the excess, or of excess annual additions and any allocable gains.

Hardship distributions from a 401(k) plan that occur after 1998 cannot be rolled over into an IRA or other eligible retirement plan. They are subject to the 10% additional tax on early distributions. However, they are not subject to the 20% withholding tax that generally applies to eligible rollover distributions that are not transferred directly to another retirement plan or IRA.

Withholding requirements.   If, during a year, a qualified plan pays to a participant one or more eligible rollover distributions that are reasonably expected to total $200 or more, the payor must withhold 20% of each distribution for federal income tax.

If, instead of having the distribution paid to him or her, the participant chooses to have the plan pay it directly to an IRA or another eligible retirement plan, no withholding is required.

If the distribution is not an eligible rollover distribution, the 20% withholding requirement does not apply. Other withholding rules apply to distributions such as long-term periodic distributions and required distributions (periodic or nonperiodic).

However, the participant can still choose not to have tax withheld from these distributions. If the participant does not make this choice, the following withholding rules apply.

1. For periodic distributions, withholding is based on their treatment as wages.
2. For nonperiodic distributions, 10% of the taxable part is withheld.

If no income tax is withheld or not enough tax is withheld, the recipient of a distribution may have to make estimated tax payments.

FASB STANDARDS RELATING TO EMPLOYEE BENEFITS

There are five current Standards applying to various facets of employee benefits—FASB 87, 88, 106, 112, and 132. See the discussion that follows.

FASB STATEMENT 87, EMPLOYERS' ACCOUNTING FOR PENSION PLANS

1. Companies using other than the prescribed plan-based benefit approach to attributing pension costs of periods were faced with a method change with potential significant effect on amounts recognized in the income statement.

2. Each significant assumption affecting the pension computation requires the best estimate of that factor alone. Under this explicit approach, the use of assumptions known to be inaccurate but with offsetting effect became unacceptable. Major assumptions that must be developed and continuously updated for significant changes include the discount rate (the current rate at which benefits could be effectively settled) used to measure pension obligations and portions of periodic pension cost; the expected long-term rate of return on plan assets necessary for the gain or loss calculation; and where determined by the plan's benefit formula, assumed future compensation levels.

3. Provided the accounting policy adopted is followed consistently, Statement 87 allows a number of choices. The market-related value of plan assets, a factor in the gain or loss computation, may be either fair market value or a calculated value that recognizes changes in fair value of plan assets over not more than five years; different methods of calculating market-related value can be used for different classes of plan assets. Prior service costs may be amortized by the declining method prescribed for general use or by an alternative that reduces any unrecognized balance more rapidly. Subject to specified conditions, unrecognized net gains or losses may be amortized by any systematic method. The measurement date for requirements can be the date of the financial statements, or a date not more than three months earlier.

4. Calendar-year companies are required to report any minimum unfunded pension liabilities, offset by intangible assets and/or reductions in shareholders' equity in their balance sheets.

5. The income statement effects of adopting Statement 87, which may include recording pension income instead of pension costs, may have unanticipated effects on bonus, profit-sharing, incentive, and similar plans. These effects should be estimated promptly and decisions made on whether the plans should be amended.

6. The rules for foreign plans are the same as the rules for domestic plans.

7. Compliance with rules for determining the tax deductibility of pension costs might require data for IRS different from that needed for reporting under Statement 87. Supplemental actuarial valuations may be needed for tax purposes.

Of the several types of pension plans covered by these rules, the most significant impact of the Standard is on single-employer defined benefit plans. (A single-employer plan is maintained by one employer. The term is also used to describe a plan that is maintained by related parties such as a parent and its subsidiaries.)

The main requirements of single-employer plans follow:

1. For calendar-year companies, balance sheet recognition of a minimum pension liability must be recognized. The "unfunded accumulated benefit obligation" equals the excess of the present value of benefits earned to date, calculated without reference to future compensation levels over the fair value of plan assets. Recording the minimum liability generates an intangible asset to the extent of unrecognized prior service cost; any excess is recorded as a reduction of equity.

2. Development of a standardized method for attributing pension cost to service periods. In requiring that the attribution method be based on the plan's benefit formula, the use of a "benefit" instead of a "cost" approach to determining periodic cost must be applied.

3. Recognition of future compensation levels in calculating the unrecognized net asset or obligation at the transition date, in determining net period cost and in disclosing the "projected benefit obligation" but not in calculating a minimum liability displayed in the balance sheet.

4. Linkage of current and delayed cost recognition to employee service periods. A liability must be recognized if net pension costs *exceeds* employer contribution. An additional minimum liability is recognized as an intangible asset. In limited circumstances, cost allocation is determined instead by the remaining life expectancy of inactive plan participants.

5. Prospective recognition of prior service cost and of the unrecognized net obligation or net asset determined at the transition date.

6. Delayed recognition of gains and losses. Those from all sources are aggregated and amortized by any systematic method consistently applied, subject to a floor set by the Standard's "corridor" approach. In an attempt to reduce volatility, the Board compounded the Standard's complexity by basing the gain or loss computation on the expected return on plan assets. That factor is determined by applying the expected long-term rate of return on plan assets to the market-related value of

plan assets, which are defined as either fair value or a calculated value that spreads change in fair value over not more than five years.

7. Separate calculation of numerous components of net periodic pension cost and separate disclosure of four items: service cost, interest cost, actual return on plan assets, and the net total of all other components.

8. Pension expense is reflected on the accrual basis.

9. Actuarial gains and losses applicable to a single event not related to the pension plan and not in the ordinary course of business are recognized immediately in earnings. (Examples are plant closing; segment disposal.)

FASB Statement 88, Employer's Accounting for Settlements and Curtailments of Defined Benefit Pension Plans and for Termination Benefits

The reason for this separate Statement to be applied simultaneously with Statement 87 was the FASB's decision that a separate Statement on employer's accounting for a settlement of a pension obligation, or a curtailment of a defined benefit pension plan, or a termination of benefits, would provide a better understanding of the accounting procedures than to include them in the scope of Statement 87. This Statement applies to an employer that sponsors a defined benefit pension plan accounted for under the provisions of Statement 87 if all or part of the plan's pension benefit obligation is settled or the plan is curtailed. It also applies to an employer that offers benefits to employees in connection with their termination of employment.

The significant requirements of this Statement follow:

1. Statement 88 requires that recognized balances of prior service costs and net gains and losses computed under Statement 87's delayed recognition model be considered to the extent specified in determining the effect on the income statement of a settlement or curtailment meeting the Standard's criteria.

2. Restatement of previously issued financial statements was prohibited, except for one provision that had a retroactive effect; e.g., at the time of transition to Statement 87 companies having deferred gains resulting from previous asset reversions were required, subject to limitations, to recognize them as income.

3. A settlement and/or a curtailment may occur separately or together.

4. The maximum gain or loss subject to recognition in earnings when a pension obligation is settled is the unrecognized net gain or loss plus any remaining unrecognized net asset existing at the date of initial application of Statement 87.

5. The projected benefit obligation may be decreased (a gain) or increased (a loss) by a curtailment. To the extent that a gain exceeds any unrecognized net loss, it is a curtailment gain. To the extent that a loss exceeds any unrecognized net gain, it is a curtailment loss.

6. An employer can provide benefits to employees in connection with their termination of employment. The benefits can be either *special termination benefits* offered only for a short period of time, or *contractual termination benefits* required by the terms of a plan only if a specified event (a plant closing, for example) occurs. The employer that gives special termination benefits must recognize a liability and a loss when the employees accept the plan and the amount can be reasonably estimated. Termination benefits can take various forms including lump-sum payments, periodic future payments, a combination of both, paid directly from the employer's assets, from an existing pension plan, or from a new employee benefit plan.

7. The Statement sets forth the events that required previously unrecognized amounts to be recognized in earnings and as adjustments to assets and liabilities. The previously unrecognized net gain or net loss and the previously unrecognized prior service cost should be recognized in the period when *all* of the following conditions are met:

    a. All pension obligations are settled.

    b. Defined benefits are no longer accrued under the plan.

    c. The plan is not replaced by another defined benefit plan.

    d. No plan assets remain.

    e. The employees are terminated.

    f. The plan ceases to exist as an entity.

FASB Statement 106, Employers' Accounting for Postretirement Benefits Other Than Pensions

FASB Statement 106 applies to all postretirement benefits other than pensions, sometimes referred to as OPEBs (other postretirement employee benefits), provided by employers to employees. The requirements of Statement 106 are similar in most respects to those in Statements 87 and 88. The product of nearly 11 years' work, Statement 106 requires large public companies to begin taking charges for the cash they expect to pay out in the future for medical and other nonpension benefits promised to retired employees and their families.

Previously, companies were given the option of using accrual accounting similar to that required under Standards 87 and 88 for the postretirement benefit plans. However, since so few employers availed themselves of the opportunity voluntarily, many were stunned by the arrival of 1993 and the concomitant necessity of facing up to the requirements of Statement 106. Private companies with fewer than 500 participants in a plan and non-U.S. plans had to be in compliance in 1995.

Until Statement 106, these costs had been recognized as expenses as they were paid each year. However, companies must now expense the costs associated with the benefits as they are earned by employees. In shifting from a pay-as-you-go cash basis to accrual accounting, companies must acknowledge a huge "catchup" liability: the total present value of future commitments already made to present retirees and employees.

Decisions about transition obligations relating to those benefits deemed earned at the time FASB 106 was adopted, but not yet expensed under cash-basis accounting, have now been weighed and considered. Subject to certain limitations, when a company converts to the accrual method, the transition obligation can be recognized immediately through a onetime charge to income. The other choice is to extend the transition obligations over succeeding years, using a straight-line method applied to the average remaining service period of active participants, or 20 years, whichever time is longer.

Regardless of which alternative has been selected, most companies have unquestionably had little awareness of the enormity of the obligations they were building up. If there were no other positive aspects, at last management has been forced to come face to face with the reality that lay ahead, particularly in relation to health care costs. However, other areas of benefits can also add substantial obligations: life insurance outside a pension plan, tuition assistance, day care, legal assistance, and housing subsidies, among other benefits.

The Statement covers both defined benefit and defined contribution-type plans. Underlying the new Statement is the assumption that postretirement benefits are a form of deferred compensation that should be recorded using the accrual method as a cost during the employee's active work life when the employer actually receives the benefits of the employee's services. The accrual of the cost under this method begins when an employee is hired, and continues until the employee becomes eligible for the full benefits under the terms of the particular plan.

In the case of defined contribution postretirement plans, the Rule requires that the postretirement cost be the annual contribution during the employee's active service period. If funding is delayed to retirement, the future estimated cost must be accrued over the employee's service life.

The estimate of the present value of an employer's postretirement benefit obligation is the principal determinant of postretirement benefit costs. An employer's postretirement obligation is the actuarial present value, as of a specific date, of the postretirement benefits expected to be provided by the employer in the future, that are attributable to current and retired employees.

Companies who must now separate the cost of retiree benefits from those of active workers could formerly combine them. To estimate future obligations in addition to current costs, company estimates will be required that could easily be far off the mark. The forward-looking estimates will necessitate a number of subjective considerations, including the projected cost of medical benefits. During the last decade, the number of retirees and the average life expectancy have increased appreciably, while the cost of health care has grown much faster than other sectors of the economy.

To add to the problem, a reduction of federal and state Medicare and Medicaid benefits has resulted in private companies having to absorb the increase in medical costs and has forced health care reimbursement plans to cover a larger share of these costs. As a result, earnings pressures may cause companies to consider reducing or canceling health care benefits, perhaps to the detriment of the company.

When taking into account years of benefit coverage, an important element in computing possible payouts, an estimate must include the number of retirees and dependents eligible for benefits, multiplied by the number of years each will be covered. These projections require using data on current employees and retirees, including age, gender, and number of dependents, as well as actuarial assumptions for retirement age, employee turnover, and life expectancy. As is readily apparent, these variables are subject to wide margins of error, but they are not the only element for errors in projections.

Another difficult determinant of plan payouts is the number of times each of the medical services covered under existing plans may be used by the retirees and their dependents and the net cost to the company. This can be projected by estimating plan variables, such as the deductible factor, level of participant contributions, number and length of hospital stays, and frequency of doctor visits by a similar sector of the population. Among important factors is the price paid by participants, net of relevant reimbursements such as Medicare. These costs must be estimated using actuarial projections of medical cost increases.

If a company changes its benefits and updates its assumptions, there will be an immediate effect on the annual service costs of employers' OPEB by producing actuarial gains and losses. Similar to pensions, a practice can be adopted that will either recognize or defer the changes. If deferral is used, amortization of the deferral is required only when the cumulative amount exceeds a prescribed minimum. The main effect of deferrals is to help eliminate volatility due to the need to use assumptions.

The major tax impact will arise from federal income taxes, although other taxes may also be affected for certain funding approaches. The deductions are governed by the tax code: "There shall be allowed as a deduction all the ordinary and necessary expenses paid or incurred during the taxable year in carrying on any trade or business, including a reasonable allowance for salaries or *other compensation* for personal services actually rendered." When postretirement benefits meet these requirements, they can be deducted when paid, as the tax code requires companies to use the pay-as-you-go method to compute their tax deduction for benefit payments. Federal tax deductions for OPEB are generally allowed only at the time the benefits are paid. Under limited conditions, deductions can be allowed when the obligation is prefunded.

Those who in the past have offered generous postretirement benefits and who have high ratios of retirees to active employees were probably already beginning to feel profit pressures even under cash-basis accounting. New, rapidly growing companies having low turnover, young workers, and few retirees may begin to feel the pressures under this rule.

However, Statement 106 does allow management, under certain circumstances, to assume it will be able to modify the company's current postretirement benefit plan to provide fewer future benefits, which will lower current obligations. Since plans with ceilings on benefits are usually less costly than plans without benefit limitations, a shift from unlimited to limited benefits appears to be one option a company faced with mounting benefits costs will consider. Such changes in the plan provisions to anticipate changes in the computation of the obligations and costs are permissible as long as the changes have been communicated to plan participants.

FASB Statement 112, *Employers' Accounting for Postemployment Benefits*

For fiscal years beginning after December 15, 1993, Statement 112 set standards for the financial accounting and reporting of the estimated costs incurred by employers who provide benefits to former or inactive employees after employment but before retirement. These postemployment benefits are of various types provided to former or inactive employees, their beneficiaries, and covered dependents.

Inactive employees are those who at a given time are not actively participating in company business or actually rendering service to the employer, but they have not been terminated. This group may consist of employees who have been laid off and those on disability leave, even though they may not be expected to return to active status. The benefits may include, but are not limited to, salary continuation, supplemental unemployment benefits, severance benefits, disability benefits including workers' compensation, job training and/or counseling, and continuation of benefits like health care and life insurance coverage.

These benefits can be provided in cash or in kind, and they can be paid as a result of death, or other event, as well as from temporary or permanent disability or layoff. They can be paid immediately upon cessation of active employment or over a specified period of time. Employees' rights to benefits may accumulate or vest as they render service.

The Statement should be considered an outgrowth, or more properly a continuation, of FASB work in developing Statement 106. While that project was underway, the members specifically declined to give consideration to the employers' accounting requirements for postemployment benefits other than pensions. They agreed to delay this specific aspect of the project and to deal with it as a separate phase. Thus, with the adoption of Statement 112, the Board's consideration of employers' accounting for pensions and all other postemployment benefits appears to be completed.

FASB 112 amends, but does not significantly alter, FASB Statement 5, *Accounting for Contingencies* and FASB Statement 43, *Accounting for Compensated Absences*. It affirms the view that generally accepted accounting principles require recognition of the cost of postemployment benefits on an accrual basis and amends the above mentioned Statements to include the accounting for these postemployment benefits.

It is necessary for employers to recognize the obligation to provide postemployment benefits in accordance with FASB Statement 43 if:

1. the obligation is attributable to employees' services already rendered
2. employees have the right to let those benefits accumulate or vest
3. payment of the benefits is probable
4. the amount of the benefits can be reasonably estimated.

If these four conditions are not met, the employer should account for postemployment benefits when it is probable that a liability has been incurred and the amount can be reasonably estimated in accordance with FASB 5, *Accounting for Contingencies*. When an obligation for postemployment benefits has not been accrued in accordance with either of these FASB Statements because the company's management feels that the amount of the obligation cannot be reasonably estimated, the reasoning behind the inability to arrive at an estimate must be disclosed in the financial statement.

The accounting for postemployment benefits provided through a pension or postretirement benefit plan, as set forth in Statements 87, 88 and 106 are not affected by Statement 112.

FASB Statement 132, *Employers' Disclosures About Pensions and Other Postretirement Benefits*

This new standard revises and improves the effectiveness of current note disclosure requirements for employers' pensions and other postretirement employee benefits (OPEBs), but does not alter the retiree benefit accounting rules. It does not deal with recognition or measurement issues, but provides additional information to facilitate financial analysis and eliminates some disclosures that are no longer useful.

Although FASB 132 reduces the disclosure burden on benefits, there is still much to be disclosed. Among the requirements are the following:

1. Retirement benefits must be accounted for on an accrual basis. Differences between net periodic retirement benefit costs and the amount funded and charged against income should be accounted for as a prepaid cost or accrued cost.
2. Reasonable estimates should be used.
3. All employees should be covered by a plan, not just certain employees.
4. When an employer contracts to pay benefits, he or she must record a liability.
5. Assumptions have to be made for accrual amounts for the forecasted rate of return time value of money expected on plan assets and future compensation levels.
6. The employer must accounting for a plan curtailment that significantly changes the accrual amounts.
7. A gain or loss in a curtailment results in the employer recognizing as a loss the appropriate remaining balance amount of unrecognized prior service cost.
8. A curtailment loss that results from terminating the accrual of additional benefits for future service will include the pro rata amount of unrecognized prior service costs in addition to a pro rata amount of any remaining unrecognized transition obligations.
9. Unrecognized amounts of prior service are recognized as a loss.
10. A loss is part of an unrecognized prior service cost that still remains.
11. The final statement date is the measurement date for plan assets.
12. Unrecognized gain or loss should be recognized in income when a postretirement obligation is settled.
13. When the effect of a net loss is estimated, the loss is recognized in income.
14. When all of an obligation is settled, any gain reduces any unrecognized transition. Any excess (if any) is included in income. All of a loss is taken into income.
15. When the effect of a net loss is estimated, the loss is recognized in income.
16. A loss that results from the termination of an accrual of additional benefits for future service consists of the pro rata amount transition of the remaining unrecognized prior service costs, in addition to the unrecognized amount of transition obligations.

17. When all of an obligation is settled, any gain reduces any unrecognized transactions. Any excess (if remaining) is included in income. All of a loss is taken into income.

18. Insurance contracts are not allowed that cover accumulated postretirement benefits.

Chapter 24
Higher Education Incentives

There are many new tax benefits for those saving for or paying higher education costs for themselves and members of their families or who are repaying student loans. Most of these benefits first became available in 1998 as a result of measures included in The Taxpayer Relief Act of 1997. The new benefits include tax credits, individual retirement account options, and a deduction for student loan interest.

IMPORTANT CONSIDERATIONS

Consideration was given in formulation of these incentives to providing coverage for assorted levels of higher education, to covering different types of costs in different plans, and to designating staggered income limits for different plans. Thus, as a result of the last element, the assortment of benefits provides step-ups to various limits rather than a blank wall which could effectively penalize the taxpayer for earning a few extra dollars. With such a varied assortment, there should be something for everyone. On the other hand, it may well take a knowledgeable accountant/adviser/tax preparer to guide the taxpayer, if he or she expects to take full advantage of the several provisions.

It would be premature to attempt to evaluate any "benefit" that may have resulted from the expanded list of tax incentives intended to raise the educational level in the U.S., but there can be no question that Congress and the Administration are trying their best to foster a better educated citizenry.

The discussion of tax benefits for persons who are saving for or paying higher education costs for themselves and members of their families includes the following:

1. Two education credits—the Hope credit and the lifetime learning credit.
2. Education individual retirement accounts (education IRAs).
3. Withdrawals from traditional or Roth IRAs.
4. Interest paid on certain student loans.
5. The cancellation of certain student loans.
6. Qualified state tuition programs (QSTP).
7. Interest earned on certain savings bonds.
8. Employer-provided educational assistance benefits.

Two of the available tax credits that have received the most publicity (along with the education IRA) are the Hope credit and the lifetime learning credit. They have many features in common, but they also differ in a number of respects. Therefore, it is important, particularly if both appear to cover a particular individual, to figure which provides more benefit.

APPLICABLE TO BOTH HOPE AND LIFETIME LEARNING CREDITS

The amount of each credit is determined by:

1. The amount paid for qualified tuition and related expenses for students.
2. The amount of the individual's modified adjusted gross income.

These education credits are subtracted from the individual's tax but they are nonrefundable. This means if the credits are more than the tax, the excess is not refunded. (Married taxpayers filing separate returns cannot claim the higher education credits.)

Qualified Expenses

The tax credits are based on qualified tuition and related expenses the taxpayer pays for himself or herself, a spouse, or a dependent claimed on the tax return. In general, qualified tuition and related expenses are tuition and fees required for enrollment or attendance at an eligible educational institution. Fees for course-related books, supplies and equipment, and student activity fees are included in qualified tuition and related expenses *only if the fees must be paid to the institution* as a condition of enrollment or attendance.

Qualified tuition and related expenses *do not include* the cost of insurance, medical expenses (including student health fees), room and board, transportation or similar personal, living or family expenses, even if the fee must be paid to the institution as a condition of enrollment or attendance.

Prepaid Expenses

When qualified tuition and related expenses for an academic period that begins in the first three months of the following year are prepaid, the taxpayer can use the prepaid amount in figuring the credit.

The Dependent

A dependent is a person for whom a dependency exemption is claimed. This generally includes an unmarried child who is under age 19 or who is a full-time student under age 24 if the taxpayer supplies more than half the child's support for the year.

Eligible Educational Institution

An eligible educational institution is any accredited college, university, vocational school, or other accredited postsecondary educational institution eligible to participate in a student aid program administered by the Department of Education. It includes virtually all accredited, public, non-profit, and proprietary (privately owned profit making) postsecondary institutions. The school should be able to inform the taxpayer if it is an "eligible educational institution."

Academic Period

An academic period includes a semester, trimester, quarter, or any other period designated by the educational institution as a period of instructional time. For purposes of the education credits an academic period begins on the first day of classes and does not include periods of student orientation, counseling, or vacation.

Special Situations

1. If a deduction for higher education expenses is claimed on a tax return, a credit cannot be claimed for those same expenses.

2. If higher education expenses are paid with certain tax-free funds, a credit cannot be claimed for those amounts. Tax-free funds could include:

    a. Scholarships.
    b. Pell grants.
    c. Employer-provided educational assistance.
    d. Veterans' educational assistance.
    e. Any other nontaxable payments (other than gifts, bequests, or inheritances) received for educational expenses.

3. A credit can be claimed for expenses paid with the student's earnings, loans, gifts, inheritances, and personal savings.

4. If a student receives a tax-free withdrawal from an education IRA in a particular tax year, none of that student's expenses can be used as the basis of a higher education credit for that tax year. However, the student can waive the tax-free treatment.

5. If, in a later tax year, the taxpayer receives a refund of an expense used to figure a higher education credit, all or part of the credit may have to be refunded.

HOPE CREDIT

For expenses paid after December 31, 1999, for academic periods beginning after that date, the taxpayer may be able to claim a Hope credit of up to $1,500 for the qualified tuition and related expenses paid for *each* eligible student. This credit may be claimed for only two taxable years for each eligible student.

Eligible Student for Hope Credit

A Hope credit may be claimed only for an eligible student who meets all of the following requirements:

1. Has not completed the first two years of postsecondary education (generally, the freshman or sophomore years of college).

2. Is enrolled in a program that leads to a degree, certificate, or other recognized educational credential.

3. Is taking at least one-half of the normal full-time work load for his or her course of study for at least one academic period beginning during the calendar year.

4. Is free of any felony conviction for possessing or distributing a controlled substance.

Amount of Credit

The amount of the Hope credit is 100% of the first $1,000 plus 50% of the next $1,000 paid for each eligible student's qualified tuition and related expenses. The maximum amount of Hope credit that could be claimed in 1999 was $1,500 times the number of eligible students. In other words, the taxpayer can claim the full $1,500 for each eligible student for whom at least $2,000 was paid for qualified expenses.

However, the credit could be reduced based on the individual's modified adjusted gross income.

LIFETIME LEARNING CREDIT

For expenses paid after June 30, 1998, for academic periods beginning after that date, the taxpayer may be able to claim a lifetime learning credit of up to $1,000 for the total qualified tuition and related expenses paid during the tax year for all students who were enrolled in eligible educational institutions. Unlike the Hope credit:

1. The lifetime learning credit is not based on the student's work load. It is allowed for one or more courses.
2. The lifetime learning credit is not limited to students in the first two years of postsecondary education.
3. Expenses for graduate-level degree work are eligible.
4. There is no limit on the number of years for which the lifetime learning credit can be claimed for each student.
5. The amount that can be claimed as a lifetime learning credit does not vary (increase) based on the number of students for whom qualified expenses are paid.

Amount of Credit

The amount of the lifetime learning credit is 20% of the first $5,000 paid for qualified tuition and related expenses for all students in the family. The maximum amount of lifetime learning credit that could be claimed for 1999 was $1,000 (20% times $5,000). However, that amount could be reduced based on an individual's modified adjusted gross income.

POINTS TO CONSIDER IN CHOOSING WHICH CREDIT TO CLAIM

The following points should be considered when deciding which credit to claim:

1. For each student, the taxpayer can elect for any tax year only one of the credits or a tax-free withdrawal from an education IRA. For example, if he or she elects to take the Hope credit for a child on a tax return, the taxpayer cannot, for that same child, also claim the lifetime learning credit or take a tax-free withdrawal from an education IRA for the same year.

2. It is permissible to take the Hope credit for the first two years of a child's postsecondary education and claim the lifetime learning credit for that same child in later tax years.

3. If qualified expenses are paid for more than one student in the same year, it is possible to choose to take credits on a per-student, per-year basis. This means that the Hope credit could be claimed for one child and the lifetime learning credit for another child in the same tax year.

4. It should be fairly obvious that in any one tax year, only one person can claim a higher education credit for a student's expenses. If the taxpayer is paying higher education costs for a dependent child, one or the other, but not both, can claim a credit for a particular year.

5. If the taxpayer claims an exemption for a child on his or her tax return, the taxpayer should treat any expenses paid by the child as if the taxpayer had paid them. These expenses should be included when figuring the amount of the Hope or lifetime learning credit.

INCOME PHASEOUT

Education credits are phased out (gradually reduced) if the individual's modified adjusted gross income is between $40,000 and $50,000 ($80,000 and $100,000 in the case of a joint return). No higher education credits can be claimed if modified adjusted gross income is over $50,000 ($100,000 in the case of a joint return).

For most taxpayers, modified adjusted gross income will be their adjusted gross income (AGI) as figured on their federal income tax return. However, each individual must make adjustments to AGI if they excluded income earned abroad or from certain U.S. territories or possessions or took a foreign housing deduction. When this applies, the individual should increase the AGI by the following amounts excluded or deducted from income:

1. Foreign earned income of U.S. citizens or residents living abroad.
2. Housing costs of U.S. citizens or residents living abroad.
3. Income from sources within Puerto Rico, Guam, American Samoa, or the Northern Mariana Islands.

The phaseout (reduction) works on a sliding scale. The higher the modified adjusted gross income, the more the credits are reduced.

Claiming the Credits

Education credits are claimed by completing Form 8863 and attaching it to the income tax return. An eligible educational institution (the college or university) that receives payment of qualified tuition and related expenses should issue Form 1098-T, Tuition Payments Statement, to each student. The information on Form 1098-T will help to determine whether an education tax credit can be claimed for any particular year.

EDUCATION INDIVIDUAL RETIREMENT ACCOUNT

The education IRA or ED IRA is another new savings device to be used in paying the qualified higher education expenses of a designated beneficiary under the age of 18. Those expenses include tuition, fees, books, supplies and equipment, as well as room and board if the designated beneficiary is at least a half-time student at an eligible educational institution.

Contributions to these IRAs are nondeductible, and earnings on the amount held in them will be nontaxable until distributed. Annual contributions by any individual, including the child, are limited to $500 per beneficiary. There is no limit on the *number* of education IRAs established for the same child; however, total contributions for a tax year may not exceed the $500 limit. Any individual may contribute to a child's education IRA if the individual's modified AGI is less than $110,000 or $160,000 for joint filers.

Excess Withdrawals

Distributions from an education IRA are excludable from income to the extent the amount *does not exceed* the qualified higher education expenses of the eligible student during the year of distribution. If the distribution is in excess of the qualified higher education expenses, only a portion of the distribution may be excluded. In addition, distributions not used for higher education are subject to a 10% penalty. The Act requires any balance remaining in an education IRA at the time a beneficiary becomes 30 years of age to be distributed and taxed as income to the beneficiary (and subject to the 10% penalty). However, the balance may be rolled over tax free to another education IRA benefiting another under-age-30 family member.

Requirements

But what *is* this education IRA? And how does one go about setting one up? It is a trust or custodial account designated as an education IRA and created for the express purpose of paying the qualified higher education expenses of the beneficiary. The document creating and governing the trust must be in writing and abide by the following requirements:

1. It must be created or organized in the U.S.
2. The trustee must be a bank, credit union, or other entity approved by the IRS.
3. The trust must provide that the trustee can accept only cash contributions made before the beneficiary reaches age 18 that would not exceed $500 in the tax year (not including rollover contributions).
4. Money in the account may not be invested in life insurance contracts.
5. Money in the account may not be combined with other property except in a common trust fund or common investment fund.
6. The balance in the account generally must be withdrawn within 30 days after the earlier of the following events.
   a. The beneficiary reaches age 30.
   b. The beneficiary's death.

Qualified Expenses

These are expenses required for the enrollment or attendance of the designated beneficiary at an eligible educational institution. Included are the following items:

1. Tuition and fees.
2. Books, supplies, and equipment.
3. Amounts contributed to a qualified state tuition program. (See below.)
4. Room and board if the designated beneficiary is at least a half-time student at an eligible educational institution. (A student is enrolled "at least half time" if he or she is enrolled for at least half the full-time academic work load for the course of study the student is pursuing as determined under the standards of the school where the student is enrolled.) The expense for room and board is limited to one of the following two amounts.
   a. The school's posted room and board charge for students living on campus.
   b. $2,500 each year for students living off campus and not at home.

Excess Contributions

A 6% excise tax applies each year to excess contributions made to an education IRA. They include the following amounts:

1. Contributions that are more than the contribution limit.
2. Contributions to the account if any amount is also contributed to a qualified state tuition program on behalf of the same child in the same tax year. The excise tax will not apply, however, if funds were withdrawn from the education IRA to be contributed to the qualified state tuition program.
3. Excess contributions for the preceding year reduced by the total of:
   a. Withdrawals (other than rollovers) made during the year, and
   b. The contribution limit for the current year minus the amount contributed for the current year.

However, the excise tax does not apply if the excess contributions (and any earnings on them) are withdrawn before the due date of the beneficiary's tax return (including extensions). If the beneficiary does not have to file a return, the tax does not apply if the excess contributions (and the earnings) are withdrawn by April 15 of the year following the year the contributions are made. The withdrawn earnings must be included in the beneficiary's income for the year in which the excess contribution is made.

The excise tax also does not apply to any rollover contribution.

Rollovers and Other Transfers

Assets can be rolled over from one education IRA to another, the designated beneficiary can be changed, or the beneficiary's interest can be transferred to a spouse or former spouse because of divorce.

Rollovers. Any amount withdrawn from an education IRA and rolled over to another education IRA for the benefit of the same beneficiary or certain members of the beneficiary's family is not taxable. A rollover to an education IRA of a family member is not taxable only if that family member is under age 30. An amount is rolled over if it is paid to another education IRA within 60 days after the date of the withdrawal. Only one rollover for an education IRA is permitted during a twelve-month period ending on the date of the payment or withdrawal.

The beneficiary's spouse and the following individuals (and their spouses) are members of the beneficiary's family:

- The beneficiary's child, grandchild, or stepchild.
- A brother, sister, half-brother, half-sister, stepbrother, or stepsister of the beneficiary.
- The father, mother, grandfather, grandmother, stepfather, or stepmother of the beneficiary.

- A brother or sister of the beneficiary's father or mother.
- A son or daughter of the beneficiary's brother or sister.
- The beneficiary's son-in-law, daughter-in-law, father-in-law, mother-in-law, brother-in-law, or sister-in-law.

WITHDRAWALS FROM TRADITIONAL OR ROTH IRAs

Withdrawals may be made from a traditional or Roth IRA for qualified higher education expenses. (A traditional IRA is an IRA that is not a Roth IRA, SIMPLE IRA, or education IRA.) Income tax must be paid on at least part of the amount withdrawn, but the 10% additional tax on early withdrawals will not apply.

Tax Liability of Withdrawals

Part (or all) of any withdrawal may not be subject to the 10% additional tax on early withdrawals. The part *not* subject to the tax is generally the amount that is not more than the qualified higher education expenses at an eligible educational institution. The education must be for the taxpayer, spouse, children, or grandchildren of the taxpayer or spouse.

When determining the amount of the withdrawal that is not subject to the 10% additional tax, the qualified higher education expenses paid with any of the following may be included:

1. An individual's earnings.
2. A loan.
3. A gift.
4. An inheritance given either to the student or the individual making the withdrawal.
5. Personal savings (including savings from a qualified state tuition program).

Expenses paid with any of the following funds may not be included:

1. Tax-free withdrawals from an education IRA.
2. Tax-free scholarships, such as a Pell grant.
3. Tax-free employer-provided educational assistance.
4. Any tax-free payment (other than a gift, bequest, or devise) due to enrollment at an eligible educational institution.

Qualified Expenses

Qualified higher education expenses are tuition, fees, books, supplies, and equipment required for the enrollment or attendance of a student at an eligible educational institution. In addition, if the individual is at least a half-time student, room and board are qualified higher education expenses.

QUALIFIED EDUCATION STUDENT LOAN DEDUCTIONS

An above-the-line maximum deduction for up to $2,500 of interest paid by taxpayers on qualified education loans was provided in the 1997 legislation. The $2,500 limit is phased in (i.e., $1,500 in 1999, $2,000 in 2000, and $2,500 in 2001).

Interest deductions are allowed only for the first 60 months that interest payments are required. The deduction is phased out for taxpayers with modified AGI between $40,000 and $55,000, or $60,000 and $75,000 for joint filers.

This deduction is an adjustment to income; therefore, it can be claimed even though the taxpayer does not itemize deductions. Married taxpayers must file jointly to take the deduction. Furthermore, the credit may not be claimed on the tax return of anyone who is claimed as a dependent by another person.

Qualifying Loan

This is a loan taken out solely to pay qualified higher education expenses. The expenses must have been:

1. For the taxpayer, spouse, or a person who was a dependent when the indebtedness was incurred.
2. Paid or incurred within a reasonable time before or after the loan was taken out.
3. For education furnished during a period when the recipient of the education was an eligible student.

Qualified Expenses

These expenses are the costs of attending an eligible educational institution, including graduate school. Generally, these costs include tuition, fees, room and board, books, equipment, and other necessary expenses, such as transportation. But these costs must be reduced by the following items:

1. Nontaxable employer-provided educational assistance benefits.
2. Nontaxable withdrawals from an education IRA.
3. U.S. savings bond interest that is nontaxable because qualified higher education expenses have been paid.
4. Qualified scholarships that are nontaxable.
5. Veterans' educational assistance benefits.
6. Any other nontaxable payments (other than gifts, bequests, or inheritances) received for educational expenses.

In addition to the definition of "eligible educational institution" given earlier, for purposes of the student loan interest deduction, the term also includes an institution conducting an internship or residency program leading to a degree or certificate from an institution of higher education, a hospital, or a health care facility that offers postgraduate training.

Eligible Student

An eligible student is one who:

1. Is enrolled in a degree, certificate, or other program (including a program of study abroad that is approved for credit by the institution at which the student is enrolled) leading to a recognized educational credential at an eligible educational institution, and
2. Is carrying at least one-half the normal full-time workload for the course of study the student is pursuing.

Related Person Loan

Interest cannot be deducted on a loan obtained from a related person. Related persons include brothers and sisters, half-brothers and half-sisters, spouse, ancestors (parents, grandparents, etc.), and lineal descendants (children, grandchildren, etc.). Related persons also include certain corporations, partnerships, trusts, and exempt organizations.

Refinanced Loan

If a qualified student loan is refinanced, the new loan can also be a qualified student loan, but refinancing a loan does not extend the 60-month period described earlier. The 60-month period is based on the original loan.

CANCELLATION OF DEBT ON STUDENT LOANS

Certain student loans contain a provision that all or part of the debt incurred to attend the qualified educational institution will be canceled if the recipient works for a certain period of time in certain professions for any of a broad class of employers. If the conditions were met and the loan was canceled, the canceled debt does not have to be included in income. The loan must be made by one of the following:

1. A governmental unit—federal, state, or local, or an instrumentality, agency, or subdivision thereof.
2. A tax-exempt public benefit corporation that has assumed control of a state, county, or municipal hospital, and whose employees are considered public employees under state law.
3. An educational institution if the loan is made:
   a. Under an agreement with an entity described in one of the categories above that provided the funds to the educational institution to make the loan.
   b. Under a program of the educational institution as part of its program designed to encourage students to serve in occupations or areas with unmet needs, and the services provided are for or under the direction of a governmental unit or a qualifying Section 501 (c)(3) tax-exempt organization. These include any corporation, community chest, fund or foundation organized and operated exclusively for one or more of the following purposes:
      • charitable
      • religious
      • educational
      • scientific
      • literary
      • testing for public safety
      • fostering national or international amateur sports competition (but only if none of its activities involve providing athletic facilities or equipment)
      • prevention of cruelty to children or animals.

A loan will also qualify if it was made by an educational institution, or a tax-exempt organization to refinance a student loan that meets these requirements. This is true if the new loan is made:

1. To assist the student in attending the educational institution, and
2. Under a program of the new lender that meets the conditions of (3)(b) above.

STATE TUITION PROGRAM

Certain states and agencies maintain programs that allow people to purchase credits or certificates or make contributions to an account to pay for future education. Contributions to a qualified state tuition program are not deductible, and withdrawals are taxable only to the extent they are more than the amount contributed to the program. (See "Excess Withdrawals" under "Education IRA.") A qualified state tuition program is one that is established and maintained by a state or agency and that:

1. Allows a person to:
   a. Buy tuition credits or certificates for a designated beneficiary who would then be entitled to a waiver or payment of qualified higher educational expenses, or
   b. Make contributions to an account that is set up to meet the qualified higher educational expenses of a designated beneficiary of the account.
2. Requires all purchases or contributions to be made only in cash,
3. Prohibits the contributor and the beneficiary from directing the amount invested,
4. Allows a rollover or a change of beneficiary to be made only between members of the same family (defined earlier in "Rollovers" under "Education IRA"), and
5. Imposes a penalty on any refund of earnings that does not meet at least one of the following conditions:
   a. The amount is used for qualified higher educational expenses of the beneficiary.
   b. The refund is made because of the death or disability of the beneficiary.
   c. The refund is made because the beneficiary received (and the refund is not more than) a scholarship, a veterans' educational assistance allowance, or another nontaxable payment (other than a gift, bequest, or inheritance) for educational expenses.

For more information on a specific state tuition program, the taxpayer should contact the state or agency that established and maintains it.

THE EDUCATION SAVINGS BOND PROGRAM

This program makes it possible to exclude from income all or part of the interest received on the redemption of qualified U.S. savings bonds during the year if the taxpayer pays qualified higher educational expenses during that same year. If married, the taxpayer can exclude the interest from income only if a joint return is filed with the spouse.

A qualified U.S. savings bond is a Series EE U.S. savings bond issued *after* 1989, or a Series I bond. The bond must be issued either in the sole owner's name or in the owner and his or her spouse's names as co-owners. The taxpayer must be at least 24 years old before the bond's issue date. The date a bond is issued can be earlier than the date the bond is purchased, because bonds are issued as of the first day of the month in which they are purchased. Any individual, including a child, can be designated a beneficiary of the bond payable on death.

Excludable Amounts

If the total proceeds (interest and principal) from the qualified U.S. savings bonds redeemed during the year are not more than the qualified higher educational expenses for the year, all of the interest can be excluded. If the proceeds are more than the expenses, part of the interest can be excluded.

The interest exclusion is phased out if the modified adjusted gross income is:

1. $53,100 to $68,100 for taxpayers filing singly or as head of household.
2. $79,650 to $109,650 for married taxpayers filing jointly.

(The individual does not qualify for the interest exclusion if the modified adjusted gross income is equal to or more than the upper limit.)

Modified adjusted gross income for purposes of this exclusion is AGI figured on the individual's federal income tax return and modified by adding back any of the following amounts that may have been deducted or excluded from income:

1. Foreign-earned income of U.S. citizens or residents living abroad.
2. Foreign housing costs exclusion or deduction.
3. Income from sources within Puerto Rico, American Samoa, Guam, or the Northern Mariana Islands.
4. U.S. savings bond interest that is nontaxable because qualified higher education expenses were paid.
5. Adoption benefits received under an employer's adoption benefits assistance program.
6. Student loan interest.

If an interest exclusion is claimed, a written record must be kept of the Series EE U.S. savings bonds issued after 1989 that are redeemed. The written record must include the serial number, issue date, face value, and redemption proceeds of each bond. Any bills, receipts, canceled checks or other documentation must be kept that show qualified higher educational expenses were paid during the year.

Qualified Expenses

Qualified higher education expenses include the following items paid for the taxpayer, his or her spouse, or a dependent for whom they claim an exemption.

1. Tuition and fees required to enroll at or attend an eligible educational institution (defined earlier). Qualified expenses do not include expenses for room and board or for courses involving sports, games, or hobbies that are not part of a degree program.
2. Contributions to a qualified state tuition program.
3. Contributions to an education IRA.

Reduced Expenses

Educational expenses are reduced by the amount of any of the following benefits the student received:

1. Tax-free scholarships.
2. Tax-free withdrawals from an education IRA.
3. Any nontaxable payments (other than gifts, bequests, or inheritances) received for educational expenses or for attending an eligible educational institution. Such benefits include:
   a. Veterans' educational assistance benefits.
   b. Benefits under a qualified state tuition program.
   c. Tax-free employer-provided educational assistance.
4. Any expenses used in figuring the Hope and lifetime learning credits.

EMPLOYER-PROVIDED EDUCATIONAL ASSISTANCE

Educational assistance benefits received from an employer under an educational assistance program are tax-free, up to $5,250 each year. This means the employer should not include the benefits with wages, tips, and other compensation.

An employee must reduce deductible educational expenses by the amount of any tax-free educational assistance benefits received for those expenses.

To qualify as an educational assistance program, the plan must be written and meet certain other requirements. The employer can inform an employee whether or not there is a qualified program in effect.

Assistance Coverage

Tax-free educational assistance benefits include payments by the employer for tuition, fees and similar expenses, books, supplies, and equipment. The payments must be for undergraduate-level courses that begin before June 1, 2000. The payments do not have to be for work-related courses.

Educational assistance benefits do not include payments for the following items.

1. Meals, lodging, transportation, or tools or supplies (other than textbooks) that the student can keep after completing the course of instruction.
2. Education involving sports, games, or hobbies unless the education has a reasonable relationship to the business of the employer, or is required as part of a degree program.
3. Graduate-level courses that began after June 30, 1996, and are normally taken under a program leading to a law, business, medical, or other advanced academic or professional degree.

Benefit Over $5,250

If the employer provides more than $5,250 of educational assistance benefits during the year, the amount over $5,250 is generally taxable. The employer should include the taxable amount in wages.

However, if the payments also qualify as a working condition fringe benefit, the employer can exclude all of the payments from wages. A working condition fringe benefit is a benefit which, had the employee paid for it, could be deducted as an employee business expense.

Expenses Paid with Benefits

If the taxpayer received tax-free benefits under an employer's qualified educational assistance program, he or she cannot take a deduction for qualified educational expenses.

Chapter 25
Mutual Funds

KINDS OF DISTRIBUTIONS

There are several kinds of distributions that a shareholder can receive from a mutual fund. They include:

1. Ordinary dividends.
2. Capital gain distributions.
3. Exempt-interest dividends.
4. Return of capital (nontaxable) distribution.

Tax-Exempt Mutual Fund

Distributions from a tax-exempt mutual fund—one that invests primarily in tax-exempt securities—can consist of ordinary dividends, capital gains distributions, undistributed capital gains, or return of capital like any other mutual fund. These contributions follow the same rules as a regular mutual fund. Distributions designated as exempt-interest dividends are not taxable.

A mutual fund may pay exempt-interest dividends to its shareholders if it meets certain requirements. These dividends are paid from tax-exempt interest earned by the fund. Since the exempt-interest dividends keep their tax-exempt character, the taxpayer does not have to include them in income, but may need to report them on his or her return. The mutual fund will send the taxpayer a statement within 60 days after the close of its tax year showing the amount of exempt-interest dividends. Although exempt-interest dividends are not taxable, they must be reported on the tax return if one is required to

500

be filed. This is an information reporting requirement and does not convert tax-exempt interest to taxable interest.

Return of Capital

A distribution that is not out of earnings and profits is a return of the investment, or capital, in the mutual fund. The return of capital distributions are not taxed as ordinary dividends and are sometimes called tax-free dividends or nontaxable distributions that may be fully or partly taxable as capital gains.

A return of capital distribution reduces the basis in the shares. The basis cannot be reduced below zero. If the basis is reduced to zero, the taxpayer must report the return of capital distribution on the tax return as a capital gain. The distribution is taxable if, when added to all returns of capital distribution received in past years, it is more than the basis in the shares. Whether it is a long-term or short-term capital gain depends on how long the shares had been held.

Reinvestment of Distributions

Most mutual funds permit shareholders to automatically reinvest distributions, including dividends and capital gains, in more shares in the fund. Instead of receiving cash, distributions are used to purchase additional shares. The reinvested amounts must be reported to the IRS in the same way as if the reinvestment were received in cash. Reinvested ordinary dividends and capital gains distributions must be reported as income; reinvested exempt-interest dividends are not reported as income.

FOREIGN TAX DEDUCTION OR CREDIT

Some mutual funds invest in foreign securities or other instruments. A mutual fund may choose to allow an investor to claim a deduction or credit for the taxes the fund paid to a foreign country or U.S. possession. The notice to the fund's investors will include their share of the foreign taxes paid to each foreign country or possession, and the part of the dividend derived from sources in each country or possession.

BASIS

The basis in shares of a regulated investment company (mutual fund) is generally figured in the same way as the basis of other stock. The cost basis of purchased mutual fund shares often includes a sales fee, also known as a *load charge.* In certain cases, the entire amount of a load charge incurred after October 3, 1989, cannot be added to the cost basis, if the load charge gives the purchaser a reinvestment right.

Commissions and Load Charges

The fees and charges paid to acquire or redeem shares of a mutual fund are not tax deductible. They are usually added to the cost of the shares and increase the basis. A fee paid to redeem the shares is usually a reduction in the redemption price (sales price) in the case of mutual funds.

Keeping Track of the Basis

The investor in mutual funds should keep careful track of his or her basis because the basis is needed to figure any gain or loss on the shares when they are sold, exchanged, or redeemed. When mutual fund shares are bought or sold, the confirmation statements should be kept to show the price paid for the shares, and the price received for the shares when sold. If the shares are acquired by gift or inheritance, the investor needs information that is different from that in a confirmation statement for figuring the basis of those shares. The basis of shares of a mutual fund is important to know in figuring a gain or loss, with the basis dependent upon how the shares are acquired.

Shares Acquired by Inheritance

If mutual funds shares are inherited shares, the basis is the fair market value (FMV) at the date of the decedent's death, or at the alternate valuation date, if chosen for estate tax purposes. In community property states, each spouse is considered to own half the estate. If one spouse dies and at least half of the community interest is includable in the decedent's gross estate, the FMV of the community property at the date of death becomes the basis of both halves of the property.

Adjusted Basis

After mutual fund shares are acquired, adjustments may need to be made to the basis. The adjusted basis of stock is the original basis, increased or reduced. The basis is increased in a fund by 65% of any undistributed capital gain that is included in the taxpayer's income. This has the effect of increasing the basis by the difference between the amount of gain included in income and the credit claimed for the tax considered paid on that income. The mutual fund reports the amount of undistributed capital gain.

Reduction of the Basis

The basis must be reduced in the fund by any return of capital distributions received from the fund. The basis is not reduced for distributions that are exempt-interest dividends.

SALES, EXCHANGES, AND REDEMPTIONS

When mutual fund shares are sold, exchanged, or redeemed, the investor will usually have a taxable gain or deductible loss. This includes shares in a tax-exempt mutual fund. The amount of the gain or loss is the difference between the adjusted basis in the shares and the amount realized from the sale, exchange, or redemption.

Gains and losses are figured on the disposition of shares by comparing the amount realized with the adjusted basis of the owner's shares. If the amount realized is more than the adjusted basis of the shares, a gain results; if the amount realized is less than the adjusted basis of the shares, a loss results. The amount received from a disposition of mutual fund shares is the money and value of any property received for the shares disposed of, minus expenses of sale such as redemption fees, sales commissions, sales charges, or exit fees.

The exchange of one fund for another fund is a taxable exchange, regardless of whether shares in one fund are exchanged for shares in another fund that has the same distributor or underwriter without paying a sales charge. Any gain or loss on the investment in the original shares as a capital gain or loss must be reported in the year in which the exchange occurs. Service charges or fees paid in connection with an exchange can be added to the cost of the shares acquired. Mutual funds and brokers must report to the IRS the proceeds from sales, exchanges, or redemptions. The broker must give each customer a written statement with the information by January 31 of the year following the calendar year the transaction occurred. The broker must be given a correct taxpayer identification number (TIN); a social security number is acceptable as a TIN.

Identifying the Shares Sold

When mutual fund shares are disposed of, the investor must determine which shares were sold and the basis of those shares. If the shares were acquired all on the same day and for the same price, figuring their basis is not difficult; however, for shares that are acquired at various times, in various quantities, and at various prices, determining the cost basis can be a difficult process. Two methods can be used to figure the basis, the cost basis, or the average basis.

Under the cost basis one of the following methods can be chosen:

1. Specific share identification.
2. First-in first-out (FIFO).

If the shares sold can be definitely identified, the adjusted basis of those particular shares can be used to figure a gain or loss. The shares can be adequately identified, even if bought in different lots at various prices and times, if:

1. The buyer specifies to the broker or other agent the particular shares to be sold or transferred at the time of the sale or transfer.
2. The buyer receives confirmation of the specification from his or her broker in writing within a reasonable time.

The confirmation by the mutual fund must state that the seller instructed the broker to sell particular shares. The owner of the shares has to be able to prove the basis of the specified shares at the time of sale or transfer.

If the shares were acquired at different times or at different prices, and the seller cannot identify which shares were sold, the basis of the shares acquired initially (first-in, first-out) is used as the basis of the shares sold. Therefore, the oldest shares still available are considered sold first. An adequate record should be kept of each purchase and any dispositions of the shares, until all shares purchased at the same time have been disposed of completely.

Average Basis

The average basis can be used to figure a gain or loss when all or part of the number of shares in a regulated investment company are sold. This choice can be made only if acquired at various times and prices, and the shares were left on deposit in an account handled by a custodian or agent who acquires or redeems those shares. The investor may be able to find the average basis of the shares from information provided by the fund. Once the average basis is used, it must continue to be used for all accounts in the same fund. However, a different method can be used for the shares in other funds.

To figure average basis, one of the following methods can be used:

1. Single-category method.
2. Double-category method.

Single-category method. In the single-category method, the average cost is found of all shares owned at the time of each disposition, regardless of how long the shares were owned. Shares acquired with reinvested dividends or capital gains distributions must be included. Even if only one category is used to compute the basis, it is possible to have short-term or long-term gains or losses. To determine the holding period, the shares disposed of are considered to be those acquired first. The following steps are used to compute the basis of shares sold:

1. The cost of all shares owned is added.
2. The result of Step 1 is divided by the number of shares owned. This gives the *average basis* per share.
3. The result of Step 2 is multiplied by the number of shares sold. This gives the basis of the shares sold.

The basis of the shares determined under average basis is the basis of all the shares in the account at the time of each sale. If no shares were acquired or sold since the last sale, the basis of the remaining shares at the time of the next sale is the same as the basis of the shares sold in the last sale.

Double-category method. In the double-category method, all shares in an account at the time of each disposition are divided into two categories: short-term and long-term. The adjusted basis of each share in a category is the total adjusted basis of all shares in that category at the time of disposition, divided by the total shares in the category.

The investor can specify to the custodian or agent handling the account from which category the shares are to be sold or transferred. The custodian or agent must confirm in writing the seller's specification. If the investor does not specify or receive confirmation, the shares sold must first be charged against the long-term category and then any remaining shares sold against the short-term category.

When a share has been held for more than one year, it must be transferred from the short-term category to the long-term category. When the change is made, the basis of a transferred share is its actual cost or adjusted basis; if some of the shares in the short-term category have been disposed of, its basis falls under the average basis method. The average basis of the undisposed shares would be figured at the time of the most recent disposition from this category.

Holding Period

When mutual fund shares are disposed of, the holding period must be determined. The period starts by using the trade date—the *trade date* is the date on which the holder of the shares bought or sold the mutual fund shares. Most mutual funds will show the trade date on confirmation statements of the purchases and sales.

INVESTMENT EXPENSES

The expenses of producing taxable investment income on a *nonpublicly* offered mutual fund during the year are generally deductible expenses; these include counseling and advice, legal and accounting fees, and investment newsletters. These are deductible as miscellaneous itemized deductions to the extent that they exceed 2% of adjusted gross income. Interest paid on money to buy or carry investment property is also deductible.

A nonpublicly offered mutual fund is one that:

1. Is not continuously offered pursuant to a public offering.
2. Is not regularly traded on an established securities market.
3. Is not held by at least 500 persons at all times during the tax year.

Generally, mutual funds are *publicly* offered funds. Expenses of publicly offered mutual funds are not treated as miscellaneous itemized deductions because these mutual funds report only the net amount of investment income after the investor's share of the investment expenses has been deducted. Expenses on the shares of nonpublicly offered mutual funds can be claimed as a miscellaneous itemized deduction subject to the 2% limit.

Expenses cannot be deducted for the collection or production of exempt-interest dividends. Expenses must be allocated if they were for both taxable and tax-exempt income. One accepted method for allocating expenses is to divide them in the same proportion that the tax-exempt income from the mutual fund is to the total income from the fund.

The amount that can be deducted as investment interest expense must be limited in two different ways. First, the interest cannot be deducted for the expenses borrowed to buy or carry shares in a mutual fund that distributes only tax-exempt dividends. Second, investment interest is limited by the amount of investment income. Deductions for interest expense are limited to the amount of net investment income. Net investment is figured by subtracting investment expenses other than interest from investment income. Investment income includes gross income derived from property held for investment, such as interest, dividends, annuities, and royalties. It does not include net capital gains derived from disposing of investment property, or capital gains distributions from mutual fund shares. Investment interest that cannot be deducted because of the 2% limit can be carried forward to the next tax year, provided that net investment income exceeds investment interest in the later year.

INDEPENDENT INVESTMENT COMPANY DIRECTORS

The Securities and Exchange Commission is proposing new rules and rule amendments that are designed to *enhance the effectiveness of fund indepen-*

dent directors. The Commission also is issuing a release that provides its views on the Commission's role in disputes between independent directors and fund management, and the views of its staff on interpretive issues related to independent directors.

These initiatives are designed to reaffirm the important role of independent directors in the following ways by:

1. Emphasizing the role they play in protecting fund investors.
2. Strengthening their hand in dealing with fund management.
3. Reinforcing their independence.
4. Providing investors with greater information to assess the directors' independence.

SEC Rule Changes

The proposed rule amendments would require that for funds relying on any of ten commonly used exemptive rules (including the rule that permits funds to charge distribution fees (or 12b-1 fees):

1. Independent directors constitute at least a majority of the fund's board of directors, rather than the 40% currently required by the Investment Company Act. The Commission is requesting comment on whether:
   a. It should adopt a simple majority requirement (as recommended by a 1992 Commission staff report), or
   b. A two-thirds super-majority requirement (as recommended by the recent Investment Company Institute Advisory Group Report).
2. Independent directors select and nominate other independent directors.
3. Any legal counsel for the fund's independent directors be an independent legal counsel; i.e., it does not also represent the fund's management or close affiliates.

Fund Disclosure Changes

The proposed *disclosure* amendments would require funds to provide better information about directors, including:

1. Basic information about the identity and business experience of directors.
2. Fund shares owned by directors.
3. Information about directors' potential conflicts of interest.
4. The board's role in governing the fund's operations.

Additional Rule Changes

The proposed new rules and rule amendments also would:

1. Prevent qualified individuals from being unnecessarily disqualified from serving as independent directors because they invest in index funds that hold shares of the fund's adviser or other affiliates.
2. Protect the independence of independent directors by requiring that joint "errors and omissions" insurance policies cover lawsuits against them brought by investment advisers.
3. Encourage the development of independent audit committees by exempting funds that have these committees from seeking shareholder approval of the fund's auditor.
4. Require funds to keep any records they rely on to assess the independence of independent directors.

Interpretive Matters Related to Independent Directors

The Commission is issuing an Interpretive Release expressing the views of the Commission's staff on interpretive matters related to independent directors. The Interpretive Release would:

1. Provide guidance about the types of material business and professional relationships that might disqualify a director from serving as an independent director of a fund.
2. Clarify that actions taken by fund directors in their capacities as directors generally would not be "joint transactions" that require prior Commission approval.
3. Provide guidance regarding when funds may advance legal fees to their directors.
4. Provide guidance concerning the circumstances under which funds may compensate fund directors with fund shares.

The Interpretive Release also would provide the Commission's views regarding its role and response in disputes between fund independent directors and fund management when there are allegations of violations of the federal securities laws.

Comment Period and Effectiveness Comments on the rule proposals were due January 28, 2000. The views discussed in the Interpretive Release would be effective when it is published.

Chapter 26

Mutual Fund "Profile" Disclosure Option

The Securities and Exchange Commission has adopted a new Rule that permits an open-end management investment company (mutual fund) to offer investors a user-friendly disclosure document called a "profile." This document summarizes key information about the fund, including the fund's investment strategies, risks, performance, and fees, in a concise, standardized format.

A fund that offers a profile will be able to give investors a choice of the amount of information that they wish to consider before making a decision about investing in the fund; investors will have the option of purchasing the fund's shares after reviewing the information in the profile or after requesting and reviewing the fund's prospectus (and other information). An investor deciding to purchase fund shares based on the information in a profile will receive the fund's prospectus with the confirmation of purchase.

The SEC also adopted amendments to Rule 497 under the Securities Act to require a fund to file a profile with the Commission at least 30 days prior to the profile's first use. At the same time, they adopted revisions to the prospectus disclosure requirements in Form N-1A, the registration statement used by funds. The revisions should *minimize* prospectus disclosure about technical, legal, and operational matters that generally are common to all funds and thus *focus prospectus disclosure on essential information* about a particular fund. The reasoning is that the simplified general information should enable the average investor to make better informed decisions about investing in that fund.

509

NEED FOR SIMPLIFIED DISCLOSURE INFORMATION

As more investors turn to funds for professional management of current and retirement savings, funds have introduced new investment options and shareholder services to appeal to investors. While benefiting from these developments, investors also faced an increasingly difficult task in choosing from the many different fund investments. The SEC, fund investors, and others realized it was in everyone's best interest to improve fund disclosure documents to help investors evaluate and compare them.

In the Commission's view, the growth of the fund industry and the diversity of fund investors warranted a new approach to fund disclosure to offer more choices in the format and the amount of information available about these investments. (Particularly, it would seem, since so many relatively "uninitiated" investors were testing the mutual fund market.)

The Profile summarizes key information about a fund, including its investment objectives, strategies, risks, performance, fees, investment adviser and portfolio manager, purchase and redemption procedures, distributions, tax information and the services available to the fund's investors.

It was designed to provide summary information about a fund that could assist an investor in deciding whether to invest in that particular fund immediately, or to request additional information about it before deciding whether or not to buy shares in it.

Rule 498 requires a fund to mail the prospectus and other information to the requesting investor within 3 business days of a request. An investor deciding to purchase fund shares based on the Profile receives the fund's prospectus with the purchase confirmation.

PROFILE REQUIREMENTS UNDER RULE 498

1. ***Standardized Fund Summaries.*** The profile includes concise disclosure of 9 items of key information about a fund in a specific sequence.
2. ***Improved Risk Disclosure.*** A risk/return summary (also required at the beginning of a fund's *prospectus*) provides information about a fund's investment objectives, principal strategies, risks, performance, and fees.
3. ***Graphic Disclosure of Variability of Returns.*** The risk/return summary provides a bar chart of a fund's annual returns over a 10-year period that illustrates the variability of those returns and gives investors some idea of the risks of an investment in the fund. To help investors evaluate a fund's risks and returns relative to "the market," a table accompanying the bar chart compares the fund's average annual returns for 1-, 5-, and 10-year periods to that of a broad-based securities market index.

4. *Other Fund Information.* The profile includes information on the fund's investment adviser and portfolio manager, purchase and redemption procedures, tax considerations, and shareholder services.

5. *Plain English Disclosure.* The Commission's plain English disclosure requirements, which are designed to give investors understandable disclosure documents, apply to the profile. The plain English rule requires the use of plain English writing principles, including short sentences, everyday language, active voice, tabular presentation of complex material, no legal or business jargon, and no multiple negatives. (For a discussion of this rule, see Chapter 21.)

PROFILES FOR TAX-DEFERRED ARRANGEMENTS

Rule 498 also permits a fund that serves as an investment option for a participant-directed defined contribution plan (or for certain other tax-deferred arrangements) to provide investors with a profile that includes disclosure that is tailored for the plan (or other arrangement).

Profiles tailored for such use can exclude information relating to the purchase and sale of fund shares, fund distributions, tax consequences, and fund services otherwise required in a profile.

PILOT PROFILE PROGRAM

The Commission tested various options for improving fund disclosure documents in a pilot program conducted with participation by the Investment Company Institute (ICI) and several large fund groups, in which the funds used profile-like summaries with their prospectuses. The Pilot Profile summarized important information about specific funds to determine whether investors found these profiles helpful in making investment decisions. Focus groups conducted on the Commission's behalf responded positively to the profile concept, indicating that a disclosure document of this type would assist them in making investment decisions. Fund investors participating in a survey sponsored by the ICI also strongly supported the profile idea.

OTHER INVESTMENT COMPANIES EXCLUDED FROM PROFILE OPTION

The Commission has decided that other types of investment companies, such as closed-end investment companies, unit investment trusts, and separate accounts that offer variable annuities do not come within the scope of Rule 498. It is available only to mutual funds.

Although the Agency recognizes that a short, summary disclosure document such as the profile could potentially benefit investors in other types of investment companies, it has concluded that it would be prudent to assess the use of profiles by mutual funds over a period of time before considering a rule to allow other types of investment companies to use similar summary documents. As the Commission gains experience with funds' use of the profile and analyzes the results of other pilot profile programs that are underway, it will undoubtedly consider expanding use of the concept to other types of investment companies if things work out as well as they anticipate.

MULTIPLE FUNDS DESCRIBED IN A PROFILE

The SEC decided that a profile that describes more than one fund can be consistent with the goal of a summary disclosure document that assists investors in evaluating and comparing funds. In fact they believe that describing more than one fund or class of a fund in a profile can be a useful means of providing investors with information about related investment alternatives offered by a fund group (e.g., a range of tax-exempt funds or different types of money market funds) or about the classes of a multiple class fund. However, profiles describing multiple funds must be organized in a clear, concise, summary manner in a format designed to communicate the information effectively. Thus, a profile that offers the securities of more than one fund or class does not need to repeat information that is the same for each one described in the document.

COVER PAGE

Rule 498 requires the cover page of a fund's profile to include certain basic information about the fund and to disclose that the profile is a *summary disclosure document.* The cover page identifies it as a "profile" without using the term "prospectus." It includes a legend explaining the profile's purpose, and displays the fund's name. A fund also could describe its investment objectives or its type or category (e.g., that the fund is a growth fund or invests its assets in a particular country). The cover page must state the approximate date of the profile's first use.

Required Legend

The new rule requires the following legend on the cover page, or at the beginning, of a profile:

"This profile summarizes key information about a Fund that is included in the Fund's prospectus. The Fund's prospectus includes additional information about the Fund, including a more detailed description of the risks associated with investing in the Fund that you may want to consider before you invest. You may obtain the prospectus and other information about the Fund at no cost by calling _____."

A toll-free (or collect) telephone number that investors can use to obtain the prospectus and other information must be provided. The fund may also indicate, as applicable, that the prospectus and other information is available on the fund's Internet site or by e-mail request.

When additional information is requested, a 3-business day mailing requirement applies. Since many funds use intermediaries in distributing or servicing their shares, revised Rule 498 also permits the legend to state that additional information in such a case may be obtained from financial intermediaries. The 3-business day rule applies here also.

RISK / RETURN SUMMARY

The first 4 items of the profile must contain information that would be substantially identical to the proposed risk/return summary at the beginning of every prospectus. The following discussion summarizes the main features of the risk/return summary required by Form N-1A and discusses specific disclosure required in the profile.

Fund Investment Objectives / Goals

To assist investors in identifying funds that meet their general investment needs, the risk/return summary requires a fund to disclose its investment objectives or goals.

Principal Investment Strategy

The risk/return summary requires a fund to summarize, based on the information provided in its prospectus, how the fund intends to achieve its investment objectives. The purpose of this disclosure is to provide a summary of the fund's principal investment strategies, including the specific types of securities in which the fund invests or will invest principally, and any policy of the fund to concentrate its investments in an industry or group of industries.

In addition, a fund (other than one that has not yet been required to deliver a semi-annual or annual report) must provide the following disclosure:

"Additional information about the Fund's investments is available in the Fund's annual and semi-annual reports to shareholders. In the Fund's annual report you will find a discussion of the market conditions and investment strategies that significantly affected the Fund's performance during the last fiscal year. You may obtain either or both of these reports at no cost by calling _____."

Principal Risks of Investing in the Fund

Summary Risk Disclosure. The risk summary gives a fund the option to include disclosure in its profile about the types of investors for whom the fund is intended and the types of investment goals that may be consistent with an investment in the fund.

Special Risk Disclosure Requirements. A mutual fund profile is required to provide a special disclosure in the risk summary for money market funds to the effect that, "An investment in the Fund is not insured or guaranteed by the Federal Deposit Insurance Corporation or any other government agency. Although the Fund seeks to preserve the value of your investment at $1.00 per share, it is possible to lose money by investing in the Fund."

A fund advised by or sold through a bank would disclose in the risk summary of its profile: "An investment in the Fund is not a deposit of the bank and is not insured or guaranteed by the Federal Deposit Insurance Corporation or any other government agency."

Risk/Return Bar Chart and Table. The risk/return summary requires a fund's profile to include a bar chart showing the fund's annual returns for each of the last 10 calendar years and a table comparing the fund's average annual returns for the last 1, 5, and 10 fiscal years to those of a broad-based securities market index.

Obviously, this provision requires a fund to have at least one calendar year of returns before including the bar chart. It requires a fund whose profile does not include a bar chart, because the fund does not have annual returns for a full calendar year, to modify the narrative explanation to refer only to information presented in the table. The provision also requires the bar chart of a fund in operation for fewer than 10 years to include annual returns for the life of the fund.

To show a fund's highest and lowest returns (or "range" of returns) for annual or other periods as an alternative, or in addition, to the bar chart, the Profile ruling requires that a fund disclose (in addition to the bar chart) its best and worst returns for a quarter during the 10-year (or other) period reflected in the bar chart. This information is aimed at disclosing the variability of a fund's returns and the risks by pointing out that a fund's shares may very well be subject to short-term price fluctuations.

Presentation of Return Information. To help investors use the information in the bar chart and table, the profile risk/return summary requires a fund to provide a brief narrative explanation of just how the information illustrates the variability of the fund's returns.

Bar Chart Return Information. The risk/return summary requires calendar-year periods for both the bar chart and table. Under Rule 498, the average annual return information in the table in a fund's profile risk/return summary must be as of the most recent calendar quarter and updated quarterly.

Bar Chart Presentation. The bar chart may include return information for more than one fund. However, the presentation of the bar chart is subject to the general requirement that disclosure should be presented in a format designed to communicate information *clearly and effectively*.

The risk/return summary requires a fund offering more than one class of shares in a profile to include annual return information in its bar chart for only one class. The ruling permits a fund to choose the class to be reflected in the bar chart, subject to certain limitations: the chart must reflect the performance of a class that has returns for at least 10 years (e.g., a fund could not present a class in the bar chart with 2 years of returns when another class has returns for at least 10 years). In addition, if two or more classes offered in the profile have returns for less than 10 years, the bar chart must reflect returns for the class that has returns for the longest period.

Fees and Expenses of the Fund

The risk/return summary requires a bar chart showing the fund's fees and expenses, including any sales loads charged in connection with an investment in the fund. The fee table must be included in both the profile and the prospectus. This emphasis underlines the SEC's belief that fees and expenses of a fund figure high in a typical investor's decision to invest in a fund. The fee table is designed to help them understand the costs of investing in a particular fund and to compare those costs with the costs of other funds.

OTHER DISCLOSURE REQUIREMENTS

The profile of a fund must include not only the risk/return summary, but also disclosure about other key aspects of investing in the fund—the other items to be disclosed in sequence: Investment Adviser, Sub-Adviser(s) and Portfolio Manager(s) of the Fund.

The profile requirements are very precise in this respect. This section requires:

1. Identification of the fund's investment adviser.
2. Identification of the fund's sub-adviser(s) (if any):
   a. A fund need not identify a sub-adviser(s) whose sole responsibility for the fund is limited to day-to-day management of the fund's holdings of cash and cash equivalent instruments, unless the fund is a money market fund or other fund with a principal investment strategy of regularly holding cash and cash equivalent instruments.
   b. A fund having three or more sub-advisers, each of which manages a portion of the fund's portfolio, need not identify each such sub-adviser, except that the fund must identify any sub-adviser that is (or is reasonably expected to be) responsible for the management of a significant portion of the fund's net assets. For purposes of this paragraph, a significant portion of a fund's net assets generally will be deemed to be 30% or more of the fund's net assets.
   c. State the name and length of service of the person or persons employed by or associated with the fund's investment adviser (or the fund) who are primarily responsible for the day-to-day management of the fund's portfolio and summarize each person's *business experience* for the last five years.

      A fund with three or more such persons, each of whom is (or is reasonably expected to be) responsible for the management of a portion of the Fund's portfolio, need not identify each person, except that a fund must identify and summarize the business experience for the last five years of each person who is (or is reasonably expected to be) responsible for the management of a significant portion of the fund's net assets. For purposes of this paragraph, a significant portion of a fund's net assets generally will be deemed to be 30% or more of the fund's net assets.

Purchase of Fund Shares

Under Rule 498, a fund must disclose the minimum initial or subsequent investment requirements, the initial sales load (or other loads), and, if applicable, the initial sales load breakpoints or waivers.

Sale of Fund Shares

Rule 498 also requires a fund to state that its shares are redeemable; to identify the procedures for redeeming shares (e.g., on any business day by written request, telephone, or wire transfer); to identify any charges or sales loads that may be assessed upon redemption (including, if applicable, the existence of waivers of these charges).

Fund Distributions and Tax Information

Rule 498 requires a mutual fund's profile to describe how frequently the fund intends to make distributions and what reinvestment options for distributions (if any) are available to its investors.

It also requires a fund to disclose whether its distributions to shareholders may be taxed as ordinary income or capital gains and that the rates shareholders pay on capital gains may be taxed at different rates depending upon the length of time that the fund holds its assets.

If a fund expects that its distributions, as a result of its investment objectives or strategies, primarily will consist of ordinary income or capital gains, it must provide disclosure to that effect. Funds subject to this requirement would include, for example, those often described as "tax-managed," "tax-sensitive," or "tax-advantaged," which have investment strategies to maximize long-term capital gains and minimize ordinary income.

If a fund has a *principal* investment objective or strategy to achieve tax-managed results of this type, the fund would be required to provide disclosure to that effect in the discussion of its investment objectives.

For a fund that describes itself as investing in securities generating tax-exempt income, it must provide, as applicable, a general statement to the effect that a portion of the fund's distributions may be subject to federal income tax.

Other Services Provided by the Fund

A fund profile should provide a brief summary of services available to the fund's shareholders (e.g., any exchange privileges or automated information services), unless this information has already been provided in earlier sections of the profile. A fund should disclose only those services that generally are available to typical investors in the fund.

APPLICATION TO PURCHASE SHARES

The profile may include an application that a prospective investor can use to purchase the fund's shares as long as the application explains with equal prominence that an investor has the option of purchasing shares of the fund after reviewing the information in the profile or after requesting and reviewing the fund's prospectus (and other information) before making a decision about investing in the fund.

FILING REQUIREMENTS

A profile is to be filed with the Commission at least 30 days before the date that it is first sent or given to a prospective investor. The first profile filing must be accompanied by the submission of a profile in the format in which it will be distributed to investors. Subsequent filings will not require the additional formatted profile. An amended form of any profile must be filed with the Commission within 5 business days after it is used.

MODIFIED PROFILES FOR CERTAIN FUNDS

Funds can tailor disclosure for profiles to be used for investments in defined contribution plans qualified under the Internal Revenue Code, and for funds offered through variable insurance contracts. The Commission believes that this revision will help to ensure that profiles contain information that investors will find meaningful and useful.

Rule 498 permits a profile for a fund offered as an investment option for a plan to include, or be accompanied by, an enrollment form for the plan. An application or enrollment form for a variable insurance contract may accompany the profile for the funds that serve as investment options; however, this is only if the form also is accompanied by a full prospectus for the contract.

The Rule also permits funds to modify the legend and other disclosure in profiles intended for use in connection with defined contribution plans, other tax-deferred arrangements described in the Rule, and variable insurance contracts.

Chapter 27

Practice Before the IRS and the Power of Attorney

EXPANDING THE CONFIDENTIALITY PRIVILEGE

The confidentiality protection for communications between a taxpayer and attorney has been expanded to communications involving tax advice between a taxpayer and any *federally authorized tax practitioners*. These tax practitioners include attorneys, certified public accountants, enrolled agents, enrolled actuaries, and certain other individuals allowed to practice before the Internal Revenue Service. This provision became effective for communications occurring after July 21, 1998.

This protection applies only to the advice given to the taxpayer by any of these individuals. Tax advice is considered to be advice in regard to a matter that is within the scope of the practitioner's authority to practice. The confidentiality protection is applied to communications that would be privileged if between the taxpayer and an attorney, and that relate to noncriminal tax matters or to tax proceedings brought in federal court by or against the United States.

This protection of tax advice communications does not apply to certain written communications between a federally authorized tax practitioner and a director, shareholder, officer, employee, agent, or representative of a corporation. It does not apply if the communication involves the promotion of the direct or indirect participation of the corporation in any tax shelter.

Practicing Before the IRS

A person is practicing before the IRS if he or she:

1. Communicates with the IRS for a taxpayer regarding taxpayer's rights, privileges, or liabilities under laws and regulations administered by the IRS.
2. Represents a taxpayer at conferences, hearings, or meetings with the IRS.
3. Prepares and files necessary documents with the IRS for a taxpayer.

Just preparing a tax return, furnishing information at the request of the IRS, or appearing as a witness for a taxpayer, does not constitute practicing before the IRS.

Becoming a Recognized Representative

Any of the following individuals can practice before the IRS. However, any individual who is recognized to practice—a recognized representative—must file a written declaration with the IRS that he or she is qualified and authorized to represent a taxpayer.

Those individuals include:

1. Any attorney who is not currently under suspension or disbarment from practice before the IRS and who is a member in good standing of the bar at the highest court of any state, possession, territory, commonwealth, or in the District of Columbia.
2. Any Certified Public Accountant who is not currently under suspension or disbarment from practice before the IRS and who is qualified to practice as a CPA in any state, possession, territory, commonwealth, or in the District of Columbia.
3. Any enrolled agent.
4. Any individual who is enrolled as an actuary by the Joint Board for the Enrollment of Actuaries. The practice of enrolled actuaries is limited to certain Internal Revenue Code sections that relate to their area of expertise, principally those sections governing employee retirement plans.
5. Any individual other than an attorney, CPA, enrolled agent, or enrolled actuary who prepares a return and signs it as the return preparer is an unenrolled return preparer. Also, any individual who prepares a return and is not required to sign it as the preparer is considered to be an unenrolled preparer.

These individuals are limited in their practice. They can represent a taxpayer concerning the tax liability only for the year or period covered by the return that he or she prepared. Also, an unenrolled return preparer is permitted to represent taxpayers only before the Examination Division of the IRS and is not permitted to represent taxpayers before the Appeals, Collection, or any other division of the IRS.

Unenrolled return preparers cannot perform the following activities for another taxpayer:

a. Sign claims for a refund.

b. Receive refund checks.

c. Sign consents to extend the statutory period for assessment for or collection of tax.

d. Sign closing agreements regarding a tax liability.

e. Sign waivers of restriction on assessment or collection of a tax deficiency.

6. Because of their special relationship with a taxpayer, the following unenrolled individuals can represent the specified taxpayers before the IRS, provided they present satisfactory identification and proof of authority to represent.

   a. An individual can represent himself or herself before the IRS and does not have to file a written declaration of qualification and authority.

   b. An individual family member can represent members of his or her immediate family. Family members include a spouse, child, parent, brother, or sister of the individual.

   c. A *bona fide* officer of a corporation (including parents subsidiaries, or affiliated corporation), association, organized group, or, in the course of his or her other official duties, an officer of a governmental unit, agency, or authority can represent the organization of which he or she is an officer.

   d. A trustee, receiver, guardian, personal representative, or executor can represent a trust or estate.

   e. A regular full-time employee can represent his or her employer. An employer can be, but is not limited to, an individual, partnership, corporation (including parents, subsidiaries, or affiliated corporations), association, trust, receivership, guardianship, estate, organized group, governmental unit, agency, or authority.

An unenrolled individual can represent any individual or entity before IRS personnel who are outside the United States.

Denial of Right to Limited Practice

The IRS Director of Practice, after giving notice and an opportunity for a conference, can deny eligibility for limited practice before the IRS to any unenrolled preparer or other unenrolled individual who has engaged in disreputable conduct. This conduct includes, but is not limited to, the list of items under Disreputable Conduct.

Authorization for Special Appearance

An individual can be authorized to practice before the IRS or represent another person in a particular matter. The prospective representative must request this authorization in writing from the Director of Practice. It is granted only when extremely compelling circumstances exist. If granted, the IRS will issue a letter that details the conditions related to the appearance and the particular tax matter for which the authorization is granted.

The authorization letter should not be confused with a letter from an IRS service center advising an individual that he or she has been assigned a *Centralized Authorization File* number which identifies an assigned representative. The issuance of a number does not indicate that a person is either recognized or authorized to practice before the IRS. It merely confirms that a centralized file for authorizations has been established for the representative under that number.

Who Cannot Practice

Individuals cannot practice before the IRS either because they are not eligible to practice, or because they have lost the privilege as a result of certain actions. The following individuals generally cannot practice before the IRS:

1. Individuals convicted of any criminal offense under the revenue laws of the U.S.
2. Individuals convicted of any offense involving dishonesty or breach of trust.
3. Individuals under disbarment or suspension from practicing as attorneys, CPAs, public accountants, or actuaries in any state, possession, territory, commonwealth, or in the District of Columbia, or before any federal court, or any body or board of any federal agency.
4. Individuals who are disbarred or suspended from practice before the IRS because they refuse or have refused to comply with the regulations governing practice before the IRS.

METHODS OF ENROLLMENT

The Director of Practice can grant an enrollment to practice before the IRS to an applicant who has demonstrated special competence in tax matters by passing a written examination administered by the IRS. Enrollment also can be granted to an applicant who qualifies because of past service and technical experience in the IRS. In either case certain application forms must be filed. An applicant must never have engaged in any conduct that would justify suspension or disbarment by the IRS.

An *enrollment card* will be issued to each individual whose application is approved. The individual is enrolled until the expiration date shown on the enrollment card. To continue practicing beyond the expiration date, the individual must request renewal of the enrollment.

RULES OF PRACTICE

An attorney, CPA, enrolled agent, or enrolled actuary authorized to practice before the IRS who is referred to as a practitioner has the duty to perform certain acts and is restricted from performing other acts. Any practitioner who does not comply with the rules of practice or engages in disreputable conduct is subject to disciplinary action. Also, unenrolled preparers must comply with most of these rules of practice and conduct to exercise the privilege of limited practice before the IRS.

Practitioners must promptly submit records or information requested by officers or employees of the IRS. When the IRS requests information concerning possible violations of the regulations by other parties, the practitioner must provide it and be prepared to testify in disbarment or suspension proceedings. A practitioner can be exempt from these rules if he or she believes in good faith and on reasonable grounds that the information requested is privileged or that the request is of doubtful legality.

A practitioner who knows that his or her client has not complied with the revenue laws, or has made an error in or omission from any return, document, affidavit, or other required paper has the responsibility to advise the client promptly of the noncompliance error or omission.

Required Due Diligence

A practitioner must exercise due diligence when performing the following duties:

1. Preparing or assisting in the preparation, approving, and filing of returns, documents, affidavits, and other papers relating to IRS matters.

2. Determining the correctness of oral or written representations made by him or her to the Department of the Treasury.
3. Determining the correctness of oral or written presentations made by him or her to clients with reference to any matter administered by the IRS.

Restrictions

Practitioners are restricted from engaging in certain practices:

1. A practitioner must not unreasonably delay the prompt disposition of any matter before the IRS.
2. A practitioner must not knowingly, directly or indirectly, employ or accept assistance from any person who is under disbarment or suspension from practice before the IRS.
3. He or she must not accept employment as an associate, correspondent, or subagent from, or share fees with, any person under disbarment or suspension by the IRS.
4. He or she must not accept assistance from any former government employee where provisions of these regulations or any federal law would be violated.
5. If a practitioner is a notary public and is employed as counsel, attorney, or agent in a matter before the IRS, or has a material interest in the matter, he or she must not engage in any notary activities relative to that matter.
6. A partner of an officer or employee of the executive branch of the U.S. Government, or of an independent agency of the U.S. or of the District of Columbia, cannot represent anyone in a matter before the IRS in which the officer or employee has or had a personal or substantial interest as a government employee. There are similar and additional restrictions on former government employees.

Disreputable Conduct

Disreputable conduct by a practitioner includes such things as:

1. Committing any criminal offense under the revenue laws, or committing any offense involving dishonesty or breach of trust.
2. Knowingly giving or participating in the giving of false or misleading information in connection with federal tax matters.
3. Willful failure to file a tax return, evading or attempting to evade any federal tax or payment, or participating in such actions.

4. Misappropriating, or failing properly and promptly to remit funds received from clients for payment of taxes.

5. Directly or indirectly attempting to influence the official action of IRS employees by the use of threats, false accusations, duress, or coercion, or by offering gifts, favors, or any special inducements.

6. Being disbarred or suspended by the District of Columbia or by any state, possession, territory, commonwealth, or any federal court, or any body or board of any federal agency.

7. Knowingly aiding and abetting another person to practice before the IRS during a period of suspension, disbarment, or ineligibility, or maintaining a partnership so that a suspended or disbarred person can continue to practice before the IRS.

8. Contemptuous conduct in connection with practice before the IRS, including the use of abusive language, making false accusations and statements, or circulating or publishing malicious or libelous matter.

9. Giving a false opinion knowingly, or recklessly, or through gross incompetence, or following a pattern of providing incompetent opinions in questions arising under the federal tax laws.

10. Soliciting employment by prohibited means.

The Power of Attorney

A power of attorney is a taxpayer's written authorization for an individual to act for him or her in tax matters. If the authorization is not limited, the individual can generally perform all acts that a taxpayer can perform. The authority granted to an unenrolled preparer cannot exceed that shown under the special rules of limited practice.

Any representative, other than an unenrolled preparer, can usually perform the following acts:

1. Represent the taxpayer before any office of the IRS.

2. Record the interview.

3. Sign an offer or a waiver of restriction on assessment or collection of a tax deficiency, or a waiver of notice of disallowance of claim for credit or refunds.

4. Sign a consent to extend the statutory time period for assessment or collection of a tax.

5. Sign a closing agreement.

6. Receive, but not endorse or cash, a refund check drawn on the U.S. Treasury. The taxpayer must specifically sign a form showing the name of the individual designated to receive the refund check.

The representative named under a power of attorney is not permitted to sign the taxpayer's income tax return unless the signature is permitted under the Internal Revenue Code and the related regulations of the Tax Regulations. The taxpayer can authorize this in the taxpayer's power of attorney.

The regulation permits a representative to sign a client's income tax return if the client is unable to make the return for any of the following reasons:

1. Disease or injury.
2. Continuous absence from the United States for a period of at least 60 days prior to the date required by law for filing the return.
3. Other good cause if specific permission is requested of and granted by the IRS.

If a taxpayer wants a representative to receive a refund check, the taxpayer must specifically so authorize it in the power of attorney. However, if the representative is an income tax return preparer, the representative cannot be authorized to endorse or otherwise cash the client's check related to income taxes.

The appointed representative can substitute a representative or delegate authority to a new representative only if this is specifically authorized under the power of attorney. A power of attorney is generally terminated if the client becomes incapacitated or incompetent. The power of attorney can continue, however, in the case of the taxpayer's incapacity or incompetency if the taxpayer had previously authorized that it be continued.

When a Power of Attorney Is Required

A taxpayer should submit a power of attorney when he or she wants to authorize an individual to represent him or her before the IRS, whether or not the representative performs any of the other acts discussed earlier. A power of attorney is most often required when a taxpayer wants to authorize another individual to perform at least one of the following acts on his or her behalf:

1. Represent the taxpayer at a conference with the IRS.
2. Prepare and file a written response to the IRS.

A taxpayer can appoint an unenrolled return preparer as his or her representative. The preparer can represent the taxpayer only before revenue agents and examining officers. Also, the preparer can represent a taxpayer concerning his or her tax liability only for the period covered by a return prepared by the preparer.

The IRS will accept a non-IRS power of attorney, but a transmittal form must be attached in order for the power of attorney to be entered into the *Centralized Authorization File*. If a power of attorney document other than the required transmittal form is used, it must contain the following information:

1. The taxpayer's name and mailing address, Social Security number, and/or employer identification number.
2. An employee plan number, if applicable.
3. The name and mailing address of the taxpayer's representative.
4. The types of tax involved.
5. The federal tax form number.
6. The specific years or periods involved.
7. For estate tax matters, the decedent's date of death.
8. A clear expression of the taxpayer's intention concerning the scope of authority granted to his or her representative.
9. The taxpayer's signature and date.

The taxpayer must also attach to the non-IRS power of attorney a signed and dated statement made by the taxpayer's representative. This statement, which is referred to as the *Declaration of Representative* is included with the transmittal form filed.

Filing a Power of Attorney

The power of attorney is filed with each IRS office with which the taxpayer deals. If the power of attorney is filed for a matter currently pending before an office of the IRS, it should be filed with that office. Otherwise, the power should be filed with the service center where the related return was, or will be, filed.

When a Power of Attorney Is Not Required

The following situations do not require a power of attorney:

1. A power of attorney is not required when a person is merely furnishing information at the request of the IRS.
2. A power of attorney is not required to authorize the IRS to disclose information concerning a tax account to an individual (whether or not the individual is authorized to practice before the IRS) or other party, such as a corporation, a partnership, or an association.

The Tax Matters Partner or Person (TMP)

A TMP is authorized by law to perform various acts on behalf of a partnership or Subchapter S corporation. This includes the power to delegate authority to represent the TMP and to sign documents in that capacity, but certain acts performed by the TMP cannot be delegated.

The Fiduciary

A fiduciary, trustee, executor, administrator, receiver, or guardian, stands in the position of the taxpayer and acts as the taxpayer. Therefore, a fiduciary does not act as a representative and should not file a power of attorney. A fiduciary should file Form 56, *Notice Concerning Fiduciary Relationship*, to notify the IRS of the fiduciary relationship.

Completed Documents

A power of attorney will be recognized after the Form 56 is received, reviewed, and determined by the IRS to contain the required information. However, until a power of attorney is entered into the Centralized Authorized File (CAF), IRS personnel, other than the individual to whom the form is submitted, may be unaware of the authority of the taxpayer's representative and request an additional copy.

When the IRS receives a complete and valid power of attorney, the IRS will take action to recognize the representative. This involves processing the document into the CAF system. The power of attorney is not considered valid until all required information is entered on the document. The individual named as representative will not be recognized to practice before the IRS until the document is complete and accepted by the IRS.

In most instances, the recognition involves processing the document by recording the information on the CAF which enables the IRS to automatically direct copies of mailings to an authorized representative and to instantly recognize the scope of authority granted.

After the power of attorney is filed, the IRS will recognize the taxpayer's representative. However, if it appears the representative is responsible for unreasonably delaying or hindering the prompt disposition of an IRS matter by failing to furnish, after repeated requests, nonprivileged information, the IRS can bypass the representative and contact the taxpayer directly.

Revoking a Power of Attorney

If a taxpayers wants to revoke an existing power of attorney and does not want to name a new representative, there are two ways to do it:

1. By sending a *revocation copy* of a previous appointment form to each office of the IRS where forms were originally filed.
2. By sending a *revocation statement* to the service center where a return was filed that was covered by the power of attorney.

Unless a taxpayer wants to revoke a power of attorney for which no form was filed, a letter can be written requesting the revocation with a copy of the power of attorney to be revoked. The letter should be signed and dated and sent to each office of the IRS where the taxpayer originally filed the non-IRS power of attorney.

Unless a taxpayer specifies otherwise, a newly filed power of attorney concerning the same matter will revoke a previously filed power of attorney, but not a previously filed tax authorization. A newly filed tax information authorization will revoke a previously filed tax authorization concerning the same matter, but will not revoke a power of attorney concerning that matter.

Chapter 28
Depreciation

Depreciation is a decrease in the value of property over the time the property is being used. Events that can cause property to depreciate include wear and tear, age, deterioration, and obsolescence. It is possible to get back the cost of certain property by taking deductions for depreciation. For example, depreciation deduction may be taken for equipment used in business or for the production of income.

TYPES OF PROPERTY

To determine if property is a depreciation deduction, the property must be defined as either tangible or intangible.

Tangible property is property that can be seen or touched. There are two main types of tangible property, real property, such as land, buildings, and generally anything built or constructed on land, growing on land, or attached to the land; and personal property including cars, trucks, machinery, furniture, equipment and anything that isn't real property.

Intangible property is generally any property that has value but cannot be seen or touched. It includes items such as computer software, copyrights, franchises, patents, trademarks, and trade names. Generally, if intangible property is depreciable the straight line method is used. It allows for the same amount of depreciation each year.

In general, only the owner using the property for business or for producing income may claim depreciation.

Only the property meeting all the following requirements may be depreciated.

1. It must be used in business or held to produce income.
2. It must be expected to last more than one year. In other words, it must have a useful life that extends substantially beyond the year it is placed in service.
3. It must be something that wears out, decays, gets used up, becomes obsolete, or loses its value from natural causes.

WHAT CANNOT BE DEPRECIATED

Property placed in service and disposed of in the same year may not be depreciated.

Tangible Property

The following are types of tangible property that cannot be depreciated, even though they are used in business or held to produce income.

1. The cost of land may not be depreciated because land does not wear out, become obsolete, or get used up. The cost of land generally includes the cost of clearing, grading, planting, and landscaping because these expenses are all part of the cost of the land itself.
2. Inventory is any property held primarily for sale to customers in the ordinary course of business and may not be depreciated.
3. Generally, containers are part of inventory and cannot be depreciated.
4. Equipment held to build capital improvements may not be depreciated.
5. Leased property may be depreciated only if the incidents of ownership for the property are retained. Leased property to use in business or for the production of income cannot be depreciated because the incidents of ownership are not retained. A lessor generally can depreciate its cost even if the lessee has agreed to preserve, replace, renew, and maintain the property. However, if the lease provides that the lessee is to maintain the property and return to the lessor the same property or its equivalent in value at the expiration of the lease in as good condition and value as when leased, the cost of the property may not be depreciated.

"Incidents of ownership" include the legal title, the legal obligation to pay for it, the responsibility to pay its maintenance and operating expenses, the duty to pay any taxes and the risk of loss if the property is destroyed, condemned, or diminishes in value through obsolescence or exhaustion.

6. Generally, a deduction for depreciation may not be taken on a term interest in property created or acquired after July 27, 1989, for any period during which the remainder interest is held, directly or indirectly, by a person related to the owner.

Intangible Property

There are two types of intangible property that can never be depreciated.

1. Goodwill may never be depreciated because its useful life cannot be determined. However, if a business was acquired after August 10, 1993 (after July 25, 1991, if elected), and part of the price included goodwill, it may be possible to amortize the cost of the goodwill over 15 years.
2. In general, trademark and trade name expenses must be capitalized. Neither trademarks nor trade names may be depreciated or amortized if acquired before August 11, 1993 (before July 26, 1991, if elected). It may be possible to amortize over 15 years the costs of trademarks and trade names acquired after August 10, 1993 (after July 25, 1991, if elected).

WHEN DEPRECIATION BEGINS AND ENDS

Property may be depreciated when it is placed in service for use in a trade or business or for the production of income. It is no longer depreciable when the cost has been fully recovered or other basis or when it is retired from service, whichever happens first.

For depreciation purposes, property is placed in service when it is ready and available for a specific use, whether in a trade or business, for the production of income, a tax-exempt activity, or a personal activity. Even if the property is not being used, it is in service when it is ready and available for its specific use.

Property permanently withdrawn from use in trade or business or from use in the production of income is considered retired from service and is no longer depreciable. Property can be retired either when sold or exchanged, when it is abandoned or when it is destroyed.

USING THE SECTION 179 DEDUCTION

The Section 179 deduction is a means of recovering the cost of property through a current deduction rather than through depreciation. Section 179 of the Internal Revenue Code allows for the deduction of all or part of the cost of certain qualifying property in the year it is placed in service. This would be done instead of recovering the cost by taking depreciation deductions over a specified recovery period. However, there are limits on the amount that can be deducted in a year.

What Costs Can and Cannot Be Deducted

The Section 179 deduction may be used for the cost of qualifying property acquired for use in trade or business, but not for the cost of property held only for the production of income.

Only the cost of property acquired by purchase for use in business qualifies for the Section 179 deduction. The cost of property acquired from a related person or group may not qualify.

If an asset is purchased with cash and a trade-in, a Section 179 deduction can be claimed based only on the amount of cash paid. The Section 179 deduction does not include the adjusted basis of the trade-in used in the purchase.

Qualifying Property

Property qualifying for the Section 179 deduction is depreciable property and includes the following.

1. Tangible personal property.
2. Other tangible property (except buildings and their structural components) used as:
   a. An integral part of manufacturing, production, or extraction or of furnishing transportation, communications, electricity, gas, water, or sewage disposal services,
   b. A research facility used in connection with any of the activities in above, or
   c. A facility used in connection with any of the activities for the bulk storage of fungible commodities.
3. Single purpose agricultural (livestock) or horticultural structures.
4. Storage facilities (except buildings and their structural components) used in connection with distributing petroleum or any primary product of petroleum.

Generally, a Section 179 deduction may not be claimed based on the cost of leased property. However, a Section 179 deduction may be claimed based on the cost of the following:

1. Property manufactured or produced and leased to others.
2. Property purchased and leased to others if both of the following apply.
   a. The term of the lease (including options to renew) is less than half of the property's class life.
   b. For the first 12 months after the property is transferred to the lessee, the total business deductions allowed on the property (other than rent and reimbursed amounts) is more than 15% of the rental income from the property.

Partial Business Use

When property is used for both business and nonbusiness purposes, the Section 179 deduction may be used if the property is used more than 50% for business in the year it was placed in service. The part of the cost of the property that is for business use is the cost of the property multiplied by the percentage of business use. The result is the business cost.

Nonqualifying Property

Generally, the Section 179 deduction cannot be claimed on the cost of any of the following.

1. Property held only for the production of income.
2. Real property, including buildings and their structural components.
3. Property acquired from certain groups or persons.
4. Air conditioning or heating units.
5. Certain property used predominantly outside the U.S.
6. Property used predominantly to furnish lodging or in connection with the furnishing of lodging.
7. Property used by certain tax-exempt organizations.
8. Property used by governmental units.
9. Property used by foreign persons or entities.
10. Certain property leased to others by a noncorporate lessor.

Electing the Deduction

The Section 179 deduction is not automatic. An individual must elect to take a Section 179 deduction. For purposes of the Section 179 deduction, property is considered placed in service in the year it is first made ready and available for a specific use. This use can be in a trade or business, the production of income, a tax-exempt activity, or a personal activity. If property is placed in service in a use that does not qualify it for the Section 179 deduction, it cannot later qualify in another year even if it is changed to business use. Records must be kept that show the specific identification of each piece of qualifying Section 179 property. These records must show how the property was acquired, the person it was acquired from and when it was placed in service.

How to Figure the Deduction

The total business cost an individual can elect to deduct under Section 179 in 2000 is $20,000; in 2001 and 2002, it is $24,000; after 2002, it is $25,000. This maximum dollar limit applies to each taxpayer, not to each business. The full amount does not have to be claimed. A percentage of the business cost of qualifying property may be deducted under Section 179. Then it may be possible to depreciate any difference in the cost not deducted under Section 179. If more than one item of qualifying property is acquired and placed in service during the same year, it is possible to divide the deduction among the items in any way, as long as the total deduction is not more than the limits.

If there is only one item of qualifying property and it does not cost more than the dollar limit, the deduction is limited to the lesser of the following.

1. An individual's taxable income from trade or business.
2. The cost of the item.

The Section 179 deduction must be figured before figuring the depreciation deduction. The amount deducted under Section 179 must be subtracted from the business/investment cost of the qualifying property. The result is called the unadjusted basis and is the amount used to figure any depreciation deduction.

Deduction Limits

The Section 179 deduction cannot be more than the business cost of the qualifying property. In addition, the following limits must be applied to the Section 179 deduction.

1. Maximum dollar limit. The total cost of Section 179 property that can be elected for deduction cannot be more than the amounts listed above.
2. Investment limit. If the cost of the qualifying Section 179 property placed in service in a year at present is over $200,000, the maximum dollar limit for each dollar over $200,000 must be reduced (but not below zero). If the business cost of Section 179 property placed in service is $200,000 plus the maximum dollar limit, or more, a Section 179 deduction cannot be taken for more than the total, and cannot be carried over.

3. Taxable income limit.The total cost that can be deducted each year is limited to the taxable income from the active conduct of any trade or business during the year. Generally, an individual is considered to be actively conducting a trade or business if he or she meaningfully participates in the management or operations of the trade or business.

THE MODIFIED ACCELERATED COST RECOVERY SYSTEM (MACRS)

The Modified Accelerated Cost Recovery System (MACRS) consists of two systems that determine how to depreciate property. The main system is called the General Depreciation System (GDS) and the second system is called the Alternative Depreciation System (ADS).

The main difference between the two systems is that ADS generally provides for a longer recovery period and uses only the straight line method of depreciation to figure a deduction. Unless specifically required by law to use ADS, GDS is generally used to figure a depreciation deduction.

Both systems simplify the way to figure the deduction by providing three preset conventions. These conventions determine the number of months for which depreciation may be claimed both in the year the property is placed in service, and in the year in which the property is disposed of. The conventions are as follows:

1. Mid-month convention. Used for all nonresidential real property and residential rental property. The property is treated for tax purposes as if use began or ended in the middle of the month.
2. Mid-quarter convention. Used if the basis of property placed in service during the last three months of the tax year is more than 40% of the total bases of all property placed in service for the entire year (excluding nonresidential real property, residential rental property, and property placed in service and disposed of in the same year). The property is treated for tax purposes as if use began or ended in the middle of the quarter.
3. Half-year convention. Used for all other property. The property is treated for tax purposes as if use began or ended in the middle of the year.

MACRS provides four methods of figuring depreciation on property:

1. The 200% declining balance method over a GDS recovery period.
2. The 150% declining balance method over a GDS recovery period.
3. The straight line method over a GDS recovery period.
4. The straight line method over an ADS recovery period.

What to Depreciate Under MACRS

MACRS applies to most tangible depreciable property placed in service after 1986. MACRS must be used to depreciate all real property acquired before 1987 that has been changed from personal use to a business or income-producing use after 1986.

Knowing Which System to Use

Most tangible depreciable property falls within the *general* rule of MACRS, which is also called the General Depreciation System (GDS). Because GDS permits use of the declining balance method over a shorter recovery period, the deduction is greater in the earlier years.

However, there are specifications for the use of each system.

Both GDS and ADS have pre-established class lives for most property. Under GDS, most property is assigned to eight property classes based on these class lives. These property classes provide the number of years over which the cost of an item in a class may be recovered.

Some examples of this:

3-year property. Any race horse over 2 years old when placed in service. Any other horse over 12 years old when placed in service.

5-year property. Automobiles, taxis, buses, and trucks; computers and peripheral equipment; some office machinery; breeding cattle and dairy cattle.

However, ADS must be used for the following property:

1. Any tangible property used predominantly outside the U.S. during the year.
2. Any tax-exempt use property.
3. Any tax-exempt bond-financed property.
4. Any property used predominantly in a farming business and placed in service during any tax year in which the individual makes an election not to apply the uniform capitalization rules to certain farming costs.
5. Any imported property covered by an executive order of the President of the United States.

What Cannot Be Depreciated Under MACRS

MACRS cannot be used to depreciate the following property.

1. Intangible property.
2. Any motion picture film or video tape.
3. Any sound recording.
4. Certain real and personal property placed in service before 1987.

Any property that can be properly depreciated under a method of depreciation not based on a term of years may be excluded from MACRS.

Property Placed in Service Before 1987. There are special rules that prevent the use of MACRS for property placed in service by anyone (for any purpose) before 1987 (before August 1, 1986, if MACRS was elected). These rules apply to both personal and real property. However, the rules for personal property are more restrictive. And although there are some exceptions to these rules, they do offer a basic guideline from which to work.

Personal property. MACRS may not be used for most personal property acquired after 1986 (after July 31, 1986, if MACRS was elected) if any of the following apply.

1. The individual or a relative owned or used the property in 1986.
2. The property was acquired from a person who owned it in 1986 and as part of the transaction the user of the property did not change.
3. The property was leased to a person (or someone related to this person) who owned or used the property in 1986.
4. The property was acquired in a transaction in which:
   a. The user of the property did not change, and
   b. The property was not MACRS property in the hands of the person from whom the individual acquired it because of (2) or (3).

Real property. MACRS may not be used for certain real property. This includes real property acquired after 1986 (after July 31, 1986, if MACRS was elected) if any of the following apply.

1. The individual or a relative owned the property in 1986.
2. The property was leased back to the person (or someone related to this person) who owned the property in 1986.
3. The property was acquired in a transaction in which some of the individual's gain or loss was not recognized. MACRS applies only to that part of the basis in the acquired property that represents cash paid or unlike property given up. It does not apply to the substituted portion of the basis.

Certain nontaxable transfers of property. MACRS does not apply to property involved in certain nontaxable transfers. This applies to property used before 1987 and transferred after 1986 to a corporation or partnership if its basis is determined by reference to the basis in the hands of the transferor or distributor. If MACRS was elected, it also applies to property used before August 1, 1986, and transferred after July 31, 1986, to a corporation or partnership if its basis is determined by reference to the basis in the hands of the transferor or distributor.

The nontaxable transfers covered by this rule include the following:

1. A distribution in complete liquidation of a subsidiary.
2. A transfer to a corporation controlled by the transferor.
3. An exchange of property solely for corporate stock or securities in a reorganization.
4. A contribution of property to a partnership in exchange for a partnership interest.
5. A partnership distribution of property to a partner.

Election to Exclude Property from MACRS

If property is depreciated under a method not based on a term of years, such as the unit-of-production method, that property may be excluded from MACRS.

Use of Standard Mileage Rate

If the standard mileage rate is used to figure a tax deduction for a business automobile, it is treated as having made an election to exclude the automobile from MACRS.

How to Figure the Deduction

Once it is determined that the property may be depreciated under MACRS and whether it falls under GDS or ADS, the following information must be known about the property.

1. Its basis. Generally, this refers to the cost plus amounts paid for items such as sales tax, freight, installation, and testing.
2. Its property class and recovery period. This refers to the member of years over which the cost "basis" of the property is recovered.
3. The date it was placed in service. This refers to the date the item was actually first used—not when it was purchased.

4. Which convention to use—mid-month, mid-quarter, or half-year.
5. Which depreciation method to use:
   a. GDS or ADS
   b. Which class the property is in.
   c. What type of property it is.

DISPOSITIONS

A disposition is the permanent withdrawal of property from use in a trade or business or in the production of income. A withdrawal can be made by sale, exchange, retirement, abandonment, involuntary conversion, or destruction. Generally gain or loss on the disposition of property is recognized by a sale. However, nonrecognition rules may allow for postponement of some gain.

If property is disposed of before the end of its recovery period, it is called an early disposition. If that property is depreciated under MACRS, a depreciation deduction for the year of disposition is allowed. The depreciation deduction is determined for the year of disposition.

With the exception of gain on the disposition of residential rental and nonresidential real property, all gain on the disposition of property depreciated under MACRS is included in income as ordinary income, up to the amount of previously allowed depreciation deducted for the property. There is no recapture for residential rental and nonresidential real property.

GENERAL ASSET ACCOUNTS

It is possible to group separate properties into one or more general asset accounts. They then can be depreciated as a single item of property. Each account can include only property with similar characteristics, such as asset class and recovery period. Some property cannot be included in a general asset account. There are additional rules for passenger automobiles, disposing of property, converting property to personal use, and property that generates foreign source income.

Once a general asset account is established, the amount of depreciation for each account is achieved by using the depreciation method, recovery period, and convention that applies to the property in the account. For each general asset account, the depreciation allowance is recorded in a separate depreciation reserve account.

Property used in both a trade or business (or for the production of income) and in a personal activity in the year in which it was first placed in service may not be in a general asset account.

How to Group Property in General Asset Accounts

Each general asset account must include only property placed in service in the same year and that has the following in common:

1. Asset class.
2. Recovery period.
3. Depreciation method.
4. Convention.

The following rules also apply when establishing a general asset account.

1. No asset class. Property without an asset class, but with the same depreciation method, recovery period, and convention, placed in service in the same year, can be grouped into the same general asset account.
2. Mid-quarter convention. Property subject to the mid-quarter convention can only be grouped into a general asset account with property that is placed in service in the same quarter.
3. Mid-month convention. Property subject to the mid-month convention can only be grouped into a general asset account with property that is placed in service in the same month.
4. Passenger automobiles. Passenger automobiles subject to the limits on passenger automobile depreciation must be grouped into a separate general asset account.

Dispositions and Conversions

Property in a general asset account is considered disposed of when any of the following occurs:

1. It is permanently withdrawn from use in trade or business or from the production of income.
2. It is transferred to a supplies, scrap, or similar account.
3. It is sold, exchanged, retired, physically abandoned, or destroyed.

Note the following:

1. The retirement of a structural component of real property is not a disposal.
2. The unadjusted depreciable basis and the depreciation reserve of the general asset account are not affected by the disposition of property from the general asset account.

3. Any property changed to personal use must be removed from the general asset account.

Unadjusted depreciable basis. The unadjusted depreciable basis of an item of property in a general asset account is the same amount used to figure gain on the sale of the property, but it is figured without taking into account any depreciation taken in earlier years. The unadjusted depreciable basis of a general asset account is the total of the unadjusted depreciable bases of all of the property in the account.

Adjusted depreciable basis. The adjusted depreciable basis of a general asset account is the unadjusted depreciable basis of the account minus any allowed or allowable depreciation based on the account.

Disposition of remaining property. If all or the last item of property is disposed of in a general asset account, the adjusted depreciable basis of the general asset account can be recovered. Under this rule, the general asset account ends and the amount of gain or loss for the general asset account is figured by comparing the adjusted depreciable basis of the general asset account with the amount realized. If the amount realized is more than the adjusted depreciable basis, the difference is a gain. If it is less, the difference is a loss. If there is a gain, the amount that is subject to recapture as ordinary income is limited.

Change to personal use. An item of property in a general asset account becomes ineligible for general asset account treatment if it is used in a personal activity. Once the property has been converted to personal use, it is removed from the general asset account as of the first day of the year in which the change in use occurs and the appropriate adjustments are made.

Chapter 29

Independent Contractor or Employee?

Whether a person is an employee or independent contractor has been an area of uncertainty for many years. In August 1996, during the 104th Congress, changing and strengthening the "safe harbor" provisions were enacted as part of the *Small Business Jobs Protection Act*. The changes allow small businesses to rely on previous IRS actions and determinations to avoid reclassification of independent contractors as employees. The legislation does, however, still leave open the key question of what exactly is an independent contractor.

To make the definition of an independent contractor as clear as possible under current law, the IRS issued a training manual for IRS personnel on the independent contractor issue; introduced procedures for facilitating rapid determinations and appeals; and reduced penalties where a business acts in good faith to classify its independent contractors.

WORKER CLASSIFICATION

With the exception of statutory employees, work classification is based upon a common law standard for determining whether the worker is an independent contractor or employee. That standard essentially asks whether the business has the right to *direct and control the worker*. The courts have traditionally looked to a variety of evidentiary facts in applying this standard, and the IRS has adopted those facts to assist in classifying workers.

Accountant's Concern?

When conducting an audit, the auditor needs to assist taxpayers in identifying all of the evidence relative to their business relationships with workers. Many taxpayers may not be aware of what information is needed to make a correct determination of worker classification. This is especially true of small business owners who may not be aware of the relief available under Section 530 of the Revenue Act of 1978, resulting from worker reclassification. An auditor's examination should actively consider Section 530 during an examination, including furnishing taxpayers with a summary of Section 530 at the beginning of an examination.

Essentially, an accountant's responsibility is similar to an IRS tax examiner's responsibility as set forth by the Treasury Department which states:

"The examiner has a responsibility to the taxpayer and to the government to determine the correct tax liability and to maintain a fair and impartial attitude in all matters relating to the examination. The fair and impartial attitude of an examiner aids in increasing voluntary compliance. An examiner must approach each examination with an objective point of view."

Primary Categories

Officially termed the *worker classification issue,* the focus is centered on three main areas that the IRS has concluded are primary categories of evidence to draw a distinction between an employee and an independent contractor. The essence of the distinction is whether or not the employer has the right to direct and control the worker. The three areas are:

1. Behavioral control.
2. Financial control.
3. Relationship of the parties.

Those three areas provide evidence that substantiates the right to direct or control the details and means by which the worker performs the required services. Training is important in this context. Significant are such workplace developments as evaluation systems and concern for customer security in conjunction with business identification. All relevant information must be considered and weighed to determine whether a worker is an independent contractor or an employee.

Virtually every business will impose on workers, whether contractors or employees, some form of instruction. How else would a worker know what he or she is supposed to do, what duties to perform? This fact alone, however, is not sufficient evidence to determine a worker's status. As with every relevant fact, the problem is to determine whether the employer has retained the right to control the *details* of a worker's performance, or instead has given up the business's right to control those details. Accordingly, the weight of evidence in any case depends on the *degree* to which instructions apply with respect to *how the job gets done rather than to the end result.*

Behavioral Control

Behavioral control concerns whether there is a right to direct or control how the worker performs the specific task for which he or she is engaged. Instructions and training are the main factors in considering the degree of behavioral control.

The degree of instruction depends on the scope of instructions, the extent to which the business retains the right to control the worker's compliance with the instructions, and the effect on the worker in the event of noncompliance. All these provide useful clues for identifying whether the business keeps control over the manner and means of work performance, or only over a particular product or service. The more detailed the instructions are that the worker is required to follow, the more control the business exerts over the worker, and the more likely the business retains the right to control the methods by which the worker performs the work. Absence of detail in instructions reflects less control.

Although the presence and extent of instructions is important in reaching a conclusion as to whether a business retains the right to direct and control the methods by which a worker performs a job, it is also important to consider the weight to be given those instructions if they are imposed by the business only in compliance with governmental or governing body regulations. If a business requires its workers to comply with established, municipal building codes related to construction, for example, the fact that such rules are imposed by the business should be given little weight in determining the worker's status. However, if the business develops more stringent guidelines for a worker in addition to those imposed by a third party, more weight should be given to these instructions in determining whether the business has retained the right to control the worker.

The nature of a worker's occupation also affects the degree of direction and control necessary to determine worker status. Highly trained professionals such as doctors, accountants, lawyers, engineers, or computer specialists may require very little, if any, training and instruction on how to perform their services for a particular business. In fact, it may be impossible for the business to instruct the worker on how to perform the services because it may lack the essential knowledge and skills to do so. Generally, professional workers who are engaged in the pursuit of an independent trade, business, or profession in which they offer their services to the public are independent contractors, not employees. In analyzing the status of professional workers, evidence of control or autonomy with respect to the financial details of how the task is performed tends to be especially important, as does evidence concerning the relationship of the parties.

An employment relationship can also exist when the work can be done with a minimal amount of direction and control, such as work done by a store clerk, or gas station attendant. The absence of a *need* to control should not be confused with the absence of the *right* to control. The right to control as an incident of employment requires only such supervision as the nature of the work requires. The key fact to consider is whether the business retains the *right* to direct and control the worker, regardless of whether the business actually exercises that right.

Evaluation systems are used by virtually all businesses to monitor the quality of work performed by workers, whether independent contractors or employees. In analyzing whether a business's evaluation system provides evidence of the right to control work performance, or the absence of such a right, an auditor should look for evidence of how the evaluation system may influence the worker's behavior in performing the details of the job.

If an evaluation system measures compliance with performance standards concerning the details of how the work is to be performed, the system and its enforcement are evidence of control over the worker's behavior. However, not all businesses have developed formal performance standards or evaluation systems. This is especially true of smaller businesses.

Training is the established means of explaining detailed methods and procedures to be used in performing a task. Periodic or ongoing training provided by a business about procedures to be followed and methods to be used indicates that the business wants the services performed in a particular manner. This type of training is strong evidence of an employer-employee relationship.

Financial Control

Financial control concerns the facts which illustrate whether there is a *right* to direct or control how the worker's activities are conducted.

Factors to be considered are the business aspects of the worker's activities; significant investment, if any; unreimbursed expenses; services available to the relevant market; method of payment; and opportunity for profit or loss. These factors can be thought of as bearing on the issue of whether the recipient has the right to direct and control the means and details of the business aspects of how the worker performs services.

A significant investment is evidence that an independent contractor relationship may exist. It should be stressed that a significant investment is not necessary for an independent contractor. Some types of work simply do not require large expenditures. Even if large expenditures, such as costly equipment, are required, an independent contractor may rent the equipment needed at fair rental value. There are no precise dollar limits that must be met in order to have a significant investment. The size of the worker's investment and the risk borne by the worker are not diminished merely because the seller or lessor receives the benefit of the worker's services.

The extent to which a worker chooses to incur expenses and costs impacts his or her opportunity for profit or loss. This constitutes evidence that the worker has the right to direct and control the financial aspects of the business operations. Although not every independent contractor needs to make a significant investment, almost every independent contractor will incur an array of business expenses either in the form of direct expenditures or in the form of fees for pro rata portions of one or several expenses. Businesses often pay business or travel expenses for their employees. Independent contractors' expenses may also be reimbursed. An independent contractor can contract for direct reimbursement of certain expenses, or can seek to establish contract prices that will reimburse the contractor for these expenses. Attention should center on *unreimbursed* expenses, which better distinguish independent contractors and employees, inasmuch as independent contractors are more likely to have unreimbursed expenses. If expenses are unreimbursed, then the opportunity for profit or loss exists. Fixed ongoing costs that are incurred regardless of whether work is currently being performed are especially important. However, employees may also incur unreimbursed expenses in connection with the services they perform for their businesses. Relatively minor expenses incurred by a worker, or more significant expenses that are customarily borne by an employee in a particular line of business, would generally not indicate an independent contractor relationship.

An independent contractor is generally free to seek out business opportunities, as independent contractors' income depends on doing so successfully. As a result, independent contractors often advertise, maintain a visible business location, and are available to work for the relevant market. An independent contractor with special skills may be contacted by word of mouth and referrals without the need for advertising. An independent contractor who has negotiated a long-term contract may find advertising equally unnecessary, and may be unavailable to work for others for the duration of a contract. Other independent contractors may find that a visible business location does not generate sufficient business to justify the expense. Therefore, the absence of these activities is a neutral fact.

The method of payment can be helpful in determining whether the worker has the opportunity for profit or loss. A worker who is compensated on an hourly, daily, weekly, or similar basis is guaranteed a return for labor. This is generally evidence of an employer-employee relationship, even when the wage or salary is accompanied by a commission. In some lines of business, such as law, it is typical to pay independent contractors on an hourly basis. Performance of a task for a flat fee is generally evidence of an independent contractor relationship, especially if the worker incurs the expenses of performing the services. A commission-based worker can be either an independent contractor or employee. The worker's status will depend on the worker's ability to realize a profit or incur a loss as a result of services rendered.

The ability to realize a profit or incur a loss is probably the strongest evidence that a worker controls the business aspects of services rendered.

Also to be considered is whether the worker is free to make business decisions that affect his profit or loss. If the worker is making decisions that affect the bottom line, the worker likely has the ability to realize profit or loss. It is sometimes thought that because a worker can receive more money working longer hours or receive less money by working less, he has the ability to incur a profit or loss. This type of income variation, however, is also consistent with employer status and does not distinguish employees from independent contractors.

Not all financial control facts need be present for the worker to have the ability to realize profit or loss. For example, a worker who is paid on a straight commission basis, makes business decisions, and has unreimbursed business expenses, likely would have the ability to realize a profit or loss, even if the worker does not have a significant investment and does not market her services.

Relationship of the Parties

There are other facts that recent court decisions consider relevant in determining worker status. Most of these facts reflect how the worker and the business perceive the relationship to each other. It is much more difficult to link the facts in this category directly to the right to direct and control *how* work is to be performed than the categories discussed above. The relationship of the parties is important because it reflects the parties' *intent* concerning control. Courts often look at the intent of the parties because the intent is most often stated in their contractual relationship. A written agreement describing the worker as an independent contractor is viewed as evidence of the parties' intent that a worker is an independent contractor. However, a contractual designation, in and of itself, is not sufficient evidence for determining worker status. The facts and circumstances under which a worker performs services determine a worker's status. The *substance* of a relationship, not a label, governs the worker's status. The contract may be relevant in ascertaining methods of compensation, expenses that will be incurred, and rights and obligations of each party with respect to *how* work is to be performed. In addition, if it is difficult, if not impossible, to decide whether a worker is an independent contractor, the intent of the parties, as reflected in the contractual designation, is an effective way to resolve the issue.

Questions sometimes arise concerning whether a worker who creates a corporation through which to perform services can be an employee of a business that engages the corporation. If the corporate formalities are properly followed, and at least one nontax business purpose exists, the corporate form is generally recognized for both state law and federal law, including federal tax purposes. Disregarding the corporate entity is generally an extraordinary remedy, applied by most courts only in cases of clear abuse, so the worker will usually not be treated as an employee of the business, but as an employee of the corporation. (It should be noted that the fact that a worker receives payment for services from a business through the worker's corporation does not automatically require a finding of independent contractor status with respect to those services.)

Employee benefits. Providing a worker with employee benefits has traditionally been linked with employee status and, therefore, can be an important factor in deciding an independent contractor-employee relationship. If a worker receives employee benefits, such as paid vacation days, paid sick days, health insurance, life or disability insurance, or a pension, this constitutes some evidence of employee status. The evidence is strongest if the worker is provided with employee benefits under a tax-qualified retirement plan, 403(b) annuity, or cafeteria plan, because by statute, these benefits can be provided to employees only. If an individual is excluded from a benefit plan because the worker is not considered an employee by the business, this is relevant though not conclusive in determining the worker's status as an independent contractor. If the worker is excluded on some other grounds, the exclusion is irrelevant in determining whether the worker is an independent contractor or an employee. This is because none of these employee benefits is required to be provided to employees. Many workers whose status as bona fide employees is unquestioned receive no employee benefits, as there is no requirement that all workers be covered.

Termination rights. The circumstances under which a business or a worker can terminate their relationship have traditionally been considered useful evidence bearing on the status the parties intended the worker to have. However, in order to determine whether the facts are relevant to the worker's status, the impact of modern business practices and legal standards governing worker termination must be considered. A business's ability to terminate the work relationship at will, without penalty, provides a highly effective method to control the details of how work is performed, and indicates employee status. On the other hand, in the traditional independent contractor relationship, the business could terminate the relationship only if the worker failed to provide the intended service, which indicates the parties' intent that the business does not have the right to control how the work was performed. In practice, businesses rarely have complete flexibility in discharging an employee. The business may be liable for pay in lieu of notice, severance pay, "golden parachutes," or other forms of compensation when it discharges an employee. In addition, the reasons for which a business can terminate an employee may be limited, whether by law, by contract, or by its own practices.

A worker's ability to terminate work at will was traditionally considered to illustrate that the worker merely provided labor and tended to indicate an employer-employee relationship. In contrast, if the worker terminated work, and the business could refuse payment or sue for nonperformance, this indicated the business's interest in receiving the contracted product or service, which tended to indicate an independent contractor relationship. In practice, however, independent contractors can enter into short-term contracts for which nonperformance remedies are inappropriate; or they may negotiate limits on their liability for nonperformance. Typical examples are professionals, such as doctors and attorneys, who can terminate their contractual relationship without penalty.

Businesses can successfully sue employees for substantial damages resulting from their failure to perform the services for which they were engaged. As a result, the presence or absence of limits on workers' ability to terminate the relationship, by themselves, no longer constitutes useful evidence in determining worker status. A business's ability to refuse payment for unsatisfactory work continues to be characteristic of an independent contractor relationship.

Permanent/indefinite relationship.   The existence of a permanent relationship between the worker and the business is relevant evidence in determining whether there is an employer-employee relationship. If a business engages a worker with the expectation that the relationship will continue indefinitely, rather than for a specific project or period, it is a factor that is generally considered evidence of an intent to create an employment relationship.

A relationship that is created with the expectation that it will be indefinite should not be confused with a long-term relationship. A long-term relationship may exist between a business and either an independent contractor or an employee. The relationship between the business and an independent contractor can be long-term for several reasons:

1. The contract may be a long-term contract.
2. Contacts can be renewed regularly due to superior service, competitive costs, or lack of alternative service providers.

A business can also have a relationship with an employee that is long-term, but not indefinite. This could occur if temporary employment contracts are renewed, or if a long-term, but not indefinite, employment contract is entered into. As a result, a relationship that is long-term, but not indefinite, is a neutral fact that should be disregarded.

A temporary relationship is a neutral fact that should be disregarded. An independent contractor will typically have a temporary relationship with a business, but so too will employees engaged on a seasonal project, or on an "as needed" basis. The services performed by the worker, and the extent to which those services are a key aspect of the regular business of the company, are germane. In considering this, it should be remembered that the fact that a service is desirable, necessary, or even essential to a business does not mean that the service provider is an employee. The work of an attorney or paralegal is part of the regular business of a law firm. If a law firm hires an attorney or paralegal, it is likely that the law firm will present the work as its own. As a result, there is an increased probability that the law firm will direct or control the activities. However, further facts should be examined to see whether there is evidence of the *right* to direct or control before a conclusion is reached that these workers are employees. It is possible that the work performed is part of the principal business of the law firm, yet it has hired workers who are outside specialists and may be independent contractors.

CHECKLIST

The 20 factors indicating whether an individual is an employee or an independent contractor follow:

1. *Instructions.* An employee must comply with instructions about when, where, and how to work. Even if no instructions are given, the control factor is present if the employer has the right to control how the work results are achieved.

2. *Training.* An employee may be trained to perform services in a particular manner. Independent contractors ordinarily use their own methods and receive no training from the purchasers of their services.

3. *Integration.* An employee's services are usually integrated into the business operations because the services are important to the success or continuation of the business. This shows that the employee is subject to direction and control.

4. *Services Are Rendered Personally.* An employee renders services personally. This shows that the employer is interested in the methods as well as the results.

5. *Hiring Assistants.* An employee works for an employer who hires, supervises, and pays workers. An independent contractor can hire, super-

vise, and pay assistants under a contract that requires their contractor to provide materials and labor and to be responsible only for the result.

6. *Continuing Relationship.* An employee generally has a continuing relationship that may exist even if work is performed at recurring although irregular intervals.

7. *Set Hours of Work.* An employee usually has set hours of work established by an employer. Independent contractors generally can set their own work hours.

8. *Full-Time Required.* An employee may be required to work or be available full-time. This indicates control by the employer. An independent contractor can work when and for whom he or she chooses.

9. *Work Done on Premises.* An employee usually works on the premises of an employer, or works on a route or at a location designated by an employer.

10. *Order or Sequence Set.* An employee may be required to perform services in the order or sequence set by an employer. This shows that the employee is subject to direction and control.

11. *Reports.* An employee may be required to submit reports to an employer, which shows that the employer maintains a degree of control.

12. *Payments.* An employee generally is paid by the hour, week, or month. An independent contractor is usually paid by the job or on a straight commission.

13. *Expenses.* An employee's business and travel expenses are generally paid by an employer. This shows that the employee is subject to regulation and control.

14. *Tools and Materials.* An employee is normally furnished significant tools, materials, and other equipment by an employer.

15. *Investment.* An independent contractor has a significant investment in the facilities used in performing services for someone else.

16. *Profit or Loss.* An independent contractor can make a profit or suffer a loss.

17. *Works for More than One Person or Firm.* An independent contractor is generally free to provide services to two or more unrelated persons or firms at the same time.

18. *Offers Services to General Public.* An independent contractor makes services available to the general public.

19. *Right to Fire.* An employee can be fired by an employer. An independent contractor cannot be fired as long as results are produced that meet the specifications of the contract.

20. *Right to Quit.* An employee can quit a job at any time without incurring liability. An independent contractor usually agrees to complete a specific job and is responsible for its satisfactory completion, or legally is obligated to make good for failure to complete it.

NEW EMPHASIS ON CATEGORIES

Since the publication of the training manual for IRS personnel on worker classification, there has been less reliance upon the common law standard or the list of 20 factors. The three categories (behavioral control, financial control, and relationship of the parties) are relied upon more heavily for the determination. However, it is wise to consider all aspects of the arrangement. In fact, the IRS cautions, "In each case, it is very important to consider all the facts—no single fact provides the answer."

And it is not only the employer who considers the independent contractor/employee situation a morass. Recently tax lawyers, CPAs and corporate tax officers have come up with a list of high priority suggestions for simplifing the tax situation: drop the minimum tax; standardize the rules on classifying workers as employees or independent contractors; clarify the eight tax incentives for education.

The following addition to the Internal Revenue Code may not help in the worker classification process, but it does provide Tax Court review rights.

NEW PROCEDURES FOR PROCESSING EMPLOYMENT TAX CASES

The Taxpayer Relief Act of 1997 (TRA'97) created Section 7436 of the Internal Revenue Code, which provides Tax Court review rights concerning certain employment tax determinations.

Code Notice 98-43 provides information about how taxpayers can petition for Tax Court review of employment tax determinations under the provision that became effective August 5, 1997. Attached to this Notice as Exhibit 1 is a "Notice of Determination Concerning Worker Classification Under Section 7436."

With respect to taxpayers whose workers are the subject of an employment tax determination as to whether they are independent contractors, or, in fact, employees, the attached Notice of Determination addressed to a taxpayer will constitute the "determination" that is a prerequisite to invoking the Tax Court's jurisdiction.

The new Section of the Code contains the following provisions:

1. The Tax Court has the jurisdiction to review determinations by the IRS that workers are employees for purposes of Subtitle C of the Code.
2. And that the organization for which services are performed is not entitled to relief from employment taxes under Section 530 of the Revenue Act of 1978.
3. The determination must involve an actual controversy relating to independent contractor/employee status.

4. The determination is made as part of an examination of worker classification.

Section 7436 can be conducted pursuant to the Tax Court's simplified procedures for small tax cases set forth in the new Section of the Code and Rule 295 of the Tax Court's Rules of Practice and Procedure. Currently, taxpayers can elect, with the concurrence of the Tax Court, to use these simplified procedures if the amount of employment taxes placed in dispute resulting from workers being designated as independent contractors is $50,000 or less for each calendar quarter involved.

Issues to Which Section 7436 Applies

Section 7436(a) provides the Tax Court with jurisdiction to review the IRS's determinations that one or more individuals performing services for the taxpayer are employees of the taxpayer, not independent contractors, for purposes of Subtitle C of the Code, or that the taxpayer is not entitled to relief under Section 530 with respect to such individuals.

Thus, 7436(a) does not:

1. Provide the Tax Court with jurisdiction to determine any amount of employment tax or penalties.
2. Provide the Tax Court with jurisdiction to review other employment tax issues.
3. Apply to employment-related issues not arising under Subtitle C, such as the classification of individuals with respect to pension plan coverage or the proper treatment of individual income tax deductions.

Additionally, insofar as 7436(a) only confers jurisdiction upon the Tax Court to review determinations that are made by the IRS as part of an employment tax examination, other IRS determinations that are not made as part of an examination, including those that are made in the context of private letter rulings or Form SS-8, "Determination of Employee Work Status for Purposes of Federal Employment Taxes and Income Tax Withholding," are not subject to review by the Tax Court under this provision.

The IRS will issue a Notice of Determination only after the IRS has determined both that:

1. One or more individuals performing services for the taxpayer are employees for purposes of Subtitle C.
2. The taxpayer is not entitled to relief under Section 530. This will provide taxpayers with the opportunity to resolve both issues in one judicial determination.

Taxpayers Eligible to Seek Review

Section 7436(b) provides that a pleading seeking Tax Court review of the IRS's determination can be filed only by "the person for whom the services are performed." Thus, workers may not seek review of the IRS's determinations under these provisions. In addition, because there must be an actual controversy, review may not be sought by a third party who has not been determined by the IRS to be the employer.

Notice of Determination

The IRS will inform taxpayers of a determination by sending the taxpayer a Notice of Determination by certified or registered mail. The Notice of Determination will advise taxpayers of the opportunity to seek Tax Court review, and it provides information on how to do so. Attached to the notice will be a schedule showing each kind of tax with its proposed employment tax adjustment for the specific taxpayer by calendar quarter.

This schedule will be provided to enable the taxpayer to determine eligibility to elect use of the small tax case procedures under Section 7436(c). Currently, the small tax case procedures may be available if the amount of employment taxes in dispute is $50,000 or less for each calendar quarter involved.

In most cases, a taxpayer who receives a Notice of Determination will have previously received a "thirty-day letter," which the IRS sends to taxpayers in unagreed examination cases. The thirty-day letter lists the proposed employment tax adjustments to be made and describes the taxpayer's right either to agree to the proposed employment tax adjustments or, alternatively, to protest the proposed adjustments to the Appeals Division within thirty days of the date of the letter.

If the taxpayer does not respond to the thirty-day letter by agreeing to the proposed adjustments or, alternatively, by filing a protest with the Appeals Division, the taxpayer will receive, by certified or registered mail, a Notice of Determination. Under normal procedures, if the taxpayer does not respond to the thirty-day letter, the taxpayer should generally expect to receive the notice within sixty days after expiration of the thirty-day period beginning with the date on the thirty-day letter. If no notice is received during this period, the taxpayer may wish to contact the local Internal Revenue Service office to check on the status of the case.

If the taxpayer responds to the thirty-day letter by filing a protest with the Appeals Division (or if the case proceeds to Appeals by way of the employment tax early referral procedures), and the worker classification and Section 530 issues are not settled on an agreed basis in the Appeals Division, the taxpayer will then receive a Notice of Determination.

Taxpayers are encouraged to resolve cases in nondocketed status by requesting use of the early referral procedures in appropriate cases.

Prerequisite for Seeking Review

Because a Notice of Determination constitutes the IRS's determination of worker classification, it is a jurisdictional prerequisite for seeking Tax Court review of the IRS's determinations regarding classification of the worker as an independent contractor or an employee, and Section 530 issues. Tax Court proceedings seeking review of these determinations can not begin prior to issuance of the notice.

Time of Filing

Section 7436(b)(2) provides that a taxpayer's petition for review must be filed with the Tax Court before the 91st day after the IRS mails its Notice of Determination to the taxpayer by certified or registered mail. If the taxpayer discusses the case with the IRS during the period before the 91st day following the mailing of the notice, the discussion will not extend the period in which the taxpayer may file a petition with the Tax Court.

A taxpayer who does not file a Tax Court petition within the allotted time retains the right to seek judicial review of the employment tax determinations by paying the tax and filing a claim for refund, as required by the Code. If the claim for refund is denied, the taxpayer may file a refund suit in district court or the Court of Federal Claims.

Appeals Jurisdiction

Cases docketed in the U.S. Tax Court will be referred by District Counsel to the Appeals Division of the IRS for consideration of settlement unless the Notice of Determination was issued by Appeals. Cases in which Appeals issued such a Notice of Determination may be referred to them unless District Counsel determines that there is little likelihood that a settlement of all or a part of the case can be achieved in a reasonable period of time. Appeals will have sole settlement authority over docketed cases referred to them until the case is returned to District Counsel.

Suspension of the Statute of Limitations

The ruling provides that the suspension of the limitations period for assessment in Section 6503(a) of the Code applies in the same manner as though a notice of deficiency had been issued. Thus, the mailing of the Notice of Determination by certified or registered mail will suspend the statute of limitations for assessment of taxes attributable to the worker classification and Section 530 issues. Generally, the statute of limitations for assessment of taxes attributable to these issues is suspended for the 90-day period during which the taxpayer can begin a suit in Tax Court, plus an additional 60 days thereafter.

Moreover, if the taxpayer does file a timely petition in the Tax Court, the statute of limitations for assessment of taxes attributable to the issues will be suspended during the Tax Court proceedings, and for 60 days after the decision becomes final.

Restrictions on Assessment

This same ruling provides that the restrictions on assessment in Section 6213 of the Code apply in the same manner as if a notice had been issued. Thus, the IRS is precluded from assessing the taxes prior to expiration of the 90-day period during which the taxpayer can file a timely Tax Court petition.

If he or she does file, this generally precludes the IRS from assessing the taxes until the decision of the Tax Court has become final. If the taxpayer does not file a timely Tax Court petition before the 91st day after the Notice of Determination was mailed, the employment taxes attributable to the workers described in the Notice of Determination can then be assessed.

Agreed Settlements

If the taxpayer wishes to settle the employment issues on an agreed basis before issuance of a Notice of Determination, the taxpayer must formally waive the restrictions on assessment. This will generally be accomplished by execution of an agreed settlement that contains the following language: "I understand that, by signing this agreement, I am waiving the restrictions on assessment provided in Sections 7436(d) and 6213(a) of the Internal Revenue Code of 1986."

The IRS will not assess employment taxes attributable to those issues unless either a Notice of Determination has been issued to the taxpayer and the 90-day period for filing a Tax Court petition has expired or, alternatively, the taxpayer has waived the restrictions on assessment.

If the IRS erroneously makes an assessment of taxes attributable to those issues without first either issuing a Notice of Determination or obtaining a waiver of restrictions on assessment, the taxpayer is entitled to an automatic abatement of the assessment. However, once any such procedural defects are corrected, the IRS can reassess the employment taxes to the same extent as if the abated assessment had not occurred.

Section 1454 of TRA '97 was effective as of August 5, 1997. Thus, assessments that were made prior to the August 5, 1997 effective date of the Act are not subject to this legislation or the procedures discussed above. All employment tax examinations involving worker classification and/or Section 530 issues that were pending as of August 5, 1997 are subject to the legislation.

Chapter 30

Taxpayer Rights

NEW IMAGE FOR THE IRS

Along with their tax bills, taxpayers receive publications delineating their rights and obligations in handling various and sundry tax problems. Some of the points made are reminiscent of those previously publicized in the Taxpayer Bill of Rights 1, 2, and 3. (The last may be better known as the *IRS Restructuring and Reform Act of 1998*, but more on that below.) These two publications emphasize some of the measures adopted in the Congressional Bills, but are also based on IRS regulations and other legislation. They are not a Taxpayer Bill of Rights 4. Regardless, it does appear that the Service is attempting to serve the public and make tax paying as painless as possible.

At some point, between the time that Congress passed the 1998 bill and the IRS started sending out information publications for the 1998 tax season, it had picked up a subtitle and become known as the *Taxpayer Bill of Rights 3*.

In fact, the IRS states, "The *IRS Restructuring Reform Act of 1998* contains the Taxpayer Bill of Rights 3. It preserves the balance between safeguarding the rights of the individual taxpayers and enabling the Internal Revenue Service to administer the tax laws efficiently, fairly, and with the least amount of burden to the taxpayer."

Under this bill, taxpayer rights have been expanded in several areas:

1. The burden of proof will shift to the IRS in certain court proceedings.

2. In certain cases, taxpayers may be awarded damages and fees, and get liens released.

3. Penalties will be eased when the IRS exceeds specified time limits between when a return is filed and when the taxpayer is notified of a tax liability.

4. Interest will be eliminated in certain cases involving federally-declared disaster areas.

5. There are new rules for collection actions by levy.

6. Innocent spouse relief provisions have been strengthened.

7. In certain situations, taxpayer-requested installment agreements must be accepted. Taxpayers will get annual status reports of their installment agreements.

Included are requirements that IRS employees are now required to be more polite and responsive. For example, any IRS correspondence not computer generated must include the name and telephone number of an employee whom a taxpayer can contact. The new law also establishes a nine-member board to oversee the general administration of the agency. And to assure that key decision making will not remain in the self-protecting hands of IRS career employees, six of the board's members will be "outsiders." Many of these provisions are contained in the material that follows.

DECLARATION OF TAXPAYER RIGHTS

The first part of this discussion explains some of a taxpayer's most important rights. The second part explains the examination, appeal, collection, and refund procedures.

I. *Protection of a Taxpayer's Rights.* IRS employees will explain and protect a taxpayer's rights throughout his or her contact with the IRS.

II. *Privacy and Confidentiality.* The IRS will not disclose to anyone the information given to the IRS, except as authorized by law.

III. *Professional and Courteous Service.* If a taxpayer believes an IRS employee has not treated him or her in a professional, fair, and courteous manner, the employee's supervisor should be told. If the supervisor's response is not satisfactory, the taxpayer should write to the IRS District Director or Service Center Director.

IV. *Representation.* A taxpayer can either represent himself or herself or, with proper written authorization, have someone else as a representative. The taxpayer's representative must be a person allowed to practice before the IRS, such as an attorney, certified public accountant, or enrolled agent.

If a taxpayer is in an interview and asks to consult such a person, then the IRS must stop and reschedule the interview in most cases. Someone may accompany the taxpayer to an interview, and make recordings of any meetings with the IRS examining agent, appeal or collection personnel, provided the taxpayer tells the IRS in writing 10 days before the meeting.

V. *Payment of Only the Correct Amount of Tax*. Taxpayers are responsible for paying the correct amount of tax due under the law—no more, no less. If a responsible taxpayer cannot pay all of his or her tax when it is due, it may be possible to make monthly installment payments. Arrangements for payments are made with the IRS.

VI. *Help with Unresolved Tax Problems*. The National Taxpayer Advocate's Problem Resolution Program can help a taxpayer who has tried unsuccessfully to resolve a problem with the IRS. A local Taxpayer Advocate can offer special help for a significant hardship as a result of a tax problem. The taxpayer may call toll-free or write to the Taxpayer Advocate at the IRS office that last contacted him or her.

VII. *Appeals and Judicial Review*. If a taxpayer disagrees with the IRS about the amount of a tax liability or certain collection actions, it is the taxpayer's right to ask the Appeals Office to review the case. The taxpayer also has the right to ask a court to review the case.

VIII. *Relief from Certain Penalties and Interest*. The IRS will waive penalties when allowed by law if a taxpayer can show he or she has acted reasonably and in good faith or relied on the incorrect advice of an IRS employee. The IRS will waive interest that is the result of certain errors or delays caused by an IRS employee.

EXAMINATIONS, APPEALS, COLLECTIONS, AND REFUNDS

Examinations (Audits). The IRS accepts most taxpayers' returns as filed. If the IRS inquires about a return or selects it for examination, it does not suggest the taxpayer is dishonest. The inquiry or examination may or may not result in more tax. A case can be closed without change, or the taxpayer may receive a refund.

The process of selecting a return for examination usually begins in one of two ways:

1. Computer programs are used to identify returns that may have incorrect amounts. These programs may be based on:

   a. Information returns, such as Forms 1099 and W-2.

   b. Studies of past examinations.

    c. Certain issues identified by compliance projects.

2. Information is used from outside sources that indicate that a return has incorrect amounts. These sources include:

    a. Newspapers.

    b. Public records.

    c. Individuals.

If it is determined that the information is accurate and reliable, this information may be used to select a particular tax return for examination.

Examinations by Mail. The IRS processes many examinations and inquiries by mail. They will send a letter to a taxpayer with either a request for more information or a reason the IRS believes a change in a return may be needed. The taxpayer can respond by mail or can request a personal interview with an examiner. If the taxpayer mails the requested information or provides an explanation, the IRS may or may not agree with the taxpayer's explanation, and will explain the reasons for any changes. The IRS urges taxpayers not to hesitate to write about anything they do not understand.

By Interview. If the IRS notifies a taxpayer that they will conduct an examination through a personal interview, or the taxpayer requests such an interview, the taxpayer has the right to ask that the examination take place at a reasonable time and place that is convenient for both the taxpayer and the IRS. If an examiner proposes any changes to a return, the examination will make clear the reasons for the changes. If the taxpayer does not agree with these changes, he or she can meet with the examiner's supervisor.

Repeat Examinations. If the IRS examined a return for the same items in either of the two previous years and proposed no change to the taxpayer's tax liability, he or she should contact the IRS as soon as possible so that the IRS can determine if the current examination should be discontinued.

Appeals. If a taxpayer does not agree with an examiner's proposed changes, he or she can appeal them to the Appeals Office of the IRS. Most differences can be settled without expensive and time-consuming court trials. If the taxpayer does not want to use the Appeals Office or disagrees with its finding, the case can be taken to the U.S. Tax Court, U.S. Court of Federal Claims, or the U.S. District Court where the taxpayer lives. If a case is taken to court, the IRS will have the burden of proving certain facts. These would include whether the taxpayer:

1. Kept audit records to show the tax liability.
2. Cooperated fully with the IRS.
3. Met certain other conditions.

If the court agrees with the taxpayer on most issues in a case, and finds that the IRS position was largely unjustified, the taxpayer may be able to recover some of the administrative and litigation costs. However, the taxpayer cannot recover these costs unless he or she tried to resolve a case administratively, including going through the appeals system, and giving the IRS the information necessary to resolve the case.

Innocent Spouse Relief.   Generally, both spouses are responsible, jointly and individually, for paying the full amount of any tax, interest, or penalties due on their joint return. However, one spouse may not have to pay the tax, interest, and penalties related to the other spouse or former spouse.

New tax law changes make it easier to qualify for innocent spouse relief and add two other ways to get relief through "separation of liability" and "equitable relief." Thus, there are now three types of relief available:

1. Innocent spouse relief which applies to all joint filers.
2. Separation of liability, which applies to joint filers who are divorced, widowed, legally separated, or have not lived together for the past 12 months.
3. Equitable relief, which applies to all joint filers and married couples filing separate returns in community property states.

Innocent spouse relief and separation of liability apply only to items incorrectly reported on the return. If a spouse does not qualify for innocent spouse relief or separation of liability, the IRS may grant equitable relief.

Refunds.   A taxpayer can file a claim for a refund if he or she thinks too much tax was levied The claim must generally be filed within 3 years from the date the original return was filed, or 2 years from the date the tax was paid, whichever is later. The law generally provides for interest on a refund if it is not paid within 45 days of the date the return was filed or the refund was claimed.

THE IRS COLLECTION PROCESS

There are steps the IRS can take to collect overdue taxes. The information in this discussion applies to all taxpayers—for individuals who owe income taxes and employers who owe employment tax. Special rules that apply only to employers are given at the end of this discussion.

By law, taxpayers have the right to be treated professionally, fairly, promptly, and courteously by IRS employees. Some of those rights are to:

1. Disagree with claims on the tax bill.
2. Meet with an IRS manager if the taxpayer disagrees with the IRS employee who handles the tax case.
3. Appeal most IRS collection actions.
4. Transfer a case to a different IRS office.
5. Be represented by someone when dealing with IRS matters.
6. Receive a receipt for any payment he or she makes.

Disagreement with an IRS Decision. If a taxpayer disagrees with a decision of an IRS employee at any time during the collection process, the taxpayer can ask the employee's manager to review the case. The employee will then refer the taxpayer to a manager who will either speak with the taxpayer then or return a call by the next work day.

If the taxpayer disagrees with a manager's decision, the taxpayer has the right to file an appeal which enables him or her to appeal most collection actions taken by the IRS, including filing a lien, placing a levy on the taxpayer's wages or bank account, or seizing a taxpayer's property.

Someone to Represent a Taxpayer. When dealing with the IRS, a taxpayer can choose to represent himself or herself, or can have an attorney, a certified public accountant, an enrolled agent, or any person enrolled to practice before the IRS as a representative.

Problem Resolution Program. This program ensures that taxpayers' problems are handled promptly and properly. If repeated attempts have been made to sort out a tax problem with the IRS, but have been unsuccessful, then the taxpayer can first ask any IRS employee or manager for help. If the problem continues, the taxpayer may ask for an appointment with the Taxpayer Advocate in the local IRS office. The Taxpayer Advocate determines whether the taxpayer qualifies for the Problem Resolution Program.

IRS Sharing Information. By law the IRS can share a taxpayer's information with city and state tax agencies and, in some cases, with the Department of Justice, other federal agencies, and with people the taxpayer authorizes to receive that information. Such information can also be shared with certain foreign governments under tax treaty provisions.

The IRS can contact other sources, such as neighbors, banks, employers or employees, to investigate a case. However, after January 18, 1999, the new law provides that before contacting other persons, the IRS must notify the individual that, in examining or collecting tax liability, they may contact third parties. In addition, the new law requires the Service to provide a list of persons who were questioned. This information is to be provided periodically and upon request.

The notification provision does not apply in the following circumstances:

1. Pending criminal investigations.
2. When providing notice would jeopardize collection of any tax liability.
3. Where providing notice may result in reprisal against any person.
4. When the taxpayer authorized the contact.

If a taxpayer is involved in a bankruptcy proceeding, the proceeding may not eliminate the tax debt, but it may temporarily stop IRS enforcement action from collecting a debt related to the bankruptcy.

If a Taxpayer Owes Child Support. If a taxpayer is entitled to a federal or state tax refund while still owing unpaid taxes or child support, the IRS can apply the refund toward the debt and send the taxpayer the remaining balance, if there is any.

When a Taxpayer Can't Pay. When a tax return is filed, the IRS checks to see if the mathematics is accurate and if the taxpayer has paid the correct amount. If the taxpayer has not paid all that is owed, the IRS will send a bill called a *Notice of Tax Due and Demand for Payment*. The bill will include the taxes, plus penalties and interest, and the IRS encourages a taxpayer to pay the tax bill by check or money order as quickly as possible.

If the taxpayer has received a bill for unpaid taxes, the entire amount should be paid, or the IRS should be notified why the taxpayer cannot pay. If the taxpayer does not pay the taxes owed and makes no effort to pay them, the IRS can ask the taxpayer to take action to pay by selling or mortgaging any assets, or getting a loan. If the taxpayer still makes no effort to pay the taxes owed or to work out a payment plan, the IRS can also take more serious action, such as seizing the taxpayer's bank, levying his or her wages, or taking other income or assets.

If a Taxpayer Believes the Bill Is Wrong. If a taxpayer believes a bill is wrong, the IRS should be contacted as soon as possible by:

1. Calling the number on the bill.
2. Writing to the IRS office that sent the bill.
3. Visiting the local IRS office.

To help IRS consideration of the problem, the taxpayer should send a copy of the bill along with copies (not originals) of any records, tax returns, and canceled checks that will help the IRS understand why the taxpayer believes the bill to be wrong. When writing to the IRS, the taxpayer should state clearly why he or she believes the bill is wrong. If the IRS finds the taxpayer is correct, the account will be adjusted, and, if necessary, the taxpayer will be sent a corrected bill.

If the total amount owed cannot be paid immediately, as much as possible should be paid. By paying that portion, the amount of interest and penalty will be reduced. The taxpayer should call, write, or visit the nearest IRS office to explain the situation. The IRS will ask for a completed form, *Collection Information Statement,* to help them consider the amount the taxpayer can pay based upon the taxpayer's monthly income and expenses. The IRS will then help to figure out a payment plan that fits the situation. The IRS will work with the taxpayer to consider several different ways to pay what is owed:

1. The taxpayer may be able to make monthly payments through an installment agreement.
2. The taxpayer may be able to apply for an offer in compromise.
3. The taxpayer may qualify for a temporary delay, or the case may be considered a significant hardship.

An Installment Agreement.   Installment agreements allow the full payment of taxes in smaller, equal monthly payments. The amount of each installment payment is based on the amount of tax owed and the taxpayer's ability to pay that amount within the time available to the IRS to collect the tax debt.

Previously, the IRS did not have to agree to accept the payment of taxes in installments. However, as of July 22, 1998, they must enter into an installment agreement for the payment of income tax if the taxpayer meets all of the following conditions on the date he or she offers to enter into the agreement:

1. The total income tax owed is not more than $10,000.
2. In the last 5 years, the taxpayer (and spouse if the liability relates to a joint return) has:
   a. Filed all required income tax returns.

    b. Paid all taxes shown on the returns filed.

    c. Not entered into an installment agreement to pay any income tax.

3. The taxpayer shows (and the IRS agrees) that the individual cannot pay the income tax in full when due.

4. The taxpayer agrees to pay the tax in full in 3 years or less.

5. The taxpayer agrees to comply with the tax laws while the agreement is in effect.

An installment agreement is a reasonable payment option for some taxpayers, but they should be aware that an installment agreement is more costly than paying all the tax owed and may be more costly than borrowing funds to pay the full amount. Why? Because the IRS charges interest and *penalties* on the tax owed and also charges interest on the unpaid penalties and interest that have been charged to the taxpayer's account. This means that while the taxpayer is making payments on his or her tax debt through an installment agreement, the IRS continues to charge interest and penalties on the unpaid portion of that debt.

The interest rate on a bank loan or on a cash advance on a credit card may be lower than the combination of penalties and interest the IRS charges. There is also another cost associated with an installment agreement. To set up the payment program, the IRS charges a $43 user fee. If a taxpayer owes $10,000 or less in tax, the taxpayer can call the number on the tax bill to set up a plan. The IRS will inform the taxpayer what has to be done to begin immediately.

If more than $10,000 is owed, the IRS may still be able to set up an installment agreement with the taxpayer based on the completed form, *Collection Information Statement*. Even though a taxpayer agrees to an installment plan, the IRS can still file a *Notice of Federal Tax Lien* to secure the government's interest until the taxpayer makes the final payment.

However, the IRS cannot levy against the taxpayer's property:

1. While a request for an installment agreement is being considered.

2. While an agreement is in effect.

3. For 30 days after the request for an agreement has been rejected.

4. For any period while an appeal of the rejection is being evaluated by the IRS.

If an installment agreement is arranged, the taxpayer can pay with personal or business checks, money orders, certified funds, or payroll deductions the employer takes from the taxpayer's salary and regularly sends to the IRS, or by electronic transfers from the employee's bank account or other means.

An installment agreement is based on the taxpayer's financial situation. If a change in the financial situation makes it necessary to change the terms of the installment agreement, the IRS will inform the taxpayer by letter 30 days before changing the established plan. The payments on an installment agreement must be paid on time; if a payment cannot be made, the IRS should be informed immediately. The IRS can end an agreement if the taxpayer does not furnish updated financial information when the IRS requests it, or if the taxpayer fails to meet the terms of the agreement.

An agreement could end if the taxpayer misses a payment, or does not file or pay all required tax returns. In that case, the IRS can take enforced collection action. In some cases, the IRS will accept an offer in compromise. On the other hand, if taxes are not paid when they are due, the taxpayer may be subject to a failure-to-pay penalty of 5% of the unpaid taxes for each month they are not paid. But if a return was filed on time, the penalty will be reduced to 2.5% for any month beginning after 1999 in which the taxpayer has an installment agreement in effect.

Offer in Compromise. In some cases, the IRS may accept an Offer in Compromise to settle an unpaid tax account, including any interest and penalties. With such an arrangement, they can accept less than the amount owed when it is doubtful that they would be able to collect all of the taxpayer's debt any time in the near future.

Temporary Delay. If the IRS determines that the taxpayer cannot pay *any* of a tax debt, they may temporarily delay collection until the taxpayer's financial condition improves. If the IRS does delay collection, the debt will increase because penalties and interest are charged until the full amount is paid. During a temporary delay, the IRS will review the individual's ability to pay, and may file a *Notice of Federal Tax Lien* to protect the government's interest in the taxpayer's assets.

A Significant Hardship. The IRS can consider whether a significant hardship exists for a taxpayer to pay a tax liability. It would be judged a significant hardship if the taxpayer cannot afford to maintain even the necessities to live day to day (adequate food, clothing, shelter, transportation, and medical treatment). Other cases that can be considered as significant hardship by law:

1. An immediate threat of adverse action.
2. Delay of more than 30 days in resolving taxpayer account problems.
3. Incurring significant costs (including fees for professional representation) if relief is not granted.
4. Irreparable injury to, or long-term adverse impact on, the taxpayer if relief is not granted.

A taxpayer may apply for emergency relief if facing a significant hardship. He or she should call the toll-free IRS Taxpayer Assistant number or visit the district's Taxpayer Advocate. A qualifying taxpayer will be assisted in filling out the form, *Application for Taxpayer Assistance Order*.

EMPLOYMENT TAXES FOR EMPLOYERS

To encourage prompt payment of withheld income and employment taxes, including Social Security taxes, railroad retirement taxes, or collected excise taxes, Congress passed a law that provides for the trust fund recovery penalty. (These taxes are called *trust fund taxes* because the employer actually holds the employee's money in trust until making a federal tax deposit in that amount.)

If the IRS plans to assess an employer for the trust fund recovery penalty, they will send a letter stating that the employer is the *responsible* person. An employer has 60 days after receiving the letter to appeal the IRS proposal. If the employer does not respond to the letter, the IRS will assess the penalty and send a *Notice and Demand for Payment*. The IRS can apply this penalty even if the employer has gone out of business.

Responsible Person. A responsible person is a person or group of people having the duty to perform and the power to direct the collecting, accounting, and paying of trust fund taxes. This person may be:

1. An officer or an employee of a corporation.
2. A member or employee of a partnership.
3. A corporate director or shareholder.
4. A member of a board of trustees of a nonprofit organization.
5. Another person with authority and control over funds to direct their disbursement.

Assessing the Trust Fund Recovery Penalty. The IRS may assess the penalty against anyone who:

1. Is responsible for collecting or paying withheld income and employment taxes, or for paying collected excise taxes.
2. Willfully fails to collect or pay them.

For *willfulness* to exist, the responsible person must:

1. Have known about the unpaid taxes.
2. Have used the funds to keep the business going or allowed available funds to be paid to other creditors.

Employment Taxes. Employment taxes include the amount the employer should *withhold* from employees for both income and Social Security tax, plus the amount of Social Security tax paid on behalf of each employee.

If the employer fails to pay employment taxes on time, or if required to but did not include payment with the return, the IRS will charge interest and penalties on any unpaid balance. They may charge penalties of up to 15% of the amount not deposited, depending on how many days late the payment is.

If withheld trust fund taxes are not paid, the IRS may take additional collection action. They may require the employer to:

1. File and pay the employee's taxes monthly rather than quarterly, or
2. Open a special bank account for the withheld amounts, under penalty of prosecution.

Award of Administrative Costs

Rules for awarding reasonable administrative costs and certain fees incurred after January 18, 1999 include:

Qualified Offer Rule. The taxpayer can receive reasonable costs and fees as a prevailing party in a civil action or proceeding when all of the following occur:

1. The taxpayer makes a qualified offer to the IRS to settle the case.
2. The IRS rejects that offer.
3. The tax liability (not including interest) later determined by the Court is not more than the the qualified offer.

The Court can consider the IRS not to be the prevailing party in a civil action or proceeding based on the fact that the IRS has lost in other courts of appeal on substantially similar issues.

Qualified Offer. This is a written offer made by the taxpayer during the qualified offer period. It must specify both of the following:

1. The amount of the taxpayer's liability (not including interest).
2. That it is a qualified offer when made.

It must remain open until the earliest of the following dates:

1. The date the offer is rejected.

2. The date the trial begins.
3. 90 days from the date of the offer.

The qualified offer period is the period beginning with the date that the 30-day letter is mailed by the IRS to the taxpayer and ending on the date that is 30 days before the date the case is first set for trial.

Administrative costs can be awarded for costs incurred after the earliest of the following dates:

1. The date of the notice of deficiency.
2. The date the first letter of proposed deficiency is sent that allows an opportunity to request administrative review in the IRS Office of Appeals.
3. The date the taxpayer receives the IRS Office of Appeals' decision

Attorney Fees. The basic rate of an award for attorney fees has been raised from $110 to $125 per hour and it can be higher in certain circumstances. Those circumstances now include the difficulty level of the issues in the case and the availability of tax expertise locally. The basic rate is subject to adjustment each year.

Attorney fees now include the fees paid for the services of anyone who is authorized to practice before the Tax Court or before the IRS. In addition, attorney fees can be awarded in civil actions taken for unauthorized inspection or disclosure of the taxpayer's tax return or return information.

Fees can be awarded in excess of the actual amount charged if all of the following apply:

1. The fees are charged at less than the $125 basic rate.
2. The taxpayer is represented for no fee, or for a nominal fee, as a pro bono service.
3. The award is paid to the taxpayer's representative or to the representative's employer.

EXPLANATION OF CLAIM FOR REFUND DISALLOWANCE

The IRS has the obligation to explain the specific reasons that a claim for refund is disallowed or partially disallowed. Claims for refund can be disallowed based on a preliminary review or on examination by a revenue agent. This means that the taxpayer must receive one of the following:

1. A form explaining that the claim is disallowed for one of the following reasons:
   a. The claim was filed late.

   b. It was based solely on the unconstitutionality of the revenue acts.

   c. It was waived as part of a settlement.

   d. It covered a tax year or issues that were part of a closing agreement or an offer in compromise.

   e. It was related to a return closed by a final court order.

2. A revenue agent's report explaining the reasons that the claim is disallowed.

TAX COURT PROCEEDINGS

Burden of Proof. Generally, for court proceedings resulting from examinations started after July 22, 1998, the IRS has the burden of proving any factual issue if the taxpayer has introduced credible evidence relating to the issue. However, the taxpayer must also have done all of the following:

1. Complied with all substantiation requirements of the Internal Revenue Code.

2. Maintained all records required by the Internal Revenue Code.

3. Cooperated with all reasonable requests by the IRS for information regarding the preparation and related tax treatment of any item reported on a tax return.

4. Had a net worth of $7 million or less at the time the tax liability is contested in any court proceeding if the tax return is for a corporation, partnership, or trust.

Use of Statistical Information. The IRS has the burden of proof in court proceedings that are based on any reconstruction of an individual's income solely through the use of statistical information on unrelated taxpayers.

Penalties. The IRS has the burden of proof in court proceedings with respect to the liability of any individual taxpayer for any penalty, addition to tax, or additional amount imposed by the tax laws.

Refund or Credit of Overpayments Before Final Decision. Beginning July 22, 1998, any court with proper jurisdiction, including the Tax Court, has the authority to order the IRS to refund any part of a tax deficiency that the IRS collects from the taxpayer during a period when the IRS is not permitted to assess, levy, or engage in any court proceeding to collect that tax deficiency. In addition, the court can order a refund of any part of a tax deficiency that is not at issue in a taxpayer's appeal to the court. The court can order these refunds before its decision on the case is final. Generally, the IRS is not permitted to take action on a tax deficiency during the following periods.

1. The 90-day (or 150-day if outside of the United States) period that the taxpayer has to petition a notice of deficiency to the Tax Court.
2. The period that the case is under appeal.

Under prior law, no authority existed for ordering the IRS to refund any amount collected during an Impermissible period, or to refund any amount that was not at issue in an appeal, before the final decision of the Tax Court.

Small Case Procedures. For proceedings beginning after July 22, 1998, small tax case procedures are available for disputes that involve $50,000 or less. Under prior law, small tax case procedures were limited to disputes involving $10,000 or less. Small tax case procedures can be used, at the taxpayer's request and with the Tax Court's concurrence, for income, estate, gift, certain employment, and certain excise taxes. The proceedings are conducted as informally as possible. Neither briefs nor oral arguments are required. Most taxpayers represent themselves, although they may be represented by anyone admitted to practice before the Tax Court.

ADDITIONAL PROVISIONS FOR TAXPAYER RIGHTS

The rules were expanded for awarding reasonable administrative costs and certain fees incurred after January 18, 1999. Reasonable costs and fees can be received as a prevailing party in a civil action or proceeding when all the following occur:

1. A qualified offer is made to the IRS to settle the case.
2. The IRS rejects the offer.
3. The tax liability (not including interest) later determined by the Court is not more than the amount of the qualified offer.

A *qualified offer* is a written offer made by a taxpayer during the qualified offer period. It must specify both of the following.

1. The amount of the liability (not including interest).
2. That it is a qualified offer when made. It must also remain open until the earliest of the following dates.
   a. The date the offer is rejected.

b. The date the trial begins.

c. 90 days from the date of the offer.

A *qualified offer* period is the period beginning with the date that the 30-day letter is mailed by the IRS to the taxpayer and ending on the date that is 30 days before the date the case is first set for trial.

Administrative costs can be awarded for costs incurred after the earliest of the following dates.

1. The date of the notice of deficiency.
2. The date the first letter of proposed deficiency is sent that allows the taxpayer an opportunity to request administrative review in the Appeals Office of IRS.
3. The date the taxpayer receives the Appeals Office of IRS decision.

Attorney Fees

The basic rate of an award for attorney fees has increased from $110 to $125 ($140 for 2000) per hour and it can be higher in certain circumstances. Those circumstances now include the difficulty level of the issues in the case and the availability of tax expertise locally. The basic rate is subject to adjustment each year.

Notice of IRS Contact of Third Parties

The IRS must notify a taxpayer *before* IRS can contact third parties when examining or collecting a tax liability. Third parties may include neighbors, banks, employees, or employers. The IRS must periodically, and upon request, provide notice of specific contacts. This is effective for contacts made after January 18, 1999.

This provision does not apply in the following circumstances:

1. When there is a pending criminal investigation.
2. When providing notice would jeopardize collection of any Tax liability.
3. Where providing notice may result in reprisal against any person.
4. When the taxpayer authorized the contact.

Last Date for Filing Tax Court Petition

Beginning in 1999, each notice that the IRS mails out must specify the last date on which a timely petition can be filed with the Tax Court. This date is the 90th day after the date that the notice of deficiency is mailed by the IRS.

Explanation of Claim for Refund Disallowance

Beginning January 19, 1999, the IRS must explain to the taxpayer the specific reasons why a claim for refund is disallowed or partially disallowed. This puts into law an existing practice of the IRS. Claims for refund can be disallowed based on a preliminary review or an examination by a revenue agent. This means the taxpayer must receive a form explaining that the claim is disallowed for one of the following reasons.

1. It was filed late.
2. It was based solely on the unconstitutionality of the revenue acts.
3. It was waived as part of a settlement.
4. It covered a tax year or issues that were part of a closing agreement or an offer in compromise.
5. It was related to a return closed by a final court order.
6. A revenue agent's report explaining the reasons that it is disallowed.

Chapter 31
Expert Witness

With the plethora of high profile legal cases which have inundated the news in the last few years, we've all become trial experts. After being briefed on a variety of cases, we're aware of all the legal terms—and ramifications.

But of a less spectacular nature has been the steady increase of experts in more dignified, straightforward, less publicized cases; in fact, to the lay person, these are often downright boring. However, to the accountant who has found his niche as an "expert witness," they are not only fascinating, but can be quite remunerative. (After all, it was accounting that finally put Al Capone behind bars.) Many accountants are discovering they can increase business, gain public awareness, and enjoy using their special knowledge and experience as expert witnesses. Their financial knowledge and ability to follow a paper trail of figures gives them importance as investigators as well as witnesses in complicated court cases involving financial dealings. There can also be pitfalls along the way.

The need for the accountant as an "expert witness" has increased proportionately with the growing complexity of business affairs. For a number of years, the courts had permitted a rather liberal use of experts in trials; however, the days of relative immunity from prosecution of the expert witness seem to have ended as litigation threatened to become a national pastime. Obviously, the more lawsuits, the more losers. And the loser has to take it out on someone. (That loser may be the opposing party—or it could be the accountant's client.) Why not go after that expert who caused all the trouble? And his firm, too!

ENGAGEMENT LETTER

Therein lies the raison d'être of a well thought-out, carefully constructed engagement agreement containing buffers against both parties. This agreement needs, at the minimum, to spell out carefully:

1. What the accountant has agreed to do.
2. What information the client *must* make available to the expert witness to enable him or her to investigate the evidence and reach an opinion.
3. Lines of effective communication with both the client(s) and the attorney(s).
4. What the client can expect if the accountant is *required* to reveal on the stand any and all information on which his opinion is based.
5. That the attorney *must* keep the accountant informed in a timely fashion of any and all legal requirements such as filing times, submission of written documents, when any graphic presentations are due, and the like.

The corollary of this is, of course, that the accountant needs to guarantee to do or not do several things of concern to the client and/or attorney. If the accountant feels that he may not "fit the bill" as an expert witness in a case, he must not accept the engagement. The accountant must:

1. Possess the necessary qualifications and background.
2. Be cognizant of the accounting profession's technical and ethical standards applicable to litigation services, specifically those applying to expert witnesses.
3. Schedule adequate time and opportunity to investigate the case thoroughly.
4. Be prepared to furnish testimony in a forceful, confident manner.
5. Be prepared to defend a position "properly taken" in a polite, matter-of-fact manner in cross-examination.
6. Keep foremost in mind that the objective is to aid the client and attorney in winning the case, but *not* at the cost of the accountant's integrity.
7. Remember that the expert witness is *not* a client advocate, but an advocate of the accountant's own opinion and point of view.
8. Be positive that there can be no taint of conflict of interest that could be detrimental to the case.
9. Steer away from any engagement where there could be a possibility of divulging privileged information.

10. Withdraw as expeditiously as possible if there are any doubts about the litigation in question.
11. Adhere to the strategy of the lawyer, but here again, *not* at the expense of the accountant's integrity.

PREP TIME

Preparing for the first trial may be the most difficult part of joining the growing number of accountants entering the expert witness niche. This is the time when the accountant, if he's been lucky or hasn't served on a jury, really becomes familiar with the down-to-earth aspects of the judicial system.

There's nothing like familiarity in developing confidence and ease of presentation; therefore, preparation should include:

1. Becoming familiar with the general rules governing real-life courtroom procedure in the locale where the testimony will be given.
2. A visit to a court, preferably one where there is a trial being held involving an accountant expert witness. In metropolitan areas, this should be relatively easy.
3. When apprised of the specific court assignment of the case, the accountant should visit the particular judge's courtroom to observe his attitude and demeanor.
4. Role playing. This activity is recommended for all sorts of therapy, where it may or may not work, but it definitely works in a situation like this. (The attorneys had to play out their role for moot court in law school. Why not the accountant turning expert witness?) Partners, staff and/or family members make great critics—as well as actors in this courtroom drama. Even a full-length mirror can ask questions and talk back.

DEFINITION OF AN EXPERT WITNESS

The courts uniformly agree that the accountant possesses the qualifications of an expert witness on any subject matter falling within the scope of his experience, training, and education.

There are perhaps as many definitions of an "expert witness" as there are statutes, judges, and writers concerned with testimony. The following definition of an expert witness is designed to cover all aspect of "expert" definitions (without any whereases or wherefores): *A witness is an expert witness and is qualified to give expert testimony if the judge finds that to perceive, know, or understand the matter concerning which the witness is to testify requires special knowledge, skill, experience, training, and/or education, and that the witness has the requisite special knowledge, skill, experience, training, and/or education deemed necessary and appropriate.*

If the opposing party offers any objection to the use of an expert's testimony, the accountant's special knowledge, skill, experience, training, or education must be shown before the witness may testify as an expert. Regardless, this information should be made known to the court. A witness's special knowledge, skill, training, or education may be shown by his own testimony, but it will probably "set" better with the jury if the lawyer elicits the pertinent information from the witness relating to his or her education, experience, and specialized knowledge.

Since the basic requirement of an expert witness is that the witness possess the ability to interpret, analyze, and evaluate the significant facts on a question concerning which just a judge or a judge and jury need assistance to resolve, it is imperative that they be aware of the accountant's background. This expertise must be demonstrated in a positive but unassuming manner to be effective. No one likes a braggart.

The courts have uniformly accepted the accountant as an expert. In the majority of cases, the primary and most significant criteria in guidance of a trial court's determination of qualifications of an expert witness are based on occupational experience. Equally significant is the judicial recognition of the special knowledge acquired by an accountant relating to a particular industry, trade, occupation, or profession to qualify her as an expert on particular business and trade practices and on other factors relating to costs and gross profit margins.

In actual practice, it is rare that the trial court will refuse to permit the witness to testify as an expert because he is insufficiently qualified. Rather, any weakness or deficiency will show up in the quality and impact of the testimony rather than its admissibility.

Therefore, it is imperative that an accountant be very cautious about accepting an assignment that may be beyond his or her area of expertise.

FUNCTION OF THE EXPERT WITNESS

The function of the expert witness is to form an opinion or inference on matters when individuals in the normal course of affairs would probably not be able to do so. Therefore, an expert witness is needed in any case where by reason of his special knowledge, the expert is able to form a valid opinion on the facts while the man on the street would—or should—not.

Courts vary in their conception of when the expert is needed. Some courts maintain that expert testimony is admissible only when the subject matter is beyond the common experience of the ordinary juror who would then be unable to reach an informed opinion or draw a valid inference from the facts. In effect, they apply a "strict" test of necessity. More often, the determination is made on the basis of whether this testimony would be of "assistance" to the judge or jury.

BASIS OF INVESTIGATION

In his investigation preparatory to giving testimony, an expert may rely upon various sources. He may:

1. Rely on known facts if such facts are material to the inquiry.
2. Obtain information gained from a demonstrably reliable source.

    This could include previous audit reports, certified financial statements, books and records of the business—even though they were not kept by the expert witness—or demonstrable customs and practices within the business or industry of the client for whom the expert is testifying.

3. If the expert has firsthand knowledge of the situation, inferences or opinions may be stated directly. However, care should be taken to be absolutely sure that the practitioner states fully the facts relied upon, the reliable source, and the permissibility of the basis upon which an opinion was founded. Otherwise, the testimony will do more harm than good. If a judge and/or jury become aware of even one instance in which the accountant has slipped up, his expertise will henceforth be open to question.

In addition, the expert witness must have a thorough knowledge of the substantive issue in the case. The investigation and subsequent conclusion may be incomplete and unrelated to the issue if he either has not been informed properly of the particulars in a case, or has not done his homework thoroughly. It is also necessary that he know the issues of the case so that he can anticipate and respond promptly and forcefully to cross-examination and avoid answers that are incomplete, confusing, and irrelevant. In other words, the expert must be made privy to all relevant facts in the case as well as to the direction of the lawyer's attack or counterattack.

The "need to know" policy should not be carried so far that the accountant appears "in the dark" or at best ill-informed. Therefore, it is important for the accountant to ascertain whether the attorney is willing to work closely with the "expert witness." If the accountant finds it impossible to work in good faith with a particular attorney or law firm, he should withdraw from the case, if possible, or at least refuse to work with that individual or firm in the future. Failure to be aware of or to consider all of the facts not only diminishes the value of the expert's testimony to the case but quite often leaves the expert vulnerable to attack on cross-examination. Not only can the accountant become surprised and confused by the additional facts, but the image as an expert will be damaged in the minds of the judge and jury. The individual's credibility and reputation could be severely damaged.

EXHIBITS

It is almost mandatory that the expert witness prepare, or have prepared, some type of exhibit for several obvious reasons, not the least of which is the fact that very few individuals can make any sense of numbers from just *hearing* them. Oversize charts, graphs, schedules, diagrams—whatever aids the court in visualizing the accountant's findings—can be useful in focusing their attention. Visual aids not only help the expert witness explain his conclusions but they can have a greater impact on the judge and jury. *If* these graphics can be presented in an interesting, imaginative way, they might also tend to lessen the tedium of often very dry facts and figures.

This "demonstrative evidence" (in the parlance of the court) must not appear to be a way of "lecturing" to the judge and jury. At the same time, these are not people preparing for the CPA exam. The visual materials must present readily understood, clearly identifiable steps the accountant took in arriving at opinions and conclusions—not just a jumble of numbers.

It may be appropriate to provide copies of the material to the judge and the members of the jury so that they can use both eyes and ears to follow the testimony of the expert. Even then, it is probably better to have too little information on a graph or schedule than too much.

UNDERSTANDABLE TESTIMONY

Expert testimony is valuable only when it is understood by the judge and jury. The expert must be able to explain and defend her opinion in language reasonably understood by the layman. Everyone complains about "legalese." What about "accountantese"? It should always be kept in mind that the very reason the expert is testifying is that the subject matter is beyond the common knowledge and experience of the average juror.

A common error committed by the accounting expert is to use technical language in testimony without offering an explanation of its meaning.

Terms like *earnings per share, stockholder's equity,* and *retained earnings* may have a nice ring to them. However, if the testimony must necessarily involve technical accounting terms and concepts of this caliber, they must be defined and explained in a clear and simple manner.

CROSS-EXAMINATION

An accountant testifying as an expert may be cross-examined to the same extent as any other witness.

Therefore, the expert should assume that his opinion will be rigorously challenged on cross-examination. The fact that the subject matter is being litigated indicates conflicting theories or facts upon which an opinion may be based. In order to preserve the value and effectiveness of testimony given as an expert, the witness should anticipate what may be brought up in cross-examination. Thorough preparation, awareness of other aspects of a case, anticipation of where the "attack" may come will all aid in the individual's holding up well in this phase of a court appearance. Now is the time when the opposing counsel will attempt to discredit the expert witness concerning qualifications, knowledge of the subject matter, the validity of the source of relevant information, and the basis for arriving at the stated opinion and conclusions.

It is important for the accountant to remember that this is the lawyer's job. Since the purpose of cross-examination is to diminish or destroy the expert's conclusions, the lawyer may be argumentative, supercilious, and aggressive in an attempt to catch the witness off balance—to make the expert react too quickly and speak before thinking. Instead, this is the time when remaining courteous, unemotional, and firmly convinced of the correctness of previous statements pays off.

One of the techniques used in cross-examination is to show a contradiction or omission of facts upon which the expert founded an opinion. For this reason, it is essential that the expert make a thorough investigation, have knowledge of all relevant theories and material facts, and be prepared to support that opinion rationally on cross-examination. If the expert has adequately prepared, she can reasonably anticipate any weak or questionable aspects of the testimony and be ready to cope with them quickly and spontaneously on cross-examination.

REBUTTAL

Rebuttal testimony provides the opposing party with an opportunity to introduce evidence that refutes the prior evidence of the other side in the case. The opposing side may decide to offer in rebuttal its own expert to directly refute the testimony of the original expert. Rebuttal testimony may not go beyond the scope of the original evidence. In other words, a party may not introduce new evidence but is limited to a direct rebuttal of prior evidence. However, there is still plenty of opportunity for accounting expert witness No. 2 to question the validity of the original expert's assumptions, opinions, and conclusions concerning alternative ways of looking at a situation.

If the original expert has considered and discussed the cause for litigation from every possible angle, the impact of a rebuttal expert witness who attempts to base opinion on opposing theories and facts has basically been forestalled, because that ground has already been covered, and discarded.

LEGAL MATTERS

What are these weighty matters which the expert witness is going to investigate, form opinions concerning, testify to, be cross-examined about or offer rebuttal to? As might be expected, there may even be a "mini-niche" within this niche where the accountant could decide to specialize. Among the more likely spots are:

1. Tax cases-civil, criminal, fraud—both state and federal. It is difficult to imagine a tax case that does not involve accounting problems. Attorneys for both the government and the taxpayer can be expected to have a general knowledge of accounting principles, but they have other responsibilities in the case. Enter the practitioner investigator and witness to refute the charge of "willful attempt to evade taxes," or just an assertion of deficiency in tax payments.
2. Divorce cases. In states with community property laws, this can become extremely involved in tracing and determining which funds are community property, separate property, proceeds from separate property, commingled funds, and separate funds of various descriptions.
3. Probate proceedings. Wills, state inheritance taxes, and federal estate taxes in states with community property laws also often need testimony from investigative accountants. In fact, the distinction between separate and community property is often crucial in figuring the amount of state inheritance and federal estate taxes owed.
4. Partnership dissolution and/or valuation of partnership interest. The accountant is frequently employed as an expert to prepare a partnership accounting of a dissolved partnership. Following is a sampling of the items that will come to the attention of the accountant in preparing her report for submission to the court:
   a. Contractual agreements among the partners expressly providing for a partnership accounting for capital or profits.

b. Capital contributions reflected in the partnership agreement, additional loans, and restrictions or limitations on the right of a partner to withdraw the profits or capital.

c. Present fair market value (FMV) of property previously contributed by a partner.

d. Allocation of profits and losses for the current year in accordance with the partnership agreement.

5. Corporate suits brought by shareholders; corporate fraud cases. These involve not only large corporations, but also very small ones that have been inundated in the flood of litigation in the U.S.

The accountant must, obviously, have an understanding of the pertinent substantive law before being competent to undertake an investigation of the facts and testify as an expert witness—giving an opinion and conclusions concerning a legal as well as a financial matter.

It becomes fairly obvious that the neophyte expert witness needs to do some investigating to determine just what laws apply to the niche he has chosen to delve into. The particular state laws are undoubtedly the place to begin the investigation since each will be somewhat different—some more than others.

Chapter 32
Tip Income

What's the big deal? An estimated $9 billion a year in unreported, untaxed tip income, that's what. Reporting all tip income has always been required by law. When the significant extent to which taxpayers were ignoring the law became evident, the IRS stepped up the emphasis on the requirements for both employee and employer to report tip income.

TIP RATE DETERMINATION / EDUCATION PROGRAM

The Tip Rate Determination/Education Program (TRD/EP) was first promoted in the gaming industry (casino industry) in Las Vegas, Nevada, and has spread to the food and beverage industry. Other industries whose employees receive tips include beauty parlors, barber shops, taxi companies, and pizza delivery establishments.

The Tip Rate Determination/Education Program created in 1993 is a national program used in all states. The employer has the option to enter into one of two arrangements under this program: the Tip Rate Determination Agreement (TRDA) or the Tip Reporting Alternative Commitment (TRAC) created in June 1995.

With the introduction of the new programs, four options became available for tip reporting:

1. Tip Rate Determination Agreement (TRDA).
2. Tip Reporting Alternative Commitment (TRAC).

585

3. The status quo—the old basic method following the requirements listed below without any "formal" agreement.

4. Examination of Tip Income Reporting.

Under the Tip Rate Determination/Education Program (TRD/EP), the employer may enter into either the TRDA or TRAC arrangement. The IRS will assist applicants in understanding and meeting the requirements for participation. Many similarities exist between the two new alternatives, but there are some differences. Following is a descriptive list of the requirements for each, particularly in reference to the food and beverage industry:

TRDA

1. Requires the IRS to work with the establishment to arrive at a tip rate for the various restaurant occupations.

2. Requires the employee to enter into a Tipped Employee Participation Agreement (TEPA) with the employer.

3. Requires the employer to get 75% of the employees to sign TEPAs and report at or above the determined rate.

4. Provides that if employees fail to report at or above the determined rate, the employer will provide the names of those employees, their social security numbers, job classification, sales, hours worked, and amount of tips reported.

5. Has no specific education requirement relating to legal responsibility to report tips under the agreement.

6. Participation assures the employer that prior periods will not be examined during the period that the TRDA is in effect.

7. Results in the mailing of a notice and demand to employer for the employer's portion of FICA taxes on unreported tips determined for the six month period used to set the tip rate(s).

8. Prevents employer (only) assessments during the period that the agreement is in effect.

TRAC

1. Does not require that a tip rate be established, but it does require the employer to:

   a. Establish a procedure where a directly tipped employee is provided (no less than monthly) a written statement of charged tips attributed to the employee.

   b. Implement a procedure for the employee to verify or correct any statement of attributed tips.

c. Adopt a method where an indirectly tipped employee reports his or her tips (no less than monthly). This could include a statement prepared by the employer and verified or corrected by the employee.

d. Establish a procedure where a written statement is prepared and processed (no less than monthly) reflecting all cash tips attributable to sales of the directly tipped employee.

2. Does not require an agreement between the employee and the employer.

3. Affects all (100%) of the employees.

4. Includes a commitment by the employer to educate and reeducate quarterly all directly and indirectly tipped employees and new hires of their statutory requirement to report all tips to their employer.

5. Participation assures the employer that prior periods will not be examined during the period that the agreement is in effect.

6. Prevents employer (only) assessments during the period that the agreement is in effect.

7. Assures that employers comply with all tax reporting, filing, and payment obligations.

8. Requires employers to maintain and make available records to the IRS.

9. Emphasizes that employees earning $20 or more a month in tips must report them to the employer.

In return, the IRS generally will not perform a tip examination on employers complying with the TRAC guidelines. In contrast, an establishment whose employees underreport their tips could be liable for back FICA taxes.

The approach has helped lead to increased tip reporting, but the IRS believes there is still ample room for improvement. In the food and beverage sector alone, tip reporting jumped from $3.9 billion in 1993 to $5.2 billion in 1995 to more than $7 billion in 1998. However, estimates placed the amount of annual tips going to those same workers at $18 billion annually.

TRAC Agreement Revised

The IRS has been working cooperatively with the restaurant industry in response to industry concerns regarding some aspects of the TRAC program. In late 1999, the IRS took steps to reduce the administrative burdens of restaurant operators by making several changes in the regulations:

1. The IRS will no longer revoke TRAC agreements in cases where employers make a good-faith effort at following the guidelines but

employees still fail to report tips. Instead of pursuing the employers in such situations, the IRS will focus on the employees who are not in compliance with tip reporting.

2. Another change involves restaurants with locations in different IRS Districts. Under the new plan, the restaurant's headquarter operations will work directly with their local IRS office on TRAC issues. This streamlined approach will be simpler and more straightforward than the old system, where different locations of a company had to deal with different people in different IRS Districts.

3. The third change involves the expiration date of the TRAC program. Instead of ending in May, 2000, the program will now run through May, 2005, with the possibility of its being extended even longer.

About 10,000 companies, representing more than 30,000 locations, have already entered the agreements, and the IRS hopes more will follow in the months ahead as a result of this shifting of more responsibility to the employee.

Instituting the Program

To enter into one of the arrangements, an employer should submit an application letter to the area IRS Chief, Examination/Compliance Division, Attn: Tip Coordinator. The Tip Coordinator can provide a letter format as well as extensive information on the two separate arrangements.

All employers with establishments where tipping is customary should review their operations. Then, if it is determined that there is or has been an underreporting of tips, the employer should apply for one of the two arrangements under the TRD/EP. Employers currently with the TRDA in effect may revoke the arrangement and simultaneously enter into a TRAC.

The particular advantage to the employer who adopts one of these programs is that no subsequent tip examination is imposed as long as terms of the arrangement have been met and all tips have been reported.

BASIC RULES RELATING TO TIP INCOME REPORTING

The following discussion concerns how tip income is taxed and how it should be reported to the IRS on the federal income tax return. The employees of food and beverage companies are the main subjects of this review; the record keeping rules and other information also apply to other workers who receive tips.

As pointed out earlier, all tips that are received by employees are taxable income and are subject to federal income taxes. Employees must include in gross income all tips received directly from customers, and tips from charge customers paid to the employer, who must pay them to the employee. In addition, cash tips of $20 or more that an employee receives in a month while working for any one employer are subject to withholding of income tax, social security retirement tax, and Medicare tax. The employee should report tips to the employer in order to determine the correct amount of these taxes.

Tips and other pay are used to determine the amount of social security benefits that an employee receives when he or she retires, becomes disabled, or dies. Noncash tips are not counted as wages for social security purposes. Future Social Security Administration (SSA) benefits can be figured correctly only if the SSA has the correct information. To make sure that an employee has received credit for all his or her earnings, the employee should request a statement of earnings from the SSA at least every other year. The SSA will send the person a statement that should be carefully checked to be sure it includes all of the employee's earnings.

Every large food and beverage business must report to the IRS any tips allocated to the employees. Generally, tips must be allocated to be paid by employees when the total tips reported to an employer by employees are less than 8% of the establishment's food and beverage sales of that employee. This necessitates the employer and employees keeping accurate records of the employee's tip income.

Daily Tip Record

The employee must keep a daily tip record so he or she can:

1. Report tips accurately to the employer.
2. Report tips accurately on a tax return.
3. Prove tip income if the taxpayer's return is ever questioned.

There are two ways to keep a daily tip record:

1. The employee can keep a daily "tip diary."
2. The employee should keep copies of documents that show the tips, such as restaurant bills and credit card charge slips.

The employee can start record keeping by writing his or her name, the employer's name, and the name of the business if it is different from the employer's name. Each workday, the employee should write and date the following information in a tip diary.

1. Cash tips received directly from customers or other employees.
2. Tips from credit card charge customers that the employer pays the employee.
3. The value of any noncash tips received, such as tickets, passes, or other items of value.

4. The amount of tips the employee paid out to other employees through tip pools, tip splitting, or other arrangements, and the names of the employees to whom tips were paid.

Reporting Tips to the Employer

The employee must report tips to the employer so that:

1. The employer can withhold federal income tax, social security taxes, and Medicare taxes.
2. The employer can report the correct amount of the employee's earnings to the Social Security Administration. This will affect the employee's benefits when the employee retires or becomes disabled, or the family's benefits upon the employee's death.

What Tips to Report

Only cash, check, or credit card tips should be reported to the employer. If the total tips for any one month from any one job are less than $20, they should not be reported to the employer. The value of any noncash tips, such as tickets or passes, is not reported to the employer because the employee does not have to pay social security and Medicare taxes on these tips. The employee will, however, report them on his or her individual tax return. The following information should be written on the report to be given to the employer:

1. Name, address, and social security number.
2. The employer's name, address, and business name if it is different from the employer's name.
3. The month, or the dates of any shorter period, in which the tips are received.
4. The total amount of tips the employee received.

The employee must sign and date the report and give it to the employer. The employee should keep a copy of the report for his or her personal records. The report is to be completed each month and given to the employer by the tenth of the next month.

Employer Records for Tip Allocation

Large food and beverage establishments are required to report certain additional information about tips to the IRS. To make sure that employees are reporting tips correctly, employers must keep records to verify amounts reported by employees. Certain employers must allocate tips if the percentage of tips reported by employees falls below a required minimum percentage of gross sales. To allocate tips means to assign an additional amount as tips to each employee whose reported tips are below the required percentage. The rules apply to premises in which:

1. Food and beverages are provided for consumption on the premises.
2. Tipping is customary.
3. The employer normally employed more than ten people on a typical business day during the preceding calendar year.

Tip allocation rules do not apply to food and beverage establishments where tipping is not customary such as:

1. A cafeteria or fast food restaurant.
2. A restaurant that adds a service charge of 10% or more to 95% or more of its food and beverage sales.
3. Food and beverage establishments located outside the United States.

The rules apply only if the total amount of tips reported by all tipped employees to the employer is less than 8%, or some lower acceptable percentage of the establishment's total food or beverage sales, with some adjustments. If reported tips total less than 8% of total sales, the employer must allocate the difference between 8% of total sales, or some lower acceptable percentage approved by the IRS, and the amount of tips reported by all tipped employees. The employer will exclude carryout sales, state and local taxes, and sales with a service charge of 10% or more when figuring total sales.

Usually, the employer will allocate to all affected employees their share of tips every payroll period. However, the employer should not withhold any taxes from the allocated amount. No allocation will be made to the employee if the employee reports tips at least equal to the employee's share of 8% of the establishment's total food and beverage sales.

Penalty for Not Reporting Tips

If the employee does not report tips to his or her employer as required, the employee can be subject to a penalty equal to 50% of the social security and Medicare taxes owed. The penalty amount is in addition to the taxes owed. The penalty can be avoided if the employee can show reasonable cause for not reporting the tips to the employer. A statement should be attached to the tax return explaining why the tips were not reported to the employer. If an employee's regular pay is not enough for the employer to withhold all the taxes owed on the regular pay plus reported tips, the employee can give the employer money to pay the rest of the taxes, up to the close of the calendar year.

If the employee does not give the employer enough money, the employer will apply the regular pay and any money given by the employee in the following order:

1. All taxes on the employee's regular pay.
2. Social security and Medicare taxes on the reported tips.
3. Federal, state, and local income taxes on the reported tips.

Any taxes that remain unpaid can be collected by the employer from the employee's next paycheck. If withholding taxes remain uncollected at the end of the year, the employee must make an estimated tax payment. To report these taxes, a return must be filed even if the employee would not otherwise have to file. If the employer could not collect all the social security and Medicare taxes owed on the tips reported to the employer, the uncollected taxes must be shown by the employer on a Form W-2. The employee must then also report these uncollected taxes on his or her return.

TIP RATES

Depending on the Occupational Category and the employer's business practices, tips can be *measured* in different ways.

1. *Actual tips* generally apply to Employees in Occupational Categories (O.C.) where pooling of tips is common. The tips are pooled during a shift and the total is split among the employees of the O.C. who worked the shift.
2. *Tip rates* generally apply to employees in O.C. where pooling of tips is not common. The rate may be a percentage of sales, a dollar amount, or other accurate basis of measurement per hour or shift, a dollar amount per drink served, a dollar amount per working hour, or other accurate measurement.

Methods for Determining Tip Rates

The employer will determine tip rates for the O.C. based on information available to the employer, historical information provided by the district director, and generally accepted accounting principles (GAAP). The rates will specify whether the tips are received as a percentage of sales, a dollar amount per hour or shift, a dollar amount per drink served, a dollar amount per dealing hour in a casino, or on another basis.

Initial Tip Rate

The initial tip rate for each O.C. is shown where pool and split tips methods are used by the employees.

ANNUAL REVIEW

The employer will review annually, on a calender year basis, changes in the tip rates assigned to its O.C. In connection with the review, the employer can review its O.C. The initial rates for each O.C. will apply to the first full calendar year of the review.

Employer Submission

If the employer believes that a revision of one or more rates or O.C. is appropriate, the employer will submit proposed revisions to the District Director by September 30. If the employer fails to submit a proposed rate revision by September 30 of the taxable year, the employee will be treated as having submitted the rate in effect for the current year.

District Director Review

The District Director will review the proposed rates and notify the employer in writing of the approval or disapproval by November 30. If the District Director does not approve one or more proposed rates, the existing rate or rates will be continued until no later than the last day of the following February.

The effective date of revised rates and O.C. will become effective on the later of January 1 of the calendar year, or on the first day of the month following the date the employer and the district director agree upon a revised rate. The district director can examine a participating employee's tip income for any period if an employee reports tips at a rate less than the tip rate for the employee's occupational category.

These amounts must be an additional tax on the employee's tax return. The employee may have uncollected taxes if his or her regular pay was not enough for the employer to withhold all the taxes the taxpayer owed, but did not give the employer enough money to pay the rest of the taxes. The employee must report these uncollected taxes on a return.

ALLOCATED TIPS

Allocated tips are tips that the employer assigned to an employee in addition to the tips the employee reported to the employer for the year. The employer will have done this only if the employee worked in a restaurant, cocktail lounge, or similar business that must allocate tips to employees, and the reported tips were less than the employee's share of 8% of food and drink sales. If allocated tips are shown on a return, and if social security and Medicare taxes were not withheld from the allocated tips, these taxes must be reported as additional tax on a return.

Allocation Formula

The allocation can be done either under a formula agreed to by both the employer and the employees or, if they cannot reach an agreement, under a formula prescribed by IRS regulations. The allocation formula in the regulations provides that tip allocations are made only to directly tipped employees. If tips are received directly from customers, the employees are directly tipped employees, even if the tips are turned over to a tip pool. Waiters, waitresses, and bartenders are usually considered directly tipped employees. If tips are not normally received directly from customers, the employee is an indirectly tipped employee. Examples are busboys, service bartenders, and cooks. If an employee receives tips both directly and indirectly through tip splitting or tip pooling, the employee is treated as a directly tipped employee.

If customers of the establishment tip less than 8% on average, either the employee or a majority of the directly tipped employees can petition to have the allocation percentage reduced from 8%. This petition is made to the district director for the IRS district in which the establishment is located. The percentage cannot be reduced below 2%.

A fee is required to have the IRS consider a petition to lower the tip allocation percentage. The fee must be paid by check or money order made out to the Internal Revenue Service. (The user fee amount for 1998 is $275; the district director in the taxpayer's area will know if this amount has changed.)

The employees' petition to lower the allocation percentage must be in writing, and must contain enough information to allow the district director to estimate with reasonable accuracy the establishment's actual tip rate. This information might include the changed tip rate, type of establishment, menu prices, location, hours of operation, amount of self-service required, and whether the customer receives the check from the server or pays the server for the meal. If the employer possesses any relevant information, the employer must provide it to the district upon request of the employees or the district director.

The employees' petition must be consented to by more than one-half of the directly tipped employees working for the establishment at the time the petition is filed. If the petition covers more than one establishment, it must be consented to by more than one-half of the total number of directly tipped employees of the covered establishments. The petition must state the total number of directly tipped employees of the establishment(s) and the number of directly tipped employees consenting to the petition.

The petition may cover two or more establishments if the employees have made a good faith determination that the tip wages are essentially the same and if the establishments are:

1. Owned by the same employer.
2. Essentially the same type of business.
3. In the same Internal Revenue Service region.

A petition that covers two or more establishments must include the names and locations of the establishments and must be sent to the district director for the district in which the greatest number of covered establishments are located. If there is an equal number of covered establishments in two or more districts, the employees can choose which district to petition. Employees who file a petition must promptly notify their employer of the petition. The employer must then promptly furnish the district director with an annual information return form showing the tip income and allocated tips filed for the establishment for the three immediately preceding calendar years.

The employer will report the amount of tips allocated to employees on the employees' Form W-2 separately from wages and reported tips. The employer bases withholding only on wages and reported tips. The employer should not withhold income, social security, and Medicare taxes from the allocated amount. Any incorrectly withheld taxes should be refunded to the employee by the employer.

If an employee leaves a job before the end of the calendar year and requests an early Form W-2, the employer does not have to include a tip allocation on the Form W-2. However, the employer can show the actual allocated amount if it is known, or show an estimated allocation. In January of the following year, the employer most provide Form W-2 if the early Form W-2 showed no allocation and the employer later determined that an allocation was required, or if the estimated allocation shown was wrong by more than 5% of the actual allocation.

If an employee does not have adequate records for his or her actual tips, the employee must include the allocated tips shown on the Form W-2 as additional tip income on the tax return. If the employee has records, allocated tips should not be shown on the employee's return. Additional tip income is included only if those records show more tips received than the amount reported to the employer.

Chapter 33

Business Use of a Home

Rules that went into effect in 1999 make it easier to claim a deduction for the business use of a home. Under these rules, a taxpayer may qualify to claim the deduction, even though never having qualified before. The following information explains these rules.

PRINCIPAL PLACE OF BUSINESS

Under the latest rules for deducting expenses for the business use of a home, it is easier for a home office to qualify as the principal place of business. Under the old rules, a taxpayer had to consider the relative importance of the activities carried out at each business location when determining if a home was the principal place of business. The place where the taxpayer conducted the most important activities was the place where meetings were held with clients, customers, or patients, or the location where goods or services were delivered. Performing administrative or management duties in the home office was considered less important.

Before 1999, an outside salesperson's home office did not qualify as a principal place of business. The place where he or she met with customers to explain available products and take orders was considered more important than the home office where administrative duties were conducted. Beginning in 1999, however, a home office qualifies as a principal place of business for deducting expenses for the use of it:

1. If the home office is used exclusively for administration or management activities of a trade or business.
2. If the taxpayer has no other fixed location for conducting substantial administrative or management activities relating to a trade or business.

There are many activities that are administrative or managerial in nature. Some of these activities are:

1. Billing customers, clients, or patients.
2. Keeping books and records.
3. Ordering supplies.
4. Setting up appointments.
5. Forwarding orders or writing reports.

The following administrative or management activities performed at other locations will *not* disqualify a home office as a principal place of business:

1. When others conduct a taxpayer's administrative or management activities at locations other than the home.
2. The conduct of administrative or management activities at places that are not fixed locations of a business, such as in a car or a hotel room.
3. The taxpayer occasionally conducts minimal administrative or management activities at a fixed location outside of the home.
4. The taxpayer conducts substantial *non*administrative or *non*management business at a fixed location outside the home.
5. Suitable space to conduct administrative or management activities is available outside the home office, but a home office is used for those activities instead.

OTHER CRITERIA FOR DETERMINING PLACE OF BUSINESS

If the newer rules do not appear to cover the taxpayer's particular situation, the older rules may give an indication of other aspects when considering deductions for business use of the home—or the IRS may add further rules for the upcoming tax season.

It is permissible to have more than one business location, including a home, for a single trade or business. To qualify to deduct the expenses for the business use of a home, the home must be a principal place of business of that trade or business. To determine the principal place of business, all of the facts and circumstances must be considered. If, after considering the business locations, one cannot be identified as a principal place of business, then home office expenses cannot be deducted. The two primary factors to consider are:

1. The relative importance of the activities performed at each location.
2. The time spent at each location.

To determine whether a home is the principal place of business, the taxpayer must consider the relative importance of the activities carried out at each business location. The relative importance of the activities performed at each business location is determined by the basic characteristics of the business. If the business requires that meetings or conferences be held with clients or patients, or that goods or services be delivered to a customer, then the place where contacts are made must be given great weight in determining where the most important activities are performed.

If the relative importance of the activities does not clearly establish the principal place of business, such as when to deliver goods or services at both the office, in the home, and elsewhere, then the time spent at each location is important. Comparison should be made of the time spent on business at the home office with the time spent at other locations.

SEPARATE STRUCTURES

Expenses can be deducted for a separate free-standing structure, such as a studio, garage, or barn, if the structure is used exclusively and regularly for the business. The structure does not have to be the principal place of business, or a place where patients, clients or customers are met.

FIGURING THE DEDUCTION

Once it has been determined that the "home office" does qualify for a deduction, the next step is determining how much the taxpayer can deduct. Certain expenses related to the business use of a home can be deducted, but deductions are limited by the following:

1. Percentage of the home used for business, i.e., the business percentage.
2. Deduction limit.

To find the *business percentage*, the taxpayer must compare the size of the part of the home used for business to the entire house. The resulting percentage is used to separate the business part of the expenses from the expenses for operating the entire home. Any reasonable method to determine the business percentage can be used. Two commonly used methods are:

1. Dividing the square foot area of the "business space" by the total area of the home.
2. Dividing the number of rooms used for business by the total number of rooms in the home. This method can be used if the rooms in the home are all about the same size.

DEDUCTION LIMIT

If gross income from the business use of a home equals or exceeds the total business expenses (including depreciation), all of the business expenses can be deducted. If the gross income from that use is less than the total business expenses, the deduction for certain expenses for the business use is limited. The deduction of otherwise nondeductible expenses, such as insurance, utilities, and depreciation (with depreciation taken last), allocable to business is limited to the gross income from the business use of the home minus the sum of the following:

1. The business part of expenses that could be deducted even if the home was not used for business (such as mortgage interest, real estate taxes, and casualty and theft losses).
2. The business expenses that relate to the business activity in the home (for example, salaries or supplies), but not to the use of the home itself.

A self-employed individual may not include in (2) above the deduction for half of the self-employment tax.

If deductions are greater than the current year's limit, it is possible to carry over the excess to the next year. Any carryover is subject to the gross income limit from the business use of the home for the next tax year. The amount carried over will be allowable only up to the taxpayer's gross income in the next tax year from the business in which the deduction arose whether the individual lives in the home during that year or not.

ASSORTED USE TESTS

To qualify under the *regular use test*, a specific area of the home must be used for business on a continuing basis. The regular-use test is not met if the business use of the area is only occasional, even if that area is not used for any other purpose.

To qualify under the *trade or business use* test requires that part of a home be used in connection with a trade or business. If part of the home is used for some other profit-seeking activity that is not a trade or business, a deduction cannot be taken for a business use.

A taxpayer who is an employee must qualify under the *convenience-of-the-employer* test. If an employer provides suitable work space for administrative management activities, this fact must be considered in determining whether this test is met. Even if expenses qualify for a deduction for the business use of a home, the deduction may be limited. If the employee's gross income from the business use of a home is less than the employee's total business expenses, the deduction for some of the expenses—utilities, insurance, depreciation, for example—is limited.

Exclusive Use

To qualify under the *exclusive use* test, a specific area of a home must be used only for a trade or business. The area used for business can be a room or other separately identifiable space. The space does not need to be marked off by a permanent partition. If the home area in question is used both for business and personal purposes, it does not meet the requirements of the exclusive use test rule.

The exclusive use test does not have to be met if space is used for the *storage of inventory or product samples*, or for a *day-care facility*. When part of a home is used for the storage of inventory or product samples, the following 5 tests must all be met:

1. The inventory or product samples are kept for use in a trade or business.
2. The trade or business is a wholesale or retail selling of products.
3. The home is the only fixed location of a trade or business.
4. The storage space must be used on a regular basis.
5. The space is an identifiably separate space suitable for storage.

Part-Year Use

Expenses for the business use of a home *may not* be incurred during any part of the year it was not being used for business purposes. Only those expenses for the portion of the year in which it was actually used for business may be used in figuring the allowable deduction.

DAY-CARE FACILITY

If space in the home is used on a regular basis for providing day care, it may be possible to deduct the business expenses for that part of the home even though the same space is used for nonbusiness purposes. To qualify for this exception to the exclusive use rule, the following requirements must be met:

1. The space must be used in the trade or business of providing day care for children, persons 65 or older, or persons who are physically or mentally unable to care for themselves.
2. The taxpayer must have applied for, been granted or be exempt from having a license certification registration, or approval as a day-care center or as a family or group day-care home under state law. An individual does not meet this requirement if an application was rejected or license or other authorization was revoked.

If a part of the home is regularly used for day care, it is necessary to figure the percentage of that part which is used for day care, as explained above under *business percentage*. All the allocable expenses subject to the deduction limit, as explained earlier, may be deducted for that part used exclusively for day care. If the use of part of the home as a day-care facility is regular, but not exclusive, it is necessary to figure what part of available time it is actually used for business.

A room that is available for use throughout each business day and that is regularly used in the business is considered to be used for day care throughout each business day. It is not necessary to keep records to show the specific hours the area was used for business. The area may be used occasionally for personal reasons; however, a room used only occasionally for business does not qualify for the deduction.

To find that part of the available time the home is actually used for business, the total business-use time is compared to the total time that part of the home can be used for all purposes. The comparison may be based upon the hours of business use in a week with the number of hours in a week (168), or the hours of business use for the tax year with the number of hours in the tax year.

Meal Allowance

If food is provided for a day-care business, the expense is not included as a cost of using the home for business. It is a separate deduction on the taxpayer's Schedule C (Form 1040). The cost of food consumed by the taxpayer or his or her family may not be deducted. However, 100% of the cost of food consumed by the day-care recipients and generally only 50% of the cost of food consumed by employees can be deducted. However, 100% of the cost of food consumed by employees can be deducted if its value can be excluded from their wages as a de minimis fringe benefit. For tax years beginning after 1997, the value of meals provided to employees on business premises is generally de minimis if more than half of these employees are provided the meals for the taxpayer's convenience.

If cost of food for the day-care business is deducted, a separate record (with receipts) must be maintained of the family's food costs. Reimbursements received from a sponsor under the Child and Adult Food Care Program of the Department of Agriculture are taxable only to the extent they exceed expenses for food for eligible children. If reimbursements are more than expenses for food, the difference is shown as income in Part I of Schedule C. If food expenses are greater than the reimbursements, the difference is shown as an expense in Part V of Schedule C.

BUSINESS FURNITURE AND EQUIPMENT

Depreciation and Section 179 deductions may be used for furniture and equipment that an employee uses in his or her home for business or work. These deductions are available whether or not the individual qualifies to deduct expenses for the business use of a home. Following are explanations of the different rules for:

1. Listed property.
2. Property bought for business use.
3. Personal property converted to business use.

Listed Property

Special rules apply to certain types of property, called listed property, used in the home. Listed property includes any property of a type generally used for entertainment, recreation, and amusement (including photographic, phonographic, communication, and video recording equipment). But "listed property" also includes computers and related equipment.

Listed property bought and placed in service in 1998 must be used more than 50% for business (including work as an employee) to be claimed as a Section 179 deduction or an accelerated depreciation deduction. If the business use of listed property is 50% or less, a Section 179 deduction cannot be taken and the property must be depreciated using the Alternate Depreciation System (ADS) (straight-line method). Listed property meets the more-than-50%-use test for any tax year if its qualified business use is more than 50% of its total use. Allocation among its various uses must be made for the use of any item of listed property used for more than one purpose during the tax year. The *percentage of investment use may not be used* as part of the percentage of qualified business use to meet the more-than-50%-use test. However, the taxpayer should use the combined total of business and investment use to figure the depreciation deduction for the property.

If an employee uses his or her own listed property (or listed rented property) for work as an employee, the property is business-use property only if both of the following requirements are met.

1. The use is for the convenience of the employer.
2. The use is required as a condition of employment.

"As a condition of employment" means that the use of the property is *necessary* for proper performance of work. Whether the use of the property is required for this purpose depends on all the facts and circumstances. The employer does not have to tell the employee specifically to have a computer for use in the home, nor is a statement by the employer to that effect sufficient.

If, in a year after placing an item of listed property in service, the taxpayer fails to meet the more-than-50%-use test for that item of property, he or she may be required to do both of the following.

1. Figure depreciation, beginning with the year the property is no longer used more than 50% for business, using the straight-line method.
2. Figure any excess depreciation and Section 179 deduction on the property and add it to:
   a. Gross income.
   b. The adjusted basis of the property.

It is not possible to take any depreciation of the Section 179 deduction for the use of listed property unless business/investment use can be proved with adequate records or sufficient evidence to support the individual's own statements. To meet the adequate records requirement, the taxpayer must maintain an account book, diary, log, statement of expense, trip sheet, or similar record or other documentary evidence that is sufficient to establish business/investment use.

Property Bought for Business Use

The taxpayer who has bought certain property to use in his or her business can do any one of the following (subject to the limits discussed below).

1. Elect a Section 179 deduction for the full cost of the property.
2. Take part of the cost as a Section 179 deduction.
3. Depreciate the full cost of the property.

Section 179 Deduction

A Section 179 deduction can generally be claimed on depreciable tangible personal property bought for use in the active conduct of business. The taxpayer can choose how much (subject to the limit) of the cost to deduct under Section 179 and how much to depreciate. The Section 179 deduction can be spread over several items of property in any way selected as long as the total does not exceed the maximum allowable. However, the taxpayer cannot take a Section 179 deduction for the basis of the business part of the home.

Section 179 Deduction Limits

The Section 179 deduction cannot be more than the business cost of the qualifying property. In addition, the following limits apply when figuring a Section 179 deduction.

1. Maximum dollar limit.
2. Investment limit.
3. Taxable income limit.

The total cost of Section 179 property the taxpayer can elect to deduct for 2000 cannot be more than $20,000; for 2001 and 2002, it is $24,000; after 2002, it is $25,000. This *maximum dollar limit* is reduced if the individual goes over the investment limit in any tax year.

If the cost of the qualifying Section 179 property is over the *investment limit*, the taxpayer must reduce the maximum dollar limit for each dollar over $200,000.

The total cost that can be deducted each tax year is subject to the total *taxable income limit*. This is figured on the income from the active conduct of all trade or business activities, including wages, during the tax year. The taxable income for this purpose is figured in the usual way, but without regard to all of the following.

1. The Section 179 deduction.
2. The self-employment tax deduction.
3. Any net operating loss carryback or carryforward.

DEPRECIATION

Part II of Form 4562 is used to claim a deduction for depreciation on property placed in service in 1998. It does not include any costs deducted in Part I (Section 179 deduction).

Most business property used in a home office is either 5-year or 7-year property under MACRS.

- 5-year property includes computers and peripheral equipment, typewriters, calculators, adding machines, and copiers.
- 7-year property includes office furniture and equipment such as desks, files, and safes.

Under MACRS, the half-year convention is generally used, which allows deduction of a half-year of depreciation in the first year the property is used in the business. If more than 40% of the depreciable property was placed in service during the last 3 months of the tax year, the mid-quarter convention must be used instead of the half-year convention.

PERSONAL PROPERTY CONVERTED TO BUSINESS USE

If property is used in the home office that was used previously for personal purposes, a Section 179 deduction cannot be taken for the property, but it can be depreciated. The method of depreciation depends upon when the property was first used for personal purposes.

Appendix A
Financial Planning Tables

The following tables, involving the effects of interest factors, are useful in various forms of future business planning.

SIMPLE INTEREST TABLE

SIMPLE INTEREST TABLE

<u>Example of use of this table:</u>
Find amount of $500 in 8 years at 6% simple interest.
From table at 8 yrs. and 6% for $1   1.48
Value in 8 yrs. for $500 (500 x 1.48) $740

Number of Years	Interest Rate							
	3%	4%	5%	6%	7%	8%	9%	10%
1	1.03	1.04	1.05	1.06	1.07	1.08	1.09	1.10
2	1.06	1.08	1.10	1.12	1.14	1.16	1.18	1.20
3	1.09	1.12	1.15	1.18	1.21	1.24	1.27	1.30
4	1.12	1.16	1.20	1.24	1.28	1.32	1.36	1.40
5	1.15	1.20	1.25	1.30	1.35	1.40	1.45	1.50
6	1.18	1.24	1.30	1.36	1.42	1.48	1.54	1.60
7	1.21	1.28	1.35	1.42	1.49	1.56	1.63	1.70
8	1.24	1.32	1.40	1.48	1.56	1.64	1.72	1.80
9	1.27	1.36	1.45	1.54	1.63	1.72	1.81	1.90
10	1.30	1.40	1.50	1.60	1.70	1.80	1.90	2.00
11	1.33	1.44	1.55	1.66	1.77	1.88	1.99	2.10
12	1.36	1.48	1.60	1.72	1.84	1.96	2.08	2.20
13	1.39	1.52	1.65	1.78	1.91	2.04	2.17	2.30
14	1.42	1.56	1.70	1.84	1.98	2.12	2.26	2.40
15	1.45	1.60	1.75	1.90	2.05	2.20	2.35	2.50
16	1.48	1.64	1.80	1.96	2.12	2.28	2.44	2.60
17	1.51	1.68	1.85	2.02	2.19	2.36	2.53	2.70
18	1.54	1.72	1.90	2.08	2.26	2.44	2.62	2.80
19	1.57	1.76	1.95	2.14	2.33	2.52	2.71	2.90
20	1.60	1.80	2.00	2.20	2.40	2.60	2.80	3.00
21	1.63	1.84	2.05	2.26	2.47	2.68	2.89	3.10
22	1.66	1.88	2.10	2.32	2.54	2.76	2.98	3.20
23	1.69	1.92	2.15	2.38	2.61	2.84	3.07	3.30
24	1.72	1.96	2.20	2.44	2.68	2.92	3.16	3.40
25	1.75	2.00	2.25	2.50	2.75	3.00	3.25	3.50
26	1.78	2.04	2.30	2.56	2.82	3.08	3.34	3.60
27	1.81	2.08	2.35	2.62	2.89	3.16	3.43	3.70
28	1.84	2.12	2.40	2.68	2.96	3.24	3.52	3.80
29	1.87	2.16	2.45	2.74	3.03	3.32	3.61	3.90
30	1.90	2.20	2.50	2.80	3.10	3.40	3.70	4.00
31	1.93	2.24	2.55	2.86	3.17	3.48	3.79	4.10
32	1.96	2.28	2.60	2.92	3.24	3.56	3.88	4.20
33	1.99	2.32	2.65	2.98	3.31	3.64	3.97	4.30
34	2.02	2.36	2.70	3.04	3.38	3.72	4.06	4.40
35	2.05	2.40	2.75	3.10	3.45	3.80	4.15	4.50
36	2.08	2.44	2.80	3.16	3.52	3.88	4.24	4.60
37	2.11	2.48	2.85	3.22	3.59	3.96	4.33	4.70
38	2.14	2.52	2.90	3.28	3.66	4.04	4.42	4.80
39	2.17	2.56	2.95	3.34	3.73	4.12	4.51	4.90
40	2.20	2.60	3.00	3.40	3.80	4.20	4.60	5.00

COMPOUND INTEREST TABLE

Example of use of this table:

Find how much $1,000 now in bank will grow to in 14 years at 6% interest.

From table 14 years at 6%   2.2609

Value in 14 years of $1,000 $2,260.9

Interest Rate

Number of Years	6%	6 1/2%	7%	7 1/2%	8%	8 1/2%	9%	9 1/2%
1	1.0600	1.0650	1.0700	1.0750	1.0800	1.0850	1.0900	1.0950
2	1.1236	1.1342	1.1449	1.1556	1.1664	1.1772	1.1881	1.1990
3	1.1910	1.2079	1.2250	1.2422	1.2597	1.2772	1.2950	1.3129
4	1.2624	1.2864	1.3107	1.3354	1.3604	1.3858	1.4115	1.4376
5	1.3332	1.3700	1.4025	1.4356	1.4693	1.5036	1.5386	1.5742
6	1.4135	1.4591	1.5007	1.5433	1.5868	1.6314	1.6771	1.7237
7	1.5030	1.5539	1.6057	1.6590	1.7138	1.7701	1.8230	1.8875
8	1.5938	1.6549	1.7181	1.7834	1.8509	1.9206	1.9925	2.0668
9	1.6894	1.7625	1.8384	1.9172	1.9990	2.0838	2.1718	2.2632
10	1.7908	1.8771	1.9671	2.0610	2.1589	2.2609	2.3673	2.4782
11	1.8982	1.9991	2.1048	2.2156	2.3316	2.4531	2.5804	2.7136
12	2.0121	2.1290	2.2521	2.3817	2.5181	2.6616	2.8126	2.9714
13	2.1329	2.2674	2.4098	2.5604	2.7196	2.8879	3.0658	3.2537
14	2.2609	2.4148	2.5785	2.7524	2.9371	3.1334	3.3417	3.5628
15	2.3965	2.5718	2.7590	2.9588	3.1721	3.3997	3.6424	3.9013
16	2.5403	2.7390	2.9521	3.1807	3.4259	3.6887	3.9703	4.2719
17	2.6927	2.9170	3.1588	3.4193	3.7000	4.0022	4.3276	4.6777
18	2.8543	3.1066	3.3799	3.6758	3.9960	4.3424	4.7171	5.1221
19	3.0255	3.3085	3.6165	3.9514	4.3157	4.7115	5.1416	5.6087
20	3.2075	3.5236	3.8696	4.2478	4.6609	5.1120	5.6044	6.1416
21	3.3995	3.7526	4.1405	4.5664	5.0338	5.5465	6.1088	6.7250
22	3.6035	3.9966	4.4304	4.9089	5.4365	6.0180	6.6586	7.3639
23	3.8197	4.2563	4.7405	5.2770	5.8714	6.5295	7.2578	8.0635
24	4.0489	4.5330	5.0723	5.6728	6.3411	7.0845	7.9110	8.8295
25	4.2918	4.8276	5.4274	6.0983	6.8484	7.6867	8.6230	9.6683
26	4.5493	5.1414	5.8073	6.5557	7.3963	8.3401	9.3991	10.5868
27	4.8223	5.4756	6.2138	7.0473	7.9880	9.0490	10.2450	11.5926
28	5.1116	5.8316	6.6488	7.5759	8.6271	9.8182	11.1671	12.6939
29	5.4183	6.2106	7.1142	8.1441	9.3172	10.6527	12.1721	13.8998
30	5.7434	6.6143	7.6122	8.7549	10.5582	11.5582	13.2676	15.2203
31	6.0881	7.0442	8.1451	9.4115	10.8676	12.5407	14.4617	16.6662
32	6.4533	7.5021	8.7152	10.1174	11.7370	13.6066	15.7633	18.2495
33	6.8408	7.9898	9.3253	10.8762	12.6760	14.7632	17.1820	19.9832
34	7.2510	8.5091	9.9781	11.6919	13.6901	16.0181	18.7284	21.8816
35	7.6860	9.0622	10.6765	12.5688	14.7853	17.3796	20.4139	23.9604
36	8.1479	9.6513	11.4239	13.5115	15.9681	18.8569	22.2512	26.2366
37	8.6360	10.2786	12.2236	14.5249	17.2456	20.4597	24.2538	28.7291
38	9.1542	10.9467	13.0792	15.6142	18.6252	22.1988	26.4366	31.4583
39	9.7035	11.6582	13.9948	16.7853	20.1152	24.0857	28.8159	34.4469
40	10.2857	12.4160	14.9744	18.0442	21.7245	26.1330	31.4094	37.7193

Compound Interest Table (*Cont'd*)

Number of Years	10%	11%	12%	13%	14%	15%	16%	17%
1	1.1000	1.1100	1.1200	1.1300	1.1400	1.1500	1.1600	1.1700
2	1.2100	1.2321	1.2544	1.2769	1.2996	1.3225	1.3456	1.3689
3	1.3310	1.3576	1.4049	1.4428	1.4815	1.5208	1.5608	1.6016
4	1.4647	1.5180	1.5735	1.6304	1.6389	1.7490	1.8106	1.8738
5	1.6105	1.6350	1.7623	1.8424	1.9254	2.0113	2.1003	2.1924
6	1.7715	1.8704	1.9738	2.0819	2.1949	2.3130	2.4363	2.5651
7	1.9487	2.0761	2.2106	2.3526	2.5022	2.6600	2.8262	3.0012
8	2.1435	2.3045	2.4759	2.6584	2.8525	3.0590	3.2784	3.5114
9	2.3579	2.5580	2.7730	3.0040	3.2519	3.5178	3.8029	4.1084
10	2.5937	2.8394	3.1058	3.3945	3.7072	4.0455	4.4114	4.8068
11	2.8531	3.1517	3.4785	3.8358	4.2262	4.6523	5.1172	5.6239
12	3.1384	3.4984	3.8959	4.3345	4.8179	5.3502	5.9360	6.5800
13	3.4522	3.8832	4.3634	4.8980	5.4924	6.1527	6.8857	7.6986
14	3.7974	4.3104	4.8871	5.5347	6.2613	7.0757	7.9875	9.0074
15	4.1772	4.7845	5.4735	6.2542	7.1379	8.1370	9.2655	10.5387
16	4.5949	5.3108	6.1303	7.0673	8.1372	9.3576	10.7480	12.3303
17	5.0544	5.8950	6.8660	7.9860	9.2764	10.7612	12.4676	14.4264
18	5.5599	6.5435	7.6899	9.0242	10.5751	12.3754	14.4625	16.8789
19	6.1159	7.2633	8.6127	10.1974	12.0556	14.2317	16.7765	19.7483
20	6.7274	8.0623	9.6462	11.5230	13.7434	16.3665	19.4607	23.1055
21	7.4002	8.9491	10.8038	13.0210	15.6675	18.8215	22.5744	27.0335
22	8.1402	9.9335	12.1003	14.7138	17.8610	21.6447	26.1863	31.6292
23	8.9543	11.0262	13.5523	16.6266	20.3615	24.8914	30.3762	37.0062
24	9.8497	12.2391	15.1786	18.7880	23.2122	28.6251	35.2364	43.2972
25	10.8347	13.5854	17.0000	21.2305	26.4619	32.9189	40.8742	50.6578
26	11.9181	15.0793	19.0400	23.9905	30.1665	37.8567	47.4141	59.2696
27	13.1099	16.7386	21.3248	27.1092	34.3899	43.5353	55.0003	69.3454
28	14.4209	18.5799	23.8838	30.6334	39.2044	50.0656	63.8004	81.1342
29	15.8630	20.6236	26.7499	34.6158	44.6931	57.5754	74.0085	94.9270
30	17.4494	22.8922	29.9599	39.1158	50.9501	66.2117	85.8498	111.0646
31	19.1943	25.4104	33.5551	44.2009	58.0831	76.1435	99.5858	129.9456
32	21.1137	28.2055	37.5817	49.9470	66.2148	87.5650	115.5195	152.0363
33	23.2251	31.3082	42.0915	56.4402	75.4849	100.6998	134.0027	177.8825
34	25.5476	34.7521	47.1425	63.7774	86.0527	115.8048	155.4431	208.1226
35	28.1024	38.5748	52.7996	72.0685	98.1001	133.1755	180.3140	243.5034
36	30.9128	42.8180	59.1355	81.4374	111.8342	153.1518	209.1643	284.8990
37	34.0039	47.5280	66.2318	92.0242	127.4909	176.1246	242.6306	333.3319
38	37.4048	52.7561	74.1796	103.9874	145.3397	202.5433	281.4515	389.9983
39	41.1447	58.5593	83.0812	117.5057	165.6872	232.9248	326.4837	456.2980
40	45.2592	65.0008	93.0509	132.7815	188.8835	267.8635	378.7211	533.8687

Compound Interest Table (*Cont'd*)

Number of Years	18%	19%	20%	21%	22%	23%	24%	25%
1	1.1800	1.1900	1.2000	1.2100	1.2200	1.2300	1.2400	1.2500
2	1.3924	1.4161	1.4400	1.4641	1.4884	1.5129	1.5376	1.5625
3	1.6430	1.6851	1.7280	1.7715	1.8158	1.8608	1.9066	1.9531
4	1.9387	2.0053	2.0736	2.1435	2.2153	2.2888	2.3642	2.4414
5	2.2877	2.3863	2.4883	2.5937	2.7027	2.8153	2.9316	3.0517
6	2.6995	2.8397	2.9859	3.1384	3.2973	3.4628	3.6352	3.8146
7	3.1854	3.3793	3.5831	3.7974	4.0227	4.2592	4.5076	4.7683
8	3.7588	4.0213	4.2998	4.5949	4.9077	5.2389	5.5895	5.9604
9	4.4354	4.7854	5.1597	5.5599	5.9874	6.4438	6.9309	7.4505
10	5.2338	5.6946	6.1917	6.7274	7.3046	7.9259	8.5944	9.3132
11	6.1759	6.7766	7.4300	8.1402	8.9116	9.7489	10.6570	11.6415
12	7.2875	8.0642	8.9161	9.8497	10.8722	11.9911	13.2147	14.5519
13	8.5993	9.5964	10.6993	11.9181	13.2641	14.7491	16.3863	18.1898
14	10.1472	11.4197	12.8391	14.4209	16.1822	18.1414	20.3190	22.7373
15	11.9737	13.5895	15.4070	17.4494	19.7422	22.3139	25.1956	28.4217
16	14.1290	16.1715	18.4884	21.1137	24.0855	27.4461	31.2425	35.5271
17	16.6722	19.2441	22.1861	25.5476	29.3844	33.7587	38.7408	44.4089
18	19.6732	22.9005	26.6233	30.9126	35.8489	41.5233	48.0385	55.5111
19	23.2144	27.2516	31.9479	37.4043	43.7357	51.0736	59.5678	69.3889
20	27.3930	32.4294	38.3375	45.2592	53.3576	62.8206	73.8641	86.7361
21	32.3237	38.5910	46.0051	54.7636	65.0963	77.2693	91.5915	108.4202
22	38.1420	45.9233	55.2061	66.2640	79.4175	95.0413	113.5735	135.5252
23	45.0076	54.6487	66.2473	80.1795	96.8893	116.9008	140.8311	169.4065
24	53.1090	65.0319	79.4968	97.0172	118.2050	143.7880	174.6306	211.7582
25	62.6686	77.3880	95.3962	117.3908	144.2101	176.8592	216.5419	264.6977
26	73.9488	92.0918	114.4754	142.0429	175.9363	217.5368	268.5120	330.8722
27	87.2597	109.5892	137.3705	171.8719	214.6423	267.5703	332.9549	413.5903
28	102.9665	130.4112	164.8446	207.9650	261.8636	329.1115	412.8641	516.9878
29	121.5005	155.1893	197.8135	251.6377	319.4736	404.8072	511.9515	646.2348
30	143.3708	184.6753	237.3763	304.4816	389.7578	497.9128	634.8199	807.7935
31	169.1773	219.7636	284.8515	368.4227	475.5046	612.4328	787.1767	1009.7419
32	199.6292	261.5187	341.8218	445.7915	580.1156	753.2923	976.0991	1262.1774
33	235.5625	311.2072	410.1862	539.4077	707.7410	926.5496	1210.3629	1577.7218
34	277.9638	370.3366	492.2235	652.6834	863.4441	1139.6560	1500.8500	1972.1522
35	327.9972	440.7006	590.6682	789.7469	1053.4018	1401.7769	1861.0540	2465.1903
36	387.0368	524.4337	708.8018	955.5938	1285.1502	1724.1855	2307.7069	3081.4879
37	456.7034	624.0761	850.5622	1156.2685	1567.8833	2120.7482	2861.5566	3851.8598
38	538.9100	742.6505	1020.6746	1399.0849	1912.8176	2608.5203	3548.3302	4814.8248
39	635.9138	883.7542	1224.8096	1692.8927	2333.6375	3208.4800	4399.9295	6018.5310
40	750.3783	1051.6675	1469.7715	2048.4002	2847.0377	3946.4304	5455.9126	7523.1638

PERIODIC DEPOSIT TABLE

Example of use of this table:
How much is $1,000 a year invested at 6% worth in 20 years?
At 6% for 20 years, the figure is   38.993
For $1,000 a year, the amount is $38,993

Interest Rate

Number of Years	6%	7%	8%	9%	10%	11%	12%	13%
1	1.060	1.070	1.080	1.090	1.100	1.110	1.120	1.130
2	2.183	2.215	2.246	2.278	2.310	2.342	2.374	2.407
3	3.375	3.440	3.506	3.573	3.641	3.710	3.779	3.850
4	4.637	4.751	4.867	4.985	5.105	5.228	5.353	5.480
5	5.975	6.153	6.336	6.523	6.716	6.913	7.115	7.323
6	7.394	7.654	7.923	8.200	8.487	8.783	9.089	9.405
7	8.897	9.260	9.637	10.028	10.436	10.859	11.300	11.757
8	10.491	10.978	11.488	12.021	12.579	13.164	13.776	14.416
9	12.181	12.816	13.487	14.193	14.937	15.722	16.549	17.420
10	13.972	14.784	15.645	16.560	17.531	18.561	19.655	20.814
11	15.870	16.888	17.977	19.141	20.384	21.713	23.133	24.650
12	17.882	19.141	20.495	21.953	23.523	25.212	27.029	28.985
13	20.015	21.550	23.215	25.019	26.975	29.095	31.393	33.883
14	22.276	24.129	26.152	28.361	30.772	33.405	36.280	39.417
15	24.673	26.888	29.324	32.003	34.950	38.190	41.753	45.672
16	27.213	29.840	32.750	35.974	39.545	43.501	47.884	52.739
17	29.906	32.999	36.450	40.301	44.599	49.396	54.750	60.725
18	32.760	36.379	40.446	45.018	50.159	55.939	62.440	69.749
19	35.786	39.995	44.762	50.160	56.275	63.203	71.052	79.947
20	38.993	43.865	49.423	55.765	63.002	71.265	80.699	91.470
21	42.392	48.006	54.457	61.873	70.403	80.214	91.503	104.491
22	45.996	52.436	59.893	68.532	78.543	90.148	103.603	119.205
23	49.816	57.177	65.765	75.790	87.497	101.174	117.155	135.831
24	53.865	62.249	72.106	83.701	97.347	113.413	132.334	154.620
25	58.156	67.676	78.954	92.324	108.182	126.999	149.334	175.850
26	62.706	73.484	86.351	101.723	120.100	142.079	168.374	199.841
27	67.528	79.698	94.339	111.968	133.210	158.817	189.699	226.950
28	72.640	86.347	102.966	123.135	147.631	177.397	213.583	257.583
29	78.058	93.461	112.283	135.308	163.494	198.021	240.333	292.199
30	83.802	101.073	122.346	148.575	180.943	220.913	270.293	331.315
31	89.890	109.218	133.214	163.037	200.138	246.324	303.848	375.516
32	96.343	117.933	144.951	178.800	221.252	274.529	341.429	425.463
33	103.184	127.259	157.627	195.982	244.477	305.837	383.521	481.903
34	110.435	137.237	171.317	214.711	270.024	340.590	430.663	545.681
35	118.121	147.913	186.102	235.125	298.127	379.164	483.463	617.749
36	126.268	159.337	202.070	257.376	329.039	421.982	542.599	699.187
37	134.904	171.561	219.316	281.630	363.043	469.511	608.831	791.211
38	144.058	184.640	237.941	308.066	400.448	522.267	683.010	895.198
39	153.762	198.635	258.057	336.882	441.593	580.826	766.091	1012.704
40	164.048	213.610	279.781	368.292	486.852	645.827	859.142	1145.486

COMPOUND DISCOUNT TABLE

This table shows the present or discounted value of $1 due at a given future time. For example, assume property which will revert to a lessor in 10 years will then be worth $1,000. The present value of this reversion, computed at an assumed rate of 4% on the investment, is found by finding the factor on the 10-year line in the 4% column. The factor .6756 is multiplied by 1000 to obtain the answer of $675.60.

Years	4%	4-1/2%	5%	5-1/2%	6%	6-1/2%	7%	7-1/2%	8%	9%	10%	11%
1	0.9615	0.9569	0.9524	0.9479	0.9434	0.9390	0.9346	0.9302	0.9259	0.9174	0.9091	0.9009
2	.9246	.9157	.9070	.8985	.8900	.8817	.8734	.8653	.8573	.8417	.8264	.8116
3	.8890	.8763	.8638	.8516	.8396	.8278	.8163	.8050	.7938	.7722	.7513	.7312
4	.8548	.8386	.8227	.8072	.7921	.7773	.7629	.7488	.7350	.7084	.6830	.6587
5	.8219	.8025	.7835	.7651	.7473	.7299	.7130	.6966	.6806	.6499	.6209	.5935
6	.7903	.7679	.7462	.7252	.7050	.6853	.6663	.6480	.6302	.5963	.5645	.5346
7	.7599	.7343	.7107	.6874	.6651	.6435	.6227	.6027	.5835	.5470	.5132	.4816
8	.7307	.7032	.6768	.6516	.6274	.6042	.5820	.5607	.5403	.5019	.4665	.4339
9	.7026	.6729	.6446	.6176	.5919	.5673	.5439	.5216	.5002	.4604	.4241	.3909
10	.6756	.6439	.6139	.5854	.5584	.5327	.5083	.4852	.4632	.4224	.3855	.3522
11	.6496	.6162	.5847	.5549	.5268	.5002	.4751	.4514	.4289	.3875	.3505	.3173
12	.6246	.5897	.5568	.5260	.4970	.4697	.4440	.4199	.3971	.3555	.3186	.2858
13	.6006	.5643	.5303	.4986	.4688	.4410	.4150	.3906	.3677	.3262	.2897	.2575
14	.5775	.5400	.5051	.4726	.4423	.4141	.3878	.3633	.3405	.2992	.2633	.2320
15	.5553	.5167	.4810	.4479	.4173	.3888	.3624	.3380	.3152	.2745	.2394	.2090
16	.5339	.4945	.4581	.4246	.3936	.3651	.3387	.3144	.2919	.2519	.2176	.1883
17	.5134	.4732	.4363	.4024	.3714	.3428	.3166	.2924	.2703	.2311	.1978	.1696
18	.4936	.4528	.4155	.3815	.3503	.3219	.2959	.2720	.2502	.2120	.1799	.1528
19	.4746	.4333	.3957	.3616	.3305	.3022	.2765	.2531	.2317	.1945	.1635	.1377
20	.4564	.4146	.3769	.3427	.3118	.2838	.2584	.2354	.2145	.1784	.1486	.1240
21	.4388	.3968	.3589	.3249	.2942	.2665	.2415	.2190	.1987	.1637	.1351	.1117
22	.4220	.3797	.3418	.3079	.2775	.2502	.2257	.2037	.1839	.1502	.1228	.1007
23	.4057	.3633	.3256	.2919	.2618	.2349	.2109	.1895	.1703	.1378	.1117	.0907
24	.3901	.3477	.3101	.2766	.2470	.2206	.1971	.1763	.1577	.1264	.1015	.0817
25	.3751	.3327	.2953	.2622	.2330	.2071	.1842	.1640	.1460	.1160	.0923	.0736
26	.3607	.3184	.2812	.2486	.2198	.1945	.1722	.1525	.1352	.1064	.0829	.0663
27	.3468	.3047	.2678	.2356	.2074	.1826	.1609	.1419	.1252	.0976	.0763	.0597
28	.3335	.2916	.2551	.2233	.1956	.1715	.1504	.1320	.1159	.0895	.0693	.0538

Compound Discount Table (*Cont'd*)

Years	4%	4-1/2%	5%	5-1/2%	6%	6-1/2%	7%	7-1/2%	8%	9%	10%	11%
29	0.3207	0.2790	0.2429	0.2117	0.1846	0.1610	0.1406	0.1228	0.1073	0.0822	0.0630	0.0485
30	.3083	.2670	.2314	.2006	.1741	.1512	.1314	.1142	.0994	.0754	.0573	.0437
31	.2965	.2555	.2204	.1902	.1643	.1420	.1228	.1063	.0920	.0691	.0521	.0394
32	.2851	.2445	.2099	.1803	.1550	.1333	.1147	.0988	.0852	.0634	.0474	.0354
33	.2741	.2340	.1999	.1709	.1462	.1251	.1072	.0919	.0789	.0582	.0431	.0319
34	.2636	.2239	.1904	.1620	.1379	.1175	.1002	.0855	.0730	.0534	.0391	.0288
35	.2534	.2142	.1813	.1535	.1301	.1103	.0937	.0796	.0676	.0490	.0356	.0259
36	.2437	.2050	.1727	.1455	.1227	.1036	.0875	.0740	.0626	.0449	.0323	.0234
37	.2343	.1962	.1644	.1379	.1158	.0973	.0818	.0688	.0580	.0412	.0294	.0210
38	.2253	.1878	.1566	.1307	.1092	.0914	.0765	.0640	.0537	.0378	.0267	.0189
39	.2166	.1797	.1491	.1239	.1031	.0858	.0715	.0596	.0497	.0347	.0243	.0171
40	.2083	.1719	.1420	.1175	.0972	.0805	.0668	.0554	.0460	.0318	.0221	.0154
41	.2003	.1645	.1353	.1113	.0917	.0756	.0624	.0515	.0426	.0292	.0201	.0139
42	.1926	.1574	.1288	.1055	.0865	.0710	.0583	.0480	.0395	.0268	.0183	.0125
43	.1852	.1507	.1227	.1000	.0816	.0667	.0545	.0446	.0365	.0246	.0166	.0112
44	.1780	.1442	.1169	.0948	.0770	.0626	.0509	.0415	.0338	.0225	.0151	.0101
45	.1712	.1380	.1113	.0899	.0726	.0588	.0476	.0386	.0313	.0207	.0137	.0091
46	.1646	.1320	.1060	.0852	.0685	.0552	.0445	.0359	.0290	.0190	.0125	.0082
47	.1583	.1263	.1009	.0807	.0647	.0518	.0416	.0334	.0269	.0174	.0113	.0074
48	.1522	.1209	.0961	.0765	.0610	.0487	.0389	.0311	.0249	.0160	.0103	.0067
49	.1463	.1157	.0916	.0725	.0575	.0457	.0363	.0289	.0230	.0147	.0094	.0060
50	.1407	.1107	.0872	.0688	.0543	.0429	.0339	.0269	.0213	.0134	.0085	.0054
51	.1353	.1059	.0831	.0652	.0512	.0403	.0317	.0250	.0197	.0123	.0077	.00488
52	.1301	.1014	.0791	.0618	.0483	.0378	.0297	.0233	.0183	.0113	.0070	.00440
53	.1251	.0970	.0753	.0586	.0456	.0355	.0277	.0216	.0169	.0104	.0064	.00396
54	.1203	.0928	.0717	.0555	.0430	.0333	.0259	.0201	.0157	.0095	.0058	.00357
55	.1157	.0888	.0683	.0526	.0406	.0313	.0242	.0187	.0145	.0087	.0053	.00322
56	.1112	.0850	.0651	.0499	.0383	.0294	.0226	.0174	.0134	.0080	.0048	.00290
57	.1069	.0814	.0620	.0473	.0361	.0276	.0211	.0162	.0124	.0073	.0044	.00261
58	.1028	.0778	.0590	.0448	.0341	.0259	.0198	.0151	.0115	.0067	.0040	.00235
59	.0989	.0745	.0562	.0425	.0321	.0243	.0185	.0140	.0107	.0062	.0036	.00212
60	.0951	.0713	.0535	.0403	.0303	.0229	.0173	.0130	.0099	.0057	.0033	.00191

PRESENT WORTH TABLE — SINGLE FUTURE PAYMENT

Example of use of this table:
Find how much $10,000 payable in 12 years is worth now at an interest rate of 6%.
From table for 12 years 6%
Present value of $10,000 in 12 years (10,000 × .4970)

.4970
$4.970

Interest Rate

Number of Years	6%	7%	8%	9%	10%	11%	12%	13%
1	0.9434	0.9346	0.9259	0.9174	0.9091	0.9009	0.8929	0.8850
2	0.8900	0.8734	0.8573	0.8417	0.8264	0.8116	0.7972	0.7831
3	0.8396	0.8163	0.7938	0.7722	0.7513	0.7312	0.7118	0.6931
4	0.7921	0.7629	0.7350	0.7084	0.6830	0.6587	0.6355	0.6133
5	0.7473	0.7130	0.6806	0.6499	0.6209	0.5935	0.5674	0.5428
6	0.7050	0.6663	0.6302	0.5963	0.5645	0.5346	0.5066	0.4803
7	0.6651	0.6227	0.5835	0.5470	0.5132	0.4816	0.4523	0.4251
8	0.6274	0.5820	0.5403	0.5019	0.4665	0.4339	0.4039	0.3762
9	0.5919	0.5439	0.5002	0.4604	0.4241	0.3909	0.3606	0.3329
10	0.5584	0.5083	0.4632	0.4224	0.3855	0.3522	0.3220	0.2946
11	0.5268	0.4751	0.4289	0.3875	0.3505	0.3173	0.2875	0.2607
12	0.4970	0.4440	0.3971	0.3555	0.3186	0.2858	0.2567	0.2307
13	0.4688	0.4150	0.3677	0.3262	0.2897	0.2575	0.2292	0.2042
14	0.4423	0.3878	0.3405	0.2992	0.2633	0.2320	0.2046	0.1807
15	0.4173	0.3624	0.3152	0.2745	0.2394	0.2090	0.1827	0.1599
16	0.3936	0.3387	0.2919	0.2519	0.2176	0.1883	0.1631	0.1415
17	0.3714	0.3166	0.2703	0.2311	0.1978	0.1696	0.1456	0.1252
18	0.3503	0.2959	0.2502	0.2120	0.1799	0.1528	0.1300	0.1108
19	0.3305	0.2765	0.2317	0.1945	0.1635	0.1377	0.1161	0.0981
20	0.3118	0.2584	0.2145	0.1784	0.1486	0.1240	0.1037	0.0868
21	0.2942	0.2415	0.1987	0.1637	0.1351	0.1117	0.0926	0.0768
22	0.2775	0.2257	0.1839	0.1502	0.1228	0.1007	0.0826	0.0680
23	0.2618	0.2109	0.1703	0.1378	0.1117	0.0907	0.0738	0.0601
24	0.2470	0.1971	0.1577	0.1264	0.1015	0.0817	0.0660	0.0532
25	0.2330	0.1842	0.1460	0.1160	0.0923	0.0736	0.0588	0.0471
26	0.2198	0.1722	0.1352	0.1064	0.0829	0.0663	0.0525	0.0417
27	0.2074	0.1609	0.1252	0.0976	0.0763	0.0597	0.0470	0.0369
28	0.1956	0.1504	0.1159	0.0895	0.0693	0.0538	0.0420	0.0326
29	0.1846	0.1406	0.1073	0.0822	0.0630	0.0485	0.0374	0.0289
30	0.1741	0.1314	0.0994	0.0754	0.0573	0.0437	0.0334	0.0256
31	0.1643	0.1228	0.0920	0.0691	0.0521	0.0394	0.0298	0.0226
32	0.1550	0.1147	0.0852	0.0634	0.0474	0.0354	0.0266	0.0200
33	0.1462	0.1072	0.0789	0.0582	0.0431	0.0319	0.0238	0.0177
34	0.1379	0.1002	0.0730	0.0534	0.0391	0.0288	0.0212	0.0157
35	0.1301	0.0937	0.0676	0.0490	0.0356	0.0259	0.0189	0.0139
36	0.1227	0.0875	0.0626	0.0449	0.0323	0.0234	0.0169	0.0123
37	0.1158	0.0818	0.0580	0.0412	0.0294	0.0210	0.0151	0.0109
38	0.1092	0.0765	0.0536	0.0378	0.0267	0.0189	0.0135	0.0096
39	0.1031	0.0715	0.0497	0.0347	0.0243	0.0171	0.0120	0.0085
40	0.0972	0.0668	0.0460	0.0318	0.0221	0.0154	0.0107	0.0075

PRESENT WORTH TABLE—PERIODIC FUTURE PAYMENT

Example of use of this table:
To find the cost now of $1,000 of income per year for 20 years at 7%.
From table for 20 years at 7%   10.5940
Cost of $1,000 per year ($1,000 × 10.5940) $10,594

Interest Rate

Number of Years	6%	7%	8%	9%	10%	11%	12%	13%
1	0.9434	0.9346	0.9259	0.9174	0.9091	0.9009	0.8929	0.8850
2	1.8334	1.8080	1.7833	1.7591	1.7355	1.7125	1.6901	1.6681
3	2.6730	2.6243	2.5771	2.5313	2.4869	2.4437	2.4018	2.3612
4	3.4651	3.3872	3.3121	3.2397	3.1699	3.1024	3.0373	2.9745
5	4.2124	4.1002	3.9927	3.8897	3.7908	3.6959	3.6048	3.5172
6	4.9173	4.7665	4.6229	4.4859	4.3553	4.2305	4.1114	3.9975
7	5.5824	5.3893	5.2064	5.0330	4.8684	4.7122	4.5638	4.4226
8	6.2098	5.9713	5.7466	5.5348	5.3349	5.1461	4.9676	4.7988
9	6.8017	6.5152	6.2469	5.9952	5.7590	5.5370	5.3282	5.1317
10	7.3601	7.0236	6.7101	6.4177	6.1446	5.8892	5.6502	5.4262
11	7.8869	7.4987	7.1390	6.8052	6.4951	6.2065	5.9377	5.6869
12	8.3838	7.9427	7.5361	7.1607	6.8137	6.4924	6.1944	5.9176
13	8.8527	8.3577	7.9038	7.4869	7.1034	6.7499	6.4235	6.1218
14	9.2950	8.7455	8.2442	7.7862	7.3667	6.9819	6.6282	6.3025
15	9.7122	9.1079	8.5595	8.0607	7.6061	7.1909	6.8109	6.4624
16	10.1059	9.4466	8.8514	8.3126	7.8237	7.3792	6.9740	6.6039
17	10.4773	9.7632	9.1216	8.5436	8.0216	7.5488	7.1196	6.7291
18	10.8276	10.0591	9.3719	8.7556	8.2014	7.7016	7.2497	6.8399
19	11.1581	10.3356	9.6036	8.9501	8.3649	7.8393	7.3658	6.9380
20	11.4699	10.5940	9.8181	9.1285	8.5136	7.9633	7.4694	7.0248
21	11.7641	10.8355	10.0168	9.2922	8.6487	8.0751	7.5620	7.1016
22	12.0416	11.0612	10.2007	9.4424	8.7715	8.1757	7.6446	7.1695
23	12.3034	11.2722	10.3711	9.5802	8.8832	8.2664	7.7184	7.2297
24	12.5504	11.4693	10.5288	9.7066	8.9847	8.3481	7.7843	7.2829
25	12.7834	11.6536	10.6748	9.8226	9.0770	8.4217	7.8431	7.3299
26	13.0032	11.8258	10.8100	9.9290	9.1609	8.4881	7.8957	7.3717
27	13.2105	11.9867	10.9352	10.0266	9.2372	8.5478	7.9426	7.4086
28	13.4062	12.1371	11.0511	10.1161	9.3066	8.6016	7.9844	7.4412
29	13.5907	12.2777	11.1584	10.1983	9.3696	8.6501	8.0218	7.4701
30	13.7648	12.4090	11.2578	10.2737	9.4269	8.6938	8.0552	7.4957
31	13.9291	12.5318	11.3498	10.3428	9.4790	8.7331	8.0850	7.5183
32	14.0840	12.6466	11.4350	10.4062	9.5264	8.7686	8.1116	7.5383
33	14.2302	12.7538	11.5139	10.4644	9.5694	8.8005	8.1354	7.5560
34	14.3681	12.8540	11.5869	10.5178	9.6086	8.8293	8.1566	7.5717
35	14.4982	12.9477	11.6546	10.5668	9.6442	8.8552	8.1755	7.5856
36	14.6210	13.0352	11.7172	10.6118	9.6765	8.8786	8.1924	7.5979
37	14.7368	13.1170	11.7752	10.6530	9.7059	8.8996	8.2075	7.6087
38	14.8460	13.1935	11.8289	10.6908	9.7327	8.9186	8.2210	7.6183
39	14.9491	13.2649	11.8786	10.7255	9.7569	8.9357	8.2330	7.6268
40	15.0463	13.3317	11.9246	10.7574	9.7791	8.9511	8.2438	7.6344

SINKING FUND REQUIREMENTS TABLE

Example of use of this table:
To find the amount of money which must be deposited at the end of each year to grow to $10,000 in 19 years at 8%.

From table for 19 years at 8%   .02413
Amount of each deposit ($10,000 × .02413) $241.30

Interest Rate

Number of Years	6%	7%	8%	9%	10%	11%	12%	13%
1	1.00000	1.00000	1.00000	1.00000	1.00000	1.00000	1.00000	1.00000
2	.48544	.48309	.48077	.47847	.47619	.47393	.47169	.46948
3	.31411	.31105	.30803	.30505	.30211	.29921	.29635	.29352
4	.22859	.22523	.22192	.21867	.21547	.21233	.20923	.20619
5	.17740	.17389	.17046	.16709	.16379	.16057	.15741	.15431
6	.14336	.13979	.13632	.13292	.12961	.12638	.12323	.12015
7	.11913	.11555	.11207	.10869	.10541	.10222	.09912	.09611
8	.10104	.09747	.09401	.09067	.08744	.08432	.08130	.07839
9	.08702	.08349	.08008	.07679	.07364	.07060	.06768	.06487
10	.07587	.07238	.06903	.06582	.06275	.05980	.05698	.05429
11	.06679	.06336	.06008	.05695	.05396	.05112	.04846	.04584
12	.05928	.05590	.05269	.04965	.04676	.04403	.04144	.03899
13	.05296	.04965	.04652	.04357	.04078	.03815	.03568	.03335
14	.04758	.04434	.04129	.03843	.03575	.03323	.03087	.02867
15	.04206	.03979	.03683	.03406	.03147	.02907	.02682	.02474
16	.03895	.03586	.03298	.03030	.02782	.02552	.02339	.02143
17	.03544	.03243	.02963	.02705	.02466	.02247	.02046	.01861
18	.03236	.02941	.02670	.02421	.02193	.01984	.01794	.01620
19	.02962	.02675	.02413	.02173	.01955	.01756	.01576	.01413
20	.02718	.02439	.02185	.01955	.01746	.01558	.01388	.01235
21	.02500	.02229	.01983	.01762	.01562	.01384	.01224	.01081
22	.02305	.02041	.01803	.01590	.01401	.01231	.01081	.00948
23	.02128	.01871	.01642	.01438	.01257	.01097	.00956	.00832
24	.01968	.01719	.01498	.01302	.01129	.00979	.00846	.00731
25	.01823	.01581	.01368	.01181	.01017	.00874	.00749	.00643
26	.01690	.01456	.01251	.01072	.00916	.00781	.00665	.00565
27	.01570	.01343	.01145	.00973	.00826	.00699	.00590	.00498
28	.01459	.01239	.01049	.00885	.00745	.00626	.00524	.00439
29	.01358	.01145	.00962	.00806	.00673	.00561	.00466	.00387
30	.01265	.01059	.00883	.00734	.00608	.00502	.00414	.00341
31	.01179	.00979	.00811	.00667	.00549	.00451	.00369	.00301
32	.01100	.00907	.00745	.00609	.00497	.00404	.00328	.00266
33	.01027	.00841	.00685	.00556	.00449	.00363	.00292	.00234
34	.00960	.00779	.00630	.00508	.00407	.00326	.00260	.00207
35	.00897	.00723	.00580	.00464	.00369	.00293	.00232	.00183
36	.00839	.00676	.00534	.00424	.00334	.00263	.00206	.00162
37	.00786	.00624	.00492	.00387	.00303	.00236	.00184	.00143
38	.00736	.00579	.00454	.00354	.00275	.00213	.00164	.00126
39	.00689	.00539	.00419	.00324	.00249	.00191	.00146	.00112
40	.00646	.00501	.00386	.00296	.00226	.00172	.00130	.00099

Appendix B
Index to Journal Entries

Standard cost variances:

Raw material price variance—62

Direct labor rate and time variance—63

Overhead variance—64

Adjust closing inventory—65

Adjust inventory for variances—66

Stock acquisitions:

Equity method—93 to 98

Consolidation—99 to 101

Stock dividend:

3% taxable dividend (to recipient)—41

Nontaxable dividend (to recipient)—42

Stock options—employee compensation entries

Stock split-up—44

effected in the form of a stock dividend—43

Subchapter S corporation:

First year's net income—27

Retitling prior retained earnings—28

New distribution—29

Summary monthly entries:

Purchase journal—7

Cash disbursements—regular account—8

Cash disbursements—payroll account—9

Sales book—10

Cash receipts book—11

Petty cash box—12

Tax loss carryback—26

Treasury stock:

Purchase of—83

Sale of—84

Voiding own check—33

SAMPLE JOURNAL ENTRIES

OPENING INVESTMENT — Sole Proprietorship:
[1]

Cash	5,000	
Building (fair value)	45,000	
A. Able, Net Worth		50,000

OPENING INVESTMENT — Partnership:
[2]

Cash	30,000	
Inventory	30,000	
B. Baker (50%), Capital		30,000
C. Charles (50%), Capital		30,000

PARTNERSHIP INVESTMENT — with Goodwill:
[3]

Building (fair value)	45,000	
Goodwill	15,000	
A. Able (50%), Capital		60,000

Able contributes building for
½ share of partnership.

PARTNERSHIP INVESTMENT — Skill, no funds:
[4]

A. Able, Capital	3,000	
B. Baker, Capital	3,000	
C. Charles, Capital	6,000	
D. Dog, Capital		12,000

Dog gets 10% of partnership
for the skill he'll contribute.
Ratios will now be:

Able	(25% less 10%)	22.5%
Baker	(same)	22.5%
Charles	(50% less 10%)	45.0%
Dog	(as granted)	10.0%
		100.0%

PARTNERSHIP INCORPORATES:
[5]

Cash	30,000	
Inventory — Raw Material	30,000	
Building (fair value)	45,000	
Capital Stock (par $10; 10,000		
shares issued; 100,000 auth.)		100,000
Additional Paid-in Capital		5,000

Shares issued: A. 2250; B. 2250;
C. 4500; D. 1,000. Note that
partnership goodwill is not carried
over to corporation.

CORPORATE INVESTMENT — with Goodwill:
[6]

Machinery & Equipment (fair value)	9,000	
Goodwill	1,000	
Capital Stock (1,000 shares)		10,000

Issuing 1,000 shares to E. Easy
@ $10 par for machinery contributed.

CORPORATION MONTHLY ENTRIES — The corporation

records all entries into the general ledger *through* summary entries made in the general journal from the books and sources of original entry:

[7] *Summary of Purchase Journal*, where all vendor invoices are entered:

Purchases — Raw Material	10,000	
Shop Supplies	2,000	
Office Supplies	1,000	
Office Equipment	3,000	
Utilities	1,000	
Freight Out	2,000	
Advertising	1,000	
Accounts Payable		20,000

[8] *Summary of Cash Disbursement, Regular Cash A/C:*

Cash — Payroll A/C	13,000	
Petty Cash	200	
Accounts Payable	14,500	
Federal Tax Deposits Made	5,100	
Bank Charges	2	
Cash — Regular A/C		32,602
Cash Discounts Taken		200

[9] *Summary of Cash Disbursements, Payroll A/C:*

Direct Labor — Shop	12,500	
Indirect Labor — Shop	1.500	
Salaries — Sales Dept.	2,000	
Salaries — G & A	4,000	
Cash — Payroll A/C (net pay)		13,000
W/H Tax Pay — Federal		4,400
FICA Tax Withheld		1,200
SUI & Disability W/H		300
State Income Taxes W/H		600
Savings Bonds W/H		500

[10] *Summary of Sales Book:*

Accounts Receivable	35,000	
Sales Returns & Allowances	500	
Sales — Product L		18,000
Sales — Product M		16,600
Sales Taxes Payable		900

[11] *Summary of Cash Receipts Book:*

Cash — Regular A/C	30,500	
Cash Discounts Allowed	500	
Accounts Receivable		30,000
Machinery and Equipment		1,000

[12] *Summary of Petty Cash Box:*

Postage	40	
Entertainment	60	
Travel Expense	30	
Misc. Expense	20	
Petty Cash		150

[13] *General Journal Entries during month:*

Depreciation — M & E	10	
Machinery and Equipment	400	
Gain on Sale of Machinery		410

To correct entry from cash receipts:

Basis	$ 600	
Deprec.	10 (1/60th)	
	590	
S.P.	1000	
Gain	$ 410	

[14]

Depr.— Bldg (1/40x45,000x1/12)	94	
Depr.— M&E (1/5 x 8,400x1/12)	140	
Depr.— OE (1/5 x 3,000x1/12)	50	
Amortization (1/40x1,000x1/12)	2	
Accum Depr.— Bldg		94
Accum Depr.— M&E		140
Accum Depr.— OE		50
Goodwill		2

[15]

Real Estate Taxes	300	
Accrued Taxes — RE		300

1/12th of estimated $3,600 for yr

[16]

Direct Labor (3125)	2,500	
Indirect Labor (375)	300	
Salaries — Selling (500)	400	
Salaries — G & A (1000)	800	
Accrued Salaries (5000)		4,000

To accrue 4/5 of last payroll in month.

[17]

W/H Tax Payable — Federal	3,300	
FICA Tax Withheld	900	
FICA Tax Expense — employer	900	
Federal Tax Deposits Made		5,100
FICA Tax Expense — employer	300	
SUI & DISAB Expense	600	
FUI Expense	100	
Accrued Taxes — Payroll		1,000

To zero deposit account against
withholding accounts and to book
employer FICA expense and estimated
unemployment tax for month.

[18]

Overhead	6,106	
Depr.— Bldg (60% of 94)		56
Depr.— M&E (all)		140
Indirect Labor (all)		1,800
Payroll Tax Exp (70% of 1900)		1,330
Shop supplies (all considered used)		2,000

Utilities (60% of 1000)		600
Taxes — RE (60% of 300)		180

To allocate expenses to overhead.
Taxes based on payroll proportion.
Other allocations based on space occupied.

[19]

Inventory — Raw Materials	(15,000)	
Inventory — Work in Process	none	
Inventory — Finished Goods	15,369	
Cost of Production — Inventory Change		369

To increase or (decrease) inventory
accounts to reflect new month-end
inventory as follows:

Raw Material:

Opening Inventory	$ 30,000
Purchases	10,000
Less used in production	(25,000)
Closing inventory	15,000
To adjust opening	$ (15,000)

Finished Goods:

Materials used (above)	$ 25,000
Direct labor costs	15,000
Overhead costs	6,106
3 units produced	46,106
1 unit unsold (⅓)	$ 15,369

(none at hand at beginning)
No work in process this month.

(The entries through here are all related with respect to the dollars shown. From here on, they are independent with respect to each CAPITAL HEADING, but related within the headed area.)

CUSTOMER'S CHECK BOUNCES
[20]

Accounts Receivable (Mr. A.)	100	
Cash (Disbursements)		100

To record bank charge for
Mr. A's check return — insufficient
funds.

[21]

Cash (Receipts)	100	
Accounts Receivable (Mr. A.)		100

For re-deposit of above, per
customer's instructions.

NOTES RECEIVABLE DISCOUNTED

[22]

Cash	9,900
Interest Expense	250

         Notes receivable Discounted   10,000
         Interest Income   150
     For proceeds from customer note discounted,
     due 90 days @ 6%, discount rate 10%.

[23]

     Notes Receivable Discounted   10,000
         Notes Receivable   10,000
     To offset. Customer note paid,
     per bank notice.

FIRST-YEAR DEPRECIATION

[24]

     Depreciation Expense — M & E   2,000
         Accumulated Depr — M & E   2,000
     For maximum first-year depreciation
     taken on 6/30 purchase of extruder.
     See next entry for regular deprec.

[25]

     Depreciation — M & E   400
         Accumulated Depr — M & E   400
     To take straight-line on above:
         Cost $ 10,000
         Less 1st yr. Depr   (2,000)
           S/L basis   8,000
         Over 10 yrs — per yr $ 800
         Six months this yr (no salvage value). $ 400

TAX LOSS CARRYBACK

[26]

     FIT Refund and Interest Receivable   106,000
         Income Tax (Current Yr. Income Statement)   100,000
         Interest Income   6,000
     To set up receivable for carryback tax
     refund due, plus interest.

SUBCHAPTER S EQUITY ENTRIES

     End of Year 1:

[27]

     Net income for Current Year   30,000
         Undistributed Earnings — Post-Election   30,000
     To close year's net income into
     new Sub-S undistributed earnings
     Equity account.

[28]

     Retained Earnings   55,000
         Retained Earnings — Pre-Election   55,000
     To retitle opening retained earnings
     account and keep it separate from
     earnings after Sub-S election.

[29]

Post-Election Dividends	10,000	
Cash		10,000

For cash distributions made of current earnings. (NOTE: State law may require a *formal* declaration of a dividend for corporations. If this is true, and there is no such declaration, this must be treated as a *loan receivable* from stockholders.)

INSTALLMENT SALES METHOD

[30]

Accounts Receivable	1,000	
Cost of Installment Sale		700
Deferred Gross Profit on Installment Sales		300

For original sale. (GP% is 30%)

[31]

Cash	300	
Accounts Receivable		300

For payment on account.

[32]

Deferred Gross Profit on Installment Sales	90	
Realized Gross Profit		90

To amortize 30% of above collection
to realized income.

VOIDING YOUR OWN CHECK (Issued in a prior period)

[33]

Cash (Ck # 1601)	1,500	
Rent Expense		1,500

To void check #1601 (last month).
Check reported lost. Payment
stopped. Replaced with this month's
check #1752. (See CD book)

INVESTMENT TAX CREDIT — THE DEFERRAL METHOD

[34]

Taxes Payable	7,000	
Deferred Investment Tax Credits		7,000

To set up investment tax credit under
the deferred method. *Note:* The tax
expense for this year on the income
statement does *not* reflect the use
of this credit.

Year 2:

[35]

Deferred Investment Tax Credits	700	
Income Tax Expense		700

To amortize 1/10th, based on 10-year
life of asset to which applicable.

ACCUMULATED PREFERRED STOCK DIVIDENDS
[36]

Dividends (Income Statement)	30,000	
Dividends Payable (Liability)		30,000

To accrue this year's commitment,
6% of $500,000. *Note:* There was
no "only as earned" provision attached
to this issue.

DIVIDEND DECLARATION — COMMON STOCK
[37]

Retained Earnings	100,000	
Common Stock Extra Dividend		
Declared — (show in Equity Section)		100,000

To segregate common stock extra dividend
from accumulated earnings (until paid),
10¢ per share, 1,000,000 shares.

PAYMENT OF ABOVE TWO DIVIDENDS
[38]

Dividends Payable	30,000	
Common Stock Extra Dividend Declared	100,000	
Cash		130,000

For payment of dividends.

APPROPRIATION OF RETAINED EARNINGS
[39]

Retained Earnings	50,000	
Reserve Appropriation for Inventory		
Declines (Equity Section)		50,000

To set aside retained earnings for possible
inventory losses — per Board resolution.

[40]

Retained Earnings — (1/1 opening)	150,000	
Accounts Payable (XYZ Co.)		150,000

To record prior year billing error made
by supplier, XYZ Co., on invoice #_____,
dated 12/10. Error not discovered by
XYZ until after closing of our books and
issuance of statements. Error is considered
material enough to treat as prior period
adjustment. Item was not in inventory
at 12/31.

STOCK DIVIDEND
Usually:
[41]

Retained Earnings (at market)	45,000	
Common Stock (par $10, 3,000 shares)		30,000
Additional Paid-in Capital		15,000

For 3% stock dividend distributed on
100,000 shares — 3,000 shares issued.
Market value $15 at dividend date.

Sometimes:

[42]

Additional Paid-in Capital	30,000	
Common Stock (par $10, 3,000 shares)		30,000
For non-taxable distribution out of		
Paid-in Capital.		

SPLIT-UP EFFECTED IN THE FORM OF A STOCK DIVIDEND

[43]

Retained Earnings (at par)	1,000,000	
Common Stock (par $10, 100,000 shs)		1,000,000
For split in the form of a stock dividend		
(to conform with state law). One share		
issued for each share outstanding.		
100,000 shares at par of $10.		

STOCK SPLIT-UP

[44]

Common Stock (100,000 shares @ $10.)	memo	
Common Stock (200,000 shares @ $5.)		memo
Memo entry only. To record stock split-up		
by showing change in par value and in		
number of shares outstanding. One share		
issued for each outstanding. Par changed		
from $10 to $5.		

STOCK OPTIONS FOR EMPLOYEES AS COMPENSATION

PARTNERSHIP WITHDRAWALS

[45]

S. Stone, Withdrawals	15,000	
T. Times, Withdrawals	5,000	
Cash		20,000
For cash withdrawals.		

PARTNERSHIP PROFIT ENTRY

[46]

Net Income — P & L a/c	100,000	
S. Stone, Capital (50%)		50,000
T. Times, Capital (50%)		50,000

To split profit as follows:	
Per P & L closing account	$ 80,000
Add back above included	
in P & L account	20,000
Profit to distribute	$100,000

[47]

S. Stone, Capital	15,000	
T. Times, Capital	5,000	
S. Stone, Withdrawals		15,000
T. Times, Withdrawals		5,000
To close withdrawal accounts		
to capital accounts.		

IMPUTED INTEREST (ON NOTES RECEIVABLE)

[48]

Notes Receivable (Supplier A — 6 yrs)	1,000,000	
Cash		1,000,000

For loan made to supplier. Received
non-interest bearing note, due 6 yrs.

[49]

Cost of Merchandise (from supplier A)	370,000	
Unamortized Discount on Notes Receiv.		370,000

To charge imputed interest of 8% on
above note, due in 6 years, to cost
of merchandise bought from A.

Year 2:

[50]

Unamortized Discount on Notes Receiv.	50,000	
Interest Income		50,000

To amortize this year's applicable
imputed interest on note.

BOND DISCOUNT, PREMIUM AND ISSUE COSTS

[51]

Cash	2,025,000	
Unamortized Bond Issue Costs	15,000	
Bonds Payable (8%, 10 yrs)		2,000,000
Unamortized Premium on Bonds		40,000

To set up face value of bonds, issue
costs and net cash proceeds received.

Year 2:

[52]

Unamortized Premium on Bonds	4,000*	
Unamortized Bond Issue Cost		1,500*
Interest Expense (difference)		2,500

To set up approximate amortization.
(*Should actually be based on present
values.)

[53]

Interest Expense	160,000	
Cash		160,000

To record actual payment of bond
interest. 8% of $2,000,000.

FEDERAL INCOME TAX — INTERIMS —
AND EXTRAORDINARY ITEM

[54]

Income Tax (on continuing operations)	350,000	
Extraordinary Loss (tax effect)		50,000
Taxes Payable		300,000

To set up FIT at end of First Quarter
based on full year's 50% rate and
to segregate tax applicable to
extraordinary item.

Statement should show:

Net from continuing operations	$700,000
Less FIT	(350,000)
	350,000

Extraordinary loss	
(net of $50,000 tax effect)	50,000
Net Income	$300,000

CAPITALIZING A LEASE (LESSEE)

At contracting:

[55]

Capitalized Leases	1,920,000	
Long-Term Lease Liability		3,600,000
Unamortized Discount on Lease		(1,680,000)

To capitalize lease of $25,000 per
month for 12 years @ 12% imputed
interest rate. Estimated life of asset
is 15 years. Present value used, since
fair value is higher at $2,000,000.

(Note: The two credit items shown are
netted and shown as *one net liability*
on the balance sheet. The liability
(at present value) should always equal
the asset value, also at present value.
Future lease payments are broken out,
effectively, into principal and interest.)

Month-end 1:

[56]

Long-Term Lease Liability	25,000	
Cash		25,000

First payment on lease.

[57]

Interest Expense	18,950	
Unamortized Discount on Lease		18,950

For one month's interest.
1% of $3,600,000 less $1,680,000,
less initial payment on signing of
contract of $25,000 *(entry not shown)* or
$1,895,000.

[58]

Depreciation Expense	10,667	
Accumulated Depr of Capitalized Lease		10,667

One month:
$1,920,000 x 1/5 x 1/12

CASH SURRENDER VALUE — OFFICER LIFE INSURANCE

[59]

Officer Life Insurance — expense	1,500	
Cash		1,500

For payment of premium. *Note:* Expense

is not deductible for tax purpose and
is a *permanent* difference.

[60]

Cash Surrender Value-Officer Life Ins.	1,045	
Officer Life Ins. expense		1,045
To reflect increase in C.S.V. for year		

[61]

Cash	5,000	
Loans Against Officer Life Insurance		5,000
(Displayed against the asset "C.S.V.")		
To record loan against life policy. No intent		
to repay within the next year.		

STANDARD COST VARIANCES

[62]

Purchases — Raw Mat (at stand)	200	
Accounts Payable — actual		188
Variance — material price		12

[63]

Direct Labor — at standard	50	
Variance — Direct Labor rate	10	
Payroll — actual direct labor		58
Variance — Labor Time		2

[64]

Overhead — at Standard	75	
Variance — overhead	15	
Overhead itemized actual accounts		90

Adjusting Inventories:

[65]

Inventory — Raw Materials at standard	100	
Finished Goods — at standard	75	
Cost of Production — at standard		175
To adjust inventory accounts to reflect		
end-of-month on-hand figures at standards.		

[66]

Variance — material price	xx	
Variance — labor time	xx	
Variance — direct labor rate		xx
Variance — overhead		xx
Contra Inventory Asset a/c (variances		
to offset standard and reflect cost)		xx

To pull out of variance accounts that
portion which is applicable to inventory,
in order to keep an isolated contra account,
which in offset to the "standard" asset
account, reflects approximate cost.
The portion is based on an overall ratio
of variances to production and inventory
figures (at standard). (If normal, apply
to cost of sales for interims.)

ADJUSTING INVENTORY FOR SAMPLING RESULTS

[67]

Cost of Sales	50,000	

Inventory		50,000

To reduce inventory by $50,000 based
on sampling results:

Inventory per computer run	$ 1,000,000	
Estimated calculated		
inventory per sample	950,000	
Reduction this year	$ 50,000	

Year 2:

[68]

Inventory	10,000	
Cost of Sales		10,000

To adjust inventory to actual
based on actual physical count
of entire inventory. Last year-end
sample error proved to be 4%,
not 5%.

ADJUSTING CLOSING INVENTORY FROM CLIENT'S STANDARD COST TO
AUDITOR'S DETERMINED (AND CLIENT AGREED) ACTUAL COST, AND TO
REFLECT PHYSICAL INVENTORY VS. BOOK INVENTORY DIFFERENCES

[69]

Inventory — Finished Goods (Standard)	25,000	
Cost of Sales		25,000

To adjust general ledger inventory
(at standard) to actual physical
inventory count, priced out at
standard. Actual is $25,000 more.

[70]

Cost of Sales	80,000	
Inventory — Finished Goods		
(Asset Contra Cost account)		80,000

To set up a contra account reducing
asset account, which is at standard
costs, effectively to audited actual
cost or market, whichever lower.

Year 2: (End of Year)

[71]

Inventory — Finished Goods (Asset		
Contra Cost account)	50,000	
Cost of Sales		50,000

To reduce the contra account to
the new year-end difference between
the "standard" asset account and the
actual cost determined for this new
year-end inventory.

PARTNERSHIP DISSOLUTION:

Balance Sheet

Cash	$ 20,000	
Assets other	35,000	

Liabilities   (25,000)
A Capital (50%)   (20,000)
B Capital (30%)   (14,000)
C Capital (20%)   4,000
                                      -0-

[72]

Cash   15,000
   Assets other   15,000
For sale of some assets at book value.

[73]

A Capital (⅝)   2,500
B Capital (⅜)   1,500
   C Capital   4,000
C cannot put in his overdraw —
to apportion his deficit.

[74]

Liabilities   25,000
   Cash   25,000
To pay liabilities

[75]

Cash   10,000
Loss on Sale of Assets other   10,000
   Assets other   20,000
A Capital (⅝)   6,250
B Capital (⅜)   3,750
   Loss on Sale of Assets other   10,000
Selling remaining assets and apportioning loss

[76]

A Capital (remaining balance)   11,250
B Capital (remaining balance)   8,750
   Cash   20,000
To distribute remaining cash
and zero capital accounts.

NOTE THE SHARING OF C'S DEFICIT
AND OF THE LOSS ON ASSET SALE
BEFORE DISTRIBUTING REMAINING
CASH.

MARKETABLE SECURITIES

Shown as Current Assets:
[77]

Unrealized Loss — to P & L   1,500
   Valuation Allowance — Current   1,500
To write down 100 U.S. Steel:
   Cost 1/1 $10,000
   Market 12/31   8,500
Unrealized Loss $ 1,500
Year 2:
[78]

Cash   4,500
Realized Loss — P & L   500

Marketable Securities — Current		5,000
Sold 50 @ 90	$ 4,500	
Cost 50 @ 90	5,000	
Realized Loss	$ 500	

[79]

Valuation Allowance — Current	1,250	
Valuation Adjustment — Current (P&L Gain)		1,250*

To adjust valuation allowance a/c
(current) for remaining securities
left in portfolio:

50 US Steel — cost 100	$ 5,000
Market, this year end — 95	4,750
Bal. should be	250 Cr.
Balance in valuation a/c	1,500 Cr.
Debit valuation a/c	$ 1,250 Dr.

*Note: Unrealized *gains* are called
"valuation adjustments." Unrealized
losses are called "unrealized losses."

Shown as Noncurrent Asset:

[80]

Unrealized Noncurrent Loss (Equity section)	1,000	
Valuation Allowance — Noncurrent		1,000

To write down 100 shares GM
from cost of 60 to market
value at 12/31 of 50.

Year 2:

[81]

Cash	2,900	
Realized Loss — P & L	100	
Marketable Securities — Noncurrent		3,000
Sold 50 GM @ 58	$ 2,900	
Cost 50 GM @ 60	3,000	
Realized loss	$ 100	

[82]

Valuation Allowance — Noncurrent	1,000	
Unrealized Noncurrent Loss (Equity Section)		1,000

To adjust valuation allowance a/c
(Noncurrent) as follows:

Cost 50 GM @ 60	$ 3,000
Market now @ 65	N/A
(Higher than cost)	
Valuation a/c should be	-0-
(Because market is higher than cost)	
Balance in valuation a/c	1,000 Cr.
Debit to correct	$ 1,000 Dr.

TREASURY STOCK

Purchase of:

[83]

Treasury Stock — at Cost	125,000	
Cash		125,000

Purchase of 1,000 shares @ 125
market. Par value $50.
No intent to cancel the stock.

Sale of:

[84]

Cash	140,000	
Treasury Stock — at Cost		125,000
Additional Paid — in Capital		15,000

For sale of treasury stock @ 140.

APPRAISAL WRITE-UPS

[85]

Building	350,000	
Appraisal Capital (Equity Section)		350,000

To raise building from cost of $400,000 to
appraised value of $750,000 per require-
ment of the lending institution.

Year 2:

[86]

Depreciation — Building	21,667	
Accumulated Depreciation — Building		21,667

To depreciate based on appraised value:
(400,000 for 40 years; 350,000 for 30 yrs)
Building was 10 years old at appraisal.

FOREIGN CURRENCY EXCHANGE

[87]

Unrealized Loss (balance sheet)	10,000	
Accts Payable — Foreign		10,000

To adjust liabilities payable in
Swiss Francs to US Dollars at 12/31:

Exchange rate at 12/31 .40	$40,000
Booked at (100,000 frs) .30	30,000
More dollars owed	$10,000

[88]

Deferred Taxes	5,000*	
Unrealized Loss		5,000*

To show deferred tax effect (50% rate
times $10,000 above)
*Less Foreign or Domestic Dividend
Credits, if Applicable

Year 2:

[89]

Accounts Payable — Foreign	20,000	
Cash		19,000
Realized gain (Books, not Tax)		1,000

For payment of 50,000 Swiss Francs at exchange rate of .38

[90]

Accounts Payable — Foreign	500	
Balance Sheet		500

To restate liability at year-end:

50,000 Frs @ .39	$ 19,500	
Booked to last yr.	20,000	
(Gain)	$ (500)	

[91]

Taxes Payable	2,000	
Income Tax Expense	500	
Deferred Taxes		2,500

To transfer to actual taxes payable (from deferred) that portion applying to the payment of $19,000. Original debt in dollars was $15,000. 50% tax rate on $4,000 or $2,000, plus $500 — to offset 2,500 booked to last 12/31.

[92]

Income Tax Expenses	250	
Deferred Taxes		250

To adjust deferred taxes to equal ½ of 4,500 (19,500 liability now, less original liability of 15,000) for $2,250 tax deferral.

THE EQUITY METHOD
[93]

Investment — Oleo Co.	275,000	
Cash		275,000

Purchase of 25% of Oleo's stock, at cost (25,000 shares @ $11).

[94]

Investment — Oleo Co.	40,000	
Deferred Good Will in Oleo		40,000

To set up additional underlying equity in Oleo Co. at date of acquisition — to write-off over 40 years.

[95]

Cash	5,000	
Investment — Oleo Co.		5,000

For receipt of 20¢ per share cash dividend from Oleo.

[96]

Investment — Oleo Co.	27,500	
Income from Equity Share of Undistributed Earnings of Oleo continuing operations		25,000
Income from Equity Share of Undistributed Extraordinary Item of Oleo		2,500

To pick up 25% of the following reported Oleo annual figures:

Net income after taxes, but before Extraordinary item	$100,000
Extraordinary Income (net)	10,000
Total net income reported	$110,000

[97]

Income Tax Expense — Regular	12,500*	
Income Tax Expense — Extra Item	1,250*	

Deferred Taxes	13,750*

To set up 50% of above income as accrued
taxes. Expectation is that Oleo will
continue paying dividends.

*Dividend Tax Credit, if any, should reduce
these Amounts

[98]

Deferred Taxes	2,500*	
Income Taxes Payable		2,500*

To set up actual liability for tax on cash
dividends received.

*Dividend Tax Credit, if any, should reduce
these Amounts

CONSOLIDATION

Trial Balances
Now-at
12/31-End of Year

	A Co.	B Co.	Fair Value Excess at Acquisition
Cash	10,000	6,000	
A/R	20,000	10,000	
Inventory	30,000	5,000	
Equip	50,000	30,000	5,000
Investment Cost	40,000		
Liabilities	(30,000)	(5,000)	(1,000)
Common Stock	(20,000)	(10,000)*	
Retained Earnings	(50,000)	(20,000)*	
Sales	(80,000)	(40,000)	
Costs of Sale	20,000	14,000	
Expenses	10,000	10,000	
	-0-	-0-	
	(Parent)	(Sub)	

*Unchanged from opening balances.

*At year-end there were $5,000 intercom-
pany receivables/payables. The parent had
sold $5,000 worth of product to the sub-
sidiary. The inventory of the subsidiary was
$1,000 over the parent's cost.*

Consolidating
Entries:

[99]

Excess Paid over Book Value	10,000	
Investment Cost		10,000

To reduce investment cost to that of the
subsidiary's equity at time of purchase (unchanged at 12/31).

[100]

Equipment	5,000	
Liabilities		1,000
· Excess Paid over Book Value		4,000

To reflect fair value corrections at time of
consolidation for the combination of current year-end trial balances.

[101]

B Co. Equity	30,000	
Investment Cost		30,000
Sales	5,000	
Costs of Sale		5,000
Costs of Sale	1,000	
Inventory		1,000
Liabilities	5,000	
Accounts Receivable		5,000
Excess paid over book value (expense)	150	
Goodwill		150

To eliminate intercompany dealings, debt,
investment, and to amortize goodwill.

Consolidated figures will then be:

Cash	16,000	
A/R	25,000	
Inventories	34,000	
Equipment	85,000	
Investment cost	—	
Goodwill	5,850	
Liabilities	(31,000)	
Common Stock	(20,000)	(Opening)
Ret. Earnings	(50,000)	(Opening)
Sales	(115,000)	
Cost of sales	30,000	
Expenses	20,150	
	-0-	

The year's consolidated net income (before
provision for income taxes) is $64,850.

PURCHASE METHOD OF BUSINESS COMBINATION

[102]

Accounts Receivable (present value)	50,000	
Inventory (current cost or market, lowest)	40,000	
Building (fair value)	110,000	
Equipment (fair value)	30,000	
Investments, non-current securities-market	5,000	
Goodwill	16,200	
Accounts Payable — (present value)		25,000
Long-term Debt — (face value)		30,000
Unamortized discount on long-term debt		

(to reflect present value)		(3,800)
Common Stock (Par $10; 10,000 shares)		100,000
Additional Paid-in Capital		100,000

To reflect, by the purchase method, the purchase of Diablo Company assets and liabilities for 10,000 shares of common stock; total purchase price of contract $200,000 based on market price of stock at date of consummation of $20 per share (1/1).

[103]

Amortization of Goodwill (1/40)	405	
Goodwill		405
Unamortized discount on long-term debt	760	
Discount Income (approx 1/5th)		760*

To amortize pertinent Diablo items, first yearend. Goodwill on straight-line basis — 40 years. *Should be calculated present value computation.

POOLING METHOD OF BUSINESS COMBINATION
[104]

Inventory	43,000	
Cash	5,000	
Accounts Receivable	60,000	
Reserve for Doubtful Accounts		7,000
Building	75,000	
Accumulated Depreciation — Building		15,000
Equipment	100,000	
Accumulated Depreciation — Building		60,000
Investments — non-current securities	4,000	
Accounts Payable		25,500
Long-Term Debt		30,000
Common Stock (10,000 shs @ par $10)		100,000
Additional Paid-in Capital		49,500

To reflect the pooling of Diablo items, per *their book value* on date of consummation.

FUND ACCOUNTING

Initial transactions:
[105]

Cash	100,000	
Dues Income		100,000

For initial membership dues received.

[106]

Building	50,000	
Mortgage Payable		40,000
Cash		10,000

Purchase of building for cash and mortgage.

[107]

Interest Expense	2,400	
Mortgage Payable	2,000	

| | Cash | | 4,400 |
| | For first payment on mortgage. | | |

[108]

Net income (100,000 less 2,400)	97,600	
Current Fund Balance		97,600
To close year's income		

[109]

Mortgage Payable	38,000	
Current Fund Balance	12,000	
Building		50,000
To transfer building and mortgage to plant fund.		

Plant Fund Entry:

[110]

Building	50,000	
Mortgage Payable		38,000
Plant Fund Balance		12,000
To set up building in plant fund.		

Note that interest expense is to be borne by the current fund every year as a current operating expense used in the calculation of required dues from members. Also, the principal sum-payments against mortgage are to come out of current fund assets, with no interfund debt to be set up, until such time as a special drive is held for plant fund donations for improvements and expansion.

MUNICIPAL ACCOUNTING — CURRENT OPERATING FUND

To book the budget:

[111]

Estimated Revenues	600,000	
Appropriations		590,000
Fund Balance		10,000

Actual year's transactions:

[112]

Encumbrances	575,000	
Reserve for Encumbrances		575,000
To enter contracts and purchase orders issued.		

[113]

Expenditures — itemized (not here)	515,000	
Vouchers Payable		515,000
Reserve for Encumbrances	503,000	
Encumbrances		503,000
To enter actual invoices for deliveries received and service contracts performed and to reverse applicable encumbrances.		

[114]

Taxes Receivable — Current	570,000	
Revenues		541,500
Estimated Current Uncollectible Taxes		28,500

To enter actual tax levy and to estimate uncollectibles at 5%.

[115]

Cash	55,000	
Revenues		55,000

For cash received from licenses, fees,
fines and other sources.

[116]

Cash	549,500	
Estimated Current Uncollectible Taxes	8,000	
Taxes Receivable		549,500
Revenues		8,000

For actual taxes collected for this year.

To close out budget accounts:

[117]

Revenues	604,500	
Appropriations	590,000	
Estimated Revenue		600,000
Expenditures		515,000
Encumbrances		72,000
Fund Balance		7,500

To zero budget accounts and adjust
fund balance.

DISCS — DEEMED DISTRIBUTIONS (Parent's Books)

1975 — under old law

[118]

DISC Dividends Receivable (previously taxed)	110,000	
Deemed Distribution from DISC (income)		110,000

To pick up ½ of DISC's net of $220,000.

1976 — under the new law.

[119]

DISC Dividends Receivable (previously taxed)	189,375	
Deemed Distribution from DISC (income)		189,375

As follows:
Facts:

Gross export receipts average for 1972-1975	$1,100,000
Gross export receipts - 1976	$1,300,000
Net DISC income - 1976 only	$ 250,000

Since the 1976 net income is over
$150,000, the graduated relief in the 1976
law does not apply, and the calculation is:

67% of 1,100,000 = 670,000

670,000 ÷ 1,300,000 = 51.5%

51.5% × 250,000 = $ 128,750

250,000 − 128,750 = 121,250

121,250 × 50% =   <u>   60,625</u>

        Total Deemed Distribution   <u>$ 189,375</u>

[120]

Capitalization of Interest Costs
Qualifying Asset   10,000
    Accrued Interest   10,000

[121]

Employee Compensation   50,000
    Accrued Vacation   50,000

Appendix C
Tax Terminology

Accountant's Report. When used regarding financial statements, a document in which an independent public or certified public accountant indicates the scope of the audit (or examination) which has been made and sets forth an opinion regarding the financial statements taken as a whole, or an assertion to the effect that an overall opinion cannot be expressed. When an overall opinion cannot be expressed, the reasons must be stated.

Accounting Method. A set of rules used to determine when and how income and expenses are reported.

Adjusted Issue Price. The issue price increased by any amount of discount deducted before repurchase, or, in the case of convertible obligations, decreased by any amount of premium included in gross income before repurchase.

Adjusted Sales Price. The amount realized, reduced by the aggregate for work performed on the old residence to assist in its sale. The reduction only applies to work performed during the 90-day period ending on the day on which the contract to sell the old residence is entered into.

Adverse Party. Any person having a substantial beneficial interest in the trust which would be adversely affected by the exercise or nonexercise of the authority which he/she possesses regarding the trust.

Affiliate. An affiliate of, or a person affiliated with, a specific person is one who directly or indirectly, through one or more intermediaries, controls, or is controlled by, or is under common control with, the person specified. (See **Person** below)

Affiliated Group. One or more chains of includable corporations connected through stock ownership with a common parent corporation which is

644

an includable corporation. (See **Includable Corporation** below). The ownership of stock of any corporation means the common parent possesses at least
80 percent of the total voting power of the stock of such corporation and has
a value equal to at least 80 percent of the total value of the stock of that corporation.

Alien. A foreigner is an alien who has filed his/her declaration of intention to become a citizen, but who has not yet been admitted to citizenship by
a final order of a naturalization court.

American Aircraft. An aircraft registered under the laws of the United
States.

American Vessel. Any vessel documented or numbered under the laws
of the United States, and includes any vessel which is neither documented nor
numbered under the laws of the Untied States nor documented under the laws
of any foreign country, if its crew is employed solely by one or more citizens
or residents of the United States or corporations organized under the laws of
the United States or of any State.

Amount. When used regarding securities, the principal amount if relating to evidences of indebtedness the number of shares if relating to shares,
and the number of units if relating to any other kind of security.

Amount Loaned. The amount received by the borrower.

Annual Accounting Period. The annual period, calendar year or fiscal
year, on the basis of which the taxpayer regularly computes his/her income in
keeping the books.

Annual Compensation. Includes an employee's average regular annual
compensation, or such average compensation over the last five years, or such
employee's last annual compensation if reasonably similar to his or her average regular annual compensation for the five preceding years.

Annuity Contract. A contract which may be payable in installments during the life of the annuitant only.

Applicable Installment Obligation. Any obligation which arises from
the disposition of personal property under the installment method by a person who regularly sells or otherwise disposes of personal property of the same
type on the installment plan. The disposition of real property under the
installment method which is held by the taxpayer for sale to customers in the
ordinary course of the taxpayer's trade or business, or the disposition of real
property under the installment method which is property used in the taxpayer's trade or business, or property held for the production of rental income,
but only if the sale price of such property exceeds $150,000.

Associate. Indicates a relationship with any person, and means 1) any
corporation or organization of which such person is an officer or partner or is
directly or indirectly the beneficial owner of 10 percent or more of any class
of equity securities, 2) any trust or other estate in which such person has a substantial beneficial interest or for which such person serves as trustee or in a

similar fiduciary capacity, and 3) any relative or spouse of such person, or any relative of such spouse, who has the same home as such person or who is a director or officer of the registrant or any of its parents or subsidiaries.

Audit (Examination). When used regarding financial statements, an examination of the statements by an accountant in accordance with generally accepted auditing standards for the purpose of expressing an opinion.

Balance. With respect to a reserve account or a guaranteed employment account, the amount standing to the credit of the account as of the computation date.

Bank. A bank or trust company or domestic building and loan association incorporated and doing business under the laws of the United States, including laws relating to the District of Columbia, or of any State, a substantial part of the business of which consists of receiving deposits and making loans and discounts, or of exercising fiduciary powers similar to those permitted to national banks under authority of the Comptroller of the Currency, and which is subject by law to supervision and examination by State or Federal authority having supervision over banking institutions.

Bank Holding Company. A person who is engaged, either directly or indirectly, primarily in the business of owning securities of one or more banks for the purpose, and with the effect, of exercising control. (See **Person** below)

Basis of Obligation. The basis of an installment obligation is the excess of the face value of the obligation over an amount equal to the income which would be returnable were the obligation satisfied in full.

Below-Market Loan. Any demand loan for which the interest is payable on the loan at a rate less than the applicable Federal rate, or in the case of a term loan (see **Term Loan** below) the amount loaned exceeds the present value of all payments due under the loan.

Bond. Any bond, debenture, note, or certificate or other evidence of indebtedness, but does not include any obligation which constitutes stock in trade of the taxpayer or any such obligation of a kind which would properly be included in the inventory of the taxpayer if on hand at the close of the taxable year, or any obligation held by the taxpayer primarily for sale to customers in the ordinary course of trade or business.

C Corporation. With respect to any taxable year, a corporation which is not an S corporation for such year.

Calendar Year. A period of 12 months ending on December 31. A taxpayer who has not established a fiscal year must make his/her tax return on the basis of a calendar year.

Capital Asset. Property held by a taxpayer, whether or not connected with a trade or business. The term does not include stock in trade of the taxpayer or other property of a kind which would properly be included in the inventory of the taxpayer if on hand at the close of the taxable year, or property held for sale to customers in the ordinary course of a trade or business.

Capital Expenditure. Any cost of a type that is properly chargeable to a capital account under general Federal income tax principles. Whether an expenditure is a capital expenditure is determined at the time the expenditure is paid with respect to the property. Future changes in law do not affect whether an expenditure is a capital expenditure. Capital expenditures do not include expenditures for items of current operating expense that are not properly chargeable to a capital account—so called *working capital* items.

Capital Gain. The excess of the gains from sales or exchanges of capital assets over the losses from sales or exchanges.

Carrier. An express carrier, sleeping car carrier, or rail carrier providing transportation.

Certified. When used regarding financial statements, examined and reported upon with an opinion expressed by an independent public or certified public accountant.

Charitable Contribution. A contribution or gift to or for the use of a corporation, trust, community chest, fund, or foundation operated exclusively for religious, charitable, scientific, literary, or educational purposes, or to foster national or international amateur sports competition if no part of its activities involves the provision of athletic facilities or equipment. A contribution or gift is deductible only if it is used within the Untied States or any of its possessions.

Charter. Articles of incorporation, declarations of trust, articles of association or partnership, or any similar instrument affecting, either with or without filing with any governmental agency, the organization or creation of an incorporated or unincorporated person (see **Person** below).

Child. Son, stepson, daughter, stepdaughter, adopted son, adopted daughter, or for taxable years after December 31, 1958, a child who is a member of an individual's household if the child was placed with the individual by an authorized placement agency for legal adoption pursuant to a formal application filed by the individual with the agency.

Child Care Facility. Any tangible property which qualifies as a child care center primarily for children of employees of the employer, except that the term does not include any property not of a character subject to depreciation, or located outside the United States.

Citizen. Every person born or naturalized in the United States and subject to its jurisdiction.

Collapsible Corporation. A corporation formed or availed of principally by the manufacture, construction, or production of property, for the purchase of property which is in the hands of the corporation, or for the holding of stock in a corporation so formed or availed of with a view to the sale or exchange of stock by its shareholders. The term includes distribution to its shareholders, before the realization by the corporation manufacturing, constructing, producing, or purchasing the property of $2/3$ of the taxable income to be derived from such property, and by the realization by such shareholders of gain attributable to such property.

Common Equity. Any class of common stock or an equivalent interest including, but not limited to a unit of beneficial interest in a trust or a limited partnership interest.

Common Trust Fund. A fund maintained by a bank exclusively for the collective investment and reinvestment of moneys contributed thereto by the bank in its capacity as a trustee, executor, administrator, or guardian, or as a custodian of accounts which the Secretary determines are established pursuant to a State law, and which bank has established that it has duties and responsibilities similar to the duties and responsibilities of a trustee or guardian.

Company. Corporations, associations, and joint-stock companies.

Complete Liquidation. (See **Distribution** below)

Computation Date. The date, occurring at least once each calendar year and within 27 weeks prior to the effective date of new rates of contributions, as of which such dates are computed.

Constructive Sale Price. An article sold at retail, sold on consignment, or sold otherwise than through an arm's length transaction at less than the fair market price.

Contributions. Payments required by a State law to be made into an unemployment fund by any person on account of having individuals in his/her employ, to the extent that such payments are made without being deducted or deductible from the remuneration of the employed individuals.

Control. The ownership of stock possessing at least 80% of the total combined voting power of all classes of stock entitled to vote and at least 80% of the total number of shares of all other classes of stock of the corporation.

Controlled Foreign Corporation. Any foreign corporation if more than 50% of the total combined voting power of all classes of stock of such corporation entitled to vote, or the total value of the stock of such corporation, is owned, directly or indirectly, by and for a foreign corporation, foreign partnership, foreign trust, or foreign estate shall be considered as being owned proportionately by its shareholders, partners, or beneficiaries.

Controlled Group of Corporations. One or more chains of corporations connected through stock ownership with a common parent corporation if stock possessing at least 80% of the total combined voting power of all classes of stock entitled to vote or at least 80% of the total value of shares of all classes of stock of each of the corporations, and the common parent corporation is owned by one or more of the other corporations.

Convertible Obligation. An obligation which is convertible into the stock of the issuing corporation, or a corporation which, at the time the obligation is issued or repurchased, is in control of (see **Control** above) or controlled by the issuing corporation.

Cooperative Bank. An institution without capital stock organized and operated for mutual purposes and without profit, which is subject by law to supervision and examination by State or Federal authority having supervision over such institutions.

Cooperative Housing Corporation. A corporation having one and only one class of stock outstanding, each of the stockholders of which is entitled, solely by reason of ownership of stock in the corporation, to occupy for dwelling purposes a house, or an apartment in a building, owned or leased by the cooperative housing corporation. No stockholder of the housing corporation is entitled to receive any distribution that is not out of earnings and profits of the corporation except on a complete or partial liquidation of the corporation.

Corporate Acquisition Indebtedness. Any obligation evidenced by a bond, debenture, note, or certificate or other evidence of indebtedness issued by a corporation to provide consideration for the acquisition of stock in another corporation; or the acquisition of the assets of another corporation in accordance with a plan under which at least two-thirds in value of all the assets (excluding money) is used in trades and businesses carried on by the corporation.

Corporation. Includes associations, joint-stock companies, and insurance companies.

Currency Swap Contract. A contract involving different currencies between two or more parties to exchange periodic interim payments on or prior to maturity of the contract. The swap *principal amount* is an amount of two different currencies which, under the terms of the currency swap contract, is used to determine the periodic interim payments in each currency and which is exchanged upon maturity of the contract.

Date of Original Issue. The date on which the issue was first issued to the public, or the date on which the debt instrument was sold by the issuer. In the case of any debt instrument which is publicly offered, it is the date on which the debt instrument was issued in a sale or exchange.

Debt Instrument. A bond, debenture, note, or certificate or other evidence of indebtedness.

Deficiency. The amount by which the tax imposed exceeds the sum of the amount shown as the tax by the taxpayer upon his/her return, if a return was made by the taxpayer and an amount indicated as the tax. *Deficiency* includes the amounts previously assessed or collected without assessment as a deficiency over the amount of rebates.

Deficiency Dividends. The amount of dividends paid by the corporation on or after the date of the determination (see **Determination** below), before filing claims which would have been includable in the computation of the deduction for dividends paid for the taxable year with respect to which the liability for personal holding company tax exists, if distributed during such taxable year. No dividends are considered as *deficiency dividends* unless distributed within 90 days after the determination.

Deficiency Dividend Deduction. No deduction is allowed unless the claim therefore is filed within 120 days after the determination.

Demand Loan. Any loan which is payable in full at any time on the demand of the lender.

Dependent. Any of the following individuals *over half* of whose support for the calendar year in which the taxable year of the taxpayer begins was received from the taxpayer or treated as received from the taxpayer:

1. A son or daughter of the taxpayer, or a descendant of either.
2. A stepson or stepdaughter of the taxpayer.
3. A brother, sister, stepbrother, or stepsister of the taxpayer.
4. The father or mother of the taxpayer, or an ancestor of either.
5. A stepfather or stepmother of the taxpayer.
6. A son or daughter of a brother or sister of the taxpayer.
7. A brother or sister of the father or mother of the taxpayer.
8. A son-in-law, daughter-in-law, father-in-law, mother-in-law, brother-in-law, sister-in-law, of the taxpayer.
9. An individual, other than an individual who at any time during the taxable year was the spouse, who, for the taxable year of the taxpayer, has as his/her principal place of abode the home of the taxpayer and is a member of the taxpayer's household.

Depositary Share. A security, evidenced by an *American Depositary Receipt*, that represents a foreign security or a multiple of or fraction thereof deposited with a depositary.

Determination. A decision by the Tax Court or a judgment, decree, or other order by any court of competent jurisdiction, which has become final.

Development Stage Company. A company which is devoting substantially all its efforts to establishing a new business and either of the following conditions exists:

1. Planned principal operations have not commenced.
2. Planned principal operations have commenced, but there has been no significant revenue therefrom.

Distiller. Any person who produces distilled spirits from any source or substance.

Distribution. A *distribution* is treated as in complete liquidation of a corporation, if the distribution is one of a series of distributions in redemption of all of the stock of the corporation pursuant to a plan.

Dividend. Any distribution of property made by a corporation to its shareholders out of earnings and profits of the taxable year, or from the most recently accumulated earnings and profits, computed at the close of the taxable year, without regard to the amount of earnings and profits at the time the distribution was made.

Domestic. When applied to a corporation or partnership, created or organized in the United States or under the laws of the United States or of any State.

Domestic Building and Loan Association. A domestic building and loan association, a domestic savings and loan association, or a federal savings and loan association.

Earned Income. Wages, salaries, or professional fees, and other amounts received as compensation for personal services rendered by an individual to a corporation which represent a distribution of earnings or profits rather than a reasonable allowance as compensation for the personal services actually rendered. *Earned income* includes net earnings from self-employment to the extent such net earnings constitute compensation for personal services actually rendered.

Educational Organization. An organization which normally maintains a regular faculty and curriculum and normally has regularly organized body of students in attendance at the place where its educational activities are carried on.

Employee. Any officer of a corporation; any individual who, under the usual common law rules applicable to determining the employer-employee relationship, has the status of an employee; any individual who performs services for remuneration for any person as an agent-driver engaged in distributing products; a full-time life insurance salesperson; a home worker performing work; a traveling or city salesperson.

Employee Stock Purchase Plan. A plan which provides that options are to be granted only to employees of the employer corporation, or of its parent or subsidiary corporation, to purchase stock in any such corporation; and such plan is approved by the stockholders of the granting corporation within 12 months before or after the plan is adopted.

Under the terms of the plan, no employee can be granted an option if the employee, immediately after the option is granted, owns stock amounting to 5% or more of the total combined voting power or value of all classes of stock of the employee corporation or of its parent or subsidiary corporation. Under the plan, options are to be granted to all employees of any corporation whose employees are granted any of such options by reason of their employment by such corporation, except employees who have been employed less than 2 years, or employees whose customary employment is 20 hours or less per week, or employees whose customary employment is for not more than 5 months in any calendar year.

Employer. With respect to any calendar year, any person who during any calendar quarter in the calendar year or the preceding calendar year, paid wages of $1500 or more, or on each of some 20 days during the calendar year or during the preceding calendar year (each day being in a different calendar week) employed at least one individual in employment for some portions of the day.

Employment. Any service of whatever nature performed by an employee for the person employing him or her, irrespective of the citizenship or residence of either within the United States; or any service in connection with an American vessel or American aircraft under a contract of service which is entered into within the United States or during the performance of which and while the employee is employed on and in connection with such vessel or aircraft when outside the United States. The term also includes any service of whatever nature performed outside the United States by a citizen or resident of the United States as an employee of an American employer, or if it is service, regardless of where or by whom performed, which is designated as employment or recognized as equivalent to employment under an agreement entered into under the Social Security Act.

Endowment Contract. A contract with an insurance company which depends in part on the life expectancy of the insured, which may be payable in full during the insured's life.

Energy Property. Property that is described in at least one of 6 categories:

1. Alternative energy property.
2. Solar or wind energy property.
3. Specifically defined energy property.
4. Recycling equipment.
5. Shale oil Equipment.
6. Equipment for producing natural gas from geopressured grime.

Property is not *energy property* unless depreciation or amortization is allowable and the property has an estimated useful life of 3 years or more from the time when the property is placed in service.

Enrolled Actuary. A person who is enrolled by the Joint Board for the Enrollment of Actuaries.

Equity Security. Any stock or similar security, or any security convertible, with or without consideration, into such a security, or carrying any warrant or right to subscribe to or purchase such security, or any such warrant or right.

Exchanged Basis Property. Property having a basis determined in whole or in part by reference to other property held at any time by the person for whom the basis is determined.

Executor. The administrator of the decedent, or, if there is none appointed, qualified, and acting within the United States, then any person in actual or constructive possession of any property of the decedent.

Farm. Includes stock, dairy, poultry, fruit and truck farms; also plantations, ranches, and all land used for farming operations.

Farmer. All individuals, partnerships, or corporations that cultivate, operate, or manage farms for gain or profit, either as owners or tenants.

Fiduciary. A guardian, trustee, executor, administrator, receiver, conservator, or any person acting in any fiduciary capacity for any person.

Fifty-Percent-Owned Person. A person approximately 50% of whose outstanding voting shares is owned by the specified person either directly or indirectly through one or more intermediaries (see **Person**).

Financial Statements. Include all notes to the statements and all related schedules.

Fiscal Year. An accounting period of 12 months ending on the last day of any month other than December; the 52–53 week annual accounting period, if such period has been elected by the taxpayer. A fiscal year is recognized only if it is established as the annual accounting period of the taxpayer and only if the books of the taxpayer are kept in accordance with such fiscal year.

Foreign. A corporation or partnership which is *not* domestic.

Foreign Currency Contract. A contract which requires delivery of, or settlement of, and depends on the value of, a foreign currency which is a currency in which positions are also traded through regulated futures contracts. The contract is traded in the interbank market, and is entered into at arm's length at a price determined by reference to the price in the interbank market.

Foreign Earned Income. The amount received by any individual from sources within a foreign country or countries which constitutes earned income attributable to services performed by such individual. Amounts received are considered to be received in the taxable year in which the services to which the amounts are attributable are performed.

Foreign Estate (Foreign Trust). An estate or trust, as the case may be, the income of which comes from sources without the United States which are not materially connected with the conduct of a trade or business within the United States.

Foreign Insurer or Reinsurer. One who is a non-resident alien individual, or a foreign partnership, or a foreign corporation. The term includes a nonresident alien individual, foreign partnership, or foreign corporation which will become bound by an obligation of the nature of an indemnity bond. The term *does not include* a foreign government, or municipal or other corporation exercising the taxing power.

Foreign Investment Company. Any foreign corporation which is registered under the Investment Company Act of 1940, as amended, either as a management company or as a unit investment trust, or is engaged primarily in the business of investing, reinvesting, or trading in securities, commodities, or any interest in property, including a futures or forward contract or option.

FSC (Foreign Sales Corporation). Any corporation which was created or organized under the laws of any foreign country, or under the laws applicable to any possession of the United States, has no more than 25 shareholders at any time during the taxable year, does not have any preferred stock outstanding at any time during the taxable year, and during the taxable year maintains an office located outside the United States in a foreign country, or in any possession of the United States. The term *FSC* does not include any corporation which was created or organized under the laws of any foreign country unless there is in effect between such country and the United States a bilateral or multilateral agreement, or an income tax treaty which contains an exchange of information program to which the *FSC* is subject.

Foreign Trading Gross Receipts. The gross receipts of any FSC which are from the sale, exchange, or other disposition of export property, from the lease or rental of export property for use by the lessee outside the United States, or for services which are related and subsidiary to any sale, exchange, lease, or rental of export property by such corporation.

Foundation Manager. With respect to any private foundation, an officer, director, or trustee of a foundation responsible for any act, or failure to act, and for the employees of the foundation having authority or responsibility, and for their failure to act.

General Partner (see **Partner**). The person or persons responsible under state law for directing the management of the business and affairs of a partnership that are subject of a roll-up transaction (see **Roll-Up Transaction**) including, but not limited to, a general partner(s), board of directors, board of trustees, or other person(s) having a fiduciary duty to such partnership.

General Power of Appointment. The power which is exercisable in favor of the decedent, his/her estate, his/her creditors, or the creditors of the estate.

Generation-Skipping Transfer. A taxable distribution, a taxable termination, and a direct skip. The term does not include any transfer to the extent the property transferred was subject to a prior tax imposed; and such transfers do not have the effect of avoiding tax.

Gift Loan. Any below-market loan where the forgoing of interest is in the nature of a gift (see **Below-Market Loan**).

Gross Income. All income derived from whatever source; income realized in any form, whether in money, property, or services; income realized in the form of services, meals, accommodations, stock, or other property, as well as in cash. Gross income, however, is not limited to the items enumerated.

Head of Household. An individual is considered a head of a household if, and only if, such individual is *not* married at the close of his/her taxable year, is not a surviving spouse, (see **Surviving Spouse**) maintains as his/her home a household which constitutes more than one-half of such taxable year the principal place of abode as a member of such household.

Holder. Any individual whose efforts created property held; any other individual who has acquired an interest in such property in exchange for consideration in money or money's worth paid to such creator of the invention covered by the patent, if such individual is neither the employer of the creator, nor related to the creator.

Housing Expenses. The reasonable expenses paid or incurred during the taxable year by or on behalf of an individual for housing in a foreign country for the individual, spouse and dependants.

Includable Corporation. Any corporation except those exempt from taxation, foreign corporations, insurance companies subject to taxation, regulated investment companies, and real estate investment trusts subject to tax.

Income Recognition. Dividends are included in income on the ex-dividend date; interest is accrued on a daily basis. Dividends declared on short positions existing on the record date are recorded on the ex-dividend date and included as an expense of the period.

Income Tax Return Preparer. Any person who prepares for compensation, or who employs one or more persons to prepare for compensation, any return of tax or any claim for refund of tax. The preparation of a substantial portion of a return or claim for refund is treated as if it were the preparation of such return or claim for refund.

A person is *not* an *income tax return preparer* merely because such person furnishes typing, reproducing, or other mechanical assistance, or prepares a return or claim for refund of the employer, or of an officer or employee of the employer, by whom the person is regularly and continuously employed.

Indian Tribal Government. A governing body of a tribe, band, pueblo, community, village, or a group of native American Indians, or Alaska Native.

Individual Retirement Account. A trust created or organized in the United States for the exclusive benefit of an individual or his/her beneficiaries, but only if the written governing instrument creating the trust meets the following requirements:

1. The trustee is a bank, or such other person who demonstrates that the manner in which such other person will administer the trust will be consistent with the requirements of this section.
2. No part of the trust funds will be invested in life insurance contracts.
3. The interest of the individual in the balance of the account is nonforefeitable.
4. The assets of the trust will not be commingled with other property except in a common trust fund or common investment fund.

Individual Retirement Annuity. An annuity contract, or an endowment contract issued by an insurance company which meets the following requirements:

1. The contract is not transferable by the owner.
2. Under the contract, the premiums are not fixed.
3. Any refund of premiums will be applied before the close of the calendar year following the year of the refund toward the payment of future premiums or the purchase of additional benefits.
4. The entire interest of the owner is nonforfeitable.

Influencing Legislation. Any attempt to have an effect on legislation by trying to impact the opinions of the general public or any segment thereof through communication with any member or employee of a legislative body, or with any government official or employee who may participate in the formulation of the legislation. It does not include any communication with a government official or employee *other than* one whose *principal purpose* is to affect legislation.

Insurance Company. A company whose primary and predominant business activity during the taxable year is the issuing of insurance or annuity contracts, or the reinsuring of risks underwritten by insurance companies. It is the character of the business actually done in the taxable year which determines whether a company is taxable as an insurance company. Insurance companies include both stock and mutual companies, as well as mutual benefit insurance companies. A voluntary unincorporated association of employees, including an association formed for the purpose of relieving sick and aged members, and the dependants of deceased members, is an insurance company.

Interest. Return on any obligation issued in registered form, or of a type issued to the public, but does not include any obligation with a maturity (at issue) of not more than 1 year which is held by a corporation.

International organization. A public international organization entitled to the privileges, exemptions, and immunities as an international organization under the *International Organizations Immunities Act*.

Investment in the Contract. As of the annuity starting date, the aggregate amount of premiums or other consideration paid for the contract, minus the aggregate amount received under the contract before such date, to the extent that such amount was excludable from gross income under prior income tax laws.

Itemized Deductions. Those allowable other than the deductions allowable in arriving at adjusted gross income and the deduction for personal exemptions.

Joint Return. A single return made jointly by a husband and wife.

Life Insurance Contract. An *endowment contract* which is not ordinarily payable in full during the life of the insured.

Lobbying Expenditures. Amounts spent for the purpose of influencing legislation (see **Influencing Legislation**).

Local Telephone Service. Any telephone service not taxable as long distance telephone service; leased wire, teletypewriter or talking circuit special service, or wire and equipment service. Amounts paid for the installation of instruments, wire, poles, switchboards, apparatus, and equipment, are not considered amounts paid for service.

Long Distance Telephone Service. A telephone or radio telephone message or conversation for which the toll charge is more than 24 cents and for which the charge is paid within the United States.

Long-Term Capital Gain. A gain from the sale or exchange of a capital asset held for more than 1 year, if and to the extent such gain is taken into account in computing gross income.

Long-Term Capital Loss. A loss from the sale or exchange of a capital asset held for more than 1 year, if and to the extent that such loss is taken into account in computing taxable income.

Long-Term Contract. A building, installation, construction or manufacturing contract (see **Manufacturing Contract**) which is not completed within the taxable year in which it is initiated.

Lottery. A numbers game, policy, and similar types of wagering (see **Wager**).

Lowest Price. Determined without requiring that any given percentage of sales be made at that price, and without including any fixed amount to which the purchaser has a right as a result of contractual arrangements existing at the time of the sale.

Majority-Owned Subsidiary Company. A corporation, stock of which represents in the aggregate more than 50% of the total combined voting power of all classes of stock of such corporation entitled to vote, is owned wholly by a registered holding company, or partly by such registered holding company and partly by one or more majority-owned subsidiary companies, or by one or more majority-owned subsidiary companies of the registered holding company.

Managing Underwriter. An underwriter(s) who, by contract or otherwise, deals with the registrant, organizes the selling effort, receives some benefit, directly or indirectly, in which all other underwriters similarly situated do not share in proportion to their respective interests in the underwriting, or represents any other underwriters in such matters as maintaining the records of the distribution, arranging the allotments of securities offered, or arranging for appropriate stabilization activities, if any.

Manufacturing Contract. A long-term contract which involves the manufacture of unique items of a type which is not normally carried in the finished goods inventory of the taxpayer, or of items which normally require more than 12 calendar months to complete regardless of the duration of the actual contract.

Material. Information required for those matters about which an average prudent investor ought reasonably to be informed.

Mathematical or Clerical Error:

1. An error in addition, subtraction, multiplication, or division shown on any return.
2. An incorrect use of any table provided by the IRS with respect to any return, if such incorrect use is apparent from the existence of other information on the return.
3. An entry on a return of an item which is inconsistent with another entry of the same or another item on the return.
4. An omission of information which is required to be supplied to substantiate an entry on the return.
5. An entry on a return of a deduction or credit in amount which exceeds a statutory limit, if such limit is expressed as a specified monetary amount, or as a percentage, ratio, or fraction, and if the items entering into the application of such limit appear on the return.

Municipal Bond. Any obligation issued by a government or political subdivision thereof, if the interest on such obligation is excludable from gross income. It does not include such an obligation if it is sold or otherwise disposed of by the taxpayer within 30 days after the date of its acquisition.

Net Capital Gain. The excess of the net long-term capital gain for the taxable year over the net short-term capital loss for that year.

Net Capital Loss. For corporations, the excess of the losses from sales or exchanges of capital assets only to the extent of gains from such sales or exchanges. For taxpayers other than a corporation, losses from sales or exchanges of capital assets are allowable only to the extent of the gains from such sales or exchanges, plus the lower of $3,000 ($1,500 in the case of a married individual filing a separate return), or the excess of such losses over such gains.

Net Earnings from Self-Employment. The gross income derived by an individual from any trade or business carried on by such individual, less the deductions allowed which are attributable to such trade or business.

Net Long-Term Capital Gain. The excess of long-term capital gains for the taxable year over the long-term capital losses for such year.

Net Long-Term Capital Loss. The excess of long-term capital losses for the taxable year over the long-term capital gains for such year.

Net Operating Loss. The excess of the deductions allowed over the gross income. In the case of a taxpayer other than a corporation, the amount deductible on account of losses from sales or exchanges of capital assets cannot exceed the amount includable on account of gains from sales or exchanges of capital assets.

Net Short-Term Capital Gain. The excess of short-term capital gains for the taxable year over the short-term capital losses for such year.

Net Short-Term Capital Loss. The excess of short-term capital losses for the taxable year over the short-term capital gains for such year.

Nonadverse Party. Any person who is not an adverse party (see **Adverse Party,** above).

Nonrecognition Transaction. Any disposition of property in a transaction in which gain or loss is *not* recognized in whole or in part.

Notional Principal Contract. A contract that provides for the payment of amounts by one party to another at specified intervals calculated by reference to a specified index upon a *notional principal amount* in exchange for a specified consideration or a promise to pay similar amounts.

Obligation. Any bond, debenture, note, certificate, or other evidence of indebtedness.

Operating Foundation. Any private foundation which makes distributions directly for the conduct of the activities constituting the purpose or function for which the foundation is organized and operated, equal to substantially all of the lesser of its adjusted net income, or its minimum investment return.

Option. The right or privilege of an individual to purchase stock from a corporation by virtue of an offer of the corporation continuing for a stated period of time, whether or not irrevocable, to sell such stock at a price determined under an option price, or price paid under the option. *Option Price* means the consideration in money or property which, pursuant to the terms of the option, is the price at which the stock subject to the option is purchased.

The individual owning the option is under no obligation to purchase, and the right or privilege must be evidenced in writing. While no particular form of words is necessary, the written option should express, among other things, an offer to sell at the option price and the period of time during which the offer will remain open. The individual who has the right or privilege is the *optionee* and the corporation offering to sell stock under such an arrangement is referred to as the *optionor*.

Organizational Expenditures. Any expenditure which is incident to the creation of a corporation, chargeable to capital accounts, and is of a character which, if expended incident to the creation of a corporation having a limited life, would be amortizable over such life.

Overpayment. Any payment of an Internal Revenue tax which is assessed or collected after the expiration of the period of limitation properly applicable thereto.

Owner-Employee. An owner of a proprietorship, or, in the case of a partnership, a partner who owns either more than 10% of the capital interest, or more than 10% of the profits interest, of the partnership.

Paid or Incurred (Paid or Accrued). Defined according to the method of accounting upon the basis of which the taxable income is computed.

Parent. Of a specified person, (see **Person**) is an affiliate controlling such person directly, or indirectly, through one or more intermediaries.

Parent Corporation. Any corporation, other than the employer corporation, in an unbroken chain of corporations ending with the employer corporation if each of the corporations other than the employer corporation owns stock possessing 50% or more of the total combined voting power of all classes of stock in one of the other corporations in the chain.

Partially Pooled Account. A part of an unemployment fund in which all contributions thereto are mingled and undivided. Compensation from this part is payable only to individuals to whom compensation would be payable from a reserve account or from a guaranteed employment account but for the exhaustion or termination of such reserve account or of a guaranteed employment account. (See **Pooled Fund**.)

Partner. A member of a partnership.

Partner's Interest, Liquidation Thereof. The termination of a partner's entire interest in a partnership by means of a distribution, or a series of distributions, to the partner by the partnership. A series of distributions means distributions whether they are made in one year or in more than one year. Where a partner's interest is to be liquidated by a series of distributions, the interest will not be considered as liquidated until the final distribution has been made. One which is not in liquidation of a partner's entire interest is a *current distribution*. Current distributions, therefore, include those in partial liquidation of a partner's interest, and those of the partner's distributive share.

Partnership. A syndicate, pool, group, joint venture or other unincorporated organization through or by means of which any business, financial operation, or venture is carried on, and is not a corporation, trust, or estate.

Partnership Agreement. Includes the original agreement and any modifications thereof agreed to by all the partners or adopted in any other manner provided by the partnership agreement. The agreements or modifications can be oral or written.

Payroll Period. A time frame for which a payment of wages is ordinarily made to the employee by the employer. The term *miscellaneous payroll period* means one other than a daily, weekly, biweekly, semimonthly, monthly, quarterly, semiannual, or annual period.

Pension Plan Contracts. Any contract entered into with trusts which at the time the contracts were entered into were deemed to be trusts and exempt from tax. Includes contracts entered into with trusts which were individual retirement accounts, or under contracts entered into with individual retirement annuities.

Person. Includes an individual, a trust, estate, partnership, association, company, or corporation, an officer or employee of a corporation or a member or employee of a partnership, who is under a duty to surrender the property or rights to property to discharge the obligation. The term also includes an officer or employee of the United States, of the District of Columbia, or of any agency or instrumentality who is under a duty to discharge the obligation.

Personal Holding Company. Any corporation if at least 60% of its adjusted ordinary gross income for the taxable year is personal holding company income, and at any time during the last half of the taxable year more than 50% in value of its outstanding stock is owned, directly or indirectly, by or for not more than 5 individuals. To meet the gross income requirement, it is necessary that at least 80% of the total gross income of the corporation for the taxable year be personal holding company income (see **Personal Holding Company Income**).

Personal Holding Company Income. The portion of the adjusted ordinary gross income which consists of dividends, interest, royalties (other than mineral, oil, or gas royalties or copyright royalties), and annuities.

Political Organization. A party, committee, association, fund, or other organization, whether or not incorporated, organized and operated primarily for the purpose of directly or indirectly accepting contributions or making expenditures for an exempt function activity. A political organization can be a committee or other group which accepts contributions or makes expenditures for the purpose of promoting the nomination of an individual for an elective public office in a primary election, or in a meeting or caucus of a political party:

1. **Exempt Function Activity.** Includes all activities that are directly related to and support the process of influencing or attempting to influence the selection, nomination, election, or appointment of any individual to public office, or office in a political organization.

2. **Segregated Fund.** A fund which is established and maintained by a political organization or an individual separate from the assets of the organization or the personal assets of the individual. The amounts in the fund must be for use only for an exempt function, or for an activity necessary to fulfill an exempt function. A segregated fund established and maintained by an individual may qualify as a political organization.

Pooled Fund. An unemployment fund or any part thereof other than a reserve account (see **Reserve Account**) or a guaranteed employment account, into which the total contributions of persons contributing thereto are payable, in which all contributions are mingled and undivided, and from which compensation is payable to all eligible individuals.

Predecessor. A person from whom another person acquired the major portion of the business and assets in a single succession, or in a series of related successions. In each of these successions the acquiring person received the major portion of the business and assets of the acquired.

Previously Filed or Reported. Previously filed with, or reported in, a definitive proxy statement or information statement, or in a registration statement under the Securities Act of 1933.

Principal Holder of Equity Securities. Used regarding a registrant or other person named in a particular statement or report, a holder of record or a known beneficial owner of more than 10 percent of any class of equity securities of the registrant or other person, respectively, as of the date of the related balance sheet filed.

Principal Underwriter. An underwriter in privity of contract with the issuer of the securities as to which he or she is underwriter.

Promoter. Any person who, acting alone or in conjunction with others, directly or indirectly, takes initiative in founding and organizing the business or enterprise of an issuer. Any person who in so doing received in consideration of services or property, or both services and property, 10 percent or more of any class of securities of the issuer or 10 percent or more of the proceeds from the sale of any class of securities. However, a person who receives such securities or proceeds with or solely as underwriting commissions or solely in consideration of property will not be deemed a promoter within the meaning of this paragraph if such person does not otherwise take part in founding and organizing the enterprise.

Property Used in the Trade or Business. That property used in a trade or business of a character which is subject to an allowance for depreciation, held for more than 1 year, and *real* property used in a trade or business, held for more than 1 year, and which is not a copyright, a literary work, musical, artistic composition, or similar property. Also *not* included in the definition is property of a kind which would properly be includable in the inventory of the taxpayer if on hand at the close of the taxable year, nor property held by the taxpayer primarily for sale to customers in the ordinary course of the trade or business.

Qualified Assets. The nature of any investments and other assets maintained, or required to be maintained, by applicable legal instruments in respect of outstanding face-amount certificates. If the nature of the qualifying assets and amount thereof is not subject to the provisions of the Investment Company Act of 1940, a statement to that effect should be made.

Qualified Individual. An individual whose tax home is in a foreign country and who is a citizen of the United States and establishes that he/she has been a bona fide resident of a foreign country (or countries) for an uninterrupted period which includes an entire taxable year, or a citizen or resident of the United States and who, during any period of 12 consecutive months, is present in a foreign country (or countries) during at least 330 full days in such period.

Qualified Pension, Profit-Sharing, Stock Bonus Plans and Annuity Plans. Compensation is paid under a deferred payment plan, and bond purchase plan. The plan is a definite written program and arrangement which is communicated to the employees and which is established and maintained by an employer.

In the case of a *pension plan*, to provide for the livelihood of the employees or their beneficiaries after the retirement of such employees through the benefits determined without regard to profits.

In the case of a *profit-sharing plan*, to enable employees or their beneficiaries to participate in the profits of the employer's trade or business, or in the profits of an affiliated employer who is entitled to deduct any contributions to the plan pursuant to a definite formula for allocating the contributions and for distributing the funds accumulated under the plan.

In the case of a *stock bonus plan*, to provide employees or their beneficiaries benefits similar to those of profit-sharing plans, except that such benefits are distributable in stock of the employer, and that the contributions by the employer are not necessarily dependent upon profits.

Real Estate Investment Trust (REIT). A corporation, trust, or association which meets the following conditions:

1. Is managed by one or more trustees or directors. A trustee means a person who holds legal title to the property of the *real estate investment trust*, and has such rights and powers as will meet the requirement of centralization of management. The trustee must have continuing exclusive authority over the management of the trust, the conduct of its affairs, and the disposition of the trust property.

2. Has beneficial ownership which is evidenced by transferable shares or by transferable certificates of beneficial interest and must be held by more than 100 persons determined without reference to any rules of attribution.

3. In case of a taxable year beginning before October 5, 1976, does not hold any property, other than foreclosure property, primarily for sale to customers in the ordinary course of its trade or business.
4. Is neither a financial institution, nor an insurance company.
5. Beneficial ownership of the REIT is held by 100 or more persons.
6. The REIT would not be a personal holding company if all of its gross income constituted personal holding company income.

Recomputed Basis. With respect to any property, its adjusted basis recomputed by adding to it all adjustments reflected on account of deductions allowed or allowable to the taxpayer or to any other person for depreciation or amortization.

Recovery. Regarding the recovery of tax benefit items, gross income does not include income attributable to the recovery during the taxable year of any amount deducted in any prior taxable year to the extent such amount did not reduce the amount of tax imposed.

Recovery Exclusion. Regarding a bad debt, prior tax, or delinquency amount, it is the amount determined in accordance with regulations of the deductions or credits allowed, on account of such bad debt, prior tax, or delinquency amount, which did not result in a reduction of the taxpayer's tax under corresponding provisions of prior income tax laws.

Registrant. The issuers of the securities for which an application, a registration statement, or a report is filed.

Related Parties. All affiliates of an enterprise, including its management and their immediate families, its principal owners and their immediate families, its investments accounted for by the equity method, beneficial employee trusts that are managed by the management of the enterprise, and any party that may, or does, deal with the enterprise and has ownership of, control over, or can significantly influence the management or operating policies of another party, to the extent that an arm's-length transaction may not be achieved.

Reorganization, A Party To. Includes a corporation resulting from a *reorganization*, and both corporations in a transaction qualifying as a reorganization where one corporation acquires stock or properties of another corporation. A corporation remains a *party to* the reorganization although it transfers all or part of the assets acquired as a controlled subsidiary. A corporation controlling an acquiring corporation is a party to the reorganization when the stock of the controlling corporation is used in the acquisition of properties.

Repurchase Premium. the excess of the repurchase price paid or incurred to repurchase the obligation over its adjusted issue price (see **Adjusted Issue Price**).

Reserve Account. A separate account in an unemployment fund, maintained with respect to a person, or group of persons, having individuals in his, her, or their employ, from which account (unless such account is exhausted) is paid all and only compensation payable on the basis of services performed for such person, or for one or more of the persons comprising the group.

Restricted Securities. Investment securities which cannot be offered for public sale without first being registered under the Securities Act of 1933.

Return. Any return, statement, schedule, or list, and any supplement thereto, filed with respect to any tax imposed by the law.

Roll-Up Transaction. Any transaction or series of transactions that, directly or indirectly, through acquisition or otherwise, involve the combination or reorganization of one or more partnerships and the offer or sale of securities by a successor entity, whether newly formed or previously existing, to one or more limited partners of the partnerships to be combined or reorganized.

Rules and Regulations. All needful *rules and regulations* approved by the Commissioner for the enforcement of the Code. Includes all rules and regulations necessary by reason of the alterations of the law in relation to Internal Revenue.

S Corporation. Regarding any taxable year, a small business corporation for which an election is in effect for such year (see **Small Business Corporation**).

Section 1245 Property. Any property, other than livestock, which is or has been property of a character subject to an allowance for depreciation or subject to an allowance for amortization and is personal property, or other property if such property is tangible, but not including a building or its structural components.

Section 1250 Property. Any *real* property, other than Section 1245 property, which is or has been property of a character subject to an allowance for depreciation.

Self-Employment Income. The net earnings from self-employment derived by an individual during any taxable year, except if such net earnings for the taxable year are less than $400.

Share. A *unit* of stock in a corporation, or unit of interest in an unincorporated person.

Short-Term Capital Gain. A gain from the sale or exchange of a capital asset held for not more than 1 year, if and to the extent such gain is taken into account in computing gross income.

Short-Term Capital Loss. A loss from the sale or exchange of a capital asset held for not more than 1 year, if and to the extent that such loss is taken into account in computing gross income.

Significant Subsidiary. A *subsidiary*, including its subsidiaries, which meets any of the following conditions:

1. The registrant's and its other subsidiaries' investments in and advances to the subsidiary exceed 10 percent of the total assets of the registrant and its subsidiaries consolidated as of the end of the most recently completed fiscal year for a proposed business combination to be accounted for as a pooling-of-interests. This condition is also met when the number of common shares exchanged by the registrant exceeds 10 percent of its total common shares outstanding at the date the combination is initiated.

2. The registrant's and its other subsidiaries' proportionate share of the total assets, after intercompany eliminations, of the subsidiary exceeds 10 percent of the total assets of the registrant and its subsidiaries consolidated as of the end of the most recently completed fiscal year.

3. The registrant's and its other subsidiaries' equity in the income from continuing operations before income taxes, extraordinary items and cumulative effect of a change in accounting principle of the subsidiary exceeds 10 percent of such income of the registrant and its subsidiaries consolidated for the most recently completed fiscal year.

Small Business Corporation. A domestic corporation which is not an ineligible corporation, e.g., a member of an affiliated group, and which does not have more than 35 shareholders, does not have as a shareholder a person, other than an estate or trust, who is not an individual, and does not have a nonresident alien as a shareholder.

Standard Deduction. The sum of the basic standard deduction and the additional standard deduction.

Straight Debt. Any written unconditional promise to pay on demand or on a specified date a sum certain in money if the interest rate and interest payment dates are not contingent on profits or the borrower's discretion, not convertible into stock, and the creditor is an individual, an estate, or a trust.

Subsidiary Corporation. (See **Parent Corporation**.)

Substituted Basis Property. Property which is transferred basis property, or exchanged basis property.

Summarized Financial Information. The presentation of summarized information as to the assets, liabilities and results of operations of the entity for which the information is required.

Support. Includes food, shelter, clothing, medical and dental care, education, etc. The amount of an item of *support* will be the amount of expense incurred by the one furnishing such item. If the item of *support* furnished an individual is in the form of property or lodging, it is necessary to measure the amount of such item of support in terms of its fair market value.

Surviving Spouse. A taxpayer whose spouse died during either of his/her two taxable years immediately preceding the taxable year, and who maintains as his/her home a household which constitutes for the taxable year the principal place of abode as a member of such household.

Tax Court. The United States Tax Court.

Tax-Exempt Obligation. Any obligation if the interest on such obligation is not includable in gross income.

Taxable Gifts. The total amount of gifts made during the calendar year, less the deductions provided.

Taxable Income. Gross income minus the deductions allowed, other than the standard deduction (see **Standard Deduction**). For individuals who do not itemize deductions for the taxable year, it is adjusted gross income, minus the standard deduction, and the deductions for personal exemptions.

Taxable Transportation. Transportation by air which begins and ends in the United States or in the 225-mile zone. The term *225-mile zone* means that portion of Canada and Mexico which is not more than 225 miles from the nearest point in the continental United States. The term *Continental United States* means the District of Columbia and the States other than Alaska and Hawaii.

Taxable Year. The taxpayer's annual accounting period if it is a calendar year or a fiscal year, or the calendar year if the taxpayer keeps no books or has no accounting period. (See **Annual Accounting Period** and **Calendar Year**.)

Term Loan. Any loan which is not a demand loan (see **Demand Loan**).

Tips. Wages received while performing services which constitute employment, and included in a written statement furnished to the employer.

Toll Telephone Service. A telephonic quality communication for which there is a toll charge which varies in amount with the distance and elapsed transmission time of each individual communication.

Totally Held Subsidiary. A subsidiary substantially all of whose outstanding equity securities are owned by its parent and/or the parent's other totally held subsidiaries, and which is not indebted, in an amount which is material in relation to the particular subsidiary, excepting indebtedness incurred in the ordinary course of business which is not overdue and which matures within 1 year from the date of its creation whether evidenced by securities or not. Indebtedness of a subsidiary which is secured by its parent by guarantee, pledge, assignment, or otherwise, is excluded.

Tract of Real Property. A single piece of real property, except that two or more pieces of real property should be considered a tract if at any time they were contiguous in the hands of the taxpayer, or if they would be contiguous except for the imposition of a road, street, railroad, stream, or similar property.

Trade or Business. Includes the performance of personal services within the United States at any time within the taxable year. Includes the performance of the functions of a public office.

Transferred Basis Property. Property having a basis determined in whole or in part by reference to the basis in the hands of the donor, grantor, or other transferor.

Trust. As used in the Internal Revenue Code, an arrangement created either by a will or by an *inter vivos* declaration whereby trustees take title to property for the purpose of protecting or conserving it for the beneficiaries under the ordinary rules applied in chancery or probate courts. Usually the beneficiaries of such a trust do no more than accept the benefits thereof and are not the voluntary planners or creators of the trust arrangement.

Undistributed Foreign Personal Holding Company Income. The taxable income of a *foreign personal holding company.*

Undistributed Personal Holding Company Income. The amount which is subject to the personal holding company tax.

United States Property. Any property which is a tangible property located in the United States, stock of a domestic corporation, an obligation of a United States resident, or any right to the use in the United States of a patent or copyright, an invention, model, or design (whether or not patented).

Unrealized Receivables. Any rights, contractual or otherwise, to payments for goods delivered, or to be delivered, to the extent that such payment would be treated as received for property other than a capital asset. Includes services rendered, or to be rendered, to the extent that income arising from such right to payment was not previously includable in income under the method of accounting employed. The basis for unrealized receivables includes all costs or expenses attributable thereto paid or accrued, but not previously taken into account under the method of accounting employed.

Unrecognized Gain. Any position held by the taxpayer as of the close of the taxable year, the amount of gain which would be taken into account with respect to such position if such position were sold on the last business day of such taxable year at its fair market value.

Valuation of Assets. The balance sheets of registered investment companies, other than issuers of face-amount certificates, which reflect all investments at value, with the aggregate cost of each category of investment and of the total investments reported shown parenthetically.

Voting Shares. The sum of all rights, other than as affected by events of default, to vote for election of directors; the sum of all interests in an unincorporated person (see **Person**).

Wager. Any *bet* with respect to any sporting event or a contest placed with a person engaged in the business of accepting such bets. Includes any bet placed in a wagering pool with respect to a sports event or a contest, if such pool is conducted for profit, and any bet placed in a lottery (see **Lottery**) conducted for profit.

Wages. All remuneration for services performed by an employee for an employer, including the cash value of all remuneration, including benefits.

Welfare Benefits Fund. Any fund which is part of a plan of an employer, and through which the employer provides welfare benefits to employees or their beneficiaries.

Wholly Owned Subsidiary. A subsidiary substantially all of whose outstanding voting shares (see **Voting Shares**) are owned by its parent and/or the parent's other wholly owned subsidiaries.

Year. Any 12 *consecutive* months.

Appendix D
The Going Concern Concept

The concept that financial statements are prepared on the basis of a "going concern" is one of the basics relating to financial accounting. There is an underlying presumption in the standards set for financial accounting that a business, once started, will continue functioning and operating. For example, the use of historical costs for building and property, which are currently more valuable, presupposes that the *use* of that property will generate more advantages than would present disposition. Deferrals to future periods through systematic allocations also indicate a presumption of longevity.

This presumption of continuance as a going concern is never stated by the independent auditor—never worded in his or her own opinion. On the *contrary*, it is when there appears to be danger of the firm's *not* being able to continue as a going concern that the auditor makes the assertion that "the statements have been prepared on the basis of a going concern," and that he or she is *unable* to express an opinion because of major uncertainties, then described. Therefore, the actual use of the terminology, "going concern," in the auditor's opinion indicates trouble.

Two types of problems may dictate against an entity's continuation as a going concern:

1. Operational uncertainties which may present two different types of situations giving cause for concern:
   a. Progressive deterioration of a firm's financial stability resulting from changing markets, outmoded or inefficient plant and facilities, inept management. This, in turn, leads to declining earnings or actual loss-

670

es, reduced cash balances and eventually an inability to meet current liabilities. Such uncertainties may result in gradual deterioration or, less frequently, in a very sudden turnaround of a previously profitable firm.

b. A start-up business that may never get off the ground. This is the enterprise that begins with high hopes but has not yet met with success nor achieved a solid financial footing. In the event of even a minor setback at this juncture, the firm's continuation may be open to question particularly in relation to the liquidity of its assets. What assets it has are probably tied up in inventories, specialized plant and equipment and deferred charges.

2. External difficulties beyond the control of an entity. These may be as a result of governmental controls, natural disasters such as earthquakes or floods, mandatory product recalls or devastating lawsuits. Any of these or other potential catastrophes could drain an entity beyond its financial capacity to recover.

Following is a random listing of factors which could be indicative of *possible* failure to continue as a going concern:

1. Inability to satisfy obligations on due dates.
2. Inability to perform contractual obligations.
3. Inability to meet substantial loan covenants.
4. A substantial deficit.
5. A series of continued losses.
6. The presence of major contingencies which could lead to heavy losses.
7. Catastrophes which have rendered the business inoperable.
8. Negative cash flows from operations.
9. Adverse key financial ratios.
10. Denial of usual trade credit from suppliers.
11. Necessity of finding new sources of financing.
12. Loss of key personnel.
13. Loss of a principal customer.
14. Work stoppage and labor disputes.

Appendix E

Guidelines for Interim Reporting

Guidelines for interim reporting by publicly traded companies have been established by the AICPA (and the SEC). For those private companies which do not bear the same responsibility for full and adequate disclosure to public shareholders, the guideline for public disclosure should be studied and followed, where feasible and relevant, for possible selfprotection against insurgent parties, since adherence to standards would probably be more defensible than nonadherence.

Following are the standards for determining applicable information and the appropriate guidelines for minimum disclosure:

1. Results should be based on the same principles and practices used for the latest annual statements (subject to the modifications below).
2. Revenue should be recognized as earned for the interim on the same basis as for the full year. Losses should be recognized as incurred or when becoming evident.
3. Costs may be classified as:
    a. Those associated with revenue (cost of goods sold);
    b. All other costs expenses based on:
        1. Those actually incurred, or
        2. Those allocated, based on: time expired, or benefits received, or other period activity.
4. Costs or losses (including extraordinary times) should not be deferred or apportioned unless they would be at year end. Advertised costs may be apportioned in relation to sales for interims.

672

5. With respect to inventory and cost of sales:
   a. LIFO basis should not be liquidated if expected to be replaced later, but should be based on expected replacement factor;
   b. Inventory losses should not be deferred because of cost or market rule; and conversely, later periods should then reflect gains on market price recoveries. Inventory losses should be reflected if resulting from permanent declines in market value in the interim period in which they occur; recoveries of such losses would be gains in a later interim period. If a change in inventory value is temporary, no recognition is given.
   c. With standard costs, variances which are expected to be absorbed by year end should be deferred for the interim, not expensed. Unplanned purchase price or volume variance, not expected to turn around, is to be absorbed during the period;
   d. The estimated gross profit method may be used, but must be disclosed.
6. The seasonal nature of activities should be disclosed, preferably including additional 12-month-to-date information with prior comparative figures.
7. Income taxes:
   a. Effective yearly tax rate (including year-end applicable tax-planned advantages) should be applied to interim taxable income;
   b. Extraordinary items applicable to the interim period should be shown separately net of applicable tax and the effect of the tax not applied to the tax on ordinary net income.
8. Extraordinary and unusual items including the effects of segment disposals should be disclosed separately, net of tax, for the interim period in which they occur, and they should not be apportioned over the year.
9. Contingencies should be disclosed the same as for the annual report.
10. Changes in accounting practices or principles from those allowed in prior periods should be disclosed and, where possible, those changes should be made in the first period of the year.
11. Retroactive restatement and/or prior period adjustments are required under the same rules applying to annual statements.
12. The effect of a change in an accounting estimate, including a change in the estimated effective annual tax rate, should be accounted for in the period in which the change in estimate is made. No restatement of previously reported interim information should be made for changes in estimates, but the effect on earnings of a change in estimate made in a cur-

rent interim period should be reported in the current and subsequent interim periods, if material in relation to any period presented, and should continue to be reported in interim financial information of the subsequent year, for as many periods as necessary to avoid misleading comparisons.

MINIMUM DATA TO BE REPORTED ON INTERIM STATEMENTS :

1. Sales or gross revenues, provisions for income taxes, extraordinary items (including related tax), cumulative effect of changes in accounting principles or practices, and net income;
2. Primary and fully diluted earnings per share data for each period presented;
3. Seasonal revenue, costs and expenses;
4. Disposal of business segments and extraordinary items, as well as unusual or infrequent items;
5. Contingencies;
6. Changes in estimates, changes in accounting principles or practices;
7. Significant changes in balance sheet items;
8. Significant changes in tax provisions;
9. Current year-to-date, or the last 12 months, with comparative data for prior periods;
10. In the absence of a separate fourth-quarter report, special fourth-quarter adjustments and extraordinary, infrequent or unusual items which occurred during that fourth quarter should be disclosed in a note to the annual financial statement;
11. Though not required, condensed balance sheet data and funds flow data are suggested to provide better understanding of the interim report.
12. If a fourth quarter is not presented, any material adjustment to that quarter must be commented upon in the annual report.

Interim reports are usually prepared by management and issued with that clear stipulation.

Accounting firms which issue reports for interim periods are to be guided by auditing standards set for "Reports on a Limited Review of Interim Financial Information" in Section 722 of Statements on Auditing Standards, April, 1981.

ACCOUNTING CHANGES IN INTERIM STATEMENTS

FASB 3, *Reporting Accounting Changes in Interim Financial Statements* amended APB Opinion No. 28, *Interim Financial Reporting* with respect to reporting an accounting change in interim financial reports that have a *cumulative effect*.

The following disclosures of accounting changes that have cumulative effects on income from continuing operations, net income, and related per share amounts for the interim period in which the change is made must be included in interim reports:

1. In the interim period in which the new accounting principle is adopted, disclosure should explain the nature and justification for the change.
2. Disclosure should be made of the effect of the change in the interim period in which the change is made.
3. The effect of the change for each pre-change interim period of that fiscal year should be disclosed.
4. The cumulative effect of the change should be shown on retained earnings at the beginning of that fiscal year, if the change is made in other than the first interim period of the company's fiscal year.
5. In the interim period in which a change is made, disclosure must include amounts computed on a *pro forma* basis for the interim period in which the change is made and for any interim periods of prior fiscal years for which financial information is being presented.
6. In financial reports for a subsequent interim period of the fiscal year in which a new principle is adopted, disclosure must include the effect of the change on income from continuing operations, net income, and related per share amounts for the post-change interim period.

Appendix F

Reporting Cash Payments of Over $10,000

Often smugglers and drug dealers use large cash payments to "launder" money from illegal activities. Laundering means converting "dirty" money or illegally gained money to "clean" money. Congress passed the Tax Reform Act of 1984 and the Anti-Drug Abuse Act of 1988 requiring the payment of certain cash payments of over $10,000 to be reported to the Internal Revenue Service. Any person in a trade or business who receives more than $10,000 in a single transaction or in related transactions must report the transaction to the IRS. The government can often trace the laundered money through payments that are reported. Compliance with the law provides valuable information that can stop those who evade taxes and those who profit from the drug trade and other criminal activities.

A "person" includes an individual, a company, a corporation, a partnership, an association, a trust, or an estate. A report does not have to be filed if the entire transaction, including the receipt of cash, takes place outside of:

1. The 50 states.
2. The District of Columbia.
3. Puerto Rico.
4. A possession or territory of the United States.

However, a report must be filed if the transaction, including the receipt of cash, occurs in Puerto Rico or a possession or territory of the United States and the person is subject to the Internal Revenue Code.

676

A transaction occurs when:

1. Goods, services, or property are sold.
2. Property is rented.
3. Cash is exchanged for other cash.
4. A contribution is made to a trust or escrow account.
5. A loan is made or repaid.
6. Cash is converted to a negotiable instrument such as a check or bond.

Payments to be reported include:

1. A sum over $10,000.
2. Installment payments that cause the total cash received within one year of the initial payment to total more than $10,000.
3. Other previously unreportable payments that cause the total cash received within a 12-month period to total more than $10,000.
4. Those received in the course of a trade or business.
5. Those received from the same buyer or agent.
6. Those received in a single transaction or in related transactions.

A DESIGNATED REPORTING TRANSACTION

A designated reporting transaction is the retail sale of any of the following:

1. A consumer durable, such as an automobile or boat. A consumer durable is property other than land or buildings that is suitable for personal use and can reasonably be expected to last at least one year under ordinary usage.
2. Has a sales price of more than $10,000.
3. Tangible property.
4. A "collectible," including works of art, rugs, antiques, gems, stamps, coins.
5. Travel or entertainment, if the total sales price of all items sold for the same trip or entertainment event in one transaction, or related transactions, is more than $10,000. The sales price of items such as air fare, hotel rooms, and admission tickets are all included.

Retail Sales

The term "retail sales" means any sale made in the course of a trade or business that consists mainly of making sales to ultimate consumers. Thus, if a business consists mainly of making sales to ultimate consumers, all sales made in the course of that business are retail sales. This includes sales of items that will also be resold.

Definition of Cash

In this context, cash is considered to be:

1. The coins and currency of the U.S. and any other recognized country.
2. Cashier's checks, bank drafts, traveler's checks, and money orders received if they have a face value of $10,000 or less and were received in:
    a. A designated reporting transaction.
    b. Any transaction in which the receiver knows the payer is trying to avoid the reporting of the transaction.

A check drawn on an individual's personal account is not considered cash; however, a cashier's check, even when labeled a "treasurer's check" or "bank check," is considered cash.

Exceptions to Definition of Cash

A cashier's check, bank draft, traveler's check, or money order received in a designated transaction is not treated as cash if:

1. It is the proceeds from a bank loan. As proof that it is proceeds from a bank loan, a copy of the loan document, a written statement or lien instructions from the bank, or similar proof are acceptable as evidence,
2. If received in payment on a promissory note or an installment sales contract, including a lease that is considered a sale for federal tax purposes. This exception applies if:
    a. The receiver uses similar notes or contracts in other sales to ultimate consumers in the ordinary course of trade or business.
    b. Total payments for the sale are received on or before the 60th day after the sale, and are 50% or less of the purchase price.
3. For certain down payment plans in payment for a consumer durable or collectible, or for travel and entertainment, and *all three* of the following statements are true:

  a. It was received under a payment plan requiring one or more down payments, and payment of the remainder before receipt of goods or service.
  b. It was received more than 60 days before final payment was due.
  c. Similar payment plans are used in the normal course of the trade or business.

TAXPAYER IDENTIFICATION NUMBER (TIN)

The receiver must furnish the correct TIN of the person or persons from whom the cash is received. If the transaction is conducted on behalf of another person or persons, the receiver must furnish the TIN of that person or persons. There are three types of TINs:

1. The TIN for an individual, including a sole proprietor, is the individual's social security number (SSN).
2. The TIN for a nonresident alien individual who needs a TIN, but is not eligible to get an SSN, is an IRS individual taxpayer identification number (ITIN). An ITIN has nine digits, similar to an SSN.
3. The TIN for other persons, including corporations, partnerships, and estates, is the employer identification number.

A nonresident alien individual or a foreign organization does not have to have a TIN, and so a TIN does not have to be furnished for them, if *all* the following are true:

1. The individual or organization does not have income effectively connected with the conduct of a trade or business in the United States, or an office or place of business or a fiscal or paying agent in the United States, at any time during the year.
2. The individual or organization does not file a federal tax return.
3. In the case of a nonresident alien individual, the individual has not chosen to file a joint federal income tax return with a spouse who is a U.S. citizen or resident.

RELATED TRANSACTIONS

Any transaction between a buyer, or an agent of the buyer, and a seller that occurs within a 24-hour period are related transactions. If a person receives over $10,000 in cash during two or more transactions with one buyer in a 24-hour period, he or she must treat the transactions as one transaction and report the payments. For example, if two products are sold for $6,000 each to the same customer in one day, and the customer pays the seller in cash, they are related transactions. Because they total $12,000, they must be reported.

Transactions can be related if they are more than 24 hours apart if the person knows, or has reason to know, that each is one of a series of connected transactions. For example, a travel agent receives $8,000 from a client in cash for a trip. Two days later, the same client pays the agent $3,000 more in cash to include another person on the trip. These are related transactions and must be reported.

When a person receives $10,000 or less in cash, the person may voluntarily report the payment if the transaction appears to be suspicious. A transaction is suspicious if it appears that a person is trying to cause the receiver not to report, or is trying to cause a false or incomplete report, or if there is a sign of possible illegal activity.

The amount received and when it was received determines when it must be reported to the IRS. Generally, a report must be filed within 15 days after receiving payment. If the first payment is not more than $10,000, the seller must add the first payment and any later payments made within one year of the first payment. When the total cash payments are more than $10,000, the buyer must file within 15 days. After a report is filed, a new count of cash payments received from that buyer within a 12-month period must be reported to the IRS within 15 days of the payment that causes the additional payments to total more than $10,000. The report can be filed in the seller's local IRS office.

A written statement must be given to each person named on the report to the IRS. The statement must show the name and address of the person who receives the payment, the name and telephone number of a contact person, and the total amount of reportable cash received from the person during the year. It must state that the information is being reported to the IRS. The statement must be sent to the buyer by January 31 of the year after the year in which the seller receives the cash that caused the information to be filed with the IRS. The individual making the report must keep a copy of every report filed for five years.

PENALTIES

There are civil penalties for failure to:

1. File a correct report by the date it is due.
2. Provide the required statement to those named in the report.

3. If the person receiving the cash payment intentionally disregards the requirement to file a correct form by the date it is due, the penalty is the larger of:

   a. $25,000.

   b. The amount of cash the person received and was required to report, up to $100,000.

There are criminal penalties for:

1. Willful failure to file a report.
2. Willfully filing a false or fraudulent report.
3. Stopping or trying to stop a report from being filed.
4. Setting up, helping to set up, or trying to set up a transaction in a way that would make it seem unnecessary to file a report.

Interference with or prevention of the filing of a report as well as actual willful failure to file a report may result in a substantial fine, imprisonment, or both. The fine can be up to $250,000 ($500,000 for corporations). An individual may also be sentenced to up to five years in prison. Both a fine and a prison sentence may be imposed.

The penalties for failure to file can also apply to any person, including a payer, who attempts to interfere with or prevent the seller, or business, from filing a correct report. This includes any attempt to *structure* the transaction in a way that would make it seem unnecessary to file a report by breaking up a large cash transaction into small cash transactions.

Index